GLOBAL POLITICAL ECONOMY

EVOLUTION & DYNAMICS

ROBERT O'BRIEN & MARC WILLIAMS

5TH
EDITION

 macmillan education   palgrave

First edition 2004
Second edition 2007
Third edition 2010
Fourth edition 2013
Fifth edition 2016

Published by
PALGRAVE

Palgrave in the UK is an imprint of Macmillan Publishers Limited, registered in England, company number 785998, of 4 Crinan Street, London, N1 9XW.

Palgrave Macmillan in the US is a division of St Martin's Press LLC, 175 Fifth Avenue, New York, NY 10010.

Palgrave is a global imprint of the above companies and is represented throughout the world.

Palgrave® and Macmillan® are registered trademarks in the United States, the United Kingdom, Europe and other countries.

ISBN 978–1–137–52312–9 hardback

ISBN 978–1–137–52311–2 paperback

This book is printed on paper suitable for recycling and made from fully managed and sustained forest sources. Logging, pulping and manufacturing processes are expected to conform to the environmental regulations of the country of origin.

A catalogue record for this book is available from the British Library.

A catalog record for this book is available from the Library of Congress.

Global Political Economy

To our daughters

Isabella and Louisa

The world is yours to explore and improve

Contents

List of Boxes, Tables, Figures and Maps

BOXES

TABLES

FIGURES

MAPS

Preface to the Fifth Edition

The aim of the book, as in previous editions, is to provide tools that will enable readers to understand and explain developments in the global political economy. As a result, the main structure of the book remains unchanged from previous versions. This structure – a discussion of theoretical perspectives and methods, a survey of the historical evolution of the world economy, and exploration of key frameworks and structures of the global political economy – has proved successful. Nevertheless, recognizing the importance of contemporary events, we have revised chapters to take account of recent significant changes in the global political economy since the fourth edition was published in 2013.

It has been a pleasure to continue working together to produce this fifth edition of our textbook. Our joint efforts are aided by many others. We would like to thank the anonymous reviewers of this and previous editions who provided detailed and helpful suggestions. A number of people were generous in responding to surveys and questions about the book. We have greatly benefited from their comments, even if we are not able to respond adequately to all the advice. We also owe an ongoing debt to present and former colleagues and students at the universities of Sussex, New South Wales and McMaster. Numerous instructors and students at other universities have also provided helpful feedback. Our textbook now also appears in Greek and Chinese translations and we thank the publishers, students and academics in those countries interested in our work. Finally, thanks go to Steven Kennedy who has now retired from the publishing industry, but who was instrumental in the initiation of this text and its subsequent editions. We have enjoyed working with his successor, Stephen Wenham. Although we greatly appreciate everyone's help, the responsibility for errors remains ours alone.

ROBERT O'BRIEN, DUNDAS
MARC WILLIAMS, SYDNEY

List of Abbreviations

APEC	Asia-Pacific Economic Cooperation
ASEAN	Association of Southeast Asian Nations
BIS	Bank for International Settlements
BRICS	Brazil, Russia, India, China, South Africa
CEDAW	Convention on the Elimination of All Forms of Discrimination Against Women
COP	Conferences of the Parties
DDA	Doha Development Agenda
ECB	European Central Bank
EEC	European Economic Community
EOI	export-oriented industrialization
EPZ	export processing zone
ERM	exchange rate mechanism
EU	European Union
FDI	foreign direct investment
FOC	flag of convenience
FSF	Financial Stability Forum
G5	Group of 5
G7	Group of 7
G8	Group of 8
G20	Group of 20
G77	Group of 77
G90	Group of 90
GATS	General Agreement on Trade in Services (WTO)
GATT	General Agreement on Tariffs and Trade
GCC	global commodity chain
GDP	gross domestic product
GHG	greenhouse gas
GNP	gross national product
GPE	global political economy
HDI	Human Development Index
HIPC	heavily indebted poor countries
HIV/AIDS	human immunodeficiency virus/ acquired immunodeficiency syndrome
IBRD	International Bank for Reconstruction and Development
ICFTU	International Confederation of Free Trade Unions
ICT	information and communications technology
IEOs	international economic organizations
ILO	International Labour Organization
IMF	International Monetary Fund
IMS	international monetary system
IPE	international political economy
IPR	intellectual property rights
IR	international relations
ISI	import substitution industrialization
IT	information technology
ITO	International Trade Organization
LDC	least developed country
MAI	Multilateral Agreement on Investment
MDGs	Millennium Development Goals
MDRI	Multilateral Debt Relief Initiative
MERCOSUR	Southern Common Market
MFA	Multifibre Agreement
MFN	most favoured nation
NAFTA	North American Free Trade Agreement
NATO	North Atlantic Treaty Organization
NGOs	nongovernmental organizations
NICs	newly industrializing countries
NIEO	New International Economic Order
NTBs	non-tariff barriers
OECD	Organisation for Economic Co-operation and Development
OPEC	Organization of Petroleum Exporting Countries
PPMs	process and production methods
R&D	research and development
RTA	regional trade agreement
S&D	special and differential treatment
SAPs	structural adjustment programmes
SARS	severe acute respiratory syndrome
SPS	Sanitary and Phytosanitary Measures
TNC	transnational corporation
TPP	Trans-Pacific Partnership Agreement
TRIMs	Trade-Related Investment Measures
TRIPS	Trade-Related Aspects of Intellectual Property Rights

TTIP	Transatlantic Trade and Investment Partnership	UNDP	United Nations Development Programme
UN	United Nations	UNFCCC	United Nations Framework Convention on Climate Change
UNCED	United Nations Conference on Environment and Development	UNHCR	United Nations High Commissioner for Refugees
UNCHE	United Nations Conference on the Human Environment	UNICEF	United Nations Children's Fund
UNCTAD	United Nations Conference on Trade and Development	WHO	World Health Organization
		WTO	World Trade Organization

Introduction

The aim of this textbook is to provide an accessible introduction to the study of international political economy (IPE). In pursuit of this aim, it follows two strategies that distinguish it from many other IPE textbooks. First, it adopts a historical approach to the study of IPE and offers students, the interested public and scholars a broad overview of how the modern global political economy has come into being. Instead of beginning with an analysis of contemporary global political and economic structures, the book seeks to provide an easily accessible but brief history that draws out important factors in the creation of our present situation. In our teaching, we have found that the best way for students to appreciate the nuances of the present is to expose them to the origins of political economy practices of the past. This is even more vital as we move from a world dominated by the US and Europe to a more multilateral future. Second, the book seeks to move beyond the repetition of the three dominant theoretical perspectives (economic nationalism, liberalism, Marxism) on IPE as a framework of analysis. It seeks to reflect both the developments in IPE scholarship in the past 30 years and the main debates between orthodox and heterodox scholars through attention to a broad range of themes, issues and perspectives in IPE. Unorthodox or heterodox approaches to IPE have become much more developed since the first wave of IPE texts in the 1980s by Spero (1981), Gilpin (1987), Strange (1988) and Gill and Law (1988). Ecological, feminist, neo-Gramscian and poststructural approaches now compete with traditional perspectives and shed new light on old problems. Central to our strategy is a framework that integrates material and ideational aspects of IPE.

PLAN OF THE BOOK

The text is divided into three parts. Part 1 examines key theories, locates the field in the broader social sciences and considers important methodological issues (Chapters 1 and 2). The complexities of the global political economy cannot be properly understood through a study of the 'facts' without recourse to theories of IPE. Because the meaning and impact of economic and political change are controversial and contested, Chapter 1 provides an introduction to the traditional competing perspectives in IPE. Economic nationalism, liberalism and Marxist/ critical theories are introduced, with particular attention to how these theories highlight different actors, dynamics and views on cooperation and conflict. In each case, the work of a prominent proponent of these approaches (Susan Strange, Robert Keohane, Robert Cox) is showcased to highlight how theoretical perspectives can be developed and deployed. The chapter concludes by offering a summary of contending perspectives. Chapter 2 locates IPE among a range of disciplines – economics, political science, political economy and international relations. It considers the methods by which IPE is studied, such as case studies, rational choice, institutionalism and constructivism. An example of how one academic (John Ruggie) furthered a particular method in his writings and his work in the UN is provided. The chapter concludes by considering the direction of IPE theory today and outlining the book's own theoretical approach.

Part 2 (Chapters 3–5) considers the evolution and eventual domination of a European-based world economy. Chapter 3 provides an overview of key historical processes that led to the transformation of regional economies and the beginnings of the creation of the contemporary global economic system. It is organized into two main sections. The first contrasts various regional political economies – the Middle East, China, India, Africa, the Americas and Europe in the early 15th century. The second charts the expansion of a European-centred international political economy into other areas of the world, namely Africa, the Americas and Asia. It stresses the variety of patterns of interaction including slavery, genocide, war and trade, and assesses the varied pattern of European–non-European interaction. Chapter 4 examines the rise and fall of a liberal world system from 1800 until 1945. It begins by looking at the domestic and international basis of British power in the mid-19th century, the development of the Pax Britannica as a structure of international governance and the rise of imperialism in the 19th century. It concludes by analysing the descent of Europe and the world into war and depression. Chapter 5 turns its attention to the post-1945 era. The first section examines the Cold War era and the distinct western, communist and southern political economies. The second part turns its attention to the post-Cold War era from 1989 to 2015. The competition between forms of capitalism and accompanying state transformation, the impact of the information revolution and the proliferation of international organization as a form of global governance are highlighted.

Part 3 (Chapters 6–15) focuses on the recent dynamics of the global political economy. In one sense, the global political economy can be treated as a single whole, as we do in Part 2 of this book, but in another sense it is also composed of various structures or frameworks, each with its own set of actors, processes, institutions and rules. Of course, many actors participate in more than one framework and there are linkages between them. Nevertheless, in common with standard texts in economics and political economy, we have classified the diverse practices in the world economy into certain key frameworks. We do not claim that any single framework is dominant, but we do suggest that the ten frameworks (trade, production, finance, labour, gender, development, environment, ideas, security and governance) analysed in this book constitute critical spheres of activity in the world economy.

The argument in each chapter in Part 3 is divided into four sections – definitions, theoretical perspectives, major developments and key issues. The section on definitions provides an introduction to some of the key terms and concepts used in analysis of the particular framework. The aim here is not to proffer definitive definitions but rather to discuss some of the key issues pertinent to an understanding of the framework. The theoretical perspectives section is important in raising key issues related to the normative elements of the global political economy framework. It shows the importance of knowledge in the construction of frameworks or structures in the global political economy. In our analysis, knowledge and knowledge claims are co-constitutive parts of the framework. In other words, knowledge is internal and integral to the structure rather than an external set of considerations. What counts as knowledge is not secondary but rather a central feature of the political economy framework. The beliefs that actors hold about cause and effect relations will influence the actions they will take. Within the world economy, states, firms, international organizations and social movement actors have conflicting views about the issues under scrutiny. In keeping with the historical focus of this book, the section on major developments provides an overview of key changes within the particular framework in the period since 1945. Finally, in each chapter we focus on three current issues (with exception of the finance chapter, which looks at four). There are other equally important issues that cannot be addressed in each chapter, but we have chosen ones that combine topicality with relevance to the evolution of the global political economy and contrasting IPE perspectives.

GLOBALIZATION

Writing at the beginning of the 21st century, it is impossible to ignore the phenomenon of globalization. An intense debate currently exists between proponents and opponents of what may be termed 'globalization studies'. The book enters the globalization debate through a number of its concerns. One of the central issues of contention in the controversy over globalization is that of historical evidence. In delineating the scope, nature, depth and breadth of change in the global economy this book contributes to this debate. Moreover, insofar as globalization is a process of historical change rather than a specific condition, the evidence here contributes to an assessment of this process. Second, in charting the evolution of the modern state, the book confronts a central issue in the globalization debate. We reveal the historical development of the modern state, and consequently challenge arguments that present essentialized portraits of the state.

Our analysis in Part 3 is informed by the evolving nature of globalization. We believe that the intensification of globalization since the early 1970s has changed the world political economy from an international to a global undertaking. While there are some who suggest that talk of globalization is overblown (Hirst and Thompson, 1996), we are of the view that the decreasing significance of time and space as barriers to human interaction is having a profound impact on the organization of production, the exchange of products and services, the circulation of finance, the gendered division of labour, the possibilities for development, the ecology of the planet, the transmission and power of ideas, the pursuit of security, the mobilization of political forces and forms of national and international governance. The spread of economic relations worldwide has had a significant impact on how people live their lives and how governance is practised. Our book explores these issues in further detail in the following chapters.

PART I
THEORETICAL PERSPECTIVES

Chapter 1

Theories of Global Political Economy

In its present form, the field of international political economy (IPE) or global political economy (GPE) is a relatively new undertaking at universities. This chapter introduces readers to three of its main theories. Chapter 2 gives readers an overview of the relationship of IPE to other fields, considers some of the methods used to study IPE and examines the future directions of GPE theory.

UNDERSTANDING THE GLOBAL POLITICAL ECONOMY

During 1996 and into 1997, a small number of investors and currency traders began to have doubts about whether Thailand's economy would be able to continue its record of remarkable growth. Fearing a reduction in economic prosperity and profit, some of these investors began to withdraw their money and investments. The outflow of money forced the Thai central bank to devalue its currency, the baht. This began a process which was later called the 1997 'Asian financial crisis'. By the time the crisis had run its course, several Asian countries experienced economic depression, the government of Indonesia was overthrown, countries previously labelled economic miracles, for example South Korea, were forced to seek loans from the International Monetary Fund (IMF) and the viability of the international financial system was called into question.

Although the 1997 Asian financial crisis was clearly a significant development in the global political economy, it was not immediately apparent what caused the events, what were its most significant aspects or what lessons might be drawn from the crisis to prevent a similar event from occurring. Indeed, a number of different stories are told about the crisis (see Table 1.1). One story, the liberal story, locates the causes of the crisis primarily in the financial policies followed by Asian states (McLeod and Garnaut, 1998). This view suggests that resources were directed to inefficient uses because of corrupt business practices and political influence over financial institutions. The term 'crony capitalism' was developed to capture this inappropriate model of political economy. The lesson to be drawn from the crisis is that financial markets will eventually punish economic activity which violates or ignores liberal economic principles. The solution is for developing countries to have more transparent financial practices and follow a more liberal economic model.

A second story stresses the significance of state power in creating and exploiting the crisis (Weiss, 1999). In this view, the problem arose because developing countries liberalized their economies prematurely and allowed large amounts of money to flow into and out of their countries too quickly. This undermined the

Table 1.1 Interpretations of the Asian financial crisis

	Liberal	State power	Critical
Causes	Crony capitalism, lack of transparency	Overrapid liberalization, reduced state capacity to regulate	Predatory liberalism, power of financial interests, systemic flaws
Key issue(s)	Corruption, lack of liberal economic practices	Clash of Anglo-American versus Asian models	Human suffering caused by financial collapse
Lessons	Increase transparency and good practice in developing countries	Limit financial speculation through state policies	Reform international financial system, defend national system

East Asian model of political economy and caused a crisis. This approach would stress how the US used the Asian crisis as an opportunity to force some states to restructure along lines that benefited American business. During the crisis, Asian states attempted to counter American initiatives at the IMF and to continue to resist the undermining of their particular form of capitalism (Higgott, 1998). The lessons from the crisis are that states need to be careful about liberalizing their economic activity and must pay attention to guarding their national interest.

A third story (critical) focuses on the role of US private business interests and the US government in creating the conditions for a financial collapse. It suggests that the US government pressured developing states into liberalizing their economies because this suited the interests of the US Treasury and leading financial firms on Wall Street (Wade and Veneroso, 1998). Once the crisis took place, the same interests pressed the IMF to demand that Asian economies restructure in a way that would open markets for US firms. This story also stresses the high degree of suffering caused by the financial collapse and the fact that its costs were unevenly distributed. For example, the collapse of the Indonesian economy pushed millions further into poverty, but left wealthy financial interests in developed countries relatively untouched. In this view, the international financial system facilitates the rapid movement of money between countries and contributes to the reoccurrence of financial crisis in many parts of the world (Walton, 2002). Action needs to be taken to curb financial speculation, such as a tax on large short-term foreign exchange transactions. States should also consider restricting the ability of investors to move their funds abroad rapidly.

This brief example of the Asian financial crisis demonstrates that the same event can be analysed in several different ways. Indeed, most major developments are interpreted through competing explanations. Facts do not exist independently of explanatory frameworks. Facts are pieces of information that are thought to correspond to reality and be true, but the way in which they are perceived and judged is influenced by theory. In order to make sense of the world and to enable us to take constructive action, humans develop theories to help determine which facts are most important and what significant relationships there are between different events. Theories are used for a variety of purposes:

▶ they can prioritize information and allow individuals to turn their attention to the most important issues
▶ they can be used to make predictions about the future so that action can be taken to prepare for upcoming events
▶ they can be used to plan action or mobilize support for particular action

Every person utilizes theory to run their life even if they do not engage in explicit theorizing. Actors in the global political economy and those studying it use a variety of theories for a variety of purposes. Some people are interested in prediction. For example, they would like to be able to predict what type of monetary system would lead to stable economic growth, or to predict the likelihood of war between democratic states. Others believe that prediction is nearly impossible because so many factors come together to influence events. These people are more likely to use theory in an attempt to understand the world rather than to predict what will happen next.

In this book, we use and describe a number of theories to guide us in understanding the world. The development of IPE is often presented as a debate between three contending schools of thought, paradigms or approaches. Some commentators refer to contending paradigms, others to different schools of thought and yet others to competing approaches. It does not really matter for our purposes whether they are seen as theories, paradigms, schools of thought or approaches. The central point is that three main contending perspectives have been used to explain developments in the global political economy. Although analysts distinguish between these three approaches, there is a wide variety of thought within each approach and much work in IPE draws on more than one of them. In addition, there are a number of other approaches, such as environmentalism, feminism and poststructuralism, which contribute to the study of IPE. These will be introduced later in the text. Let us begin by looking at the oldest approach – economic nationalism.

THE ECONOMIC NATIONALIST PERSPECTIVE

One school of thought brings together analysts who focus on the role of the state and the importance of power in shaping outcomes in the international political economy. These theories stress the importance of the interest of the nation or the state in understanding activity in international relations (IR). This grouping is variously termed 'mercantilist', 'neomercantilist', 'statist', 'state-based theory', 'power politics' or 'economic nationalist'. The equivalent in IR theory is realism. We use the term 'economic nationalism' to refer to this perspective because at the centre of such analyses is the protection of the national unit. The underlying economic argumentation may alter, for example, but the objective of economic intercourse remains the same.

The origin of this school of thought can be traced back to the emergence and expansion of the nation-state in Europe in the 15th century. Mercantilism was a doctrine of political economy that governed the actions of many states until the liberal revolution in Britain in the mid-19th century. Mercantilists believed that there was only a limited amount of wealth in the world and that each state must secure its interests by blocking the economic interests of other states. This is known as a 'zero-sum game'. One state's gain is another state's loss. From the 15th until the 19th centuries, European states strove to establish overseas empires that would be as

self-sufficient as possible. Trade between neighbouring colonies of rival empires was discouraged.

Two famous advocates of mercantilist theory were Alexander Hamilton ([1791]1991) and Fredrick List ([1885]1991). Hamilton was a founding father of the United States. Writing in the 1790s, he urged Americans to protect their manufacturers from foreign competition so that they could industrialize and increase their power. Almost a hundred years later, List argued that Germany should industrialize behind trade barriers so that it could catch up with the economic might of Great Britain. He believed that only the economically strong advocated free-trade policies because other states would lose out in the ensuing competition. While Great Britain led the Industrial Revolution in the early 1800s and opened up its borders to free trade, both Germany and the US followed more economic nationalist policies.

One central question for students of the contemporary global economy relates to the persistence of mercantilist thought. It could be assumed that an economic perspective based upon unrivalled state power is of limited relevance in a world characterized by globalization. While this may be correct, contemporary economic nationalist thought should not be dismissed as some atavistic throwback to an earlier era. It reflects, on the one hand, an acknowledgement that states remain at the centre of power within the global political economy and, on the other, that there is an intimate connection between power and wealth. Economic nationalist thinking, whether it is termed 'neomercantilism' or 'statism', remains important in both analysis and practice in the contemporary global economy. For example, states may protect strategic industries against foreign rivals or attempt to export more than they import for long periods of time. Japan has been accused of being a mercantilist state because in comparison with other advanced industrialized countries its economy is relatively closed. Even states that are generally seen to follow liberal policies, such as the US, will pursue economic nationalist policies in particular sectors. For example, the US uses defence spending to support its commercial aerospace industry.

Key actors

Economic nationalist or mercantilist theories view the state as the main actor in the global political economy.

A major assumption of economic nationalists is the primacy of the political over other aspects of social life. Statist writers focus on the group (the state or nation) rather than the individual. Economic nationalist thought begins from two major assumptions. The first is that the inter-state system is anarchical and it is therefore the duty of each state to protect its own interests. At the core of the various historical versions of economic nationalism is the belief that an economic community persists and acts for the good of all its members. The second assumption concerns the primacy of the state in political life. As the state is the central instrument through which people can fulfil their goals, it follows that the state remains the preeminent actor in the domestic and international domains. Economic policy should be used to build a more powerful state.

From this perspective, the state is prior to the market and market relations are shaped by political power. Economic nationalist thought is both descriptive and predictive. Descriptive economic nationalists maintain that production, consumption, exchange and investment are all governed by political power. Markets are not 'natural'; they can only exist within a social context. For mercantilists, political needs and purposes are seen largely as being achieved through the form of the state. It remains at the core of social life. But economic nationalists move beyond description and also provide policy advice. Given their analysis of the dynamics of political economy, such advice is geared towards supporting and maintaining state power.

Economic nationalists recognize the importance of market-based actors such as firms, but subordinate their importance to that of the state. Within this perspective, the economic power of transnational corporations (TNCs) is acknowledged, but the overall power of such firms remains limited. In the end, firms are subject to the dictates of states. Insofar as firms have become important economic actors, this is only because states have abandoned regulation or lessened controls on the movement of capital. When firms encounter economic or political trouble, they quickly turn to their home states for protection.

Key dynamics

From an economic nationalist perspective, international political economy is constituted through the actions of rational states. If international relations are conceived as a struggle for power, international political economy is a struggle for power *and* wealth. The determination of a state's fate resides in its ability to ensure that its citizens reap advantages from international production and exchange. Market relations are important indicators of power and wealth but the market is governed by the activities of states. Economic activity is subordinate to political goals and objectives. Furthermore, economic actors are subject to political authority. The consequence of the salience of the state is that international economic relations are international political relations. The global economy in this view is subordinate to the international political system.

IPE scholars working in this perspective argue that the nature of the global economy reflects the interests of the most powerful states. For example, Krasner (1976) has suggested that systems of free trade are most likely when a single power dominates the international system. This dominant, or hegemonic, power is needed to provide leadership and absorb the short-term costs of maintaining a free-trade regime. Analysts such as Gilpin (1981) have argued that changes in the distribution of power between states increase the chances of conflict in the international system. Because of this view, considerable time can be devoted to contemplating the rise and fall of great powers (Gilpin, 1987; Kennedy, 1987).

In the heated debate over globalization, both defensive and sceptical economic nationalist perspectives can be heard. The defensive posture arises from a fear that globalization may prevent state actors from fulfilling their goals. This is, of course, merely the continuation of the long-held suspicion of economic exchange held by economic nationalist thinkers. Unlike proponents of free trade, economic nationalists believe that the gains from trade are unequally distributed and favour those with greater economic and political power. Thus, defensive economic nationalists can recognize globalization as a threat and seek to counter its impacts. On the other hand, sceptical economic nationalists reject many of the current liberal arguments about globalization. They contend that globalization is largely a myth and that the power of the state remains undiminished. Since economic actors are subordinate to political power, these analysts argue that the policy environment conducive to globalization has been created by states. It therefore follows that states can alter this environment by changing their policies. Moreover, it can be claimed that since states remain powerful actors and the only legitimate centres of authority in the modern world, nothing significant has occurred in the global political economy.

Conflict and cooperation

Within IR theory, realism, with its focus on the primacy of the state, the anarchical nature of international relations and the inevitability of conflict, provides the foundation for economic nationalist thought. If realism is the perspective in international politics, economic nationalism is its equivalent doctrine in political economy. Both share a commitment to the state and to the role of power in social life. Power-based theories such as economic nationalism and realism view the world as anarchic – lacking any central authority. Relations between states are thus characterized by unending conflict and the pursuit of power.

International economic relations are therefore perceived as a zero-sum game where the gain of one party necessitates a loss for another party. The system's structure is perceived in conflictual terms. While economic nationalists believe that market relations can be positive, they think that such activity can also be negative. Since participating in markets is potentially negative, economic nationalists argue in favour of state control of key economic activities or for state assistance to central economic sectors. The continued salience of economic nationalist perspectives is easily visible today in production, consumption, trade and investment. In terms of production, economic nationalist sentiment is visible in arguments concerning the continued production of some good or service within particular national borders. This can be seen in terms of security concerns; that is, a state should not be reliant on the import of a specific good, because in times of conflict, this good may become unavailable. Some countries, such as France, protect their agricultural sector, while the US defends defence technology. It can also be seen in terms of the preservation of the cultural values of the nation. For example, many economic nationalists believe that it is vital to maintain the production of certain cultural products, such as films and music, within national borders. In relation to consumption, economic nationalist arguments have been made against cultural imperialism, that is, in favour of the view that the import of some products pollutes the nation through the introduction of foreign values. Whereas a liberal would argue that the sovereignty of the consumer is paramount, economic nationalists maintain that the values of the nation are more important. From the foregoing, it is easy to see how, in the sphere of exchange, economic nationalists support the protection of domestic industries. Furthermore, economic nationalist thought is behind arguments that seek to restrict foreign investment, and supports the 'rights' of local investors over foreigners.

Economic nationalism today

Although the dominant approach to global political economy as espoused by the leading international institutions and economic theorists is liberalism, economic nationalism continues to inform thinking and action. Countries continue to protect their markets from foreign competition even though they have committed themselves to free trade. Although protectionism has been reduced as countries have lowered tariffs, many other mechanisms are used to keep out foreign products. Chapter 6 reviews how states have used a variety of reasons to restrict trade, for example health and safety, environmental, cultural, employment, infant industry. Trade in services such as education and healthcare is a particularly sensitive subject, with many states unwilling to open up to foreign competition.

States have actively involved themselves in supporting particular industries, contrary to liberal theory. Many developing countries have relied on their states to boost economic activity, shield domestic industries from competition, and direct finance to selected industries. China has enjoyed remarkable economic growth, but has imposed strict conditions on foreign investment, intervened to make sure its currency is relatively cheap and guided finance into particular activities through five-year plans. While benefiting from a generally liberal and open economic system, China has engaged in economic nationalist policies in pursuit of development.

Concerns about economic nationalism increase in times of economic downturn. Politicians and the public may wish to increase discrimination against foreign economies and firms when growth slows in the belief that steps should be taken to support national economies. Such an approach risks retaliation and the closing of world markets, which damages the interest of all

---

Box 1.1 Profile: Susan Strange – unorthodox realist

Susan Strange (2002) admitted that she never meant to become a professor, but ended up in the role after stints in journalism (with the *Observer* and *The Economist*) and working at Chatham House, a British foreign affairs research institute. She eventually became a professor at the London School of Economics and Warwick University.

Strange's theoretical approach is difficult to characterize neatly (Tooze and May, 2002). It contains a strong element of power politics or economic nationalism because it focuses on the exercise of power and pays considerable attention to key state policies in structuring the global economy. Strange takes a realist approach by advising students to focus on the role of interests and to constantly ask the question 'Who benefits?' Yet, her work is also unorthodox because she urges observers to take account of the role of markets, corporations and technological innovations in changing the environment in which the state operates. In a series of exchanges with US IPE scholars, Strange continually went against the mainstream by variously arguing that the study of regimes was faddish and mistaken (1982), that US hegemony was not declining in the 1980s (1987) and that globalization was transforming the nature of state authority (1996).

Strange viewed IPE as a method of understanding the world that focused on the relationship between markets and authority. She argued that IPE should be an interdisciplinary area that brought together IR and international economics. Her broad approach is set out in a 1988 textbook called *States and Markets*, which argues that in addition to relational power (A forces B to do A's will), power resides in structures. Structural power is the ability to shape the rules of the game in a particular area. Those who create the operating framework for everyone's activities exercise power by eliminating some possibilities and making some outcomes more likely than others. Strange maintained that there were four key structures of power (security, production, finance, knowledge) and numerous secondary structures (transport, trade, energy, welfare). Strange reasoned that since the US exercised considerable structural power in the key structures, talk of decline was mistaken.

In the 1990s, Strange increasingly turned her attention to non-state actors. A major collaboration with a business school professor (Stopford and Strange, 1991) argued that traditional notions of diplomacy being an inter-state practice had to be expanded to include state–firm and firm–firm interactions. In a following book, Strange (1996) identified other actors such as business associations, bureaucrats and even mafias that were operating transnationally and undermining the authority of states. Most of Strange's empirical work was in the area of finance and credit. She argued that the creation and control of credit was a significant source of power in the global economy. True to her realist roots, she traced the liberalization and globalization of finance to particular decisions or non-decisions of the most powerful states. Finance was globalized because it suited the interests of the most powerful states (principally the US and the UK). However, Strange also worried that the failure of states to exercise proper regulatory control over financial flows was turning the system into a form of 'casino capitalism' (1986). Her fear was that a widespread financial collapse would lead to a closing of the global economy (1998).

Strange played a prominent role in founding and supporting the study of IPE as an interdisciplinary field in Britain. Her pioneering studies in the field of finance inspired a new generation to examine the power relations flowing around credit issues. Strange's insistence that IPE be an open field of intellectual enquiry influenced the development of the field in Britain by bringing in work from a number of different disciplines. Her stinging criticism of US intellectual trends provided room for British scholars and students to ask different types of questions and use different methodologies from their US counterparts.

---

states because it reduces the possibility of growth through trade. Protectionist policies of the 1930s are often blamed for worsening the Great Depression and this lesson is used against those advocating economic nationalist policies.

Visually, the economic nationalist approach can be represented by a game of marbles (Figure 1.1). The marbles are states, with different attributes, varying in their design, size, strength and beauty. They crash into each other in a competition to determine a winner.

Figure 1.1 Economic nationalism as marbles

THE LIBERAL PERSPECTIVE

In contrast to the economic nationalist theories, liberals focus either on the individual or on a wide range of actors from the state to the corporation to interest groups. They do not see the state as a unitary actor, but as influenced by numerous factors. Rather than stress the inevitability of conflict, liberals search out the conditions for cooperation. They tend to play down the role of force and coercion in human affairs and emphasize the ability of individuals to choose between attractive courses of action or negotiate their differences. Liberals see the world system as one of interdependence rather than anarchy. States and peoples can cooperate for mutual benefit in the liberal view. Rather than a zero-sum game where one's gains are the other's losses, liberals see a positive-sum game where the pie grows bigger and everyone gains. Box 1.2 examines the debate over relative verses absolute gains.

Liberal theories of political economy emerged in 18th- and 19th-century Britain alongside the Industrial Revolution. They offered a critique of economic nationalist thought by arguing that protectionism and restriction of economic activity were actually impoverishing states. Scottish moral philosopher Adam Smith ([1776]1983) advocated freeing up commerce and creating larger national and international markets as a method of generating wealth for everyone. Englishman David Ricardo ([1817]1992) introduced the revolutionary theory of comparative advantage, which demonstrated that all nations can benefit from free trade even if they are not as competitive as other states.

Today's global economy is governed largely according to liberal principles. The trade regime is based upon

---

Box 1.2 Relative versus absolute gains

In many ways, disagreements between economic nationalists and liberals can be traced back to differences over relative and absolute gains. Relative gains refer to one actor doing better or worse compared with another actor. Absolute gains refer to whether an actor is better off compared with a previous point in time. Economic nationalists and their international relations cousins (realists) argue that since states are in competition with each other, their primary concern is how a state performs relative to its rivals. Does a particular arrangement increase or decrease the gap between states? In contrast, liberals believe that states are rational and will support measures that will increase their absolute wealth by the greatest amount.

As an example, imagine that the US and China were presented with two economic agreements that would govern their relationship for 20 years. Under agreement A, which involves carefully managing trade between the two countries, the US will grow at an annual rate of 2 per cent and China will grow at an annual rate of 2 per cent. Under agreement B, which involves a broad free-trade deal, the US will grow at an annual rate of 5 per cent and China will grow at an annual rate of 10 per cent.

An economic nationalist would opt for agreement A because it delivers similar benefits to both countries, whereas agreement B causes China to grow much faster than the US. Liberals would disagree, arguing that the US should sign agreement B because it would increase growth by 5 per cent each year rather than the meagre 2 per cent of agreement A. The free-trade arrangement will make the US richer and more prosperous than the managed trade agreement. A focus on relative gains would lead policy makers to prefer agreement A, while a focus on absolute gains would lead policy makers to choose agreement B. Which do you think the US should sign?

the goal of free trade, money flows into and out of most countries without great difficulty and all forms of economic activity are increasingly liberalized. However, there is a wide variety of liberal thought. It ranges from those who see the state fading away in an emerging borderless world dominated by corporations (Ohmae, 1990) to liberal institutionalists (Keohane and Nye, 1977), who stress the continuing importance of the state, but see it enmeshed in webs of interdependence and international organization. The book by Landes (1998), mentioned in Chapter 3, takes a particular type of liberal approach. It argues that those with liberal values have been most successful in the global economy and implies that these values were freely chosen by people in Europe and the West. However, Landes parts ways with those liberals who argue that individual choice is more significant than cultural institutions.

Key actors

Within the liberal perspective there are a number of key actors. For liberals, the starting point of analysis is the individual. Liberal economic theory, of which neoclassical economic theory is a variant, begins from the analysis of individual wants and preferences and constructs a powerful explanatory framework on this basis. In the context of analysis of the global economy, liberal theorists focus on the behaviour of individuals, firms and states. In contrast to economic nationalism, the key economic actor is the individual rather than the state. Individuals in pursuit of self-interest will maximize the benefits of economic exchange for society. Within liberal theory the firm also plays an important role. Unlike mercantilists who view the firm with a degree of suspicion, liberals see the firm as a source of economic wealth. The state is viewed with hostility by many liberals since it brings politics into the realm of economics. Liberals believe that if individuals are left freely to engage in production, exchange and consumption, all will benefit and that the insertion of state control distorts benefits and adds costs to participants in the market. People engaged in free economic exchange pursuing their own interests create a society-wide harmony of interest. From a liberal perspective the transnational corporation (TNC) is a positive force. TNCs bring advantages to both home and host countries. From the perspective of the home country, the TNC represents an optimal mix of technology, managerial skill and capital. For host countries, TNCs

boost their economies through the transfer of capital, technology and access to markets.

Key dynamics

For liberal theorists the market lies at the centre of economic life. Economic progress results from the interaction of diverse individuals pursuing their own ends. While liberals acknowledge that market relations are not always optimal, they tend to argue that intervention in the market is most likely to produce suboptimal outcomes. There is, of course, a broad spectrum of liberal thought. It ranges from John Maynard Keynes (1936), whose economic theories laid the foundation for interventionist welfare governments in the immediate postwar period, to Friedrich Hayek (1944), whose free-market philosophy guided the neoliberal revolution of the 1980s. They both subscribe to a belief in the positive role of markets and the ability of the market to lead to prosperity. However, they differ over the importance of market imperfections and the policies that ought to be implemented to deal with market failure.

For liberal theorists, IPE is constituted by a search for wealth. On the whole, open markets will enhance growth and wealth, and firms will disseminate material wealth across the globe. Economic failure in this perspective is often the result of government intervention. Many liberal theorists have been at the forefront of the debate on globalization. For what can be termed 'hyper-liberals', globalization is not only a reality (indeed, an inevitability), it is a positive force for good. Globalization breaks down artificial (for which read political) barriers and by unleashing the force of production, it can contribute to enhanced happiness for humankind. Thus, hyper-liberals welcome globalization. Keynesian-influenced liberals or those of a reformist stance perceive certain problems with the unfettered operation of the free market and are, therefore, sensitive to some unwanted consequences of globalization. They support globalization but emphasize the need for attention to market reform.

Conflict and cooperation

Liberal theorists view international relations and the international political economy as essentially cooperative. Indeed, they believe that market relations will lead to positive outcomes for all. In other words, economic relations are positive sum. A standard liberal theory that exemplifies this belief is the theory of comparative advantage, which shows that even in a situation where one country enjoys a superiority in the production of all goods and services over a second country, trade between the two countries will benefit both countries. This is explained in more detail in Chapters 4 and 6.

One persistent liberal belief has been that economic nationalist policies lead to conflict. Unlike Marxist writers who denounce the growth of global capitalism as a cause of war, liberal theorists view increased international interaction as a source of prosperity and peace. The liberal belief in the connection between protectionist policies and conflict and the reverse argument, namely that capitalism favours peace, are central to liberal critiques of the international economic order. The German philosopher Immanuel Kant ([1795]1991) foresaw an era of perpetual peace when systems of free trade, a coalition of republican states and the fear of destructive warfare would bring about an era of calm and prosperity. Towards the end of the First World War, US president Woodrow Wilson ([1918]1986) advocated liberal principles of free trade, self-determination and the use of international organizations to settle disputes between states.

The framers of international economic institutions after the Second World War were supporters of this view. It was argued that the war had its origins in the economic nationalist policies of the 1930s. As a consequence of the Great Depression, governments resorted to a series of protectionist measures that eroded confidence in international cooperation. As a result of economic nationalist policies, the basis of collective security was shattered and an atmosphere conducive to dictators was created. The shift from economic competition to military conflict was, in this view, inevitable. Hence, there was the need after the war to design institutions to foster international economic cooperation and to include within those institutions mechanisms to prevent states from resorting to competitively nationalist policies.

Within the study of IR, liberal theories of world politics and of political economy share assumptions concerning the pluralist nature of the international system and the feasibility of cooperation. Theories of interdependence developed in the 1960s to explain the connection between increased economic exchange and interconnectedness and the long peace among Western nations after 1945. They echo classical liberal political economy. These theories emphasized the economic and political benefits of economic interchange. Interdependence was proffered as both a description of events and a prescription for the solution of conflict.

In the 1980s and 90s, liberals continued to argue that international cooperation was both possible and desirable. In contrast to economic nationalists or realists, liberals argued that international agreements or regimes would maintain international economic order even if hegemonic states declined (Keohane, 1984). With the end of the Cold War and the rapid spread of liberal economic models to many states in the 1990s, it appeared that the liberal faith in cooperation and progress was justified. Some even went so far as to claim that history had ended because the liberal democratic model had triumphed over other forms of social organization (Fukuyama, 1992).

Liberalism today

Liberal neoclassical economics, which stresses the importance of rational decision makers in free markets, dominates the field of economics. International institutions such as the World Trade Organization (WTO) are founded on liberal principles of free trade, while the IMF and the World Bank preach liberal prescriptions to those seeking development funds or loans to see them through financial crises. TNCs urge state leaders to open their markets to the free flow of investment and many government officials eagerly comply. Indeed, many states have bound themselves to an ever more liberal economy through participation in international organizations and international economic agreements such as regional or bilateral free-trade agreements. The market continues to expand by bringing in more and more countries as participants (such as China) and by encompassing a wider range of activities such as services (healthcare, education, childcare, housework).

Despite the dominance of liberalism, there are challenges to liberal theory and practice from within and without. Within liberalism, the 2008 financial crisis reopened the debate among liberals about regulation and the role of government in economic crises. Does self-regulation of financial firms lead to economic efficiency or corruption and financial collapse? Should governments bail out banks with taxpayers' money or

Box 1.3 Profile: Robert Keohane – liberal institutionalist

Robert Keohane was born into an academic family and began a US teaching career after graduating from Harvard in 1966 (Keohane, 1989a). His academic career has taken him to Stanford, Brandeis, Harvard, Duke and Princeton universities. His research has had a major role in influencing the study of IPE and IR in the US and beyond.

Keohane is a central figure in what has become known as the liberal institutionalist approach to IPE and world politics (1989b). This approach suggests that institutions or sets of rules and norms can have a significant effect upon state behaviour if they have mutual interests. Institutions include formal international organizations, international regimes or conventions and customs. Liberal institutionalism was developed as a critique of realist / power politics / economic nationalist approaches to IR and IPE. The emphasis is on how institutions can help states overcome barriers to cooperation. Although Keohane himself prefers to be known simply as an institutionalist (2002, p. 3), the adjective 'liberal' is still useful because it refers to some of the liberal attributes that underlie his approach. These include a focus on the individual and a belief that properly designed international institutions can go some way to creating a more humane global system.

Keohane's first major work was written with Joseph Nye and it argued that there were certain times and issue areas when the assumptions of realist or power politics approaches did not hold sway (Keohane and Nye, 1977). They labelled these situations as 'complex interdependence' and suggested that under certain circumstances states could use international institutions to bolster cooperation. They also argued that in such situations cross-border links between officials could lead to outcomes different from those that power politics approaches would have predicted.

In 1984 Keohane published *After Hegemony*. It sought to explain why, contrary to realist assumptions, states continued to cooperate and participate in international agreements even after the major power that sponsored the agreements entered a period of relative decline. This was a significant issue because many analysts were worried about the decline of US power relative to that of other states and feared that this would make the international political economy increasingly unstable. Keohane argued that the benefits of arrangements in issue areas (such as money, oil or trade) or regimes continued independent of the rise or decline of the power of particular states. Regimes exist because they facilitate negotiations between states and allow states to overcome barriers to collective action such as uncertainty. Keohane's work helped to spark increasing attention to the issue of regime creation and maintenance. Indeed, regime theory became a mainstay of US IPE scholarship.

Another important aspect of *After Hegemony* was Keohane's use of economic theory to explain the activity of states. Drawing inspiration from economic theories that claimed to explain the activity of corporations, Keohane analysed state behaviour in terms of market failure, transaction costs and uncertainty. Market failure refers to a situation where transactions do not take place because the market is arranged in such a way as to make otherwise rational activity irrational. In the case of IPE, states might not agree to cooperate because they are unsure of the motives of other states. Regimes help to resolve this market failure by providing information about other states' behaviour and an element of predictability in inter-state interactions. States cooperated in international regimes because these regimes solved particular problems such as lack of information and uncertainty about other states' intentions and behaviour. Keohane's use of economic models and theories of rational choice coincided and blended well with the importation of economic models in other areas of US political science. The success of his book and persuasiveness of his argument helped to bolster rational choice methodology in US IPE.

Keohane's work has been important in the field of US IPE because it has advanced understanding of how states are able to cooperate through international regimes.

should they be allowed to go bankrupt? How should governments respond to financial and economic crises? Is government's role to balance budgets or spend to jump-start economic growth? What should governments do if economic growth stalls?

There are also challenges to liberalism from those who do not accept its claims. States may be happy to export into an open liberal market, but reluctant to expose their own industry to competition, as we will see in the chapters on international trade and

Figure 1.2 Liberalism as a cobweb

development. Harmed by rapid capital flows, other states may seek to intervene in the financial markets to slow the movement of money between countries or restrict the conditions under which investment takes place. Other groups may challenge liberalism because they advocate different agendas, such as labour rights (Chapter 9), gender equity (Chapter 10) or environmentalism (Chapter 12). A common criticism is that the liberal view underestimates the significance of powerful firms and states and their ability to distort and manipulate markets.

A visual representation of liberal IPE theory is the cobweb (Figure 1.2), where a giant web of interdependence connects actors such as states, corporations and people in a complex set of relations.

THE CRITICAL PERSPECTIVE

Marxist theory emerged in the 19th century in reaction to liberal thought. Marxism's critical approach to liberalism can be seen in a number of other bodies of thought that move away from the individual and states to consider other units of analysis. They are sometimes called 'critical theories' because they question the way the world is organized and seek to change the world. They are sometimes labelled as 'radical' because they challenge established forms of organization. The three most common variants of critical thought in IPE are

Marxist, feminist and environmentalist theories. Poststructuralist and cultural political economy approaches have also recently been applied to IPE. This chapter concentrates on Marxist theories, while feminist theories will be highlighted in Chapter 10, environmental theories in Chapter 12 and poststructuralist theories in Chapter 13.

Marxist theories focus on class and the interests of workers rather than state interests. Writing during the English Industrial Revolution, Karl Marx took issue with the idea of a harmony of interests that the liberals advocated. Marx and his co-author, Engels, discerned an ongoing conflict between workers and capitalists that would only be resolved when the workers seized power (Marx and Engels, [1848]1977). Feminists also see a world of exploitation but their theories look at gender relations between women and men. They seek to uncover how our ideas about what men and women are supposed to be shape the ways in which society is organized. Mary Wollstonecraft ([1792]1992), an 18th-century early feminist writer, criticized male liberal theorists for ignoring the role and interests of women in their political theories. Green theories have taken the environment and the planet as the objects to be highlighted. They examine how people shape and are shaped by the environment. Neo-Gramscian theories, which evolved out of Italian Marxism, stress the role of transnational classes and ideology in their efforts to understand the global economy. We use the term 'critical' as a label for these theories because they are united by a critical attitude to prevailing social arrangements. Here, we focus on Marxism since it is the oldest of the theories grouped under the critical perspectives heading.

These critical theories stress the nature of oppression within and across societies and the struggle for justice waged by or on behalf of workers, women and the environment. Frank's (1998) study, *ReOrient: Global Economy in the Asian Age*, is close to this form of analysis because he stresses European exploitation of others' resources in the 'rise of the West'. However, he differs from traditional Marxists who have seen Western civilization as being at the forefront of human development because it was the birthplace of capitalism. Frank disputes both the claim that capitalism originated in Europe and that European developments are more significant to world history than developments in Asia.

Key actors

Marxist writers begin with a focus on class as the main 'actor' in the global political economy. They reject the individualism of liberal theory and embrace the collectivist approach of economic nationalist perspectives. However, Marxist theory rejects statism and focuses instead on the significance of class. This focus arises from the Marxist account of capitalist relations, which are predicated on exploitation. The Marxist concept of class has been open to various interpretations and critiques. We define class simply as arising from one's position in the structure of production. Marx defined class in relation to the structure of production, which creates owners of the means of production (the bourgeoisie) and the labourers who sell their labour power to the bourgeoisie (the workers).

Within Marxist writing the firm is an instrument of exploitation. TNCs contribute to the exploitation and oppression of the working class. The centralization and concentration of capital visible in the form of TNCs is a key feature of imperialism, whereby dominance is expressed in the global political economy. In this perspective, the state is the representative of class interests rather than the expression of the harmony of communal interests posited by economic nationalists.

Key dynamics

Dominance and exploitation among and within societies provide the main dynamic for Marxist theories of IPE. Unlike liberals, Marxists view market relations as inherently exploitative. Under capitalism, workers are denied a fair remuneration because capitalists pay workers less than their labour is worth. Marxists view international economic relations as inherently unstable and conflictual because of three tendencies of capitalism:

1 The tendency for the rate of profit to fall sees capitalists engaged in fierce competition with each other, which tends to drive down workers' wages.
2 Capitalism leads to uneven development as some centres increase their wealth and growth at the expense of others. Uneven development sows the seeds of conflict between countries.

3 Marxists argue that capitalism leads to overproduction or underconsumption, giving rise to fluctuations in the business cycle and undermining social stability.

A revision of Marxist thought called 'dependency theory' has been used to explain the persisting poverty of many states. Dependency theory suggests that poor countries faced immense obstacles to development because they were vulnerable to economic exploitation from developed states (Dos Santos, 1970). The links between the rich and the poor were thought to make the poor poorer and the rich richer. Underdevelopment of some parts of the world was caused by development in other parts of the world. This school of thought informed developing countries' attempts to create a New International Economic Order (NIEO) in the 1970s (Cox, 1979). This approach was undermined in the 1980s as many developing states adopted liberal economic policies in the wake of the debt crisis.

Radical theorists have tended, for a variety of reasons, to oppose globalization. It has been argued, for example, that globalization is a myth or merely imperialism in modern clothes. According to this argument, globalization represents an ideological intervention into political economy. It ostensibly describes changes in the world but, in reality, it is a set of prescriptions in support of free markets and an instrument to increase the power of capital over labour, the West over other states, and an instrument designed to further the interests of the leading capitalist power, the US. In this sense, globalization has to be resisted since it too maintains and increases exploitative relations. At the heart of the radical argument is the view that globalization is not distinctive, that is, discussion of globalization is merely the contemporary version of imperialism. To discuss political economy in terms of globalization may mask real power relations.

In the 1980s and 90s, Marxist IPE was reinvigorated by the work of scholars drawing inspiration from Antonio Gramsci. Writers such as Robert Cox and Timothy Sinclair (1996) and Stephen Gill (1993) focused on the role of social forces and ideology in liberalizing and globalizing economic relations. They argued that globalization based on neoclassical liberal economic principles was a political project that transformed national states into instruments of global liberalization and economic management. Part of this project involved convincing people that neoliberal policies were actually in their best interest. In this view, the hegemony of a particular world order requires an ideological dominance that secures the broad consent of those ruled in an unequal and unjust manner.

Conflict and cooperation

Critical writers tend to perceive international economic relations as a zero-sum game. The structure of global capitalism is fundamentally conflictual. Two forms of conflict are prevalent in the global economy. Within states, capitalists and workers have competing interests and the state is the scene of a class struggle as the workers and bourgeoisie clash. According to Marxists, this conflict is objective and arises from the law of motion of capital. In the international arena, the clash between workers and capitalists is often obscured by nationalism and the intervention of the state. Through the mechanism of imperialism, dominant states oppress weaker ones and this sets up an international struggle between imperialists and their victims.

International conflict is inevitable because of the drive for profit. Different capitalists seek the protection of their state and this leads to war. Marxist theories of imperialism have, in different ways, accounted for the tendency of capitalist states to go to war. Lenin's theory of imperialism, the most well known of these theories, combined two different explanations of capitalist development. One part of his theory focused on underconsumption in domestic markets. Because of underconsumption, capitalists were compelled into overseas adventures since they could not maintain their rates of profit on the basis of domestic demand. Another part of his theory focused on the growth of finance capital and the merger between finance and industrial capital to form monopoly capital that sought to gain profit through overseas lending. He argued that conflict and war are a necessary end result of this competition.

At the turn of the 21st century, conflict between social forces was also seen to take place on a global scale. Elites attempting to constitutionalize neoliberal principles in institutions such as the WTO and the IMF met with opposition from social movements trying to safeguard environmental regulation, raise labour standards, improve gender equity and lobby for economic justice (O'Brien et al., 2000). Critical analysts depict a global conflict that takes place within, above and across states (Gill, 2003).

Critical theory today

With the demise of the Soviet Union and communism, Marxist states ceased to exist. The critical perspective lives on in a number of areas, however. As a form of analysis critical of capitalism's inequalities and recurring crises, Marxism continues to have adherents. Although Russia and China eventually embraced a capitalist model, many of the problems of capitalism have not been resolved. The financial crisis and ongoing austerity since 2008 have led to renewed interest in Marxist critiques of capitalism, such as Harvey's (2011) *The Enigma of Capital*. In particular, the political power of financial capital is a subject of vigorous debate, as financial institutions have prospered in the face of the crisis, while populations have borne the brunt of austerity. To give just one example, many Wall Street bankers continued to receive financial bonuses on top of their salary, while the wealth of the average American family declined by 40 per cent between 2007 and 2010 (Lee, 2012).

Other groups that also question the power imbalances and inequality in the global economy often draw on some version of critical approaches. For example, development groups struggling against rules of trade or finance that disadvantage poor countries highlight the rigged nature of the game. Social movements organizing against the lack of education and employment opportunities for girls can draw on a feminist analysis. Environmentalists concerned about the devastating effects of economic growth and runaway consumption put the health of the planet ahead of individuals or the state. We will return to these variants later in the book.

A visual representation of critical IPE theory is the layer cake (Figure 1.3), where groups are stacked in layers across the global political economy with some classes (or genders, or races or species) on the top and others on the bottom.

Figure 1.3 **Critical theory as a layer cake**

Box 1.4 Profile: Robert Cox – historical materialist

For Canadian-born Robert Cox, academic life was a second career after spending 25 years in the International Labour Organization (ILO). At the ILO, Cox served as a staff officer to the director general, chief of the programme and planning division, and as director of the International Institute for Labour Studies. After leaving the ILO, Cox took a teaching position at Columbia University in New York before settling at Toronto's York University in 1977.

Cox describes his approach to IPE and IR as historical materialist (2002a, pp. 27–9). The historical part involves recognizing that each historical era has a particular sensibility and set of institutions and understandings. This contrasts with approaches claiming that there are universal laws of human behaviour which apply across time. The materialist part places the organization of production and the social relations around production at the centre of analysis. In other words, class and class conflict play an important part in understanding political economy. Central to Cox's work has been the idea that 'production generates the capacity to exercise power, but power determines the manner in which production takes place' (1987, p. 1). He takes a particular approach to historical materialism, which mixes theoretical insights from Marx with those of scholars such as Vico, Sorel, Weber, Gramsci and Polanyi. The result is that many liberals and economic nationalists label Cox a Marxist, while many Marxists argue that he has deviated from the Marxist path (Schechter, 2002).

As the title of a collection of Cox's essays indicates, his primary interest has been *Approaches to World Order* (1996). Cox's experience at the ILO and his study of international organizations prompted him to think about the nature of power and dominance in the global economy. Cox (1983) theorized that powerful states exercise a form of hegemony that goes far beyond military strength. Hegemonic states, such as Britain in the 19th century or the US in the 20th century, drew their power from a particular form of production and social relations. Hegemony requires dominance in the economic, political, social and ideological realms. A hegemonic power is able to convince others that their interests are the same as those of the dominant power. As a result, hegemonic states try to express their interests as universal norms and use international organizations to influence other states.

Cox (1986) also argued that it was a mistake to focus on the state and ignore the role of social forces. Social forces are groups of people who occupy a particular place in the global economy by virtue of their role in the organization of production. Some social forces, such as the people who own or work in an internationally competitive industry, advocate free trade, while other social forces will oppose free trade as a threat to their interests.

In the theoretical realm, Cox (1986) was significant for highlighting the differences between critical theory and problem-solving theory. Problem-solving theory looks at the world as it is and concentrates on how issues can be addressed in the existing system. Critical theory stands back from the existing order and asks how that order came about and under what conditions it could be changed to a different form of order. Critical theorists seek to contribute to a better social order, thus they embrace emancipatory strategies. Problem-solving theory is about managing the system and critical theory is about changing the system. Most radical analyses that call for major changes in the global political economy fit into this critical category.

Cox's most significant impact in the study of IPE has been to raise critical questions about the system of international order and to contemplate how one might achieve a more egalitarian and sustainable system. This has led him to disagree with the normative and practical implications of economic liberalism, the fatality of economic nationalism and the dogma of fundamentalist Marxism.

CONTENDING PERSPECTIVES: A SUMMARY

The question arises as to why there are so many theories and what the relationship is between various theories. There are several reasons for the existence of multiple theories. According to Cox (1986, p. 207): 'Theory is always *for* someone and *for* some purpose.' Each theory has a different goal in mind. For example, economic nationalist theories are concerned with the security of the state, liberal theories with building wealth or cooperation and critical theories with pursuing economic, gender or environmental equity. While they are all trying to understand the world, they are looking at different aspects of human existence. A second and related reason is that a particular theory usually advances the causes or interests of a particular group. Richer, more satisfied people and states tend to favour liberal theories that do not threaten their interests, while those disadvantaged by the system are more likely to espouse critical theories. A third explanation is that it is impossible to prove a theory right or wrong. Evidence is often disputed and interpreted in different ways. Moreover, unlike the laws of nature, people are able to reflect upon their behaviour and change their form of organization and interaction. People may act according to mercantilist theories in some eras or situations and along liberal principles in others.

Table 1.2 presents a summary of the perspectives. In the discussion so far, our intention has been to highlight the existence of various interpretations. But what is the relationship between various theories? Are they in conflict or can they be made compatible? At their core, theories about IPE are incompatible because they have different basic assumptions about the units of analysis, the nature of the system and the motivation of actors. Yet, each theory can point to some evidence to support its existence and each seems to be useful in explaining some aspect of the global political economy. Some theorists (Strange, 1988) have suggested that people take an eclectic approach to theory – picking and choosing as they wish. This can have some advantages, but risks incoherence as one jumps from perspective to perspective. Readers should consider some systemized form of integration, where various theories may be used under particular circumstances or in a hierarchy. For example, one could have a general power politics approach while conceding that the system is also characterized by class and gender exploitation and that there are times when cooperation can be more beneficial than conflict. Alternatively, some theories may be more applicable in selected time periods.

IPE brings together knowledge from a number of fields and disciplines to increase our understanding of

Table 1.2 Comparing the perspectives

Aspect	Economic nationalist	Liberal	Critical
Historical origins	15th century	19th century	19th century
Major figures	Hamilton, List, Krasner, Gilpin, Strange	Smith, Ricardo, Kant, Wilson, Keynes, Hayek, Keohane, Nye	Marx, Lenin, Frank, Cox
Variants	Mercantilism, realism	Free trade, interdependence	Marxism, feminism, environmentalism
Human nature	Aggressive	Cooperative	Malleable
Units	States	Firms, states, NGOs, IGOs, individuals	Class, gender, planet, global capitalism
View of the state	Unitary actor	Pluralist state: diverse interest	Representative of class interest groups
View of TNCs	Beneficial/harmful	Beneficial	Exploitative
Behavioural dynamic	State as power seeking rational actor	Individual as rational actor but outcomes not always optimal	Dominance and exploitation within and between societies
Market relations	Potentially negative	Positive	Exploitative
System structure	Anarchy/conflictual	Cooperative/interdependence	Hierarchy/conflictual
Game metaphor	Zero sum	Positive sum	Zero sum
Hegemony	Importance of a dominant state	Post-hegemonic cooperation	Hegemony in state and society
International institutions	Not very significant	Important	Serve interests of wealthy (states, firms and classes)

the relationship between economics and politics across the national/international divide. Economic nationalism, liberalism and critical theories are three broad schools of thought in the field, which both explain the behaviour of actors and offer prescriptions about what states and people should do in the global political economy. In Chapter 2, we turn our attention to the evolution of the field and methods used to study it.

Further Reading

A wide-ranging and eclectic collection of articles examining IPE theory can be found in Ronen Palan (ed.) *Global Political Economy: Contemporary Theories*, 2nd edn (2012). Susan Strange outlined her critique of runaway finance in *Mad Money: When Markets Outgrow Governments* (1998), while an overview of her work is presented in Roger Tooze and Chris May (eds) *Authority and Markets: Susan Strange's Writings on International Political Economy* (2002). Robert Keohane's groundbreaking work on regimes is found in *After Hegemony* (1984), while a collection of important essays is contained in his *International Institutions and State Power: Essays in International Relations Theory* (1989). Many of Robert Cox's most influential writings are contained in (with T. Sinclair) *Approaches to World Order* (1996). A critical feminist take on GPE is V. S. Peterson's *A Critical Rewriting of Global Political Economy: Integrating Reproductive, Productive and Virtual Economies* (2003).

Two journals that publish a great deal of IPE analysis are *Review of International Political Economy*, and *New Political Economy*, both journals available at tandionline.com

International Political Economy and its Methods

This chapter takes a step back from the three usual approaches to IPE (economic nationalist, liberal, critical) to consider how IPE fits with other fields of study, what kinds of methods can be used in IPE and where the field is going in theoretical terms. We also outline the approach we have taken in writing the book.

LOCATING THE FIELD

IPE emerged as a subject of study in universities in the mid-1970s. From its tentative beginnings as one course within a degree programme, IPE has developed into a distinct sub-field of international relations (IR). In some universities it has outgrown political science departments to take on a larger interdisciplinary flavour (see Box 2.1). Similar to its 'parent' disciplines, IPE remains a field in which different theoretical traditions present the student with competing descriptions of 'reality' and conflicting explanatory frameworks. A review of the teaching and study of IPE in the 1990s identified both continuities and change in the issues considered important by scholars (Denemark and O'Brien, 1997). Some issues, such as the impact of TNCs, international finance and international trade, have remained central to the core issues covered in IPE courses. The centrality given to issues such as Third World development or North–South conflict has varied considerably over the past three decades. Meanwhile, issues such as East–West relations, energy and the impact of producer cartels have vanished to be replaced by a focus on environmental concerns and gender. In terms of a broad overview of the international political economy, analysis has shifted from a concern with interdependence to an obsession with globalization.

To situate the study of IPE among other subjects, it is useful to make some preliminary comments about the organization of knowledge in the social sciences. Although Western knowledge and universities are separated into distinct subjects, fields and departments, this was not always the case. Before 1900, intellectuals often worked in a number of different fields that would not fit into today's compartments. Thus, in the late 1700s, Adam Smith, who is often seen as the founder of liberal economics, was a professor of moral philosophy rather than an economist. As knowledge has grown, so fields have become more specialized. Those interested in the culture of other societies drift into anthropology departments, those interested in the operations of society into sociology, people concerned with the study of power and politics into political science departments and those focused on the economy into economics departments.

Each field has developed its own theoretical and methodological approaches to answering a particular set of questions. The same subject can be examined in different disciplines from a variety of perspectives.

The specialization of knowledge in the social sciences corresponded with the solidification of nation-states in western Europe. Social sciences disciplines increasingly became national disciplines. People would study the French society or the US economy in isolation from other societies or economies. In some respects this made sense. National states were becoming more developed and their regulatory activity was having an increasingly significant impact on the people within the hardening borders. However, this methodological nationalism meant that the connections between societies and their relationship to the outside world were neglected.

IPE tries to bridge some of these historic divides. It crosses the boundaries between the study of politics and economics, as well as the national and the international. Depending on the approach, it will also draw on other fields such as geography or history. We'll briefly examine some of the neighbouring fields to develop our understanding of global political economy's place.

Box 2.1 IPE or GPE?

The terms 'international political economy' and 'global political economy' are often used interchangeably. In this text we use them in specific ways. Since the term 'international political economy' is the most common way to refer to the academic field of study that examines the interaction of economic and political phenomena across state borders, we will use 'IPE' when discussing the field of study. We will also use 'international political economy' when discussing the history of economic and political activity across state borders up until the last quarter of the 20th century. When using the term 'global political economy' (GPE), we are referring to the environment from the last quarter of the 20th century until today. This is an era where states, corporations and citizens struggle to order their environment in a world characterized by intensified globalization.

Economics

The word 'economics' comes from the Greek *oikonomia*. In its original use it meant the management of the household. Over the centuries, study of the economy has varied greatly. Today the discipline is dominated by a particular approach to the economy known as 'neo-classical economics'.

The central problem for neoclassical economists is how to allocate scarce resources. Human desires are seen as unlimited, while the resources to fulfil them are finite. The problem then becomes how to allocate those resources most efficiently. The solution to this problem is to be found in the efficient operation of markets. Markets are places where informed individuals can make mutually advantageous exchanges. Consumers are important in this approach. Well-informed individuals acting in their own economic self-interest will send signals about what should be produced. Left alone, the sum of these individual choices will result in the most efficient allocation of resources.

Neoclassical economists seek to fashion their subject into a science and separate it from the study of politics and philosophy. Whereas political decisions might be influenced by emotions, economic decisions are based on rationality. Politics and politicians are often seen to block the operation of the free market and prevent it from operating efficiently. In an attempt to make the discipline of economics more scientific, many modern economics departments have turned increasingly to using mathematical models to analyse the economy and advance arguments in favour of particular policy options.

Neoclassical economics tends to view governments and government intervention in the economy as inefficient. Governments are needed to provide some basic public goods such as police forces, armies and institutions which ensure that a free market is able to function. However, they should be confined to as small a role as practically possible.

Although neoclassical economics dominates many economics departments, there are other approaches to the field (Stilwell, 2002). Keynesian economics sees government as being crucial to a well-functioning economy. Keynesians believe the government should provide a wider range of public goods (such as healthcare) and that government spending is needed to move economies out of recession or depression. Their view is that when businesses fail to invest for economic growth, governments must step in. Institutional economics is another variant; it argues that markets are not 'natural' but are the result of a series of institutions such as the legal structure, the financial system and social values. These economists argue that the discipline should focus on the real world rather than abstract models of a free market that does not actually exist. Both Keynesian and institutional economics have a much more expansive and positive view about the role of government. There are other approaches to economics such as Marxist, feminist and ecological perspectives, but these tend not to be taught in economics departments because they challenge many of the rationality assumptions of traditional economics.

While neoclassical economics purports to be based on how a free market really works, some have suggested that the study of economics actually changes how people think and behave. Neoclassical economists and their students may behave the way their models predict people should behave. One study comparing economics students with those in maths, law, science and business found that economics students trained in the use of mathematical models were far more likely to resolve a conflict between profit maximization and worker welfare in favour of profit maximization than their colleagues in other departments (Rubinstein, 2006). A series of other studies have suggested that the field's focus on self-interest prompts its students to be less charitable, have fewer concerns for fairness and be more accepting of greed than other students (Grant, 2013). The possibility that theories help shape reality rather than only explain it will be considered when we look at constructivist approaches.

The field of economics brings many useful ideas and concepts to the study of GPE. Key theories explaining macroeconomics, comparative advantage, supply and demand and the operation of markets can explain particular events and have informed the actions of decision makers. In terms of the perspectives outlined in this book, liberal theory draws heavily on the field of economics.

Political science

The use of power and politics is the subject of political science. However, there is a wide variety in what is actually studied and how it is studied in the various subfields. For example, political theory examines key political and philosophical texts about how societies should be governed. Comparative politics considers how different countries are governed and tries to learn general lessons from the varying political institutions or cultures. German, US or British politics examine the political systems of those countries. For example, US politics can examine the operation of the US Congress, the presidency, voting patterns and the influence of lobbying and pressure groups on public policy. Public administration studies the state bureaucracy and the implementation of particular policies.

Despite these varieties in the field, many political science studies share a number of common characteristics. First, they are concerned with power or the ability of one set of actors to have their preferences implemented. This is a different world from that of the economists, who see decision-making as being the result of well-informed, equal and free individuals expressing their rational preferences. In the world of politics, decision-making is influenced by argument, ideology, institutional features and the threat of violence. Second, many political studies focus on institutions, most notably the state or the machinery of government. Whereas neoclassical economists are obsessed with the operation of the market, political scientists often cannot tear their vision away from the operation of the state.

As a result of this perspective, political science brings a number of elements to the study of GPE: the focus on power, the state and the welfare of particular communities (as opposed to all communities).

Political economy

If economics has become increasingly abstract and detached from the economy as it actually operates, and political science tends to ignore the economy by focusing on political institutions, then the answer must be to integrate these two fields into the study of political economy. Unfortunately, the term 'political economy' has meant a number of different things to different people over time. Prior to the rise of neoclassical economics, political economy referred to the work of scholars such as Adam Smith, David Ricardo and Karl Marx. However, the neoclassical turn stripped the political from the economic. Some scholars who did not share this desire continued to examine how politics structured the economy and how the economy influenced politics. For this strand of thinking, politics and economics are inseparable.

However, *The Oxford Handbook of Political Economy* takes a different approach to the subject matter. Rather than view the field as the interrelationships between economics and politics, it defines the subject matter as consisting of 'the methodology of economics applied to the analysis of political behaviour and institutions' (Weingast and Wittman, 2006, p. 3). In this approach, the unit of analysis is the individual and that individual follows a rational decision-making behaviour to maximize their goals. Game theory or mathematical models are used to inform the analysis, while statistical tools or experiments are used to demonstrate the validity of particular propositions.

So, within the mainstream, political economy can mean an attempt to integrate politics and economics along the line of institutional economics, or it can mean the application of neoclassical economics assumptions and methods into the study of politics. Outside these understandings, another version of political economy survived the shift to neoclassical economics. A Marxist political economy tradition flourished but was ignored by many Western academics. Indeed, the association of political economy with Marxism was one of the reasons for the continued neglect of political economy in university economics departments. Some of these Marxist studies, such as Baran and Sweezy's *Monopoly Capital* (1966), provided important insights into the dynamics of political economy.

International relations

The field of IR is often located in political science departments. Its origins as a distinct area of study date back to the aftermath of the First World War. European leaders and publics were shocked at the length and devastating loss of life of that conflict. As part of their attempts to prevent the outbreak of another disastrous war, efforts were made to increase understanding about the causes of war and the operations of the international system. The field of IR was given this task, and as a result, it has tended to focus on issues of war and peace, the foreign policy of various states and the operation of international organizations.

Whereas many of the other fields have stressed the importance of developments internal to the state, IR concentrates on interactions between states. The focus is on how the international system operates rather than the internal workings of particular states. There is some examination of the making of foreign policy, but the emphasis is on its interaction with the foreign policy of other states.

The dominant IR theoretical approach has been realism. This theory stresses the lack of any overreaching power in the international system (anarchy) and the continuous competition for power between states. More liberal approaches have focused on the possibilities of states to cooperate, the role of international organizations and law to foster cooperation, and the significance of regional integration, free trade and democracy to foster peaceful relations between states.

In the 1970s, as US power seemed to be decreasing and economic issues were becoming more significant, some scholars turned their attention to international economic issues. The early 1970s witnessed a major change in the international monetary system, as fixed rates were abandoned, the price of energy rapidly escalated during the oil crisis and inflation and unemployment plagued Western countries. Efforts to include 'economic' issues alongside the traditional security concerns of international relations were the beginning of the study of international political economy.

Over the past 20 years, the field of IR has moved in many different directions. IPE or GPE has carved out a place in the study of IR. While realist and liberal approaches are still important, other theoretical orientations have proliferated. Feminist approaches stressing the role of gender, Marxist approaches emphasizing class, constructivist and poststructural approaches emphasizing the role of language and culture and postcolonial approaches focusing on the legacy of imperialism have broadened the subject matter and methods of the field.

IPE studies can, and do, draw on a range of fields other than economics, political science and IR. Some authors, such as ourselves, may have a historical bent and draw on the work of historians to explain today's developments. For example, Chapter 3 draws on the work of Janet Abu-Lughod and her analysis of early world economies in the 1400s. Geography is increasingly relevant for GPE as insights from geographers about the importance of space and scale are absorbed. For example, geographic approaches can be used to explain the factors that determine the geographic location of foreign direct investment and production (Dicken, 2007) or how workers use local advantages to frustrate the ambitions of global companies (Herod, 2001). Sociological studies can assist in our understanding of particular groups in the global economy, such as studies on transnational classes or globalizing elites (Sklair, 2001) that highlight how particular groups benefit from and drive economic globalization (Box 2.2). As the GPE has become more

Box 2.2 What is globalization?

The term 'globalization' is used widely, but people often mean different things when they use the term. For example, some people use the term to imply internationalization – an increase in the volume of economic flows across borders – while others use it to indicate liberalization – the removal of restrictions to cross-border flows, such as the elimination of trade or investment barriers. Both internationalization and liberalization are often used in the context of economic activity. The term 'globalization' can also be used in the realm of knowledge or ideational dissemination. For example, some analysts focus on universalization – particular ideas or principles being accepted by all people – while others emphasize Westernization – the increasing prevalence of ideas and practices originating in Europe or the US. These terms are most often used when discussing the spread of principles such as human rights or culture, such as the expansion of the US film industry.

The term 'deterritorialization' highlights the changing nature of geography and the creation of new relationships between different groups of people. Following Scholte (2000a), we understand globalization to mean a process of relative deterritorialization. Territory is not disappearing, but it is becoming less important to human affairs. Deterritorialization involves the shrinking of time and space, as well as the creation of new sets of social relations and new centres of authority. We can see that time and space have become less significant obstacles to human interaction as technologies make it easier and quicker to travel across large distances or communicate with people around the world. The lowering of time and distance barriers allows people to become involved in the lives of other people in other parts of the planet much more easily. However, this compression is extremely uneven. Some areas of the globe are left behind as advanced areas exploit technology and upgrade communication and transport infrastructure. Globalization is not occurring at the same rate and same pace in all countries or regions.

institutionalized, legal studies are of increasing significance. Legal analysis of the WTO helps scholars understand the powers and limitations of that organization's dispute settlement mechanism (Jackson, 2006). More recently, insights from cultural studies and the humanities, which emphasize the constructed nature of our reality and the important role of discourse in shaping that reality, have been developed.

In summary, GPE, as presented in this text, crosses the fields of economics, political science, political economy and IR and draws on work in geography, history, sociology, law and cultural studies. Now that we have provided you with its location in the social sciences, let us turn our attention to how we can study IPE (methodological issues).

METHODOLOGICAL ISSUES

Interested observers of global political economy who have first familiarized themselves with some of the basic approaches to the field must then decide how they will study the events and processes that interest them. They must decide what method is most suitable for their investigation. However, the question of method is complicated by three issues:

1   Different methods demand different skills and training.
2   Methods themselves embody particular theoretical assumptions and may be more value laden than they initially appear.
3   Adherents of particular methods may dismiss the arguments of people using different methods because they do not accept their research as valid (due to faulty methods).

Here, we briefly examine four methods: case studies, rational choice, institutionalism and constructivism.

Case studies and large n studies

One of the most common approaches to studying IPE is to use case studies. A case study is a detailed investigation of a particular event or issue. The event is studied to determine why a particular thing happened the way it did. A detailed analysis is designed to reveal causal factors that can either be applied to similar situations or serve as a starting point for theory building.

There are a number of different types of case studies and each has its particular use (Odell, 2001). Descriptive case studies describe a particular event, but do not provide analysis or engage in theoretical debates. They are useful as evidence for other types of studies. They can provide the raw material or data for other scholars and students. Other cases are chosen because they may help evaluate the plausibility of a particular theory. A 'least likely' case study is one where a particular theory is unlikely to seem applicable. If the theory actually holds in that unlikely case, the theory is considerably bolstered. Alternatively, a 'most likely case study' examines a case that is very likely to support a theory. If it can be shown that the theory does not hold in such a supportive case, great doubt is shed on whether the theory will apply in any other case. Comparative case studies are undertaken in the hope that different cases will shed light on when particular theories hold and when they do not. Comparing and contrasting cases can often shed more light than a single case.

'Large n studies' is a name given to statistical investigations which use a database to find common features or causes across a large number of cases. For example, there might be a hypothesis that free trade makes countries wealthy. One could investigate a particular case to see if the proposition held true in that instance, but scholars (and public officials) are likely to be interested in whether or not it holds true as a general rule across a wide variety of cases. Can it be shown that, under most circumstances, free trade brings wealth and thus should be a policy that most countries should follow? Rather than do a case study of every country in the world, it makes more sense to examine the data from a large number of countries. Countries could be evaluated according to the degree to which they engage in free trade, and their wealth per capita could then be compared. The study would then show whether there was any relationship between the wealth of a country and its openness to trade. If a relationship was found, then there could be a debate about whether free trade created the wealth or wealthy countries prefer free trade or whether some other factor generated both wealth and free trade.

Case studies and multi-country statistical studies have their advantages and disadvantages (Odell, 2001). The advantages of case studies are that they are useful for generating theories, concepts, typologies and hypotheses. They provide rich empirical material for investigation. They help us understand how particular things happen. In areas where no statistical data is available, the case study is often the only possible method of studying a phenomenon. The biggest disadvantage to the case study is that one can never be certain about how representative the case is. Does it represent a general trend or is it the exception to the rule? Does it have any applicability to other cases or is it unique? Large n studies help us determine whether a particular proposition is generally applicable or limited to a small number of cases.

Rational choice

The rational choice approach to understanding politics was pioneered in the study of US politics, especially the operation of its legislature. The method then spread to the analysis of comparative politics, IR and IPE. It explains outcomes as the result of the choices of individual actors – either an individual person or a group considered to be acting as an individual, such as a state. Within this framework, actors are assumed to be utility maximizers, that is, they attempt to maximize their gains and minimize their losses. Individuals try to improve their situation by calculating costs and benefits before choosing the best path of action.

Rational choice theories have generated significant insights into political behaviour, especially concerning how the aggregation of individual choices can lead to surprising outcomes (Geddes, 2003, pp. 193–7). One insight is that systems of majority rule do not always result in implementing the policy preferences of a majority of citizens. Although a political system may be a relatively fair and competitive democracy, majority preferences may be ignored. Smaller, wealthier interest groups are more likely to have the resources and motivation to influence public policy than poorer unorganized sectors of the population. In addition, if the benefits of a public policy are highly concentrated, but the costs are spread widely throughout the population, those reaping the benefit are highly motivated to lobby, while the many individuals paying a very small cost are unlikely to put much effort into opposing the policy. This type of logic is often used to explain trade protectionism, where an industry can reap profits from tariff protection, but individual citizens pay such a low cost that they do not mobilize to defend their interests.

Rational choice theories have also highlighted the problem of collective action in the areas of public goods and common pool resources. Public goods have two characteristics:

1 They can be enjoyed by more than one person without any reduction in the good.
2 People cannot be excluded from their consumption.

Clean air and water are examples of public goods. The problem with such goods is that it may not be rational for any individual to do the work required to provide a public good because it will be consumed by others with only a small benefit returning to the initiator. Thus, a corporate polluter may gain economic benefits from dirty production, but any individual will be reluctant to bear the cost of cleaning up the mess. Common pool resources refer to environments, such as oceans or air, which are shared by a large group of people but not owned by anyone. Here the incentives are for each person to make maximum use of the resource to everyone's detriment. This phenomenon can be seen in the overgrazing of common sheep pastures and the overfishing of ocean stocks. Rational choice theory shows how what is rational for the individual leads to poor outcomes for the group or society.

An offshoot of rational choice is game theory. Whereas rational choice looks at the strategic behaviour of individuals, game theory examines the decision-making of actors who are heavily influenced by the possible behaviour of other parties. These actors calculate their own interest in the light of what they believe others will do. It concerns the strategic interaction of a number of actors. Theorists have constructed a number of scenarios or games such as prisoner's dilemma, chicken, and stag hunt. The rules of the games differ, forcing players to behave in particular ways. For example, the prisoner's dilemma discourages players from cooperating, which leads to a poor overall outcome (see Box 2.3). In contrast, in the stag hunt, players who can manage to cooperate will be rewarded with such large benefits that there is a great incentive to maintain cooperation.

How can these abstract games contribute to understanding GPE (Carlson, 2000)? The prisoner's dilemma can help explain why countries keep protectionist measures in place even though free trade would benefit them more. A country (country A) may be concerned that if it opens up its domestic market to foreign producers, other countries may keep trade barriers, resulting in an economic loss for country A. While all countries may be better off under free trade, any individual country can gain from keeping trade barriers. So, if country A keeps its trade barriers, it will gain if other countries reduce their barriers because it can export to them. On the other hand, if other countries do not reduce their barriers and country A keeps its barriers, country A protects its own market. The problem of one country seeking the benefits of free trade but not liberalizing its own trade is one of free riding. It wants the benefits of the system, but will not itself participate in bearing any costs. Since the same logic applies to all countries, there is very little incentive for countries to reduce their trade barriers even though everyone would be better off if they did.

The prisoner's dilemma does not mean free trade is impossible. Games can change over time as the rules are changed. For example, there is a tendency for actors to change their behaviour if they play the same game a number of times. They learn the costs of cooperation and non-cooperation. Alternatively, the game can be changed if the rules are altered. The players might create an institution such as the WTO, which reduces the ability of countries to cheat or free ride and takes away the cost of cooperating. The WTO encourages all countries to adopt free trade and provides information to its members about who does not abide by the rules. This gives member states increased confidence that other countries will not free ride. It changes the calculations that each state makes so that cooperation seems like a much more rewarding policy.

Institutionalism

As a methodology, institutionalism focuses on the importance of formal and informal institutions in producing political outcomes. It shares an affinity with institutional economics mentioned in Chapter 1, because both focus on the rules and institutions that shape human behaviour. At the core of institutionalism is an emphasis on the importance of rules. While rational choice methods highlight individuals pursuing self-interest, institutionalists focus on the broader rules of the game. The global economy is conceived not as the result of the actions of diverse individuals but as the outcome of the interaction of simple and complex

Box 2.3 Prisoner's dilemma

A simple prisoner's dilemma illustrates how some environments can lead rational actors to make decisions that lead to poor outcomes. Imagine the police arrive at the scene of a robbery and discover a dead body. They arrest two suspects (person A and person B) who have stolen articles in their possession. At the police station, the suspects are put into separate rooms and interrogated. The prisoners are given the following options:

1 If both suspects keep silent, each will be convicted of robbery and given a one-year sentence.
2 If one person confesses and identifies the other as the killer, the informer will be freed and the killer will go to prison for life.
3 If both confess and identify the other as the killer, they will both be sentenced to ten years for manslaughter.

Both prisoners are assured that the other prisoner will not know of their decision until the trial. What is the most likely outcome of this scenario? The game can be shown in the table below.

The best joint strategy for both prisoners is to stay silent and get a relatively light sentence of one year. However, each prisoner knows that if the other informs and they stay silent, they will stay in prison for the rest of their life. They also know that the other player has a large incentive to inform because they could earn their freedom. Thus, the best individual strategy is to inform on the other. Prisoner A knows that if B stays silent and A informs, A will win freedom. On the other hand, if B chooses to inform, A also needs to have informed or A will go to prison for life. Prisoner A's best option, no matter what B does, arises when A informs. Both A and B follow a similar logic of informing and end up with a prison sentence of ten years, which is far longer than the 1 year if they had both stayed silent. The dilemma is that if each player responds to their individual incentives, they end up being much worse off than if they had adopted a coordinated strategy (staying silent).

	Prisoner A stays silent	Prisoner A informs on B
Prisoner B stays silent	Robbery conviction – one year each	Prisoner A – freedom for informing
		Prisoner B – life for murder
Prisoner B informs on A	Prisoner A – life for murder	Prisoner A – ten years for manslaughter
	Prisoner B – freedom for informing	Prisoner B – ten years for manslaughter

When one changes the rules of the game, the outcome can also change. For example, if both prisoner A and B were members of the mafia, they would have a large incentive to stay silent, fearing reprisals from other members of the criminal organization. This would lead them to a better outcome of staying silent and spending one year in jail rather than ten.

institutions that shape individual decisions (Spruyt, 2000). In IPE, institutionalism is most familiar in the writings of liberal scholars who emphasize the powerfully constraining and beneficial impact of institutions.

One area where institutionalism has been prominent is in discussion about the varieties of capitalism (Hall and Soskice, 2001). What accounts for different forms of capitalism and will these grow or shrink over time? Do different parts of the world exhibit distinct forms of capitalism that will evolve along divergent paths or are countries bound to converge around a

particular superior form of capitalism? Institutionalists have pointed to distinct forms of political, social and economic arrangements to explain continuing variation between countries. Some have stressed the role that finance has played in different systems. An Anglo-American market where firms raise money on the stock market has been contrasted with a German model where banks have more direct relationships with corporations, or a Japanese model that links manufacturing and finance in large conglomerates. Neocorporatist work contrasts models where labour was included in government decision-making to models where labour was excluded or suppressed. Countries have also been examined with regard to the nature of their welfare regimes (Esping-Andersen, 1990).

As the varieties of capitalism literature illustrate, many institutionalists come from a comparative politics background. They tend towards using case studies and stressing the differences between political economies and the distinctive role that institutions play in shaping behaviour.

Constructivism

Constructivism begins from the premise that there is an intimate and reciprocal connection between human subjects and the social world (Palan, 2000). Whereas rational choice analysis takes values and beliefs for granted, constructivists see beliefs and values as things that have to be explained and are crucial in shaping and determining 'reality'. Whereas institutionalists focus on rules as the driving forces in constraining and shaping behaviour in a context where identity is essentially fixed, constructivism posits that norms and values go beyond shaping actors' interests – in themselves, they constitute identities and hence interests. From this perspective, the global political economy is a set of material conditions and practices, a set of normative statements about the world and an academic discipline. It is not reducible to one of these but is always constructed as the interaction of these three 'structures'. This is also true for any 'issue' in IPE. For example, to understand development, we have to look at development in relation to material privation, the values attached to economic growth and prosperity (as well as negative values attributed to poverty), and the ways in which development is studied and analysed.

A constructivist approach to IPE encourages analysts to look in different places for explanations other than rational choice or institutionalism. They call into question the preferences that are assumed in rational choice approaches (Abdelal, 2009). Constructivists ask: 'What are actors' preferences, how have they been created and how might they change?' They direct attention to the role of ideas, norms, identities and social understanding in guiding behaviour. How is it that at one point in time the pressing economic issue is thought to be inflation, while at other times it is unemployment? Why do some people and institutions preach the value

of the market as a decision maker and others stress political institutions? What is the impact of the dominance of one idea over another and how do such things come about?

There are two complicated and divisive issues surrounding debates about method. The first has to do with the dominance of particular methods and the second has to do with the relationship between method and theory. Some scholars fear that a narrow set of methods is beginning to dominate IPE and marginalize other methods, scholars and research. Rational choice and the use of statistical methods have become extremely popular in many US universities and leading journals. Scholars using case study and constructivist methods can feel that their work is taken less seriously because they use different standards of evidence.

A second issue is that while some scholars view methods as value neutral, others believe that methods are infused with particular theoretical and value assumptions. Adherents of the different theoretical perspectives can, in principle, use any methodology, but it has tended to be the case that economic nationalists and liberals favour rational choice or institutionalism, while critical theorists favour variants of constructivism. Many rational choice studies share the basic assumptions of neoclassical economists about rational utility maximizing actors and therefore seem closely aligned with liberal assumptions. Constructivist approaches stress the shifting nature of social reality so they tend to be less conservative than approaches that take existing meaning as given, such as rational choice perspectives. Constructivist approaches are more likely to be used by analysts seeking to critique or change the existing system.

Methods like rational choice and constructivism do indeed contain theoretical assumptions. Some may even argue that they are theories rather than methods. However, our perspective is that they are better viewed as methods that can be used with a variety of theories. For example, although rational choice methods draw on many liberal assumptions, they can be used by people of a very different theoretical bent. During the 1980s, a branch of Marxism – analytical Marxism – used rational choice methodology (Elster, 1985). In a similar way, although constructivism points one to look at how reality is made through people's ideas and understandings, one could take a realist, liberal or Marxist view of what influences a particular construction. Box 2.4 shows how a constructivist has influenced policy at the UN.

Box 2.4 Profile: John Ruggie – constructivist practitioner

John Ruggie emigrated to Canada from Austria in the 1950s. He studied politics and history at McMaster University in southern Ontario before earning a Political Science PhD at the University of California, Berkeley. He subsequently taught at the universities of California, Columbia and Harvard. He also worked with the United Nations at very senior levels.

Ruggie wrote a series of important articles on a variety of topics in IR and IPE from the 1980s to the 1990s. In 1982, his article on international regimes and embedded liberalism argued that the international arrangements in trade and money were limited by the domestic normative preferences of key states (Ruggie, 1982). The US and the UK both wanted full domestic employment so they created international rules that would support such strategies. The international system reflected the social desires or social purpose of the actors that created these rules. The international liberal system was embedded in a series of national deals and priorities that prevented the system from moving in a purely liberal direction. In contrast to approaches that predicted the nature of international order from the power capabilities of various states, Ruggie argued that one must go further to determine what the identities of particular states were. In his view, a US-centred hegemony would look very different from a Russian-centred or British-centred hegemony.

In examining international regimes, agreements and organizations, Ruggie also argued that analysts need to examine actors' understandings of institutions, as well as the institutions themselves. Behaviour needs to be interpreted. For example, the norm of an international trade agreement might be that countries do not raise tariffs on manufactured goods. In one particular year, several countries might raise tariffs on cars. Evaluating the health of this agreement through an examination of actors' behaviour would lead to the conclusion that the agreement is broken or very weak. However, actors themselves may have a different understanding of each other's behaviour and view the agreement in a more positive light. It may be that in that particular year a recession forced governments into temporary protectionist measures and this was understood by all concerned as a temporary reaction. An interpretive or constructivist account would discern that the regime was still intact, while a rationalist approach would consider the regime to have been weakened.

A thread running through Ruggie's work is his concern with social constructivism in the field of international organization and IPE (1998). In his view, ideas about appropriate behaviour, the rules governing behaviour and the institutions that embody particular ideas and norms all play a significant part in shaping the global political economy.

In the late 1990s, Ruggie took on a policy role working for the UN as assistant secretary-general for strategic planning, where he helped establish and oversee the UN Global Compact and worked on the UN General Assembly's proposal and ratification of the Millennium Development Goals (MDGs). This policy role fits well with Ruggie's scholarly work, which stresses the idea of social construction. The Global Compact is a set of principles for businesses in the fields of environmental and human rights. The MDGs set out targets for improving development indicators such as education and health. Both initiatives are meant to highlight key priorities in the hope that this will shift the behaviour of key actors. In the case of the Global Compact, the hope is that peer pressure and information will encourage business to behave ethically. For the MDGs, the goal is to encourage states to direct more resources and aid towards meeting the basic needs of citizens.

Ruggie's work advanced understanding about the intersubjective nature of regimes and opened the door for constructivism as an approach to understanding global order. In the policy field, his work has advanced projects that attempt to shift the norms and practices of actors in the fields of global business ethics and development.

Concerns about the dominance of particular methods or the value-laden assumptions inherent in various methods mean that what might otherwise be a dry discussion about how to conduct research can often be a much more lively and animated debate about the nature of knowledge and political orientations.

TRENDS IN CONTEMPORARY GPE THEORY

Given the theories laid out in Chapter 1 and our discussion about IPE in the social sciences and methodological issues above, are there any patterns in how the field is developing? We observe three trends that we term 'consolidation', 'integration' and 'expansion':

▶ *Consolidation:* undertaken by scholars who view the subject matter as being the politics of international economic relations. The task here is to build on a presumed consensus concerning the key questions to be investigated and methods for pursuing that investigation.

▶ *Integration:* the attempt to combine IPE with other broad political economy traditions such as those in comparative political economy or classical political economy. This group is not as certain as the first group that there is a consensus on key questions and methodologies.

▶ *Expansion:* the expansion of subject matter in terms of geographic scope (to developing countries), new subjects such as consumption and new theoretical approaches such as poststructuralism. This trend drifts even further from the consensus articulated by the first group.

Consolidation

One trend in the field is the attempt to consolidate a politics of international economic relations approach to IPE. In this approach, the boundaries and subject matter of the field are relatively clearly identified. The suitable theoretical approaches and methodologies are generally agreed on. Interventions seeking to contribute to theoretical reflection in this tradition emphasize similar methodologies rather than challenge the methodological and epistemological convictions of scholars in the field. A recent plea for greater engagement with behavioural economics (Elms, 2008) is a case in point. The task facing scholars and students is to build on each other's work by solving a number of agreed-upon problems.

A good general statement of this position has been provided by two US specialists outlining the field of IPE in 2003. Frieden and Martin (2003) argue that the subject matter of IPE is the politics of international economics. The issue areas of trade, monetary policy and international institutions have been the central focus of the field, but other areas such as international investment are ripe for investigation. Theoretically, the key challenge is specifying the relationship between domestic and international levels of analysis. To what degree and how does domestic politics influence state decisions at the international level? How does interaction between states impact on the domestic politics of international economic issues?

This textbook has not adopted a consolidating approach to IPE. A consolidated approach is in evidence in texts such as Grieco and Ikenberry's (2003) *State Power and World Markets*. They focus on the relationship between states and markets and ask a bounded set of questions such as: What accounts for openness and stability in the world economy? How do states shape the economic environment to promote national interests? How are states challenged by the international market? How do states manage openness?

A significant element of this consolidated approach is that, while it claims to reflect 'the principal focuses of North American scholarship … it is not reflective of much European scholarship' (Frieden and Martin, 2003, p. 118). Indeed, the consolidation consensus reflects the views of a rather small number of prominent US specialists. Many of these specialists work at elite US universities and publish their work in journals such as *International Organization*. This 'American' approach to IPE is contrasted with the work of a variety of other scholars (in both the US and other countries) working on very different agendas with different methodologies (Murphy and Nelson, 2001). Contributors to a special issue of the journal *Review of International Political Economy* (RIPE, 2009) that focused on the 'American School of IPE' support the thesis that consolidation around a narrow set of questions and restricted methodology characterizes the dominant scholarship in the US.

The consolidation of IPE has both rewards and costs. The acceptance of a narrow range of questions for investigation and agreement on a shared method allows researchers to make progress on a number of specific issues. The problem is that a narrow vision robs IPE of its critical edge. The field becomes a tool for problem-solving and ignores many crucial questions such as how the world should be transformed, what the good life would look like and how we might get there. This text has cast a wide net to catch a larger number of issues and perspectives than the consolidation approach. This may have come at the cost of some precision and focus, but two other trends in IPE suggest that it is a price worth paying.

Integration

Rather than consolidating the politics of international economics, a different approach has been to try to integrate IPE with other variants of political economy. One effort has been focused on bringing comparative and international political economy together, while another effort has been made to connect IPE with classical political economy.

If it is perhaps an overstatement to claim that IPE developed in the shadow of comparative political economy, IPE research has, nevertheless, been heavily influenced by comparative political economy perspectives, even if this has not been explicitly acknowledged. In many ways, IPE is a heterodox discipline willing to borrow liberally from other fields. The interchange between IPE and comparative political economy has to date largely been taken for granted. In other words, to a large extent this development has gone unnoticed. If the main focus of IPE is on global structures, comparative political economy places emphasis on national diversity and varieties of capitalism. However, the IPE literature has given attention to the salience of domestic structures and the changing nature of capitalism.

Concern with the impact of globalization and recognition of the differential impact of globalizing processes orient students of IPE to the importance of institutions and policy regimes in explaining outcomes. And globalization has impacted on studies of comparative political economy as analysts have become increasingly aware of the ways in which global processes affect competition and regulation in national political economies. Thus, IPE researchers and comparative politics specialists have increasingly been engaged in the study of similar issues (Graz, 2001). For example, the debate on the future of the state has engaged comparative political economy specialists (Weiss, 1998, 2003) and IPE scholars (Cerny, 2000).

There are two reasons why linkages between IPE and comparative political economy are likely to become more explicit in the near future. First, increased attention to regionalism and regional processes by students of IPE (Boas et al., 2005; Soderbaum and Shaw, 2003) brings to the fore the importance of regional and domestic structures. The complexity of the new regionalism necessitates comparative analysis as well as a focus on systemic structures. Second, renewed emphasis on the public–private interface directs attention to developments at national, regional and global levels. Thus systemic-level IPE is unable to analyse issues relating to accountability, authority and governance in the absence of a detailed assessment of national structures.

IPE developed as a distinct sub-field in the context of IR. As such, debates in IPE have tended to reflect wider debates in IR, and the growth of IPE has influenced further research in IR. A tradition of classical political economy, which can be traced back to the writings of liberal theorists such as Smith and Ricardo, and a radical tradition dating from Marx remained open to IPE theorists and, while not part of the mainstream, has influenced scholarship in IPE. IPE shares with classical political economy a commitment to integrating politics and economics. While all perspectives in IPE make some claim to descend from classical political economy, there have been calls for a return to classical political economy. As the editors of *New Political Economy* declared: 'What is needed is a new political economy which combines the breadth of vision of the classical political economy of the 19th century with the analytical advances of 20th-century social science' (Gamble et al., 1996, p. 1). This insistence on a return to classical political economy has been heeded by Watson (2005), who seeks foundations for IPE in the works of Adam Smith, Thorstein Veblen and Karl Polyani.

There are two reasons for recent interest in classical political economy. First, some of the key questions in contemporary economic governance are the same as those preoccupying the classical economists. At the centre of contemporary concerns are the twin issues of relative national wealth and continuing inequality. The failure of both mainstream economic theory and traditional IPE to provide satisfactory answers to these questions has revived interest in classical political economy. Second, global capitalism as a system is under the microscope in a way that it has not been since the middle of the 20th century. It has become increasingly difficult to merely assume capitalism to be a standard and neutral feature in analyses of political economy. Thus, institutional and cultural variables are now to the forefront.

Expansion

A third trend has been the attempt to expand the subject matter of IPE. One strategy has been to take the adjective 'global' seriously and pursue a subject of *global* political economy. A second approach has been to expand by developing new issues of enquiry. Promising new issues include race and consumption in the global political economy.

Phillips (2005, p. 1) has claimed that: 'Despite its pretensions to "global" scope and relevance, the study of International Political Economy (IPE) remains entrenched in a highly specific and narrow set of theoretical, conceptual and empirical foundations.' She argues that this restrictive IPE arose from a concern with the economies of the advanced industrial countries and resulted in two kinds of limitation. First, IPE's empirical scope was too narrow (this is a theme we will return to below but in a different manner from Phillips) since it focused on the problems and concerns of these 'core' countries. Second, by privileging and universalizing the historical experiences of western Europe, Japan and the US, IPE scholars were transferring concepts of bounded utility to the rest of the world. The concerns raised by Phillips were shared by her co-authors in a volume dedicated to globalizing IPE. These sentiments have also been echoed by Taylor (2005), who contends that the neglect of the developing world by IPE theory and analysis impoverishes IPE. He argues that IPE will only become fully global if it incorporates knowledge about the varied developing societies into its central concerns.

Both Phillips and Taylor acknowledge that, despite claims to the contrary, IPE has for the most part been limited in its concerns. In an age of globalization, a discipline that strives to provide explanations for global processes can no longer be based on a narrow empirical and conceptual focus. The globalizing IPE project outlined by Phillips specifically rejects an approach that simply involves giving greater attention to other regions of the world. She contends that such a project should include

> not only an empirical broadening to widen the focus outside the 'core' parts of the world and their experiences, but also, crucially, a serious reflection (then) on the theoretical implications of this broadening and the ways in which we might act on them in order to 'globalize' the study of IPE.
>
> (Phillips, 2005, p. 7)

This project remains at an early stage and the ways in which this challenge will be developed remain unclear. Nevertheless, there are two reasons that suggest increased attention will be given to this aim in the near future. First, it has become increasingly obvious that globalizing processes are unequal and therefore affect different countries, regions and peoples in diverse ways. The failure of IPE to provide adequate explanations for global diversity starkly exposes not only its empirical but also its conceptual limitations. From the understanding of the state and sovereignty at the centre of much IPE analysis to the conceptualization of market activity, the simple imposition of concepts developed in the advanced industrial countries is likely to prove unproductive. Moreover, the recognition in the discipline of IR that it has characterized much of the world as 'the people without history', to use Eric Wolfe's felicitous phrase, and has therefore neglected them has led to recent scholarship engaging with this marginalization of the developing world (Gruffydd Jones, 2005; Lavelle, 2005). Second, the developing world (or more broadly the non-core societies) is currently perceived to be the source of most instability and violence in the world. The traditional security paradigm and newer approaches to security such as human security perspectives both locate threat and danger, whether from religious extremism, collapsed states, refugee flows or environmental collapse, as stemming from the non-Western world. Thus, IPE's focus is likely to be concerned with (in)stability in the developing world.

IPE scholarship emerged in IR at a time when traditional realist and liberal theories struggled to explain interdependence. IPE has expanded the IR agenda both theoretically and empirically and yet, as we have shown above, IPE remains constrained and limited. One of the many ways in which IPE remains bounded is in its narrow agenda. Initially, this focused principally on trade and financial issues. Recently, there has been some change, in that, conceptually, IPE analysts have incorporated the role of corporate actors and civic groups, have shown awareness of social orders and have been sensitive to the interrelationship between domestic and international structures. Empirically, IPE has embraced an expanded agenda that includes gender, the role of transnational issues and transnational actors.

However, IPE remains relatively silent concerning issues relating to culture, race or leisure. Unlike gender, which has been integrated into studies of the political, race remains undertheorized in IR and IPE (Box 2.5 on p. 35).

Box 2.5 American, British and other forms of IPE

Some have suggested that the study of IPE is divided between UK and US approaches (Cohen, 2007). The US approach is said to draw heavily on liberal economic theory and use rationalist and quantitative methods, while the British are more likely to use qualitative methods (case studies and so on) and be more open to critical theories. As a broad generalization, there is some accuracy in this statement, but it hides more than it reveals.

Even though many of the most prestigious US universities tend to have a quantitative bent and scholars take a generally liberal approach, constructivism is also widely employed in US IPE. The US system is diverse, so labels of a 'US' approach are misleading. Conversely, liberal assumptions and quantitative methods have made inroads in some academic departments in the UK and Continental Europe. Moreover, the world of IPE goes far beyond the US and the UK, making the geographic focus of the labels parochial or not very global.

Studies of the leisure industry, whether sport or fashion, are neglected in IPE. In this respect critical scholarship is no different from conventional approaches. A survey of the two leading British journals of IPE – *New Political Economy* and the *Review of International Political Economy* – for the period 2000–8 finds one article on culture (Drache and Froese, 2006), one on the leisure industry (Milanovic, 2005) and none on race.

There are three reasons why these non-traditional issues are likely to become more important for IPE in the near future:

1 The attention to globalizing processes has ensured that lawyers, economists, sociologists, anthropologists and other social scientists have been theorizing the global and have not been as restricted in their choice of subjects as IPE analysts. For example, a legal scholar has explored the racialized nature of the global economy (Gott, 2000) and an economist has written about fashion and style in the world economy (D. Brown, 2005). An expanded IPE that gives attention to culture, race and leisure is likely to result from conversations between IPE, development studies and comparative political economy.

2 Material change in the global political economy is directly related to the three issues under discussion. Processes of global inequality are not only gendered, they are also inherently racialized; leisure consumption accounts for billions of dollars in production and exchange; and cultural issues pervade discussions in national polities.

3 Advances of poststructuralist approaches into IPE highlight the degree to which language, culture and identity contribute to the creation and functioning of a global political economy (De Goede, 2006).

Three of the issues discussed above – globalizing IPE, IPE and classical political economy, and comparative political economy and IPE – reflect scholarly discontent with IR and IPE. The final topic discussed, that is, the silence and marginalization of subjects such as culture, race and leisure, is only starting to spark similar theoretical reflection. Nevertheless, we identify these topics as important for the future development of IPE. We argue that theoretical debates in IPE are essentially the product of two forces. On one hand, they reflect the engagement of IPE scholars with real-world changes. In this respect, current debates are a reflection of the experience of globalization. On the other hand, developments in IPE theory are an outcome of theoretical debates among scholars concerning the precision and adequacy of theories and concepts. On both counts we see room for growth in the scope of IPE.

While one branch of IPE (the consolidation approach) is narrowing the field, other trends are opening up the field to new subject matter. This raises the question about the appropriate boundary for GPE. If the subject is continually widening, will it expand to encompass all the social sciences? Will this result in it trying to say so much that nothing of importance is uttered? Poststructuralist approaches in particular run this risk.

Our own view is that GPE does have a core – it revolves around issues of power and inequality in a global economy. Given the complex, multifaceted and protracted nature of the problems facing the world's population, each of the trends outlined above has something to contribute to our understanding.

APPROACH OF THE BOOK

We have seen that IPE is often conceived as a debate between three contending schools of thought. We have also seen that different scholars pursue particular research agendas and that methodological issues can loom large in designing and reporting research findings. Scholars (and practitioners) of IPE tend to base their analysis on sets of assumptions common to a specific paradigm. As argued above, all IPE analyses are written from a particular theoretical perspective. Theoretical assumptions guide choices about which theories and events should be highlighted and which will not make it into the study. Our purpose in this book is to provide readers with the theoretical tools and empirical knowledge needed to develop their own understanding of how the global political economy works. This is a challenging task, as this chapter has already demonstrated. We do it on the basis of a framework of analysis indebted to the insights of the three IPE perspectives, but not fully ascribing to the assumptions and propositions of any one of these perspectives. We will return to the three main approaches when they are helpful for understanding particular developments. For example, liberal theories help us understand some of the elements of British policy in the 19th century and the thinking behind multilateral trade institutions in the 20th century.

This text takes an eclectic approach to the theory and method surrounding IPE. We draw on a number of different theories and methods to address a wide range of IPE topics. Strange (1991) argued that an eclectic IPE approach should have three elements: openness to many disciplines, openness to conceptual synthesis, and recognition of the key role of firms. Writing 20 years later, Sil and Katzenstein (2010) have suggested that an eclectic approach to world politics plays down metaphysical divides in favour of policy and practice, takes on wide complicated problems, and offers complex causal stories that draw on a range of explanatory theories, models and narratives from competing research traditions. Both of these approaches share the inclination to draw on multiple disciplines and theoretical traditions to address a wide range of issues.

> **Box 2.6** Approach of this book
>
> This text pays particular attention to:
>
> **1** historical change
> **2** structure–agency dynamics
> **3** integration of cognitive structures
> **4** political–economic interaction
> **5** dynamic institutionalism
> **6** salience and variety of domestic structures.

Out text also integrates key concepts and theoretical insights from different approaches into an overarching, multidimensional approach. The framework of analysis outlined below and developed in the remainder of the book is intended to allow students to organize and simplify in a systematic manner the theoretical approaches and empirical evidence necessary to explain contemporary developments in the global political economy. It allows them to investigate a wide range of issues and draw on a variety of theoretical approaches. The framework is an organizing device and not itself a theory.

First, our approach is historicist in that it is sensitive to historical change. The nature of political economy, its major institutions and ideas about how it operates change over time (Cox and Sinclair, 1996, pp. 49–59). This book places historical development at the centre of its explanatory framework, and recognizes history as both the context or framework within which meaning is located, and an ideological concept that is evident in various perspectives on political economy. Theories about how the world works arise in particular historical contexts and need to be linked to those contexts. Theories can be more or less helpful depending on when they are created and how they are used. A historical sensitivity is also important to understanding the path-dependent nature of the evolution of the global political economy. Some states and groups of people have become locked into particular development patterns because of events that took place many years ago. For example, many developing countries export low-value commodities because their economies were oriented to this task during the age of imperialism.

The role of historical practices in development raises a second point, which is the relationship between structure and agency. Put simply, this is the question of whether overarching structures such as the organization of production or the institution of patriarchy determine the action of agents (states, firms, people) or whether agents engage in free choice and construct their own environments (Wendt, 1987). We view the relationship as dynamic and do not privilege either systemic or unit-level variables. There are dangers in reifying structures on one hand and in reducing complex events to individual action on the other. In rejecting structural determinism and methodological individualism, we seek to understand the ways in which structures constrain action and agency impacts on structural constraints. The existence of a structure of patriarchy does not, for example, determine that all males will exploit women.

Third, we recognize the salience of ideas or cognitive structures as significant elements in the global political economy and examine the role of ideas in structuring outcomes (Finnemore and Sikkink, 1998). Norms, values, ideologies and ideas are constitutive elements of the global political economy. This means that they help to make the world the way it is rather than only reflecting how we think about the world. While ideas are linked to material developments and interests, they are not derived solely from the material structures of the global economy. On the contrary, ideas shape, mould, facilitate and constrain the activities of economic agents. For example, if it is believed that inflation is the economic problem most destructive of stability, harmony and progress, this becomes an economic 'fact' and redistributivist policies are subsumed to the dictates of the fight against inflation. Fighting inflation ceases to be perceived as a policy choice and instead is taken to be a central and natural feature of economic governance. Another example would be the ideas supporting patriarchy. It might be assumed that women are naturally docile and dextrous, thus making them the ideal choice for particular types of employment. The importance of ideas, intellectual schemes and ideologies will therefore be investigated rather than taken as given. Certain claims to the contrary notwithstanding, political economy is not value free and arguments over economic theories cannot be dismissed as rhetoric.

Fourth, we stress the inseparability of economics and politics, and therefore reject the separation of the economic from the political at the core of liberal and mercantilist approaches. Whereas liberalism separates the economic from the political and mercantilism subsumes the economic to the political, we insist that the economic constitutes the political and the political constitutes the economic. One of the ways this becomes apparent in the text is that we link events in the field of economic development with the deployment of organized violence and the ramifications of warfare.

Fifth, we view institutions as constantly undergoing change. Perspectives that take the institutional context as a given are deficient. Recently, economics and political science literatures have recognized the importance of social institutions in structuring market behaviour. We begin from the recognition that formal and informal institutions play significant roles in structuring outcomes in the international system. We therefore investigate the impact of institutions and emphasize the contribution of formal organizations to the evolution of the global economy. Two of the significant institutions we examine in the text are the changing nature of the state and the organization of international or world order. For example, the states discussed in Chapter 3 have mercantilist and imperialist characteristics, while the Industrial Revolution sees the emergence of a liberal British state. Following the Second World War, many Third World countries were characterized by developmental states and Western countries adopted some form of the Keynesian state.

Finally, our view of the global political economy is sensitive to the relationship between changes in domestic social orders and structures of international order and global political economy (Cox, 1986; Skidmore, 1997). Social and class conflict in key states can bolster or undermine the principles and institutions on which a particular world order rests. A leading explanation for the success of European expansionist activity in the 16th and 17th centuries was the greater relative autonomy that merchants enjoyed in Europe compared with empires in other parts of the world. Another example is the role that mobilized populations played in thwarting the attempts to build a stable liberal international system between 1918 and 1939. Changes in citizen expectations about government behaviour made it impossible to impose the economic medicine that liberal theory demanded.

Keeping the main approaches and our own blend of important characteristics in mind, we now turn our attention in Chapter 3 to the evolution of the global political economy beginning in the early 1400s.

Further Reading

A good overview of the contribution that economics makes to IPE is provided by Andrew Walter and Gautam Sen's *Analysing the Global Political Economy* (2008). John Ruggie's key articles are found in *Constructing the World Polity: Essays on International Institutionalization* (1998). A more recent application of constructivism is Rawi Abdelal, Mark Blyth and Craig Parsons, *Constructing the International Economy* (2010). A useful overview on the debates surrounding IPE including the US versus British approaches is Nicola Phillips and Catherine Weaver (eds) *International Political Economy: Debating the Past, Present and Future* (2011). Jacqueline Best and Matthew Paterson provide an overview of cultural approaches in *Cultural Political Economy* (2012). Other contributions can be found in the pages of the journal *Review of International Political Economy*.

PART 2
EVOLUTION

Chapter

3

Forging a World Economy: 1400–1800

Why do we inhabit a world where there are such great inequalities of wealth and life chances between regions? Why do some countries seem to be caught in a trap of producing products whose value declines over time, such as sugar or coffee? What accounts for the racial hierarchies in countries such as the US and South Africa? Why do some societies and countries seem suspicious of the foreign and economic policies of Western states, corporations and civic associations? The answers to these questions are partially rooted in the origins of the global economy. Indeed, a full understanding of today's global economy requires a familiarity with patterns that were initiated hundreds of years ago.

Croce's argument that 'however remote in time events there recounted may seem to be, the history in reality refers to present needs and present situations wherein those events vibrate' (Croce, 1941, p. 19) implies that history is constantly rewritten in light of existing debates and sensibilities. New histories often tell us as much about the times in which they were written as they do about the historical events themselves. An interesting example of this can be seen in the last decade of the 20th century when several prominent scholars engaged in a debate about the 'rise of the West'. They tried to explain why political and economic power was concentrated in the hands of several Western states (western Europe and the US). On one side of the debate were those who congratulated today's winners in the global economy by arguing that the rich were wealthy because they had the most virtuous social, economic and political institutions. We can call this the 'cultural approach'. The rich are rich because they have a culture that supports success. A prominent exponent of this view is Harvard historian David Landes in his book *The Wealth and Poverty of Nations* (1998). The other side of the debate argued that Western success was accidental and temporary, built on force and expropriation as much as any positive cultural attributes. We can call this the 'global historical approach', because it stresses the role of other civilizations and refutes the historical claims of the culturalists. Such an approach challenges the notion that history has ended because Western states have discovered the ultimate model for structuring economic, social and political relations. A prominent illustration of this approach is Hobson's *The Eastern Origins of Western Civilization* (2004).

The debate between cultural and global historical explanations about the 'rise of the West' became heated because it concerned the present and the future as much as it did the past. Participants claimed that they had discovered the secrets to why some are rich and others are poor. Such knowledge can be used by others to restructure their societies in the hope of similar success. The practical implications are immense. The culturalists see the cause of poverty as the behaviour of the poor, while the global historicist side sees it as a result of the relationship between the poor and the rich. The policy implications of the first view are that the poor are themselves primarily responsible for improving their position, while the implication of the second view is that the system of political and economic relations must be changed to create greater equity. The first message offers comfort to those already enjoying economic success, while the second urges mobilization and change.

How far back in history should we go to gain a better understanding of today's patterns of inequalities and wealth generation? In his bestselling book *Guns, Germs, and Steel: The Fates of Human Societies*, Diamond (1997) argued that we need to go back 11,000 years to find the ultimate causes of differences in economic development between people and regions. In his view, environmental and geographic factors such as differences in plant and animal species, rates of migration and diffusion within and between continents and total area/population size of continents privileged the peoples of Europe and Asia over people in other parts of the world. The ability to produce food and domesticate animals allowed for the creation of civilizations that overwhelmed societies with less complicated divisions of labour.

Our investigation will begin in the late 1400s when Spanish adventurers forcefully integrated sections of the Americas into an intercontinental economy that already linked parts of Europe, Africa and Asia. This chapter focuses on the period when the major regional economies in Asia, Africa, Europe and the Americas were brought into increased contact through the persistence of European expansionism. It is the beginning of the first truly worldwide or global economy. This will be accomplished in two steps. First, we will provide a brief overview of the major economic areas before the Spanish conquest of the 1500s. This will give us an understanding of the diversity of political economy arrangements around the world and will lay the groundwork for understanding the varying pattern of European–non-European interaction in subsequent centuries. Second, we will look at the pattern of European engagement with other parts of the world from the 1490s until the early 1800s. The conclusion analyses the historical record in terms of the key frameworks used in Part 3 – trade, production, finance, labour, gender, development, environment, ideas, security and governance.

The chapter has two major arguments. First, the regional political economies that were connecting during this period varied greatly in terms of social, political and economic organization. Second, this heterogeneity

created a variety of interactions from free exchange to open warfare and slavery. A third point, explored in following chapters, is that these interactions would have long-lasting effects.

REGIONS OF THE WORLD ECONOMY

This section provides a snapshot of several areas of the world prior to European contact with the Americas, which created the first truly worldwide political economy. In the year 1400, there was little hint that the residents of Europe would have such an influence on the majority of people who lived in other regions. As the Portuguese, Spanish, Dutch, English and French steadily moved outwards from their own continent, they encountered a variety of people and social organizations. Rather than expanding into a vacuum, the Europeans interacted with established civilizations, economic systems and military forces.

There are several points to keep in mind. First, with few exceptions, economic activity was on a local level. Agricultural production was the norm and this was usually centred on a market town with an agricultural hinterland of about 30 kilometres (Schwartz, 1994, p. 13). Second, despite the predominance of this local activity, intercontinental trade routes moving luxury goods had existed for thousands of years. Third, at the heart of these trade routes lay very different civilizations with distinct political economies. Indeed, some approaches to international relations and global history take different civilizations as their starting point (Braudel, 1994; Cox, 1996).

Janet Abu-Lughod (1989) has provided an interesting account of the world system before Europeans began their transatlantic voyages. Her research reveals a system of trade and economic exchange reaching from China to Europe. The system was composed of eight overlapping regions. Economic activity was concentrated within these regions, but they were linked to neighbouring regions, allowing products to move from eastern Asia to western Europe. Map 3.1 reproduces Abu-Lughod's diagram showing the regions, but it also adds four additional regions that will be discussed below under 'Africa' and 'the Americas'. Moving from west to east on the Eurasian continent, the first area is the region that brought together northern and southern

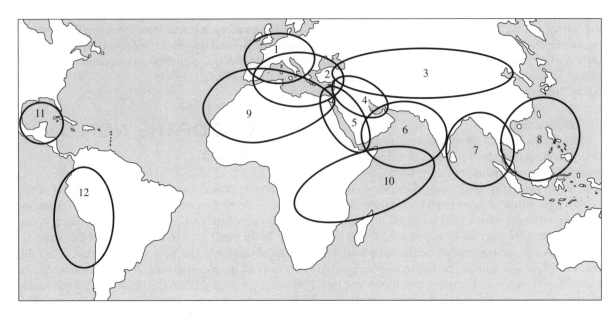

Map 3.1 **Regions of the 15th-century world economy**

Europe. The second region sits above the Mediterranean, crossing the divide between Christian southern Europe and the Islamic centres of Egypt. This Mediterranean region overlapped with three central regions. Region 3 covered the overland trade routes that stretched across central Asia to China and were maintained by the Mongols. Region 4 included the territory around the Tigris and Euphrates rivers (modern-day Iraq) down to the Persian Gulf. Region 5 also joined the Mediterranean and the Indian Ocean, but through Egypt and the Red Sea. Products making their way into the Indian Ocean were then transported across Region 6, which covered the Arabian Sea, linking Arabia with the western coast of India. Region 7 linked India with South-east Asia, while Region 8 finished the route by taking in China and South-east Asia. This meant that there were three routes for products to move from China to Europe. The northern route moved goods overland from China via central Asia through the Mediterranean into the European region. Alternatively, products could move by sea through South-east Asia, the Indian Ocean and then into the Mediterranean either through the Persian Gulf or the Red Sea.

Abu-Lughod's work omits African trading regions, so we have added two regions that cover certain areas of sub-Saharan Africa. Region 9 brought goods from sub-Saharan Africa into northern Africa and the Mediterranean/European world. Region 10 brought African

goods into the Middle East and Asia via the Indian Ocean. Our map also includes two regions in the Americas that were not joined to the African-European-Asian system. These are Region 11, which belonged to the Aztec Empire, and Region 12, ruled by the Incas.

Although it would have taken years to travel around this circuit of trade in the 1400s and the volumes of trade were minuscule by today's standards, economic activity was increasing across the system. Let's turn our attention to each of these regions to get a brief idea of their nature. We are particularly interested in the types of economic activity and political relations that characterized each region.

The Middle East

In Abu-Lughod's diagram of 14th-century regions, the Middle East acts as the key gateway between the Mediterranean/European and the Eastern worlds. Indeed, the desire to get around this gateway was one of the key motivations driving European merchants into the Atlantic Ocean, around Africa and across to the Americas. By the time of Christopher Columbus's voyage across the Atlantic, there had already been a 700-year history of bloody and lucrative interchange between European Christendom and Middle Eastern Islam. Islamic and Christian clashes took place from the south of France, through modern-day Egypt, Israel and Turkey, to the gates of Vienna. Yet, this rivalry was balanced by many instances of cooperation, with alliances and economic interchange between Europeans and Middle Easterners. For example, the Genovese sold Christian and pagan slaves to the Mamlukes in Egypt who then trained them as soldiers to be used against the Crusaders, while the Venetians financed an Ottoman fleet to battle the Portuguese in the Red Sea.

For almost 1,000 years Islamic warriors waged successful military campaigns against European forces. Behind those Middle Eastern armies stood a dynamic economy, extensive trade networks, bustling cities and great centres of learning. In retrospect, we can see that the 15th century was a period of transition in the Middle East. While the religion of Islam was dominant, forms of political authority were the objects of intense rivalry. Although ultimate political authority eventually came to rest in the hands of the sultan of the Ottoman Empire, this occurred only after a period of conflict with and between Turkish tribes, Mongols, Persians and Mamlukes. The competition between rival sources of political power characteristic of Europe was not absent in the Middle East. However, by the early 1500s, the Ottoman Empire held the upper hand. It proceeded to extend its rule eastwards and westwards towards Europe. On land and at sea the Europeans had great difficulty matching the might of Islamic forces. It would not be until the second siege of Vienna in 1683 that European militaries would start to win consistent victories.

The Mamlukes, followed by the Ottomans, presided over a thriving trading economy. In the 14th century, Cairo had a population of approximately half a million, which was only exceeded by one or two cities in China (Abu-Lughod, 1989, p. 212). The Mamlukes developed a structured and prosperous trading relationship with the Venetians. Through force of arms they prevented Europeans from seizing Egyptian territory that would have granted direct access to the wealth of India and China via the Red Sea. Venetians docked in Alexandria to wait for access to spices, dyes, pepper, silk, cotton and porcelains from Malaysia, India and China.

Outside the Mediterranean, Arab traders pursued economic activity along the coast of eastern Africa, the western coast of India and into South-east Asia. Zanzibar, off the coast of eastern Africa, was occupied by Arab traders as early as the eighth century. The cultural remnants of this early commercial activity can be seen in the Muslim populations of countries such as Malaysia and Indonesia (the largest Muslim country in the world).

China

Of all the great civilizations of the 15th century, China was the largest and most powerful. It produced products that were greatly desired by the elite in other regions of the world, chief among these being ceramics and silk. China contained the world's largest cities, advanced technology and impressive military forces. Indeed, the wonders of China were so great that when the Italian Marco Polo returned from his travels to that land in 1295, his observations were often dismissed as being fanciful. Some of his tales were exaggerated, but there is no doubt that China was a world leader in technology and inventions many years before the European Renaissance (see Box 3.1).

During the 14th and 15th centuries China was also undergoing dramatic changes. In 1370, the Chinese had finally succeeded in driving out Mongol rulers and re-established a Chinese emperor. This line of rulers was called the Ming Dynasty (1368–1644). Initially, the Mings launched several long-range trading voyages as far as the eastern coast of Africa. Their ships were five times as large as later Portuguese ships and they contained far more cargo space and cannons. They would have been capable of crossing the Pacific Ocean if they had attempted the task (McNeill, 1982, pp. 44–5). Indeed, had the voyages continued, it is possible that the Chinese might have sailed around Africa and reached Portugal, as well as 'discovered' the Americas. However, expeditions to the west (1405–33) were eventually halted by the Ming emperors and the seagoing fleet decommissioned. For the next several hundred years, the Chinese were less engaged with the outside world and fell behind, relative to the expanding Europeans.

There are several possible explanations for why the naval excursions were ended. One has to do with court politics. The leader of the expeditions (Zheng He) was both a Muslim and a eunuch and eventually lost the support of the emperors. Another explanation is that although the voyages brought back interesting goods, there was little the Chinese found that they actually needed. Unlike the Europeans, who were desperate for spices and silks, the Chinese did not find anything so attractive that it would justify the expense of further

Box 3.1 Ancient Chinese technology

Archaeological discoveries point to the origins of Chinese civilization as early as 7,000–8,000 years ago. Traditionally, the Chinese view the greatest technological contributions of ancient China to the world as the Four Great Inventions: the compass (AD 1040–44), gunpowder (AD 800–900), papermaking (AD 105) and printing (AD 868). Not only have the four discoveries had an enormous impact on the development of Chinese civilization, but also a far-reaching global impact as other peoples adopted these innovations. A closer examination of China reveals a whole series of inventions that had their origins in that civilization (Needham, 1954–1995). These include:

▶ Metal casting (1800 BC)
▶ Decimal system (1200 BC)
▶ Row planting (c. 500 BC)
▶ Seed drill (c. 202 BC – AD 220)
▶ Iron ploughs (202 BC – AD 220)
▶ Deep drilling (202 BC – AD 220)
▶ Ship's rudder (202 BC – AD 220)
▶ Abacus (200 BC)
▶ Paper money (140–87 BC)
▶ Harness for horses (AD 220–581)
▶ Porcelain (AD 581–618)
▶ Mechanical clock (AD 732).

exploration. Finally, the centre of gravity in China shifted towards the north and internal development. The Mings moved the capital from Nanjing northwards to Beijing and became more concerned with land rather than sea threats. In addition, new locks on the Grand Canal joined the Yangtze and Yellow River valleys, securing year-round rice transport in internal waters. This greatly reduced the importance of any maritime threats to Chinese stability and hence the need for a powerful navy (McNeill, 1982, p. 47).

In terms of political structures, the Ming emperor was the sole source of law. His views might be restrained by appeal to precedent and scholarly discussions or debates, but his power was absolute (Mote, 1999, p. 637). China was governed by a single political authority, unlike the rival states that fought continuously in Europe. The court sat in Beijing and governors of provinces reported to the bureaucracy and the court in the capital city. The emperor was supported by a well-trained bureaucracy that was selected through a process of examination. Confucian scholar-officials played the major role in running the bureaucracy and advising the emperor. Increasingly during the Ming Dynasty, eunuchs played a key role in running the court and providing services to the emperor. In some cases, they advanced their interests over that of the empire and cut the emperor off from developments in his realm.

India

Like China, India also possessed an ancient civilization, considerable economic wealth and military might. However, India was a more diverse and decentralized political economy than China. The northern section of India had experienced a series of invasions from Persian, Mongol, Turkish and Afghan tribes. In the 15th century, the northern region, known as the Delhi Sultanate, was ruled by descendants of invading Islamic forces, but they were constantly under attack from new waves of invaders. The sultanate was ravaged by the Mongol descendant Timur (Tamerlane) in 1388 and Delhi was sacked in 1398. Internal cohesion was difficult to maintain. In 1526, Barbur, a descendant of Timur, invaded India and founded the Mughal (Mongol) dynasty. Many of India's architectural wonders, such as the Taj Mahal, date from the Mughal era.

Other parts of India were ruled by independent kingdoms. The southern region was dominated by the Hindu kingdom of Vijayanagar from 1336 to 1565. It was often engaged in conflict with its neighbour, the Bahmani Sultanate. The eastern province of Bengal was usually controlled by independent rulers and the western coastal area of Gujarat also enjoyed independence. There were numerous other smaller kingdoms during this period.

Ports in coastal areas of India enjoyed a great deal of autonomy from the inland empires and economic activity was conducted by a wide range of social and economic groups. In Kerala, external trade was conducted by Jews and Christians who had been resident since the sixth century. In other parts of India, Jains, Buddhists, Muslims and Hindus were involved in trade (Bouchon and Lombard, 1987). On the western coast of India, the state of Gujarat dominated trade moving from the Middle East to the east coast of India. On the east coast, Bengal played a major part in moving goods on to South-east Asia. However, these coastal areas were relatively peripheral to the land-based empire. For example, it is reported that when the Mughal Emperor Akbar visited the recently conquered Indian ports of Cambay and Surat in the late 1500s, it was the first time he had ever seen the ocean (Risso, 1995).

Reflecting on the experiences of the Middle East, China and India, it is noteworthy that while these civilizations engaged in maritime activity, it was difficult for maritime interests to influence political power. The large land-based empires engaged in seaborne trade and established wide-ranging activity crossing the Mediterranean, Red Sea, Persian Gulf, Indian Ocean and around the seas to China. However, the Ottomans, Chinese and Mughals were primarily concerned with events within their existing empires and concentrated most of their effort in land-based expansion and defence. This was a very different pattern from the maritime-dependent Portuguese, Spanish, Dutch and British Empires.

Africa

To Abu-Lughod's diagram of trading networks we added two regions to cover interaction with sub-Saharan Africa (see Map 3.1). Region 9 covers land on either side of the Sahara Desert and the difficult trade across that arid territory. In western Africa, gold mines supplied European demand for currency while pepper was shipped north for consumption in food seasoning. This trade eventually encouraged the Portuguese to sail around the desert to establish direct trading contacts. Region 10 integrates the trade of eastern Africa with that of the Indian Ocean. In eastern Africa, trading posts exported slaves, ivory, iron, rhinoceros horn, turtle shell, amber and leopard skins to India and beyond. Both networks had existed for thousands of years.

Africa contained a large variety of political groups (Shillington, 1995). Northern African states were integrated into the Islamic empire. In Ethiopia, a Christian kingdom was founded in the fourth century and maintained its independence until the late 1930s. In the Shona state of Great Zimbabwe, 10-metre-high stone enclosures surrounded the king's residence. Around the great lakes area of central Africa, the Luba and Lunda Empires concentrated on fishing and hunting. They purchased iron and salt from the north and copper from the south, which was made into rings, bracelets and necklaces. In summary, the large continent contained a number of different political economies linked together through trade.

It is important that Africa is not viewed as static or stagnant in this period. Briefly we can note three main characteristics of the African political economy at that time. First, as noted above there was significant variation among different regions. Different ecological regions gave rise to differing factor endowments and thus the production of different goods and services. Second, over the period covered, commercial activity shifted as new commercial centres rose and old ones declined. For example, control over the gold trade made Hausaland a major commercial centre in the 16th century. But as gold declined in importance and the trade in people increased, Dahomey (modern day Benin) became the new hub of activity in the 17th century. Third, African economic activity was frequently disrupted by drought and famine. These 'limits to growth' both spurred technical innovation and also limited consistent development.

The Americas

Although the existence of the Americas came as a surprise to Europeans, many areas were marked by advanced civilizations. Advanced civilization, in terms of intensive agricultural activity and large cities with complicated architecture, took place in two regions of the Americas. One region was the Inca Empire in the Andes in Peru and Bolivia, which stretched from Ecuador to Chile. The other was in Mesoamerica – Mexico and Guatemala. This was the home of the Maya who were starting to decline and the Aztecs who were in the process of creating a large empire.

The Spanish encountered a well-developed empire when they began contact with the population of Mexico in 1519. The Aztecs ruled Mexico and were the successor to a series of civilizations, which included the Olmec, Teotihuacan and Toltecs. Although there were differences between these civilizations, some continuities are noticeable (Davies, 1982). Similar to Old World civilizations, the native Americans demonstrated an ability to build and maintain cities, erect large monuments and support sophisticated forms of art. Tenochtitlan, the Aztec capital, dazzled the Spanish invaders because of its large population and elaborate beauty. Its population was more than ten times that of leading Spanish cities of the same era. Unlike the Europeans and Asians, the native Americans faced greater transportation difficulties. They lacked beasts of burden, so most goods were carried on foot. Water transport was also limited due to the presence of mountain ranges (Andes) or inland empires. This meant that more energy had to be expended on transportation than in other parts of the world.

Exchange of goods was primarily in the form of tribute rather than trade. Goods were traded, but the empires tended to accumulate things by demanding them as tribute from weaker states. Dominated cities provided goods for the elite of the empire. Under the Aztecs, political relations were characterized by the use of force. There was severe punishment for disobeying the king, and the Aztecs engaged in the practice of human sacrifice to appease the gods. The Aztec civilization exploited conquered peoples to amass wealth. Thus, when the Spaniard Cortés began his conquest of Mexico, he found willing local allies eager to throw off Aztec oppression.

Europe

The political economy of the area now known as western Europe underwent significant changes during the 13th to 15th centuries, which placed a series of European states in a much stronger position in relation to outside powers. The two most significant changes were increased economic activity and integration across Europe, and the consolidation of European political authority into rival states. We'll examine the increased economic activity by considering new trading patterns and the role of money and finance. Under consolidation of rival states, we'll review the emergence of nation-states and the consequences of changing forms of European warfare. The combination of these changes set the stage for European expansion.

New patterns of trade

The 14th and 15th centuries saw the western-European economy build bridges between its southern and northern centres. In the south, a handful of small Italian cities (Venice, Amalfi, Pisa and Genoa) began to develop their commercial roles, while in northern Europe, economic activity developed in the Low Countries of present-day Belgium and the Netherlands and in the North Sea and the Baltic Sea. Gradually, economic activity began to link together these two poles of European commerce (see Map 3.2).

Map 3.2 European political economy, 1400–1500

The Italians amassed wealth by tapping into the lucrative trade in the Mediterranean. They gathered silk from China, ivory from Africa and spices from India, Africa and South-east Asia. Spices were in high demand among the European elites because they masked the taste of rotten food in an era before refrigeration. Key spices included ginger, saffron, mace, cinnamon, sugar, cloves and nutmeg. The favourite spice, however, was pepper. Some years, a million pounds of pepper would pass through Venice. In return for such goods, the Italians were required to either pay in gold and silver, or ship goods to other regions in the Mediterranean. These products included timber, grain, linen, cloth, salt and slaves from the European interior (Braudel, 1994, p. 107).

Although the Italians were developing their commercial and financial skills, the rise of the Italian city-states depended as much on war as on trading skills. It was the Crusades that launched the trading fortunes of Christendom and especially Venice. The men of northern Europe spent large sums of money in Italy as they paid for their passage to the Holy Land. Christian states in the Middle East opened an additional gateway to secure pepper, spices, silk and drugs. For the struggling Italian city-states, the main battle was not between Christians and Muslims, but with their fellow Italians. Venice and Genoa engaged in a long and difficult commercial rivalry across the Mediterranean.

Simultaneously, a commercial network was developing in northern Europe, with the Belgian city of Bruges emerging as a second Venice. Bruges participated in a series of Flemish fairs by 1200, exploited its English contacts and welcomed Genovese ships in 1277. Its population grew from 35,000 in 1340 to 100,000 by 1500 (Braudel, 1994, p. 99). Its textile industry thrived and, by 1309, Bruges had set up its own stock market, the Bourse. Outside Belgium, northern economic activity was facilitated by the seaborne commercial triumph of the 'Hansa' (a group of merchants), which operated in the Baltic Sea, the North Sea, the English Channel and the Irish Sea. In 1356, the Hanseatic League, an alliance of trading ports, was created. The products of the north and east (wood, wax, fur, rye and wheat) were sent west in exchange for salt, cloth and wine. In contrast to the Italian luxury trade, most northern products were bulky items such as Polish grain, herring, salt, wine, wood or Swedish iron. Raw wool was the most valued product, much of it finding its way into the manufacturing of textiles in Flemish industry or into Italy.

There were some northern luxury products, however. These included fine Flemish cloth, furs, amber for jewellery, beeswax for candles, and honey.

Although this economic activity increased wealth in many parts of Europe, there was an imbalance in trade. Money drained from the north of Europe to the south and eventually to the east of the Mediterranean and beyond. High-priced and desirable goods came into Europe from China, India, the Middle East and Africa. In return, the Europeans had some large bulk goods to offer, but this was often not sufficient. Luxury goods that could not be offset with trade had to be purchased with silver or gold. However, there was a limit as to how much silver or gold Europeans were able to mine. Eventually this would leave Europeans with three choices: they could find new sources of silver and gold; they could try to seize the goods they wanted by force; or they could develop more desirable goods for trade purposes. As we shall see in later chapters, all these strategies were pursued with varying degrees of success. Their biggest breakthrough was seizing American silver to buy Asian products.

Money and finance

Now that we have raised the issue of finance and money, it is appropriate to take a detour to consider the growth of financial innovation in Europe. New forms of money, credit and the control of money developed in this period and were crucial to the growing wealth and military power in Europe and beyond. For people today, living in the age of electronic banking and credit cards, it is easy to take the presence of money and credit for granted. Yet, these institutions have not always existed as they do today. Moreover, the existence of an accepted form of money that is easily interchangeable and the instrument of credit is essential for anything more than a primitive economy (see Box 3.2).

Although various forms of money have been in existence for approximately 4,000 years (iron, tobacco, cattle, shells, beads, whisky, stones), it is only in the last century or so that the value of money has been readily accepted by the public without intense scrutiny (Galbraith, 1996). There has often been doubt about how much value was stored in the commodities used as money. In the case of metal coins, there has always been the risk that the issuing authority would debase the currency. Debasement occurred when the person minting the coins diluted the gold or silver with other metals

Box 3.2 The utility of money

Consider a fanciful, but useful example from an era before money existed. In this context, money can be defined simply as an object that is commonly offered or received for the purchase or sale of goods or services. When there is no money, economic activity must take place on the basis of barter. One product is exchanged for another product rather than for money. For example, your neighbours might give you some firewood if you baked some bread for them. Now, imagine a gathering of four people seeking to exchange products in a society that does not have money. One is a farmer who has brought several bushels of wheat, another is a shepherd bringing some wool from his sheep, a third has brought a horse for exchange and the fourth is a blacksmith with some simple tools such as knives. One problem arises when people try to exchange products of unequal value. Suppose that the person with the horse would like to barter for a single knife. The trade may not take place because the blacksmith can't make change for a horse. Another problem could arise if one person does not want the product of another. For example, the shepherd may want the farmer's wheat, but the farmer may not want the shepherd's wool. The shepherd might have to trade his wool for a knife and then trade the knife for the wheat. Alternatively, he may not be able to barter for a product that the farmer wants and the economic exchange is frustrated. The problem is only solved if all these people value a single commodity. They could sell their own products for that commodity and use it to purchase other people's goods. That valued commodity is called 'money'.

over time as it became debased. A modern form of debasement is inflation, where money loses its value as prices for goods rise.

Another difficulty in the age of multiple coins was the problem of exchanging money from various jurisdictions. How could one be sure of the value of a foreign coin? Even more serious was the possibility of counterfeit coins. When people from diverse jurisdictions met at trading centres, they would often prefer to be paid in coins that had a better reputation for keeping their value than others. The result was that traders would take the valued ones and keep them for private use while the debased ones were passed on. This habit of hoarding good currency led to Thomas Gresham's famous observation in 1558 that bad money always drives out good. The problem of creating a stable international monetary system, which facilitates the exchange of foreign currencies and trade, continues to this day. We will explore some of its dimensions in Chapter 8.

A key advance in financial history was the development of banking and the provision of credit. Today, we tend to encounter three types of banks:

1 *Deposit banks* (sometimes called clearing or commercial banks) take deposits and give loans to individuals and corporations. Examples include Citibank, Barclays or Deutsche Bank. These banks project a serious image and rely upon their reputation for sound finance to attract and keep customers.
2 *Investment or merchant banks* make deals between rich individuals or companies to finance business investments and corporate takeovers. They tend to be more aggressive than deposit banks.
3 *Central banks* are the bank of the country. They are run by the government and are tasked with printing and distributing money and controlling the supply of money within a country (see Box 3.3).

and passed it off as a pure product. For example, rather than issuing a gold coin that contained 100 per cent gold, a ruler might be tempted to claim that it was 100 per cent gold but put in 15 per cent copper. The hope was that the coin would still purchase the same amount of goods as the original gold coin, but cost less to make because there was a smaller gold content. Eventually, users of the coins would discover the change and demand more of it to pay for the same amount of goods. The amount of goods the coin could buy would decrease

The creation of credit greatly facilitated the growth of European economic activity. Credit notes were paper that allowed a person to buy now and pay later. This facilitated economic growth as some people and enterprises were able to conduct business that otherwise would not have taken place. A modern example of such activity is the house mortgage. Very few people would be able to buy a house if they were required to pay for it in cash. However, by taking a loan and paying it off over a long time period, many people can own houses. A similar mechanism was needed to finance long-distance trade.

> ## Box 3.3 Banks and financial instability
>
> Although banks and credit allow people to undertake more economic activity, they also pose a financial risk. People, companies or states can take on too much debt and have difficulty repaying the loan. In the case of the banking industry, there is always the risk that customers will panic and cause the collapse of a bank. Banks lend money out of their deposits via currency or notes of credit. However, there is a problem if all depositors come to the bank at once to ask for their money back. The bank will be unable to pay because the money has been distributed to other customers in the form of loans that cannot be instantly recalled. If there is a hint that a bank may be in financial trouble, depositors will rush to withdraw their money, thereby guaranteeing the bank's collapse. A bank must be able to retain the confidence of its depositors if it is to survive. In national banking systems, the central bank often acts as a lender of last resort. The lender of last resort is a financial institution that guarantees to pay a proportion of depositors' money in the hope that this will prevent a run on the bank. There is no official lender of last resort in the international system.

Another significant development in this area was the beginning of companies with partners or shareholders rather than a single owner. For example, in Italy there was an arrangement called the *commenda*. When launching a trading voyage, one merchant would supply two-thirds of the capital while another would supply one-third and manage the enterprise abroad. Both would share the profits. This allowed young adventurous merchants to trade with other merchants' capital. As trade was conducted over greater distances and time periods, there was more demand for pooling investment in the form of the corporation. Large infrastructure projects such as canal-building and, later, railways contributed to the rise of share-holding companies and eventually the creation of stock exchanges (Kindleberger, 1993, pp. 190–8).

The development of accepted forms of money, credit and banks was a precondition for financing European economic, political and military expansion from the 1400s until today.

Rise of sovereign territorial states

Having survived the threat of foreign invasions (see Box 3.4), Europe began a transition from feudal forms of organization to new political structures to the eventual emergence of sovereign territorial states between the 15th and 17th centuries. The push for political formations such as city-states, leagues and sovereign states came from merchants in cities seeking greater economic freedom to capitalize on growing long-distance trade (Spruyt, 1994). In Italy, the wealth of the luxury trade with the East allowed particular cities to develop resources great enough to guarantee their economic and military independence. In France, merchants allied with the king to undercut the power of the nobility and free up commerce. This led to the creation of the centralized state. In Germany, the king sided with the nobles, forcing cities such as Lubeck and Bremen to band together in the Hanseatic League.

Over time, the state form of organization proved to be more successful than the league or city-state. The state differed from other forms of medieval political organization because it was both sovereign and territorial. Sovereignty meant that there was no higher form of political authority than the states. The king or the parliament was the ultimate legal authority, concentrating law-making and the use of violence in their hands. This contrasts with the feudal system, where sovereignty was diffuse and authority was shared or contested among various actors such as the church, the empire, cities and lords. It also contrasted with leagues of cities where decision-making was difficult to achieve and more difficult to enforce.

The state was also territorial, which means that its authority was confined to a particular geographic area. Unlike universalistic organizations such as the church, which claimed authority over all Christians, states limited their jurisdiction to confined borders. The French king claimed authority over people living in France, but recognized the authority of the English king over people living in England. France and England might dispute the specific borders of each country or even try to conquer each other, but there was no question that they recognized each sovereign's right to govern their own people as they wished.

Box 3.4 Europe on the precipice: the Mongol invasion

Two hundred and fifty years before the Spanish arrived in the Americas and began to conquer the continent, Christian Europe barely survived a challenge to its existence (Marshall, 1993). In April 1241, two great European armies were decisively defeated by a more mobile, astute and deadly enemy – the Mongols. Duke Henry of Silesia led a force of Teutonic Knights, Knight Templars and Hospitallers from France to their death in Liegnitz, Poland, while in Hungary a force of 100,000 was destroyed by a force of 40,000 Mongols led by Prince Batu (later Khan Batu of the Golden Horde).

Whereas the European knights were weighed down by heavy armour and lacked any flexibility in strategic thinking, the Mongol armies were swift and versatile. Veterans of successful campaigns in China, central Asia, Persia and Russia, the Mongol armies were a foe the Europeans could not defeat. As the Mongols prepared to advance from Hungary, panic swept European leaders and peoples. European kings and princes were unable to field a united army, while religious leaders warned of an end of times brought about by the hammer of God – the 'Tartars'. Suddenly, in May 1242, the Mongol forces halted their invasion of Europe and returned to Russia, leaving a trail of death and destruction. The Great Khan Ogedei had died and subsequent internal rivalry prevented a resumption of the conquest of Europe. If Ogedei had lived longer or there had been a different successor, European expansion to other parts of the world would have ended before it began.

The emergence of the sovereign territorial state had several important consequences. First, it proved to be more efficient at mobilizing economic resources than other forms of organization. A single power with a given territory was gradually able to create national markets for commerce. This involved the destruction of the numerous barriers to economic activity that had grown up in the feudal era. Prominent among these barriers were varying customary laws, dangerous travel conditions, tolls on roads or waterways, a multitude of currencies and diverse weights and measures. By standardizing coinage, weights and measures, developing common laws protecting private property and ensuring safe and easier transit, states were able to increase economic activity and bring resources into their own treasuries.

A second important consequence was the competition created by a system of sovereign states. European states engaged in deadly economic and military competition with each other for hundreds of years. At times this weakened their position with the rest of the world, as in the aftermath of the First and Second World Wars. However, this state rivalry and the inability of any single European state to create a lasting empire over Europe (with the brief exception of Napoleon) injected a certain dynamic into European relations. Innovation in one European state would often be copied in others seeking to keep up in the competitive battle. City-states and states turned to the external world to gain an advantage over their European rivals. For example, as Venice grew stronger, Genoa supported Portuguese and Spanish attempts to break Venetian power by sailing around Africa or across the Atlantic. Although Columbus sailed from Spain, he was originally from Genoa and had approached the Portuguese for support.

As Tilly (1999) points out, wars drove European state formation. Conflict between European political authorities and their need for capital to finance ever more destructive wars contributed to the rise of nation-states. Nation-states proved to be more efficient at raising revenue and mobilizing military forces than either the city-states of Italy or leagues of cities such as the Baltic-based Hanseatic League. The centralization of violence within a state's control was so significant that the sociologist Max Weber concentrated on this feature when he defined a state as 'a human community that (successfully) claims the monopoly of the legitimate use of physical force within a given territory' (cited in Gerth and Mills, 1958, p. 78).

This competitive European state system often had negative implications for people outside Europe.

Where they were strong enough, Europeans used other parts of the world either as a battleground for their struggles or as venues to mobilize resources that they could use to further their rivalry. The strength of the Europeans depended on their ability to reap the benefits from increased trade, financial innovation and military developments.

In summary, the early 1400s witnessed numerous thriving and dynamic civilizations. China, India and the Ottoman Empire stood out as powerful land-based powers. Regional economies in Asia, Africa, Europe and the Americas varied in terms of political structures and economic activity. There was little indication at the time that Europeans would become as influential as they did in later centuries. Indeed, Europeans desired foreign products much more than other parts of the world desired European goods. Europe appeared economically weak. In political terms, Europe was composed of fragmented and warring political authorities. European technology and military forces were on a par with those of some other areas, but did not overshadow the military might of other civilizations. Despite these seemingly inauspicious indicators, the age of European expansion began in the 15th century.

EUROPEAN EXPANSION

In the middle of the 1400s Portugal, and then Spain, began a process of European exploration, expansion and conquest that would continue in various forms and guises for over 500 years. In time, the Portuguese and Spanish were surpassed by the Dutch, French and English states. Europeans launched a three-pronged attack on the political, economic and cultural foundations of the societies they encountered (Abernethy, 2000). Where they could exercise power over other groups, Europeans established new political structures ruling over local peoples in the form of colonies. They restructured local economies, transferring new forms of production oriented to satisfying European demands and tastes. They also transformed local cultures by introducing Christianity, notions of European racial superiority and, eventually, Western political ideologies such as nationalism, liberalism and Marxism. This section sketches out the reasons for this expansion and the varying patterns of interaction established between Europeans and Americans, Africans and Asians, from the Italian Renaissance until the Industrial Revolution.

The causes of European expansion have generated considerable academic and political debate. This chapter highlights several important factors: greed, fear, knowledge and biological good fortune. The greed was for valued products from outside Europe. Fear was created by the competition from other European powers

and the Islamic forces of Egypt blocking trade routes to the Far East. Knowledge was contained in the crucial technologies enabling the development of the seagoing, cannon-carrying sailing ship. The biological good fortune of the Europeans lay in their possession of a stock of threatening diseases and productive domesticated animals.

The waves of European expansion are summarized in Table 3.1. It lists the major expansionist powers, their period of greatest activity, the regions they operated in, the types of local activity they conducted and the major economic sectors they dominated. The first four countries are prominent in this chapter, while the other five countries are featured in following chapters.

Into the Americas

We begin our survey of European expansion in the Americas because this is the area of the world where Europeans had an early and dramatic success in subjugating the peoples and environment of another continent. In the 15th century, the sailors of Portugal and Spain sailed west into the Atlantic Ocean in an effort to secure the luxuries of the East. As will be discussed below, the Portuguese sailed down the African coast and eventually into Asia. The Spanish headed west across the Atlantic, hoping to reach China. Rather than reaching China, they encountered the Americas and quickly went about plundering its wealth. The resulting collision of European and American civilizations can be compared to an avalanche. A combination of European diseases, livestock and force of arms swept American civilization before it, creating waves of destruction.

A key factor in explaining this swift collapse of American civilization is the role played by the introduction of European diseases. Diseases such as smallpox, measles and, to a lesser extent, malaria ravaged indigenous populations, causing up to 100 million deaths in less than 100 years. It has been estimated that the pre–Spanish conquest population of Central America and Mexico of 25 million declined to 1.5 million by 1650. Similarly, the population of Peru may have declined from 5 million to 300,000 in the 1780s (Wolf, 1982, p. 134).

Prior to the Spanish arrival, the indigenous people were a healthy group of people. Their migration to the American continent via the frozen Bering Strait and subsequent isolation from other parts of the world

Table 3.1 **Summary of European expansionist activity**

European power	Most active years	Countries/regions	Local interaction	Economic activity
Portugal	Mid-1400s to late 1600s	Brazil, West and southern Africa, coastal ports in India and China	Conquest, trade, coastal ports	Fish, spices, sugar, slaving, intra-Asian trade
Spain	Late 1400s to late 1700s	North Africa, the Americas, Philippines	Conquest	Silver and gold extraction
Holland	Early 1600s to late 1700s	Indonesia, North America	Trade, port seizure, conquest	Spices, intra-Asian trade, slaving
Great Britain	Early 1700s to mid-1900s	North America and the Caribbean, Africa, Middle East, South and South-east Asia, Australia, New Zealand	Conquest, settler colonies, trade	Fish, furs, raw materials, sugar, cotton, slaving, drugs
France	1600s to mid-1900s	North America, the Caribbean, North and West Africa, India, South-east Asia, Oceania	Conquest, trade	Spices, furs, sugar, slaving
Belgium	Late 1800s to 1960s	Congo	Conquest	Rubber extraction
Germany	Late 1800s to 1940s	South, West and East Africa	Conquest	Minor economic interests
Italy	Late 1800s to 1940s	Libya, Ethiopia	Conquest	Minor economic interests
United States	Early 1800s to ?	North and Central America, the Caribbean, Hawaii, Philippines, Vietnam, Middle East	Conquest, occupation, trade	Natural resources

meant that the humans living there developed free of the numerous deadly pathogens breeding on the Euro-Afro-Asian land mass. The peoples of the Old World had created crowded civilizations, engaged in extensive agriculture and domesticated large numbers of animals. Each of these steps resulted in the creation and spread of new forms of disease. For example, living in dirty cities close to human garbage bred cholera and dysentery, while close human contact with cows, sheep and chickens led to the spread of animal diseases into the human population in the form of tuberculosis and smallpox (Nikiforuk, 1996).

When the Spanish arrived in the Americas, they unknowingly unleashed their pathogens on the vulnerable indigenous population. Smallpox was the most devastating disease, exterminating villages and tribes. The spread of disease was facilitated by bringing large numbers of native inhabitants together as slaves for the mines. Living in unhealthy conditions, they were made even more vulnerable to illness. Smallpox spread across the continent, preceding the arrival of Europeans into the American interior. The continent seemed empty to many European settlers as they spread across the Americas, partly because so much of the population

had already been killed. European diseases were part of a broader ecological imperialism (see Box 3.5).

The Euro-American political economy

European political and economic strategy in what they termed the 'New World' was both mercantilist and imperialist. Europe's relations with the Americas were imperialist, in that they subjugated local economies to the power of the European states and reoriented economic activity to serve only the interests of those states. Leading European states used the Americas as a resource for their empires. Many local economies and polities were destroyed and refashioned to serve the Spanish, Portuguese, French and English crowns. With regard to relations between European states, commercial activity was mercantilist. Economic activity was designed to increase the wealth and power of particular states and economic barriers were created to keep out contact with other states. For example, efforts were made to prevent Spanish and Portuguese or English and French colonies from trading with each other. Economic activity was viewed as a zero-sum game. Each country tried to be as self-sufficient as possible and to

Box 3.5 Ecological imperialism

Europe's ecological imperialism was not confined to disease. Another element in the success of the European invaders was the livestock they introduced into the Americas. Horses provided power for agricultural development and military advantage over the native population; pigs, rabbits and cattle provided for food and changed the environment to pasture land; bees provided the settlers with honey. All these animals were strangers to the Americas and provided their owners with a significant advantage in surviving in a new environment. Europeans came to the Americas not only as individual warriors, settlers or traders, but also as 'part of a grunting, lowing, neighing, crowing, chirping, snarling, buzzing, self-replicating avalanche' (Crosby, 1996, p. 194). That avalanche buried the majority of the native population and set the groundwork for the creation of a 'New World' shaped to benefit Europe, Europeans and the European settlers in the Americas.

deny their rivals the opportunity of creating wealth. The British and French crowns licensed private individuals to raid the fleets of opposing nations. The Spanish viewed such activity as piracy.

The Spanish initially came to the Americas seeking a route to China and India. In their first encounters with the native Americans, it was gold that caught their eye, and although it continued to be a source of fascination for the Spanish and other Europeans, it was silver that accounted for the majority of the wealth confiscated from the Americas. Spanish silver did not flow only to Europe: large quantities were also shipped across the Pacific. Silver was shipped from Acapulco in Mexico to the Spanish-controlled Philippines where it was exchanged for Chinese goods, especially textiles (silk). In 1797, more Spanish bullion went from Acapulco to Manila than was transferred across the Atlantic. Between 1570 and 1780, it is estimated that 4,000–5,000 tons of silver went to the Far East to pay for goods (Wolf, 1982, p. 154). The Americas had been forcibly entered into the world economy and Europeans were consuming the benefits of the integration.

The effort to mine silver led to a transformation of the American economy. The Spanish needed labour for

their mines, and supplies to maintain the mining industry. Labour was provided by native American and African slaves. Silver processing was exceedingly dangerous as it involved the use of mercury and resulted in mercury poisoning. The mines were at high altitude and work was conducted under physically draining conditions. Desperate for relief, the native working population increasingly turned to a substance previously confined to Inca religious ceremonies – coca leaf. Chewing the leaves dulled the workers' pain and the Spanish were happy to democratize coca consumption to keep the silver flowing (Pomeranz and Topik, 1999, pp. 156–8).

Mining also shifted the local economy away from pre-Hispanic agriculture to the silver veins of the Sierra Madre and Bolivian and Mexican mountains. It created a demand for food and supplies. Drawing on their feudal heritage, the Spanish introduced a system of large landholdings called 'haciendas'. These were landed estates worked by labourers settled on them and directly dependent on the estate owners. The highly unequal pattern of land ownership and resulting political influence of a landholding elite frustrated economic and political transition for hundreds of years.

After the Spanish conquest, the surviving native American communities played a vital but unequal role in what is now Latin America. Spain and Portugal focused on resource extraction and never engaged in large-scale emigration to the Americas. In contrast to what became the United States and Canada, the Spanish relied on local labour and integrated native Americans into their society in a hierarchical manner. The former native nobility often supervised local communities but were deprived of power. Locals were converted to Christianity, although Christianity itself was forced to accommodate local forms of worship and myths. In general, native Americans were integrated into the Spanish system as reservoirs of labour and sources of cheap agricultural and craft products. They were often subject to Spanish tribute or taxes and were forced to hire themselves out to pay their forced debts.

Spanish settlement in the Americas, similar to European settlement in other territories, created a racial division of labour that would last for centuries. In the Spanish case, relatively few Europeans emigrated to the Americas. Europeans and their descendants dominated the elite levels of society, with the children of Spanish/native American unions taking a secondary role. At the bottom of the society were native Americans, excluded from the political system, but providing essential labour. In the north of America, the pattern was different as native Americans were excluded from society and Africans were imported for the intensive labour role.

Spain was not the only European state to carry out economic activity in the Americas before the Industrial Revolution. Two years after the Spanish contact with the Americas, Portugal and Spain signed a treaty that granted Spain all the lands 370 leagues west of the Cape Verde Islands and Portugal all lands east. Portugal took Brazil and the South Atlantic, which led to Asia, while Spain took the rest of the Americas. In Brazil, the Portuguese concentrated on the production of sugar on large plantations as an export crop. This activity spread to the Caribbean, where it was copied by the Dutch, French and English who became rivals. This will be dealt with in greater detail in the following section on relations with Africa.

In the north of America, a number of states were engaged in economic activity. The Portuguese were attracted by the fish off the banks of Newfoundland and New England. They were followed by French and English fleets. As Portuguese and Spanish maritime power decreased around 1600, the French, British and Dutch were able to establish permanent settlements along the eastern seaboard and pursue a four-legged form of gold – the beaver. The demand for beaver to make expensive and fashionable hats for the European upper classes drove Europeans further into the American continent. As a result of the beaver trade, indigenous peoples in the interior became involved in hunting the increasingly scarce mammal. Over time, the local inhabitants moved from being partners in the fur trade to subordinate producers (Wolf, 1982, p. 194). As Canada and the US became settler colonies for an overflow of Europeans in the 18th and 19th centuries, an even worse fate awaited aboriginal inhabitants. Some groups were eliminated through genocidal warfare, while others were made economically dependent and herded onto reserves.

Along Africa: the triangular trade

In contrast to the Americas, Europeans did not enjoy a pathogen advantage in their relations with Africa. In fact, the presence of malaria on the African continent dictated a very different relationship. Europeans were confined to the coasts of sub-Saharan Africa, dependent on Africans being willing to engage in trade. Attempts to proceed further into the continent (with the exception of southern Africa, which had a more moderate climate) met with disease and death for most Europeans. Large-scale colonization of Africa would not occur for another 400 years, until the development of improved rifle technology and the antimalarial drug quinine.

Europe's maritime engagement with sub-Saharan Africa began with the Portuguese. The initial desire to sail along the African coast came from the hope that they could secure gold without having to rely on the trans-Saharan trade, which brought the commodity up from Senegal. In addition to gold, the Portuguese sought pepper, ivory, dyewoods, beeswax, leather and timber, as well as some slaves from Africa. In return, they exchanged textiles, wheat, brass utensils and glass beads. In later years they brought Brazilian tobacco. Slaves purchased from African traders were originally sent back to Portugal. Since slavery marked the prime economic interaction between Europe and Africa in the period under discussion, it is useful to focus on this activity.

Slavery was not a new institution to either the Europeans or the Africans. In African tradition, slaves were usually acquired as a result of unpaid debts, the judicial process or war. They were not used as the basis for economic activity. In Europe, the Roman and Greek Empires rested upon slave power. During the Crusades, Europeans and Muslims enslaved each other. In the 13th century, Venetians and Genovese imported Turkish and Mongol slaves. Slaves were used to grow sugar cane in Cyprus and Sicily and to work in mines. In the 14th century, Europe imported Slavs and Greeks. In Scotland, miners and saltpan workers were still enslaved in the 17th and 18th centuries.

Thus, the beginning of the slave trade was not unusual for either party. The transatlantic slave trade took the form of a joint European–African operation. Europeans financed, organized and drew the primary benefits from the trade. The capture, delivery, control and maintenance before the voyage was primarily an African affair. Europeans took over for ocean transport and beyond. Although some Europeans seized Africans directly as slaves, they usually exchanged metal, firearms, textiles, rum and tobacco for their human cargo.

As Europeans began to mine for silver and gold and introduce new crops into the Americas, the nature and size of the slave trade changed dramatically. Slaves were required for mining silver and gold. Portugal introduced sugar from the Mediterranean into Brazil and it later spread to the Caribbean. American tobacco was exported to Europe, while cotton plantations were introduced from Asia. All these products required a large workforce for their harvesting.

A number of forms of labour were harnessed to this activity. To state the obvious, this was backbreaking work that few people would freely choose. The Europeans first enslaved the local population. Their numbers were limited, however. Many died from disease while others escaped to form rebel communities. The Europeans also tried indentured labour from their home countries. Impoverished Europeans would agree to work for a number of years as labourers in return for their eventual freedom and an opportunity for a new life in the Americas. However, many European labourers died before their term was up and it became an increasingly unattractive option.

The solution for plantation and mine owners was to move labour in large numbers from Africa to the Americas in the form of slaves. Many Africans would die in the plantations, but they were replaced by more slaves. Why did Africa become the source of slave labour? As mentioned earlier, there was already trade in slaves before the introduction of plantation economies into the Americas, which provided a precedent. Furthermore, Africans transported across the Atlantic were at a greater disadvantage than indigenous enslaved people. It was virtually impossible for Africans to return home, while some of the local inhabitants were able to flee to neighbouring areas. Those Africans who survived transport to the Americas faced years of hard labour before dying in poverty. Their descendants could expect much the same fate. When slavery was finally abolished, Africans would remain on the bottom of the socioeconomic scale, stigmatized by poverty and racism for generations.

Similar to many historical events, there is some dispute about the number of Africans who were forcibly moved from their homes to slavery in the Americas. In the period 1450–1900, it is estimated that somewhere between 9 million and 13 million Africans were transported to the Americas (Iliffe, 1995, p. 131). The trade began relatively slowly, with some 275,000–370,000 being sent from 1451 to 1600. Almost 2 million were sent in the following 100 years and about 6 million between 1700 and 1800 as the plantation economies grew. An additional 3 million were transported in the 19th century. Mortality rates from the brutal methods of transportation were high – as much as 14 per cent on Dutch ships. Exact figures are difficult to establish, but one estimate is that for every 100 Angolans taken as slaves in the 18th century, 10 died during initial capture, 22 died on the way to the coast, 10 in coastal holding areas, 6 died on the voyage and 3 in the Americas before starting work (Iliffe, 1995, p. 135).

This horrendous economic activity was one side of what was called the 'triangular trade' (see Map 3.3). Europeans manufactured various goods such as textiles, guns, beads and semi-precious stones and exchanged them for slaves in Africa. The slaves were transported across the Atlantic, where they worked on plantations and in mines. The products of their labour – silver, cotton, sugar – were then exported at great profit to Europe and beyond. English cities such as Bristol and Liverpool became major slaving ports until Britain ended its participation in 1807. Large fortunes were created on the backs of slave labour.

The triangular trade allowed Europeans to export more products to Africa and use cheap labour to produce commodities in the Americas. The growing slave plantations and American colonies also served as a market for European manufactured goods. In a controversial book, Williams (1944) suggested that the profits from the slave trade fuelled the Industrial Revolution in Britain. While Williams may have underestimated the importance of the European market to the Industrial Revolution, the triangular trade certainly did contribute to the European economic take-off in the 1800s (Wolf, 1982, pp. 199–200).

On a personal level and in terms of specific communities, the consequences of the transatlantic slave trade were horrific. Individuals suffered immense deprivation, families and communities were shattered and millions died. The effects on African civilization were more mixed. In western Africa, groups along the coast were able to use trade with the Europeans to strengthen their hands against interior rivals. For example, the Asante were able to build an empire in the 18th and 19th centuries by using Dutch weapons to enlarge their territory and acquire more slaves. In the Niger Delta, it transformed society into slave-accumulating organizations and subjugated people further inland. In the Congo, it had the opposite effect, devastating the polity and creating rival groups engaged in slavery and war. In general, Africa suffered from the slave trade as its political economy was rearranged and millions were transported to another continent. However, Africans continued to resist European encroachment and would do so for many years.

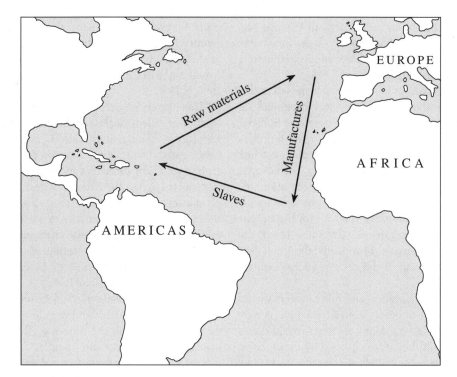

Map 3.3 **Transatlantic triangular trade**

On the peripheries of Asia

Voyages to America and Africa grew out of the European search for new trade routes to Asia. In the 1490s, Vasco da Gama finally sailed around Africa and reached India, with the help of an Arab navigator. A new route to the wealth of Asia was opened. However, the pattern of interaction with Asian political economies was far different from European experience in the Americas and Africa. The Asian empires were often larger, more densely populated and more productive than the European countries. For several hundred years Europeans were confined to seaports and trading posts. In some cases, they faced military defeat and in others they were frustrated by the lack of goods of sufficient quality to trade with Asians. Unfortunately, Eurocentric histories can give us a distorted view of this era by downplaying the significance of Asian activities (see Box 3.6).

The Portuguese were the first Europeans to sail around Africa. They immediately came into contact with an expanding Muslim trade network. The Portuguese could not hope to compete with Asians in a head-to-head

struggle so they attempted to control strategic pressure points, such as Goa, Hormuz and Malacca. Their attempt to expand into China was defeated in battle in 1521. The pattern of seizing coastal ports to gain a foothold in lucrative Asian trade was repeated by the Dutch and the British.

The Europeans were confined to working the sea lanes between trading outposts in Asia. The Portuguese, then the Dutch and the English moved cargo between Asian ports and back to Europe, amassing wealth for their own countries, but making limited progress into the Asian heartland. Although mercantilist economic theory posited a world where European states would trade with their colonies on a North–South basis, the economic realities dictated a much more profitable trade for Europeans in facilitating economic relations between different parts of the non-European world.

The success the Europeans did enjoy was due to the gun-bearing sailing ship. Around AD 1400, the Europeans combined the square rig of their designs with the lateen rig of the Arabs. They then equipped this with cannon. After 1500, cannons were installed below decks

---

Box 3.6 Ayutthaya versus Venice

Ayutthaya is located in Thailand just outside Bangkok. Its historical significance is that it was the capital of Thailand for over 400 years (1351–1767) and was one of the wealthiest cities in South-east Asia (Gamier, 2005). This wealth facilitated the building of an impressive city marked by beautiful temples. A city surrounded by rivers, Ayutthaya served as a crossroads for Chinese, Malay, Indonesian, Indian and even Persian goods. European merchants also set up trading posts in the city. It acted as a key centre of exchange linking eastern and southern Asian trade.

Despite its significance, far fewer people have heard of Ayutthaya than of the European city of Venice. This is partially because Venice is still a thriving city that attracts tourists from around the world, while Ayutthaya is less of a tourist destination and no longer a major international centre. However, another explanation lies in the fact that histories of the global economy usually emphasize Western locations and developments while ignoring significant developments in other parts of the world. 'Eurocentrism' is the term used to describe a view of the world that places Europe and her offspring settler colonies (the US, Canada, Australia, New Zealand) at the centre of world history without understanding the role of other countries and peoples.

---

and the galleon made its appearance – half warship, half merchant ship. It overwhelmed Arab and Asian naval opposition in direct confrontations, but could do little to subdue large land empires or stop the local trade conducted by smaller vessels.

Early Portuguese and Dutch economic activity in South-east Asia relied heavily on a relatively egalitarian gendered division of labour between European traders and native businesswomen (Pomeranz and Topik, 1999, pp. 28–31). The European merchants encountered existing commercial networks that were often run by local women. Local women had well-established business connections and a familiarity with the economy that proved invaluable to the Europeans. The business opportunities provided by these women, combined with the extreme difficulty of attracting European women to the colonies, led to widespread intermarriage between Portuguese/Dutch merchants and Asian businesswomen. In many cases, local women were able to continue amassing wealth as their sickly European partners succumbed to tropical diseases. This state of affairs lasted for about 200 years until the 19th century. As technical innovations took hold, such as the Suez Canal, the telegraph and vaccinations, it became more possible to pursue a 'European' lifestyle in Asia. This resulted in European men bringing their European wives to the colonies, causing the marginalization of native women and increasing differentiation between Europeans and non-Europeans. As Europeans became more entrenched and powerful, their need and tolerance for local cultures decreased.

The British followed the Portuguese and Dutch into the Indian Ocean and eventually gained direct control over a large Asian land-based power – India. The colonization of India proved to be a financial windfall for the British, which enabled them to build a much larger empire. As British children were taught, the sun never set on the empire because it spanned the globe. The British began modestly in India. The British East India Company initially accepted the sovereignty of local Indian rulers. However, in 1757, the company intervened in a local power struggle in Bengal and ended up taking power in the territory. At about this time, the Muslim-dominated Mughal Empire entered a stage of crisis. This allowed the English to defeat local Indian forces in battle at Hyderabad in 1789 and Mysore in 1799.

British participation in Indian trade created large private fortunes, which were brought back to England. With each new success the Indian economy was reorganized to pay for English warfare and conquest. Indian agriculture was switched to export crops that would benefit Britain, such as cotton, sugar, tobacco, jute, indigo and opium. The English also imposed new patterns of tax and introduced English law. English machine-produced cottons were introduced after 1814, destroying the high-quality Indian textile industry. A new army was created with English officers and Indian troops. The British forces succeeded in suppressing an 1857 revolt against the company's rule in India, but the British government was so concerned that it relieved the East India Company from ruling India and took direct control.

Although the British had succeeded in subjugating India, they were unable to make much progress with China. The Chinese were not very interested in trade with red-haired barbarians. The English were confined to the trading port of Canton and sought silks, porcelain and medicines. In exchange for these products, the English had to pay in silver, since they possessed no goods that the Chinese wanted. The situation became more serious as the English developed a taste for tea. Tea-drinking had begun in England in 1664, introduced by the Dutch. By 1783, consumption was worth £6 million a year, later rising to £15 million (Wolf, 1982, p. 255). All this consumption had to be paid for in silver, which originated in the Americas. China became the tomb of American silver.

England desperately needed to find a commodity that it could exchange for desired Chinese goods, as it could not export silver to China indefinitely. British harvesting of sandalwood devastated the forests of Fiji between 1804 and 1810 and Hawaii between 1811 and the 1830s, but this was not sufficient to pay for Chinese products (Pomeranz and Topik, 1999, p. 161). The answer to British problems was to export drugs grown in India. The drug of choice was opium, which is highly addictive and is known in another form as heroin. In 1773, the East India Company established a monopoly over the opium trade and smuggled it into China. US traders also became involved, shipping opium from Turkey to New York to China. The Chinese declared the trade illegal, but this did not stop British and American entrepreneurs. By 1828, the British had been able to reverse the flow of silver so that more left China than entered it. Not content with smuggling drugs, British and US merchants pushed for the right to sell them openly to China. The Chinese market was finally opened as a result of British victory over the Chinese in the Opium Wars (1839–60). British gunboats were the crucial ingredient in persuading the Chinese to open their border to drugs. The European drug strategy was a success for their trade balances, but a disaster for China. It shifted the economic balance in favour of Europe and created millions of opium addicts in China. The present-day export of cocaine from Colombia to the US, which has sparked a 'drug war' in the US and Latin America, pales in comparison with this historical episode.

It was in this era that we see the beginnings of the modern corporation in the form of the Dutch and British East India Companies (Pomeranz and Topik, 1999,

pp. 163–6). These companies were different from other forms of business such as family firms or temporary companies in several ways. First, they were impersonal in the sense that partners in the company did not have to all know each other. Second, the owners of the companies did not directly control the companies. Directors were elected to run the companies and owners or investors either accepted their decisions or sold their share of ownership. Third, the companies were designed to be permanent. They would survive change in owners and were founded for an unlimited time period. Earlier ventures were usually created for a limited time such as the completion of a single voyage or for a series of voyages. The expectation of the East India Companies was that they would engage in commercial activity for as long as it was financially viable.

This new type of economic organization was needed because the commercial activity undertaken demanded large amounts of capital over a long time period. Return voyages from Europe to Asia could take up to three years. Capital invested would often need to be spread over several voyages due to the possibility that any single trip would not be successful. Another significant reason for huge capital expenditures is that much of the commercial activity was combined with expensive military action. In this mercantilist era, European intercontinental trade was typified by the seizure of territory, building of forts and provision of armed vessels. This greatly increased the cost of commercial activity, but was essential if merchants were to ward off their European rivals and cling to their footholds on the Asian mainland.

CONCLUSION

The early era of forging a world economy from the 1400s until the mid-1800s was not a savoury process. Coercion was often more in evidence than cooperation. European expansion decimated civilizations with disease, enslaved millions of Americans and Africans, worked millions of others to death, reoriented local economies to serve European elite interests and trafficked in drugs to undermine other civilizations. The period saw a great transformation in the key frameworks of political economy as Europeans increasingly collided with other centres of wealth and power. Here, we review these changes using the frameworks that serve as separate chapters in Part 3 – trade, production, finance, labour, gender, development, environment, ideas, security and governance.

Trade

It has been said that trade is an activity as old as human civilization and this chapter has outlined various trading systems in existence over the period 1400–1800. Apart from forms of local exchange, international trade (that is, cross-border trade) is a significant feature of this period. We showed the importance of long-distance trade and intercontinental trade routes to a number of societies. No simple or single imperative accounts for this trade, although it was mainly stimulated by the desire to attain goods not produced domestically. This differs from the current international trading system where developed states import goods that are also produced locally. The trade discussed above varied from the exotic to the tragic; from the sale of spices and metals to the sale of human beings. This chapter shows some of the continuities in the history of international trade and some of the contingent features of trade. Among the continuities are the search for exotica and mass consumption goods. On the other hand, the chapter alerts us to the fact that goods considered moral in one epoch may not be perceived as such at another period in history. For example, while slavery and the trade in slaves still exists, it is universally condemned as a practice.

The push and pull of markets played a key role in driving European expansion. European lust for luxury goods from the East motivated states and merchants to find new sources of supply. It was the European inability to produce particular products such as silk and spices that drove them out of their regional shell. When they could not take what they wanted by force (which was most of the time), Europeans engaged in trade. However, in several locations, trade that originally was conducted on the basis of relative equality eventually had disastrous effects on local economies. The fur trade in the north of America eventually undermined the independence of indigenous peoples, while the slave trade devastated large parts of Africa as it evolved from a minor activity to a large-scale operation.

Production

During the four centuries covered in this chapter, production remained primarily agricultural and was largely designed for local use. Although there were no great advances in the technology of production, there were significant changes in who produced what and for whom. European conquest of the Americas radically altered the production structure of two continents. Native economies were either destroyed or reorganized to supply raw materials (metals, crops, furs) to European states. In the southern US, Latin America and the Caribbean, the patterns of production relations consisted of a small wealthy landholding class and a large disempowered and often enslaved labouring class working in agriculture or mining. In the northern US and parts of Canada, settler colonies were set up with a more equal distribution of land and an industrial base was slowly nurtured. In Africa, the capture and export of slaves grew from a relatively minor practice to a large economic activity, which destabilized some societies and brought resources to others.

Finance

Long-distance trade led to and was facilitated by financial innovation. An important element in European expansion was the development of financial instruments to fund exploration, trade and war. The development of banking and the provision of credit was a key advance. In some cases, the financial innovations outpaced people's ability to handle them (see Box 3.7). Money had to be lent over long periods of time so that risky but highly profitable trade could take place. Economic activity over great distances and long time periods also encouraged the development of impersonal and long-standing corporations. Giant economic actors such as the British and Dutch East India Companies were required to engage in intercontinental trade. They were also needed because economic activity often required military security from foreign rivals and local populations. As a result, these companies employed military forces to protect and extend their interests.

Labour

The reorientation of production in various continents led to the emergence of a division of labour that increasingly grouped the export sector of countries into particular tasks. Europeans took on the roles of producing manufactured goods, shipping goods between continents and running plantations and mines on several continents. Africans were incorporated into the

---

Box 3.7 Tulip mania in the 17th century

The great tulip bubble or tulip mania is one of the earliest reported financial bubbles in human history and refers to the extreme change in prices for several breeds of tulip bulbs in Holland between 1634 and 1637 (Garber, 1989). Tulips were introduced to western Europe from Turkey during the 16th century and rapidly came to be prized much more highly than all other flowers. In 1554, Ogier Ghiselin de Busbecq, the ambassador of the Holy Roman Empire to Turkey, sent the first tulip bulbs and seeds to Vienna. In 1593, Carolus Clusius, a Flemish botanist, brought tulips from Constantinople (now Istanbul) to Holland for research. In the beginning of the 17th century, the tulip gained popularity in Holland as a product for garden decorating and medical use. The huge interest in the flower dramatically increased the tulip's price. Some hybrid breeds were seen as rarities and a sign of high status. In late 1636 and early 1637, a manic demand for tulips swept through Holland. Some varieties cost more than a house in Amsterdam and most of the Dutch, including many non-professionals, took part in the tulip business. For example, at the height of the speculation, a single Semper Augustus bulb was sold for 5,500 guilders, a weight of gold equal to $50,000, evaluated at $450 per ounce (Mackay, 1852). High speculative values attracted large amounts of foreign funds and people from all walks of life hurriedly liquidated other assets to participate in the tulip market. As a result, the bulb prices rose steadily throughout the 1630s and the market price far exceeded rational values. Finally, the price bubble burst and even the rarest bulbs could find no buyers at 10 per cent of their previous prices (Garber, 1989). Fortunes had been made, but many Dutch people suffered as the price of tulips collapsed. The economic frenzy over tulips may seem strange from today's vantage point, but the dynamics of greed and irrationality are similar to our own recent financial crisis.

---

division of labour as providers of slaves. Native Americans were either exterminated, marginalized on reserves or poor land, or integrated into subordinated labour relations. In Asia, large land empires ensured more balanced relations with the European adventurers and traders. Indian, South-east Asian and Chinese producers continued to make highly desirable products and insisted on fair compensation for their goods.

Gender

Gender relations were central to the interaction between Europeans and non-European societies. In cases where the two communities were of equal strength, European men often relied on women from other cultures for assistance. An example given above was of business arrangements between Portuguese men and Indonesian businesswomen. However, in areas where Europeans exercised power over other peoples, a more unequal and fiercely contested set of gender relations emerged (Mies, 1998, pp. 90–110). Europeans worked to undermine the place of women in Asia, Africa and the Americas, seeing independent women as a sign of a 'backward' society. In plantation societies, Europeans engaged in a struggle with female slaves to increase or decrease their birth rate according to the economic demands of the owners.

Development

In this era, we can see the origins of some of today's development dilemmas. The economies of what are now Latin America and the Caribbean were forcefully integrated into the world economy in the role of natural resource producers. European and Asian crops, for example cotton and sugar cane, were introduced and the economy was organized to benefit Western capitalists. This resulted in two developments: certain areas were locked into producing products whose value would decrease over time, and wealth was transferred from the producers of the products (often native Americans or slaves) to the owners of the mines and plantations (European landholders, capitalists and settlers). In Africa, the slave trade allowed some tribes to increase their power relative to African rivals, but it destroyed other societies and weakened the continent as a whole. In Asia, the European impact was far less significant until the 19th century. Indeed, it is likely that the transfer of European silver (taken from the Americas) to pay for goods stimulated Asian industry.

Environment

During this period, the natural environment in the Americas went through massive change. European introduction of crops and animals shifted the existing balance between people and nature to a new dynamic, which saw the increasing subjugation of nature to human economic activity.

Ideas

Ideas played an important part in the period 1400–1800 as a world economy was in the process of formation. At the simplest level, the knowledge structure provides the technology and know-how of societies and civilizations. We have shown how different societies, empires and civilizations had developed various levels of technological sophistication at the beginning of this period and how the technological bases of these societies changed over the course of these four centuries. During this period, Europe rose from a subordinate position to a potentially dominant one.

The knowledge structure also provides what can be termed 'worldviews', that is, the meta-structure determining the reception of knowledge and structuring perception of human–environment relations. Once again, this period provides an example of the wide diversity in human thought and behaviour. It also shows how some worldviews proved more adaptable to changing environmental conditions, while others failed to cope with advances in technology.

The third aspect relating to the role of knowledge pertains to ideas about the relationship between humans. The organization of society, economics and politics rests on ideas about social relations. From the Incas to the Chinese, Africans and Europeans, different systems were developed during this period. And yet at the end of this period, we stand on the verge of the global dominance of just one of these systems of thought.

The analysis above has attempted to provide some answers to the rise of Europe, while acknowledging that no definitive answer can be given. It has shown that in all three areas of the knowledge structure identified – technical, rational and social – the world in 1400 exhibited greater diversity than our world at the beginning of the 21st century. It has also demonstrated that working on different principles, peoples were able to develop functioning polities and economies. By the end of this period the ideational structure of one group of people was becoming dominant. This chapter has argued that this is not because these ideas were, in themselves, superior but that, in combination with other themes examined, they contributed to the transformation of Europe in a manner that resulted in European dominance and expansion as other societies experienced conquest, decay and decline.

Security

The security structure was crucial to influencing the international economy in this period. Some historians (Parker, 1996) have argued that European military superiority was the key variable in explaining the success of European endeavours, but this is debatable. Spanish military technology was not much more advanced than that of the native Americans. In Asia, the Indian and Chinese military were for centuries more than capable of resisting European arms. It is true that Western naval technology proved crucial for securing coastal ports, but Western land forces would have to await the invention of better rifle, artillery and machine gun technology in the 19th century before gaining a decisive edge over non-Europeans.

The relative equality in arms suggests that European military success was often dependent on the cooperation of local collaborators (Thompson, 2000, p. 79). Americans, Africans and Asians were in competition with other Americans, Africans and Asians just as European states were struggling against each other. Alliances between locals and Europeans against other locals or other Europeans were common. For example, the Spanish conquistador Cortés relied on local tribes to help defeat the Aztecs. Europeans needed Africans to supply slaves to their coastal stations. The British allied with Indians who opposed Mughal rule to gradually take over the whole country. Thus, European success depended on local cooperation.

Governance

The growth of the international economy cannot be separated from developments in domestic and international governance arrangements, including the use of organized violence. In terms of domestic governance arrangements, the most significant political development was the rise of the modern state in Europe. As the reigning monarchs of Europe fought each other, they needed to finance their wars. The discovery that the centralized state was more efficient at raising revenue for the purposes of conducting military campaigns contributed to the demise of city-states and the various leagues of states. Competition spurred innovation within states and resulted in other areas feeling the impact of European struggles.

The emergence of a new form of political organization was intimately linked with developments in the market. First, the territorial state was effective in the removal of barriers to economic activity across space and place. A multiplicity of political authorities had resulted in an often insurmountable range of barriers to commerce, for example customs duties and tolls. The creation of a single political authority, similar to the creation of a common market or free-trade area today, breaks down barriers within the same territorial space. Second, the emergence of the state not only abolished various barriers to commerce but also encouraged trade through legislation. The development of law, common currencies and various methods of standardization, for example of weights and measures, facilitated economic exchange and the development of the market.

The pattern of European interaction and the rules that governed interaction across civilizations varied greatly according to the ability of other groups to resist European dominance. In the case of the Americas, Europeans imposed their own form of political economy as they overwhelmed local groups. In Africa, Europeans were prevented from moving in much beyond the coastal regions, but their thirst for slaves reshaped African societies. In most parts of Asia, Europeans were confined to coastal trading cities by larger and more powerful Asian empires. Some European advance was made in India after 200 years, but China resisted European power well into the 19th century. European expansionism also resulted in widely diverse patterns of cultural transformation in the societies they encountered (Curtin, 2000). In some cases, such as southern Africa, new racial hierarchies were introduced through migration, while in other cases, such as Mexico, European and native cultures fused into a new entity.

Interactions brought about by European expansion had great implications for Europe, as well as for those it encountered. 'Discovery' of the Americas caused Europeans to re-evaluate their place in the cosmos and reconsider their relationship to other peoples. Did these other peoples have similar rights to Europeans? Were they equal in the eyes of God? While European actions often seemed to answer these questions in the negative, a more egalitarian view of non-Europeans would eventually emerge in the late 20th century. In commercial terms, new products flooded into Europe, changing social and political organizations. One example was the introduction of the potato, which allowed millions of poorer Europeans to have a richer diet. More significantly, the flow of American silver allowed Europe to engage in greater trade with Asian centres.

Entering the 19th century, Europe had increased its wealth and power relative to other parts of the world. It had wrought destruction on the Americas, weakened Africa but was held at a distance in much of Asia. It would await the Industrial Revolution before European expansion could make further inroads. We begin with this development in Chapter 4.

Further Reading

Janet Abu-Lughod provides an excellent overview of the pre-1400 world system in *Before European Hegemony: The World System A.D. 1250–1350* (1989). The ecological factors in European expansion are detailed by Alfred Crosby in *Ecological Imperialism: The Biological Expansion of Europe, 900–1900* (1996). French historian Ferdinand Braudel provides a detailed examination of the early European economy internationalizing in *The Perspective of the World: Civilization and Capitalism 15th–18th Century*, vol. 3 (1979). David Landes argues that European values account for the rise of the West in *The Wealth and Poverty of Nations* (New York: W. W. Norton, 1998), while John Hobson argues against a Eurocentric perspective on global economic history in *The Eastern Origins of Western Civilization* (2004). A good introduction to the origins and role of money is John Kenneth Galbraith's *Money: Whence It Came and Where It Went* (1996).

Chapter

4

Industry, Empire and War: 1800–1945

This chapter examines the emergence of a liberal and imperialist international economy in the 19th century and its destruction in the early 20th century. The first part of the chapter investigates the origins of the Industrial Revolution in Britain and the factors that facilitated it. The second section focuses on the international system that was created as a result of the advantages the revolution gave to Great Britain and other Western powers (Pax Britannica). The third section examines one of the consequences of the increased power flowing from the Industrial Revolution – the era of renewed imperialism. The fourth section examines the breakdown of the liberal system during the First World War and the futile attempt to re-establish it during the 1930s.

There are several points we can take from this historical overview of the 19th and early 20th century. First, both wealth and power flowed to the elites of states who were able to harness innovation in production technologies. The Industrial Revolution increased British power and wealth to such an extent that some scholars describe the mid-1800s as a period of British hegemony or Pax Britannica. The German and US lead in the second Industrial Revolution at the end of the 19th century propelled them into prominent roles in the early 20th century. Technological innovation and the ability to adapt to new methods of production are important.

Second, the liberal market of the 19th century was created at some human cost. Within Britain, people were herded into cities and factories; vulnerable women and children were the initial factory labour force until a 'free' labour market eventually dragged in male workers. In the international arena, the wealth generated by the British textile industry relied on US slave labour to produce the input of raw cotton. Progress had its costs and they were distributed very unevenly.

Third, although the benefits of free trade were loudly proclaimed, the practice was much more limited. Bolstered by the productivity increases of the Industrial Revolution, Britain led the way in pursuing free trade unilaterally. Some countries followed the example in order to secure key technologies. However, once other countries felt themselves in direct competition with Britain, they often erected protectionist barriers. Britain was eventually surpassed in the second Industrial Revolution by two highly protectionist countries – the US and Germany.

Fourth, the international order required particular domestic arrangements to function smoothly. Two important mechanisms of the 19th-century system relied on the exclusion of public opinion from policy-making. The gold standard required automatic social and economic adjustment to trade flows, while the balance of power necessitated strategic decisions based on the calculation of interest to the exclusion of ideology or affinity. These practices were possible because most people were excluded from political participation. However, as democratization continued in the 19th century and a rising tide of nationalism spread across all European states, it was much more difficult to control policy options.

Fifth, the developments in European industrial innovation shifted the balance of power between Europeans and non-Europeans, sparking a renewed bout of expansionism and competition. Large parts of Africa and Asia, which had previously resisted European expansion, succumbed to the force of European arms and industrial might. Once again, economies were reoriented to serve foreign interests, often with disastrous consequences for local populations.

Sixth, competition between European states eventually degenerated into open warfare, leading to tremendous human and financial losses. The destruction of the liberal imperial system was violent and efforts to rebuild it proved largely futile. Ideologies and movements unleashed by the First World War made a return to the old system impossible. Indeed, it was not until the aftermath of the Second World War that a stable system was rebuilt.

THE INDUSTRIAL REVOLUTION

What was the Industrial Revolution?

To simplify a complex phenomenon, the Industrial Revolution involved the application of machinery to production, the introduction of new energy sources to power the machines and the reorganization of the labour force into factories. The first Industrial Revolution began in Britain and lasted about 100 years from the mid-1700s until the 1870s. Changes began in the textile industry with cotton and were followed by the steel industry, especially in the form of railways. In the 1870s, a second Industrial Revolution focusing on new products and technologies swept the Western world, led by Germany and the US. Elsewhere, the results were much more varied. A few states such as Japan, Russia and Canada successfully mimicked the British example, while some states are still attempting to industrialize their societies in the 21st century.

Let us begin by looking at the British textile industry in the 1700s. At this time, the British were engaged in serious competition with Dutch and Indian textile producers. While they were able to combat Dutch production because of cheaper products and labour costs, they were unable to compete with Indian products, which were cheaper and a better quality than those produced in England. The solution to this competitive problem was the protection of the domestic market by forbidding the British East India Company to import Indian textiles into the UK.

The British wanted to improve their productivity, but ran into a serious technical barrier. The key problem was the lack of synchronization between spinning and weaving. It took a long time to use a spinning wheel to spin the cotton into thread and a relatively short time to weave it into a garment. Thus the pace of weaving depended on the speed at which cotton could be spun. A series of inventions in the late 1700s remedied these problems. The invention of the spinning jenny allowed a spinner to spin several threads of yarn simultaneously. The water frame drew out fibres on rollers and wound them on upright spindles. The 'mule' combined the features of the water frame and jenny. By 1790, steam power was applied to the mule, massively increasing the amount of cotton that could be processed in a specific time. Box 4.1 provides some examples of increased productivity generated by the Industrial Revolution.

The introduction of mechanized production meant that the labour force had to gather in a single place to work with the machines. This resulted in the development of the factory system. The factory system concentrated a large number of workers engaged in different

> **Box 4.1** Increased productivity in the Industrial Revolution
>
> ▶ Number of hours to process 100 pounds of raw cotton into thread: 50,000 in 1700, 2,000 in 1775, 300 in 1795 and 135 in 1825
> ▶ Railway construction: 5,000 miles in 1840, 228,000 miles in 1880
> ▶ Overland freight rates declined 90 per cent in countries with railways
> ▶ Tripling of British railway and steel exports 1845–75, export of machinery increased ten times
> ▶ Voyage of a sailing ship with 1,000 tons of cargo from London to China: 120–130 days in 1800. In 1865, the same voyage on a steamship carrying three times as much cargo was 77 days (Wolf, 1982, pp. 273, 291–3).

technical operations on one site. It took over from the putting-out system, whereby producers distributed raw materials to be assembled or processed to individual households/workers and awaited the finished product. This was not an ideal system from the owner's perspective because they had little control over work intensity, the duration of labour, pilfering or quality, which all resulted in delays in processing and delivery. It was more advantageous for workers, who would sometimes spend most of the week engaged in other activities and then work very hard for a couple of days to fulfil their quota.

The cotton factories of the Industrial Revolution were essentially spinning mills. Weaving kept pace by a multiplication of hand looms and manual weavers. From 1805, the working day was lengthened by introducing artificial light with gas lighting. Factory work was extremely unpopular with the British population, who exhibited a general unwillingness to work in factories. Although factory wages were sometimes higher than those in other unskilled industries, male workers were originally reluctant to enter the workforce because they lost independence. As a result, the bulk of the factory workforce came from the more exploitable sector of the population – women and children. It is estimated that in 1838 only 23 per cent of textile workers were adult men (Hobsbawm, 1987, p. 68). As the factory system progressed, more men entered the workforce and women were gradually confined to the domestic sphere. Early unions were often male dominated and saw women workers as competition. Many men who lost control over their work by being reduced to factory automatons reasserted control through domestic violence at home or against women in the workplace (Stearns, 1993, p. 62). The difficult working conditions in factories sparked waves of resistance, ranging from the activity of Luddites destroying machines to the formation of trade unions and the growth of democratic and Chartist movements.

The growth of textile and other types of factories had a number of effects on British society. In some locations it led to the creation of great metropolitan areas. For example, the population of Manchester expanded from 24,000 people in 1773 to over 250,000 by 1851 (Wolf, 1982, p. 276). According to Hobsbawm (1987, p. 65), the Industrial Revolution ushered in a new economic relationship between people, a new system of production, a new rhythm of life, a new society and a new historical era. This new system had three primary elements:

1 The industrial population was divided into capitalist employers, who owned the factories and materials, and workers, who owned nothing but their labour, which they sold for wages.
2 Production was organized in the factory with specialized machines and specialized labour.
3 The entire economy became dominated by capitalists pursuing profit.

There was a crucial international dimension to the Industrial Revolution in terms of both supply and demand. In terms of supply, the cotton came from outside Europe. In the late 1700s, most came from the Caribbean, but by 1807 more than 60 per cent came from the US. Between 1815 and 1860, cotton proved vital to US economic health as it accounted for more than half the total value of US exports (Wolf, 1982, p. 279). The production of this vital input to the Industrial Revolution was undertaken through the use of slave labour and the removal of indigenous peoples from their land as the plantations moved further west in the US. On the demand side, Western states created foreign markets for their products. For example, once British manufacturers held the competitive advantage (spinning cotton in 1/370th of the time of Indian spinners), they were able to destroy the Indian textile industry by exporting machine-made cloth and yarn at prices far lower than those of their handicraft rivals (Wolf, 1982, p. 273). By 1840, the Indian industry was destroyed and India was reduced to providing raw cotton as a British export to China.

The second phase of the Industrial Revolution was characterized by developments in iron and coal power, and the most visible aspect was the tremendous growth in railway-building. After Britain, the US became the centre of railway growth (Wolf, 1982, p. 292). England turned to coal as the energy source for this economic activity. Railways became the shock troops of industrialization from Argentina to the Punjab. They opened up vast new areas to further economic activity and tied parts of the world closer together. On the seas, shipping also underwent a transformation. Steel ships powered by steam power dramatically reduced the time required to transport goods. Alongside the triumph of steamships came the building of canals across Egypt and Panama. The Suez Canal in Egypt was completed in 1869 and cut the sailing time from England to Asia in half. Unfortunately for Egypt, it also resulted in their bankruptcy and virtual rule from Britain. Approximately 50 years later, US companies would overcome even greater obstacles (primarily malaria) to finish the Panama Canal in 1915 through the use of Jamaican and Chinese labour. From this time on, the US actively intervened in the operation of Central American states to ensure the safety of 'its' canal.

The advent of the railway also saw the rediscovery of a particular form of business enterprise – the corporation. As outlined in Chapter 3, today's transnational corporations were foreshadowed by the British and Dutch East India Companies. Although the early phase of the Industrial Revolution was conducted by family businesses, a more permanent and long-term organization such as the corporation was needed for the railway expansion. This was because large sums of money were needed for investment and the time frame for realizing profits was long term (Pomeranz and Topik, 1999, p. 164).

Why Britain? Why then?

The Industrial Revolution catapulted Britain into becoming a world power and decisively tilted the balance between Asia and Europe. The question arises as to why it occurred in Britain and why it happened at this time. Although there is a great debate on the subject, most analysts highlight three factors: the growth in European knowledge and technology, the rise of the liberal state, and Britain's unique role in the international economy. We will deal with these in turn.

Landes (1998, pp. 200–9) puts a great deal of emphasis on the development of a culture of knowledge in Europe and Britain. He stresses the European scientific revolution and the Enlightenment, which sought to move understanding beyond religious interpretation. Europe developed three key characteristics. First, there was a growing autonomy of intellectual enquiry. Scientists were gradually able to break free of the church and state to pursue their discoveries according to scientific principles rather than theocratic dogma. Second, a language of proof was developed in the scientific method. This required that knowledge be backed up by verifiable experiments. Finally, there was a routinization of research, which turned the pursuit of invention into a regular practice.

Technical expertise was not the preserve of Europeans or the British; it was shared by other civilizations. In order to prosper, technological changes had to be supported by a political and economic structure. The Industrial Revolution required tremendous changes in many aspects of people's lives. What type of environment facilitated such changes? In Britain, it was the advent of the liberal state, which gave more power to markets and rewarded or punished behaviour that assisted or retarded the efforts of the emerging industrial capitalists. The liberal state and economy were created through the use of force (Polanyi, 1957). People were forced out of home production and into factories so that cotton mills would have a workforce (Box 4.2). This was called creating a free labour market. The political power of agricultural labour and landholders was curbed so that the rising merchant class would be free to import and export products and hire and fire labour.

While the creation of the liberal state was supported by a particular class alliance, it was informed and inspired by liberal ideology. An ideology is a worldview that advocates a particular way of organizing social, political and economic life. Nineteenth-century Britain saw the blossoming of liberal ideology. On the economic side, liberalism promoted the ability of economic agents to engage in activity with limited interference from state authorities. Adam Smith ([1776]1983), the Scottish philosopher, is even today well known for expounding the doctrine of 'laissez-faire, laissez-passer'. The English translation (from French) is 'let it be, let it pass'. This refers to letting goods pass between points

---

Box 4.2 Encouraging factory work

During the Industrial Revolution people were extremely reluctant to work in factories, so legal changes and force were needed to create a workforce. An example of this type of change was the 1834 Reform of the Poor Law Act. This law repealed the previous system of poor relief, which had stipulated that individual parishes were responsible for their own poor people. Removing support at the local level meant that people would have to travel to find work to survive. Under the new system, the poor were encouraged to move to cities to work in the new industrial system rather than face even more horrendous conditions in poorhouses. A national police force was also assembled to deal with the violence caused by forcing people into new forms of labour. A liberal state is not necessarily a less active state.

without hindrance such as tolls, taxes or other state interference. On the political side, liberalism was known for advancing the civil rights of individuals against the powers of the state. Theorists such as John Stuart Mill ([1859]1980) pushed for responsible and representative government that respected individuals' civil and political rights. Although such rights were articulated in universal terms, in practice they excluded the majority of Britain's population by being limited to property-owning men. As Mary Wollstonecraft ([1792]1992) had pointed out in the previous century, the emerging liberal system was seriously flawed because it did not extend rights to women.

The horrors of the Industrial Revolution caused a reaction on the part of those forced to bear the cost. This period saw the formation of trade unions and democratic movements. In the ideological realm, Karl Marx emerged as the dominant theorist of class relations. His writings urged the working class to unite and overthrow the capitalist class. The publication of the *Communist Manifesto* served to inspire millions of people around the world struggling for a more equal society. Marx and Engels ([1848]1977, p. 224) described an expanding worldwide system in which: 'The need of a constantly expanding market for its products chases the bourgeoisie over the whole surface of the globe. It must nestle everywhere, settle everywhere, establish connections everywhere.' This captured the dynamic of the Industrial Revolution, but also resonates with global activity in the early 21st century. Marx envisioned a new form of society (communism) that would be based on the common ownership of production, which would distribute the fruits of people's labour evenly throughout society.

In addition to benefiting from a scientific base and a liberal state, Britain was located in a favourable international position. Due to its naval supremacy, it was able to import cotton easily from the American hemisphere and transport slaves across the Atlantic. Once textile production picked up, it was able to access foreign markets. This was important because many people in Britain were too poor to afford the volume of products being produced. The navy also acted as a source of demand for the emerging iron industry because of its need for weapons.

Following on the heels of the Industrial Revolution and the transformation of transportation technology, the world economy experienced tremendous growth. For example, whereas international trade increased in value by 30 per cent from £300 million to £400 million between 1800 and 1830, it jumped five times to £2,000 million between 1840 and 1870. Whereas in the early 1840s, Britain accumulated £160 million in credits abroad, this rose to £250 million in the 1850s and exploded to £1,000 million by 1873 (Hobsbawm, 1987, p. 139). People joined the increasing international flow of goods and capital. Whereas more than one million Europeans emigrated to the US between 1800 and 1840, more than seven million emigrated between 1840 and 1870.

While we can identify various factors that contributed to the Industrial Revolution taking place in Britain in the 19th century, it is more difficult to determine if this is the only mix that would have led to such a dramatic increase in productivity. Scientific knowledge was necessary for the application of machinery to production, but other societies had such expertise. It is harder to say whether a particular place in the international economy was a prerequisite for the Industrial Revolution. Increasing demand and supply in a national market may have been sufficient, allowing a more national economy to experience these changes. A liberal state facilitated the required social transformation, but less market-oriented states could also transfer resources. The spread of industrialization to several different types of societies at different times suggests that the British were the first to hit on one of potentially several different mixes of factors that catapulted humanity into a new era.

Hobson (2004, pp. 190–218) has gone as far as to argue that in a longer historical perspective, Britain was simply one stop on a long, multi-country technological innovation path. Britain successfully adapted Chinese technologies with some local knowledge and was able to hold the technological lead for a brief period in the 19th century. Its place in the history of the global economy depends very much on one's historical and geographic perspective.

What did the others do?

The surge of industrial activity in Great Britain caused considerable concern in other states. British industry was becoming more productive and competitive, while the British state was becoming more powerful. European rivals and the newly emergent US struggled to catch up. The race to catch up created a wide series of policy mixes from industrial sabotage to brief periods of free trade, to protectionist policies to defend industry.

In the early part of the Industrial Revolution, France was Britain's most serious rival. The French monarch tried to modernize his own economy by importing British technicians to update industrial techniques. The commercial rivalry was overshadowed as France plunged into revolution and confrontations generated by the Napoleonic Wars. The two countries that surpassed British accomplishments and led the way into the second Industrial Revolution of chemicals and electricity were Germany and the US. Both followed protectionist paths towards industrialization. German theorist Fredrick List ([1885]1991) was critical of the British notion that free trade was the best method to advance economic growth. He argued that if Germany was to catch up with Britain, it must protect its fledgling industries or risk being confined to primary products. List's writings echoed the mercantilist views of an earlier era and foreshadowed protective policies such as strategic trade theory in the 1980s.

The US used British capital to finance its industrialization. The US Civil War gave a boost to northern arms manufacturers that contributed to further industrialization in the 1870s and 80s. Increasing immigration and westward expansion fed continued economic growth behind high tariff barriers. By the early 1900s, the US was leading in many industries and introducing new forms of production such as mass production of the automobile.

Japan was the only Asian state able to respond rapidly to the challenge of Western industrialization. Following the abolition of feudalism, and the political reform known as the Meiji Restoration (1868), the Japanese government began a process of state-led industrialization (Stearns, 1993, pp. 113–29). Government-led companies began the initial investment in railways, mines, shipping and textiles. Private enterprise followed government action. For example, Mitsubishi, which was run by former samurai warriors, launched itself into the shipping industry. Japanese industrialization relied even more heavily on female labour than European industrialization and the working conditions for most Japanese workers were worse for a longer period of time than for their European counterparts. The success of its efforts were proved when, much to the shock of Europe, Japan defeated Russia in the Russo-Japanese War of 1905. Japan's industrial prowess was felt by much of the rest of Asia in the Second World War.

PAX BRITANNICA

The rise of British industrial and military power led to a particular form of international system that is sometimes called the 'Pax Britannica' (1815–1914). This translates into the 'British peace' and is an allusion to the famous Pax Romana, which was the relative peace and order characteristic of the Roman Empire at its height. The term is clearly an exaggeration because there were many areas where British power was limited and there were many violent wars. However, it does focus attention on an emerging European-centred international system that reached further than previous attempts at international order. The period is significant because it was generally based on liberal principles that are similar to the guiding principles of today's dominant powers and institutions. Three of the international arrangements that Britain tried to make the basis of the international system were the gold standard, free trade and the balance of power.

The gold standard and capital flows

Economic activity such as the exchange of goods and services is facilitated by a recognized form of money. Just as sound money helps move a local or national economy past the shortcomings of barter, a sound international monetary system will assist the exchange of goods and services across borders. In the international sphere, there is no international money and no international central bank. The international monetary system (IMS) is the mechanism for exchanging one currency for another. This is necessary because in order to import a product, you need to pay the exporter in a currency they can use. If they are not intending to buy one of your products, they will probably want to be paid in their own currency. The IMS helps to determine on what terms and by what methods others will accept your currency.

It is useful to outline some of the key elements of the IMS before explaining the 19th-century arrangement. A monetary system must address three issues (Cooper, 1987, p. 4):

1 *The role of exchange rates:* Will they be fixed in relation to other currencies or will they float, with their value changing in response to the market?
2 *The nature of reserve assets:* This refers to the commodity or form of money that the central bank

will hold on-hand to meet demands for payment of currency. A bank's reserves could be composed of gold or foreign currencies.

3 *The control of capital movement:* Does a state allow money to flow freely in and out of its borders or are there restrictions as to how much can be moved over a particular period?

In Chapter 7, we will see systems that vary from the gold standard in each of these areas.

A major problem for countries participating in an international monetary system is the balance of payments. The balance of payments is the total of the value of goods and capital flowing in and out of a country. Crudely, do you sell enough to pay for what you buy abroad? If you are buying more than you are selling, you have a balance of payments deficit: You run the risk of running out of money. There are several steps that can be taken in this situation. You can reduce imports or increase exports. In economies that are heavily influenced by state policy, it is possible to increase or decrease the amount of imports by command. In more open economies, one can either deflate the economy, devalue the currency or increase the competitiveness of local products. Increasing the competitiveness of domestic products is the most attractive strategy: better products will sell more easily, increasing revenues. However, this may take time or may be difficult to achieve. A second possibility is that the economy may be deliberately deflated or slowed down. If the economy slows, imports will decrease and the balance of payments should improve. The third option is to devalue or lower the value of your currency in relation to that of your trading partners. This should make the cost of your products cheaper to foreigners and lead to an increase in sales. Both deflation and devaluation have costs. Deflation puts people out of work and devaluation lowers real wages by making imports more expensive. It also risks inflation or price rises as foreign products become more expensive.

The era of British economic prominence in the 19th century is noted for its particular solution to the problems of exchanging currencies and balance of payments. It was called the 'gold standard'. Although the British were on a gold standard from the end of the Napoleonic Wars to 1914, the heyday of the international gold standard was 1875–1914. The gold standard was never completely respected, but many

states adhered to its principles in a consistent manner. In order for the gold standard to work, three factors had to hold true. First, countries were required to fix their currencies in relation to gold. This meant they had to declare that their currency was worth a particular amount of gold and then be willing to exchange it for gold. The second requirement was to allow the relatively free movement of gold across state boundaries. The third requirement was that currencies would be able to change value in relationship to each other while staying fixed to gold. An example of the operation of the gold standard is provided in Box 4.3.

This system had two prerequisites if it was to function smoothly. The first was an international system of credit that circulated funds between countries to finance economic activity in different parts of the world (Germain, 1997). Wealth from the centre of the world economy would have to be circulated or reinvested in other countries if a large number of states were going to be able to engage in international economic activity. In the 19th century, this role of credit provision was played by London. Private banks channelled the wealth produced by the Industrial Revolution into foreign investments. After 1815, London became the financial centre of the world, as its banks were able to draw in British money and invest it where the profit was greatest in Britain or abroad. In 1873, deposits in London banks were £120 million compared with £40 million in New York, £13 million in Paris and £8 million in Germany (Hobsbawm, 1987, p. 152).

A second important element was that the national state and society must be willing to accept automatic deflation. This required a politically inert population where the lower classes were shut out of decision-making. In Britain this was accomplished by only allowing a minority of the population to vote. This kind of system often exposed class divisions. In general, political and economic elites favoured the gold standard because it came close to automatically maintaining balance of payments equilibrium. However, the working class resisted the mechanism because they bore the cost of deflation and unemployment.

The presence of London as a financial anchor and the creation of the gold standard facilitated the movement of money from one country to another (Germain, 1997, pp. 44–58). Indeed, the 19th century saw the beginning of large capital flows through the international system. In the 1800s, French money poured into Russia, and

Box 4.3 The gold standard

Imagine two countries who are members of the gold standard and their trade is in balance. Let us choose England and France. Remember that their currencies are fixed to gold, but can freely move in relationship to each other. The values are not historically accurate, but serve to illustrate the principle. Their situation is illustrated in Stage 1 below.

Now consider a change in their trading relationship. The British begin to import more from France than they export to it. This might be because the drinking of French wine becomes more fashionable in Britain. This change in trade increases the British demand for French francs (FFs) because they are required to pay for more French imports. However, the French don't have as strong a demand for British pounds sterling (£s) because they have not increased their consumption of British goods. The French must be encouraged to sell their FFs for £s by offering a greater rate of exchange. Thus it costs more £s to buy FFs on the market. The hypothetical result is that the British must now give £15 for FF10. This is illustrated in Stage 2.

If this state of affairs were to last for too long, the eventual result would be a gold drain from Britain. An entrepreneurial French citizen could use their FF10 to buy £15. This could then be exchanged in Britain for 1.5 oz of gold. The gold could then be brought back to France and exchanged for FF15. The money-changer would make a profit of FF5 minus the cost of exchanging money and transporting the gold. If this was done on a large enough level, the profits could be great. This is an early version of a common practice in today's global financial markets – making a profit from the changing value of a currency's foreign exchange rate.

The next part of the process contained the element that would bring the system back into balance. In each country, the supply of money was determined by central banks based on the ratio of gold they held. When gold started to flow out, the bank would have to call money in or reduce the amount it loaned out by raising interest rates. This, in turn, slowed growth and reduced imports. In our example, as the British had less money to spend, they would reduce their import of French wine, reduce the need for French francs, restore the exchange rate and stop the outflow of gold. In France, the inflow of gold would have the opposite effect, expanding their money supply, increasing imports and depreciating the currency.

The result would be Stage 4, which is the same as Stage 1. This equilibrium would hold only for a brief moment in time as tastes and competition quickly moved the flows of trade and gold again. The model becomes more complicated as other countries are added. The two key points are that the gold standard tended towards re-establishing balance and it provided the security for people to exchange currencies, knowing that they were backed by gold.

	French currency		British currency
Stage 1:	1 oz gold = 10FF	trades for	£10 = 1 oz gold
Stage 2:	1 oz gold = 10FF	trades for	£15 = 1.5 oz gold
Stage 3:	10FF exchanged for £15	exchanged for	1.5 oz gold exchanged for 15FF
Stage 4:	1 oz gold = 10FF	trades for	£10 = 1 oz gold

German capital moved into the Americas and Africa. As previously mentioned, British money helped the US industrialize. Japan also benefited from British loans and modernized, quickly becoming a world power.

There were differing views as to the political impact of such capital flows. Lenin ([1917]1969), the communist theorist and revolutionary, saw these flows as leading to imperialism and eventually war. Polanyi (1957) saw the interest of capitalist investors or *haute finance* as contributing to peace among the major powers. The wealthiest investors who had a stake in the prosperity of many different countries would lobby their national governments for the cause of peace. Although bankers appeared to have limitless power, when the clouds of war gathered in the early 1900s, they had a minor political role compared with mass nationalism.

Free trade

The 19th-century international system was notable for the appearance of the doctrine and practice of free trade. This doctrine is even more prominent today. The key date in the 19th century was 1846, the year Britain repealed the Corn Laws, which had protected British aristocrats and farmers from imported corn. At the time, corn was used to make bread. The dispute pitted industrialists and many workers against landowners and farmers. The industrialists wanted cheap corn so that the cost of bread could be lowered and they could reduce or limit their workers' wages. This would give their products a competitive advantage in international markets over products from countries where food was more expensive and, therefore, wages were higher. British workers also supported the repeal of the Corn Laws because they wanted to pay less for bread. The farmers and landowners feared that foreign competition would lower or eliminate their profits.

David Ricardo, a stock trader and Member of Parliament, articulated the liberal theory of comparative advantage, which made the intellectual case for free trade. It remains in force today and is the bedrock of those arguing for economic integration and free trade. Prior to Ricardo, many liberals believed that you should engage in trade if you had an absolute advantage in a product. If you made the best cloth or wine, you would gain from a system that allowed for the freer trade of goods. Ricardo's ([1817]1992) theory was more revolutionary. He suggested that by specializing in the product you make best and engaging in free trade, you can benefit even if other people make the products better than you do. Under this theory, even countries that are economically weak will benefit from a free-trade system because their resources will be used more efficiently. Free trade was a universal good.

For many people at the time, and even today, the notion of comparative advantage is counterintuitive. How is it possible that one can benefit from trade with a country that is more efficient? Box 4.4 illustrates how Ricardo's theory operates.

Although the British state signed on to the free-trade economic policy, international acceptance of the doctrine was mixed. The golden era lasted for about 25 years from 1846 to the 1870s. Some European states initially participated, but the US did not. Once states had acquired some basic ingredients of the Industrial Revolution, protectionist policies were seen by most countries as the key to matching and surpassing Britain's economic power. Renewed moves to free trade would have to await the post-1945 US-led trading system, which is examined in Chapter 6.

The last third of the 19th century combined a number of apparently contradictory trends. As the world fragmented into rival imperialisms, capital and human mobility were at record levels. Britain lost its productive advantage, but maintained its commitment to economic liberalism because of the strength of its financial industry. Germany and the US, which were becoming more advanced in production, remained protectionist rather than embracing free trade as the British did at the height of the Industrial Revolution.

In the recent debate about globalization, some scholars have pointed to this era as evidence that today's openness is not unique. For example, Hirst and Thompson (1996) argue that the high rates of migration, trade and investment just before the First World War indicate an open system. While there was indeed a great deal of activity, it often took place in the context of empire and at much slower speeds than in the 21st century.

Balance of power

The 100 years from the end of the Napoleonic Wars in 1815 until the outbreak of the First World War in 1914 passed without a major war involving all the European powers. There were localized wars, such as the Crimean War, which pitted Britain, France and Turkey against Russia, and the Franco-Prussian War, but not the kind of systemic conflict such as raged in the early 19th and 20th centuries. Under the balance of power system, violence was not ruled out. Force could be used to contain rivals or, in the case of the popular revolutions of 1848, to support particular regimes against democratic movements. The key was to prevent conflict from degenerating into a system-wide war. This relatively peaceful era contributed to an international system that favoured growth in international trade and finance.

We are interested in why the leading European military states were able to prevent a general war. The security arrangements or structure at this time, known as the 'balance of power', had three characteristics:

1   There was a general agreement on what was called the 'Concert of Europe'. This was an arrangement between the major European powers following the

Box 4.4 Comparative advantage

Stage 1: no trade

In the first stage, two countries (the US and the UK) produce two products, but do not engage in trade. Each country employs 100 workers in the steel industry and 100 workers in the textile industry. The Americans have newer plants, so they are more productive. Thus, 100 US workers make 900 units of steel, while 100 British workers only make 400 units of steel. One hundred US weavers make 300 units of cloth, while 100 British weavers make only 200 units of cloth.

Country	Resources	Products
US	100 steel workers	900 units steel (1:9)
UK	100 steel workers	400 units steel (1:4)
Total		1,300 units steel
US	100 weavers	300 units cloth (1:3)
UK	100 weavers	200 units cloth (1:2)
Total		500 units cloth

The US makes steel and cloth more efficiently.

Stage 2: specialization

In preparation for trade relations, each country shifts resources to specialize in products in which they are comparatively stronger. While the US makes both products more efficiently, it has a greater advantage in steel (9 units per worker vs. 4 units per worker) than cloth (3 units per worker vs. 2 units per worker). The US will shift workers into its strongest product, while the UK will shift workers into the product that it is most competitive in, compared with the US. The UK will move more resources than the US because it needs to make a greater adjustment due to its relative inefficiency. The US shifts 10 workers out of cloth to steel, while the UK shifts 20 workers out of steel to cloth.

Country	Resources	Products
US	110 steel workers	990 units steel (1:9)
UK	80 steel workers	320 units steel (1:4)
Total		1310 units steel
US	90 weavers	270 units cloth (1:3)
UK	120 weavers	240 units cloth (1:2)
Total		510 units cloth

Stage 3: trade

However, the US still needs 30 units of cloth and the UK needs 80 units of steel. So the US can trade 80 units of steel for 30 units of cloth from the UK.

Stage 4: results after trade

US: 990 units of steel produced – 80 units traded = 910 units of steel, *an increase of 10 units of steel*

270 units of cloth produced + 30 units imported = 300 units of cloth, same as pre-trade number

UK: 320 units of steel produced + 80 units traded = 400 units of steel, same as pre-trade number

240 units of cloth produced – 30 units exported = 210 units of cloth, *an increase of 10 units of cloth*

Even though the US had an absolute advantage (it could produce both products more efficiently), both countries were still able to gain from trade after specializing in their areas of comparative advantage. Both countries are wealthier after specializing in the products in which they have a comparative advantage.

turmoil of the Napoleonic Wars. It provided for communication and consultation between the powers to ensure that no single state grew too strong.

2 States would shift alliances and allegiances to balance the growing power of any particular state. If any state seemed to be getting too powerful, a coalition would emerge to contain that state. This led a British statesman (Castlereagh) to famously declare that there are 'No permanent alliances, just permanent interests'.

3 Consideration of other states' ideology and domestic public opinion had to be excluded from the decision-making process. If alliances and military action were designed for keeping a balance of power, cooperation with any form or nature of state would be pursued if this kept the balance. Maintenance of the balance might require constitutional democracies to cooperate with absolute monarchies against other constitutional democracies. Public opinion would also be excluded because it might be necessary to ally with a state that had recently been an enemy. The general public might not support sudden shifts in diplomacy so their views would have to be ignored. This was not a difficult task since none of the states in question would qualify as democracies by today's standards.

The primary balancing role in this environment went to Britain. It had two considerable weapons that it could launch against the growing power of rival states. The first was the British navy, which enjoyed supremacy over the waters of the world. During the mid-19th century, the Royal Navy was as powerful as the next three or four navies combined (Kennedy, 1987, p. 154). The navy could be used to interfere with opponents' supplies, support allies or raid coastal waters. The second advantage was Britain's wealth, which could be funnelled to allies on the continent. The British government was able to provide financing to other states to keep armies in the field against Britain's rivals.

While this system appeared stable and lasted for 100 years, it went through a series of changes, becoming rigid in the first decade of the 20th century (Craig and George, 1983, pp. 28–48). As the century progressed, states continued to build their overseas empires, and engaged in imperialist rivalry. The industrialization of Germany threatened British dominance as the two

countries engaged in naval and imperial competition. The system of flexible and shifting alliances gradually hardened as Europe became divided into two camps. The Triple Entente of France, Britain and Russia confronted the Triple Alliance of Germany, Austria-Hungary and Italy. Formal treaties were bolstered with secret treaties pledging one state to come to the aid of another. States committed themselves to disastrous policies without understanding the severe consequences. The assassination in August 1914 of Archduke Ferdinand of the Austro-Hungarian Empire sparked a series of events that gradually drew European states, the US and the British Commonwealth into a long and bloody war. Ignoring the example of the US Civil War, which previewed industrial warfare, leaders foolishly predicted speedy victory.

The notion of a Pax Britannica helps us understand some aspects of an evolving global political economy but obscures others. One problem is that it tends to focus on inter-European affairs and fails to consider a crucial aspect of the Industrial Revolution, which was a new wave of European imperialism sweeping over the African continent and parts of Asia. Second, it overstates the degree to which liberal principles governed the system and downplays the flaws that led to its demise. These shortcomings are so serious that the next section is devoted to considering the new imperialism and the breakdown of the liberal system.

An additional problem with the Pax Britannica approach is that it ignores the large-scale violence taking place in several parts of the world that was linked to the growth of the international market. In the US, tensions between the export-oriented, commodity-producing south and the protectionist north erupted in the US Civil War. This was the most violent and costly war in American history. In China, the social dislocation from the Opium Wars provided the background for a Christian-influenced rebellion against the emperor (Waley-Cohen, 1999, p. 159). It is estimated that 10–20 million Chinese died during the Taiping Rebellion (1850–64) and the ensuing conflicts (Pomeranz and Topik, 1999, p. 169). In the Congo, King Leopold of Belgium carved out his own private empire (see Box 4.5), and approximately ten million Africans died in the effort to harvest rubber for export (Hochschild, 1999). These are the forgotten lives in a Western-centred view emerging with the Pax Britannica. One needs to ask: peace and wealth for whom?

Box 4.5 Imperialism in the Congo

One of the most horrific events in the new wave of imperialism was Belgian King Leopold II's exploitation of the Congo. Belgium's activity in the Congo was somewhat unique because a vast area of land became the personal property of a king rather than of the state. It was horrific because millions of Africans died, and brutal methods such as severing people's hands were used to force local people into labour.

Through clever diplomacy during the Berlin Conference of 1884–5, King Leopold II was able to establish a personal protectorate over large areas of central Africa (Pakenham, 1991, pp. 239–55). This area became known as the Congo Free State. It was more than 70 times the size of Belgium itself and about one 13th of the whole of Africa. The king was tasked with developing the Congo for the benefit of its people, but used the territory to amass a large personal fortune and to finance monuments and buildings in Brussels.

King Leopold of the Belgians became very rich and millions of Africans died because of the international desire for a new, modern commodity – rubber (Hochschild, 1999, pp. 158–66). The demand for rubber increased dramatically in the 1890s as the technology to refine rubber into a host of products was perfected. Rubber was needed for tyres, hoses, tubes and electrical wiring covers. Demand for rubber could be met most efficiently by planting and cultivating rubber trees in Latin America and Asia. However, this required considerable care and years before a harvest would be ready. The Congo contained wild rubber trees that could be harvested immediately to meet the spiralling demand. This was the source of Leopold's wealth.

In order to harvest wild rubber, workers had to venture into the forest and engage in the difficult and dangerous practice of draining sap from rubber vines. African males were pressed into this labour by rubber agents who took their families hostage until a certain amount of rubber was harvested. Another common practice in this 'rubber terror' was to chop off the hands of Africans who failed to meet their quotas or who resisted European demands for more rubber. Although it is difficult to establish the numbers of lives lost because of the rubber trade, one credible estimate is that up to ten million people died through a combination of murder, starvation, exhaustion, disease and a plummeting birth rate (Hochschild, 1999, pp. 225–33).

The horror of this Western atrocity comes down to us in English literature through Joseph Conrad's ([1902]1999) novel *The Heart of Darkness*. Conrad worked for four months on a steamship travelling the Congo River. The terrible events he saw caused him to write a novel about the voyage of a man going up a river to find a European who had crossed the line into brutal insanity. The same story was later adapted as the film *Apocalypse Now* in 1979.

A final interesting note about the sad history of Belgian intervention in the Congo is that it gave rise to the first international human rights campaign of the 20th century (Hochschild, 1999). In 1904, the Congo Reform Association was formed to lobby against the human rights abuses in that country. It campaigned in Europe and the US until 1913, when it was determined that the Belgian government, which had taken over running the Congo from the king, had instituted sufficient reforms.

RENEWED IMPERIALISM

Is it a coincidence that the era of unprecedented economic growth known as the Industrial Revolution was quickly followed by an era of unprecedented imperial expansion? Was this 'new imperialism' an inevitable consequence of capitalism or the result of political rivalry between European states? We will first review the events surrounding the new imperialism and then consider some alternative explanations.

As described in Chapter 3, European expansion began in the 1400s and proceeded with varying speeds and intensities in different parts of the world. In the first half of the 1800s, European powers relinquished formal control in the Americas, but created new colonies in southern Africa, Algeria, India and southern Vietnam. In the Americas, Spanish colonies were able to assert their independence, but remained economically vulnerable to Europe and later the US. European expansion accelerated in the last quarter of the century. Between 1878 and 1913, Europeans extended their control over an additional one-sixth of the earth's surface (Abernethy, 2000, p. 81). Moving from coastal settlements, Europeans expanded into the interior of the

African and Asian continents. No longer satisfied with economic exchange, European traders and states insisted on formal political control in the form of new colonies. China was not colonized, but Western powers carved out spheres of influence in the country.

This era of expanding Western powers brought four significant developments (Abernethy, 2000, pp. 84–7). First, traditional European powers enlarged their empires. Holland expanded its reach in what is today known as Indonesia. Portugal pushed out from its coastal areas in southern Africa to take over Angola and Mozambique. France established colonies in northern and western Africa, as well as in Madagascar, Indochina and islands of the Pacific. Britain expanded its hold over India and attempted to dominate a portion of African territory stretching from Egypt to southern Africa. Spain was an exception to this trend as a series of wars of independence deprived it of its Latin American colonies.

Second, three new European states entered the colonial movement. Following their own unification as nation-states, Italy, Belgium and Germany rushed to seize colonies in Africa. The Italians were the least successful, suffering defeat at the hands of the Ethiopians in 1896, but managing to conquer Libya. Belgium carved out an immense territory in the Congo. Germany, riding the power derived from the second Industrial Revolution, seized territory in southern, western and eastern Africa.

Third, two Western states outside the European core completed continental expansions, subduing native populations and creating large states. In the Americas, the US rolled over indigenous peoples as it completed its drive to the Pacific Ocean. It then engaged in a policy of expanding overseas by seizing the Spanish colonies of Puerto Rico and the Philippines and invading Cuba. Control of the Hawaiian Islands was also taken from their native inhabitants. This expansion had its counterpart in Asia as Russia extended eastwards, dominating large stretches of land in its drive to the Pacific Ocean.

Finally, one Asian state was able to adapt to the Industrial Revolution, and began its process of empire-building. In the 1890s, Japan seized Taiwan, and took control of Korea in 1905. Japanese interests in Manchuria continued to grow and its imperial ambitions were later pursued in the 1930s, leading to war with the US.

The most dramatic bout of this expansionism was called the 'scramble for Africa'. This was literally a race among European powers to divide the African conti-

nent among themselves. Over a period of approximately 35 years, the African continent was transformed from being relatively independent, with Europeans confined along its edges, to being completely under foreign control, with the sole exception of Ethiopia (see Map 4.1). When the scramble was over, 10 million square miles, 110 million people and 30 colonies were added to European possessions (Pakenham, 1991, p. xxiii).

The subjugation of Africa was marked by what Pakenham (1991) calls the four Cs: commerce, Christianity, civilization and conquest. Europeans first engaged with Africa because of commerce. During the scramble, immense fortunes were made. Consider the case of Cecil Rhodes, the diamond and gold magnate. His actions resulted in the accumulation of vast wealth, the subjugation of an African people (the Ndebele) and the creation of a country by him and named after him (Rhodesia; modern-day Zimbabwe). In addition, his name lives on through the establishment of the Rhodes Scholarship at Oxford University. Christianity also played a role as missionaries flocked to Africa. They moved deeper into the interior, converting natives in the hope that this might save their souls and spare them from the Arab slave trade. European troops soon followed as one group or another of missionaries had to be saved from the local inhabitants. European explorers, settlers and traders justified their activity in terms of civilizing the Africans. It was claimed that they were bringing the virtues of advanced civilization to Africa.

As Africans resisted, it became increasingly necessary to use military force or conquest to establish European goals. There were some African successes in resisting European imperialism. For example, the Zulus defeated a British force at Isandlwana in 1879. For almost 20 years (1880s and 90s), Samori Touré led African resistance to French colonialism in western Africa. In 1896, 100,000 Ethiopian soldiers maintained the independence of their state by defeating an Italian force of 15,000 at the Battle of Adwa. However, the overall trend was one of European imperial armies and their African conscripts inflicting large-scale defeats and harsh reprisals on African forces. Examples include the Battle of Omdurman (1898), where a British force killed 10,000 Sudanese warriors at a cost of 26 British soldiers. The Germans dealt with rebellion by the Hereros in south-west Africa by exiling a tribe of 20,000 to die in the desert in 1904. With the exception of Ethiopia, all Africa fell to European arms.

Map 4.1 **Pre- and post-scramble Africa**

Many different explanations have been advanced to help us understand the imperialism of the late 19th century. Some stress developments in European countries, while others focus on developments outside Europe; some see the imperial drives as motivated by economic factors, while others stress the role of military competition.

The two most prominent explanations centre on Europe and financial factors. John Hobson (1902), an economist and a liberal, argued that imperialism was caused by underconsumption in Western states. The mass of the population were kept poor and could not buy the goods being produced. Economic interests such as the finance industry, arms exporters and shipping pushed government into expanding overseas so that these interests could continue to make a profit. Hobson's solution to this situation was a redistribution of income within Western states. This would allow people to buy the goods being produced and would end the need for imperialism in other parts of the world. For Hobson, the design of the Western economic system promoted imperialism, but this could be reversed by changing public policy.

Lenin's ([1917]1969) famous analysis of imperialism was informed by Marxism. Similar to Hobson, he thought that imperialism was caused by the economic system in Western states. Industrialists and bankers combined their interests in pursuing overseas markets. Lenin saw this as the highest and last form of capitalism. Unlike Hobson, he argued that this imperialist impulse was an inevitable feature of capitalism and could only be ended by revolution in the colonized world and in the imperial metropole. He contributed to this development by leading the Russian Revolution and creating the Soviet Union in 1917.

Another European-focused explanation argues that the imperialist upsurge was the result of military and strategic competition between European states. The scramble for colonies was the result of European competition between Britain, France, Germany, Italy, Portugal, Belgium and Spain. Colonies were seized not because they were economically profitable, but because they blocked the ambitions of rival states or served as a symbol of power and prestige. Africa was carved up as the great power game extended to new regions of the world.

Racism also played a significant role in facilitating renewed imperialism (Hobson, 2004, pp. 219–42). European imperialists convinced themselves that they had a moral obligation to civilize other parts of the world. Inhabitants of other countries were not capable of handling their own affairs. This civilizing mission involved seizing other people's lands to make them more productive, converting non-Christians so that they would recognize the 'true' God, and replacing local political and educational structures so that the colonized would benefit from improved institutions. It was this frame of mind and view of other peoples that allowed many European individuals and groups to exploit other peoples while believing that they were actually behaving in a moral fashion. In some cases, such as the handling of famine relief, racist attitudes had lethal consequences (Box 4.6).

Other analysts have tried to locate relevant explanations in the colonized societies instead of Europe. For example, Robinson (1972) suggested that the fate of imperial adventures was determined, to a large extent, by the nature of local collaborators rather than European power or abilities. He argued that European powers relied on local elites (collaborators or mediators) to manage relations with the local population. When these elites were weakened or in danger from local forces, Europeans had to expand their participation into outright rule. When the Europeans ran out of local collaborators, a process of decolonization began.

Box 4.6 Global famines

In the last quarter of the 19th century, three large-scale famines (1876–9, 1889–91, 1896–1902) devastated much of what is today referred to as the developing world (Davis, 2001). It is likely that changes in the temperature of ocean currents (El Niño) disrupted rainfall patterns in many tropical countries. The lack of rain generated crop failures. At the same time, government policy was unwilling or unable to mitigate famine conditions. The result was the death of 30–50 million people. India, China and Brazil were particularly badly hit. In India, the British rulers refused to intervene, believing that the free market would resolve food shortages. There was little sympathy for the local population. The ability of people in England to pay higher prices for grain actually resulted in food being exported from India to the UK as millions of Indians died from starvation. In most famine-struck countries, grain surpluses were available but were not distributed to the population because they could not afford to pay for them. While weather conditions created shortages, it was poverty and state inaction that caused millions to perish in horrible agony.

The upsurge in imperialism in the late 19th century was such a widespread phenomenon that a combination of factors and theories is necessary to gain a full understanding. We can begin by agreeing with Barraclough (1967, pp. 43–64) that the process of industrialization enabled Western states (and Japan) to dominate areas of the world that had previously been beyond their reach. Scientific advance gave some states, societies and businesses the means to dominate other states, societies and businesses. Racist ideologies provided the political and moral justifications for intervention in other societies. However, to explain why a certain imperial power expanded in a particular area, one needs to assess the factors in Europe, in the target states, and the ties that bound the two areas together (Doyle, 1996).

WAR AND ECONOMIC DISORDER

The 19th-century liberal and imperialist order came to an end with the onset of the First World War in 1914. Over 30 years passed between the end of the 19th-century system in 1914 and the beginning of a new world order in 1945. These three decades were marked by the two world wars and an interwar economic collapse. The wars and economic turmoil had a profound impact on the nature of the post-1945 system in which we now live. The two world wars dramatically weakened western Europe on the world stage and led to the creation of new forms of state in Europe and other continents. The economic turbulence of the interwar years encouraged the US to play a prominent role in the post-1945 era and contributed to the creation of a series of international organizations to monitor the global economy. This section examines the impact of two world wars and years of economic dislocation on the international political economy. The painful lessons learned from these years were significant factors shaping the design of the post-1945 system.

The world wars

The First and Second World Wars were massive shocks to the international economy, forcing a retreat from liberal and imperial policies. The First World War disrupted trade and finance patterns, leaving European states much weaker in 1918 than they had been before the war. The pattern of international trade suffered two effects. First, there was a change in the direction of trade as countries switched trading partners. Second, there was a change in the composition of exports as domestic production was switched from the export sector to war production. Denied access to European goods, many countries turned to domestic production or alternative suppliers. This allowed some areas of the world such as Latin America to accelerate their own industrialization. Following the war, the task of European reconstruction was thus made more difficult since old markets were no longer open.

Capital movements were also affected as the prewar pattern of the export of capital to primary commodity-producing areas was reversed, with capital directed to Europe to aid in the war effort. Moreover, the international gold standard was abandoned and international financial dealings became a destabilizing element. Some short-term investment was temporarily not recoverable and some previously attractive investments were no longer available. The war turned a number of debtor nations into creditors and some creditor nations into debtors. For example, the US, which had started the war as a debtor nation, had a healthy surplus of over £1,000 million by 1922 as a direct result of its role in financing the war in Europe. On the other hand, Germany entered the war as a creditor and emerged as a debtor. The major European belligerents (Britain, France and Germany) ended the war with a vastly reduced stock of foreign investments.

The appalling destruction of the First World War discredited the balance of power, secret treaties and power politics as tools of organizing the international system. After exacting revenge against Germany for beginning the war, the victorious powers attempted to create a security system that relied on international law and international organizations. For various reasons, this system proved inadequate to maintain peace and the world was plunged into another war 20 years later. The economic roots of this failure are outlined below; this section considers the political framework that proved woefully inadequate.

Following the lead of US president Woodrow Wilson, the victorious allies outlined a more liberal system of peace and security that rested on free economic relations and international organization. President Wilson ([1918]1986) outlined this liberal strategy in his famous Fourteen Points speech to the US Congress in January 1918, which set the agenda for the interwar international order. He called for the end of secret treaties and for free

trade, arms reduction, national self-determination and an international organization for settling disputes between states. At the centre of this system was an international organization called the League of Nations (Bennett and Oliver, 2002, pp. 27–45). Many states belonged to it, although, ironically, the US did not join. The US Senate responded to isolationist pressure and refused to give the president permission to join. This weakened the institution, depriving it of the financial and military resources of the most powerful state in the international system. The League was supposed to foster a sense of common security reflecting a general interest in peace (Box 4.7).

The most devastating criticism of this form of international order was provided by Carr (1939) on the eve of the outbreak of the Second World War. He argued that the liberal notion of harmony of interest was utopian. Peace was not a shared interest when some states were dissatisfied with the status quo and could benefit from war. Similarly, the notion of collective security is misleading because states that did not feel threatened by an aggressive act would not use force to repel it. Carr advanced a realist critique of the liberal naivety of the dangers of aggressive states. However, he also warned that realism without some dose of utopianism was power without a purpose.

The Second World War produced greater change for the world economy than its predecessor. One result was that it fundamentally altered the balance of global economic power and effectively marked the shift of power from Europe to the US. The war finally put an end to the Great Depression in the US as the country increased production for its war machine. Both the size of productive plant and the physical output of goods increased by more than 50 per cent. At the end of the war, the US accounted for more than half of the world's manufacturing output. Another important factor in the rise of the US was its dominance of international finance. The US lent enormous sums to the Allies during the course of the conflict. At the end of the war, the Allied powers were thus heavily indebted to the US.

A second development was the creation or elaboration of welfare states in western Europe. Within Europe, leftist groups such as the communists and labour parties emerged with massive electoral support because of their opposition to fascism. Conservative and business parties were placed on the defensive as large numbers of people demanded a redistribution of resources following the defeat of Germany, Italy and their collaborators in other states. The result was that European states

---

Box 4.7 The League of Nations

The League's primary task was to keep international peace. It had a system of negotiation, arbitration and adjudication to encourage states to resolve their conflicts peacefully. Member states agreed to respect each other's territorial integrity. In addition, they professed belief in a system of collective security. Any attack on a member state was to be considered an attack on the international community as a whole. The League had the ability (on paper) to institute immediate economic and political sanctions on any aggressor state. It could also raise military forces from member states to repel the aggressor's military action.

A series of crises in the 1930s demonstrated the League's shortcomings in preventing and containing war. Its first major failure was in September 1931 when Japan invaded China and occupied Manchuria. Although Japan was criticized for its aggression, the League was unable to reverse its occupation. In 1935, the fascist Italian government launched an invasion of Ethiopia. Ethiopia had already successfully fended off European imperialism during the 'scramble for Africa'. Although Ethiopia appealed to the League for help and fought the invaders, it was conquered by Italian forces. League sanctions were half-hearted and temporary. Following failure against Japan and Italy, the League proved unable to halt Hitler's annexation of Austria and Czechoslovakia. It proved similarly incapable of preventing the outbreak of the Second World War, as Japan renewed its invasion of China and Germany attacked Poland.

---

were forced to prioritize building domestic economies and introducing legislation that distributed benefits more broadly than before the war.

A third impact of the war was the large-scale destruction of property and infrastructure, especially in Europe and Asia. Physical destruction and consequent social and administrative chaos resulted in a loss of production and export capacity. Key economic actors such as Germany and Japan ended the war unable to play the role they had performed in the prewar economy. Moreover, they became a burden on the victorious coalition. The scale of devastation was such that it posed a serious problem for postwar reorganization. The destruction of physical plant and the shortage of capital devastated large regions. The gap between former great powers and the US increased because the American continent had been spared the ravages of war.

A fourth impact was the shift in relative power between Europe and the societies in its colonies. Similar to 1918, European states emerged economically drained from world war. Japanese wartime victories in Asia highlighted the vulnerability of European colonial armies. The end of the Second World War also marked the beginning of the end for most of Europe's colonies.

Interwar economic failure

The interwar period of international economic relations was marked by change, uncertainty, erratic growth and depression. Leading states were unable to re-establish a stable international economic order. In Western states the era was divided into three phases. The first phase lasted from the end of the war until the mid-1920s. Domestically, states struggled to revive their economies. Internationally, the values of currencies floated freely against each other and states attempted to liberalize economic relations between themselves. In some countries, such as Germany, this was a period of great inflation. The second phase was characterized by a return to the gold standard and rising unemployment in many states. This period stretched from the mid-1920s until the early 1930s. The third phase occurred from 1932 until the outbreak of the Second World War and was marked by retreat from the international economy to regional economies as states attempted to deal with economic problems on a unilateral basis.

Following the First World War, elites in the victorious countries were eager to re-establish a liberal trading and financial system. Their failure to acknowledge the changed reality of the international political economy led to financial disaster and eventually war. There were several problems with the attempt to re-establish open economic relations. First, in creating rigid and punitive international monetary and credit systems, leading states failed to recognize the economic damage caused by the war and the heavy burden of war reparations on the system. This weakened already-damaged economies. Second, international economic arrangements did not take into account the views and interests of the mass societies mobilized by the First World War. As a result, there was a popular backlash against liberal policies and a movement to state-led development. Finally, the largest power in the system was not fully committed to making the sacrifices needed to maintain an open international economy. The lack of US support weakened the system as it headed into crisis. We will consider these problems in turn.

Rigid monetary and financial systems

There are two aspects of the international monetary and financial system that proved to be problematic. The first was the decision to re-establish the gold standard at prewar levels and the second was the system of war reparations from Germany to France in compensation for the First World War.

States were eager to move back to the security of the gold standard, which would give people confidence in the value of their currency and facilitate international trade. A problem emerged when states were so committed to the gold standard that they disregarded the harm it caused to their national economies. Several states fixed their currency to gold in ways that damaged their national economies. For example, Britain fixed its currency to gold at the same rate as it was before the war even though the economy was weaker. This meant that the British currency was overvalued and its exports were expensive for other states. This reduced employment as British exporters lost business and jobs. In Germany, the government eventually succeeded in curbing runaway inflation, but restricted the money supply until the economy ground to a halt, causing a massive increase in unemployment. The fixation with monetary stability and unwillingness to adjust the value of currencies and money supply to boost economic growth prevented governments from responding positively to recession and depression.

The punitive side of the international economic system can be seen in the Treaty of Versailles (28 June 1919), which laid out the terms of the peace for defeated states in the First World War. It stipulated that Germany make reparation payments to the victorious countries because it was guilty of starting the war. This, in turn, created some of the conditions for the financial crisis of 1931 and the collapse of the liberal international economic order. This political decision was taken without serious reflection on its impact on the international economy. The reparations issue became an important one in immediate postwar European economic and political relations.

International financial crisis broke out in 1931. In May 1931, Austria's largest bank (the Creditanstalt) was discovered to be insolvent, partly as a result of depreciation of its assets and partly because of the withdrawal of foreign funds. Because the German and Austrian financial systems were relatively close, the crisis spread to Germany. Britain wanted to aid Germany, but needed US financial assistance to do so. The US would only help if the French also contributed. The French government would only help Germany if it granted further political concessions to France. The German government, already under pressure from the National Socialist Party (Nazis) for being too weak, was unable to accommodate the French government. Rather than face the possibility that their currency would collapse, the German government instituted capital controls (prevented people from selling German currency) and began to close their economy to the outside world. The events in Germany put pressure on other states and eventually both Britain and the US left the gold standard and concentrated on improving their domestic economies. By 1932, major states had retreated into economic relations with states that used a common currency. Thus, Germany traded with its neighbours in central Europe in the mark zone, Britain concentrated its trade with the empire in the sterling area, the Americans operated in the dollar zone and French worked in the franc zone.

As states restricted economic relations with each other, the world tumbled into recession. Kindleberger (1986) suggests that the Great Depression of the 1930s was widespread, deep and long because Britain and the US failed to undertake several key tasks of international economic management. In addition to failing to keep an open market for goods through free-trade policies, the states were unable to provide credit to countries in need. There was no lender of last resort. When financial crisis hit the international system, there was no lender who could step in with capital to stabilize the system. Domestically, the lender of last resort is the central bank. Britain played this role in the international system of the 19th century, but the isolationist US refused to play a similar role in the interwar system.

Popular mobilization and new forms of state

The interwar period is a good example of how a particular form of international order rests on the balance of social forces between and across states (Cox, 1986). Polanyi (1957) used the phrase 'double movement' to describe the dynamic at work in the early 20th century. The first part of this movement was the attempt to create a liberal market system. This involved the creation of a labour market where people sold their labour for wages with little welfare protection, some degree of free trade, and adherence to the gold standard. The second part of the double movement was the political reaction to the suffering caused by this liberal market. Social groups mobilized and put pressure on governments to protect them from the ravages of the market.

What was the problem with the liberal market? The main problem was the assumption that people were a commodity adjusting to the supply and demand of the market in the same way that commodities such as land or capital might adjust. People were viewed as 'labour' and policies assumed that they would freely participate in lowering their wages and income according to the economic models. However, the adjustments demanded by the market were so great and so brutal that people refused to accept lower standards of living and demanded governments take action to protect them.

Several alternatives to the 19th-century economic liberal state emerged, which limited economic and political participation by the majority of its citizens (Cox, 1987, pp. 164–209). During the First World War, a major challenger emerged in the form of communism. Taking advantage of Russia's disastrous performance in the war, the Bolsheviks were able to seize power in Russia. They began a process of seizing the means of production (factories, farms) and turning them into state-run economic enterprises. Russia became a command economy, where products were produced according to a series of government plans that set targets and dictated what should be produced. The free market of supply and demand was extinguished. The communist form of organization was popular among many of the workers who had been excluded from the benefits of capitalist production. Later in the century, communism was taken up by many peasant-based societies in the developing world, such as China, Vietnam and Cuba.

A second alternative to the liberal system was fascism. Fascism came to power after 1930 when the market system was in crisis (Polanyi, 1957, pp. 237–48). The fascist solution to the difficulties of re-establishing liberal economies was to keep a market economy, but to eliminate all democratic institutions in the industrial and political realms (see Box 4.8). Fascist strongmen offered their services to conservative forces threatened by the rise of socialism and communism. Capitalists were protected from leftists in the parlia-

> **Box 4.8** Fascism vs. liberalism in 1930s Germany
>
> Because of the horrors of genocide and war unleashed by fascism in the 1930s and 40s, it is possible to overlook just how successful Nazism was in dealing with economic challenges. On coming to power, Adolph Hitler rejected the debt of war reparations that had been agreed at the Treaty of Versailles. Contrary to liberal prescriptions, the Nazis instituted strict exchange controls and signed bilateral trading arrangements to create a restricted trading zone. Also contrary to liberal economic opinion at the time, the Nazis undertook massive spending on public works and military rearmament. Between 1933 and 1938, they were able to send an estimated 6–7 million Germans back to work, virtually eliminating unemployment. In contrast to previous liberal politicians who presided over runaway inflation and unemployment, the fascists seemed to have the solution to economic depression. While the fascists were not wedded to a particularly detailed and specific economic model, they were eager to assert political control over the economy to further their nationalist and racist agendas (Baker, 2006).

ment and in the streets in return for handing the political realm over to fascist parties. This appeal was particularly powerful in states such as Germany and Italy, where fascism used unsolved national issues to gain power.

Finally, in the liberal states themselves, governments were pushed towards taking a greater role in the economy and responsibility for the economic welfare of their citizens. Both the US and Britain experimented with what would later be known as Keynesian policies, that is, those advocated by the British economist John Maynard Keynes (1936). Keynes suggested that when businesses lost confidence in the economy and refused to invest, governments should spend money to ensure economic growth. After 1933, the US took some steps in this direction by expanding credit, increasing payments to the unemployed and raising public investment through Roosevelt's New Deal policies. The British cheapened credit and protected their home market, but did not engage in large public works. The real success of the Keynesian policy would not come until the Allied countries inflated their economies by preparing for war in the late 1930s and early 1940s.

US role

The US played a critical role in the establishment of the international financial system and its unravelling in the 1930s. Within the US, the financial community argued strongly for US financial leadership in international affairs, the reconstruction of Europe, free trade and the League of Nations (Frieden, 1987). They helped found professional schools such as Columbia University's School of International Affairs (1946) and Princeton's Woodrow Wilson School of Public and International Affairs (1930). Bankers took the lead in institutions such as the Carnegie Endowment for International Peace and the Council on Foreign Relations, as well as the new journal *Foreign Affairs*. All this was done to help spread the message that the US needed an activist foreign policy.

Internationalist forces, led by the financial community, had some success in extending finance to Europe in the 1920s. However, they suffered a series of defeats on issues such as the League of Nations, freer trade and the cancelling of war debts. A coalition of manufacturers, some trade-sensitive agricultural interests and the isolationist Republican Party proved too strong. The internationalism of the banking community was out of step with most Americans, who were repelled by the European war and entanglement. When the international financial crisis struck in the early 1930s, the US raised its trade barriers even higher with the Smoot-Hawley Tariff Act of 1930. This worsened the economy within the US and in other countries. Rather than showing leadership by leading coordinated action against the Great Depression, the US retreated within its own borders. This economic isolationism was matched by political isolationism.

Some international relations theorists have been so influenced by the contrasting roles of Britain and the US in the 19th and early 20th centuries that they developed a theory of international stability from these cases called 'hegemonic stability theory' (Krasner, 1976). It suggests that a superpower or hegemonic power is required for the maintenance of an international liberal economic system. Economic openness is most likely to occur when a hegemonic state is in the ascendancy and the system is likely to become less liberal as that state's power decreases relative to other states.

Advocates of this view point to the fact that the liberal economic system of the mid-19th century was backed by British financial and military might. During the interwar years, Britain no longer exercised the same degree of dominance and the US was unwilling to commit itself to maintenance of the system. While the US had the power, it lacked the will. The result was a slide to rival economic areas and eventually war. Following the Second World War, the US took up the role of hegemonic power and created a liberal international economic system.

CONCLUSION

Looking back at the 19th-century international system from today, we see elements that are strikingly similar to those in our own time. Some parts of the international economy were characterized by large-scale flows of capital, goods and people across state boundaries. Several advanced countries were experiencing a revolution in production, which increased inequality within and between countries. Liberal economic principles dominated in some states, while others sought to develop through more mercantilist policies. Several Western states possessed the military capability to intervene or dominate affairs in other continents.

The differences are also notable. In our present era, the formal political control that characterized the imperial activities of Western states has largely disappeared. Information technologies have accelerated the speed of economic activities and created new channels of communication within firms and between peoples. Rules for international activity have been formalized into international law and a host of international organizations facilitate coordination between states, firms and citizens. Finally, a series of global issues such as human rights, economic justice and environmental sustainability have created new transnational coalitions.

Trade

The 19th century is known as the century of free trade, although our analysis shows that this is an overstatement since the practice was often not observed by many states. Nevertheless, from the mid-19th century, Great Britain, the dominant power, led the way in promoting and supporting free trade. The British did so not seeking reciprocity but on a unilateral basis. But many countries, feeling unable to compete with British economic dominance, erected protectionist barriers. However, the practice of free trade only tells part of the story. Equally crucial in the emergence of a global economy was the ideology of free trade. It was during the 19th century that this pervasive modern economic ideology was born.

Production

There were important changes in the production structure in this period. The most important was the Industrial Revolution and its attendant developments, including the development of industrial capitalism and the export of capital from Europe to North America, South America and Asia. Capitalism emerged as a dominant economic, political and social system in the mid-19th century in the aftermath of the Industrial Revolution. The new power of industrial production, with its division of labour and emphasis on new technological improvements, initiated fundamental changes in the relations between individuals and communities. The developments in production were harnessed by national elites to supplement their power domestically in intra-state struggles and to enhance the power of their state in international competition. The Industrial Revolution also provided the material resources that allowed Western states to extend their dominance over other parts of the world.

Finance

Finance played an important part in the construction of an international economy in the 19th century. It was important in the industrialization of all countries that managed to make the transition to self-sustaining economic growth. For example, the US used British capital to build its railways. The export of capital is seen by many as a key instrument in the development of imperialism. During this period, financial flows increased and the geographic spread of finance expanded. The interests of financiers and industrialists frequently came into conflict but in the latter half of the century, in many countries, alliances developed between financial capital and industrial capital. Another major innovation in the development of market capitalism was the advent of the joint stock corporation. The shift from the family business as the main form of private enterprise to the modern corporation was attendant on the growth

of the railways, since the sums of money needed for investment were very large and the time frame for realizing profits was long term.

Labour

The Industrial Revolution fed an increasing differentiation in the division of labour. Within industrializing states, the wealth accumulated by the new industrial classes stood in sharp contrast with the living conditions of the new industrial proletariat. The transformation of the workforce from a primarily agricultural one to an industrial one and the changes in the gender division of labour were crucial features of economic, social and political change. The exploitation of the working classes and the conflict between capital and labour became the subject of political agitation and the domain of novelists and poets. At times it was feared by some social critics (and hoped for by others) that capitalist exploitation of the workforce would destroy the social and moral fabric of society.

The Industrial Revolution also sharpened the international division of labour between countries. Western states, led by Britain and then the US and Germany, raced ahead, producing manufactured goods. Other parts of the world were increasingly incorporated into European colonial empires as the producers of raw materials for industrialized countries. For some countries, this role continues today.

Gender

Countries industrialized in a manner that had distinct gender patterns. Initial factory work was usually performed by the most vulnerable elements of the population – women and children. They did not share in the vast sums of wealth being created, but were a crucial element of the increased productivity that gave power to others. The exploitation of gender relations for colonial benefits outlined in Chapter 3 spread with the renewed imperialism of the late 19th century.

Development

The states that were able to industrialize in the 19th century became the developed countries of the 20th century, while those that were unable to industrialize faced major development challenges in the 20th and 21st centuries. The only Asian state able to take Western technology and successfully industrialize was Japan. Today, Japan is a leading advanced economy. The fate of non-industrializers was to fall behind their Western competitors. After keeping Western states at bay for hundreds of years, India became a British colony, while China was forced to grant spheres of influence to a series of Western powers. Today, the information revolution may be playing a similar role in creating inequalities between different parts of the world.

Environment

The process of industrialization polluted the environment of the cities and countryside in Europe and Japan. A similar pattern occurred wherever industrialization took place. Globally, the process of industrialization changed the earth's ability to regulate the atmosphere because of the amount of carbon released into the air. Climate change is the legacy of the pollutants created by the Industrial Revolution.

Ideas

Ideas and knowledge were essential to the evolution of the world economy in the 19th century. We can see three different ways in which ideas were critical to that evolution. First, in a technical sense the Industrial Revolution was based on scientific and technological innovation. The series of events we refer to as the Industrial Revolution are inconceivable without reference to the development of scientific and technological expertise. In short, the Industrial Revolution involved the application of scientific and technological developments to production, the introduction of new energy sources to power the machines, which, in turn, was linked to the reorganization of the labour force into factories.

However, underlying the specific inventions and technological breakthroughs were ideas about science, technology and religion. In other words, the specific inventions depended on developments in underlying worldviews. At this second level of the impact of ideas, we can highlight the role of the Enlightenment, which ushered in new ways of thinking about the natural and social worlds. The spirit of enquiry unleashed by the Enlightenment was critical to fostering change in the international economy. This was mainly through freeing intellectual enquiry from the theocratic straitjacket in which it had been encased. This growing autonomy

of the mind to pursue intellectual enquiry ushered in a new way of scientific thinking and the development of the modern scientific method, with its emphasis on independent proof and verification.

A third set of ideas about the social world and social relations also helped to transform the international economy. Three ideologies – liberalism, nationalism and racism – were especially important in this process. Liberal ideology and the rise of the liberal state underpinned an international economic system committed, at least in principle, to liberal economic values. At the domestic level, liberal ideas supported the growth of capitalism and the development of laissez-faire policies. At the heart of 19th-century liberalism was the belief in progress. Nationalism was responsible for both redrawing the map of Europe and stimulating the economic growth of countries determined to catch up with the leading states. On the one hand, nationalism helped to maintain domestic stability as populations identified themselves with their (emerging) states, but, on the other, it also led to a backlash against liberal economic ideology as some states resorted to economic nationalist policies in their drive for industrialization. Racist ideology was also crucial in shaping 19th-century developments as racist ideas permeated European imperial expansion. European imperialism was based on myths of European superiority and whether articulated in terms of the white man's burden to civilize inferior races or as the right of Europeans to rule lesser races, this racial ideology helped mould and shape relations between European states at the centre of the world economy and peoples on the periphery.

Security

In the area of security, the 19th century has often been seen as a period of relative peace because the balance of power prevented any pan-European war for almost 100 years. However, this view reflects a Eurocentric bias. Violence in the international system was rampant for many non-European peoples subject to various forms of European imperialism. Many of Africa's population were subject to violence as European countries scrambled to take over the continent. China was shaken by the Taiping Rebellion alongside the turbulence of the Opium Wars, while famine relief in India was hindered by British authorities. The US itself was torn apart by civil war in a conflict pitting the industrial and protectionist north against the agricultural free-trading southern states.

Governance

In terms of national governance, this period saw the rise of the nation-state and the development of a liberal state. The liberal state presided over capital accumulation through its regulation of capital and labour. It was through the instrumentality of the liberal state that rights and responsibilities were assigned. The liberal state was essential to the growth of domestic capitalism and the emergence of an international economy through the role it played in increasing the power of markets and the formulation of policies designed to reward or punish behaviour that assisted or retarded the efforts of the emerging industrial capitalists.

The liberal state and Pax Britannica rested on a specific domestic political settlement in which the majority of the population was disenfranchised and played no role in policy-making. As the century progressed, working people began to agitate for increased access to political participation. One of the main differences between the 19th-century and 20th-century international economic systems resides in the role played by the working class (and peasantry) in political decision-making. With the advent of universal franchise, greater attention was given by governments to the needs of workers. Of course, as detailed above, there were gains and the domestic settlement in 1914 was different from that of 1815. Nevertheless, for most of this period, governments represented elites and could ignore the demands of most of the population. Importantly, this period saw increased conflict between the interests of rural landowners and industrialists. As the century progressed, these conflicts tended to be resolved in favour of the industrial bourgeoisie. One way in which working-class agitation was quelled was through the rise of nationalism. Although socialist parties emerged committed to class struggle in which national borders were supposed to be transcended, the nationalist myth proved more potent as an organizing device.

Chapter 5 outlines how we moved from the wreckage of the 19th-century system to a 21st-century global political economy, which shares some of its predecessor's characteristics, but has many new dimensions.

Further Reading

David Landes' *The Unbound Promethus* (2003) is a useful guide to the Industrial Revolution in Britain and Europe. The imperialist race in Africa is detailed in Tom Pakenham's *The Scramble for Africa 1876–1912* (1991), while the horrific case of colonialism in the Congo is examined in Adam Hochschild's *King Leopold's Ghost: A Story of Greed, Terror and Heroism in Colonial Africa* (1999). Karl Polanyi's *The Great Transformation* (1957) is a classic book still widely discussed today. He argues that the 19th-century liberal system led to its own downfall in the 20th century. Charles Kindleberger examines the causes of the Great Depression in *The World Depression 1929–1939* (1986).

Growing a Global Economy: 1945–2015

This chapter examines the transformation of the international political economy from the middle of the 20th century into a global political economy in the first decade and a half of the 21st century. The first section examines the period 1945–89 when international relations were marked by Cold War divisions and distinct political economies. The second section highlights developments that have taken on increasing significance since the end of the Cold War. These include competing capitalisms and state transformation, the information revolution, and developments in international organization and global governance.

It is common to refer to the Cold War system of 1945–89 as being composed of three worlds. The First World comprised the US and its allies in western Europe, Canada, Australia, New Zealand and later Japan. The Second World comprised the communist states of Eastern Europe and the Soviet Union. The Third World was the term used for the rest of the world's states that were occupied with the process of development. Some countries such as China might fall into two camps – the Second and Third Worlds. The following sections examine the relationship within and among these three worlds.

THE COLD WAR ERA: 1945–89

The US-led Western political economy

Following the Second World War, the US and its allies created a new international system to provide security and economic growth for members of the Western alliance of capitalist states. Drawing on the perceived lessons from the 1930s and 40s (see Box 5.1), the US provided a security umbrella for its allies, and new international institutions were created to foster democracy and economic growth. This section considers the security structure and economic structures of the Western system.

Cold War confrontation

The wartime alliance between the Western Allies and the Soviet Union was already under strain as Germany and Japan were in the process of being defeated. Indeed, it had always been a temporary alliance subject to rivalry and tension (Thorne, 1978). Following the war, Europe was divided between the two camps and a lukewarm alliance turned into a Cold War. The Soviet Union placed friendly regimes in power in Eastern Europe and the US led Western states in the creation of economic and military alliances against the Soviet Union.

Box 5.1 Five lessons Western powers drew from the Second World War

1 International financial chaos played a key role in facilitating the rise of fascism in Germany, leading to a breakdown in the international system. Some mechanism would be needed to maintain a stable international monetary system and facilitate the flow of liquidity. This view led to the creation of the International Monetary Fund (IMF), the World Bank and the Marshall Plan.

2 An economic system divided into competing regions could prove dangerous. Some effort would need to be made to liberalize trade between states. After a failed attempt at creating an International Trade Organization, the response was the establishment of a multilateral trading system in the form of the General Agreement on Tariffs and Trade (GATT).

3 The power of the masses and workers would need to be accommodated in some form or another. Leftist political forces could only be blunted if some of the concerns of their constituents were taken into account. The answer to this problem was the Keynesian state, which redistributed income to the broad population.

4 These economic arrangements would require more robust security arrangements than had existed under the League of Nations. States would need to be prepared to fight at an early stage in order to prevent a larger war at a later date. The post-1945 period saw the emergence of the Cold War, a series of military alliances such as NATO, and reliance on nuclear weapons to prevent wars between the superpowers.

5 The above four points could only be implemented if the US played a more active international role than it had in the 1920s and 30s. Contrary to the interwar period, the internationalists won the battle within the US and it assumed a role as a major international power and leader of the Western bloc. Indeed, the period from the mid-20th until the mid-21st century may well be remembered as the American century.

The US pledged both economic and military resources to confront the Soviet Union. In the economic realm, US funds helped with the reconstruction of western Europe and Japan. In military affairs, the US stationed troops in foreign countries and agreed to the creation of a Western military alliance – the North Atlantic Treaty Organization (NATO). At the heart of NATO was the threat that the US would use nuclear weapons to deter Soviet aggression in Europe. Canada and the US stationed troops in Europe so that any Soviet invasion would force a united defence. Once the Soviet Union also developed nuclear weapons, a balance of terror called MAD (mutually assured destruction) froze confrontation in Europe and made the prospect of direct conflict between the USSR and the US daunting (Freedman, 1985). Colonial powers France and Britain maintained the ability to intervene around the world and also developed nuclear weapons.

One of the effects of a relatively stable US–USSR confrontation was that conflict between the superpowers was played out in other parts of the world.

When the US supplied arms to Israel, Saudi Arabia and Iran (before the revolution of 1979), the USSR supplied Syria, Iraq and Egypt. The Soviet Union supplied arms to the Vietnamese in their struggle against the US,

and the Americans funded Afghan Islamic guerrillas against the Soviet Union. The US supported the racist government of South Africa, which was engaged in fighting Cuban-backed forces in Angola. In Central America, the US backed right-wing governments against left-wing insurgent movements. The US and the Soviet Union became involved in a series of national revolutions and wars of independence, greatly exacerbating local conflicts (Halliday, 1983).

The military and economic impact of this global competition varied across countries. Some East Asian states benefited from US attention and aid. For example, Japan, South Korea and Taiwan were able to use US investment and the security umbrella to develop their economies (Stubbs, 1999). However, in many other countries, Cold War rivalry fed the flames of local conflicts, contributing to escalating violence and increasing poverty. Southern Africa, Central America and Indochina bore the brunt of Cold War conflict between the US and the USSR. They served as proxy battlefields and paid the price in terms of human casualties and stunted economic development. In addition, authoritarian regimes of the left and right were able to maintain power to the detriment of their populations, due to sponsorship of one or the other of the superpowers.

These proxy wars and other violent conflicts led to death, destruction, devastation and famine for millions of poor people, while maintaining the semblance of a peaceful world in Western countries.

The Western economic system

The US used its unparalleled economic and military dominance to construct a set of institutions to manage the world economy. The international trade and payments order, constructed as the Second World War drew to a close, was in theory a negotiated order with the principal participants, the US and the UK. However, in reality, the order was largely shaped by US power and thus reflected US interests. Unlike the economic nationalism of the 1930s, this rejected bilateralism. The key features of the order were liberalism, legalism and multilateralism. The new order was based on liberal economic principles but not the laissez-faire liberalism that had characterized the 19th-century international economic order. In the wake of the political mobilization of the working class and the experiences of the Great Depression, policy makers attempted to balance social welfare concerns with a commitment to market principles. This multilateralism rested on domestic political economies that were interventionist. There was no automatic adjustment as in the gold standard nor was free trade unrestricted. The goal was to create a system that had liberal attributes, but did not undermine domestic stability. Ruggie (1982) termed this order based on Keynesian principles one of 'embedded liberalism'. Embedded liberalism was committed to a liberal international economy, but the liberalism was tempered by domestic state intervention to support social purposes such as full employment.

Western states participated in a number of economic institutions designed to free economic exchange. Three international organizations were created to oversee the liberal international economic order. While ostensibly committed to universal membership, the IMF, the International Bank for Reconstruction and Development (otherwise known as the World Bank) and the GATT restricted membership to countries committed to following free-market principles in their domestic economic management. The IMF and the World Bank were designed in 1944 to support a stable monetary system and fund postwar reconstruction. Additional funding to aid reconstruction was provided by the US in the form of the Marshall Plan. The attempt to create the International Trade Organization failed, but GATT served as a framework for gradually liberalizing trade. These three institutions were created to overcome the persistent economic problems that had arisen in the 1930s.

An important development in the postwar global political economy has been the creation of regional economic institutions. The most elaborate of these regional organizations arose and matured in western Europe. Sheltering behind the security umbrella of the US and NATO, European states created the European Economic Community (EEC), or common market, through the Treaty of Rome in 1957 to assist with economic integration. This was the continuation of a process of closer cooperation initiated by the European Coal and Steel Community in 1951. The EEC evolved into the European Union (EU) and in the process brought European states much closer to political union. The unprecedented levels of economic cooperation leading to monetary union have not translated into effective harmonization of foreign and security policies, but EU states collectively have emerged as rivals to US dominance in a number of issue areas.

Sheltered by the nuclear umbrella and supported by sympathetic economic institutions, the US, western Europe, Japan and other allies followed policies of economic growth in the postwar era. Government policy redistributed income, supported industry and maintained full employment. The provision of credit and a series of technical innovations facilitated a golden era of economic growth in Western states from the 1950s until the early 1970s. This system then came under strain as US spending on the Vietnam War and rising oil prices caused inflation and recession.

Beginning in the 1970s, northern states increasingly moved from providing welfare to preparing their citizens for global economic competition (see below). The US and the UK pushed for reforms to the trade, financial and monetary regimes, which were designed to give greater play to market forces and reduce the ability of the state to intervene in the economy. These reforms undermined the balance of embedded liberalism, pushing the economic system in a more neoliberal direction. These neoliberal ideas were captured well by the term 'Washington Consensus'. This consensus in liberal economic policy was applied domestically and also exported to developing countries through international organizations and transnational policy networks.

The communist political economy

In contrast to the Western system where individuals and corporations owned property and the allocations of resources were largely determined by the supply and demand of the market, the communist system eliminated private property and allocated resources through central planning of the state. The communist system began in Russia following the 1917 revolution. With Russia's defeat of the Nazis in eastern and central Europe, the soviet form of communism extended to countries such as Ukraine, Poland, Romania and East Germany. Social revolutions led by communist parties in cooperation with peasant movements brought central planning to countries as diverse as China, Cuba, Vietnam, North Korea, Ethiopia and Angola. Communist states were also authoritarian, one-party states where other forms of political expression were suppressed by the Communist Party.

Communist states achieved a number of notable successes, but these were often accompanied by a horrendous human cost and eventual failure. Following the Russian Revolution, the Soviet Union was able to industrialize its primarily rural economy. By the mid-1960s, its technology had advanced to such an extent that it posed a serious military threat to western Europe and was engaged in a space race with the US. The Soviet Union also made considerable headway in women's equality, literacy and healthcare for its population. However, the collectivization of agriculture in the Soviet Union was accomplished through a combination of force and starvation at the cost of many millions of lives. In economic terms, the Soviet Union enjoyed some success in intensive growth, but fell short in creating growth in other areas. It was able to show progress in areas of the economy that required people or resources in the production process, but less successful in areas that required increasing application of technology and innovation. While the Soviet Union was able to produce heavy industry and basic goods, it was unable to develop consumer goods on a par with Western states. Unable to produce consumer goods desired by many of its population and increasingly falling behind in the arms race with Western states, the Soviet growth model had reached its limit by the early 1980s. A series of largely peaceful revolutions swept the communists from power in eastern Europe in 1989. The 1990s saw eastern European states, Russia and the former republics of the Soviet Union struggle to establish functioning capitalist economies and liberal democratic states with varying degrees of success.

The Chinese communist model enjoyed less success than its Russian counterpart. A series of failed five-year plans and the Cultural Revolution, which turned on many of its own citizens, led to industrial stagnation and agricultural shortfalls. By 1979, the Chinese leadership had concluded that economic development would require a gradual opening up to Western economies. Special economic zones were created to attract investment from Western states. Over the next 35 years, China transformed many areas of its economy into capitalist forms, with large inflows of Western investment and the introduction of private property. Unlike the Soviet Union, China did not adopt political liberalization and continued an authoritarian form of state, with strict censorship, one-party rule and minimal space for political dissent.

By the early 1990s, Russia and China, the two largest communist states, had abandoned the tenets of communism. Russia evolved into a fully capitalist state fuelled by wealth from natural resources, with the institutional form of a democracy, but strains of authoritarianism in its political culture. Its transition to capitalism was marred by the rise of wealthy oligarchs who stripped the assets of the former state during a time when the rule of law was not firmly established. In China, tremendous wealth was generated in some areas of the country, lifting millions out of poverty. However, the challenges of social stability at a time of rapid economic transformation and under an authoritarian state were intense.

The southern political economy

As the Soviet Union and the US struggled for advantage in the Cold War, another historic process was taking place. This was the decolonization process and emergence of the 'Third World' as a political and economic actor. The states of the Third World embarked on a struggle for development that, to this day, has had only limited success.

Decolonization

The post-1945 period saw an impressive process of decolonization as the European empires discussed in Chapters 3 and 4 crumbled. In some cases, European states recognized the difficulty of continuing to rule foreign countries, while in other cases local populations had to wage violent campaigns to force the colonialists to relinquish control.

The nature and pace of decolonization varied considerably. For example, France tended to be more committed than Britain to using force to maintain its empire (Chamberlain, 1985, pp. 55–72). France waged long, bloody and ultimately futile wars in Vietnam and Algeria (see Box 5.2). In Vietnam, nationalists defeated the French at Dien Bien Phu in 1954. The Algerians secured their independence in 1962 after years of fighting. The French retreat in sub-Saharan Africa proceeded more peacefully as states were granted independence, but kept close economic and political ties with France. The US played a complex role in the process of decolonization. It granted the Philippines independence in 1946 and urged its European allies to abandon their empires. During the Suez crisis of 1956, it opposed the British/French/Israeli invasion of Egypt. However, as the Cold War intensified, the US itself became involved in old colonial struggles, such as preventing the reunification of Vietnam.

There are a number of competing explanations for the onset of decolonization. The Second World War was a major factor (Abernethy, 2000, pp. 345–60). For the second time in 30 years, European states inflicted damage on each other's productive and military capacities. France, Britain and the Netherlands emerged in a greatly weakened condition, much less able to hold on to territory by force. At the same time, Japanese success early in the war against the US and Europeans in Asia revealed the vulnerability of their empires. The war itself had the effect of mobilizing and uprooting millions of people in the colonies. Similar to the European masses after the First World War, these people were not willing to return to the prewar status quo.

Another important explanation is the growth of nationalist movements within the colonies and the increasing economic drain that colonies posed for European states (Darwin, 1988, pp. 17–24). Within countries such as India, Vietnam and Indonesia, educated local leaderships mobilized local populations to change the calculus of empire. Through a variety of means they demonstrated to the European colonizers that the project of empire was no longer sustainable. In the case of India, Gandhi's campaign of nonviolent resistance highlighted the potential ungovernability of South Asia. In the cases of Vietnam, Indonesia and Algeria, wars of independence were required.

The impact of decolonization was dramatic. A large number of new states came into being, shifting the balance in international institutions such as the UN General Assembly. In some cases, new organizations such as the United Nations Conference on Trade and Development were created to serve the interest of developing countries. In the 1970s, developing countries pushed for a change in the rules governing the global economy, which was called the New International Economic Order. Many of the new states, although formally independent, were highly dependent on their former metropoles for economic ties. In the security field, many of the newly independent states tried to steer a third way in the Cold War between the USSR and the US. This initiative was called the Non-Aligned Movement and was led by India, Indonesia, Ghana and Yugoslavia in the 1960s and 70s. Finally, decolonization pushed the question of development onto the international agenda, where it continues to be a significant issue.

Box 5.2 Decolonization and violence

The effects of violence on the colonizer and the colonized were starkly illustrated by Frantz Fanon in the early 1960s. Writing in the shadow of Algeria's brutal struggle for independence from France, Fanon (1963, p. 94) argued that the use of violence against the colonizer served to cleanse the colonized from years of humiliation and oppression. What Fanon did not anticipate was that, once independence was won, it was often difficult for independence leaders to abandon the use of violence in ruling their new countries.

Development success and failures

The issue of development and growth will be examined in Chapter 11, but a brief overview is required here. Some states have experienced success in their attempts to develop their economies in the post-1945 period. Japan was able to rebuild its economy after US occupation, while the four Asian tigers of South Korea, Taiwan, Hong Kong and Singapore achieved incredible progress in terms of growth rates, education levels and advances in particular economic sectors. The rise of these centres of economic power and the oil-producing states in the 1970s was so dramatic that some analysts in the US feared that American dominance or hegemony was in decline (Gilpin, 1987; Keohane, 1984). Some Asian leaders also began to believe that they had developed a political economy superior to the US and began to advance the notion of a distinct and better set of Asian values as the explanation for their success (Zakaria, 1994). Both of these trends were diminished by renewed US growth in the 1990s and the Asian financial crisis of 1997.

In contrast to some Asian success stories, many of the world's most populous states such as China, India, Indonesia, Brazil and most of Africa have suffered a series of setbacks in their pursuit of development. In some cases, such as China, until the reform process embarked on in the 1970s, disastrous central planning destroyed agricultural and industrial productivity. In other cases, such as sub-Saharan Africa, countries were trapped into producing products that declined in value over time (coffee, tin and so on). Insecurity within and between states led to resources being diverted to fighting other states or internal guerrilla movements. In many instances, the debt crisis of the 1980s halted development projects and forced states into a series of structural adjustment programmes that opened and undermined local economies.

Despite these setbacks, especially in sub-Saharan Africa, a number of developing countries emerged as thriving political economies early in the 21st century. China's export performance, India's liberalization and trade in services, Brazil's industrialization and natural resources, and Russia's oil wealth raised the spectre of a new set of emerging economies willing to finally challenge the leaders of the Western economic system.

THE POST-COLD WAR ERA: 1990–2015

Three trends have been increasingly visible as the Cold War era fades into history. The first trend is a continuation of a competition between rival forms of capitalism and its extension to emerging powers. The second is the pervasive impact of the information revolution. The third is ongoing developments in the field of international organization.

Competing capitalisms and state transformation

Simultaneous with the worldwide competition between communist and capitalist forms of political economy, rivalry and competition between differing models of capitalism was occurring among Western states. Depending on the analyst, the systems were categorized in different ways. Some saw a competition between different financial systems, such as the Anglo-American model of stock markets versus continental European models, which relied more heavily on banks to raise money for firms, versus an Asian (mainly Japanese and Korean) model of close government/industry/finance ties. Others perceived the significant difference in the various forms of capitalisms as being the manner in which they provided welfare to their citizens. The US model provided a minimal welfare state, the continental Europeans had an extensive government welfare state while Japan provided extensive welfare (such as lifetime employment) for those lucky enough to be working for key corporations (Esping-Andersen, 1990).

The Western competition between capitalisms did not provide a winner. Each model had strengths and weaknesses, periods of success and times of economic turbulence. The European system provided broad-based welfare for its citizens, but struggled with relatively high levels of unemployment. The US system generally had lower levels of unemployment, but a disturbingly high number of its citizens lacked access to basic welfare such as affordable healthcare. The Japanese economy enjoyed great success in the 1980s, sparking fears in the US of an economic rival. However, in the 1990s, it was the US economy that led a wave of technological innovation and the Japanese economy entered a decade of economic stagnation. From 2008 to 2012 both the US and European economies suffered severe financial crises. While the US showed signs of a reviving economy in 2015, Europe remained in austerity and economic stagnation.

At the close of the first decade of the 21st century, the competition between capitalisms had become more global and diverse. The welfare capitalism of western Europe and the Anglo-Saxon liberal models were joined by a host of competitors with a variety of models. The BRICS countries (Brazil, Russia, India, China and South Africa) emerged as areas of increased economic activity and political influence. First among these competitors was China, which possessed an extensive manufacturing sector and considerable capital from its export surpluses. It combined an authoritarian domestic state with strict internal labour discipline and a mercantilist approach to economic policy through regulation of foreign investment and active intervention in financial and production systems. China enjoyed tremendous economic growth, but struggled to disperse gains amongst a large and diverse population. India pursued a different model. It maintained a democratic government with leading sectors in information technology (IT) and services, but faced a substantial challenge in transforming its large subsistence agricultural sector and developing its infrastructure. A renewed and semi-democratic Russian state imbued with immense wealth from natural resources cast a shadow over increasingly energy-dependent Europe. However, a collapse in oil prices in 2014 showed the fragility of the Russian resource-dependent development model. In Latin America, Brazil, buoyed by reinvigorated industrial and agricultural sectors and led by governments committed to addressing its horrendous rates of economic inequality, offered an alternative model in the Western hemisphere. By 2015 its development model was also challenged by slow growth. In South Africa, initial optimistic hopes that a post-apartheid state would lead an African renaissance wilted in the face of stubborn inequalities and unemployment worsened by premature economic liberalization.

Alongside the competition between forms of capitalism, we also see a change in the nature of the state within various models. The function and nature of states at the beginning of the 21st century are different from those of the middle of the 20th century. In the 1950s, states in the First World were characterized by Keynesian economics or Fordism (the system of mass production and consumption). They were committed to fostering full employment and cushioning economic turbulence within their borders. In the Second World, Soviet command economies marshalled resources to feed industrialization and competition with the West. In much of the Third World, 'developmental states' intervened in the economy to protect infant industries and begin the process of industrialization. By 2000, most of the centrally planned states had disappeared, leaving the field to versions of the welfare and developmental states and the competition state.

From welfare to competition in the North

In advanced industrialized countries, considerable concern has been expressed that the nature of the state has changed from providing welfare to its citizens to preparing both citizens and corporations for international competition. The idea of a 'competition state' captures this dynamic.

Cerny (2000) suggests that the transformation of the state's role includes several major policy changes. One change is that, rather than supporting particular industries or sectors, states are more likely to ensure that national economies provide a competitive environment. This involves initiatives at the macro and microeconomic levels. At the macro level, states put a priority on low inflation to attract investment. At the micro level, steps are taken to increase organizations' competition and flexibility. This might include deregulating or privatizing industries or changing labour legislation to permit more flexible (and less secure) employment practices. Finally, governments increasingly shift from maximizing general welfare, through policies such as full employment and universal social programmes, to targeting programmes designed to increase citizens' employability, such as training, or reducing welfare benefits to encourage work at lower wage levels.

The concept of a competition state is a useful tool to think about policy innovations in Western states. However, a wide range of models continues to exist from relatively welfare-oriented Scandinavian states to the increasingly competition-oriented US and UK.

Liberal and authoritarian competition in the South

States outside the developed world have not been immune from the pressures of the global marketplace. Two developments dating back to the late 1970s and early 1980s have increased economic competition in developing states. One was the unilateral decision by the government of China that it would begin opening up to Western states by seeking trade and foreign direct investment (FDI). Although this was a slow process at the beginning, China grew to become the major recipient of FDI in the 1990s. This diverted investment from other developing countries and resulted in the growth of exports that competed with the products of other developing countries. For example, China, India and Indonesia might all be trying to sell the same product in the US market.

The second development was the debt crisis, which forced many states to abandon inward-looking development strategies in search of finding a niche in the global market. Biersteker (1992) refers to developing states turning towards liberal economic policies as 'the triumph of neoclassical economics'. From a different perspective, McMichael (1996) describes the change as the abandonment of a national development project for a globalization project of fitting into the global economy. The crucial point is that this turn towards increased openness and economic competition is taking place under a variety of political frameworks. Communist China is aggressively courting FDI and trade, but retains an authoritarian state system that suppresses dissent and independent trade unions. In the 1970s, Chile began its liberalization under the right-wing authoritarian rule of Augusto Pinochet. However, the 1990s also saw a number of southern states democratize (South Korea, South Africa, Brazil, Mexico) and continue the pursuit of a policy of insertion into the global economy.

While many southern states have liberalized, the notion of the development state attracted renewed interest in the wake of financial crisis in Western states between 2008 and 2012. Western countries seemed to have suffered from excessive liberalization and deregulation of their financial sectors, whereas states that kept the financial sector subservient to developmental goals (such as China) emerged relatively well. Developing countries continue to pursue a range of models, embracing liberalism to varying degrees and in a multitude of ways.

The rise of offshore

Another striking development in the state system was the growth of offshore regulation. The term 'offshore' refers to areas of the global economy where states create territorial or juridical enclaves characterized by a reduction in regulation (Palan, 1998, p. 626). One of the most significant developments in the offshore world has been the growth of tax havens (see Box 5.3). Tax havens are usually located in small states, such as the Cayman Islands. They allow companies and banks to move large sums of money through paper companies to avoid taxation and regulation. Some estimate that half the world's money resides in or passes through tax havens (Palan, 2002, p. 151).

Similar offshore developments can be seen in other economic sectors. Different forms of regulation have been applied to specific territories within states to foster investment and economic growth. For example, China has created special economic zones to attract FDI. Many developing and developed states have created export processing zones (EPZs) or tax-free zones. In developed states, these EPZs are likely to be in depressed areas desperate for economic growth such as inner cities. What all these areas share is that a different type of economic regulation is applied within them from that in the rest of the economy. In some cases, the EPZs may give companies tax holidays for a number of years in return for investment. In others, the main attraction may be the prohibition of independent trade unions from production in the zones.

The rise of a new political jurisdiction provides some business actors with greater economic flexibility to increase profits by reducing the costs of complying with regulation. Some states have benefited from offshore activity because it has allowed them to attract investment to their territory. However, other states have lost investment and the ability to tax or regulate in the public interest.

The information revolution

In Chapter 4, we examined the advent of the Industrial Revolution and how this changed the course of history. The last decades of the 20th century witnessed another

---

Box 5.3 Sheltering wealth offshore

A 2012 estimate of the amount of wealth hidden by rich individuals in offshore accounts placed the figure at between $21 trillion and $32 trillion (Tax Justice Network, 2012). The lower figure is as large as the GDP of the US and Japan combined. About half the total amount is owned by just 92,000 people. Since most of this wealth is not taxed by governments, an estimated $190–280 billion in tax revenue is lost. This is more than Western countries give in aid to the developing world (H. Stewart, 2012).

The drain of wealth by rich individuals out of their countries is particularly serious for states where a small number of people own most of the nation's wealth. Countries where a few individuals or families control vast oil wealth or where dictators plunder the nation's wealth are particularly damaged. However, even rich countries are harmed as states struggle to raise tax revenue without adequate contributions from their wealthiest citizens.

dramatic technological revolution, this time based on information rather than machine power. Some have suggested that we are experiencing the third great wave of human progress (Toffler, 1980). The first wave was the agricultural revolution and the second the Industrial Revolution. We are too close to the beginning of the information revolution to determine its final form and implications, but some initial points can be developed.

Technological

Most readers of this text will be familiar with the information revolution because it has become an everyday part of their lives. Western university students may not be able to imagine a world without personal computers (PCs), mobile phones and the internet. Yet, these communication and information technologies only began their diffusion in the 1970s with the invention of the microprocessor (computer chip). In 1977, the first highly successful mass-produced PC was introduced by Apple and user-friendly software was soon marketed by Microsoft.

Since the mid-1970s, the application of information and knowledge to innovation and production has accelerated technological change. PCs have become smaller and more powerful. The internet has broadened the number of people exchanging information, products and entertainment. Digital technology has allowed for improved communications through voice (phones, radio) and visual devices (television, film).

Economic

The economic impacts of the information revolution are still working their way through the global political economy. IT has certainly facilitated the globalization of economic activity. For example, financial transactions such as foreign exchange or the purchase or sale of stocks and bonds can take place 24 hours a day almost instantaneously. Improved communication between different parts of corporations allows for production to be dispersed across a wide geographical area.

The information revolution offers the prospect of increasing productivity as information and computers are applied to the production process. New economic sectors are being created with the advent of new forms of consumer electronics, medicine and agriculture. The ability to map and track genes holds out the possibility of new medical cures for diseases. Genetic manipulation has led to the creation of genetically modified crops,

Table 5.1 Decline in value of selected high-tech stocks, 2000–3

	10 March 2000	7 March 2003
Yahoo!	$178.06	$19.62
Intel	$120.19	$16.01
Nortel Networks	$180.5*	$ 3.20
724 Solutions	$304.90*	$ 0.55

Note: * Canadian dollars.
Source: Data from Bloom (2003), B1

which are more productive and more resistant to disease and insects. However, the advent of these technologies has also brought about ethical and political controversies. Concerns have been raised about the ethical implications of human cloning or using genetic tests to select designer babies. In food production, popular fears have been expressed at the dangers of genetic modification of foods and plants.

In some cases, new technology may allow some countries to leapfrog development stages. For example, mobile phones allow developing countries to create a telephone network without the cost of laying cables. Despite such optimism, concerns have been expressed about the digital divide (Norris, 2001). Advanced industrialized societies are rapidly diffusing the technology among their citizens, but many developing countries face the prospect of being left even further behind. While a country such as Canada may be worrying about how they can bring the internet to rural populations, some countries in Africa are still struggling to provide electricity or safe drinking water. The danger is that rather than allowing disadvantaged groups to catch up with developed countries, the gaps grow wider.

The enthusiasm for the information revolution created a bubble in the stock market in the late 1990s. Investors poured money into a wide range of IT firms, inflating the stock market and creating instant paper fortunes for some entrepreneurs. Like all bubbles, this one burst leaving a wreckage of sour investors and broken companies (Table 5.1). The revolution continues, but with a more realistic appraisal of the time it will take for changes to work their way through the economy.

Social

Manuel Castells (1996) has suggested that the advent of the information revolution is having profound effects on social life. He argues that new forms of communication allow people to organize themselves through networks rather than hierarchies. In the network society, people build direct links with each other rather than working through institutions that have layers of authority. For example, people concerned about the environment may form a small environmental group rather than work through a political party. Companies may opt for flexible work teams rather than a workforce divided into rigid roles and tasks. Universities might turn to distance learning rather than gather students in a classroom.

The advent of the internet and email has certainly provided the tools for groups of people to form networks around the world in order to advance their views about how society should be ordered. Citizen associations in the fields of the environment and women's issues, as well as peace campaigners, development advocates and labour groups, have used the new technology to share information and mobilize support. Given the influence of the internet, it is not surprising that governments and corporations have moved to exercise control over its content when civic groups or individuals threaten their interests (see Box 5.4).

Military

The information age is also thought to be creating a revolution in warfare (Cohen, 1996). The US has harnessed IT to bolster its surveillance and attack capabilities. The US military is better able to identify targets and strike them from a distance than any of its opponents. The advantage might be compared to European use of cannon or repeating rifles against locals in the wars of empire in the 19th century. US success in the Gulf Wars of 1991 and 2003 (also known as the Iraq Wars), as well as Afghanistan in 2001–2, indicates that a combination of new technologies and new tactics has made American military power much more effective. It is not invulnerable, but the US certainly has an edge over any possible contender.

International organizations and governance

A striking feature of the global political economy has been the rise in international organizations in the second half of the 20th century. The number of international organizations has grown, and so has their importance in organizing the global economy. In this section we'll briefly examine three sets of organizations – the UN, international economic organizations and corporate and civic associations.

The UN

The United Nations was created in 1945 as a successor to the League of Nations. There are two elements that

---

Box 5.4 Corporations, states and control of the internet

In 2010, the transparency group Wikileaks used the internet to publish US diplomatic cables and video footage showing American helicopter gunships shooting at civilians in Iraq. Some have credited this information with sparking unrest in the Middle East, which contributed to the Arab Spring of 2011 and increasing opposition to the US war in Afghanistan. The distribution of this information sparked fierce criticism from some US politicians and commentators, including calls for the assassination of the Wikileaks founder, Julian Assange. More interesting and damaging action was taken by several large transnational corporations. In December 2010, Amazon refused to continue hosting Wikileaks on its servers, while financial organizations PayPal, VISA, MasterCard, Western Union and Bank of America refused to process financial transactions, including donations that funded the organization's activities (Naughton, 2010). In the same month, Apple removed the Wikileaks app from its App Store. The financial boycott of Wikileaks threatened its survival because of its reliance on internet donations and transactions for operational funding. Many of the corporations claimed that they could not do business with Wikileaks because the organization violated their terms of service. Others suggested that the denial of service might be related to Wikileaks' activism against financial institutions or in response to requests from US politicians. This case is a good example of how the freedom of the internet is contested by corporate and state interests.

have particular significance for the global political economy. The first is the Security Council and the second, the UN's specialized agencies. The UN Security Council is composed of five permanent members and ten rotating members who are elected for two-year terms. The Security Council can make international law, compelling states to respond to its wishes. The permanent members each have a veto over proposals before the Security Council. The Security Council does not usually address strictly economic affairs, but it does influence the security structure and can authorize the employment of economic sanctions against states. Since the end of the Cold War rivalry between the US and the Soviet Union, the Security Council has taken a more active role in peacekeeping and monitoring elections (Weiss et al., 2001, pp. 65–110).

The UN contains a host of specialized agencies designed to promote cooperation and address particular issues. The World Health Organization attempts to improve global public health, the United Nations Children's Fund concentrates on improving the welfare of children and the United Nations High Commissioner for Refugees provides assistance to refugees. In general, these agencies attempt to cope with the casualties of the global political economy. While doing excellent work, they have relatively less power to influence overall economic structures than international economic institutions.

International economic organizations

The multilateral framework created after the Second World War has proved remarkably resilient in the half-century-plus since it was constructed. Because a number of chapters in Part 3 explore the role of these organizations in the context of trade, finance and development, we will only provide a brief review of the continued relevance of the multilateral framework at this point. Three themes have dominated the postwar multilateral framework – adaptation, challenge and expansion. International economic institutions have taken on increased significance in world affairs, especially since the 1980s. These institutions influence behaviour by providing advice on economic policy and demanding policy change in return for financing or settling economic disputes between actors.

In the wake of the debt crisis in the 1980s, the IMF and the World Bank took on enlarged roles in the global economy. The relevance of the IMF was underscored during the global financial crisis (2008–9) where,

despite some reservations concerning the adequacy of its lending capacity and strength of its surveillance mechanisms, it was given a central role to play in coordinating responses to the crisis. The financial assistance and policy advice of the Bretton Woods institutions have been critical in dealing with states in financial crisis. In return for assistance, the institutions have demanded that states adopt adjustment policies by liberalizing their economies and opening up to trade and foreign investment.

In the trade area, the World Trade Organization (WTO) was created in 1995. The WTO is a significant change from the GATT because it provides the trade regime with a permanent institution, opens up new areas of economic activity (for example services) to liberalization, and provides a strong dispute settlement mechanism. This last feature means that states are much more likely to be bound by trade rules after the creation of the WTO than before. Despite the long drawn out Doha Round of trade negotiations, governments appear unwilling to contemplate the collapse of the WTO.

How do we explain the longevity of these institutions? For most of this period, these organizations have enjoyed the support of the leading states within the global economy. Successive US administrations, EU countries and Japan may at times push specific agendas that weaken one or other of these regimes, but they have consistently provided support for a renewed and reinvigorated multilateralism. In other words, the postwar consensus concerning the necessity for an open, multilateral economic system has not been eroded despite shifts in economic policy. Indeed, while the rise of the BRICS has heralded a demand for increased influence in these organizations it has not signalled a threat to their existence. The postwar multilateral framework will have to adapt to a changed power structure but the precise form of the new multilateralism is not apparent at the present time. The increased influence of these institutions has sparked a debate concerning their relevance and legitimacy, with many civil society groups claiming that they are too powerful.

The IMF, the World Bank and the WTO are the most visible international economic institutions, but there are many others. The Group of Eight (commonly known as the G8) brings together the seven most advanced industrialized economies and Russia to discuss economic management of the global economy. In the wake of the global financial crisis, the Group of 20 (G20) which had traditionally focused on financial issues such as financial stability widened its scope to more general economic matters. It includes the G8 plus a number of prominent developing countries. The Bank for International Settlements, located in Geneva, is the forum for central bankers. The Organisation for Economic Co-operation and Development (OECD) is an advisory organization that brings together the industrialized countries of the world. Alongside these organizations can be added numerous regional groupings and economic integration treaties, such as the North American Free Trade Agreement (NAFTA), Southern Common Market (MERCOSUR), European Union (EU), Asia-Pacific Economic Cooperation, Economic Community of West African States, South Asian Association for Regional Cooperation, and Association of Southeast Asian Nations (ASEAN).

The multiplication of inter-state organizations means that states, corporations and citizens are increasingly governed through international organizations. In some cases, the impact is slight. For example, the OECD might publish a report urging a particular economy to spend more money on training. In other cases, the impact is greater. For example, the IMF may demand that a country cuts the amount it spends in its budget, before giving desperately needed loans. Alternatively, the WTO might rule that a domestic environmental regulation violates trade law and must be modified.

Corporate and civic associations

Both the for-profit and not-for-profit sectors have also been busy expanding their international contacts and forming international or transnational organizations. Boli and Thomas (1999, p. 41) estimate that almost 60 per cent of international nongovernmental organizations (NGOs) are concentrated in the economic or scientific fields. NGOs have been particularly active in international development. Although most publicity is given to the advocacy role of many of these organizations as they lobby governments and international organizations, NGOs have become increasingly important in the implementation of development projects (Sklias, 1999). In the 1980s, Western governments increasingly used development NGOs as a channel for the provision of economic aid (Gordenker and Weiss, 1999, p. 25). Not-for-profit citizens' organizations have also increased their international presence, and have created transnational advocacy networks to lobby TNCs, multilateral economic institutions and the

governments of nation-states (Keck and Sikkink, 1998). This activity has been enhanced by the revolution in communications, which enables activists to build networks at relatively low cost. The anti-globalization protests at meetings of the WTO, the World Bank, the IMF and G8 summits provide evidence of non-state actors attempting to influence international economic policy-making. Thus, NGOs and citizen groups have become important as actors in the normative and material structures of the global political economy.

In some areas where states have not set up appropriate regulatory frameworks, industries have formed their own associations and brought in rules or norms. For example, in the area of environmental standards, leading TNCs have established the ISO 14000 set of regulations (Clapp, 1998). The role of industry associations in the construction and maintenance of global governance structures is becoming increasingly visible. While industry associations have long played a part at the domestic level in influencing national legislation, as the appropriate levels of decision-making move beyond the state, so national and transnational industry bodies have sought to influence global policy-making (Sell, 2000; Smythe, 2000).

CONCLUSION

The key frameworks of the global political economy in the 21st century will be explored in Part 3. This conclusion provides an overview of their evolution in the 20th century and contrasts them with the historical eras examined in Chapters 3 and 4.

Trade

The post-1945 era saw an increase in both the volume and type of trade. Trade liberalization took place under a series of negotiating rounds of the GATT. Tariffs were gradually reduced and in the 1970s an effort was made to address non-tariff barriers to trade. In 1995, the creation of the WTO marked the next step in trade as countries began to liberalize trade in services and agriculture, as well as agreeing to submit their disputes to a binding dispute-settlement mechanism. Alongside these multilateral trade initiatives, a series of regional agreements were created to facilitate the movement of goods and services among neighbouring countries. The most significant of these were in Europe (EU), North America (NAFTA), South America (MERCOSUR) and Southeast Asia (ASEAN). As trade agreements intruded more directly on national political economies, trade initiatives became the subject of extensive national and international debate. Concern has been expressed about their economic, environmental and social impacts. Unlike earlier eras, trade and investment take place under an elaborate system of rules and formal international organizations.

Production

The most visible development in the area of production has been the growth of transnational corporations. TNCs account for the majority of the global production structure and 50 per cent of world trade. In 1998, 53,000 TNCs with 450,000 foreign subsidiaries had total sales of $9.5 trillion. By 2015 the top 2,000 TNCs had combined revenues of $39 trillion. The largest TNCs have annual sales greater than the GDP of most countries. This results in the investment decisions of TNCs having an enormous impact on the economic fortunes of particular states. The influence of these corporations has led to suggestions that the state is losing power to economic actors and that democracy is threatened by their growing power. Since most large TNCs originate in and invest in developed states, the problem of development continues to plague many countries.

Another significant trend has been the increasing importance of East and South-east Asia as a site for international production. The development of the four tigers has been followed by the industrialization of the coastal Chinese mainland. China's government created special economic zones to lure foreign investment and build its export base. If it can maintain its political integrity and manage the inequalities brought about by industrialization, China has the potential to become a leading international power. Indeed, an influential publication predicted that by 2050 China would become the world's leading economy (HSBC, 2011).

Finance

The financial field has witnessed a transition from the immediate postwar period, where markets were restricted and government actors played a large role, to today's global system where capital is extremely mobile and private firms take the lead role. The international monetary system has moved from a system of fixed exchange rates to a system of fluctuating rates. Thus, we have a system of capital mobility and floating exchange rates, but the currencies are not tied to an accepted commodity such as gold. The 1970s was the transition decade from a system of national Keynesianism or embedded liberalism to a more open, neoliberal state and global economy. The openness of the global financial field is not unprecedented, but its particular form has not been seen before. Information technologies allow for a much more rapid movement of funds across state boundaries, while the flow of news has the financial markets reacting immediately to the latest current events. A financial crisis in one country can spill over into neighbouring countries and around the globe in a matter of days.

Labour

The postwar years have seen a shift from an international to a more global division of labour. The concept of a global division of labour captures a form of organization that reaches around the world, but where work is not confined to particular states. In a global division of labour, activities that in the past might have been thought of as being confined to particular states now exist in very different types of states. Labour that one might associate with a developing country flourishes in a developed state and jobs thought to be the preserve of advanced industrialized countries exist alongside labour-intensive jobs in developing states. For example, an expanding computer software industry has developed in India alongside the majority of the population that lives on subsistence agriculture. The distinctive feature of these jobs is that they are plugged into a transnational production process and they are not confined to particular parts of the globe, although they may be more concentrated in some areas than others.

Gender

The gendered nature of the post-1945 global political economy has become clearer with increasing research into the subject. Economies of all states relied on women to provide free labour to care for family members so that men could participate in the paid workforce. In addition, economic restructuring in response to financial crisis demands that women provide even more services as states cut back on social provision. At the same time, the increasing globalization of the economy is bringing more women into the global workforce in particular roles – as domestics or nannies, entertainment or sex workers, or workers in labour-intensive factories in the developing world. While some women pursue desirable career opportunities in the global economy, most struggle to make ends meet.

Development

Development has become a significant issue in the post-1945 era with the process of decolonization. Although a large number of countries gained their independence in the postwar period, the struggle for development has been much more difficult. In this period we have witnessed uneven development within and among countries. The recent rise of Brazil, China and India may be the precursors to sustained economic development elsewhere. We have seen too many false dawns to make firm predictions. Nevertheless, we can note that these are not the only countries contributing to what has been termed the 'Rise of the South' (UNDP, 2013a). At the end of the 15-year period marked by the Millennium Development Goals, some progress in human development has been made. But meaningful development continues to evade many people on the planet.

Environment

Environmental degradation became a large issue in the latter part of the 20th century. One of the consequences of European, North American, Japanese and Soviet industrialization programmes has been the poisoning of the natural environment. In the 21st century issues such as global warming have become prominent. The proposed solutions, such as the Kyoto Protocol, have sparked heated debate within developed states and between developed and developing states. In the developing world, poverty has led to economic practices that contribute to, among other things, deforestation and pollution.

Ideas

In the realm of ideas, the postwar era has seen a prolonged struggle over the superior method of organizing domestic political economies. In Western states, Keynesian welfare policies dominated. Central planning in the Soviet model offered an alternative vision of

society until the end of the Cold War in 1989. Although the capitalist system emerged triumphant in 1989, vigorous debates continue about what form of capitalism is appropriate for any particular economy. Usually the liberal Anglo-American systems are contrasted against more welfare-oriented European arrangements or Asian corporatist practices, which integrate business, government and subordinate labour organizations. Another significant development in thinking has been the rise of the concept of globalization. Over the last quarter of the 20th century, the term 'global' was increasingly used to describe a range of activities in the cultural, economic and political realms. Globalization concerns the growth of supraterritorial relations between people (Scholte, 2000a). These relations can be found in engagement with and response to mass media (for example, pressure for humanitarian intervention following a TV broadcast), developed through economic structures (global production and finance) or aroused in response to shifting centres of authority.

Security

On the security front, most of the postwar era was dominated by the Cold War between the US and the USSR. This competition structured political and economic relations around the world. Conflicts between the superpowers were often channelled to developing countries, which resulted in losses and gains for those states. With the end of the Cold War in 1989, the security issues of terrorism, nuclear proliferation and conflict within states took on increased prominence. The US continued to build its military advantage by applying technological innovation to its armed forces. Increasingly, the developed world was characterized as a zone of peace (with the exception of occasional terror attacks), while much of the developing world faced the prospect of inter-state or civil war. For most of the world's citizens, premature death was much more likely to come from poverty, disease or malnutrition than war.

Governance

There are two governance developments that set this era apart from its predecessors. One element has been the proliferation of formal international organizations dedicated to coordinating policy on a wide range of issues. Institutions such as the IMF, the World Bank and the WTO exercise considerable influence over policy formation in the areas of trade, finance and development, especially in weaker and poorer states. A second feature has been the democratization of state institutions. Greater public influence over decision makers (compared with previous eras) complicates foreign economic and diplomatic policies. Economic arrangements, such as NAFTA and the operation of the WTO, have become issues for debate in many states. This indicates that global governance structures increasingly need to be rooted in the politics of democratic states. The automatic economic adjustment demanded in the gold standard era is no longer possible.

Having provided readers with a general introduction to theories and methods in GPE in Part 1, and an overview of the historical emergence of a GPE in Part 2, we now turn our attention in Part 3 to a more detailed analysis of key GPE frameworks in the post-1945 era. The following chapters examine definitions, theories, major developments and key issues in the areas of trade, production, finance, labour, gender, development, environment, ideas, security and governance.

Further Reading

John Ruggie's concept of embedded liberalism was elaborated in his 1982 article 'International Regimes, Transactions and Change: Embedded Liberalism in the Postwar Economic Order', *International Organization*, 36(2): 379–415. Thematic overviews of various aspects of post-1945 IPE can be found in the edited collections by Richard Stubbs and Geoffrey Underhill (eds) *Political Economy and the Changing Global Order*, 3rd edn (2005), and John Ravenhill (ed.) (2011) *Global Political Economy*, 3rd edn.

PART 3
DYNAMICS

International Trade

Trade across borders inflames passions and creates controversies that are absent in discussions of trade within countries. Early chapters of this book demonstrated the importance of trade in the evolution of the contemporary global economic system. This chapter provides an introduction to understanding the political economy of the modern global trading system. One striking feature of the contemporary international trading system arises from the conflict between the continuing political importance of the national border and its declining economic relevance. Political conflicts over trade exist simultaneously with the growth of transnational production (see Chapter 7), wherein production by firms is less restricted by national frontiers than at any time in history.

This chapter provides an introduction to international trade through an examination of the material and normative structures that constitute the international trading system. It begins with a brief definition of some key terms, and an introduction to the importance of the means of exchange. Next, we discuss some of the more important theoretical disputes and examine empirical claims made by various proponents in key debates concerning the evolution and impact of free trade. We then examine the major developments in the postwar international trading system. These include the tremendous expansion in trade, the development of new forms of protectionism, and the emergence and development of the regulation of trade through, first, the General Agreement on Tariffs and Trade (GATT) and, latterly, the World Trade Organization (WTO). The key issues considered in this chapter are the special needs of developing countries, the growth of regionalism and the debate over the legitimacy of the trading system.

DEFINITIONS

Simply speaking, trade refers to the exchange of one commodity for another. Whenever two or more individuals exchange goods and services, they are engaged in trade. Thus we can see that trade has been a feature of all civilizations. Trade as an activity takes place domestically when two or more individuals exchange goods and services. International trade arises when the exchange is conducted across national borders.

However, the content of what are considered tradeable commodities and hence part of the international trading system has changed historically. While current definitions of international trade highlight it as consisting of the exchange of goods and services, the latter has only recently been integrated into the international trading system with the creation of the General Agreement of Trade in Services (GATS) at the conclusion of the Uruguay Round of trade negotiations. Traditionally, many parts of the services sector were seen as principally confined to the domestic economy and not subject to trade policy considerations. The increasing importance of the services sector in national output, the deregulation of many service sectors previously held to be the domain of government policy, and technological change leading to removal of existing (national) barriers to entry created conditions that led to changed attitudes concerning the content of international trade and the need for international regulation. Pressure for GATS came from governments in the developed world mainly, the European Union and the United States, and leading companies in the financial and telecommunications services sectors.

In any discussion of international trade, two issues are important: the existence of barriers or restrictions to trade, and the medium of exchange in which trade is conducted. There are a number of different barriers to trade and we will be concerned here with political rather than technical barriers such as travel and distance. Political barriers to trade are erected wherever different political authorities decide to prohibit or restrict their citizens' access to foreign goods and services. In other words, for a variety of reasons, the goods and services from one political region may be prohibited from entering, or leaving, another region; or they may be made more costly for a country's citizens in comparison with similar domestic goods and services. Within the global political economy, therefore, the national border has added significance, insofar as different national authorities may attempt to control the activities of their citizens in making transactions across borders. Protectionism refers to policies designed to restrict the import of goods and services. In recent history, discussions of protectionism have referred to national forms of protection, but this need not be the case. For example, until Federation in 1901, the Australian colonies had systems of protection against imports from each other.

Protection can take many forms, but the most common has traditionally been tariffs. Tariffs are a tax imposed on imports of particular products. The tax revenue goes to the government of the importing state. More recently, protection has increasingly taken the form of non-tariff barriers (NTBs), such as:

1   *Quotas:* the application of a quantitative restriction against goods and services from another country or region, as well as health and safety requirements. In other words, quotas are specific limits on the quantity of imports or their value.

2   *Subsidies:* payments made to particular industries to help them to be competitive on the international market. Examples of subsidies include depreciation allowances, cash grants and tax holidays.

3   *Currency controls:* limit the availability of foreign currency for the purchase of foreign goods.

4   *Administrative regulations:* include bureaucratic procedures, systems of advance payment, minimal domestic content rules, special marketing standards and health and safety provisions.

5   *Voluntary export restraints:* whereby one country agrees to limit its exports to a third country (or countries). This agreement is usually made because the importing country (countries) threatens to place barriers against the goods of the exporting country.

When two or more parties decide to engage in trade they have to agree on a medium of exchange. There are essentially two means of facilitating exchange – barter and money. As described in Chapter 3, under a barter system a direct exchange of commodities takes place. For example, person A swaps cows for goats with person B. When trade becomes more complex, either through the number of traders involved or because of the range of commodities traded, money tends to replace barter as the most efficient means of exchange. Money need not take the form we know today: historically, many commodities, including cowrie shells and gold, have played the role of money, that is, as a store of value and a means of exchange. In Chapter 8, we will consider how different international monetary systems facilitate or hinder international economic activity such as trade.

THEORETICAL PERSPECTIVES: FREE TRADE AND PROTECTIONISM

Is trade beneficial or harmful? Should traders be free to move goods and services across national frontiers? And if trade is to be subject to restrictions, what kinds of barriers should be imposed and for what reasons? These questions have confronted policy makers, citizens, businesspeople and scholars for centuries. In the era of globalization these questions take on an increased relevance.

Within the contemporary global economy, international trade touches many societies and communities through direct and indirect effects. It reaches into our homes, workplaces and recreational venues. Depending on where we live and how deeply our society is integrated into the global economy, we can find daily reminders of the importance of international trade through the consumption patterns of our families and friends. At its simplest level, the food we eat and the clothes we wear provide evidence of the tremendous importance of trade across national frontiers. But despite this importance, there is no consensus concerning the costs and benefits to countries from engaging in the pursuit of trade. Perhaps we should say that conflicting views exist because of the salience of trade. Given the conflicting values and interests in this structure of the global political economy, it is not surprising to discover the absence of agreement on the answers to the questions posed above.

We will now explore contrasting perspectives on the costs and benefits of international trade, beginning with arguments that emphasize the benefits of free trade before moving on to examine critical perspectives. Liberal political economy emphasizes the benefits of trade. For liberals, free trade benefits everyone, increases efficiency and raises productivity. In sharp contrast, nationalist and radical critics argue that free trade can undermine national economies, create uneven development and damage the environment.

Proponents of free trade

Within academic and policy contexts, liberal trade theory provides the framework for the analysis of international trade. This is a sophisticated and substantial body of work that has emerged since its tentative origins in the 19th century. Liberal trade theory appears counterintuitive since it propounds a positive-sum view of something that many people perceive as being zero sum. A common-sense view of transactions sees one side as gaining while the other one loses. Many people are sceptical of the notion that both sides to a transaction can make a profit. The liberal case for free trade, that is, a situation in which all can gain, is based on the theory of comparative advantage. According to the theory of comparative advantage, countries should specialize and produce the goods and services in which they are most efficient.

The theory of comparative advantage thus lies at the centre of neoclassical trade theory. Prior to the development of the theory of comparative advantage (or comparative costs, as it is sometimes known) by the British political economist David Ricardo in the 19th century, the dominant approach to trade focused on absolute advantage. Mercantilist theories argued that the aim of a country was to increase its trade relative to that of its rivals, thus increasing its wealth. For mercantilists, trade was a zero-sum game with one country's gain equivalent to a loss sustained by its trading partner. Since mercantilists believed there was a fixed amount of gold in the world, it therefore followed that a country with a trade surplus received more gold and hence an increase in its wealth. Adam Smith provided an answer to mercantilist theorists with his concept of absolute advantage. Smith argued that two countries could benefit from trade if they specialized in the goods they produced better than their rivals and traded with each other. Smith's theory of absolute advantage was an advance on mercantilist thought, but Ricardo's singular achievement was to demonstrate that trade was a positive-sum game in which all parties benefited even if one party had an absolute advantage in the production of all goods and services. Stated simply, the theory of comparative advantage shows that if a country specializes in the production of those goods and services in which it is relatively efficient (or alternatively, relatively less inefficient) compared with its competitors, it will be better off. As illustrated in Chapter 4, Ricardo's model discussed two countries and two products and showed how, given different cost structures of production, trade was beneficial for both countries since it enabled them to consume more than they would be able to without trade.

Under a liberal order, trade would be undertaken by countries according to their comparative advantage. Countries would improve their economic growth, and become more stable, powerful and efficient since they would be specializing in the production of goods and services in which they were the most efficient producers and enabling their consumers to buy foreign goods at the lowest prices. Specialization in accordance with comparative advantage promotes efficiency since, by definition, a small market is an obstacle to growth. Ricardo's theory provides the basic principles underlying modern trade theory. However, its assumption that differences in labour productivity were the sole determinant of comparative advantage is too limiting, and modern trade theory focuses on factor endowments (capital, land and labour). Developed by Eli Heckscher (1919) and Bertil Ohlin (1933), factor endowment theory states that comparative advantage arises from the different relative factor endowments of countries. Countries will have a comparative advantage in those industries that concentrate on the natural advantages or endowments of that country. For example, a country that has a large poor population will be most efficient in industries that require cheap labour (such as textile production), while a country with a large amount of fertile land and a small population will be better off specializing in farming. Following this theory, it is not surprising that Bangladesh has a comparative advantage in textiles and New Zealand has one in sheep and dairy products. Bangladesh has greater factor endowments in labour, while New Zealand has the factor endowment advantage in land. In this case, the Heckscher-Ohlin theorem would predict that New Zealand will export sheep or dairy products to Bangladesh in exchange for textiles.

Liberal trade theory has been further refined to take account of the growth of intra-firm and intra-industry trade, but these refinements do not challenge the basic underlying assumptions of the liberal paradigm. Liberal trade theory does not enquire into the origin of comparative advantage, that is, it does not ask how the different cost structures were established initially. It is also prescriptive, since it suggests that the welfare of an individual country and that of the world as a whole will be improved if countries specialize according to their comparative advantage. This theory therefore prescribes free trade and warns of the dangers of protectionism. From a liberal perspective, protectionism is inefficient, since it reduces competition and increases the monopoly power and thus the profits of the industries (or companies) that benefit from protection. On the other hand, free trade increases the amount of products available to consumers, although ultimately it may reduce the level of product differentiation in each country. The gains from trade come partly from greater product variety and partly from the lower price per product.

Free-trade theory emphasizes the gains or benefits from trade for a nation. There are two aspects to the gains from trade: the static benefits deriving from specialization according to comparative advantage and those deriving from and contributing to the process of economic growth and development over time. In this view, trade is an engine of growth and generates a number of dynamic, educative effects, including the diffusion of knowledge of production and organizational techniques, and changed patterns of demand. Specialization leads to an increase in productivity and economic growth. The theory of comparative advantage, it is argued, is relevant for all countries. Free trade offers hope for low-income countries, whereas protectionism harms poor countries (see Box 6.1). Liberal trade theorists argue that specialization brings the likelihood of an improvement in skills and an increase in workforce productivity. They contend that since the export sector can act as a stimulus to the economy as a whole, and foreign investment accompanies increased trade, developing countries will be better off under a free-trade regime. Liberal economists argue that the evidence shows that technological progress has been faster, all other things being equal, for countries that have been increasing their openness to the international flow of goods, services, capital, labour, technology and ideas. Low-income, developing countries can import technologies and information at virtually zero cost, whether explicitly (the actual process or plan) or implicitly (through the goods themselves). They insist that the process of innovation and the diffusion of knowledge is linked to international trade and is crucial for growth.

Although the theory of comparative advantage is theoretically elegant, it has consistently been attacked by critics. Despite these attacks, the theory has been sufficiently robust to withstand these various critiques. We will now discuss two schools of thought critical of the liberal arguments in support of free trade. First, we will examine the approaches of writers who can, broadly speaking, be grouped together under the umbrella of mercantilism and neomercantilism. We will then look at variants of critical theory.

Critics of free trade

Mercantilist and neomercantilist writers advocate the regulation of economic life to enhance state power or protect a variety of national groups from competition. Support for protection comes from groups who argue that protection of local production increases national (usually economic) welfare. Many people are willing to forgo absolute gain for relative gain; that is, in an anarchical international system, states in pursuit of power may give primacy to the relative gains from trade and

Box 6.1 The costs of protectionism: a liberal perspective

Many opponents of liberal trade argue that further liberalization damages the interests of people in poor countries. However, the liberal theories examined above suggest the reverse. In other words, it is protectionism rather than free trade that hurts the global poor in both developing and developed states. Protectionism may be in the interests of some producers but overall it has a negative impact on consumers in rich and poor countries.

While there is no agreement on the precise amount by which protectionism in the rich countries negatively affects poorer countries the general consensus is that it is significant (Tokarick, 2008) and negatively impacts both trade and growth (OECD, 2010). Furthermore, studies show that protectionism or unfair trade practices hit precisely those sectors where poor countries have the greatest potential to reap gains from trade, and thus impact the poorer segments of society (Goldin and Reinert, 2007, p. 61). An International Food Policy Research Institute study has calculated that rich countries' agricultural protectionism costs developing countries around US$24 billion in lost income (Diao et al., 2003, p. 2). The authors note that trade-distorting measures account for another US$40 billion of lost agricultural exports from the developing world. Another study has concluded that although reform of the EU's Common Agricultural Policy has reduced its trade-distorting impact on world markets, heavy subsidies to European farmers nevertheless result in significant losses for some developing countries' producers (Matthews, 2008).

Liberal theorists contend that protectionism in OECD countries also has a detrimental effect on the host country. For example, it has been estimated that American protectionist policies cost US consumers $70 billion in 1990, more than 1 per cent of gross national product (GNP) (Hufbauer and Elliott, 1994). Another study of US protectionist practices claimed that the loss suffered by consumers was three times greater than any gains to workers (Krol, 2008).

adopt protectionist measures in order to stabilize their economies even though it diminishes their absolute gains from trade.

Some state-based critiques of liberal trade theory have focused on the prescriptive power of the theory, and others on the accuracy of its empirical claims. Two arguments have been made consistently since the 19th century diminishing the desirability of free trade. The first argument is the so-called 'infant industry' case. Supporters of industrialization argue that predominantly agricultural countries will experience obstacles in their attempts to industrialize, since comparative advantage dictates that they continue to import industrial products whereas they may well have a future comparative advantage in the production of industrial products. The infant industry argument makes the case for temporary protection for industries likely to become competitive on the world stage. This perspective is not simply about individual industries but is tied to a wider societal vision. The process of industrialization, in this view, will be hindered in the absence of effective protection of fledgling local industries, thus providing support for a policy of tariffs and other protections for new domestic industries. In other words, protection should

be given to these industries until they become competitive and can reap the benefits of comparative advantage. Historically, protectionist policies, by providing the opportunity to develop economies of scale and domestic market stability, have been important and perhaps necessary components of government-led strategies of economic growth and restructuring (Chang, 2002) in countries such as Germany and the US. According to advocates of this form of protection, governments should intervene to protect those industries that have the potential to develop efficient production but which at the moment would be destroyed by fierce international competition. In societies that have already industrialized, infant industry arguments are mobilized in favour of postindustrial areas of economic activity. For example, a country might be concerned about entering markets in the industries of the future such as nanotechnology or biotechnology.

Some liberal theorists are willing to accept the infant industry argument as an exception to standard comparative advantage theory. However, while providing support for temporary forms of protection, they stress an inherent problem with the infant industry argument. Domestic producers are unlikely to willingly renounce the protection from which they benefit, and agreement on the point at which protection is to be discontinued may therefore prove politically difficult even though the economic arguments are compelling. How is a government able to determine what needs protection and for how long? Is a government likely to make a better decision than the market?

The second historical argument against free trade claims that the dictates of national security take precedence over trade. In other words, countries need to be self-sufficient in the production of certain strategic industries. These may be related directly to the waging of war or they may refer to foodstuffs. Whether items are necessary for the direct defence of the nation or food security, dependence on external markets can threaten a nation's security. In the interests of national security, countries are urged to temper support for free trade with policies protective of national security. It is widely accepted that if free trade jeopardizes other non-economic objectives such as national security, it is necessary for governments to impose restrictions in order to protect society. From this perspective, the real income gains that motivate free trade cannot be separated from the security externalities that can either impede or facilitate it. Trade with an adversary can be harmful to a nation's security, while trade with an ally can support a nation's security. Although states resort to economic warfare and use economic sanctions in cases of conflict, it can be argued that the security dimension of trade is always present.

The infant industry argument and the national security argument have a long historical pedigree. Two further arguments for protection have emerged to lend support to the state-based critique of free trade. First, strategic trade theory (Krugman, 1986, 1987) argues that countries should pursue competitive advantage in those industries of future economic benefit to the nation where the economic and social costs of falling behind competitors are huge. Second, a number of governments and domestic groups concerned about the impact of globalization on their culture have argued that protectionist measures should be implemented to protect the national culture. In the face of globalization, many analysts warn that distinctive cultural practices will be swamped by the import of goods and ideas from abroad. Cultural protection in relation to films, media and communications technologies is therefore supported by those who want to resist what they see as the undesirable consequences of globalization.

We can identify three different strands of the critical or radical critique of free trade. The one with the longest historical legacy is the unequal exchange perspective. Writers in this perspective have a Marxist heritage and provide a powerful social justice critique of liberal trade principles. Although a single unequal exchange perspective does not exist, broadly speaking, we can discern three main parts to this critique. First, these writers stress the importance of historical power relations in the creation of comparative advantage (Frank, 1967). Unlike liberal analysts who take comparative advantage as a given, unequal exchange theorists enquire into the construction of different cost structures across national borders and argue that many have been determined by imperialist plunder. The second aspect of the unequal exchange perspective is an emphasis on the redistributional benefits of free trade. They emphasize the unequal gains to participants in international exchange, which, they argue, freeze the status quo and make it difficult for poorer countries to develop, and the concentration of economic power in the hands of the wealthy (Coote, 1992; Oxfam International, 2002). Within the current world order, trade from this perspective sustains the activities of TNCs and large bureaucracies (government departments or regional organizations) at the expense of peasants and workers (Madeley, 1992). A third variant of this perspective was developed by Arghiri Emmanuel (1972), an Italian Marxist, who argued that trade systematically discriminated against developing countries because of the lower wage rates in developing countries. Emmanuel assumed that labour productivity did not vary between rich and poor countries and therefore the product of labour was equal in rich and poor countries. But since the prices of goods produced by rich countries reflected their high wages and those produced by poor countries reflected their low wages, the exchange was inherently unequal since goods produced by rich countries commanded a higher price internationally.

Another radical argument in favour of protection is made by environmental activists (Ekins, 1989; Morris, 1989), who claim that free trade contributes to environmental degradation. They argue that the externalities of trade are omitted from standard trade theory (Clapp and Dauvergne, 2011, pp. 129–30). Environmentalists contend that current trading practices are unsustainable and they campaign for a return to local trade (Shrybman, 1990). This is discussed in more detail in Chapter 12. Feminist scholars have also turned their attention to the gendered nature of trade, arguing that trade is not gender neutral (Samson, 1995; Van Staveren et al; 2007). In common with human rights and environmental activists, feminists argue that trade theory has ignored the social costs of trade (Fontana et al., 1998). Similarly, scholars and activists wanting the incorporation of labour rights (Verma, 2003) and human rights issues into trade (see Abbott et al., 2006; Dommen, 2002) have also explored ways of incorporating these concerns into the traditional paradigm.

In this section, we have examined competing perspectives on the relationship between free trade and national and/or world welfare. We have argued that modern international trade theory provides a normative framework for the conduct of international trade. It furnishes both an explanation of, and justification for, trade. Thus, despite the claims of standard neoclassical economics, trade theory is ideological and political. This does not mean that its analytical tools, prescriptions and conclusions are to be rejected as biased and unscientific. Rather, this recognition brings to the fore the fact that trade theory is not only socially constructed but is the subject and object of its own analysis. Actors in the trading system are influenced by the writings of trade theorists. While this captures part of the argument being made here, it fails to fully extend its implications. The crucial point is that the 'reality' examined by trade theory is itself partly constructed by trade theory.

Moreover, it is arguable that even if the principle of comparative advantage is applied on a global basis, the gains from trade will be evenly distributed. In the short term, it is likely that free trade will result in an unequal distribution of costs and benefits, thus undermining the basis for adherence to free-trade policies since those countries losing out will resort to protectionist measures such as tariffs or subsidies.

MAJOR DEVELOPMENTS

There have been two notable developments in the world trading system since the end of the Second World War. One has been a large increase in the volume of world trade and accompanying changing forms of protectionism as states struggle to cushion the dislocations caused by trade liberalization. The second has been the transformation of the institutional arrangements governing

world trade. The failure of states to create an International Trade Organization (ITO) after the Second World War left the GATT as the primary international framework governing trade relations. In 1995, the GATT gave way to the new WTO, an indication of a further institutionalization of trade rules.

Growth and protectionism

Since the end of the Second World War, trade has increased more rapidly than production, which is a clear indicator of the increased internationalization of economic activities and the greater interconnectedness that has come to characterize the world economy. Between 1945 and 2007, growth in world trade consistently outstripped growth in world production. In this period, world production doubled but international trade grew more than fourfold.

The onset of the global economic recession in 2008 led to the largest contraction in world trade (in 2009) since the Great Depression of the 1930s (see Table 6.1). The impact of the recession on trade was short-lived with trade volumes increasing by 14 per cent in 2010 (WTO, 2012, p. 21) before returning to levels around the long-term trend by 2013. In this section we will

Table 6.1 Growth in the volume of world exports and production by major product groups, 2005–13 (percentage change)

	2005–13	2009	2011	2013
World merchandise exports	3.5	-12.0	5.5	2.5
Agricultural products	3.5	-2.5	6.0	3.0
Fuels and mining products	1.5	-5.5	2.0	0.5
Manufactures	4.0	-15.0	7.0	3.0
World merchandise production	2.0	-2.5	3.0	2.0
Agriculture	2.0	0.5	2.0	5.5
Mining	0.5	-1.5	1.5	0.5
Manufacturing	2.5	-4.0	4.0	1.5
World GDP	2.0	-2.5	2.5	2.0

Note: World merchandise production differs from world GDP in that it excludes services and construction.

Source: WTO (2011b, p. 19; 2014a, p. 21)

review the developments in international trade between 1945 and 2014.

There are some noticeable features of world trade growth in the postwar period and these will be discussed below. We will focus on the magnitude of trade, its geographical concentration, the commodity composition of trade and the growth in intra-industry and intra-firm trade.

The growth in trade has been uneven and there have been periods of recession when trade growth slowed, but overall the trend has been positive. For example, the WTO (1998) calculated that merchandise exports grew on average 6 per cent per annum between 1947 and 1997, and that total trade in 1997 was 14 times the level of 1950. These trends continued in the early 21st century until the onset of the global financial crisis in 2008. Between 2000 and 2005, world merchandise trade grew approximately 10 per cent (WTO, 2006, p. 11); although there was some slowdown in 2006 and 2007, with annual increases of 8 per cent and 5.5 per cent, respectively (WTO, 2007, p. 2; 2008, p. 2). Trade growth has since fluctuated with sizable increases in 2010 before falling again in 2011 and 2012 (United Nations, 2013a, p. vi). These figures indicate that trade has been an important sector in the contemporary global economy and a main agent of economic growth.

The relationship between trade and growth has been intensely debated during this period, especially since it is an important consideration for countries trying to promote economic development. The consensus among economists is that trade promotes growth. Countries with an open economy engaging in international trade have performed better than those countries where policy has restricted domestic access to foreign products. The relation between trade and economic growth is twofold. First, trade acts as a stimulus to the local economy, providing it with resources cheaper than it would cost to produce them domestically. Trade thus raises the production possibility frontier, enabling countries to consume more than they would have done in the absence of trade. The relationship between consumption and growth will be discussed below where we will show the importance of consumption to contemporary economic growth. Second, trade forces domestic producers to manufacture goods to world market standards, thus increasing productivity and product quality. This leads to a more efficient use of resources. In the light of these arguments, it is possible to see one of the reasons for the failure of Soviet-style communism.

Instead of embracing trade, communist authorities approached trade with suspicion, viewing it as a source of economic leakage rather than, as it turned out, a source of economic strength. Trade remained a residual element in national economic plans where the drive was for self-sufficiency. Even the attempt at integration through the Soviet-dominated trading organization, the Council for Mutual Economic Assistance, was predicated less on exploring dynamic comparative advantage through the benefits of specialization than on protecting what were perceived to be national interests.

Not only has overall trade growth been uneven, it has also been so in respect of different countries and regions (see Table 6.2). However, the historical imbalance in shares of world trade between developed and developing countries appears to be shifting. A steady increase in developing countries' share of world trade was further stimulated by the recent global economic crisis. In 1980 developing countries accounted for 34 per cent of world trade but this had risen to 47 per cent by 2011 (WTO, 2013, p. 5). Both exports and imports from the emerging market economies have benefitted from increased trade volumes (UNCTAD, 2013, p. iii). Moreover, South–South trade grew from 8 per cent of world trade in 1980 to 24 per cent in 2011 (WTO, 2013, p. 6).

Whereas the theory of comparative advantage predicts that trade will grow fastest between unlike economies, postwar trade growth has seen the reverse of this proposition. In the 1950s and 60s, trade grew fastest in manufactured products. In 1945, the commodity composition of international trade reflected the sectoral composition of output in the leading economies and was therefore mainly composed of merchandise trade.

Table 6.2 **Percentage share of world merchandise trade by region, 2013**

Exports	Region	Imports
100	World	100
13.2	North America	17.4
4.0	South and Central America	4.2
36.3	Europe	35.8
3.3	Africa	3.4
7.4	Middle East	4.2
31.5	Asia	31.8

Source: WTO (2014a, pp. 24–5)

But as services became the dominant sector in industrialized economies, so the trade in services has expanded, with the result that one of the major developments in the international trading system has been the rise of trade in services. While trade in services is not the largest sector in world trade, it has been the fastest growing sector.

The term 'intra-industry trade' refers to the situation where trade occurs within the same industry rather than between industries. One of the main features of postwar trade growth has been the phenomenon of intra-industry trade. Countries have exchanged similar products where price and product differentiation have played an important part. In consumer goods, we have seen the exchange of consumer durables so that although the UK, for example, produces motor vehicles and washing machines, it has also imported these items from other OECD member countries. International trade has supported both horizontal and vertical integration. The growth of intra-industry trade has also been matched by the growth of intra-firm trade. The rise of the TNC and a global production system (see Chapter 7) has stimulated intra-firm trade. An increasing percentage of world trade takes place within firms rather than between separate, individual firms. One of the crucial implications for trade theory and for national governments is that if trade takes place within a TNC, pricing policies will not reflect real costs. In such cases, trade is driven not by comparative costs but by the management decisions of the firm.

The period 1947–73 was one of unprecedented expansion for the world economy, with output and trade growing faster than in any previously recorded period. Global output expanded at an annual average of 5 per cent, while exports grew at 7 per cent per annum. This provided an economic climate conducive to trade liberalization, and it was against this background that protectionism was reduced on manufactured products. A number of significant structural changes took place between 1947 and 1973. The most important change in the context of the trading system was the shift away from a traditional dependence on the export of primary commodities to the increasing specialization in labour-intensive, low-tech manufactured products by a number of developing countries, such as India, Brazil and the East Asian newly industrializing countries. These developing country exporters took advantage of expanding markets in the developed economies and the contraction of productive capacity in some sectors in the OECD countries as the dynamic comparative advantage of developing countries became evident. Industries such as textiles and footwear were initially developed in the industrialized countries but during this period the technological know-how associated with these activities was diffused to some developing countries.

During the long boom (1947–73), it was relatively easy for developed countries to make the necessary adjustments to imports of manufactures from the developing world because the employment-creating effects of international trade outweighed the employment-displacing effects. The outcome of these developments was that the benefits of trade were obvious and, by and large, consumers and producers willingly acquiesced in the trade liberalization process. Thus, protectionist pressures were specific rather than general.

With the downturn in the world economy following the first oil crisis in 1973–4, unemployment grew and became a critical political issue in the industrialized world. The importance of the recession of 1973–7 was to focus the attention of various pressure groups on the perceived connection between foreign trade and domestic employment, that is, on the link between employment displacement and import penetration. Employment preservation through the restriction of imports became an acceptable means of preventing unemployment from rising. What characterized this period was the resort to non-tariff instruments of policy. Countries abandoned the use of old protectionism in the form of tariffs for new protectionism using NTBs. Because they were the most vulnerable, discrimination against developing countries grew at an alarming rate. As an OECD report declared: 'developing countries have in practice been most exposed to discriminatory export restraint agreements and other trade distorting measures, with the incidence of this discrimination being greatest in those sectors in which they have a comparative advantage' (Goldin et al., 1993, p. 22).

If structural change accounted for the onset of protectionism, it was the existence of the GATT that shaped the forms the new protectionism would take. The 1947 GATT Articles provide for the introduction of restraints under certain designated circumstances. For example, Article XIX condones the use of import controls for the emergency protection of domestic industry. Recourse to these 'escape clauses' became increasingly prevalent in the 1970s, as the major developed countries made more frequent usage of the protectionist option. However, recourse to Article XIX was rather limited, since many countries taking protectionist action preferred to evade GATT stipulations on non-discrimination and reciprocity and therefore turned to extralegal alternatives that suited their purposes better than Article XIX. These provisions are central to the explanation of a reluctance to use Article XIX and a willingness to look for alternatives outside the GATT framework. The most widely used NTBs were voluntary export restraints, import quotas, product standards, including regulations pertaining to health and technical safeguards, and anti-dumping measures and countervailing duties, which are still drawn on today. An example of the use of health standards to discriminate against imports is given in Box 6.2. The negotiation of a voluntary export restraint allowed action to be taken on a discriminatory basis, a facility unavailable under Article XIX. In order to appease pressure groups at home while doing little to impair export prospects, governments followed the path of least resistance. This period also saw the mushrooming of administrative controls such as the use of health,

safety and environmental standards. Protectionism also took the form of subsidies and government procurement policies. This move from GATT's rule of law brought with it a heightened absence of transparency, given that non-transparency is a property of NTBs.

The rise of new protectionism and the failure of the GATT to remedy these developments contributed to dissatisfaction with the organization's performance. This issue will be addressed in the next section. While the new protectionism is no longer a major issue since the creation of the WTO gave a boost to liberalizing forces, the confrontation between advocates of trade liberalization and those of protectionism remains an important issue in the contemporary global economy.

The growth in world trade in the early years of the 21st century has been uneven, reflecting the global economic cycle. Nevertheless, it is possible to discern the emergence of a new geography of trade centred on the rapid growth of developing economies. Concomitant to rising growth rates and increased shares of global GDP, developing countries as a group have developed a larger stake in the world trading system (UNCTAD, 2013,

Box 6.2 Health risks and hormone-treated beef

The EU first banned the importation of hormone-treated meat in 1989, arguing that injecting livestock with bovine somatropin (BST) posed a health risk to humans. BST, a growth hormone produced by beef cattle, was in use by major meat-producing countries including Canada and the US. Scientists from meat-exporting countries that used BST argued that it was safe, but consumer groups in the EU and the European farm lobby protested that hormonal irregularities or cancer would result from its consumption. Was this a genuine health issue or a form of disguised protectionism? The EU claimed it was a health issue, but producers affected by the ban argued that it reflected an attempt to protect the inefficient EU meat industry. At the centre of the dispute is whether the EU's ban is in compliance with the WTO Agreement on Sanitary and Phytosanitary Measures (SPS).

In 1997, the WTO's dispute settlement panel found the EU ban to be incompatible with its obligations under the SPS Agreement; and in 1998 the WTO's Appellate Body confirmed that the European ban on hormone-fed beef violated its rules, but noted that the EU ban would be justified if convincing scientific proof could be provided concerning the health risks of hormone-treated beef. The outcome from the WTO process supported the contention of meat exporters to the EU who had lost revenue as a result of the EU ban. For example, US red meat exports to the EU fell from $231 million in 1988 (a year before the ban) to $98 million in 1994. Despite this ruling, deep scepticism remains among EU consumers. The EU has, since 2003, cited new scientific evidence as the basis for its import restrictions in an attempt to make the EU ban consistent with the WTO's ruling, and to evade trade sanctions that had been imposed since July 1999. In October 2008, the Appellate Body permitted the EU to maintain its restrictions but also granted Canada and the US the authority to impose trade sanctions totalling in excess of US$125 million annually. In March 2012, the EU settled the beef dispute with Canada and the US by agreeing to increase the imports of non-hormone-treated US beef by 25,000 tonnes (EUbusiness, 2012).

Sources: Bridges Trade BioRes (2009); EUbusiness (2012)

p. 6). Of course, these trends are uneven with some countries such as Brazil, China and India at the forefront of the increased growth. In the last decades, China, India and Brazil, among others, have emerged as important hubs of economic growth and trade in manufacturing, services and agriculture and commodities. As the 2013 WTR notes, 'especially China, but also India and Brazil have transformed the balance of power in the multilateral trading system' (p. 268). These changes have taken place in both merchandise trade as well as trade in services. Developing countries' share in world services exports reached 31 per cent in 2012, and their share of service imports was around 37 per cent (United Nations, 2014a, p. 51).

Changing institutional arrangements

The origins of the postwar international trade regime are to be found in Anglo-American cooperation during the Second World War. The liberal trade regime that was created reflected primarily US interests. American preference for open market arrangements and for the imposition of a multilateral rule-based system to limit national action is at the centre of the regime. Two particular issues were of concern to American policy makers – British imperial preferences and the system of protection that had developed in Latin America during the war. The US therefore proposed a non-discriminatory, multilateral system of trade and payments. In practice, this meant provision for reciprocity, international supervision of tariff and exchange rates, outlawing of quantitative restrictions, freely convertible currencies and the generalization of tariff reductions to all members of the regime. The trade regime is, to use a term coined by Ruggie (1982), one of 'embedded liberalism'. In other words, its main features subscribe to liberal trade principles, but nevertheless recognition is made of deviations from the standard principles to support key domestic goals.

Thus, the international trade regime is not purely a laissez-faire system but has many elements of managed trade. The trading regime is based on four key principles: non-discrimination, reciprocity, transparency and multilateralism. These have been the guiding principles for a series of international institutions designed to govern postwar international trade:

1 *Non-discrimination* is enshrined in the most favoured nation (MFN) clause. The MFN principle ensures that any concession granted to one member must be extended to all other members. Under MFN provisions, all members of the GATT/WTO are treated in a non-discriminatory manner. A tariff on an import from a GATT/WTO member had to be placed on all other GATT/WTO members in a similar manner, with the exception of customs unions or free-trade areas. This principle is therefore at the centre of the multilateral trading system.

2 *Reciprocity* is intended to ensure that when one country lowers its tariffs against the exports of another country, it will, in turn, be granted equal trade concessions. The principle of reciprocity that is applied through multilateral bargaining means that, in theory, one country's concessions are paid for by a third country, which then passes them on to another country and the process repeats itself.

3 *Transparency* refers to the fact that any discrimination must be clearly visible. The system is based on the principle that tariffs are the only permissible form of discrimination. NTBs such as import quotas are banned and countries are urged to replace them with tariffs.

4 *Multilateralism* is a commitment to the creation of a broadly based trade regime including the maximum number of countries committed to cooperation through a rule-based system and engaging in periodic rounds of tariff-cutting.

The Conference on Trade and Employment held in Havana, Cuba in 1948 created the ITO as the institutional framework of the postwar international trading system. However, in the US many business groups opposed the ITO, fearing that it was not sufficiently liberal and offered too many concessions to countries trying to protect their own industries. Given the preponderance of the US in the world economy, most governments delayed ratification until the US Congress gave its assent. In 1951 President Truman, aware of widespread domestic hostility to the ITO, decided not to seek congressional assent, thus consigning the ITO to history. With the failure of the ITO, the GATT became the institutional focus of the world trading system. The GATT was the result of a tariff-cutting exercise by 23 nations prior to the Havana conference. Meeting in Geneva in March 1947, the delegates

Table 6.3 **GATT negotiating rounds**

Name	Dates	Number of countries participating
Geneva	1947	23
Annecy	1949	13
Torquay	1951	38
Geneva	1956	26
Dillon	1960–1	26
Kennedy	1964–7	62
Tokyo	1973–9	102
Uruguay	1986–93	123

decided on a series of tariff reductions, and a temporary mechanism to oversee these cuts. Instead of withering away as initially envisaged, the GATT was given permanence. The GATT provided a code of rules, a dispute settlement mechanism and a forum for trade negotiations. Its main importance lay in its role as a forum for trade negotiations. In eight rounds (see Table 6.3) of multilateral trade negotiations between 1947 and 1994, it presided over a period of unprecedented growth in world trade.

Until the Kennedy Round, negotiations were conducted on an item-by-item basis, but in that round the negotiators moved to an across-the-board approach. The GATT enjoyed uneven success in its quest to reduce trade barriers. It was most successful in tackling barriers to manufactured goods but less so in preventing agricultural protectionism. Three main features of trade liberalization are visible in the GATT period.

First, the GATT achieved considerable success in reducing tariffs on manufactured goods. Beginning with the Geneva conference in 1947, significant tariff rounds were negotiated in successive multilateral trade rounds on some 45,000 products, constituting approximately half of world trade at that stage (Williams, 1994, p. 150). Progress slowed somewhat between this first conference and the Kennedy Round, but substantial tariff reductions were achieved. The new approach used in the Kennedy Round yielded average tariff reductions of 36–39 per cent, and despite the unfavourable economic circumstances, tariff cuts in the Tokyo Round averaged 33–38 per cent.

Second, the process of trade liberalization under GATT was uneven. Trade liberalization was almost solely confined to manufactured products – the most

dominant growth sector. In 1947, at the first round of GATT negotiations, the average tariff on manufactured goods was around 40 per cent. By the end of the Kennedy Round, these tariffs had been lowered to an average of 10 per cent. The tariffs of the industrial countries were reduced by a further 35 per cent as a result of the Tokyo Round (Winham, 1986, p. 17). To illustrate the significance of tariff reductions to the industrial countries, tariffs on industrial products in the US declined from around 50 per cent in 1947 to about 4 per cent in 1979, and those in the UK moved from around 40 per cent to about 4 per cent in the same period (Greenaway and Hine, 1991). Industrial countries were willing to liberalize in sectors that were expanding but reluctant to do so in those in which they had lost or were losing comparative advantage and felt most under threat. Agricultural protection continued unchecked until the Uruguay Round, where a start was made on phasing out the protection afforded to farmers in the developed world. Reform of agricultural trade proved difficult and continued to be a sensitive political issue in future trade talks. Developed countries also devised a series of restrictive measures in relation to textiles and clothing. Under the guise of ensuring orderly market behaviour, in 1974 the GATT sanctioned the Multifibre Agreement (MFA) to regulate trade in textiles and clothing. This was, in effect, a protectionist device limiting particular developing countries' exports of textiles to developed states. It was not phased out until 2005 as a result of decisions made during the Uruguay Round negotiations.

Third, whereas trade liberalization was initially limited solely to trade in merchandise goods, beginning with the Tokyo Round, additional issues have been placed on the agenda. The Tokyo Round negotiations were conducted during the period known as the 'new protectionism', where states prohibited from a recourse to tariff barriers through their GATT commitments began to impose significant NTBs. At the conclusion of the Tokyo Round, negotiators agreed six voluntary codes to prohibit the use of NTBs, but implementation was poor. They also attempted to develop a framework to regulate anti-dumping measures. During the Uruguay Round, the agenda of the world trading system was further expanded to include services, intellectual property rights (IPR), investment, environment, labour standards and domestic (nontrade) policies.

The GATT also provided a normative framework and a dispute settlement mechanism. Assessment of

GATT's impact as a normative framework is difficult but two issues can be examined. It is undeniable that GATT made a major contribution to the development of international economic law (Jackson, 1969; Kock, 1969). The GATT treaty is a legal document, and it provided a code of rules that set the framework for international commercial transactions. Additionally, governments used the existence of GATT disciplines as a mechanism to resist domestic demands for protection. One of GATT's major failures was its dispute settlement mechanism. Because the recommendations of the dispute panel required unanimous consent, contracting parties could block the decisions of GATT panels.

At the end of the Uruguay Round of negotiations, a new trade organization, the WTO, was created and officially commenced on 1 January 1995. The WTO is the successor to the GATT and owes its existence to perceived deficiencies of GATT. Dissatisfaction with GATT grew because of the organization's failure to reverse the growth of protectionism, the weakness of its dispute settlement procedures and the uneven nature of its trade liberalization process. In an effort to reverse protectionism and bolster trade liberalization, the WTO was created as a permanent international organization with greater scope than the GATT. The WTO is the legal and institutional foundation of the world trading system. It is a legal agreement specifying the rights and obligations of its members. The WTO consists of a series of interlocking legal agreements and membership requires acceptance of these agreements as a single undertaking. On accession to the WTO, a state must adhere to the following agreements:

▹ the agreement establishing the WTO
▹ GATT 1994 and other multilateral trade agreements for goods, including the SPS Agreement, the Agreement on Technical Barriers to Trade, and the Agreement on Trade-Related Investment Measures (TRIMS)
▹ the General Agreement on Trade in Services (GATS)
▹ the Agreement on Trade-Related Aspects of Intellectual Property Rights (TRIPS)
▹ the Understanding on Rules and Procedures Governing the Settlement of Disputes
▹ the Trade Policy Review Mechanism.

The WTO also consists of plurilateral agreements governing civil aircraft, government procurement and dairy and bovine products, but the acceptance of these agreements is not mandatory for membership.

While the GATT was essentially a contractual agreement among its member states, the WTO is an international organization with a legal personality akin to other intergovernmental organizations such as the IMF and the World Bank. The sole formal actors in the WTO are the member states and the principal decision-making body is the Ministerial Conference, which meets every two years. To date, eight Ministerial Conferences have been held. The Ministerial Conference is empowered to make decisions on any issue covered by the WTO agreements. Since it only meets every two years, it has delegated its competence to the General Council. The General Council, consisting of all WTO members, is the highest decision-making body in the interval between Ministerial Conferences. The General Council also acts as the Dispute Settlement Body and the Trade Policy Review Body. The organizational structure of the WTO is completed by three councils, each with a functional area of specialization: the Council for Trade in Goods, the Council for Trade in Services and the Council for Trade-Related Aspects of Intellectual Property Rights; and by various committees and a number of working groups and working parties.

In an attempt to improve the functioning of the world trading system under the WTO, the procedure for settling trade disputes was considerably strengthened. The Dispute Settlement Understanding provides the machinery for settling members' differences on their rights and obligations. It consists of a first-stage panel adjudication followed by an appeals process (the Appellate Body), and a clear schedule for the processing of disputes. Moreover, decisions from the dispute settlement process are based on a negative consensus, that is, they can only be overturned by the General Council if all members are in agreement. As a centre for the settlement of disputes, the WTO contributes to the stability and further evolution of the world trading system, since liberalization will not take place in the absence of effective dispute settlement procedures.

Furthermore, compared with the GATT, the WTO has transformed the management of world trade in three crucial respects:

1 It engineered a shift from trade liberalization based on tariff concessions (shallow or negative integration) to discussions of domestic policies, institutional practices and regulations (deep or positive integration).

Table 6.4 **World merchandise trade (billion US dollar, current prices)**

	1948	1953	1963	1973	1983	1993	2003	2013
Exports	59	84	157	579	1,838	3,684	7,380	18,301
Imports	62	85	164	594	1,883	3,800	7,696	18,409

Source: WTO (2014a, pp. 24–5)

2　It constructed a new agenda expanding the scope – through the inclusion of services, TRIPS and domestic (nontrade) policies – and changing the character of negotiations from a focus on bargaining over products to negotiations over policies that shape the conditions of competition.

3　It initiated a movement towards policy harmonization, for example in the areas of subsidies, trade-related investment measures and services.

The WTO's extensive powers have given it a much higher profile than its predecessor.

Trade liberalization since 1947 has been accompanied by a rise in international trade (see Table 6.4), which supporters of further liberalization claim is a result of the process of removing restrictions to trade. They argue that the institutional framework creates liberalization and this in turn enhances increased trade (Finlayson and Zacher, 1981). Structuralist critics, on the other hand, claim that trade expansion would have taken place without these governing arrangements since the growth of trade has principally been a response to structural change in the world economy (Strange, 1985).

Prior to an examination of key underlying issues in the international trading system we will conclude this review of changing institutional arrangements with a brief discussion of the state of the Doha Round of multilateral trade negotiations as of June 2015. Some observers fear that failure to arrive at a satisfactory outcome of the Doha Round will lead to the collapse of the WTO. The extent to which the stalled Doha negotiations will be concluded and development concerns addressed remains unclear. The Ninth Ministerial Conference of the WTO in Bali (3–7 December 2013) brought signs of hope that the long drawn out negotiations were eventually heading to a successful conclusion (McClanahan, 2013). This resulted in two important decisions taken by the WTO in the post-Bali period. First, a decision was reached on the thorny issue of public stockholding for food security purposes (WT/L/939). The G33 coalition had called for a

relaxation of the rules on public stockholding of food because the existing regulation meant that the domestic support policies of many developing countries could be in breach of WTO regulations. At the Bali meeting a 'peace' clause was agreed which effectively shielded government action from legal challenges. Second, an agreement has been reached on trade facilitation (WT/L/940) to expedite the movement, release and clearance of goods; make provision for special and differential treatment for developing (and least developed) countries; and lead to the creation of a trade facilitation committee in the WTO (additionally members must create national committees to ensure coordination and implementation). July 2015 was the date set as the deadline for agreement on the work program agreed at the Bali Ministerial Conference.

KEY ISSUES

There are numerous trade issues on the contemporary international agenda. However, the future of the liberal trading system and the role of the WTO as the key institutional node of the trade regime lie at the centre of current discussions. The long delays in concluding the Doha Development Agenda (DDA) is a pertinent reminder of the central crisis of the multilateral trade system. Here, we discuss three broad issues that are relevant to the lengthy Doha negotiating process and the future of world trade. The first is the place of developing countries in the world trading system, and the second concerns the significance of regional trade agreements. The third issue is the question of the legitimacy of regional trade agreements.

Developing country interests

Although the economic structures of developing countries are diverse, a set of interests specific to them have emerged within the world trading system. Central to this development has been the self-identification of developing countries, and the limited political influence they exert in international trade negotiations. While no single developing country coalition exists in the context of the WTO, developing countries have identified common interests (Narlikar and Tussie, 2004) and have at times created formal negotiating groups (see Box 6.3). Issue-based coalitions amongst developing countries

---

Box 6.3 Developing country coalitions in the WTO

Individually, many developing countries are too small and have limited bargaining power in international trade negotiations. Coalitions frequently arise on a specific issue or emerge at a particular conference. Some major developing countries seek to enhance their bargaining power through joining a coalition and other smaller countries join groups for defensive purposes. Examples of developing country coalitions include:

▶ The Like-Minded Group of developing countries was formed in 1996. It has been active in opposing progress on the so-called new issues, such as TRIPS and GATS, and insists on implementation of the Uruguay Round agreements. Its main members are African and Asian countries.

▶ The G20 emerged in response to the Cancún agenda in 2003 and was initiated by Brazil and India. The G20's core membership is influential developing countries such as Brazil, China, India, South Africa, Pakistan, Egypt and Nigeria, and spans the various regions of the developing world. The focus of the G20 is agricultural negotiations.

▶ The G90 was created at the Cancún conference and brings together some of the poorest developing countries. Its membership is made up from the least developed country (LDC) group, the African, Caribbean and Pacific Group of States, the Small Island Developing States Group and the African Group.

▶ The Cotton-4, formed prior to the Cancún conference in 2003, brings together the main African cotton producers – Benin, Burkina Faso, Chad and Mali.

---

coincided with the adoption of 'integrative' or 'value-creating' negotiating strategies, which involve 'actions designed to expand rather than split the pie' (Hurrell and Narlikar, 2006, p. 423).

Two issues have consistently emerged at the centre of the debate. The first concerns the benefits of a liberal trading order, and the second relates to the continuation of protectionist forces in the postwar trading system. In relation to the first issue, a debate exists between those who contend that trade promotes development and those who maintain that industrialization is best achieved behind protectionist barriers. A related debate exists between those who argue that the reform of trading arrangements will benefit developing countries and those who contend that the trading system is inherently exploitative. We will not revisit these debates here. Instead, we will examine the ways in which developing countries have articulated their interests and the response to these concerns.

In the debates on trade liberalization since the creation of the WTO, the developing countries have attempted to define and promote specific sets of interests. In November 2001, the first major round of multilateral trade negotiations since the Uruguay Round was launched at the Doha Ministerial Conference of the WTO. The DDA was specifically targeted at the interests of developing countries. As the *Doha Ministerial Declaration* stated: 'The majority of WTO members are developing countries. We seek to place their needs and interests at the heart of the Work Programme adopted in this Declaration' (WTO, 2001, para. 2). The hopes and aspirations enunciated in 2001 have been frustrated by a tortuous negotiating process that remains unfinished. The failure to make significant progress on the talks reflects both the inability of developing countries to impose their will and the continued veto power possessed by the EU and the US in trade negotiations.

Agricultural trade liberalization has been an issue of central concern to the developing countries during the Doha negotiations. Many developing countries remain dependent on the export of agricultural commodities, and even in those countries in which agriculture is not the major export sector, agriculture remains a significant employer of labour (see Table 6.5).

Whereas the industrialized countries have embraced liberalization in manufactured products, they have been reluctant to fully liberalize agricultural trade. Indeed, until the Uruguay Round, agriculture was kept off the negotiating agenda. Despite the progress made

Table 6.5 GDP composition by sector: agriculture, 2014 (per cent)

Country	Share of GDP in agriculture
Somalia	60.2
Central African Republic	55.1
Comoros	50.4
Ethiopia	47.7
Sierra Leone	42.5
Congo, Democratic Republic	40.4
Burkina Faso	38
Mali	38
Niger	37.7
Burma	37.1
Rwanda	32.5
Cambodia	32.1
Benin	31.8
Malawi	30.1
Nepal	30
Kenya	29.3
Mozambique	28.9
Madagascar	28.1
Togo	27.6
Tajikistan	27.2
Tanzania	26.9
Sudan	26.8
Papua New Guinea	26.3
Cote d'Ivoire	25.9
Pakistan	25.1

Source: CIA (2014)

during the Uruguay Round, agriculture in the industrialized countries continues to enjoy high levels of protection. The agricultural support policies of the developed countries have an overall negative impact on developing countries. This is an area in which the developed world abandons its support of comparative advantage and, for a number of economic, political and social reasons, implements discriminatory policies. When protection leads to excess domestic production, this results in lower world prices, thus reducing the incomes of producers in the developing world. Protection, in the form of import levies and quotas, removes a large part of agricultural trade from the world market, increasing

the volatility of international prices. The persistence of impediments to market access in agriculture therefore remains a major policy concern of many developing countries. The persistence of subsidies on major agricultural exports from the developed countries, continued domestic support to agriculture and high tariffs resulting from tariffication (the process whereby NTBs are converted to tariffs) have conspired to restrict the gains made by developing countries. The issue of agricultural protection is also of interest to some developed country exporters and has given rise to a grouping of developed and developing country producers. The Cairns Group (see Box 6.4) is an intergovernmental pressure group for agricultural reform linking developing countries and developed countries.

Although agriculture was prioritized as a key issue in the Doha talks and WTO members were committed to a significant reduction in trade-distorting subsidies and other forms of agricultural protection, the negotiations were characterized by countless disagreements, shifting deadlines and eventually a failure to reach compromise. The slow pace of the agricultural negotiations prompted the development of solidarity among developing countries (Clapp, 2006). It also led to an unprecedented move by four West African cotton producers and the reshaping of the agenda to meet their specific interests (see Box 6.5).

Box 6.4 The Cairns Group

Largely an Australian invention under the Hawke government, the Cairns Group comprises 19 agricultural exporting countries. Formed in 1986, the Cairns Group has effectively put agriculture on the multilateral trade agenda after decades of stalemate over the reduction in the protection received by agricultural products. It was largely as a result of the group's efforts that a framework for reform in farm products trade was established in the Uruguay Round and agriculture was, for the first time, subject to trade liberalization rules. These rules are set out in the WTO Agreement on Agriculture. Membership of the Cairns Group comprises Argentina, Australia, Bolivia, Brazil, Canada, Chile, Colombia, Costa Rica, Guatemala, Indonesia, Malaysia, New Zealand, Pakistan, Paraguay, Peru, the Philippines, South Africa, Thailand and Uruguay.

Box 6.5 The cotton initiative

The slow progress of the agricultural negotiations frustrated many LDCs who were aware that failure further weakened their fragile trading positions. In June 2003, prior to the WTO Ministerial Conference in Cancún, four West African countries – Benin, Burkina Faso, Chad and Mali (the Cotton-4) – submitted a paper to the WTO's Trade Negotiations Committee calling for the abolition of developed country cotton subsidies, and financial compensation to be paid to the four countries while the subsidies remained. The proposal was submitted to the Cancún conference in September 2003 but no agreement was reached. There were objections by various states to both parts of the draft document – treating cotton as a separate issue, and the provision of financial compensation. These disagreements were overshadowed by the disdainful attitude of the US delegation to the proposal. In the charged atmosphere of Cancún, the cotton initiative became a key symbol of developing countries' anger and disappointment. In the discussion post-Cancún to get the multilateral trade negotiations back on track after the 'failure' of two successive Ministerial Conferences, the cotton initiative was placed on a separate negotiating track. A cotton subcommittee was created in November 2004 under the framework of the agricultural negotiations. Along with the rest of the Doha Round, negotiations have stalled and no further progress has been made.

The varying interests of developing countries were visible in the scramble for export markets following the end of the MFA on 1 January 2005. The phasing out of the MFA has had a differential impact on developing country exporters. The limited research available on the post-MFA textile industry has produced inconclusive findings. An analysis of the export performance of Asian countries post-MFA argues that the short-term impact of the end of restrictions has been small (Whalley, 2006). Another study argued that while a small number of countries will benefit, a large number of (smaller) developing countries will be significantly worse off (Heron, 2006). Inevitably, a number of other developing countries have expressed concern that the textile industries in their area might close as production is concentrated in China. Several sub-Saharan African countries are particularly vulnerable (Dinesh and Little, 2004). With the ending of MFA protection, Taiwanese or Hong Kong businesses that invested in Africa to find a way around import quotas are now able to close down their African plants and locate production in the Chinese mainland.

The expansion of the multilateral trade agenda during the Uruguay Round to include new issues has remained controversial and has created difficulties for WTO trade governance. It has been argued that three issues – trade in services, IPR and investment measures – separately and together limit the policy autonomy of developing country governments (Wade, 2003). The most frequently discussed services – tourism, business services and finance – provide greater returns for the developed world. However, in some cases such as business services in publishing and data processing, developing countries have been able to build up exportable services. This is particularly the case in India. The concern is that in the overall trade in services, developing countries are at a disadvantage. While developing countries were able to safeguard some of their interests by insisting that the GATS be based on a positive list, that is, countries must list the services to be liberalized, the impact of liberalization in services on developing countries remains a hotly debated topic (Wiener, 2005).

The issue of IPR is also of great importance to developing countries (also see Chapter 13). Until the Uruguay Round, copyrights, patents and other forms of intellectual property were not treated as trade or even trade-related issues. They were brought into the Uruguay Round on the insistence of US TNCs, who insisted that exports of counterfeit goods, especially from South-east Asia, were responsible for large revenue and profit losses (Sell, 2000). Moreover, pharmaceutical companies had long complained that their profits and research and development were harmed by the local production of their products without payment of a licence, and usually justified under national health guidelines. The TRIPS Agreement gives greater influence to foreign investors and provides increased international patent protection to a range of products and processes previously exempt from patent protection (Hoogvelt, 1997, p. 136). It requires countries to accept the substance of existing international conventions on copyright (Berne Convention) and patents (Paris

Convention). Bringing these agreements under the WTO subjects them to WTO dispute settlement procedures and enforcement mechanisms. The agreement forces two kinds of costs upon middle- and low-income countries: revenue losses due to the increased cost of drugs, and the administrative costs of introducing relevant legal frameworks to protect patents.

The likely detrimental impact of the TRIPS Agreement has been most clearly visible in the area of public health, where drug companies holding the patents to medicines can dictate the price of essential drugs. Concerns of developing countries over the availability of generic (cheaper) drugs led to the Declaration on the TRIPS Agreement and Public Health at the Doha Ministerial Conference. This concession was an attempt to meet the concern many developing countries felt about the price of medicines. However, it has been argued that the declaration has made no significant difference to either importing countries or those with the capacity to manufacture pharmaceuticals (May, 2005, p. 173). Moreover, pharmaceutical companies can take out new patents and thus deprive developing country producers of revenues. In other words, local knowledge that is currently free will cease to be so if a foreign company takes out a patent on that knowledge. The costs of introducing the required legal and administrative mechanisms will be highest for LDCs. It has been claimed that 'the main beneficiaries will be the core group of less than a dozen seeds and pharmaceuticals companies which control over 70% of the world's seeds trade' (Hoogvelt, 1997, p. 136). The issue of drug patents and HIV/AIDS is discussed in greater detail in Chapter 13.

Some critics are worried that the move towards giving foreign investors unfettered access to global markets will undermine the sovereignty of host governments. The issue surfaced in the negotiations on TRIMS (Trade-Related Investment Measures). TRIMS is designed to limit the ability of governments to set performance requirements for FDI. Although an agreement with the potential to override national law does not exist, it is believed by many that it is only a matter of time before such an agreement is signed. The attempt to create a regulatory code for foreign investment in the OECD met vociferous opposition from critics in the developed world, and also from groups claiming to speak for the developing world. Opposition to the Multilateral Agreement on Investment from social movement activists was instrumental in the failure by governments to agree on it (Goodman and Ranald, 2000).

Another issue of interest to developing countries relates to their special status in trade negotiations. Developing countries have been concerned since the 1960s with ensuring that their participation in international trade meets with their development needs. The demand for special and differential treatment (S&D) was based on the claim that the demands of development are incompatible with the free operation of market forces. The demand for S&D was first formally accepted in 1965 with the addition of a new chapter to the GATT. Part IV of the GATT, 'Trade and Development', gave legal sanction to the principle of S&D and provided the developing countries with a specific focus from which to mount further campaigns for reform. While the Tokyo Round extended S&D, the creation of the WTO has seen a move away from treating developing countries as a special case. Within the WTO, increased emphasis is given to the trade needs of the LDCs; and developing countries, while given some concessions, are expected to conform to the general rules. S&D under the WTO can be classified into five main groups:

1 provisions aimed at increasing trade opportunity through market access
2 provisions requiring WTO members to safeguard the interests of the developing countries
3 provisions allowing flexibility to developing countries in rules and disciplines governing trade measures
4 provisions allowing longer transitional periods to developing countries
5 provisions for technical assistance.

Within each of these groups, additional provisions are made specifically for the LDCs. The aim of the WTO is to include developing countries as full participants in the system, that is, to move to a position where it will be possible to withdraw any special and differential status. The provisions noted above with regard to the S&D of developing countries have largely been ineffectual. For example, the developed countries are not taking the special needs of developing countries into account in preparing and applying sanitary and phytosanitary measures, technical regulations, standards and conformity assessment procedures. Moreover, the transitional periods do not always give sufficient time to deal with specific shortfalls in capacity that are faced by individual members or those with precise development needs. Finally, many developing countries emphasize the critical and continued need for technical assistance. They call for better coordination of technical assistance from all sources, and have asked for increased funding of technical assistance in the core WTO budget. Taking cases before the dispute settlement mechanism usually requires the payment of large fees for specialist legal advice.

The special emphasis of the DDA on development brought increased prominence to S&D. The *Doha Ministerial Declaration* reaffirmed 'that provisions for special and differential treatment are an integral part of the WTO Agreements' (WTO, 2001, para. 44). Moreover, it was agreed that 'all special and differential treatment provisions shall be reviewed with a view to strengthening them and making them more precise, effective and operational' (WTO, 2001, para. 44). To date, there has been limited progress in meeting these objectives.

Regional trade agreements

The past two decades have witnessed an avalanche in the creation of regional trade agreement (RTAs). There are currently over 260 RTAs in force, with most of these created since the establishment of the WTO. Between 1948 and 1995, the GATT received notification of 124 RTAs, but the WTO received notification of 449 RTAs between January 1995 and April 2015 (WTO, 2015). Box 6.6 provides an example of the evolution of RTAs as part of the trade strategy of a middle power with a strong commitment to multilateral trade. An acceleration in the creation of RTAs seems to be concurrent with the slow pace of multilateral negotiations. Recent major RTA developments include the launch of negotiations on a Trans-Atlantic Trade and Investment Partnership (TTIP) between the United States and the EU, and continued negotiations on the Trans-Pacific Partnership Agreement (TPP) (see Box 6.7).

Regional economic organizations have multiple objectives, of which the promotion of trade liberalization is frequently only one aim. Other aims can include investment liberalization, the managing of economic conflict, domestic economic restructuring and political integration. Current RTA negotiations often involve multiple parties and/or parties accounting for major shares of world trade; they aim at high-standard integration through WTO-plus or WTO-extra provisions

---

Box 6.6 Australia and its regional trade agreements

Existing free trade agreements (FTAs)

- Australia–New Zealand Closer Economic Relations (1988)
- Singapore–Australia FTA (2003)
- Australia–United States FTA (2005)
- Thailand–Australia FTA (2005)
- ASEAN–Australia–New Zealand FTA (2009)
- Australia–Chile FTA (2009)
- Malaysia–Australia FTA (2013)
- China–Australia FTA (2014)
- Korea–Australia FTA (2014)
- Japan–Australia Partnership Agreement (2015)

FTAs under negotiation

- Australia–Gulf Cooperation Council (GCC) FTA
- Australia–India Comprehensive Economic Cooperation Agreement
- Australia–Indonesia Comprehensive Economic Partnership Agreement
- Pacific Agreement on Closer Economic Relations (PACER) Plus negotiations
- Regional Comprehensive Economic Partnership Agreement (RCEP)
- Trans-Pacific Partnership Agreement (TPP)

---

on behind-the-border regulatory measures, such as technical regulations, standards, conformity assessment systems, sanitary and phytosanitary regulations, services, investment, intellectual property, state aid and state-owned enterprise (SOEs), public procurement, competition policy, environment, or labour market regulations.

Nevertheless, whether trade liberalization is a central objective or the means towards an end, the development of regionalism is a crucial feature of the trading system. Central to discussions of RTAs is their likely impact (positive or negative) on global welfare. Since members of RTAs are also members of the WTO, implicitly national governments are indicating compatibility between the pursuit of regionalism and multilateralism.

Analysts tend to place the development of regionalism into two phases. It is widely agreed that the creation of the European Economic Community (EEC) in 1957

Box 6.7 The Trans-Pacific Partnership Agreement (TPP)

The first round of TPP negotiations was held in Melbourne in March 2010. As of 2015 there were 12 negotiating parties: Australia, Brunei, Canada, Chile, Japan, Malaysia, Mexico, New Zealand, Peru, Singapore, the United States and Vietnam. Together these countries make up 11.2 per cent of world population, 36.2 per cent of world GDP and 25.5 per cent of world trade (DFAT, 2015). Envisaged as a comprehensive trade agreement, the TPP has the aim of addressing *inter alia* traditional trade issues such as trade in goods and services, and new issues such as investment, competition and state-owned enterprises, regulatory coherence, and transparency.

The political and economic elites supporting the TPP have argued that it is vital in securing future economic prosperity. As the delegates to the November 2011 meeting on the TPO stated,

We are confident that this agreement will be a model for ambition for other free trade agreements in the future, forging close linkages among our economies, enhancing our competitiveness, benefitting our consumers and supporting the creation and retention of jobs, higher living standards, and the reduction of poverty in our countries.

(TPP Leaders' Statement,
November 2011)

However, the TPP has been opposed by various groups including environmentalists, labour unions and health professionals. The scope of the treaty and the secrecy of the negotiations have drawn extensive criticism from civic groups and elected officials in various legislatures. An issue of particular concern is possible investor protection provisions which would allow companies to sue states in the event that public policies hinder their pursuit of profits. The TPP negotiations were successfully concluded on 5 October 2015. It now remains for national legislatures to ratify the agreement in order for the provisions to be implemented.

initiated the first phase. The second period is dated from the mid-1990s. The impact of the two phases of regionalism on world trade is different. In the first phase, regionalism was relatively inward. In the developing world, the aim of regional economic arrangements was to stimulate industrialization, which meant that such organizations were more concerned with trade diversion than trade creation. Trade diversion refers to the process where low-cost suppliers from outside the union are replaced by high-cost suppliers within the regional grouping. Trade creation refers to the situation where, as a result of dismantling barriers within the region, trade is stimulated. In Europe, the scene of the two most successful early attempts at regional integration (the European Free Trade Association and the EEC), regionalism was concerned with dismantling barriers among the participants. In the second phase, many of the new associations have adopted a policy of open regionalism, making the reductions to trade more compatible with multilateral commitments.

Although regionalism can be seen in most parts of the world, specific regional agreements vary greatly in their goals and terms. This has led to some debate about the internal nature of regions and the relationship between regions. Internally, political struggles have been waged over the degree to which specific regions should have strong or weak institutions and the scope of policy-making that should be considered at the regional level. These struggles have influenced the different nature of the regions. For example, the EU has some supranational institutions that oversee common rules. It also has provisions for regional development funding and labour rights. Most of its members have gone even further and adopted a single currency. In contrast, the North American Free Trade Agreement (NAFTA) tends to enforce existing national legislation, has no development funding and very weak provisions for the respect of labour and environmental standards. Whereas in Europe there is discussion about eventual political union, this subject is of little interest in North America. Moving to the Asia-Pacific area, we encounter an even looser regional organization – Asia-Pacific Economic Cooperation (APEC). APEC is more of a coordinating body between countries on the Pacific Rim than an attempt to build strong regional ties with robust institutions. Asian states' fears that a more developed institution would allow the US to influence their domestic economies or political regimes have led to a minimalist structure and trade liberalization agenda.

Some economists have raised fears that increasing regionalization will undermine the multilateral trading system (Baldwin and Thornton, 2008). It is argued that these regional agreements are inherently inefficient and discriminatory. RTAs will erode the MFN principle, increase barriers to products from other regions and divert the natural flow of free trade. Such actions could cause economic damage and undermine political support for a multilateral system. For example, Europeans and Americans disagree about how much risk should be accepted in the production of food. This has led to conflicts at the WTO over the EU banning the imports of products such as cattle that the Americans have injected with growth hormones. Other observers have argued that RTAs can be compatible with the multilateral trading system (Griswold, 2003). The issue is sometimes phrased as a debate between those who see regions as building blocks for global free trade and those who see them as stumbling blocks that create incompatible areas of regional economies.

A final issue is the fate of those areas of the world that are left out of the prominent regional trading areas. Regional integration is proceeding with some speed in Europe, North America and East Asia through the activity of governments and firms. This excludes large areas of the world such as Africa, Latin America and South Asia. Developing-country non-parties with limited capacity may run risks of marginalization and damage to their competitiveness, particularly if they do not substantially participate in world trade or are unable to conform to higher standards embedded in RTAs. There have been several responses. In Latin America, Chile has lobbied for admission to NAFTA. In contrast, Brazil has put its energy into building MERCOSUR, the common market of several South American countries. Sub-Saharan Africa and South Asia have a series of regional agreements, but these are underdeveloped because they lack a powerful motor economy such as Germany, the US or Japan. Their efforts at successful regional integration face large obstacles.

Legitimacy

As trade agreements at the multilateral and regional level have proliferated and influenced domestic political economies, increasing concern has been voiced by various segments of civil society in many states (Williams, 2005a). A wide range of issues has attracted attention. Some groups worry that regional and global institutions are insulated from democratic control. They contend that business and political elites have considerable input into the structure of such agreements, but citizens find it difficult to hold their governments accountable for the decision-making authority transferred to international institutions. It should be noted, however, that firms are also formally excluded from the WTO. The influence of the corporate sector comes from its influence at the national level (and inclusion on national delegations) rather than directly at the multilateral level. Nevertheless, the democratic credentials of the WTO and RTAs have been a subject of considerable debate. It has become widely accepted that democracy is a universal norm and in the context of a debate on democratization, a focus has arisen concerning the representative nature of multilateral trade agreements.

This issue has been raised most vociferously in relation to the WTO but it has also surfaced in relation to existing regional institutions such as the EU and NAFTA, and proposed RTAs such as the TPP. At the European level, support for further integration has been diminished in a number of member countries, and nationalist sentiments gathered around right-wing parties have made some electoral gains. The so-called 'democratic deficit' in the EU became a topical issue in the mid-1990s and has remained so ever since. The debate on the WTO has focused on issues related to transparency, accountability and participation (Williams, 1999, pp. 158–60). Essential features of this debate are summarized in Box 6.8. The WTO has been responsive to criticism but this has not silenced its critics. In efforts to bolster its legitimacy, the WTO has derestricted documents, held consultations with NGOs, and accepted submissions from outside parties (known as amicus briefs) during disputes. Nevertheless, critics maintain the WTO is undemocratic, claiming that decisions are frequently made in secret and that the visible part of proceedings is a mere masquerade with little relation to the real exercise of power that takes place outside the public gaze (Kwa, 2003). Moreover, they argue that access to information on which decisions are made should be more readily available. In response, supporters of the WTO point out that the organization is an intergovernmental forum in which decisions are based on consensus and subject to ratification by

Box 6.8 Democracy and the WTO

Is the WTO an undemocratic organization? The scale and ferocity of protests against the international trading regime in general and the WTO in particular suggest that the organization is undemocratic and therefore illegitimate. What are we to make of such claims?

First, we can observe that no consensus exists on the definition, meaning or practice of democracy. It can be argued, however, that the WTO (with its 157 members and 27 observer governments) is one of the most democratic international organizations, because:

1 Its large and diverse membership represents most of the trading nations in the world and a variety of economic and political systems.
2 The consensus method of decision-making in the WTO gives each country a voice, and goes some way towards providing small, poorer countries with some source of influence.
3 The WTO is relatively transparent in terms of making access to its documents easy to obtain. Insofar as negotiations are conducted in secret, it should be recalled that trade negotiations do involve complex and often controversial trade-offs.

Critics of the WTO reject these points and argue that the organization fails to provide sufficient access for civil society groups in its deliberations. Increased participation of social movement representatives will, it is claimed, provide high-quality information, balanced input into policy-making, public education, and increased public support for the organization. These steps are needed to counter the alleged influence of transnational capital.

At the centre of the debate, therefore, is the intergovernmental nature of the WTO. But the solution is not a simple one. On the one hand, if we accept the intergovernmental character of the WTO, the representative nature of national governments can be questioned. How legitimate are the agreements entered into by states that are themselves authoritarian? Another issue relates to the size of population. Is a system that gives China and Norway the same formal representation democratic, given the vast differences in population? On the other hand, if we agree that an intergovernmental organization fails to capture the range of stakeholders affected by developments in the global trade regime, it does not follow that increased representation of NGOs necessarily makes the WTO more democratic, since it cannot be assumed that NGOs are more representative than national governments. Indeed, developing countries are hostile to increased representation of (largely northern) NGOs from social movements because they see them as representing narrow privileged interests.

national parliaments. In this sense, the organization is fully representative of its membership. A report by One World Trust, an independent British NGO, on the accountability practices of five intergovernmental organizations, six TNCs and seven NGOs investigated the decision-making practices of the WTO. Although the report placed the WTO second in its category, it argued that 'the reality is that some members lack the capacity to engage meaningfully in decision-making' (Kovach et al., 2002/3, p. 14). In respect of access to information, the report noted that 'Information on the WTO's trade activities is excellent' (Kovach et al., 2002/3, p. 15).

Other groups concern themselves with the detrimental effects of these agreements on social policies, environmental degradation and labour standards (Wal-lach and Woodall, 2004). Attention to global and regional trade organizations has developed as citizen attention has turned to the increasingly influential role these organizations play in a globalized world economy. The opposition to international economic agreements (including trade agreements) grew in the late 1990s and the first two years of the 21st century. The 1997 APEC meeting in Vancouver was marked by Canadian police pepper-spraying protesters, while the 1999 Seattle WTO Ministerial Conference was also disrupted by public protests. As one activist noted in the wake of the Seattle protests: 'What civil society, North and South, should be doing at this point is either pushing for the abolition of the WTO or overloading or jamming it so that it cannot function effectively' (Bello, 2000). In Europe, citizens expressed concern about the direction of integration through a number of referenda and the support given to nationalist, especially right-wing, political parties. In the US, President Clinton and initially President Bush found it difficult to secure negotiating authority from the US Congress to continue the liberalization process. Under President Obama, trade liberalization was not a priority area.

Increasingly, publics are concerned about further economic integration and trade agreements. Multilateral and regional trade organizations face a legitimacy problem because they are seen to place the values of liberalizing economic activity or protecting private interests above other values and interests. Some critics perceive the projects sponsored by such bodies as promoting economic globalization and social injustice. We will return to these issues in Chapter 15, which examines governance in the global economy.

reason why protectionism remains a central feature of the world economy is that all economies need some degree of protectionism in order to develop in ways that they value.

One of the major changes in the international trading system since the end of the Second World War has been the expansion of the trade agenda beyond a concern with market access and market expansion to provide coverage of issues such as intellectual property rights, government procurement, investment protection, and labour and environmental regulations. This expanded agenda has brought increased scrutiny to trade policies.

In this chapter we have examined some of the key controversies attendant on the globalization of trade. In Chapter 7 we turn our attention to transnational production, an equally controversial issue in the global political economy.

CONCLUSION

Experience with tariff negotiations has led to the observation that most countries favour trade liberalization in principle but are reluctant to undertake unilateral reduction of trade barriers because it would open their markets, leaving them vulnerable to international firms. Therefore, protectionism remains a prominent issue in the world economy. Protectionism is an attractive policy for domestic markets, and it is here that pressing demands originate. The demands for protection reflect structural changes bound up with the growth of transnational capitalism. It can also be seen as part of a process of structural change in the global economy, which may reinforce the strength of social forces favourable to the maintenance of open trade. The demand for protection comes from rational actors in the economic process that are concerned with their nations' interests, which would suffer from free trade. The most obvious

Further Reading

For a spirited defence of trade liberalization see Anne O. Krueger (2004), 'Wilful Ignorance: The Struggle to Convince the Free Trade Skeptics', *World Trade Review*, 3(3): 483–93. For a wide ranging text that examines the legal, political and economic aspects of the WTO see Amrita Narlikar, Martin Daunton and Robert M. Stern (eds) *The Oxford Handbook on the World Trade Organization* (2012). Lisa Martin (ed.) *The Oxford Handbook of the Political Economy of International Trade* (2015) provides a comprehensive introduction to key aspects of contemporary trade politics. A succinct introduction to the importance of regional trade can be found in David A. Lynch, *Trade and Globalization: An Introduction to Regional Trade Agreements* (2010).

Chapter

7

Transnational Production

Hundreds of books, theses, government reports and thousands of papers in academic and professional journals have been written on the subject of transnational production, the causes of foreign direct investment (FDI) and the costs and benefits of inbound foreign investment for a host country. Scarcely a day goes by without a newspaper or magazine article praising or blaming what is now often referred to as the 'globalization of business activity'. Despite, or perhaps because of, the extensive literature on transnational production, no consensus exists on either the causes or impact of this phenomenon, although it is widely agreed that the growth of transnational production has profoundly shaped the evolution of the global economy. For example, the current rhetoric of globalization assigns a crucial role to changes in the global production structure. However, it should also be noted that attention to the role of large international firms first arose in the 1960s. Prior to the current interest in globalization, students of the global political economy had developed an awareness of the impact of the changing production structure on international relations.

The global production system is a complex process, with millions of workers and workplaces integrated into diverse local, national, regional and global systems. The relationship between discrete centres of production and the global economy cannot be captured through any simple model. The link between sites of production and wider patterns of social, political and economic integration forming part of the global economy raises problems of comprehension for the student of IPE. One way of trying to provide an entry to understanding the global production structure is by focusing on the role of the principal agents of this process, namely, the large international firm, referred to as the 'transnational corporation' (TNC). The literature on transnational production tends to focus on the role of the large international firm as the key agent in this process and this chapter will adopt this standard approach. The TNC is one of the defining features of economic life in the contemporary global economy. TNCs account for the major part of the global production structure and approximately 50 per cent of world trade. The Fortune Global 500, an annual ranking of the 500 leading TNCs, estimated that in 2014 the combined revenue of these companies was $31.1 trillion and their profits stood at $2.1 trillion (Fortune, 2014). Significantly, over half the world's 500 largest corporations are located in only three countries – 128 in the US, 95 in China and 57 in Japan. The increasing number of Chinese firms in the Global 500 is another indication of the rise of China as a global economic power. Another pertinent conclusion that can be derived from the survey of the leading international firms concerns the global gendered division of labour (see Chapter 10). Of the top 500 companies a mere 17 companies have appointed a woman chief executive officer (CEO). While Walmart, a retail giant, remains the top company the petroleum sector dominates the Fortune Global 500 (see Table 7.1).

Table 7.1 **The 25 largest corporations by revenues, 2014 (millions of dollars)**

Rank	Name	Country	Industry	Revenue	Profits
1	Walmart Stores	US	Retailer	476,294	16,022
2	Royal Dutch Shell	Netherlands	Petroleum	459,599	16,371
3	Sinopec Group	China	Petroleum	457,801	8,932
4	China National Petroleum	China	Petroleum	432,007	18,504
5	Exxon Mobil	US	Petroleum	407,660	32,580
6	BP	UK	Petroleum	396,217	23,451
7	State Grid	China	Power	333,386	7,982
8	Volkswagen	Germany	Automobiles	261,175	12,071
9	Toyota Motor	Japan	Automobiles	256,454	18,198
10	Glencore International	Switzerland	Commodities	232,194	-7,402
11	Total	France	Petroleum	227,882	11,204
12	Chevron	US	Petroleum	220,356	21,423
13	Samsung Electronics	South Korea	Conglomerate	208,938	27,245
14	Berkshire Hathaway	US	Conglomerate	181,250	19,478
15	Apple	US	Electronics	170,910	37,037
16	AXA	France	Financial services	165,893	5,950
17	Gazprom	Russia	Energy	165,016	35,769
18	E.ON	Germany	Conglomerate	162,560	2,843
19	Phillips 66	US	Petroleum	161,175	3,726
20	Daimler	Germany	Automobiles	156,628	9,083
21	General Motors	US	Automobiles	155,427	5,346
22	ENI	Italy	Petroleum	151,408	6,850
23	Japan Post Holdings	Japan	Postal and financial services	152,125	4,782
24	EXOR Group	Italy	Investment	150,986	2,768
25	Industrial & commercial Bank of China	China	Financial services	148,802	42,718

Source: Fortune (2014)

Another key statistic confirming the globalization of production is that relating to flows of FDI. And although below the record high achieved prior to the global financial crisis, in 2014 the total global inflow of FDI was estimated to be $1,452 billion (see Table 7.2).

We begin this chapter with a discussion of the various terms, such as 'transnational' or 'multinational' corporation, that have been used to describe large international firms. In the next section, we consider competing explanations for the emergence and growth of transnational production, and the impact of TNCs on national societies. The following section outlines the globalization and changing organizational forms of production. The final section examines three key issues addressed in the contemporary global production system: the benefits and costs of TNCs, especially for developing countries; the changing relationship between the state and the firm; and the international regulation of TNCs.

Table 7.2 **World FDI flows, 2007–13 (billions of US dollars)**

Year	2007	2008	2009	2010	2011	2012	2013
Inflows	1,964	1,754	1,131	1,391	1,760	1,330	1,452
Outflows	2,169	1,855	2,169	1,139	1,712	1,347	1,411

Sources: OECD (2012); UNCTAD (2014, p. xiv)

DEFINITIONS

Economists distinguish between two types of foreign investment – foreign direct investment and indirect foreign investment, also termed 'portfolio investment'. The transformation of the global production system has been brought about by rising levels of FDI. FDI refers to investment made outside the home country of the investing company in which control over the resources transferred remains with the investor. It consists of a package of assets and intermediate goods such as capital, technology, management skills, access to markets and entrepreneurship. Foreign indirect (portfolio) investment refers to specific assets and intermediate products, for example capital, debt or equity, technology, which are separately transferred between two independent economic agents through the modality of the market. In this instance, control over the resources is relinquished by the seller to the buyer. Only financial resources are transferred.

Two examples will help to clarify the difference between FDI and portfolio investment. If French carmaker Renault bought a controlling interest in US carmaker General Motors by buying its shares in the US stock market, this would be FDI. Renault would control GM and could decide to shut down plants or introduce new models of cars in the US. In the 19th century, when British financiers bought bonds to fund the construction of US railways, it was portfolio investment. Control over corporate decisions stayed with the railway builders. The British financiers did not tell the Americans which cities the railways would connect. FDI entails control of business decisions, while portfolio investment does not. In this chapter, we will follow conventional usage and use FDI as an indicator of the growth of international production.

Before 1914, long-term portfolio investment was more important than FDI, and FDI was relatively short term. FDI began to grow extensively after the Second World War. In the 1950s and 60s, FDI was predominantly in the manufacturing sector, and the largest amount of FDI flowed from the US (Vernon, 1977). As a consequence of postwar recovery and the attainment of high productivity, the growth of the Eurocurrency market and improvements in transport and communications, FDI flows from Europe and Japan began to grow. FDI continued to grow rapidly in the 1980s and 90s (Julius, 1990; UNCTAD, 1999). For example, in the early 1980s, the annual growth rate of FDI was approximately 14 per cent and between 1986 and 1996, FDI rose 350 per cent. Global FDI inflow continued to grow between 2000 and 2007, when it reached a historic high of $1,964 billion. This growth in FDI, fuelled by investment in services as well as manufacturing, was brought to a halt by the global financial crisis and economic recession (2008–2010). Since the global economic crisis FDI inflows have been unstable. They fell between 2008 and 2010 before modest recovery in 2011, fell again in 2012 but recovered in 2013 (see Table 7.2).

While the distinction between foreign direct investment and indirect foreign investment is relatively non-contentious, no agreement exists on the term to be applied to firms engaging in transnational production or FDI. These firms are variously called multinational, international, transnational or global. It is now common to speak of multinational corporations or multinational enterprises, international firms, transnational corporations or transnational enterprises and global corporations. Most writers make no distinction between these terms and have settled for one terminology rather than another without any seeming reflection on the implications of these terms. The most commonly used term is 'multinational corporations' but this chapter will refer to these economic agents as TNCs for reasons that will be explained below.

Serious attention was first given to the rise of transnational production in the late 1960s and early 1970s. At this stage, both political and popular interest (Bannock, 1971; Servan Schreiber, 1968) and academic attention (Kindleberger, 1969; Vernon, 1971) turned to describing and assessing the importance of what was perceived as a new international actor, although large international firms had existed for centuries. The term 'multinational enterprise' was first given prominence by the Harvard Multinational Project, which produced a number of important studies including Wilkins' (1970) analyses of the growth of American business. These studies did much to establish the term 'multinational' to describe this new phenomenon. At the same time, others from various perspectives, for example Penrose (1968) in her magisterial study of the oil industry, preferred to use the term 'international corporation'. Vernon, in his widely influential book *Sovereignty at Bay* (1971), although based at Harvard, followed Penrose in using the term 'international corporation', as did Radice (1975) in an influential collection of critical essays.

While the term 'multinational' first gained widespread usage to describe large international firms, it was challenged from the mid-1970s by the term 'transnational corporation' or 'transnational enterprise' (Lall and Streeten, 1977; Vaitsos, 1975). The term 'transnational' reflected UN usage, and proponents of its use argued that whereas 'multinational' suggested a merger of capital from more than one nation-state, with a few notable exceptions, for example Royal Dutch Shell and Unilever, most large international firms are owned and controlled by nationals of one country and conduct activities across national borders. The term 'transnational corporation' (or 'transnational enterprise') more accurately reflects the fact that these firms are usually owned and controlled by the nationals of one country and enter into direct production activities abroad. Thus, the term 'multinational corporation' appears inappropriate and that of 'transnational corporation' more accurate, since these firms operate trans (that is, across) borders, so giving greater weight to that term than to 'international'. Another term sometimes used to refer to these large firms is 'global corporation'. The term 'global corporation' was popularized in the 1970s by Barnett (Barnett and Muller, 1975). His central concern was the global reach of these firms and he coined the term to reflect the impact of their activities.

These choices revealed no essential differences in the operation of the firms so described. The distinctions arise from those who want to emphasize the issue of ownership and those analysts who prefer to stress the reach of these actors. Despite the differences in nomenclature, most analysts would agree that the firm they are describing could be defined as one with production facilities in two or more countries. Thus, in reality, a single definition can suffice whether these firms are called multinational, international, transnational or global. A TNC is a firm that owns and controls production (value-added) facilities in two or more countries. It follows that all TNCs are not huge, uncontrollable firms, and TNCs will vary in size, resources, organizational structure (see Box 7.1) and influence potential. Furthermore, the estimation of the size, resources and power wielded by a TNC will vary depending on the standpoint of the analyst.

THEORETICAL PERSPECTIVES: EXPLAINING THE GROWTH OF TNCS

Two issues have dominated discussions of transnational production, namely the growth of the TNC and its impact on sovereign states. In this section we begin by reviewing some of the most influential theories devised to explain the growth of transnational production. We then provide a brief introduction to competing perspectives on the impact of TNCs. The three perspectives on IPE discussed in Chapters 1 and 2 provide broad interpretations of the issues discussed below.

Box 7.1 Vertical, horizontal and conglomerate TNCs

One way to differentiate among TNCs is by their structure – vertical, horizontal or conglomerate integration (Grimwade, 2000, pp. 124–33):

▶ *Vertical integration* occurs when different stages of the production process are incorporated into one firm. For example, an oil company such as British Petroleum might own oil wells in the Middle East and the petrol stations in the UK that sell the final product. This form of investment may occur because a corporation wants to ensure security of supply or reduce transaction costs within the firm.

▶ *Horizontal integration* takes place when a company makes the same product in a number of different countries. For example, Toyota has plants in the US and Europe to avoid protectionism and gain access to local markets.

▶ *Conglomerate integration* occurs when a company produces a number of different product lines in a variety of countries. For example, Procter & Gamble produces beauty, home, health, baby and pet products, which allows it to diversify risk and make profits in a number of different sectors.

Thus, different organizational structures and activities can lead TNCs to adopt a variety of global strategies for different reasons.

Economic nationalist perspectives emphasize the importance of state behaviour in creating the conditions necessary for the emergence of global production and focus on the ability of states to control the activity of TNCs. Liberal theory gives greater weight to the relevance of the market both in terms of explaining the growth of transnational production and in assessing the impact of TNCs on the state. Critical or radical theorists emphasize the changing nature of capitalist relations and retain a scepticism concerning the impact of TNCs on host economies.

The growth of transnational production has attracted attention across the spectrum of the social sciences, with contributions from economics, geography, political science, sociology and business studies. Within the array of studies emanating from this profusion of disciplinary, interdisciplinary and cross-disciplinary research, three approaches (economic, organizational and motivational) to the study of TNCs are discernible. Economic approaches tend to emphasize the market characteristics that have given rise to the decision to invest abroad. Organizational perspectives give more emphasis to the internal structure of the corporation and seek explanations in terms of the decision-making structure of the firm. Motivational perspectives provide explanations in terms of the individuals and the belief systems they hold. It is not our intention to examine the wide range of theories that have been developed. Instead, we will briefly outline some of the theories that have been most influential in the study of international political economy. These can be classified as liberal, structuralist and radical.

Two of the most important liberal theories were proposed by Vernon and Dunning. The first widely cited theory was the product life cycle model developed by Raymond Vernon (1966), which provided an explanation for the expansion of American business overseas. Vernon argued that, through advances in technology, companies are able to gain competitive advantage in the American domestic market. In the initial stage, these firms are content to sell their products abroad. However, the importers of US products begin to acquire the appropriate technology and start producing these goods domestically, thus providing products at a cheaper rate than the imported goods since they do not face transport costs. In order to protect their markets, US producers are forced to establish factories abroad. The third stage of the product life cycle occurs when foreign firms begin producing the product cheaper than US companies and begin exporting to the US. According to this model, the main motivation for FDI arises from the desire to exploit technological comparative advantage and maintain market share. Critics of the product life cycle theory pointed to its inability to explain non-American FDI (Caves, 1974).

Another liberal theory was developed by John Dunning, one of the most prolific writers on the TNC. Drawing on economic and managerial factors, Dunning developed the ownership, location and internationalization model, a comprehensive theory focusing on the decision to invest abroad, with emphasis on ownership characteristics and the desirability of the foreign location (see, for example, Dunning, 1973, 1981, 1988).

Strange (1991, 1994) has provided a structuralist alternative to the liberal theories, which shifts the emphasis from the decisions of firms to major structural change in the global economy. Strange lists three key structural changes that have accelerated transnational production: falling real costs of transport and communication; development of new technologies; and the creation of new financial instruments. She argues that structural changes in technology, communications and finance created the growth conditions for TNCs. She claims that a rapid increase in technology spurred by the IT revolution has quickened the pace of globalized production; increased capital mobility has facilitated the dispersion of industry; and changes in the knowledge structure have made transborder communication and transportation cheaper and faster.

Marxist writers, with their traditional focus on the centralization and concentration of capital, were well placed to provide explanations for the growth of transnational production. An interesting contribution to the radical literature was made by Stephen Hymer. In his seminal study, *The International Operation of National Firms* (1976), he argued that the dominance of American business ventures abroad arose from the oligopolistic business structure. In later works such as *The Multinational Corporation: A Radical Approach* (1979), he drew on Lenin's theory of imperialism and he gave more attention to systemic factors and emphasized the uneven development of capital.

The theoretical dispute over the causes of transnational production is mirrored in the conflict concerning the impact of this activity on the nation-state and national societies. Two broad positions are discernible – the positive and the negative. Some analysts have developed arguments that emphasize the positive results of FDI but these findings are disputed by those who claim that, on balance, the net effect of TNC investment is negative for host countries. The positive case stresses the net positive benefits of FDI. For the most part, it can recognize the possibility of costs but tends to put the emphasis on the favourable aspects of foreign investment. The negative case coming out of radical and dependency analyses places the focus on the negative impact of foreign firms. Although some analysts in this tradition are willing to admit some gains from FDI, others are unwilling to accept a positive role for transnational capital under any circumstances. These writers tend to stress the size of these firms vis-à-vis governments.

It is not surprising that it should be liberal economists and the business community who contend that the net impact of TNC activity is positive. These analysts argue that both the direct and indirect effects of FDI are, on the whole, beneficial for host countries.

It is argued that FDI provides five main *positive direct effects*:

1 FDI provides additional resources and capabilities, that is, capital, technology, access to markets and management skills.
2 It provides additional tax revenues through the increase in economic activity in the host country.
3 FDI increases GDP, thus increasing the tax base.
4 By better linking the host economy with the global marketplace, TNCs help to advance economic growth by fostering a more efficient division of labour.
5 FDI improves the balance of payments through import substitution, export generation or efficiency-seeking investment.

It is claimed that FDI provides three *positive indirect effects*:

1 TNCs inject entrepreneurship, new management styles, new work cultures and more dynamic competitive practices.
2 By bringing more efficient resource allocation, competitive stimulus and spillover effects to suppliers and/or consumers, TNCs can help upgrade domestic resources and capabilities, and the productivity

of local firms, and also foster clusters of related activities to the benefit of participating firms.
3 TNCs enhance national welfare by more directly exposing the host economy to: the political and economic systems of other countries; the values and demand structures of foreign households; superior attitudes to work practices, incentives and industrial relations; and the many different customs and behavioural norms of foreign countries.

The critics document four main *negative direct effects*:

1 TNCs transfer too few or the wrong kind of resources or assets. TNCs can cut off foreign markets, that is, those serviced by domestic firms; can fail to adjust to localized capabilities and needs; and may not provide an addition to capital at all.
2 TNCs use transfer pricing and other devices to lower taxes paid. Also, by restricting growth, there is an overall loss of tax revenue.
3 FDI promotes a division of labour likely to be in the company's interests and this can be detrimental to the country's comparative advantage. The division of labour is likely to be based on what the firm perceives to be in its global interests, which may be inconsistent with dynamic comparative advantage as perceived by the host country.
4 TNCs worsen the balance of payments through limiting exports and promoting imports, and outcompeting local firms that export more and import less.

The critics claim that TNCs bring four *negative indirect effects*:

1 Foreign entrepreneurship, management styles and working practices fail to accommodate or, where appropriate, change local business cultures. The introduction of foreign industrial relations procedures may lead to industrial unrest. By the pursuit of anti-competitive practices, TNCs may bring an unacceptable degree of market concentration.
2 Foreign firms can limit the upgrading of local resources and capabilities by restricting local production to low-value activities and importing the major proportion of higher value intermediate products. They may also reduce the opportunities for domestic economies of scale by confining their linkages to foreign suppliers and industrial concerns.

3 TNCs may cause unrest by introducing conflicting values through advertising, business customs, labour practices and environmental standards.

4 TNCs may exercise direct interference in the political regime or electoral process of the host country.

Below we will argue that the rise and development of the TNC is to be understood as the result of a changing political, economic, technological and managerial context. We will also try to suggest a way not of reconciling competing views on the impact of TNCs but of going beyond them. Instead of adhering to either a positive or negative overview, this perspective recognizes that the costs and benefits of FDI vary from case to case and that what constitutes costs and benefits will vary depending on the values of the observer. Our intention in putting forward this perspective arises from what we see as key flaws in the competing approaches to state–firm relations. The pro-TNC approach fails to think about power in the market. In viewing TNCs as wholly beneficial, these writers pay limited, if any, attention to non-economic factors, and minimize the role of market failure and market distortions. The anti-TNC perspective, in demonizing the firm, gives no credence to governments' ability to shape economic policy, and fails to fully appreciate the structural changes that have taken place in the world economy.

MAJOR DEVELOPMENTS

There have been two major changes in the global production structure. The first has been the globalization of production. There has been a proliferation of corporate activity and business networks around the world. The second major development has been the change in the underlying principles of the organization of production and key features of the global production system.

The globalization of production

The globalization of production is aptly captured by phrases such as 'from national production to global production', and 'from local markets to global markets'. It refers to the proliferation and stretching of corporate activity and business networks across the globe.

The globalization of production is a consequence of structural change in the global economy, the changing organizational forms and strategies of TNCs and the policies of national governments. While initially the spread of transnational production was viewed as a distinctly US phenomenon, the overseas expansion of European and Japanese firms followed by TNCs originating from developing countries, such as China, India and Brazil, has demonstrated that it is a truly global event. For many analysts, the creation of US hegemony in the aftermath of the Second World War brought with it the beginnings of globalized production 'based on offshore low-wage assembly' (Bernard, 1994, p. 221). This was also partly the consequence of US foreign policy, which encouraged manufacturing firms to invest in anti-communist countries to support its position during the Cold War. In the past three decades, however, transnational production has escaped its early origins in US economic growth and policy choices and has become a driving force in the global economy. Major enterprises in industrialized countries have found that they have 'outgrown national markets, national laws and national financial markets' and, in response, have begun producing 'for a global market according to a global corporate strategy' (Strange, 1991, p. 246).

The postwar spread of the capitalist mode of production and free trade has led to the development of a complex and highly integrated world economy in which international trade and investment flows occur on a massive scale at increasingly rapid rates. International economic structures based on finance and trade have led to increasing interdependence and closer ties between countries. An important part of this process is associated with the growth of transnational production, with the increasing ability of firms to locate parts of their production overseas while still maintaining direct control over the activities of foreign subsidiaries. This move by many enterprises to spread their activities into other countries has bolstered the globalization process, broadening the links between countries. The organizational form of the TNC has undergone extensive change, leading to the development of deep integration (Dicken, 1992) and these developments will be discussed in the next subsection. First, we will consider structural changes in technology, communications and transport, finance, and the political conditions attendant on these developments.

Technological change

The global production system is dominated by rapid developments in the technological environment. New technologies have placed innovation at the centre of profitability, and the creation, implementation and diffusion of new technology are now critical to economic efficiency and international competitiveness. The new production techniques are characterized by cutting-edge technological innovation, sophisticated coordination of operations and more efficient means of meeting the needs of customers. With these developments, production has grown in scale and become more cost-effective.

The accelerating pace of technological change has enhanced the capacity of successful producers to supply the market with new products and/or make them with new materials or new processes. At the same time, the accelerating rate of technological change in the production process has been central to creating the world market system. Technological change has prompted the emergence of global markets for goods and services by contributing to greater homogeneity in consumer tastes worldwide, by causing firms to seek wider markets, and by making it easier for firms to produce and market products globally. Additionally, new technology contributes to the processes whereby product and process lifetimes have shortened, sometimes dramatically. As companies are required to satisfy consumer demands and win strategic alliances, new technologies are being applied across a wider range of goods and services, making them easily available at more affordable prices.

Technologies have been at the forefront of the process whereby new products replace old ones at a rapid rate. This process can be illustrated through a brief overview of some of the developments in home entertainment for consumers around the globe, but especially in advanced industrial countries. At the beginning of the 20th century, musical entertainment at home was produced by manual means with the use of piano, wind and string instruments. At the beginning of the 21st century, we have access to electronic and digital technology to aid us in our production of music. The vinyl record and the cassette tape were supplanted by the compact disc and this is being surpassed by digital music. In 2014 the revenue from digital music matched those accrued from physical formats for the first time, with music subscription services being the major driver of growth in the digital music market (IFPI, 2015). The

videotape, a development which came into widespread usage less than 20 years ago, was replaced by the DVD and it too may disappear in favour of online or streaming videos. Since 2012, digital sales have been increasing with revenue from DVD sales falling and Blu-ray sales experiencing slow growth. Statistics from Digital Entertainment Group, the industry advocacy group, show that in 2014 in the US (the largest market) revenue gained from DVDs and Blu-ray discs stood at $6.93 billion, while digital spending was $7.53 billion (DEG, 2015).

Meanwhile, the cost to the firm of investment in research and development (R&D) and therefore innovation has risen. The time it takes to recoup profits from national markets is too long to keep up with the costs of developing and installing new technology, products and processes. To keep products competitive, especially when other companies may already be transnational, firms are having to gain access to overseas markets to increase the volume of their sales. Despite the growth of liberal trade, it can still be difficult to access foreign markets, and the risk that trade barriers may be raised is always a problem. To overcome this, firms have directed their efforts towards producing locally in the markets they wish to sell in, and this has proved to be more cost-effective (Strange, 1991, pp. 247–8).

Communications and transport

One of the major reasons for the growth of transnational production has been the accelerated reduction in international transport and communications costs. The decrease in communications and transport costs has benefited strategic planning from headquarters and also facilitated the growth of outsourcing in industrial production. Reduced communications costs allow new systems of global information management to become feasible. Information and transport technologies lower the real costs and risks of management at a distance. Better communications networks, which are reliable, fast and efficient, have meant that TNCs can be in constant contact with all their subsidiaries and allow information to flow relatively freely within the firm, despite geographical distance. Transport systems are also faster and more reliable so resources and products can be moved cheaply and easily from primary extraction to processing plants to markets. In the mid-1980s, for example, Apple computers 'travelled' around two million miles before reaching the final customer (Kaplinsky,

1991). These global assembly lines are extremely fluid, with the production organization being 'centrally coordinated' (McMichael, 1996, p. 89). Communications networks also give TNCs greater access to markets: television, radio, magazines, newspapers and the internet have allowed firms' advertising to reach millions of people around the world, tapping into global markets at a relatively low cost to the firm. Telecommunications technology allows firms to organize along global lines, moving components and software among offshore sites and selling products in world markets. As digital and communications technology has become more accessible and integrated into daily life, it has become embedded in all areas of existence, thus pushing us further towards a global marketplace.

Finance

Central to transnational investment is the acquisition and deployment of capital. Developments in international finance have created integrated financial markets that facilitate global production (Stopford and Strange, 1991). Firms have been able to finance their production operations overseas as a result of the internationalization of finance. This globalization in the financial market is the result of three factors. The first factor leading to an expansion in the availability of capital is technological innovation, which has produced reductions in cross-border transaction costs and facilitated private international capital transactions. The second is the removal of governmental, legal and technical barriers to the movement of capital, thus easing cross-border capital flows. There has been a widespread liberalization of capital markets around the world. This partial and incomplete transformation began with the creation of the Eurocurrency market in the 1960s and continued with the deregulation initiated by the US in the mid-1970s and early 1980s. As barriers went down, the mobility of capital went up. The old difficulties of raising money for investment in offshore operations and moving it across the exchanges vanished. While flows declined during the global financial crisis no major new barriers were erected.

The third factor is the growth of innovation in financial instruments. A variety of financial instruments and capital mobility support the globalization of production and cross-border transactions of TNCs in global financial markets. Not surprisingly, these developments have been most widely exploited among the developed countries where the barriers to integration have been the least. But they have also been important for developing countries. These instruments include interest rates, currency and stock market index futures and over-the-counter instruments such as derivatives, swaps, options, futures, forward transactions, bond-lending and reinsurance. As a result, capital moves across borders and boundaries in places where previously it was difficult for it to do so. The impact of these developments transcends capital markets, in that capital mobility has introduced major changes in international trade and the organization of the TNC. This sustained growth of commerce and international investment is a central element in the globalization of production because it has provided the financing for the expansion of TNC operations.

The expansion of international finance has radically reshaped the structural and institutional composition of the world economy. The integration of capital markets into one worldwide market for savings and credit means that TNCs can enjoy far greater possibilities by raising money wherever they operate without having to transfer funds across frontiers and exchanges. It is either unnecessary for the TNCs to find new funds, or they can do so locally.

Attendant on these changes is the impact of capital flight on host countries. Short-term capital flows have caused instability in the international financial market and played a part in the Mexican crisis of 1994, the Asian financial crisis of 1997 and the Argentinian crisis of 2001. The relationship between national governments and foreign investors can move from one of accommodation and cooperation to a hostile and adversarial one. Crucially, capital does not operate in a vacuum and the determination of the impact of capital on nation-states is linked to government–business relations. Box 7.2 provides an exploration of one such relationship.

Political

The globalization of production has also been influenced by the policies of national governments. The policy decisions taken by states cannot be seen simply as automatic reactions to structural change or as arising solely from competitive pressures. There is a mix of motives and pressures acting on national governments. We will mention three aspects in which political factors contributed to the globalization of production. First, we see the influence of political factors in the construction and maintenance of the liberal system of trade and payments ushered in after the Second World War, which formed the background to the early development of transnational production. We mentioned at the outset of this chapter the importance of US interests and US foreign policy in the outward expansion of US business enterprises. Of central importance in the development of transnational production was the US military and political power underpinning the Bretton Woods system of liberal trade and payments, and a US foreign policy supportive of an expansive capitalist system in the Cold War conflict with the Soviet Union. Second, we note that the liberalization in financial markets that stimulated changes in the production structure after 1973 was the result of political decisions taken by states. The degree, content and timing of liberalization in the US and Europe shows varying influences of competitive pressure rather than a necessary correspondence between structural change and governmental regulation.

Third, we note that the relocation of manufacturing production to Third World states during the 1960s and 70s was in response to various nationalist projects. A major, and often overlooked, reason for the shift in industrial production was the policies of governments of developing countries to attract foreign investment.

As some East Asian states embarked on their model of export-oriented industrialization, they sought massive foreign investment. One such incentive was through the creation of export processing zones (EPZs). An EPZ is an area of land created especially for export production in which national regulations are modified or relaxed to attract foreign investment. For example, in Mexico, one investment firm was offered 100 per cent tax exemption for the first ten years and 50 per cent exemption for the following ten years, as an incentive to locate an EPZ near the border with the US (McMichael, 1996, p. 94). EPZs are attractive to TNCs since they offer low-wage labour with minimal external costs, while governments reap the benefits of capital investment and foreign currency earnings from exports. Of course, this was not the only determinant of these flows of investment. Other reasons included the desire of firms to break into growing markets. The best way to do this was to locate all or part of their production in these Third World countries. Moreover, at this point, firms were also encountering market saturation and a reduction in profits in the industrialized world.

EPZs remain controversial, with supporters and critics engaged in dispute concerning their negative or positive impacts. For supporters, they provide a link to global markets and contribute to employment and income generation. For critics, they are exploitative

---

Box 7.2 Government regulation, international capital and financial instability: the case of South Korea

Until the late 1980s, government intervention in the economy, and in particular the financial sector, was important for South Korea's development process. Interference in major financial activities including interest rates and credit allocations enabled the state to support growth in strategically chosen industries. Following partial deregulation of South Korea's capital controls, the economy's exposure to unregulated international capital flows made it vulnerable to capital flight and the whims of foreign speculators. Direct financing includes issuing bonds and stocks, and it increased from 15 per cent of financing in 1970 to 45.2 per cent in 1990.

In the 1990s, the government's deregulation of the short-term commercial paper market moved faster than the long-term interest rates of the banks, which led to a large expansion of short-term borrowing. Between 1992 and 1996, these short-term liabilities accounted for a massive 84.4 per cent of total capital flows into South Korea and, by 1996, they amounted to one-third of its GDP. When economic growth is high, this 'hot money' is useful for investments in capacity that is used by buoyant demand. However, when demand becomes sluggish, the high level of investment becomes excess capacity and the loans, which require repayment in the short term, become harder and harder to service. This increase in non-performing loans causes foreign investors to lose confidence in the economy and massive capital outflow ensues. Thus, the South Korean 'bubble economy', inflated by short-term investment, was at the mercy of world economic growth, in particular export demand, and the confidence of foreign investors. Short-term capital flows constituted a major destabilizing factor to the South Korean economy in the mid-1990s.

Box 7.3 Export processing zones: an ILO perspective

The ILO study, *Labour and Social Issues Relating to Export Processing Zones* (1998a), reported exponential growth in EPZs in the 1980s and 90s, and the geographic spread of EPZs. The largest numbers of EPZs are in North America (320) and Asia (225). But the concentration of EPZs is rising in developing regions such as the Caribbean (51), Central America (41) and the Middle East (39) and the figures are likely to increase throughout the world. The report noted that while EPZs are traditionally associated with manufactured products, variations to this pattern have arisen in a number of places. For example, in Islamabad, a number of agri-export zones specializing in the export of cut flowers and rose onions had been established. On the central issue of the impact of EPZs on overall economic growth, a press release about the report stated that there is a 'pervasive absence of meaningful linkages between the EPZs and the domestic economies of most of the host countries' (ILO, 1998b). Moreover, the main author of the report, Mr Auret Van Heerden, noted 'the frequent absence of minimal standards and poor labour-management relations have predictable outcomes, such as high labour turnover, absenteeism, stress and fatigue, low rates of productivity, excessive wastage of materials and labour unrest which are still too common in EPZs' (ILO, 1998b).

The report concluded that while some countries had capitalized on the presence of EPZs in their territory, others had not. Whether or not an EPZ had benefited its host country is related to the degree of sophistication of the goods produced in the zone. Malaysia and Singapore attracted quality investment in high-tech manufactures and have utilized the presence of such industries to qualify their own workforce in highly skilled sectors. Other states, including Bangladesh, Pakistan and Sri Lanka, that host the more labour-intensive zones are finding that rather than increasing the quality of the workforce, EPZs are perpetuating a stagnant skill level in their workers. In textiles, garment manufacturing and electronics assembly, women account for 90 per cent or more of the workers and it is in these processing and assembly operations where companies see labour as a cost to contain rather than an asset to develop.

enclaves that fail to produce the hoped-for benefits and increase dependency on external agents. The impact of EPZs has been studied by governments, independent researchers and international organizations. Box 7.3 presents the findings of a study conducted by the International Labour Organization (ILO).

Changing organizational principles

The globalization of international production is a response to structural change and governmental policies. It is also the consequence of changing organizational patterns within firms, and changes in the wider system of production.

In the past, each phase of the production process was completed by a different firm. Over time, firms came to realize that by merging, so that one firm controlled several steps, they could reduce costs and improve production efficiency. Between each step of production there are transaction costs between firms. If these firms merged they could internalize these

costs, resulting in an overall saving on external costs. Vertical integration or internalizing production flows is one of the major economic incentives that has led to the growth in TNCs. When a firm decides to move part of its production process overseas, it retains control and reduces its costs by keeping the flows of 'globally-applicable technology and marketing expertise' (Casson, 1991, p. 271) within the company, thus eliminating the necessity of licensing out to firms within the host country. This internal trade serves only to redistribute income between different divisions of the company, eliminating the possibility that one parent of the transaction may default. This provides added security and control to the central managing body and prevents external forces from interrupting the production process. Much of the world's trade is now internalized in TNCs with the movement of components between foreign subsidiaries and parent companies during the production process. The benefits of internalizing transaction costs are an incentive for firms to transnationalize their production. The decision by one firm in an industry puts pressure on other firms to go global in order to remain competitive.

Another development has been in the creation of an integrated trans-border production system. This arises when the entire production process is spread across widely dispersed locations within and between countries. Facilitated by supraterritorial coordination, which links the components, machinery, finance and services of a company anywhere in the world, a global production operation emerges. The emphasis in this environment is on the transfer of production to points of optimum conditions. Additionally, electronic networks have facilitated global alliances of manufacturing companies to allow more efficient outsourcing of production of parts or products to suppliers throughout the world.

From Fordist to post-Fordist production

The expansion of TNC activity in the 1950s and 60s was in accordance with what has come to be called the 'Fordist production system'. Named after the American industrialist Henry Ford, production under a Fordist system conformed to two simple principles, namely, mass production and mass consumption. The standard system for production was the factory system based on semi-skilled labour using specialized equipment to mass produce standardized goods. Competitive advantage accrued from cutting costs and this was achieved through an assembly line system. Firms achieved economies of scale through mass production and increased efficiency by training workers to perform routine tasks. Under this system, workers earned sufficient wages to boost consumer demand, thus ensuring factory production maintained a high rate of turnover. However, from the late 1970s, there was a change in the organization of manufacturing activities, which shifted the priorities of TNCs from labour costs and mass production to product innovation. Changes in the nature of consumer demand have meant that product innovation quality is more important than price competitiveness, although price is still an important factor. Companies now tend to look for flexible specialization, competitive differentiation and quality control as the main features of their production process. This means that the mass production of goods that are very similar to the products of other companies will not necessarily give the competitive advantage required in today's market.

In the 1980s, the Japanese car company Toyota developed the just in time (JIT) system, in which component parts are delivered by Toyota's suppliers two hours before assembly – just in time. JIT permits Toyota to hold no inventory and allows design and production to be changed quickly in response to consumer demand and changes in the consumer market (McMichael, 1996, p. 107). These new systems of production reduce the ability of companies to mass produce goods that can then be stored until they are required in the market, and the workers often need to be more skilled so that design and managerial decisions can be made on the factory floor. Furthermore, with the need to produce goods speedily in response to demands in the market, suppliers and assembly plants need to be in close geographical proximity. Now the advantage of low wages is not as important in the location choice for production as it was under Fordist manufacturing systems. Factors that now affect location choice include proximity to suppliers and markets, and the availability of skilled labour and specialized technology. Post-Fordist production also has greater infrastructure requirements, which many countries specializing in cheap labour are unable to meet.

Under these new conditions, many TNCs need to have entire production chains occurring in one region. For example, this shift gives East Asia a competitive advantage over Africa. In East Asia, tremendous efforts had been made to increase the skills of the labour force and much of the required infrastructure had been built during industrialization in the 1960s and 70s, with large networks of firms established, mostly already within TNC production lines. For much of Africa, however, these developments mean that it is unlikely that there will be a significant amount of investment by TNCs in the foreseeable future, given the lack of infrastructure, geographical distance and poorly educated population. While under post-Fordism, the demand for mass-produced goods is still a feature of markets, the need for more flexible and innovative products has changed the direction of foreign investment.

Mergers, strategic alliances and joint ventures

If the shift from Fordist to post-Fordist production captures the key organizing principle of capitalist production in managerial terms, there have also been changes in the ways in which TNCs organize in the emerging world market. The attitudes, organizational structures and behaviour of business corporations have adapted to changes in the global economy and governments' policies. One development from the 1980s onwards was a rapid increase in mergers and acquisitions, joint ventures and other strategic alliances. Such activity reached a peak in 2007 but as the business cycle contracted there has been a sharp fall in mergers and acquisitions. The value of mergers and acquisitions in 2013 was one-third of the level reached in 2007 (see Table 7.3). The creation of strategic alliances, joint ventures and the resort to increased incidence of mergers and acquisitions is partly a response to the impact of technological change on product life cycles (as discussed above), partly the result of the development of new markets and partly a consequence of the expansion in the services sector. A single firm may lack the combination of technological know-how, funds for R&D, local market knowledge, access to finance and market share necessary to remain competitive in this rapidly changing environment. Thus firms have adapted organizationally to these developments.

Another development has been the emergence of new attitudes and strategies towards foreign investment. In the past, firms tended to either increase investment or reduce investment sequentially, whereas in the past 15 years or so, firms have used both investment and disinvestment strategies at the same time. They have expanded in one sector or territory while simultaneously contracting in another sector or territory. This is also a response to the rapid shortening of product life cycles and the segmentation of market structures.

A third change has been the requirement under conditions of post-Fordist production to pay more attention to both the relationship between market integration and the specialized nature of local markets. For example, McDonald's, the global burger chain, serves standard fare in most of its global outlets, while developing products specifically designed for the local market. Customers in Singapore can order burgers with rice buns, Germans can have bratwurst, Indians can consume curry, Israelis can devour falafels, Norwegians can eat salmon wraps and Spaniards can sample gazpacho with their Big Macs (*Chicago Tribune*, 2012). Firms are aware that they possess certain advantages or core competencies that have given them a competitive advantage, but that these general characteristics are likely to be of limited utility unless their production is sensitive to the demands of consumers, and the shifting cultural context in which they operate.

Global supply chains

The forces underlying the globalization of production discussed above have given rise to yet another shift in the organizational principles of transnational production. Firms are now increasingly organizing their production into global supply chains. There are varied definitions of the term 'supply chain' (see Box 7.4 for discussion of a frequently used alternative term). A simple definition proffered by the OECD can be adapted for use here. A global supply chain is the (global) 'network of organizations that cooperate to transform raw materials into finished goods and services for consumers' (OECD, 2012, p. 4). In other words, a global supply chain connects suppliers, manufacturers, distributors, retail outlets and customers. It links the global sourcing of components with global manufacturing and global markets. Key characteristics of global supply chains are outsourcing some of the firm's activities to third parties and offshoring parts of their supply chain outside their home country.

The rise of global supply chains is driven by the search for higher profits, a desire to expand business operations and easier access to markets. The creation of global supply chains has brought a number of benefits to TNCs. These include reduced total costs; a reduction in the inventory they hold; increased productivity; enhanced speed and efficiency of business operations and access to new markets. However, the rise of global supply chains has brought attendant problems and risks. There are added risks of operating in a global environment. These include risks arising from geographic distance coupled with different cultural and political systems; increased security risks; ensuring adequate ethical standards at overseas partners and relevant technical and technological capacity. The pursuit of short-term profit may not yield long-term

Table 7.3 Cross-border mergers and alliances, by sector, 2007–8, 2012–13 (millions of dollars)

Year	2007	2008	2012	2013
World	1,045,085	625,235	331,651	348,755
Primary Sector	93,918	88,682	3,427	27,229
Manufacturing Sector	329,135	195,847	138,230	96,165
Services Sector	622,032	340,706	189,993	225,361

Source: UNCTAD (2014, pp. 213, 216)

Box 7.4 Global value chains and global value chain analysis

A global value chain (GVC) has been defined as 'the full range of activities that firms and workers perform to bring a product from its conception to end use and beyond' (Gereffi and Fernandez-Stark, 2011). The integration of supply chains across multiple sovereignties raises issues of mutual dependency. A GVC analysis shifts attention away from the simply economic or managerial aspects of supply chain management to broader issues of power and control. For example, it raises issues not only about cost-structures and efficiency but also about corporate social responsibility and sustainability. A GVC analysis follows the processes involved in a single industry, enabling the analyst to grasp the range of actors (e.g. producers, subcontractors, small companies and large TNCs); the regulations; the technologies and the markets involved in the process of adding value to a product across diverse geographical locations. By following a chain or network of connections, GVC offers distinct insights into the global production structure. It enables analysts to examine an industry from the 'top-down' or the 'bottom-up'.

sustainability. The CEO of a Fortune 500 company put the issue starkly: 'The world's supply chain forms the backbone of our global economy, security and health, and the risks it faces are many. The five "P's" of powerful weather, pandemic, political instability, port closures, and primary sourcing can easily cause disruption, potentially triggering a cascading effect for millions' (Bergman, 2013). In other words, outsourcing and off-shoring are not cost-free. This new organizational form has given rise to the study of global supply chain management.

Inevitably, the rise of global supply chains has given rise to studies of their economic and political impact. It has been argued that while offshoring can raise wages in developing countries that attract new investment, there are limited benefits of diffusion within the wider economy (Levy, 2005). From a critical management perspective Levy (2005, p. 692) concludes that offshoring leads to 'a shift in the distribution of resources and the balance of power between and among firms, countries, and social groups'. A study by Kate Macdonald agrees with the contention that economic power is being dispersed away from the state in favour of corporations. However, she argues that marginalized workers are not automatically disadvantaged by these changes with the outcome dependent on struggles of contestation at the local level (Macdonald, 2014). And a study of the agricultural sector argues that the governance of supply chains is affected by the characteristics of the commodity, thus making vast generalizations unsafe (Swinnen, 2007). Nevertheless, the study found that trade liberalization and the replacement of state-controlled agricultural production in the developing

world by TNCs increases market opportunities for farmers in the developing world and may therefore contribute positively to economic growth, rural development and poverty reduction.

KEY ISSUES

This section examines three key issues surrounding TNCs. The first concerns the evaluation of the benefits of FDI and we argue that this needs to be done on a case-by-case basis. Second, we examine the continuing debate over state–firm interactions. Third, we consider capital regulation.

Re-evaluating the benefits of FDI

As we pointed out in the section exploring theoretical perspectives, there are competing views concerning the impact of TNCs on national societies. These debates between supporters and opponents of FDI erupted in the 1960s and continue today (see the discussion on transnational land acquisitions in Chapter 12). During the 1970s, when the Third World's demand for a New International Economic Order was at its peak, and dependency analyses were fashionable, the views of the critics were given greater prominence. But with the triumph of neoliberalism and the imposition of adjustment policies in the developing world, it is the views of FDI proponents that have been in the ascendancy. It is difficult to reconcile these contrasting views, and analysts use selective statistics and case studies to support their respective arguments. An example of an ongoing and intense discussion is the debate swirling around Walmart, the world's largest corporation (see Box 7.5).

The approach taken in this text rejects the overgeneralization of both perspectives. Instead, it begins from the observation that FDI can have negative or beneficial impacts but that this is essentially an empirical question, which can only be answered in relation to concrete circumstances. This requires analysts to focus on specific country and firm characteristics rather than assuming a general orientation of firms and countries. Here, we consider the ways in which governments may seek to increase the benefits for their societies from inward FDI. In other words, we raise some of the key issues that should be examined in the context of specific case studies through an exploration of the interactions between governments and TNCs.

It is not always apparent if many of the objections to TNCs stem from their size and control over economic resources or whether the main objections are made in respect of the foreign ownership of productive assets. The benefits and costs of FDI have been assessed through the use of economic, political and cultural criteria. Economic criteria include the balance of payments, economic growth and tax revenues; political issues include interference in domestic politics and the effect on sovereignty; and crucial cultural issues focus on taste transfer and protecting traditional national culture. The evaluation of the costs and benefits of TNC investment in a host country will therefore vary depending on which of these criteria the analyst thinks is most important. Different conclusions may be reached depending on the starting point of the observer. For example, if the main objection is to foreign ownership, then even if it can be shown that economic growth has been positive, the critique of TNC involvement still retains its force.

What determines the net benefits of FDI? What can governments do to ensure that such investment best contributes to economic growth and development? The answers to these questions depend on the policies followed by host governments, the economic and social context of investment, the type of firm and the sector in which the investment is located.

The impacts that TNCs have on their host countries will be strongly influenced by the host government's

---

Box 7.5 Walmart, the TNC

The American retailer Walmart is the largest corporation in the world in terms of revenues and in terms of employees. The size of this global corporation is captured on its website which states that it operates more than 11,00 retail units in 28 countries, e-commerce websites in 11 countries and employs 2.2 million people (http://corporate.walmart.com/our-story/our-business/). Walmart's Facebook page has 32 million 'likes', its Twitter feed has almost 21,000 followers and its Google+ account has more than 61,000 followers. The resort to social media by Walmart is a necessary response by a large corporation to the varied sources of information available in a digital age.

As the largest retailer in the world, Walmart exercises immense influence and generates considerable controversy. Because of its large size and effective economic power, its decisions about which suppliers to use or what wages and benefits it will pay can set standards for local and global labour markets and industries.

Making Change at Walmart is an activist coalition bringing together Walmart associates, union members, small-business owners, religious leaders, community organizations, women's advocacy groups, multiethnic coalitions, elected officials and ordinary citizens. Supported by the United Food & Commercial Workers Union, Making Change at Walmart campaigns for changes in Walmart's corporate policies. The campaign focuses on Walmart's employee policies, working conditions, wages and benefits paid to workers, its relations with suppliers, environmental impact and impact on local communities (see http://makingchangeatwalmart.org).

The company has also been the subject of negative activist documentaries such as Robert Greenwald's *Wal-Mart: The High Cost of Low Prices* (2005). Walmart counters these criticisms by asserting that it creates economic opportunity, enhances environmental sustainability and builds strong communities (see Walmart, 2015).

policies. While we recognize that the impact of FDI is also dependent on a range of economic and societal variables not necessarily subject to governmental control, we focus on governmental policies. In deciding to welcome FDI, unless states promote policies designed to achieve greater economic and social welfare for their citizens from TNCs' activities, they will fail to reap sufficient benefits. This is not solely an issue of governments becoming more accommodating to the needs of foreign firms. States need to maintain a certain level of control and input into the activities of foreign investors to ensure that they maximize the benefits to the host country. The different results available from studies on the impact of FDI, especially in developing countries, reflect the success or failure of governments to direct foreign investment to productive activity (Stopford and Strange, 1991). While in some countries little attention has been paid to this issue, others have made consistent efforts to direct TNCs' activities in fulfilment of their national development plans. In Singapore, for example, TNCs have been directed towards investing in 'higher than average value-added activities' and upgrading 'the quality of labour' (Dunning, 1985, p. 415). This has resulted in greater levels of development and economic growth in Singapore and has now allowed it to develop stronger national industries, with a more skilled labour force to draw on. While some countries have actively promoted EPZs to attract foreign investment, others are careful to avoid export enclaves by ensuring that at least a proportion of the sales are produced or subcontracted locally (Dunning, 1985, p. 418). The nature of the host government's policies towards TNCs is thus a crucial factor in determining if a TNC enhances or inhibits the development of local industries.

One of the major points of contention over the net benefits of FDI for developing countries concerns the transfer of technology. Indeed, this is one of the main reasons why many governments allow greater foreign investment, as they realize that in the absence of the finance and knowledge provided by TNCs, it would be much harder, and in many cases almost impossible, for them to gain access to industrial technologies. While in some cases this transfer of technology by TNCs has led to much faster diffusion of technology than would otherwise have been the case, it is unlikely to achieve maximum impact unless governments upgrade human and technological capabilities. However, as will be discussed below, government policies are only one side of the picture. No amount of regulation by a government or national policies to enhance the technological capability of the population will help to provide value-added FDI if the technology transferred is less advanced compared with the technology being developed and used in home countries at any given time. Studies have shown that the technology frequently transferred from industrial countries to developing countries is designed to maintain low-level production activities in those countries (Bernard, 1994, p. 251). On the other hand, in advanced countries, the transfer of technology tends to be more effective, with their better capabilities allowing them to 'absorb leading edge technologies' from foreign investors (Lall, 1991, p. 251).

The overall economic impact of TNCs through the provision of additional capital, a positive impact on the balance of payments, increased tax revenue, and diffusion of skills and technology is dependent on governmental policies. Governments can devise a broad macroeconomic framework, and institute legal and administrative reforms that ensure positive linkages between local firms and foreign capital. Within the developing world, there exists a vast array of governmental attitudes, skills and ability to design and implement the requisite changes. In these circumstances, the impact of FDI is likely to vary depending on the country in question. We do not intend to imply that the implementation of effective policies is a simple matter and that governments that fail to do so are simply incompetent. On the contrary, the domestic political economy of reform is a complex and difficult process. We do not have the space to explore the economic, political, cultural and institutional dimensions of domestic policy reform. In the context of this chapter, the important point is that the benefits of FDI will vary depending on the local context.

The evidence does seem to suggest that those developing countries that have been open to foreign investment and allowed TNCs to establish export-oriented plants have generally industrialized at much greater rates than their more restrictive counterparts (Lall, 1991, p. 251). This is supported by figures on international trade, which show that between 1960 and 1979, Third World countries increased their share of world trade from 6 per cent to 10 per cent (McMichael, 1996, p. 86), most of which was due to the export of manufactured goods produced by TNCs; evidence from post-communist economies also supports these findings. As mentioned above, government policies also play an important role in this industrializing process. It is vital that the state promotes integration with global structures by creating the necessary infrastructure, thus ensuring that even if the TNCs were to withdraw from the country, domestic firms would have sufficiently developed the capabilities for continued participation in world trade and production.

While the above suggests that the net effects of TNCs' participation in the local economy can contribute positively to development when accompanied by suitable government policies, the likelihood that governments will be in a position to maximize bargaining with the firm also has to be discussed. The structural power of TNCs can lead to situations where sound macroeconomic policies followed by governments may not always produce positive net benefits. For example, while export levels and visible industrialization may take place, the actual development of the host country may be inhibited. There is concern in both developed and developing countries that the plants established by TNCs in host countries serve only as 'offshore satellites for the main activities' in home countries (Dunning, 1985, p. 415). The result is that few benefits accrue to the host country since the profits are, for the most part, returned to the parent company. Even more importantly, high value-added activities, R&D activities for example, tend to remain concentrated in home countries and few of the cutting-edge technologies are transferred to foreign subsidiaries, thus limiting the opportunities for host governments to establish industries capable of producing high-end exports, or in some cases moving beyond basic component manufacture. It has been argued, for example, that the export-oriented industrialization achieved by some Third World countries was more a result of the First World 'shedding the production of consumer goods' (McMichael, 1996, p. 86), rather than a positive attempt to assist developing countries along the path of industrialization.

R&D within enterprises has also tended to remain in home countries. A study of TNCs from Japan, Germany and the US, the three largest sources of foreign investment, showed that 'an overwhelming share of their R&D spending' is maintained at home (Pauly and Reich, 1997, p. 22). Any R&D that does occur overseas is generally directed towards studies of the local markets for the customization of products or to collect knowledge which is then sent back to the home country (Pauly and Reich, 1997, p. 12). Nike, for example, produces most of its shoes in Asia but all product design and sales promotion are done at the company's headquarters in the US (McMichael, 1996, p. 98). As Lall (1991, p. 253) puts it, by receiving the know-how (operational procedures) but not the 'know-why' (research and innovation capabilities), combined with the internalization of technology markets within TNCs, developing countries are restricted from moving their own technological base 'beyond that needed for adaptive activity ... and research'. Lall further claims that evidence from Taiwan and South Korea has shown that know-how has developed far more in industries in which TNC entry has been restricted. In short, there is compelling evidence to suggest that TNCs from the advanced industrial countries continue to exercise a tight rein over their technological knowledge.

Moreover, from a nationalist perspective, if the entry of foreign firms into local markets results in local firms being squeezed out despite an improvement in efficiency, this will be seen as a negative development that will ultimately undermine the economic development of the country. During the industrialization of the West, infant industries were often given the benefit of protectionist government policies to allow them to establish themselves before they faced competition. With the involvement of TNCs and the liberalization of international trade, however, new local industries in developing countries are not provided with similar opportunities. By the early 1970s, the amount of manufacturing exports that was controlled by TNCs ranged from 20 per cent in Taiwan to 43 per cent in Brazil to 90 per cent in Singapore (McMichael, 1996, p. 82). Without careful management and effective policies by the host government, the technological transfer and industrializing promises of TNCs do not actually help developing countries come any closer to catching up with industrialized states. While some benefits have accrued to developing countries from investment by TNCs, it has been argued by many critics that this is only a by-product of the move away from manufacturing and unskilled production by the advanced industrial countries. Thus the Third World became an inexpensive source of consumer goods that are no longer viable to produce in highly industrialized nations.

State–firm interactions

The issue of the net impact of FDI on host societies is intimately connected with the wider question of the changing relations between the state and the firm. The central issue often debated here concerns the relative power of the state and the TNC. A number of commentators and social groups are concerned that the globalization of production has created or is creating a situation in which the state is losing some of its authority and power and is being replaced by the TNC in many areas.

TNCs act as the producers of wealth within the global political economy and as such have increased their ability to influence political systems. When firms were generally confined within national borders, they relied on the state to represent their interests at the international level. Now, however, TNCs are becoming important actors within the global political economy (Stopford and Strange, 1991) and it is arguable that, at times, their influence can be greater than that of states. States are more and more involved in bargaining with TNCs in order to attract foreign investment (Strange, 1994). Increasingly, in both developed and developing countries, states need to cooperate with TNCs to achieve their economic, political and social goals. Trying to control the activities of many large firms through regulatory policies can be difficult and risky, considering that the opportunities offered by foreign investment can be an important part of economic planning and growth.

States have therefore moved into a new policy environment in which they must try to find a balance between attracting and encouraging investment and still maintaining a range of social goals and promoting the so-called 'national interest'. Within this new environment, states still retain territorial control and firms require access to territory in order to conduct their business activities. As such, states enjoy a degree of legitimacy that is denied to firms. However, states can also clash with each other as they attempt to regulate TNC activity (see Box 7.6). The changing context of state–firm interactions has raised a number of issues. Here, we focus on four: changing attitudes of governments towards TNCs; decision-making and national autonomy; the transformation of state policies; and the impact on labour.

Changing attitudes

An important factor in determining the evolution of state–firm interactions is the views and attitudes held by the political elite concerning the net benefits of FDI. The attitudes of governments to TNCs have changed considerably over the past 40 years. With the onset of the North–South dialogue in the 1960s, many Third World governments were highly critical of, if not downright hostile to, foreign investment. Attitudes began to change in the 1980s, with most governments in the developing world acclaiming FDI as good news. In the earlier period, it was generally believed that the economic power of TNCs and their affiliates had adverse

---

Box 7.6 Spain defends its TNCs

To what degree do states see the interests of TNCs with home offices in their territory as also being the interests of those states? While the US government has often been identified as pursuing a foreign policy that favours its TNCs, the trend goes beyond a single state. An interesting example of this activity was provided by the Spanish government in April 2012. At that time Argentina's President Kirchner announced that her government would nationalize the local oil assets of a company called YPF. Argentinian politicians expressed dissatisfaction with the company's performance and alleged that it was not operating in the national interest. YPF is Argentina's largest oil company and had been government owned until it was privatized in the early 1990s. In 1999, the company was acquired by a Spanish firm, Repsol. Nationalization entails putting the company under government control through purchasing its stock.

The Spanish government took offence at Argentina's treatment of a Spanish company and threatened to break off economic and fraternal relations with Argentina. The Spanish prime minister Mariano Rajoy made it clear that the interests of the Spanish state and Spanish TNCs were one and the same. He boldly declared that: 'Wherever there is a Spanish company, the Spanish government will be there defending its interests as its own' (Macalister and Goñi, 2012).

effects on national economies through such practices as transfer pricing and restrictions on the sources of imported components (Dunning, 1991, p. 231). In response, government policies attempted to bolster domestic industries while restricting the activities of foreign firms. Governments also used planning to allocate resources, rather than markets.

There are a number of reasons for this change of heart. The first is the triumph of neoliberal economic ideology and the resort to neoliberal economic policies by most governments. The renewed faith of most countries in the workings of the market economy is demonstrated, for example, in the wholesale privatization of state-owned assets and the deregulation and liberalization of markets since the mid-1980s. The move to remove structural market distortions has been played out all over the developing world, and was initiated in the US and western Europe. For some analysts, this development arises from the proven superiority of the liberal order, while for others this is the result of the imposition of structural adjustment policies by international financial institutions and multilateral development banks following the debt crisis.

The second explanation is the increasing globalization of economic activity and the integration of international production and cross-border markets by TNCs. This has led many countries to re-evaluate the costs and benefits of FDI and the opportunities provided by TNCs for increased participation in international trade and labour markets. In the Third World, in particular, industrialization policies based on import substitution were replaced with export-oriented policies using TNC systems of production and distribution. The third reason is that the key ingredients of contemporary economic growth of created assets, such as technology, intellectual capital, learning experience and organizational competence, are not only becoming more mobile across national boundaries, but also becoming increasingly housed in TNC systems.

The fourth reason why governments have modified their attitudes towards FDI is the successful industrialization of a number of countries, particularly in East Asia. As a result, the competition for the world's scarce resources of capital, technology and organizational skills is becoming increasingly intensive. The fifth is that the economic structures of the major industrialized countries are converging, one result of which is that competition between firms from these nations is becoming more intra-industry and more pronounced.

The sixth explanation is that the criterion for judging the success of FDI by host governments has changed over the years, and changed in a way that has made for a less confrontational and more cooperative stance between themselves and foreign investors. More particularly, the emphasis of evaluating inbound TNC activity over the past two decades has switched from the direct contributions of foreign affiliates to its wider impact on the upgrading of the competitiveness of a host country's dynamic comparative advantage. And, finally, the learning experience of countries about what TNCs can and cannot do for host countries has created a belief in many governments that they can take action to ensure they more efficiently promote their economic and social goals. This appears to be a belief that has limited application in reality and many governments in the developed world find it difficult to fulfil these goals. For example, in 2001, the British government was confronted with its abject failure to protect jobs after two TNCs, Corus and Motorola, decided to disinvest. This happened despite the fact that investment was in depressed regions of the UK and the government tried to persuade the companies to maintain production.

Decision-making and national autonomy

The ability of TNCs to transfer resources abroad in response to changing national and international conditions affects the autonomy of state decision-making authorities. An inherent conflict exists between the political organization of authority based on national governmental structures and the economic organization of value based on growing economic interdependence. The limits to effective public policy are partly determined by the capacity of a state to promote a climate for investment favourable to transnational capital.

The globalization of production presents extraordinary challenges to the economic management of a country. Economic development is no longer restricted to the national territorial forms that prevailed for most of the past two centuries. Instead, national production is now located within world production systems. Countries can no longer rely on natural comparative advantage to win them a place in the global economy. Corporate decisions are made on the basis of global production strategies and relative efficiency. The utilization of high levels of technology and policies that encourage efficiency and promote competition are the new imperatives to international competitiveness.

Although most economic activity is not global in this sense, nevertheless, this is an emerging trend and governments increasingly have to adjust to international demands and pressures. The innovation of financial instruments and the development of multinational banks and other financial institutions have made regulation of the economy more difficult. The integration of national economies and communication systems thus creates a global system of interaction in which the state is but one player among many and state borders are losing their significance.

Moreover, firms themselves can sometimes disregard the domestic regulation of governments. Given their global production and distribution systems, firms are not dependent on government policy in a single state. They can, for example, evade restrictive credit policies by borrowing on international capital markets, and escape taxation of corporate profits through timely inter-firm transfers of resources. In the autumn of 2012, a committee of British MPs accused Amazon, Google and Starbucks of manipulating the tax system to eliminate or minimize their tax bills (Syal and Wintour, 2012). Despite seemingly successful UK business operations, numerous US TNCs were paying extremely little tax. A series of consumer actions and bad publicity resulted in Starbucks 'volunteering' to pay corporate tax. Insofar as TNCs are no longer constrained by the regulation of particular states, they are effectively footloose. The issue of corporate and individual tax abuse is considered in more depth in Chapter 8.

This problem of diminished or diminishing national authority is particularly relevant in the developing world (see Box 7.7 for a discussion of the problem of illicit financial flows from developing countries). The sheer size and resources of many TNCs in comparison with developing countries provides an unequal relationship between the two. This predisposes developing states to modify the demands they make of TNCs. Additionally, the capacity of firms to locate anywhere in the world exerts an inordinate amount of pressure on countries to acquiesce to their demands, or suffer negative consequences in their macroeconomic stability. The mobility of capital increases the alternatives available to firms while circumscribing those available to states. Thus, for many, the benefits that developing countries derive from FDI will remain negligible, given the structural imbalance between TNCs and Third World governments.

Transforming state policies

The globalization of production has altered the attitudes of governments, shifted the bargaining power between states and TNCs and also transformed the nature of the state. This change is captured by the phrase 'the competition state' (Cerny, 1995). States have become increasingly compelled to liberalize because of competitive deregulation pressures resulting from the mobility of capital (Cerny, 1993). Boundaries are shifting as resources are linked with indistinct borders, while industries shift and react to changed circumstances and new technologies. The threat of shifting production from one country to another causes countries to compete against each other. This has produced

---

Box 7.7 Illicit financial flows from the developing world

In discussing illicit financial flows here we do not intend to suggest that TNCs are implicated in all of the various activities that make up illicit financial flows. However, money laundering, tax evasion and international bribery – key aspects of illicit financial flows – may be the result of TNC activity. Recently, the scourge of illicit financial flows from developing countries has garnered attention at G8 and G20 summits, and the Fourth High Level Forum on Aid Effectiveness in Busan in 2011 agreed to increase efforts to tackle illicit financial flows.

The most authoritative source on the scale of illicit financial flows is Global Financial Integrity (GFI), a Washington-based NGO. Their latest annual report estimates that between 2003 and 2012 illicit financial flows from developing countries totalled $6.6 trillion (2015). Their statistics show that after a slowdown due to the global financial crisis, illicit outflows have risen, reaching a peak of $991.2 billion in 2012 (Kar and Spanjers, 2014). A joint report by the African Development Bank and Global Financial Integrity (2013) concluded that the level of illicit outflows from Africa surpassed the level of development assistance received by African countries, making the continent a net lender of resources to the world.

the phenomenon of competitive deregulation between states as they attempt to maintain their attractiveness to investors and sustain global competitiveness. The competitive processes between states can lead to a situation in which wages, working conditions and environmental standards become depressed. This is a consequence of increased liberalization as states seek TNC investment.

The globalization of production and internationalization of finance have enhanced the capacity of the holders of capital to evade the jurisdiction of what is often perceived as hostile economic management. States must therefore be increasingly sensitive to the regulatory policies of their neighbours, since they are now effectively competing for the right to regulate investment. Further, this new competitive dynamic is propelling states to accommodate the preferences of market actors, and to actively court international investors by introducing more liberal regulatory standards (Andrews, 1994, pp. 193–218). States will only be able to influence this process and regulate FDI by assigning or delegating to supranational institutions some of their power and authority. The development of offshore markets is another instrument that has eroded national financial barriers. These changes provide investors with prospects for minimal levels of taxation and regulation, thereby allowing for the unconstrained movement of financial resources. These instruments have also been critical in providing a wider source of funding for TNCs engaged in the process of globalizing their businesses.

Labour

The issue of the impact of transnational production on labour is examined in Chapter 9. However, we cannot leave the topic of state–firm interactions without a brief mention of the debate concerning the state's role in protecting workers. Many TNCs have transferred production processes using low-skilled and unskilled labour to developing countries to take advantage of these low wages. But they were not only escaping higher wage rates, they were also trying to circumvent minimum health and safety requirements and reap the benefits of working with a largely non-unionized workforce. Instead of protecting their workers, many Third World governments colluded with transnational capital to maintain poor working conditions. In a popular study of the impact of transnational production, Klein (2001, p. 217) argues that: 'When the actual manufacturing

process is so devalued, it stands to reason that the people doing the work of production are likely to be treated like detritus – the stuff left behind.'

This shift to low-wage economies with poor working conditions has, at times, hurt the reputational capital of major firms and led to social movement campaigns against sweatshop labour. One affected firm was Nike, which in response to a number of high profile campaigns against its employment practices in Southeast Asia devised a code of conduct for its contractors and opted into a number of international corporate social responsibility initiatives. But as an article published in 2014 reveals, balancing cost and worker safety remains an ongoing struggle (Banjo, 2014).

Shifting global production also impacts on labour in the developed world. From the perspective of some workers in particular industries in advanced industrial countries, the shift of labour-intensive production overseas altered the economic structure, causing economic and social decay in the wake of high levels of unemployment.

Regulating capital

The impact of TNCs on states and societies and the difficulty that individual governments face in controlling these firms have led to calls for greater international regulation of the activities of international business. While civil society actors call for the regulation of international business, both government and private sector interests have been increasingly resistant to such demands. Corporate interests are oriented to promoting forms of international regulation conducive to the accumulation of profits.

There are two contentious issues, one on each side of the regulatory agenda, that encapsulate the current dilemmas. Those groups trying to subject the behaviour of TNCs to greater scrutiny and to impose state sovereignty on firms' taxation provide an interesting example of the failure of both domestic and international regulatory power. Through diverse accounting procedures, firms have devised strategies to evade taxation and as a result the corporate tax contribution to the finances of governments has been declining. There is an attempt to reduce the power of firms to evade taxation at the national level through the introduction of international surveillance and cooperation between national governments. This is not a radical proposal and is supported by many liberal and conservative governments in the OECD. However, the attempt in 2001 by the OECD to develop guidelines for international taxation policies was defeated through the lobbying efforts of TNCs. They were successful in persuading the US government to oppose the OECD guidelines. On the other hand, a contrasting OECD set of regulations favourable to the expansion of international business was defeated by a coalition of civil society groups who felt that it increased the power of firms relative to that of governments. The Multilateral Agreement on Investment aimed to set standards that would further liberalize national investment regimes. Thus, while TNCs have influenced global regulation, they are unable to dictate its content.

To some observers of the contemporary global economy, TNCs are increasingly exercising a parallel authority alongside governments in matters of economic management affecting the location of industry and investment, in the direction of technological innovation and in the extraction of surplus value (May, 2015). Corporations have actively sought through industry associations and individual contacts with governments to influence the architecture of national, regional and global regulation. Firms have, to date, argued successfully for minimal regulation, and for self-regulation rather than public authority control in situations where some direct form of regulation is required (Clapp, 1998). The TNC has become endowed with a greater political role as it uses more diverse means of achieving its objectives. Not only have TNCs resorted to using access to the highest levels of decision-making with national governments, but also access to the WTO and other multilateral institutions to ensure the corporate agenda is prioritized everywhere (Sell, 2000; Smythe, 2000).

To some extent, TNCs have joined states as the authorities exercising power (whether or not affirmed by them) over the course of national and global economic development. Moreover, companies exert considerable influence over the global economy as they account for an increasingly larger proportion of international intercourse than governments. This development, facilitated by technological change, has redefined state sovereignty by reducing the magnitude of authority claims asserted by the state. Despite this, governments remain the decisive holders of authority in regard to the territories over which other states recognize their

supremacy, but are restrained in their capacity to affect economic decisions within their borders.

CONCLUSION

The spread of TNCs since the 1950s and the creation of a global production structure have had significant effects on international economic and trade structures, industrial development and government policies. The growth and nature of transnational production have changed over time, especially with the development of global supply chains, and TNCs have greatly affected national and regional developments around the world. Much of the uneven development and industrialization that occurred in the final years of the 20th century can at least partly be explained by differences in TNC involvement and government policies towards foreign investment. The shift towards transnationalization by many enterprises has also changed traditional state–firm relations, with policies of cooperation essential to the economic planning of both actors. The large amounts of capital owned and controlled by TNCs combined with their participation in virtually every national economy in the world have given them a great deal of strategic power in the global political economy, and their role in influencing international trade negotiations and other international agreements is an important issue in the contemporary global political economy.

The role of TNCs in creating a new international division of labour will be examined in Chapter 9. It will discuss the ways in which transnational production has affected mature industrial economies and developing countries. TNCs have been the major actors organizing a shift of unskilled and semi-skilled manufacturing production from the advanced industrial countries to the semi-periphery. Many developing countries were integrated into global production systems because of their large pool of low-wage labour.

Having examined how trade has increased in importance in Chapter 6 and how production has become increasingly globalized in this chapter, in Chapter 8 we detail how finance has become a global undertaking that both drives economic growth and threatens prosperity in times of crisis.

Further Reading

A framework for the analysis of value chains is provided by Gary Gereffi and Karina Fernandez-Stark in *Global Value Chain Analysis: A Primer* (2011). A useful survey of theories of TNCs and FDI can be found in Grazia Ietto-Gillies' *Transnational Corporations and International Production: Concepts, Theories and Effects*, 2nd edn (2012). The literature on Chinese firms in the global economy is rather sparse but see Craig C. Julian, Zafa U Ahmed and Junqian Xu (eds) *Research Handbook on the Globalization of Chinese Firms* (2014) for an introduction to the topic. For a study examining the relationship between national interest and FDI, see Vivienne Bath (2012), 'Foreign Investment, the National Interest and National Security: Foreign Direct Investment in Australia and China', *Sydney Law Review*, 34(5): 5–34.

Chapter 8 | The Global Financial System

This chapter considers the global financial system by focusing on its two most significant parts. Although they will be treated separately for analytical purposes, they have evolved in tandem and influence each other. We will look at the international monetary system (IMS), which governs how one national currency is exchanged for another, and the global credit system, which determines who gets to borrow money and on what terms.

Both systems have undergone dramatic changes since they were established in the mid-1940s. The IMS has evolved from a system of fixed exchange rates to using floating exchange rates. Recently, a number of states have abandoned their national currencies in favour of regional currencies, for example the euro. In the global credit system, the creation and supply of credit has moved from being the responsibility of public authorities (governments) to being provided by corporations. In addition, advances in IT and the deregulation of financial flows have resulted in much more rapid transfer of capital across state boundaries. The consequence of these developments is that many states, even the most powerful, are increasingly sensitive to market fluctuations.

We begin the analysis by providing some definitions and background about transformations in the global financial system. The next section outlines a key theory concerning the relationship between capital flows, exchange rates and domestic policy (Mundell-Fleming model). This proposition is used to find our way through other parts of the chapter. The third section outlines major developments in the global financial system since the Second World War. In the IMS, these are the move from fixed to floating exchange rates and the rise of regional currencies, while in the credit system they are financial innovations and repeated financial crises. The key issues examined in this chapter are: global credit crisis, future of the US dollar, European debt crisis, corporate and individual tax abuse.

DEFINITIONS AND BACKGROUND

In this section, we consider the nature of the international monetary and credit systems as they were created after the Second World War. We begin by focusing on the IMS as a set of arrangements that govern the exchange of one nation's currency for another. A sound IMS is necessary if economic activity across state borders is to proceed smoothly. Importers and exporters need to be able to conduct business in their clients' currencies and to take profit in their own. The post-1945 IMS has undergone two dramatic changes. The biggest alteration was a move from fixed rates to floating rates. The second major change has been the growth of regional currencies replacing some national currencies. We'll examine the major developments in the next section.

Reviewing the turmoil of the interwar period, US and British postwar planners were convinced of the need for a stable international monetary system for international economic activity and peace. The attempt to fix countries' currencies to gold proved disastrous following the First World War, but so did the system of competitive devaluation that followed the breakdown of the gold standard. Planners wanted a system that would provide stability in exchange rates, but would allow for some adjustment from time to time. Their solution was the gold exchange system of Bretton Woods.

The postwar IMS was negotiated at Bretton Woods in the US in 1944. The two most influential participants were the US and Great Britain. In general, the British favoured a system that would restrict capital flows and provide for strong international monetary institutions, whereas the US pushed for a more liberal system with less regulation. Since the British were in debt to the US because of borrowing to finance their participation in the Second World War, the US was able to secure an agreement that fell closer to its desires (Block, 1977, pp. 32–69).

The core of the system was the US dollar, which was fixed to gold at a rate of $35 to one ounce of gold. Similar to the classic gold standard discussed in Chapter 4, this would encourage people to have faith in the unchanging value of the key currency. However, in contrast to the gold standard, other currencies were not fixed to gold. They were fixed to the US dollar, but provisions were made to allow for their rate to be occasionally adjusted. The thinking behind this was that if the underlying productivity of other countries' economies changed, the value of their currency should also change. For example, if a country experienced a natural disaster that destroyed their industrial base, they should be allowed to lower the value of their currency. This would encourage exports and help rebuild the economy.

The Bretton Woods conference created two international institutions to help oversee the operation of the international financial system: the International Monetary Fund (IMF) and the International Bank for Reconstruction and Development (IBRD, later known as the World Bank) (see Box 8.1). The monetary system was to be supported by the IMF. Its purpose was to help countries that had temporary balance of payments problems. If, for some reason, a country was unable to pay for its imports, the IMF could loan money to help them through a temporary cash shortage. This money would be repaid when the difficulty had been overcome.

The Bretton Woods system relied on people having faith that the US currency would be exchanged for gold at the fixed rate if there was a demand to do so. There was no reason to doubt this assumption in the 1950s. The US possessed large gold reserves as a result of its role as a safe haven and creditor during the two world wars. Many people and states wanted to hold US dollars because they were backed by gold, but were more valuable since you could earn interest on the dollars.

An economist named Robert Triffin noticed that there was a problem at the heart of this system (Eichengreen, 1996, p. 116). The problem, known as 'Triffin's dilemma', suggested that the world needed US dollars to participate in the international economy, but as US dollars flooded out into the world through the Marshall Plan, US defence spending and Americans buying foreign goods, the balance between dollars and gold would deteriorate until people lost faith that the US would be able to honour its commitment to gold. Eventually, there would be more dollars outside the US than gold inside and the US government would not be able to redeem dollars for gold. The outflow of dollars was needed to provide money or liquidity to other parts of the world, but this would eventually undermine the US's attempts at keeping its currency fixed to gold. Foreigners would begin to worry that the US would run out of gold and would start to cash in dollars for gold to make sure that they secured full value for their currency. In 1960, US foreign monetary liabilities first exceeded US gold reserves. In 1971, the US broke the link with gold. This subject is taken up in the major developments section.

Turning to the issue of credit, readers will recall from Part 1 that the credit mechanism is vital for economic growth and bestows a certain degree of power on those who issue it. In 1945, war-torn countries needed credit to rebuild, so US and British planners devised a system to funnel money to Europe. The centrepiece was the IBRD, which was designed to lend states money for long-term rebuilding projects. Despite these plans, the Western economies faced a serious problem. There was a severe liquidity shortage. The IBRD did not have enough funds to enable European states to rebuild and purchase goods, especially US goods that required US dollars. Other mechanisms had to be found to transfer capital. The US ended up transferring money through three mechanisms: the Marshall Plan, military spending and foreign investment. The Marshall Plan transferred about $13 billion in grants from the US government to western Europe. These

Box 8.1 Bretton Woods institutions

The IMF and the World Bank are sometimes referred to as the Bretton Woods institutions. The IMF's original role was to assist countries with short-term balance of payments problems. The IMF would lend money to countries that needed short-term financing to meet their external obligations. With the onset of the debt crisis in 1982, the IMF took on an expanded role, acting as a stamp of approval for countries undergoing structural adjustment programmes (SAPs). Countries in financial difficulty that wanted to resume borrowing from private banks would have to negotiate structural reforms with the IMF before they could access IMF and private bank funds. IMF programmes were based on the liberal 'Washington Consensus', which preached the value of open markets and balanced budgets. Although the IMF usually lends to developing countries, it also provides funds for developed states in financial difficulty, as can be seen in its loan to Britain in 1976 and loans to Greece in 2010–12.

The IMF is controlled by the board of governors, which comprises a representative of each of its 188 member states. The day-to-day running of the institution is performed by a smaller executive board of 24 members, which represents all the countries. Large countries such as China and the US have their own seats, while other countries are grouped into regions with a representative on the executive board. The board uses weighted voting, with percentages reflective of the amount of money the country pledges to the institution.

In addition to its lending activities, the IMF runs surveillance and technical programmes. Surveillance entails monitoring and producing reports on the global and national economies. Technical assistance involves providing advice to states (usually low- and middle-income countries) on topics such as managing central banks, designing tax policies, macroeconomic, monetary and exchange rate policies.

In contrast to the IMF, the World Bank was originally created to assist with long-term lending aimed at reconstructing countries after the Second World War and contributing to the development of poorer countries. Over past decades, it has adapted a number of different strategies to guide its work, from focusing on large infrastructure projects to providing for basic human needs, from SAPs similar to the IMF to sustainable development. The World Bank's role will be considered in more detail in Chapter 11 on economic development.

---

grants were used to assist reconstruction and bolster investor confidence.

The Marshall Plan was far more than a financial transaction as it was deeply rooted in Cold War politics. The US Congress was only persuaded to release the money for Europe following the communist coup in Czechoslovakia in 1948. The threat of a communist takeover in Europe was required before US legislators came to Europe's financial assistance. The strings attached to the grants were also influenced by Cold War rivalry. On the surface, the grants were available to any European state, including the Soviet Union and communist Eastern European states. However, a condition of disbursement was that the accepting state had to commit itself to liberalizing its economy and engaging in freer trade. This was impossible for any Eastern European state to accept because their policy of a planned economy could not be combined with an open economy. As a result, communist states were excluded from the inflow of liquidity that the US provided to its European allies. The US also insisted that recipients

cooperate in the administration and dispersal of funds. A new organization, the Organisation for European Economic Co-operation, was created to manage Marshall funds. This was one of the first postwar organizations facilitating European cooperation and integration. It was later expanded to states outside Europe and renamed the Organisation for Economic Co-operation and Development (OECD).

The immediate response to demands for reconstruction funds was met by public sources, primarily the US government. However, the trend until the end of the century would be for larger and larger percentages of international liquidity and credit to be distributed by private sources. A key element of this shift was the rise of the eurocurrency markets, which will be examined further below. The increased liberalization of financial markets also brought increased challenge for states managing their balance of payments (see Box 8.2). Before tracing the major developments in the monetary and credit systems, we'll pause to consider a theoretical insight from the field of economics.

> **Box 8.2** Balance of payments confusion
>
> The balance of payments is a record of the economic transactions between one country and the outside world. It comprises two parts – the current account and the capital account. The current account records the sum of the flow of goods and services between one country and the rest of the world. The capital account records the movement of short- and long-term capital. Any transaction that will lead to a payment to another country is registered as a debit. This includes purchasing imports and investing abroad. Any transaction that will lead to payment from another country is registered as a credit. Exports, inflow of FDI and profits on foreign investments all lead to credits. The balance of payments should always balance or be equal to zero because outflows of money to foreigners must be matched or financed by inflows. However, there are two complicating factors. First, no state is able to record all its trans-border economic transactions so the national balance of payments accounts do not balance on paper – there is always an error factor.
>
> Second, even though the payments balance, there is often reference to a balance of payments deficit when countries go through financial crisis. What does this mean? People are usually referring to a country being unable to pay for the goods and services it would like to import. In economic terms, the current account (goods and services) is in deficit and can no longer be financed by the capital account. The country is using internal resources such as the money held at the central bank to finance its external activity. Since foreign activity cannot be financed solely from limited domestic resources, a long-term balance of payments 'deficit' requires some action to restore the balance, such as reducing imports, devaluing the currency or structural adjustment.

THEORETICAL PERSPECTIVES: THE MUNDELL-FLEMING MODEL

There are three primary approaches to understanding the global financial system. Many in the financial community subscribe to a liberal view of the way the system should operate. The liberal view is that the exchange of currencies and provision of credit should be determined by private actors in the marketplace. As described below, the liberal view has picked up the label of the 'Washington Consensus'. This consensus is sometimes challenged by a more social democratic view, which attempts to temper market mechanisms and build in safeguards for financial stability and redistribution. This might involve slowing down the rate at which financial transactions occur or regulating the behaviour of private firms. Outside the corridors of power, variations of neoMarxist thought are highly critical of the liberal financial system because of instability and the promotion of inequality between and within states. Dependency analysts focus on how northern states are able to use the financial system to retain great influence in the economies of developing countries. For example, US

companies made considerable progress in Asian markets following the 1997 Asian financial crisis.

These different understandings of how the financial system operates will be recalled in the following sections. However, for now, we will focus on a theoretical proposition known as the 'Mundell-Fleming', which stresses the tension between maintaining the ability of money to cross borders freely (capital mobility), the existence of fixed or minimally floating currencies (stable exchange rates) and the ability of a country to set its own interest rates to influence domestic economic growth and employment (monetary policy). This relationship is important because it has implications for regional currencies, financial crises and national autonomy, which are all key issues of debate.

As far back as the 1960s, Mundell and Fleming (two economists) theorized that states could not simultaneously have an independent monetary policy (supply of money and interest rates), stable exchange rates (either fixed or with gradual movement) and free flows of capital in and out of the country (see Box 8.3). Two of these objectives might be pursued, but the third could not be achieved for any length of time because it would violate the other two. Governments have to choose their priorities. For example, if a

Box 8.3 Mundell-Fleming model summary

This models suggests that it is difficult to simultaneously pursue an independent monetary policy, a stable exchange rate and free capital flows. Why?

▶ If independent monetary policy and capital flows, the exchange rate will move.
▶ If independent monetary policy and a fixed exchange rate, capital flows must be curbed.
▶ If capital flows and a fixed exchange rate, monetary autonomy must be sacrificed.

government favours capital mobility to attract investment, then it must choose between a fixed exchange rate, which will facilitate trade and investment, and an autonomous monetary policy, which will support domestic economic conditions. If it chooses a fixed exchange rate, interest rates must support that policy by providing investors with returns that will keep their money in the country. If interest rates do not support the currency and instead target domestic concerns, such as unemployment, investors may move money out of the country, putting pressure on the exchange rate. The exchange rate comes under pressure because investors sell the currency as they move their money into other currencies and assets. This creates an excess supply of the currency, lowering its value and cost. If enough investors sell the currency, it will be devalued, as happened in Britain in 1992 and Thailand in 1997 (more on this below).

Alternatively, if a state chooses to control its own interest rates based on the domestic economy in an environment of capital mobility, the exchange rate will fluctuate. This fluctuation in exchange rates may influence trade flows as the costs of a country's exports rise or fall in line with currency fluctuations. Countries such as Australia, Canada, the US and the UK have capital mobility, floating exchange rates and interest rates responding to the domestic economy. However, if a country wants an independent monetary policy and fixed exchange rate, it will have to reduce capital flows. After the 1997 Asian financial crisis, Malaysia limited capital mobility by imposing capital controls so that it

could pursue domestic monetary priorities and stabilize the exchange rate.

The term 'monetary autonomy' refers to the ability of a country to control its own money supply and interest rates in a way that responds primarily to domestic economic conditions. In the 1950s and 60s, the decision about interest rates and money supply was usually taken by central banks under the direction of national governments. In the 1980s and 90s, many states made their central banks independent of government instruction and directed them to achieve low inflation. In times of slow economic growth and low inflation, central banks would lower interest rates and raise them when inflation increased. Committing to a fixed exchange rate means abandoning this policy tool because interest rates must be high enough to prevent investors from selling the currency.

These theoretical observations have moved from the academic world into difficult policy decisions for state leaders. Many states welcome capital mobility because it allows them to access more funds for investment and economic growth. Some states (mainly developing countries) have pursued fixed or stable exchange rates in order to reassure investors that the value of their money will not be lost through a depreciating currency, while others have wanted to avoid the uncertainty of fluctuating currencies. States also like to be able to have interest rates that respond to their own economies so that rates will be lowered during recessions to fight unemployment. However, these policies cannot be pursued simultaneously. As capital mobility has increased, it has become much more difficult for states to stabilize exchange rates *and* pursue nationally focused monetary policies (Pauly, 2000). In practice, most governments have opted for freeing capital flows and then struggled to strike a balance between having some domestic autonomy and an exchange rate that is either fixed or does not fluctuate too greatly. The goal of capital mobility has been easier to achieve than that of either exchange rate stability or domestic autonomy. We'll see just how difficult it has been to manage this trinity of factors when we consider financial crises below. In some cases, this has led to increasing turbulence in financial markets, in others it has contributed to deflationary national policies. The contradictions radiating from an increasingly liberal and global financial system have led to an intense search for new methods and institutions to govern an increasingly volatile system.

MAJOR DEVELOPMENTS

There have been dramatic changes in both the IMS and the provision of credit on a global basis since the post-war system was created. Here we highlight several major changes. In the IMS a major change has been the move from fixed to floating exchange rates. We also examine how regional currencies have arisen in response to the challenges of floating exchange rates. In the credit system, financial innovation has greatly accelerated the flow of money around the globe, while many states have experienced financial crises.

IMS: from fixed to floating and regional currencies

The system of fixed exchange rates was eventually undermined by the Triffin dilemma and the failure of countries to voluntarily adjust their exchange rates. In the late 1960s, the amount of dollars held outside the US exceeded the amount of gold held by the US government. Dollars had flowed out of the US because of the investment of US TNCs abroad, US military spending and the desire of foreigners to use the US currency. The excess of US dollars compared to gold made some states and investors nervous. For example, the French government insisted on turning in its dollars for gold. Investors sold dollars for other currencies, fearing that the US would be forced to break its link with gold. The US increasingly relied on foreign central banks to support the US currency by buying dollars and on foreign governments to stimulate imports from the US. One of the underlying problems was that even though European and Japanese economies were now much stronger, they were unwilling to revalue their currency against the dollar. By keeping rates fixed their industries gained an advantage over US industries. The overvalued dollar meant that foreign products were cheap for US consumers and US products were expensive in other countries. This contributed to a deterioration in the US trade balance.

In the summer of 1971, President Richard Nixon initiated what was called the 'Nixon Shock', when the US unilaterally changed the monetary system by ending the link between the US dollar and gold and simultaneously imposed a temporary 10 per cent tax on imports.

Cutting the link with gold resulted in a devaluation of the dollar as it began to float against other currencies. This was meant to restore the competitiveness of the US economy. Although there were attempts to re-establish a fixed system, it was clear by 1973 that currencies would float for the foreseeable future. Two lessons can be drawn from the ending of the system of fixed exchange rates (Eichengreen, 1996). The first is the difficulty of maintaining fixed or pegged exchange rates in the face of increasing capital mobility. The second is that a fixed system required considerable international cooperation, which had its limits.

No one was quite sure what the consequences of moving to floating rates might be. Some predicted that it would ease economic tensions because currencies would find their proper value in the market and adjustment would be automatic. Others feared chaos as fluctuating currencies made planning and trading more difficult. The result was somewhere in the middle. Exchange rates proved to be more volatile than advocates of floating rates suggested, but they did not result in immediate financial chaos. Governments intervened in the market by buying and selling currencies in an attempt to halt large swings.

Another significant change brought about by floating rates was that over time more and more exchange rate transactions were taking place to make a profit rather than to finance international trade or investment. The move to floating exchange rates, combined with the easing or eliminating of restrictions on exchanging currencies and financial innovation (discussed below), led to increased capital mobility and vastly increased activity in foreign exchange markets. The existence of floating rates highlighted the opportunity to make profits from large-scale currency transactions. As currencies changed in value, money could be made by buying currency A at one price and selling it when it appreciated (see Box 8.4). Alternatively, a currency that was going to be devalued could be sold at one point and then repurchased at a profit when its value declined.

Floating rates turned out to be more of a problem in the 1980s. In 1979, the Federal Reserve, the US central bank, moved against rising domestic inflation by dramatically raising interest rates. The hope was that higher US interest rates would slow the economy and stop price rises (inflation). If credit was more expensive, people and industries would borrow less and spend less, reducing demand. This reduced demand would stop

Box 8.4 Foreign exchange trading

Although the variations can be complicated, the underlying principle is simple. Profit can be made by selling a currency that will decline in value and then buying it back at a later time, or buying a currency at a low value and selling when it increases. For example, imagine that Susan has a dollar and wants to buy a euro. In this example, the dollar and the euro are equal in value, so Susan sells her $1.00 (US) for €1.00. If, by the next day, the euro rises in value or appreciates 10 per cent (10 cents) against the dollar, Susan can sell her €1 for $1.10, making a profit of 10 cents. If Susan had bought €100,000, her profit would be $10,000 for a minute of work. If these numbers are multiplied many times, the time period shortened from a minute to seconds, and losses as well as gains are factored in, one begins to get an idea of the frenzy of activity on foreign exchange markets.

inflation because people would be less able and willing to pay higher prices.

The effects of this change on exchange rates was dramatic. The higher US interest rates attracted investors into the US dollar, causing its value to rise. Between 1980 and 1982, it rose in value compared with other currencies by about 30 per cent. At the same time that the Federal Reserve tightened monetary policy through high interest rates, US president Ronald Reagan loosened fiscal (budgetary) policy by increasing military spending and cutting taxes. This gave Americans more money in their pockets to buy imports. President Reagan ignored the international consequences and pursued tight monetary and loose fiscal policy. The implications for US trade were dramatic. Other countries were able to increase their exports to the US and the US found it harder to sell its exports abroad. The result was a rising US trade deficit and calls for greater protectionism.

A system of ad hoc cooperation trying to coordinate the economies of Europe, North America and Japan emerged as a result of turbulence in the foreign exchange markets (Eichengreen, 1996, pp. 145–52). At the Plaza meeting in September 1985, the G5 (the US, Japan, Germany, the UK and France) agreed to take action to reduce the value of the dollar. All countries

wanted to head off the threat of increasing US protectionism. The markets responded to this initiative and the dollar fell rapidly, losing 40 per cent from its peak against European and Japanese currencies. Two years later at the Louvre meeting of the G7 (G5 plus Canada and Italy), the Japanese agreed to stimulus measures, the Germans to tax cuts and the US to stabilize the dollar through adjustments in domestic policy. In the second half of 1988, the dollar resumed its decline.

The western European response to increasing exchange rate volatility was to try to create their own zone of currency stability called the European Monetary System. European leaders were dissatisfied with floating rates because of the problem of overshooting. When investors moved out of the dollar, they tended to rush to the German deutsche mark (DM), knocking it out of line with European currencies. At these times, the DM experienced severe currency appreciation (an increase in value compared with other currencies), which made it difficult for Germany to export its goods, while the depreciation of other currencies caused inflation in those states. The Germans wanted to take pressure off the DM. If there were fixed rates, an investor would be just as happy to hold French francs as German marks. It was also hoped that fixed rates would build confidence and investment, encouraging transnational European companies (Swann, 1992, pp. 181–220).

The European solution was the creation of the ECU and the exchange rate mechanism (ERM). The ECU was a composite currency for bookkeeping purposes. States committed themselves to limiting the fluctuation of their exchange rate to the ECU by no more or less than a given percentage below the central rates. Once a currency reached its bilateral limit, the central banks of each country intervened in the foreign exchange markets by buying or selling currencies to support the one in difficulty. For example, if the Irish punt was about to fall out of the band, the Irish and other central banks would sell their foreign reserves to buy punts. In some cases, such as the UK (see Box 8.5), countries were unable to maintain the required level and were forced out of the ERM by massive capital flows. Nevertheless, the ERM laid the groundwork for the eventual introduction of a single currency, the euro.

On 1 January 2002, 12 EU member states (Austria, Belgium, Finland, France, Germany, Greece, Ireland, Luxembourg, the Netherlands, Italy, Portugal, Spain) introduced the euro and began to phase out their

---

Box 8.5 Black Wednesday: UK forced out of the ERM

When Britain joined the ERM in 1990, its currency was fixed at a relatively high level compared with the other ERM countries. This hurt British exports to Europe and had a depressing effect on the British economy. In an environment of capital mobility, Britain was forced to keep interest rates high to attract investors into the pound to maintain its level in the ERM. In the late summer and early autumn of 1992, investors began to doubt that the British government would be able to continue to support a high pound in the face of deepening recession in the UK. They began to sell the pound for other currencies, fearing that the UK government would eventually drop out of the ERM and their investments would decrease in value as the currency depreciated. Even though the British government was committed to defending the pound by raising interest rates and the Bank of England used its foreign currency reserves to buy pounds on the market, investors continued to sell the currency. On 'Black Wednesday' (16 September 1992), the British government gave up its defence of the pound and withdrew from the ERM.

During this period, investors, sometimes labelled 'speculators', bet that the British currency would be devalued so they sold pounds for other currencies. It was a safe bet. If the government succeeded in keeping the pound in a narrow band through the ERM, the investors would only lose the money that it cost them to exchange currencies. However, if the pound did fall out of the ERM, it could decline significantly and vast fortunes would be made. The most famous speculator in this event was George Soros who was rumoured to have made $1 billion by selling the pound. Some view this activity as damaging speculation. Wealth is created without anything actually being produced. It is also suggested that massive flows of money in and out of countries weaken otherwise healthy currencies and economies, creating economic hardship. An opposite, more liberal view is that foreign exchange fluctuations serve a positive role by signalling when economies are pursuing harmful policies. This encourages governments to adopt corrective measures. A third position might hold that currencies react to real problems, but that because of the volume and speed at which they operate, a herd mentality among investors can cause unnecessary economic damage.

---

national currencies. Five other member states joined in following years (Slovenia, Cyprus, Malta, Slovakia, Estonia). By 2012, 17 of the 27 EU member states, covering over 330 million people, used the euro rather than national currencies. States joining the euro sacrificed national monetary autonomy in return for currency stability. The operation of the euro is overseen by the European Central Bank (ECB). After consultation with representatives from the national central banks, the ECB sets a single interest rate for all member states. It also manages the exchange rate between the euro and other currencies. The primary goal of the ECB is price stability, which means low inflation. In response to fears that some countries might not respect low inflation levels and might be tempted to run budget deficits, EU members agreed to a Stability and Growth Pact in June 1997. This stipulated that national governments must not run an annual budget deficit of more than 3 per cent of GDP. In theory, fines could be applied to states that did not comply, but in practice states were easily able to violate the pact.

The drive to adopt the euro prompted considerable public debate. A number of objections were raised. One issue was that countries would lose the ability to devalue their currencies if an economic shock hit their country. For example, a country reliant on oil exports such as Britain or Norway might be hit by low oil prices. With their own currency, Britain would probably devalue, letting exports in other industries make up for employment losses in the oil industry. Under a single currency this would not be possible. The result might be that particular areas of the EU could stagnate as they lost the ability to adjust their currencies. Another objection was that a single monetary policy and interest rate may not suit such a diverse continent. For example, the Irish economy might expand while the German economy stagnated. Because of the large size of the German economy, it is likely that in such a situation European interest rates would be lowered to boost German economic growth. This would help Germany, but hurt Ireland. The low interest rates in Ireland would fuel consumer and business spending and cause inflation. It could create economic bubbles in the Irish housing market as wealthy consumers and investors took advantage of low interest rates.

Opponents argued that the mechanisms that allowed federal states such as the US to overcome these problems were absent in Europe (Feldstein, 1992). The lack of labour mobility and absence of transfer payments were striking. Because of language and cultural barriers, Europeans were much less likely to migrate to jobs in another part of Europe. Many would stay in a stagnant area rather than move. Another difference with federal states is that there was little transfer of funds from richer to poorer areas for development or equalization payments. In the end, although there were economic arguments in favour of and against the euro, the decision to push forward was taken by those wishing to form a closer political union. The single currency was seen as a way of increasing the bonds between European citizens in preparation for closer political ties.

The creation of the euro was undertaken as much for its contribution to political union as its alleged economic benefits. In other parts of the world there is not the same desire for political union. Nevertheless, there have been moves by some states to reduce or eliminate their national currency in favour of a foreign currency. The general name for this trend is 'dollarization', although it can occur with a number of different currencies, not just the US dollar. Here we will look at dollarization in the Americas, where it does in fact occur through use of the US dollar.

Dollarization can take place in two ways and for two reasons (Dean and Globerman, 2001). The two ways it can take place are de facto (in fact) and de jure (in law). De facto dollarization means that national currencies still exist, but a large number of people use the dollar in practice. It is dollarization in fact. De jure dollarization means dollarization in law. This occurs when the national currency is legally replaced with the US dollar. Since the 1980s, de facto dollarization has occurred in many countries of the Americas, while de jure dollarization has occurred in Panama, Ecuador and El Salvador.

Why would a country give up or reduce the use of its own currency? One reason is that individuals and businesses may lose faith in their own currency. High inflation or repeated devaluations may encourage people to hold their money in foreign currency as a preferred store of wealth. Fearing that their money may

lose its value, they choose to hold a safer currency, in this case the US dollar. A particularly severe case of this occurred in Zimbabwe in 2009 (see Box 8.6). A second reason for adopting another currency is to facilitate trade relations with a dominant economic partner. For example, Canada's economy is heavily reliant on trade with the US. If Canada adopted the US dollar, it would increase economic exchange and eliminate problems of fluctuating currencies. In this case, Canadians (especially businesses) might favour the US dollar as the best medium of exchange.

In the case of Latin American countries, dollarization would bring some economic benefits. Foreign investors would no longer fear that they would lose money when a currency declined. It would be less risky to invest in Latin America. This should lead to more foreign investment and growth. Money would also become cheaper in dollarized countries. At the moment, Latin American states must pay an interest premium when lending domestically. This means that they must pay higher interest rates than the US to encourage

---

Box 8.6 Dollarization, 'randization' and 'pulaization' in Zimbabwe

One reason why countries may be tempted to accept foreign currencies rather than produce their own is to combat runaway inflation. In early 2009, Zimbabwe experienced an upsurge in its rate of hyperinflation. Its inflation rate was approximately 89 sextillion per cent (89 followed by 21 zeros). Prices in stores doubled every day. The central bank printed so much money that the Zimbabwean dollar lost almost all its value. The central bank actually printed a note whose face value was a hundred trillion dollars ($100,000,000,000,000). Faced with hyperinflation and a collapse in the value of its currency, the Zimbabwean government essentially abandoned its own currency by announcing that all domestic purchases could be made in foreign currencies. Retailers and shops instantly began to accept US dollars, South African rand and Botswana pulas. The sudden appearance of viable currencies led to a reopening of shops and a rapid increase in economic activity (York, 2009).

investors to buy government bonds and securities. This is necessary because their currency is a riskier investment. By adopting the US dollar, this risk premium would disappear.

Despite obvious advantages, there are serious disadvantages to the dollarization process. Unlike the European example, there is no effort to make US monetary policy sensitive to the needs of other countries. There would be no central bank of the Americas similar to the ECB in Europe. Countries that enter into dollarization will have their money supply and interest rates controlled by the US. This may reduce economic growth if the US pursues a monetary policy that is contrary to the needs of the dollarized country. If a dollarized economy experiences some form of economic shock, it will be unable to devalue its currency to restore competitiveness. Adjustment will have to take place by further depressing real wages and reducing incomes.

In a dollar bloc, it is likely that most of the financial institutions will be from the US. These institutions may not have much interest in lending money to small local businesses, poorer individuals, farmers and local governments. Clients of the formerly national institutions could well be starved of credit, hampering economic growth. On the other hand, dollarization may feed speculative bubbles as funds flow into particular sectors and flow out again with similar ease.

In short, dollarization offers some advantages, but creates more restraints on state policies. It reduces their flexibility and policy levers. If there are no funds to help with the process of adjustment (none are proposed), the economic costs of dollarization could prove to be very high. This in turn would probably lead to increased domestic political conflict as the costs of adjustment are distributed unequally through the national economy.

The advent of the euro and the dollarization process indicates several things about the IMS. First, many states are willing to consider the benefits of abandoning their national currency in favour of joining a currency bloc. In the European case, this is part of a deep process of economic and political integration. In the Americas, the motivation is primarily economic gain. Second, the existing IMS is not serving the interests of many of its members. Many developing countries cannot trade or borrow unless they do so in a major currency such as the US dollar. They must pay for goods in dollars and loans are denominated in dollars. Countries must continually earn more dollars to engage in international economic transactions. This means that they are vulnerable to any shock that upsets their economic relationship with the outside world.

In the 2000s, currency misalignment was once again a major issue, but this time between the US and China. The US ran a record trade deficit with China and argued that China should allow its currency to float freely against the dollar. A floating currency would rise in value against the dollar, making American products cheaper in China and Chinese products more expensive in the US. However, the issue of the 'proper' value of the Chinese and US currencies is complicated. The US relies on China to fund its budget deficits and China relies on the US to buy its exports. A deterioration in their financial relationship could hurt both countries.

Credit: financial innovation and repeated crises

Two remarkable features of the global financial system have been the degree of innovation and the repeated instances of financial crises. Advances in telecommunications such as fax, high-speed telephone lines, satellite connections and the internet have allowed financial transactions to take place at a much faster pace and greater volume. New types of financial products have been introduced to provide investors with more options. Despite, or perhaps because of, such advances, financial crises have spread to every region of the world.

One of the major financial innovations was the creation of offshore financial markets, sometimes called eurocurrency (or eurodollar) markets. The term 'eurocurrency markets' is a bit misleading because the market does not just consist of European currencies. 'Eurocurrency markets' refers to a wide series of financial transactions that take place in currencies other than the currency of the state in which the business is being conducted. For example, the eurocurrency market was initially composed of the exchange of US dollars in London. The eurocurrency market in New York operates in funds other than US dollars. The market in the Cayman Islands operates in any currency other than the local one. The primary reason why financial operators do not use the local currency is because state authorities do not regulate their activity if they are working with foreign currencies.

The eurocurrency market began in London after the Second World War and met several needs. The British state supported its expansion because it brought financial business back to London and helped the city re-establish its role as an important financial centre. The Soviet Union made use of the market as a place where it could store and exchange US dollars beyond the reach of its Cold War rival, the US. US corporations investing in Europe increasingly used the market to escape restrictive US laws on banking activity. However, the big jump in the euromarkets' size came with the 1973 oil crisis and the increase in revenues flowing to OPEC states (Organization of Petroleum Exporting Countries). Many of these states turned to the euromarkets to conduct their banking. Estimates of the money put into the markets show it rising from $3 billion in 1960 to $75 billion in 1970 to $1,000 billion by 1984 (Strange, 1988, p. 105).

Alongside the rise of currency markets, the 1970s and 80s saw a global financial revolution. Capital was increasingly flowing between countries in larger volumes and at faster speeds. Technological advances allowed for cheap, instantaneous, constant communication. In the late 1970s and early 1980s, a number of key states eliminated capital controls, allowing individuals and corporations to move their money freely in or out of their country. The US took this step in 1974 and the UK followed in 1979. In 1986, the UK increased liberalization in its financial industry through what was called the 'Big Bang'. This was the name given to financial deregulation in Britain. It involved two major elements. The first was allowing any foreign company to enter the UK's stock market and foreign exchanges.

The second step was to allow banks, stockbroking firms and insurance companies to compete in each other's industries. This broke down the barriers that had formerly stipulated that only banks could engage in banking, insurance companies in insurance and stockbrokers in selling stocks. The advantage of this deregulation was that it increased competition in the financial industry. The disadvantage was that this competition might push some firms into more risky behaviour, possibly leading to financial crises.

The liberalization of financial activity resulted in both increased competition and a series of financial crises. Financial products proliferated, with a range of new instruments coming onto the market. These included currency swaps, futures, options and derivatives.

However, financial problems also arose. In the UK, an economic boom followed on the creation of new wealth from the enlivened financial markets. However, the boom turned to bust in 1988 following the 1987 stock market crash and the collapse in the housing market. Fuelled by the expansion in credit, many people bought houses at overinflated prices and suffered the consequences when the economy slowed.

The financial liberalization and innovation of the 1980s accelerated in the 1990s. Large sums of money were expended to manage and profit from the increasing risks of the volatile financial markets. An increasingly popular method of coping with the risks (the possibility that exchange rates, the rate of inflation or the price of commodities might change) was the use of derivatives. The two most common forms are futures and options. These are derived or spun off from stocks or bonds. A future commits someone to buying a stock or a commodity at a specified time in the future for a price set today. Futures can be bought on margin, which means that the purchaser only has to put down a percentage of the purchase price when committing to the deal and the rest when the future comes due. Futures have been very common in the agricultural field where someone would agree to buy a farmer's product six months before it was available. This gave the farmer a guaranteed price and some security against the risk of planting a crop and then receiving a low price during the harvest period. One might also buy oil futures if there was fear that oil prices would rise in the future. An option requires someone to pay a small fee for the opportunity to buy a stock or bond at a specified price at a specified time. If the price of the commodity goes down, the trader can back out of the purchase, but lose their fee. If the price goes up, they can buy the commodity and sell it for a profit.

Used wisely, derivatives can insure businesses and individuals against the risks of falling or rising prices. However, they are also used to make money in themselves. Traders and investors use them to make money by betting on the value of a product at some time in the future. If they are correct about the price movement, they can sell at a profit. If they are incorrect, they suffer a financial loss. Since these products can be bought on margin, large sums of money can be pledged without having the ability to pay at the time of purchase. This kind of a system encourages investors to take risks for potentially large pay-offs. We'll consider some of the dangers of rapid innovation in the key issues section. In general, financial innovation has been aimed at wealthy clients, but this is not always the case (see Box 8.7).

The 1990s and 2000s also saw the rise of two other large financial players – sovereign wealth funds and hedge funds. Sovereign wealth funds are investment companies created and controlled by national governments. They are economic nationalist instruments that allow governments to gather revenues and direct them into strategic foreign investments. Sovereign wealth funds are dominated by countries that have large surpluses of cash (oil exporters or countries with large trade surpluses) and favour state intervention in the economy. The biggest sovereign wealth funds are controlled by the United Arab Emirates, Singapore, Norway, Kuwait, Russia and China. It was estimated in 2007 that these funds held $2.5–3 trillion in assets (Weissman, 2007). In some countries, the rise of such funds has caused concern because they do not behave in the same manner as private companies, may threaten other states' national interests, and are accused of engaging in transnational 'nationalization' rather than transnational investment.

Hedge funds are financial companies that engage in complicated financial transactions in which combinations of assets are bought and sold over short and long time frames (Krugman, 2008, pp. 120–2). Along with other financial innovations, their abuse has contributed to a number of private sector financial crises (see Box 8.8). Buying 'short' positions involves borrowing a stock from its owner for a period of time. The stock is initially sold and then bought at a future date and returned to the owner. If the value of the stock falls during this period, the hedge fund makes money because it sold the stock when it was high and bought it back when it dropped in value. A 'short' position is taken when one believes the value of the asset (oil, currencies) will fall over time. The profit is usually invested in a long position or an asset whose value will increase over time. Hedge funds have three characteristics that led them to play an important role in the financial crisis:

1 The hedging is done with very little capital, allowing the funds to take very large positions in the markets.
2 Hedge funds offer large financial returns when they do well, but imprudent bets can result in financial disaster since the funds are so heavily leveraged.
3 Hedge funds largely operate beyond government regulation so that government officials have been largely unaware of their massive size and extensive holdings.

Box 8.7 Microcredit: financial innovation for the poor

Not all financial innovation is for rich people. Microcredit was created to improve poor people's access to credit. Poor people are often not able to access credit and if they can get it, it is usually on very poor terms and at extremely high interest rates. Women find it particularly difficult to secure credit because they often do not have assets to secure loans or are seen as poor lending risks by bankers. In the 1970s, an innovative credit programme, which distributed small loans directly to poor people (often women), began in Bangladesh. The Grameen Bank (www.grameen.com) pioneered small loans (about $100) to poor people so that they could generate income from self-employment. These loans were usually distributed to groups of borrowers and given without asking for collateral. The philosophy was that poor people could improve their circumstances with a small amount of credit to kick-start economic activity.

The Grameen model enjoyed considerable success in channelling credit to poor people. By the 1990s, it had been taken up as a model form of finance by the UN and the World Bank. A Microcredit Summit was held in February 1997 in Washington DC, which brought together microcredit participants from around the world. Their goal was to launch a campaign to bring microcredit to 100 million of the poorest people through financing self-employed poor women (www.microcreditsummit.org). In October 2006, the Grameen Bank and its founder Muhammad Yunus were awarded the Nobel Peace Prize for their development work.

While microcredit has attracted considerable positive publicity, concerns have also been raised about its role in the global economy. Some critics have argued that while microcredit might make poverty slightly more bearable, it does nothing to tackle the larger political and economic structures that foster poverty (Elahi, 2004). Others see microcredit as an attempt to suppress political opposition to poverty by improving the welfare of a few people, while discouraging attempts at broader-based social change (Weber, 2004).

Box 8.8 Financial innovation and crisis in the private sector

Two financial collapses of the 1990s illustrate that the proliferation of financial instruments is difficult to regulate through market mechanisms and that they are also risky to employ even for the most brilliant financial and mathematical minds. In 1995, Barings Bank collapsed because it was unable to detect the irregular activity of one financial trader. Over the summer of 1995, Nick Leeson, an employee of Barings Bank in Singapore, used derivatives to place a series of bets that the Japanese economy would prosper in the following years. Unfortunately for Japan and Barings Bank, economic recession continued and Japan was struck by a large earthquake. When the dust had settled and the margins were called, Barings could not cover its losses. The bank collapsed and Leeson spent time in prison in Singapore. Criminals can be found in any organization, but what is striking is that the bank was unable to monitor its employee's actions and that it gave so much financial power to individual traders.

An even more cautionary tale is that of Long Term Capital Management. This was an investment firm set up by leaders in the financial field, including two economics Nobel Prize winners, numerous mathematics PhDs and people with backgrounds in Wall Street firms and the Federal Reserve. They created a hedge fund that used derivatives to make large sums of money for their wealthy clients and banks. All their mathematical models proved of no assistance when Russia experienced economic difficulty in 1998 and the fund's assets disappeared. The US financial system teetered on the brink of collapse before a number of private financial institutions stepped in to pick up the pieces at the urging of the US government (Blustein, 2001, pp. 305–36). A system that encourages financial risk led a group of talented financial minds to financial ruin and almost caused a national and international financial crisis.

For developing states, the liberalization of capital markets created the enabling conditions for the 1980s' debt crisis. A combination of supply and demand factors help us understand why developing countries became exposed to large debt (Lever and Huhne, 1986), but decisions about interest rates in developed states led to the onset of the crisis. On the supply side, vast sums of money became available for lending purposes in the 1970s. The rise in oil prices had a dramatic effect on the international credit market. It caused a shift in wealth from oil consumers to oil producers. The producers, primarily OPEC members, invested some of their money in the eurodollar markets. This money then had to be lent out if the banks were to turn a profit. Bankers were flooded with cash and eagerly looked around for potential customers. Fortunately for the banks, there was a great demand for credit. Developing countries were desperate for funds to help them industrialize their economies. In some cases, developing countries were oil consumers and required loans to help pay for rising oil prices. In other cases, a decision had been made to follow a strategy of indebted industrialization (Frieden, 1981). This meant that states borrowed money to invest in industrialization and hoped that they could pay off the loans from the profits of their new industries. Loans were an attractive option because they did not come with the influence of foreign TNCs that accompanied FDI, and most states had few funds of their own to invest.

In the late 1960s and early 1970s, developing states appeared to be a sound investment because many had indeed enjoyed high growth rates up to that point. The market appeared to be working well by bringing together the capital rich and the capital poor to the benefit of both. However, events at the end of the 1970s took a turn for the worse and the debt crisis erupted in 1982. In 1979, Ayatollah Khomeini was able to overthrow the Shah of Iran in the Iranian revolution. Not long afterwards, war erupted as Iraq invaded Iran in a misjudged attempt to take advantage of the political turmoil. The result was a second oil shock. The US response to this oil shock was considerably different from that in 1973. Rather than let the higher prices move through the US economy via inflation, a decision was taken by the chairman of the US Federal Reserve to fight inflation by raising interest rates. Interest rates would reduce the rise in prices because credit would be more expensive and people would have less money to spend or invest. This would reduce the amount of money chasing goods and services, reducing demand, leading to a slowdown in price rises (deflation).

The effect of this policy in the US was the onset of recession. The effects in other parts of the world were much more serious. The cost of international money went up, following the increase in US interest rates. Whereas interest rates on international loans were about 2 per cent in the early 1970s, they rose to over 18 per cent in the early 1980s. This greatly increased the interest charges to developing states on their international loans. At the same time that developing states were facing higher interest charges, it became more difficult for them to sell their products to developed states. The recession that swept the developed world reduced imports in two ways. Recession meant that demand for imports went down in general. In addition, recession fed protectionist forces in developed states, resulting in the restriction of imports to support domestic jobs.

The consequences for many developing countries were disastrous. Those states that were oil importers were faced with massive bills to cover their debts. Those developing states that were oil exporters (such as Mexico and Venezuela) were hurt because they had borrowed heavily to industrialize and were then caught as oil prices fell in response to lower demand during the recession. In August 1982, Mexico announced that it could no longer service its debt. This meant that it could no longer cover the cost of interest payments, much less hope to repay the debt. Mexico's announcement burst the bubble and ushered in the debt crisis, as banks recognized their exposure to a series of bad loans. Private funds flowing into Mexico and some other states halted. Before long, it was evident that states such as Brazil, Venezuela, Argentina and many sub-Saharan African countries were in equally difficult financial positions.

It was in these circumstances that the IMF began to play a more prominent role. It negotiated standby loans with debtors, offering temporary assistance to states in need. In return for the loans, states agreed to undertake economic reforms. These SAPs required countries to liberalize trade, attract foreign investment and reduce state subsidies and bureaucracies to balance national budgets. The phrase 'Washington Consensus' was coined to capture the agreement on economic policy that was shared between the two major international financial institutions in Washington (the IMF and the World Bank) and the US government itself. The Washington Consensus stipulated that the best path to economic development was through financial and trade liberalization and that international institutions should persuade countries to adopt such measures as quickly as possible. Although the Washington Consensus referred to conventional wisdom, critics of the IMF and the World Bank associate the term with all that is wrong with rapid economic liberalization. In their eyes, it stands for harmful and arrogant policies determined by financial and Western elites and imposed on developing states. The rise and stall of the Washington Consensus is developed in more detail in Chapter 13.

The effects of these policies on the population in developing countries were devastating. The 1980s is known as the 'lost decade' of development. Many developing countries' economies were smaller and poorer in 1990 than in 1980. Over the 1980s and 90s, debt in many developing countries was so great that governments had few resources to spend on social services and development (see Table 8.1).

The effects of the debt crisis went well beyond financial indicators. In sub-Saharan Africa, debt burdens greatly complicated responses to the AIDS crisis. Approximately 5,000 people die every day from AIDS in Africa and the disease has rolled back previous gains in life expectancy and development. SAPs designed to

Table 8.1 National expenditure on social services versus debt

Region/country	Year(s)	Percentage of central government expenditure on	
		Basic social services	Debt service
Africa			
Tanzania	1994–5	15	46
Kenya	1995	13	40
Uganda	1994–5	21	9
South Africa	1996–7	14	8
Asia			
Philippines	1992	8	31
Sri Lanka	1996	13	22
Nepal	1997	14	15
Thailand	1997	15	1
Latin America and Caribbean			
Jamaica	1996	10	31
Brazil	1995	9	20
Costa Rica	1996	13	13
Chile	1996	11	3

Source: Adapted from UNICEF (1999), p. 32

address debt problems led to the downsizing or privatization of health and educational services (Cheru, 2002). This weakened governments' ability to provide healthcare and information about AIDS to their populations. Money that might have gone into public health campaigns was diverted to pay off external debt. Efforts by the World Bank and the IMF in 1996 to reduce the debt loads of heavily indebted poor countries (the HIPC Initiative) freed up some money for some countries. However, given the extreme health emergency, broader and more rapid cancellation of external debt was required.

The debt crisis sealed the 'triumph of neoclassical economics' in most developing countries (Biersteker, 1992). Starved of international finance, states had little choice but to open their economies to foreign investors and trade. Mexico is the most dramatic example.

Following its revolution in the early part of the 20th century, Mexico had tried to follow a development strategy that stressed the building of a national economy. It was a leading advocate of import substitution industrialization. Mexico erected tariff barriers against imports and tried to produce its own goods behind these barriers. However, following the debt crisis, Mexican policy concentrated on integrating itself into the international market. As the 1980s and 90s progressed, more and more developing countries followed a similar path. McMichael (1996) has described this as a transition from a development model of national economic growth to a globalization model of searching for a 'niche' in the world market. The Mexican liberalization process was capped and solidified when it signed the 1993 North American Free Trade Agreement (NAFTA) along with Canada and the US. NAFTA locked in Mexico's liberal reforms because it acted as an economic constitution for North America. However, despite the policy changes in many developing states, the burden of debt compared with gross national product (GNP) continued to grow in the 1980s and 90s (see Figures 8.1 and 8.2).

While the debt crisis was severe and had a long-lasting impact, it was followed by a series of other crises – another one in Mexico (see Box 8.9), one in formerly prosperous East Asia (see Box 8.10) and in the financial system itself with the collapse of private companies. One leading observer of the operation of the global financial markets termed it 'casino capitalism' (Strange, 1986). Strange argued that the increased volatility in most markets and the lack of sensible regulation over transactions had turned the financial markets into one large casino. Investors placed bets on the future of company profits, commodity prices, exchange rates, interest rates and many other economic indicators. The large sums involved and the rapidity with which money travelled encouraged investors to take risks and increased the possibility that crises would occur. Crucially, this casino has many involuntary players. People not placing the bets suffer the consequences when the financial wheel of fortune takes a bad turn. The citizens of developed states bear the cost of financial bailouts through their taxes, and the population of developing states pay through reduced living standards and, in some cases, malnutrition and death.

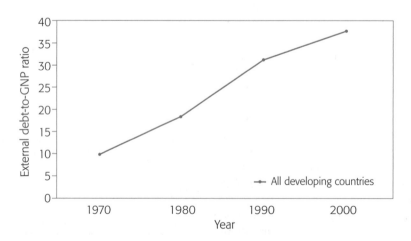

Figure 8.1 Developing country external debt as a percentage of GNP

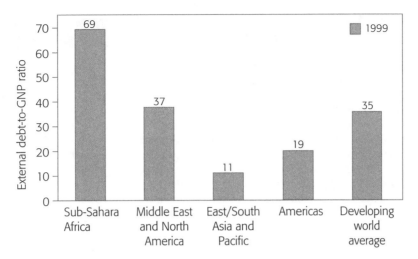

Figure 8.2 Regional averages: external debt as a percentage of GNP

Box 8.9 Financial crisis: Mexico

Although Mexico underwent massive restructuring as a result of the 1980s' debt crisis, it plunged into another crisis in the mid-1990s. The decade had started well enough for Mexico. Its negotiation and signing of NAFTA had convinced investors that the government was committed to liberalization. Between 1990 and 1993, $91 billion flowed into Mexico, a fifth of all capital going to developing states (Strange, 1998, p. 103). Money flowed into the stock market, boosting share prices and creating a sense of increasing wealth. However, a series of events, including higher US interest rates, rebellion in the state of Chiapas and the assassination of a presidential candidate, caused investors to doubt whether Mexico could maintain its fixed exchange rate with the US dollar. In December 1994, investors sold the Mexican peso in such large quantities that the government ran down its foreign currency reserves and was forced to abandon the link with the dollar. Although Mexico was committed to capital mobility (to attract investment) and exchange rate stability (to keep the investment), it was unable to withstand the destruction caused by rapid capital flows. When it was over, the Mexican government owed over $55 billion, mostly to private foreign investors such as pension funds. The US government, over the objection of the Congress, committed $20 billion to a rescue package and pressed the IMF and the Bank for International Settlements (BIS, the central bankers' central bank, based in Basel, Switzerland) to contribute another $32 billion. The effects of the crisis on Mexicans were disastrous as living standards were cut in half. The poor suffered enormously and the middle class faced huge debts because of skyrocketing interest rates and the diminishing of their savings when the peso devalued.

The Mexican crisis was notable for several reasons:

1 It spilled over into other countries such as Brazil and Argentina, forcing them to take defensive measures such as raising their interest rates to stop capital flight. This became known as the 'Tequila effect'.
2 Mexico suffered a severe financial crisis despite having undergone over a decade of liberalization and economic restructuring after the first debt crisis.
3 The dangers of the flow of short-term capital into and out of a developing country were highlighted by the Mexican events.
4 The players on the creditor side had changed. In the 1982 crisis, it was banks that were involved and eventually had to accept some losses on their loans. In 1994, it was non-bank actors such as pension funds, mutual funds and stock market investors that pulled the money out. Thanks to the US/IMF/BIS loan, investors escaped with relatively little financial loss. The Mexican people were not as fortunate.

Box 8.10 Financial crisis: East Asia

East Asia's financial crisis was surprising because it hit a group of countries that had been held out as success stories – the newly industrializing countries of East and Southeast Asia. In 1997, South Korea, Malaysia, Thailand and Indonesia suffered serious financial crisis. Hong Kong, Taiwan and even China were threatened by turmoil as well. Yet, only a few years earlier, the World Bank (1993) had issued a report praising the 'development miracles' of East Asia. How could this have come about?

In July 1997, investors started to have doubts about whether the government of Thailand would be able to maintain the value of its currency against the US dollar. Similar to events in Mexico in 1994 and Britain in 1992, they began to sell the local currency, betting that the government would eventually have to devalue. After defeating the Thai peg, attention turned to other countries in Asia. Successful speculative attacks were mounted against Indonesia, Malaysia and South Korea, and unsuccessful attacks took place against China and Hong Kong. States formerly thought to be in good shape were forced to turn to the IMF for financial assistance.

There are several interesting aspects of the Asian crisis:

1 It revealed the degree to which almost any developing state could be subject to a financial crisis in a very short period of time.
2 The states affected by capital outflows adopted very different policies. Thailand closely followed advice from the IMF, as did Indonesia and South Korea later. In contrast, the Malaysian government blamed foreigners for provoking the crisis and instituted capital controls to prevent rapid inflows and outflows of funds.
3 Although many in the US government saw the reforms requested of states in crisis as natural and advisable, many in Asia saw them as an opportunity for US businesses and state elites to take advantage of Asian weakness (Higgott, 1998).

These repeated crises led to a questioning of the stability of the global financial system. Investors, alarmed by a crisis in one part of the world, had the tendency to remove money from other parts of the world, thus spreading panic beyond the initial problem cases. This is known as 'contagion' and is a considerable source of worry for money managers and state elites. The official response to these fears was to begin a discussion about new forms of governance in international finance. Hundreds of studies and many hours of meetings were devoted to the topic of a 'new financial architecture'. The two substantial institutional innovations that emerged out of this process in 1999 were the Financial Stability Forum (FSF) and the Group of Twenty (G20).

The FSF brings together officials from the G7 with representatives of a wide range of international financial institutions and regulators. Representatives from the IMF and the World Bank are joined by those from the OECD, the BIS, the Basel Committee on Banking Supervision, the International Organization of Securities Commissions, the International Association of Insurance Supervisors, the Committee on the Global Financial System and the Committee on Payments and

Settlements. The FSF has concentrated its work on three issues: offshore financial centres, cross-border capital flows and highly leveraged institutions (hedge funds). Its investigation of offshore financial centres confirmed the view that these areas contributed to systemic instability. It proposed that more information about offshore centres should be gathered and that they be pressured to comply with international standards.

A more politically oriented body was created with the founding of the G20 in September 1999. The G20 is composed of the finance ministers and central bank governors of the G7 states plus a further 12 countries – Argentina, Australia, Brazil, China, India, Indonesia, South Korea, Mexico, Russia, Saudi Arabia, South Africa, Turkey – and a representative of the EU. G20 meetings also invite representatives of the key international institutions such as the IMF, the World Bank and the WTO to participate in their discussions. The G20 accounts for over 85 per cent of the world's GDP and 65 per cent of the world's population. Whereas the FSF is essentially a gathering of the most economically developed states, the G20 includes several of the largest developing states (Brazil, China, India and Indonesia).

This is an attempt to bolster the legitimacy of financial reforms by having a broader base of countries participate in decision-making. The G7 countries suffered from the accusation that they were a rich man's club.

Initially, the G20 concentrated on reviewing codes and standards for financial transactions and exchange rates. It was thought that the institution could serve as an arena where policy could be formulated and implementation followed up. The larger multilateral institutions of the IMF and the World Bank could take formal decisions after the G20 reached a consensus. At its second annual meeting in Montreal in October 2000, the G20 broadened its future agenda to include issues of social safety nets, infectious diseases, the environment and debt relief (G20, 2000). It is doubtful whether the G20 framework has the resources to handle these issues, but public concern about the consequences of financial liberalization has forced it to take up a broader agenda. In the wake of the 2008 US credit crisis that spread to many other countries, the G20 was given an expanded role.

Returning to the Asian financial crisis, a crucial aspect of the debate around the Asian financial crisis and the stability of the international monetary system was whether the primary problem was with the units or the structure of the system. A problem with the units would mean that there was something wrong with the policies that individual states were following. They might be spending their money in a wasteful manner, following inefficient economic policies, borrowing excessively or have a financial system that lacked transparency. A system fault would mean that there was something wrong in how international finance was organized. This could stem from markets that moved too rapidly, or incentives to firms to engage in unwise lending, or a trading system that made it difficult for countries to earn sufficient resources. If the problem was at the unit level, the solution would be found in domestic reform. If the problem was at the systemic level, the solution would require changes to the rules governing the exchange and flow of money. These changes could take place at the level of international organizations or in the states that regulated the largest financial markets (such as the US or the UK).

It is often the case that creditors and advanced industrialized countries believe that the problems of financial stability arise because of poor policies at the unit level. Efforts to increase stability are therefore aimed at reforming developing countries (again).

During the 1980s, Latin American countries were criticized because their economies were not sufficiently export oriented. In the late 1990s, formerly successful Asian states were blamed for practising a corrupt form of capitalism – crony capitalism. In contrast, many developing countries and NGOs believe that the fault lies in a global financial system that rewards speculation and the rapid flow of capital.

Development groups and social democratic critics of the liberal global financial system have suggested that capital mobility needs to be slowed down to provide greater stability. One proposal to do this has been the Tobin tax. The Tobin tax would levy a charge on foreign exchange dealings. The idea is that the tax would discourage those people trading currencies just to make money, but would not deter foreign exchange transactions for purposes such as medium- to long-term investment, buying imports or tourism. Although there are technical objections to the Tobin tax and other measures to slow the flow of capital, the primary obstacles are political. Vast fortunes are generated by the free flow of capital. Those who benefit from the system are adept at using their influence to prevent measures that might reduce their potential for increased wealth. The beneficiaries of capital mobility are those who have money to invest. This includes wealthy individuals, the financial industry itself and corporations with a need for investment or which are investing in financial instruments or the stock market.

In the 1990s, the group of actors interested in a buoyant stock market expanded from corporations and wealthy individuals to a large number of less wealthy individuals. Beginning in the 1980s, large numbers of people from modest economic backgrounds in the developed world entered the stock market as governments privatized pension systems. As a result, more individuals relied on a healthy stock market for pensions and savings. This meant a large growth of individual investment in the stock market through mutual funds or unit trusts. In addition, employer pension funds of civil servants or teachers have become major stock market participants as they search for the best return for their customers. These organizations are called 'institutional investors' and their investment decisions can move markets. The number of people in advanced industrialized countries committed to open financial markets has grown, making attempts to curb such openness much more politically difficult (Harmes, 1998). At the same time, the number of people vulnerable to a stock market slump has also grown. This opens the possibility of an anti-liberal backlash if prolonged recession destroys millions of investors' retirement funds.

KEY ISSUES

This section focuses on four key issues that have dominated the global financial system in the first part of the 21st century. The first issue is the global credit crisis, which began in the US in 2008 and spread to numerous countries in the following years. The second issue is the fate of the US dollar and the possibility that another currency may emerge as its global rival. The third issue is the sovereign debt crisis, which swept over Europe in 2010 and threatened the economic models and currency of Europe. The final issue is the prevalence of corporate and individual tax abuse which deprives states of revenue and workers of decent salaries.

Global credit crisis

In 2008 and into 2009, the world was buffeted by yet another financial crisis. The systemic consequence of this crisis has been so severe that it merits discussion as a key issue in its own right. However, unlike the financial crises of the 1980s and 90s, this one did not begin in developing countries. The origins and, indeed, causes lay in the US. This section highlights the causes of that crisis, reviews its global consequences and considers the issues it poses. In the broadest sense, the financial crisis of 2008 came about because loans were extended to people who could not carry the debt load and the risk for these loans extended deep into the US financial system (O'Brien, 2009). A market fundamentalist philosophy and powerful political interests ensured that there was minimal regulation as a series of financial institutions took on greater and greater risk in a search for increased returns (see Chapter 13).

After the bursting of the tech bubble in 2001, the US Federal Reserve kept interest rates low to stimulate growth. Low interest rates encouraged people to buy houses. As demand for loans grew, the financial industry responded by creating new instruments – subprime mortgages – that extended loans to people previously excluded from borrowing because they had low credit ratings and were therefore seen as more risky. Wall Street investment banks took home mortgages, divided them up into smaller slices, bundled them up as mortgage securities and then sold them off to other investors. The advantage of this system was that the risk of the original mortgage could be spread among a large number of investors. If a few mortgages went bad, the large number of investors would easily be able to absorb the small fragments of financial loss.

These financial instruments and many others were popularized by 'parallel' or 'shadow banks' (Krugman, 2008, pp. 158–62). Shadow banks are financial institutions that engage in banking activity – taking deposits and lending out money – but are not classified as banks. Because they are not classified as banks, these institutions are not regulated like banks. They do not have to keep a similar percentage of their capital on reserve to pay out to borrowers and they do not have to pay into the deposit insurance system like banks do. Since they do not bear the regulatory costs of banks, they can make more profit, but they are exposed to more risk than deposit banks. Key shadow banks include investment banks, hedge funds and even insurance companies.

As the housing boom took off (house values doubled between 2000 and 2006), a number of worrying trends developed. Because the financial units that originally dispersed the mortgages (mortgage originators) sold the risk on to other parties, they became more willing to take on riskier and riskier customers. For example, the term 'Ninja loans' stood for 'no income, no job, no assets' and referred to mortgages that did not require customers to demonstrate that they were creditworthy (Dodd and Mills, 2008). Mortgages were offered to customers with little or no money for down payments (deposits) and without due regard to their financial health. The link between the lender and borrower was broken because risk was passed on to other investors in the financial system. Those making the loans would not be held accountable for their actions because the loans were sold off to others.

By the end of 2006, the housing market had reached its peak and prices started to decline. Unfortunately, a very large number of individuals and financial institutions had structured their economic activity around inflated house prices and were now financially vulnerable. The emerging crisis was first seen in the subprime market. As house prices declined, subprime lenders lost money as clients defaulted on their mortgages. Over the next year or two, financial firms faced financial collapse from exposure to bad mortgages and the mortgage derivatives that had become so common. Credit markets tightened up and the crunch hit banks in other countries. Banks and investment vehicles such as hedge funds declared large losses over the year.

The use of derivatives had not only spread the risk associated with bad mortgages, it had hidden the extent and scope of the risks. No one knew how bad the financial mess was or could be. In September and October 2008 the crisis intensified, causing the Republican and conservative US president George W. Bush to embark on one of the largest government interventions in US history. In October, the US Treasury Secretary and the chairman of the Federal Reserve lobbied Congress for $700 billion to buy up toxic mortgages. After initially losing a vote in Congress, the administration was given the authority to put in place a rescue package. However, this initial plan was overtaken by events and the government soon changed course to follow the initiative of the UK government. Rather than focusing on buying up bad mortgages, the government directly infused $250 billion of capital into banks by taking shares in the largest US banks (Citigroup, Wells Fargo, JPMorgan Chase, Bank of America and Morgan Stanley). Further bailouts followed, with the Federal Reserve eventually creating a 'bad bank' to buy up the toxic loans of financial institutions in 2009.

The financial crisis spilled over into the 'real economy' as the US plunged into recession. Turbulence in the financial markets reduced credit to consumers and businesses. As economic activity slowed, lay-offs began and unemployment rates rose. Pensioners also suffered devastating losses as their stock market funds dropped by a third. Consumers who funded their activity through credit or based on the inflated value of their homes or land values were being forced to cut back drastically on consumption. Attempts to reduce poverty by broadening home ownership suffered a serious reversal as the credit crisis forced economically vulnerable people from their homes. Economic conservatives (neoliberals) in the US were outraged over the massive government intervention in the markets and the drift to 'socialism' evident in the government's stake in banks, mortgage and insurance companies. Commentators on the left and right asked: 'Is this the end of American capitalism?' (Faiola, 2008).

The US financial crisis rapidly spread to other countries. With its large international financial services industry, Britain was especially hard hit. Many British financial institutions teetered on the brink of insolvency and the government was forced to mount massive bailout packages. Several small states that had nurtured oversized financial industries were plunged into economic turmoil. Iceland went bankrupt and Ireland's economy was hard hit. The prime minister of Iceland was charged with criminal negligence over the collapse of its banking system. In eastern Europe, governments, companies and individuals who had taken out loans with western European banks in euros or Swiss francs suffered when their currencies weakened. Both Hungary and Ukraine turned to the IMF for emergency loans. Countries heavily reliant on exports for economic growth such as China suffered from the reduction of economic activity in major export markets such as the US. Developing countries faced the prospect of reduced exports, as well as more difficult access to credit, investment and development assistance.

While the international impacts of the US financial crisis unfolded at an accelerating rate, a coherent international response did not. Initially, many states viewed the financial problem as a US concern and left it up to the US to devise a solution. As the impact spread, some momentum built for global coordination, but agreement was difficult. The US and China embarked on large domestic spending initiatives to stimulate their economies, but Continental Europe did not. A G20 meeting in London in April 2009 signalled the increasing importance of that institution, but failed to adopt new rules for global financial regulations. The G20 did announce the provision of more funding to developing countries, but was unable to secure from its members common programmes to stimulate economies, deal with toxic loans or provide a new framework for regulation. In the UK, the greatest impact of the meeting was the fallout from heavy-handed policing of demonstrators, including the death of one individual. In September 2009, G20 leaders decided that the G20 would take over from the G8 as the major forum to guide the global economy.

One result of the crisis has been increased attention to the IMF. As was the case with the 1980s' debt crisis, world leaders turned to the IMF as a key instrument in combating the crisis. At the G20 summit in April 2009, world leaders pledged to boost IMF lending resources to $750 billion to support lending to emerging markets, and provide assistance to low-income countries. But a renewed role for the IMF is linked to reform of the institution. This will be a slow and difficult process but one step in this direction was the decision to ratify the Fourth Amendment of the IMF's Charter, thus making the allocation of special drawing rights more equitable. Special drawing rights allow countries to borrow more money than would otherwise be available.

The failure to develop a common response to financial crises opens a number of difficult questions. If new regulations are not put in place, what is to prevent a similar crisis developing at another time and in another place? If countries do not coordinate their responses, is it possible that they will adopt policies that are temporarily attractive, but damage the interests of other nations? Is it possible that countries will become more protectionist as a response to economic slowdown? Could this undermine global growth and recovery?

Future of the US dollar

The financial crisis that swept the US in 2008 and spread to other countries gave added weight to a discussion that had been emerging about the role of the world's major reserve currency – the US dollar. The world's reserve currency is the currency that is most used by central banks as a reserve asset and is the currency most often used in the provision of loans or the purchase of products. Many countries in the world hold a large share of their foreign currency reserves in US dollars. Many products traded on the international market are priced in US dollars – the most important of these is oil. Many international loans are also denominated in dollars. The existence of a world reserve or international currency facilitates international economic activity because it serves as a medium of exchange, a unit of account and a store of value (Helleiner, 2008). Acting as a means of exchange involves being the medium that is used to settle economic transactions. It allows people to pay for imports in a currency their trading partners want to hold or allows governments to purchase other currencies. The role of serving as a unit of account means that calculations of value are undertaken in that currency. For example, oil is priced in a certain number of dollars per barrel. A store of value means that firms and states will use the currency to hold their wealth, rather than using gold or investing in housing.

The US dollar has been the world's primary reserve currency since the end of the Second World War because investors and states have had more faith in the US economy than that of any other country. This has been a source of power and substantial benefit to the US (Kirshner, 2008). Because of the high demand for the dollar, the US has had to pay relatively low interest rates when it sells its government bonds to foreigners. Investors will take less in interest payments because of the security of their investment. This has allowed the US to fund large budget deficits relatively cheaply. Low interest rates have meant that the US government and US consumers have been able to live beyond their means and consume more than otherwise would have been possible (see Box 8.11). Since US borrowing is done in dollars, there is no risk of the US debt increasing if the value of the dollar falls. In such a situation, the creditors would lose money as they saw the value of their loans fall in relation to their own country. This is the opposite of the situation that many developing countries face when they borrow in dollars and then have to make ever larger payments if their currency weakens. The pricing of other key assets (such as oil) in dollars has also insulated the US from other price fluctuations. For example, if the euro declines in value against the US dollar, Europeans must pay more for oil that is sold in US dollars. However, if the US currency loses value, it does not pay more for oil since oil remains priced in US dollars.

Box 8.11 Government deficits and debt

A government runs a budget deficit when it spends more than it raises in taxation and revenue. It finances this deficit by borrowing money. A government's debt is the total of all the money it owes from accumulated annual deficits, including the ongoing interest it owes from annual borrowing to cover the deficits. Debt can be productive if the money is being invested to generate new economic activity. For example, spending might go towards building large infrastructure projects, such as roads or schools, which contribute to long-term economic growth. Debts used to finance consumption, such as tax breaks to consumers, may generate an initial burst of economic activity but do not generate long-term growth to pay back the debt. A high level of government debt can drain an economy by diverting government revenue from other expenditures, such as health or education, to servicing the debt (making interest payments).

In the wake of the near collapse of the US financial system in 2008, a number of voices have been raised questioning the future role of the US dollar. In March 2009, the head of China's central bank suggested that the dollar be replaced as the world's reserve currency. China was unhappy with the uncertain position of the dollar and the possibility that it might lose money on its investments in US debt if the dollar entered a decline (see Box 8.12). If countries began to move away from the dollar by switching to another currency, Americans would have to pay more for imported goods as the value of the dollar declined. The US would also have to raise interest rates on government and private debt to support the value of the dollar. A weaker dollar would challenge the US to reduce consumption, restore fiscal balance and invest in infrastructure and human capital

(Roubini, 2009) to become more competitive. Simultaneously, it would shift the power and privileges of the reserve currency to another state or population.

A movement away from the US dollar as the top international currency will require more than simply weakness in the US economy. Because so many firms and states already use the dollar for many different tasks, a viable alternative needs to be in place for a switch to happen. Surveying the leading contenders, Eichengreen (2011, p. 7) found no single alternative, declaring that one rival is a currency without a state, while another is a currency with too much of a state. The currency without the state is the euro. Since its creation in 1999, the euro has been taking on a larger international role. It has gained an increasing role as a foreign reserve currency for central banks, bonds have

Box 8.12 The US–China financial relationship

In the early 2000s, the financial relationship between the US and China became complicated and volatile (Krugman, 2005). China attracted large amounts of capital in the form of foreign investment as US, European and Asian companies invested in Chinese production. Money also flowed into China because it was running trade surpluses with many countries, especially the US. This should usually take care of itself because an inflow of money should raise the value of the Chinese currency, which would make China's trade surpluses shrink.

However, the Chinese government did not allow its currency to rise in value. It took the money flowing into China and sent it right back to the US by buying dollar assets such as US government bonds. The easy inflow of Chinese money into the US has meant that the US can keep its interest rates low and easily fund large budget deficits. Budget deficits allowed the government to pursue a war in Iraq and cut taxes. At the same time, low interest rates encouraged US consumers to spend and facilitated a housing boom.

This arrangement benefited both China and the US. China was able to base its economic development on exporting to the US and Americans were allowed to enjoy high rates of consumption. However, the model is unsustainable and faces major problems (Samuelson, 2009). Americans used borrowed money to consume rather than invest in new productive capacity. This raised questions about how the money would be paid back. The Chinese government became heavily dependent on export growth to provide employment and prevent social unrest. The relationship became more strained in the wake of the 2008 US financial crisis. The US government needs continued Chinese investment to finance its spending and budget deficits, which are designed to save financial institutions and reflate the US economy. However, the weakness of the US economy threatens the value of Chinese investments. If China starts to shift its money away from the US, the Federal Reserve will be forced to raise interest rates to attract investors. This, in turn, will slow the US economy and reduce growth. At that point, Americans will have to pay the true cost of their budget deficits. If the adjustment happens slowly, the economy will be able to adapt, but a rapid change in money flows could cause considerable economic turmoil in the US and the global economy.

There are risks for China, as well. It is heavily dependent on the US for an export market. A severe downturn in the US economy threatens Chinese exports and employment levels. This, in turn, could increase social instability in China. China is trying to avoid these dangers by increasing consumer spending in its domestic market. This is being done by spending on infrastructure programmes and reducing the need for citizens to save for health expenses by introducing a wider safety net and social programmes.

increasingly been issued in euros and international transactions can be conducted in euros (McNamara, 2008). On many measures the euro has been catching up with the dollar as an international currency. However, the euro does not have the unqualified backing of a large powerful state willing to deploy its financial and political power in defence of the currency. The euro is the creation of an alliance of states that may or may not be willing to support the currency in a crisis. This became painfully evident with the onset of the European sovereign debt crisis in 2010. European states were unable to agree on a quick and effective course of action in response to Greece's economic problems, throwing the future of the euro into doubt (more on this below). Without the backing of state power, it is unlikely that the euro can replace the dollar as the key international currency.

The currency with too much state is the Chinese renminbi. Because of its large trade surpluses, China has accumulated large amounts of foreign currency reserves, including a considerable holding of US dollar debt. Although large areas of China remain poor, the export-oriented parts of its economy have generated enormous wealth. The trade surpluses and foreign currency reserves would ordinarily cause China's currency to play a larger international role. However, the Chinese state plays an active role in managing its currency for domestic policy reasons, which makes it unsuitable to serve as a major international currency. The Chinese government does not allow its currency to float on the international market because it insists on controlling the currency's value. A rise in the value of the renminbi is seen as a threat because it would reduce Chinese exports, risking the social stability created by economic growth (Bowles and Wang, 2008). Although full convertibility of the renminbi is unlikely until 2017 at the earliest, the Chinese government has been taking steps to internationalize its currency. The People's Bank of China has signed bilateral currency swap agreements with other central banks including the European Central Bank; Chinese trade is increasingly being settled in renminbi; investors are adding it to their portfolios and some central banks are adding it to their reserve currency stocks (Financial Times, 2014). In 2013 the renminbi became the ninth largest traded currency (BIS, 2014).

The weakness of the US dollar, combined with the lack of a serious alternative, suggests two possible scenarios. The first is a gradual shift from a world with one world reserve currency (the US dollar) to an environment where several currencies share the role. This would see a continued role for the dollar, but an increasing international role for the euro and the renminbi as countries and firms diversified their holdings of currencies. In addition, the euro and renminbi would increasingly serve as the dominant currencies in their regions, with the euro in Europe, North Africa, the Middle East and Russia, and the renminbi exercising influence in Southeast and East Asian economic relations. Such an arrangement would necessitate more coordination among the US, Europe and China on international monetary affairs. It would also imply that the US would be under increasing pressure to reduce its levels of consumption through reducing its budget and trade deficits because the days of unlimited and relatively cheap credit would be curbed.

A less positive scenario is that despite the lack of an alternative to the dollar, markets or states could rapidly lose faith in the dollar, causing a panic and a flight from the currency. This would cause the US to go into an economic tailspin as its cost of borrowing would skyrocket and pressure to service its debt would become intense. The economic impact would spill over to many other countries that rely heavily on the US as an export market. Currency markets would be disrupted and international economic activity would suffer. The trigger for such a panic could be in the political or economic realm. For example, a confrontation between the US and China over Taiwan might cause the Chinese to sell US Treasury Bills as a form of economic pressure, which would then cause an unintended financial panic. Alternatively, the inability of the US Congress to take steps to balance the budget could cause a loss of confidence among institutional investors, leading to a sell-off of US debt that triggers a wider panic. The history of the US credit crisis indicates that once there is panic in the market, the result is unpredictable.

The European sovereign debt and euro crisis

Following the credit crisis of 2008, a number of states experienced problems with servicing their debt. The most serious problem occurred in Europe. A country's debt is the total amount of money it owes creditors. It is the sum of money owed from the financing of annual budget deficits. These budget deficits are the result of governments spending more in a year than they raise in tax revenue. Governments raise money from creditors by selling government bonds. As bonds mature or become due, governments must pay them from tax revenue or issue new bonds and roll over the debt (see Box 8.13).

Between 2010 and 2012, a dual financial crisis emerged in Europe. One part of the crisis was the threat that several European countries appeared unable to service their government debt. The other element was the impact of these debt problems on the viability of the European currency, the euro. It was a combination of a credit and monetary system crisis.

The groundwork for the dual crisis was laid with the introduction of the euro in 2002. A number of European countries that relied heavily on selling government bonds to fund their budget deficits suddenly experienced reduced borrowing costs. Creditors demanded less interest because these countries were now issuing debt in euros and it was perceived that the currency risk was lower. It was thought that the debt of these countries was supported by the economic weight of the EU. Heavy borrowers, such as Portugal, Ireland, Italy, Greece and Spain, experienced a surge of relatively cheap credit. These indebted European countries were sometimes referred to as the PIIGS. Public and private sector borrowing increased to levels that would not have been possible prior to the euro. The cheap credit sparked increased property speculation in Spain and rapid expansion of Irish banks.

The crisis began in October 2009 shortly after the election of a new left-wing government in Greece. The new government examined the finances it had inherited and announced that the previous calculation of Greek government deficits had been underreported. Rather than being 6 per cent of annual GDP, they were actually closer to 13 per cent of GDP. This figure was subsequently increased to 15 per cent. The doubling of the calculated value of Greece's deficits startled the credit rating agencies and bond sellers. Suddenly, Greek government debt looked much riskier. The significance of the size of Greece's debt became serious for several reasons:

1 Revised calculation of yearly deficits increased the overall size of the debt.
2 Economic crisis increased the yearly deficits as the economy slowed and the government was unable to raise as much revenue.
3 The cost of servicing the debt increased as credit rating agencies downgraded Greek bonds in December. This meant that the Greek government was forced to increase the interest it paid to borrow money to refinance the debt.

The combination of these factors caused Greek debt to dramatically increase in relation to the value of the

---

Box 8.13 How do government bonds work?

Governments sell bonds to investors who promise to pay back the face value of the bond at a set time in the future. Short-term bonds will be sold at a discount, which means that the government accepts a payment less than the face value of the bond. For example, a six-month $100 bond is sold to investor A for $95. In six months' time, the bond matures and the investor gets $100. Longer-term bonds pay an interest rate (also called a coupon) usually semi-annually to the investor. Bonds are issued in the government's currency, so foreign investors are potentially exposed to a currency risk. If the value of the country's currency declines, so does the return on the bond. Bonds are also sold on a secondary market, which means that a bondholder can sell their bond to someone else. The value of the interest rate and the secondary market of the bond is determined by how much confidence investors have that the bonds will be repaid. The greater the confidence, the lower the coupon. Confidence is increased if governments have a growing economy, a low level of debt compared to the size of their economy and a plan to reduce deficits or run surplus budgets.

The US funds its debt primarily through the sale of its government bonds. The name of these bonds changes according to the time period for which they are issued. The shortest term bonds are called 'Treasury Bills' and come due in either three-month, six-month or one-year maturities. They are sold at a discount from their face value. 'Treasury notes' pay an interest rate (or coupon) every six months and have maturities that range from one to ten years. Treasury bonds are usually sold with 20- or 30-year maturity and also pay interest semi-annually.

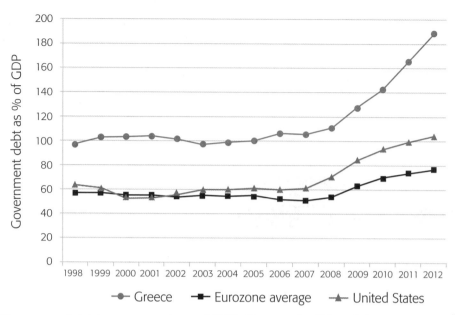

Figure 8.3 **Government debt as a percentage of GDP: Greece, the US and the eurozone**

products and services that Greece produced (Figure 8.3). Unless some action was taken, it appeared that Greece would not be able to service its debt.

As the cost of Greek debt rose, it became more difficult for the government to rollover the debt by issuing new bonds. Private sector banks in other parts of Europe, which had lent to the Greek government, private sector and individuals, became nervous that they would not be paid back. With private sector investors demanding ever increasing rates of interest, the Greek government needed to borrow from other governments in order to issue new debt. Public institutions such as the IMF and European states like Germany agreed to 'bail out' Greece in a series of deals in return for assurances that Greece would slash its budget deficits by reining in government spending. In 2010 and again in 2011 and 2012, Greece agreed to these demands and implemented an austerity plan, which cut government spending, reduced the size of the public services and curbed pensions in return for loans. In the spring of 2012, private sector bondholders agreed to take a lower return on the value of their government bonds as part of a refinancing deal. However, the austerity programme of cuts in government spending plunged Greece into economic depression. Lack of growth worsened the Greek budgetary situation and public protests paralysed the political process. Lenders

demanded austerity, which the people rejected after taking several doses.

The original design of the euro came back to haunt Europeans as they struggled to deal with the Greek crisis. The German government insisted that the European problem was not one of slow growth, but of member states with out-of-control budget deficits. The weak measures designed to restrain national spending at the euro's origin had not succeeded. A single monetary policy for Europe was not matched by similar budgetary policies in the member states. Germany was reluctant to propose sweeping European-wide financial packages such as issuing European-wide bonds which would be at a relatively low rate of interest and could be used to calm investor fears about Greek debt. The currency without a state had run into severe problems.

Greece's budget issues spread to other states. One concern was that the country would leave the euro. If Greece was unable to keep to its austerity programme and secure new credit by reassuring public and private creditors, it could default on its debt. Greece might determine that it was impossible to service its debt as a member of the single currency. Outside the euro, with a devalued currency Greece might be able to experience some economic growth and begin the process of recovery. A devalued drachma would make Greek exports and tourist attractions attractive to members of the single currency and could restart economic growth. If this happened, would the euro be able to survive? In 2015 after much political conflict, Greek politicians opted to continue in the Euro and accepted continued harsh austerity measures, although the story is still unfolding (see Box 8.14).

A second concern was the knock-on effects on other countries. Investors burned by the Greek experience

---

Box 8.14 The euro vs. Greek economic growth

In 2015 Greeks were forced to choose between two deeply desired policy objectives – easing austerity and staying in the euro. After years of punishing austerity the Greek people elected an anti-austerity left-wing party (Syriza) which declared in January 2015 the end of the 'vicious cycle of austerity' (Guardian, 2015a). However, this turned out to be an inaccurate reading of the situation. Other European governments, especially Germany, refused to renegotiate Greece's loan conditions. Greece's creditors made it clear that easing austerity would result in the end of vital loans, forcing Greece into bankruptcy and withdrawal from the euro. Greeks were not prepared to leave the euro as there were fears about the economic turbulence it would bring and the euro had become important to Greek identity, representing membership in the modern, democratic European community. Thus, although Greeks rejected the creditors' tough austerity measures in a popular referendum on 5 July the government was forced to perform a volte-face and accepted (even tougher) austerity conditions as the Greek economy slid further into crisis in the following week. The government did not have a mandate to leave the euro, forcing it to break its promises about ending austerity. On 21 August 2015 the government resigned and new elections were called. Dramatic events are likely to continue as new austerity measures create further economic downturn and political conflict. In addition, the IMF warned that European failure to provide Greece with debt relief makes Greece's position unsustainable and prevents the Fund from providing further financing (Graham-Harrison, 2015).

---

turned their attention to other countries such as Portugal, Italy, Spain and Ireland. These countries also suffered from high levels of debt and stagnant domestic economies. Governments in these countries also implemented austerity policies in an attempt to settle financial markets. However, increased austerity choked off economic growth, sending unemployment, especially youth unemployment, soaring. The social and political costs were high, with the massive growth in popularity of the extreme right-wing Golden Dawn party in Greece, increased support for regional separatism in Spain, and rising social tension in Spain and Portugal. Given the relatively large size of the Italian and Spanish economies, financial crisis in these states would be more difficult to solve than Greece's tribulations.

A final concern was the fragility of the global financial system. The global system had not recovered in 2012 from the 2008 credit crisis. Europe and North America continued to experience slow growth and budgetary challenges. Indeed, government budget cutting was reducing economic growth and worsening debt problems. Confidence remained fragile and an economic collapse in Greece spreading to other European countries could plunge the global system back into crisis. US banks were tied to European financial institutions and many developing states continued to rely on the EU and US markets for export revenues. Sovereign debt crises were now not just a concern of developing countries (see Box 8.15).

Corporate and individual tax abuse

Governments rely on tax revenue to finance programmes such as healthcare, education and defence, but in the early 21st century increasing concern has been expressed about wealthy individuals and transnational corporations using the global financial system to avoid paying tax (Bernards et al 2015). A number of different terms are used to describe this: tax avoidance, effective tax planning, aggressive tax planning, tax evasion, tax abuse. Tax avoidance involves arrangements which legally minimize tax. This involves both effective tax planning which is consistent with the intent of the law and aggressive tax planning which is judged to violate the intent of the law, but is still legal. Tax evasion involves activities which are clearly illegal. In practice, the line

Box 8.15 Sovereign debt crisis: Argentina

In December 2001, the Argentinian government declared that it could not pay its debts, causing the largest government default in history. Half the debt the government owed was to foreign bondholders. In previous cases of this sort, the IMF would have negotiated a stringent SAP with Argentina and forced the government to begin paying back money to bondholders. However, a number of factors led to a different outcome:

1 Within Argentina, the financial crisis created widespread chaos and a political mood that was hostile to paying back debt. A left-wing government came to power that was unwilling to give in quickly to the IMF or private bondholders.
2 The IMF had lent so much money to Argentina that it was vulnerable if Argentina refused to pay. This weakened the IMF's bargaining position.
3 There was a change in US foreign economic policy. The George W. Bush administration was heavily influenced by right-wing economic views, which were not in favour of using government money to bail out private investors (until the US had its own crisis in 2008). They believed that IMF support for governments in crisis created a moral hazard problem. The hazard was that private investors could recklessly invest in risky countries because they knew that the IMF would get their money back if things went wrong. The Bush administration wanted to force private investors to bear some of the economic loss of poor investment decisions. As a result, a right-wing US government supported a left-wing government in Argentina as it resisted IMF demands for immediate repayment of foreign bondholders at favourable rates (Helleiner, 2005). When Argentina finally did settle with bondholders, they received only 30 cents for each dollar they had invested in Argentina's government debt.

Argentina's sovereign debt story took another turn in 2014 when a New York judge ruled that the country could not pay the reduced amounts agreed with most of its creditors unless it also paid full value to a number of hold outs that had not agreed to the deal. The hold-out investors were mainly US hedge funds. These funds were described as 'vulture funds' in Argentina, but portrayed as investors seeking legitimate debt repayment in the pages of the *New York Times* (Gilbert, 2015). Argentina tried to repay its debts to the creditors who had previously agreed a deal by rerouting transactions through its own capital markets and avoiding the New York markets. It also turned to China for financial support. Despite the US legal ruling and financial pressures from the international capital markets, Argentina continued to offer the vulture funds only 35 cents on the dollar.

between these different tax avoidance strategies is blurry and schemes can be retroactively shifted from one category to another by national tax authority rulings. A further complication is that activity which is illegal in one state may be legal in another.

States often use the tax code to further particular policy objectives such as supporting economic development in particular fields. Thus, lowering one's tax bill in the form of effective tax planning can be consistent with national goals. In contrast, aggressive tax planning and tax evasion are designed to avoid legitimate tax burdens and undermine the revenue-gathering powers of the state. Since measures that are 'legal' can still have negative impacts on states and societies we follow the advice of the tax justice network and focus on tax

abuse – the anti-social organization of one's affairs to avoid paying a fair share of tax (www.taxjustice.net). The primary method for corporations to minimize tax is profit shifting, while for individuals it is asset shifting.

Corporate profit shifting involves reporting profits in low-lax or no-tax foreign jurisdictions by artificially reallocating income and expenses in order to reduce the overall tax liability. The goal is to show expenses in high tax jurisdictions and profits in low tax jurisdictions so that the amount of tax paid is minimized. The specific ways of shifting profit vary depending on different situations but they can include: transfer pricing, contract manufacturing, relocation of property rights, debt allocation, hybrid entities, conduit companies and treaty shopping (see Table 8.2).

Table 8.2 **Corporate profit shifting strategies**

Strategy	Description
Transfer pricing	Control the pricing of goods and services sold between affiliates within an enterprise.
Debt allocation	Apportionment or assignment of debt for tax purpose between affiliates within an enterprise.
Contract manufacturing	Contract with a third-party manufacturer through a shell company in low-tax or no-tax jurisdiction to produce items that will be sold in a high-tax market.
Relocation of property rights	Relocate property rights to an affiliate in low-tax or no-tax jurisdictions.
Hybrid entities	Entities can be recognized as a corporation in some jurisdictions but not in others.
Conduit	Incomes are paid by a company to a conduit company in low-tax or no-tax jurisdiction and then redistributed by that company to its shareholders as dividends, interest, royalties, etc.
Treaty shopping	A corporation establishes a foreign subsidiary in one of the countries that signed a favourable tax treaty and thus enjoys a favourable tax rate in all these countries.

Files released by the International Consortium of Investigative Journalists (the Luxembourg files) in 2012 showed that more than 350 multinationals around the world, including FedEx, Pepsi, Ikea, Skype and Disney, used these various profit-shifting strategies to dodge taxation of their home countries. For example, Caterpillar changed the address of its global parts business to Switzerland from the US and thus escaped paying $2.4 billion tax from 2002 to 2012 (Rubin, 2015). The magnitude of corporate profit shifting and resultant revenue cost is immense. The largest US-based companies transferred about $206 billion to their stockpiles of offshore profits in 2013 (Rubin, 2014).

The implications for developing countries can be serious. Oxfam (2009) estimates that developing countries lose around $124 billion from offshore assets held in tax havens, which outweighs the $103 billion overseas aid that developing countries receive annually. An example of how this can have a devastating impact on people comes from South Africa. On 16 August 2012, 34 miners were killed by police near the Lonmin platinum mines in Marikana. The deaths were the result of an intense struggle for improved wages between groups of workers, the mining company and the South African state (Chinguno, 2013). Tax avoidance played a role in this tragedy because the company claimed it could not raise wages due to low profits when in fact it was transferring large amounts of its profit to a related company in Bermuda for 'marketing services' (Forslund, 2014). Tax avoidance means less money for governments and workers, which can have serious consequences on people's lives.

For wealthy individuals the strategy is to hide personal taxable assets in low-tax or no-tax jurisdictions by either transferring taxable assets offshore or not reporting overseas assets in their home country. The specific ways of transferring are varied, complicated and veiled, but the destinations of these assets are well known – tax havens. The Tax Justice Network estimated that as of 2010 at least $21 trillion to $32 trillion of private financial wealth has been invested virtually tax-free through tax havens (Henry, 2012). This figure is equivalent to the size of the US and Japanese economies combined (BBC, 2012).

Tax havens are political jurisdictions which attract capital flows from other countries because of their low levels of taxation. According to the OECD (1998) they charge no or only nominal tax rates, lack effective exchange of financial information with other countries, lack transparency and are designed to help clients avoid paying tax. International competition encourages some states to act as tax havens while others engage in a race-to-the-bottom tax-cutting policy to retain investment. Switzerland and Luxembourg have played the role of tax haven in Europe, while countries such as the Cayman Islands, Seychelles and Mauritius use it as a development strategy.

An important feature of corporate and individual tax abuse is the crucial role played by banks and professional accounting companies in facilitating this activity. Large accounting firms help corporations arrange their affairs to avoid tax, taking advantage of national tax loopholes, eased international capital flow and harmful national competition discussed above. The biggest accounting firms have provided some governments with expert accountants to draw up tax laws *and* simultaneously, or shortly afterward, offered advice to multinationals and individuals on how to exploit loopholes of these laws (Syal et al., 2013).

The response of international institutions and national authorities is one of high rhetoric and low achievement. International institutions and governments proclaim a desire to fight tax abuse but their measures have minimal impact. Effective international state tax cooperation is difficult. National taxation systems are to a considerable extent determined by national economic and political systems. Disputes about appropriate levels and subjects of taxation open the field to corporate tax arbitrage. Harmonizing national taxation systems treads on national sovereignty. As a result, international cooperation can be reduced to information exchange. The steps that have been take focus on four areas.

1 Closing loopholes in national tax systems. Largely responding to the astounding figures disclosed on corporate and international tax avoidance, many tax authorities are more actively working on scrutinizing their systems and closing loopholes. For example, the US tax authority announced plans to close a tax loophole that allows US firms to avoid paying taxes on overseas profit by imposing a one-off 14 per cent tax on US profits located overseas as well as a 19 per cent tax on any future profits (BBC, 2015).

2 Addressing harmful tax competition and tax havens. Following the 2008 global financial crisis, the G20 demanded that tax havens meet international standards for information-sharing and transparency. Since the launch of the international crackdown on tax havens in 2009, offshore centres have signed dozens of information-exchange agreements. However, the success of such measures is in doubt since the wealth held in offshore financial centres grew by hundreds of billions dollars in 2012 (Houlder, 2013).

3 Increased scrutiny of giant banks and professional accounting firms. Bank secrecy in countries such as Switzerland, Luxembourg and some other tax havens has been gradually eroding. In 2009, G20 leaders called for ending the era of bank secrecy as a crucial part of its global initiative to fight tax avoidance and evasion. In response the OECD issued a *Standard for Automatic Exchange of Financial Account Information in Tax Matters*, which provides a framework for governments to obtain and share detailed account information.

4 Several recent projects and reports have highlighted the need to reform international taxation rules. The OECD, mandated by the G20, launched a Base Erosion and Profit Shifting (BEPS) project to curb profit shifting. It has held numerous meetings, made recommendations and issued a regular series of reports, but its impact is unclear at the moment (OECD, 2015). In February 2015, the High-Level Panel on Illicit Financial Flows from Africa released its report with a series of recommendations (AU/ECA, 2015). The report argued that illicit or illegal transfers of money out of Africa were equivalent to all of the development aid flowing into the continent. It also suggested that the reduction of illicit flows and tax evasion and the recovery of stolen assets become part of the Post-2015 Development Agenda.

Unfortunately, at the national level the will to prosecute tax abuse is often lacking. The UK serves as a useful example. After it was revealed that there were 1,000 cases of British citizens using the Swiss subsidiary of the world's third largest bank (HSBC) to hide money from British tax authorities, only one person was prosecuted (Guardian 2015b). The British tax authority, HMRC, prefers to have wealthy tax cheats confess and pay back portions of their theft rather than prosecute them for illegal activity. HMRC has also refused to open a criminal investigation into HSBCs activities. The policy of ignoring financial crime or allowing offenders to buy themselves out of prosecution stands in stark contrast with the threat of jail that hangs over poor people caught abusing the benefits or welfare system. The degree to which tax abuse is even engrained in the operating procedures of the state itself is provided in a Canadian example. A government-controlled entity the Public Sector Pension Investment Board has used Luxembourg shell companies to avoid German tax when purchasing real estate in Berlin (CBC, 2014). Government entities are using offshore companies to deprive other states of tax revenue!

The lack of state commitment to curbing tax abuse can be seen in the fact that very little information on these activities comes from police investigations or prosecutions. The public must rely on individuals working at financial institutions to leak confidential information to begin to get a sense of the extent of the problem. Widespread tax abuse coupled with a series of financial scandals (see Box 8.16) raises serious doubts about the fairness and efficiency of the global financial system.

Box 8.16 Financial institution crime

The years since the onset of the US credit crisis in 2008 have seen a stream of allegations and occasionally prosecutions of financial crimes by large financial institutions (Sky, 2015). These include:

▸ The pushing of hundreds of billions of dollars of 'liar loans' or 'ninja loans' on people who could not afford them
▸ Questionable credit rating of these loans by credit rating agencies
▸ Facilitation of money laundering for Latin American drug cartels
▸ Fixing foreign exchange rate trading
▸ Allegations of manipulating the rate at which banks lend to each other – the Libor or London inter-bank rate
▸ Bank and accounting firm assistance and advice for corporations and individuals seeking to hide income from national tax authorities.

Despite seemingly widespread financial crime in the banking sector, few bankers face prison terms and the fines imposed amount to only a tiny percentage of the financial institutions' profits.

CONCLUSION

Underlying many of the technical debates about the global financial system are the issues of autonomy, convergence and democracy. The openness of financial markets has sparked a debate about whether all states are being forced to pursue similar policies (convergence) or whether there is still room for different economic strategies (autonomy). Following on from this is the question of the tension between the demands for financial restructuring and policy preferences articulated through the democratic process.

The idea that governments and populations have lost power to the market and business leaders is captured by the phrase 'increased structural power of capital' (Gill and Law, 1993). This means that the organization, or the structure, of the financial system gives more power to those who possess wealth and those who can move their money around the global system. Because financial markets operate around the clock and transactions can take place almost instantaneously, investors can move their money out of countries that adopt policies which might threaten their profits. For example, a government that runs budget deficits to fund welfare policies may threaten the profits of investors. Investors may then transfer money out of that country, hurting businesses and the government's finances. Financial interests are not able to dictate state policies, but they increase the cost of following policies that are seen to be against investors' profits. This reduces the autonomy of states and societies that have different priorities from investors. Although this line of argument started before discussion of globalization became fashionable, many people see globalization increasing the influence of financial markets.

One of the interesting kinds of organization that has received more attention at this time of financial globalization is the credit rating agency, such as Moody's and Standard & Poor's (Sinclair, 1994, 2005). These private firms rate the creditworthiness of governments and corporations. If your rating goes down, the price of money goes up. A government or firm with a low bond rating must pay investors higher interest to compensate them for risk. Governments need to pay attention to the judgement of these agencies because a poor rating will influence the terms on which they can access money. They raise or lower the cost of certain policy options. Even though credit rating agencies were not able to accurately access the risks involved in mortgage-backed securities that sparked off the 2008 credit crisis, they continue to pronounce on the creditworthiness of states and firms.

The notion that state policy has been restricted by mobile capital has been challenged by scholars who maintain that states still make significant choices. They argue that policies are not converging on a particular liberal financial model. Sturdy domestic institutions and the power of organized labour and leftist political parties are factors that blunt the power of investors (Garrett, 2000). Liberal financial policies are implemented by particular governments who must be held responsible for those policies. For these analysts, power still resides at the state level and the attempt to find the cause of changing state policies at the global level is mistaken.

The debate about convergence and the structural power of capital has important implications for the practice of democracy. If the structural power of capital perspective is correct, democracy can be undermined because financial interests are having an increasingly large say over public policies. Voters may elect a government on a programme of economic growth and lowering unemployment, but the government may not follow these policies because of the financial implications. The will of the people is undermined by the power of the dollar. On the other hand, if analysts who discount the power of global financial markets are correct, then talk of globalization and structural power only serves to shift responsibility from governments to shadows beyond the state. Democracy can suffer because people give up trying to hold governments accountable for their actions. We will return to issues of governance and accountability in Chapter 15.

As governments moved to reassert control over their financial institutions in the wake of the US 2008 financial crisis, it initially appeared that those arguing that states have not been weakened by financial globalization were vindicated. Yet, the financial crisis also highlighted the tremendous inequality generated by neoliberal regulation. Governments moved quickly to shore up the institutions that had generated the problem, but the costs were often borne by those who had little voice in designing the rules. In the US and other developed countries, citizens lost homes, retirement savings and jobs. In many developing countries, the shortage of capital and development aid threatened development strategies and social policies. Governments

in many countries adopted austerity policies that prolonged the economic downturn. Whereas the debate about state power has receded, the issue of inequality and democratic control of financial regulation is more pressing than ever.

The globalization of trade, production and finance has had immense implications for how people live and work in the global economy. Chapter 9 focuses directly on people and their experiences by discussing the global division of labour.

Further Reading

Barry Eichengreen provides an excellent overview of the international monetary system in *Globalizing Capital: A History of the International Monetary System* (1996) and a thoughtful investigation into the future of the US dollar in *Exorbitant Privilege: The Rise and Fall of the Dollar and the Future of the International Monetary System* (2011). An early warning about the problems of unregulated finance was produced by Susan Strange in *Casino Capitalism* (1986), while a more recent consideration of the governance dilemmas of global finance is Tony Porter's *Globalization and Finance* (2005).

Chapter 9

Global Division of Labour

When studying international economics or global political economy, it is easy to concentrate attention on the activity of corporations or states and lose sight of the fate of particular people or groups of people. This chapter focuses on how people are caught up in a division of labour created by the global political economy. Where a person fits in this division of labour has a significant role in determining how long they will live and what their quality of life will be. The focus on the division of labour reveals gross inequalities and great injustices that may not be as visible when examining other aspects of the global political economy.

The chapter begins by outlining some of the variations in terms surrounding the division of labour such as the international, global, gendered and racial division of labour. In the next section, we consider the liberal theory of division of labour and objections to this from economic nationalist and critical perspectives. Under major developments we consider changes in the production process (how things are made) and the move from an international to a global division of labour. The key issues considered in the chapter are the integration of Chinese and Indian workers into the global economy, the global struggle for workers' rights, and the relationship between workers' rights and global stability.

DEFINITIONS

The 'division of labour' refers to the roles that people occupy in the production process. Different societies and economic systems have different ways of organizing who does which particular job. Some societies have relatively simple divisions of labour where many people do similar tasks, while other societies may have a detailed division of labour where people specialize in doing only one or two tasks. Take the example of the difference between people who live on farms and those who live in cities. Most farmers must take on a number of different jobs in order to survive. In addition to planting crops, they may have to be able to fix their machinery, preserve their own vegetables, bake their own bread and even take a second job in the city. Most city dwellers specialize in a particular job and then pay others to do tasks such as baking bread, growing crops, fixing machinery or even caring for children. In this case, the city dwellers have a more specialized division of labour than the farmer.

There can also be different approaches to allocating tasks to particular individuals or groups. In some cases, a division of labour may be based on race, such as in the apartheid era in South Africa or the pre-Civil War era in the southern US. In both examples, violence was used to enforce the allocation of tasks. In other cases, unofficial discrimination or lack of skills may maintain a racial division of labour. Many Western societies aspire to a division of labour based on merit and operating in response to impartial market forces, but ethnic, racial, class and gender divisions continue.

Moving beyond local communities, one can speak of an international division of labour. The international division of labour is a process whereby countries specialize in the production of particular things for export. Your geographic location has a great influence on what type of job you do in the international economy. For example, if you are participating in the global economy and happen to live in Honduras, you would probably be involved in the export of bananas; if you lived in Bangladesh, it would likely be textiles, in China it could be toys, in California it could be aerospace or the entertainment industry.

The concept of a global division of labour captures a form of organization that reaches around the planet, but where work is not confined to particular states. In a global division of labour, you find activities that in the past might have been thought of as being confined to particular nation-states now existing in very different types of states. Labour, which one might associate with a developing country, flourishes in a developed state and jobs thought to be the preserve of advanced industrialized countries exist alongside very labour-intensive jobs in developing states. For example, an expanding computer software industry is developing in India alongside the majority of the population that lives on subsistence agriculture. Alternatively, textile sweatshops thrive in Los Angeles and New York. The distinctive feature of these jobs is that they are plugged into a transnational production process and they are not confined to particular parts of the globe, although they may be more concentrated in some areas rather than others. Most computer software jobs are in advanced industrialized countries and the textile industry has a much greater presence in developing states. Yet, some developing countries have IT jobs and developed countries have immigrants working in the textile industry.

There is another important aspect of the division of labour and that is its gendered character (see also Chapter 10). Men tend to be grouped in different jobs from women. A gendered division of labour refers to the ideas societies have about what social roles and forms of employment are most appropriate for men and women. For example, if you look around a university, it appears that most professors are men and most secretaries are women. In the global economy, women are the majority of workers in export processing zones and men are the majority of the managers. In the finance industry, men are a majority of the stockbrokers, women the majority of bank tellers.

The interesting thing about the gendered division of labour is that it is not preordained or 'natural' but changes over time depending on social and economic circumstances. For example, in Canada and the US before the Second World War, women were largely confined to domestic tasks. However, with the shortage of male workers during the war, many women were called upon to work in factories where they were more than capable of doing 'male' work. Once the war ended, women were encouraged to return to the domestic role so that men could resume their 'natural' employment patterns.

A major issue in the global division of labour is the fate of the gendered division of labour. In some nation-states, considerable progress has been made to break down the barriers between 'women's work' and 'men's work'. However, progress has been uneven and falls short in even the most progressive countries. On the global level, women occupy particular places in the division of labour and they are affected in particular ways. Every society has a distinct pattern of gendered work. The tendency is for women's work to be less well paid than work dominated by men. Women are often concentrated in particular types of employment. Women are overrepresented in the 'caring' and support professions such as clerical, teaching, nursing, counselling and childcare. Women usually combine this paid work with the unpaid work of maintaining the family home and childcare (see Figure 9.1). Finally, the vast majority of people engaged in prostitution are women or children. Being a woman in the global economy entails a much greater chance of being poorer, working harder and under worse conditions than a man. Further discussion of the gendered division of labour and its implications will be the subject of Chapter 10.

There can also be a racial and ethnic division of labour. In these cases, groups of people from particular ethnic backgrounds or with visible physical differences are confined or corralled into specific forms of labour. The racial division is used to justify the different legal status and economic exploitation of these groups of workers (Persaud, 2001). The practice of slavery in the Americas was a brutal example of a racial division of

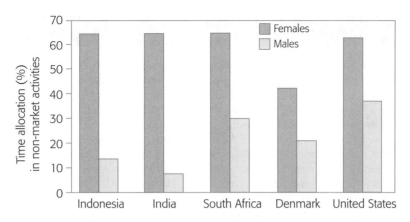

Figure 9.1 **Gender inequality in economic activity**

labour. However, racial divisions have also been crucial to the employment relations of Koreans in Japan, Indonesians in Malaysia, Mexicans and Central Americans in the US, Turks in Germany, Algerians in France, West Indians in Britain, and Indians and Chinese in many countries.

While it is often clear how national economies can be built on a racial division of labour (e.g. slavery in the US or apartheid in South Africa, immigrant labour in many countries), it has been less common to think about how race and class intersect in a global context. Bonacich (2008) and her colleagues have argued that the racialization of labour occurs when a particular group's race or ethnicity is seen to make them less important and less worthy of equal treatment than others, or they are denied citizenship rights and are seen as being outside the political community that matters. One can think of denying legal protections or decent wage rates to particular groups because their 'local culture' makes them more accepting of poor wages. Alternatively, the prevalence of certain nationalities in particular industries, such as young Asian women in electronics assembly, segments people of particular races into particular jobs. There is often an overlap between racial and gender categories as women of a particular race are seen to be the most suitable for certain tasks in the global economy. An example would be women from the Philippines in the global domestic and care industries. Cruise ships provide a vivid example of racial and gendered divisions of labour in the global entertainment and leisure industry (see Box 9.1).

THEORETICAL PERSPECTIVES: ADAM SMITH AND HIS CRITICS

The economic benefits of an advanced division of labour both nationally and internationally are at the heart of liberal economic theory. The 'naturalness' of the existing division of labour has been criticized by those who highlight the role of power in creating and maintaining particular divisions of labour. Theorists and practitioners interested in the welfare of a particular nation-state have tried to influence the division of labour by supporting the development of particular forms of industry such as manufacturing or high-tech. Feminist theorists have tried to undermine the gendered division of labour by revealing its manufactured nature.

We'll spend some time considering the liberal theory in detail before turning to alternative views. The liberal philosopher Adam Smith ([1776]1983, p. 109) chose to begin his famous work *The Wealth of Nations* by explaining the benefits of an increasing division of labour: 'The greatest improvement in the productive powers of labour, and the greater part of the skill, dexterity, and judgment with which it is anywhere directed or applied, seem to have been the effects of the division of labour.' Smith illustrated his point by contrasting a system of production where individuals made pins versus a system where the various tasks of making pins were broken down between a group of people. He suggested that a single person may only be able to make one pin in a day. If they were especially skilled, they

---

Box 9.1 Gender and ethnicity in a cruise ship crew

A cruise ship provides an interesting example of the global division of labour because one can clearly see the role that gender and ethnicity play in allocating particular roles to people from different parts of the world. At first glance, the crew of a cruise ship seems to be a 'mini UN', with a wonderful multicultural blend of people from all over the world. Cruise ships have been able to source labour from many different countries because of the widespread use of the flag of convenience. However, a closer look reveals that the makeup of the crew is not simply in response to the market forces of supply and demand, but is heavily influenced by the ethnic and gender identities of applicants and the assumptions of employers (Chin, 2008). Although there is variation over time and between cruise lines, patterns are visible. Cruise ship officers tend to be from northern countries such as Italy, the UK and the US. Employees from these countries also tend to hold the more skilled jobs such as doctors and managers of various types (casino, hotel, entertainment). Asian, eastern European and Caribbean staff tend to work as bar, cabin, restaurant and galley stewards. Non-English speaking crews work in the most menial jobs such as kitchen staff and janitors. Asian staff are often seen by employers to be culturally suited to providing friendly service (Chin, 2008, p. 12). Most of the women crew are concentrated in two roles: either providing frontline reception services or engaged in cleaning cabins. However, there is an additional distinction between women from rich and poor countries. Women from the North tend to work in better jobs on the cruise lines and see it as a chance to mix work with tourism by visiting different ports of call. In contrast, women employees from the South are uninterested in the travel dimension, but are focused on the opportunity to earn money to care for their families. The ethnic and gendered division of labour matters because the working conditions for these groups vary so significantly. Lower-level workers are required to sign longer-term contracts at lower wages with few to no holidays. In many cases, their wages are kept low with the assumption that the remainder depends on passenger tips.

---

might be able to make as many as 20 a day. However, if the job was to be broken down into tasks and assigned to individuals, many more pins could be made. One person could draw out the wire, another could cut it, and yet another could make the points. Smith divided the task of pin-making into 18 distinct operations. Under his system, ten people could make 48,000 pins, the equivalent of one person making 4,800. One can certainly doubt the various numbers that Smith used, but the point is significant. The division of labour increases productivity.

Smith attributed this increase in productivity to three factors:

1 Practice at a particular task increases dexterity, which increases speed. The more someone does a task, the better and faster they can do it.
2 Time is saved by eliminating the need to move from one job to another.
3 By simplifying the production process through task specialization, machinery can be applied to the tasks. They can then be performed more quickly.

Smith also believed that the causes of the division of labour had three sources:

1 People's natural propensity to 'truck, barter and exchange': He believed that it was part of people's nature to want new products and things they could not provide for themselves.
2 'Self-love': People's interest in furthering their own position encouraged them to trade and engage in the division of labour.
3 'Habit, custom and education': Some people were more skilled in particular trades, others had better education and still others were raised in particular tasks.

Recognizing the benefits that could be derived from a division of labour, Smith and other liberals moved on to some other points. In general, they believed that the more advanced a society, the greater the division of labour. Thus, states should take steps to support the division of labour. One thing they could do was to enlarge the size of the market. The larger the market, the more different types of products would be created and the greater the division of labour. Local markets could be expanded to national markets which could then be expanded by engaging in an international market through international trade.

Central to Smith, and liberal ideology, is the idea that the benefits of the division of labour and liberal policies flowed down to the lowest members of society. Smith argued that the difference between a prince and a peasant in Europe is not as great as between a peasant and an African king. The debatable point he wanted to make was that the worst off in the most advanced society fared better than the best off in a less advanced society. While this is clearly untrue, one can see the link between Smith's view of the benefits of an international division of labour and David Ricardo's theories of comparative advantage discussed in Chapters 4 and 6. Ricardo's view was that if each country specialized in the product that it could produce best, all countries could benefit from international trade. These benefits flowed from shifting national resources into the most competitive industries, thus increasing the degree of specialization in the international division of labour.

Modern liberal economic theory and many international institutions propagate these views by suggesting that countries and peoples will prosper by engaging in free trade and tasks that the market rewards. Thus, one sees that the IMF's structural adjustment programmes encourage developing states to open their economies and produce for the export market. The WTO was established to encourage states to reduce barriers to trade and facilitate an increasingly specialized division of labour.

Critiques of the liberal approach come from those who suggest that the division of labour is not natural and is shaped by power relations. There are three slightly different versions of this critique. Scholars working out of the dependency tradition note that countries are locked into particular forms of labour because their economies were the victims of imperialist expansion. A second set of theorists focusing primarily on advanced industrialized states argue that particular economic sectors are strategic and vital to state interests. States must shape the division of labour to ensure that they remain active in these areas. This second group shares some of the assumptions of the first about power relations shaping economic activity to the benefit of some states rather than others, but focuses on the struggle between advanced industrialized states rather than the gap between North and South. Feminist scholars are

the third group and they argue that the gendered division of labour is caused by patriarchy and the unequal distribution of power between men and women.

Looking back at history, one finds considerable support for the claims of dependency theorists that the division of labour is not 'natural' but is based on historical conflict that locks countries into particular roles (Dos Santos, 1970). An examination of the international system in the 19th and early 20th centuries reveals that there was a limited form of a division on an international basis, with areas, countries or even continents specializing in particular tasks. In general, countries that had gone through the Industrial Revolution made manufactured goods and other states supplied raw materials or food. A crucial question is: When did the division of tasks begin and why? Was it, as Smith might have suggested, something natural? Or did force and conquest play a large role in establishing an international division of labour? Unlike liberal theory, which suggests that the division is an outcome of some natural process, French historian Braudel (1979, p. 50) argues that the 'past always counts'.

Let us review the fate of the triangular trade across the Atlantic and the resulting division of labour. Europeans exchanged manufactured textiles and guns for African slaves. These slaves were then forcibly transported to plantations in the Caribbean and the US. The products from the Caribbean and the southern US were then sold at immense profit in Europe and further east. In the case of cotton, the raw material was transformed into textiles and sold on. This division of labour increased productivity and helped to feed the Industrial Revolution, but how did it come about? It is clear that the process, which resulted in the African continent 'specializing' in slaves, the Americas specializing in raw materials and Europe in manufactures, was not simply a product of different skills. America's resources were exploited through the use of force and slave labour. Many of the products in which the Caribbean and Latin America 'specialize', for example sugar, were transplanted by European colonists from other parts of the world.

Another good example of force of arms shifting the division of labour is the textile industry in Britain and India in the 18th and 19th centuries. When Britain had the superior navy and inferior textiles, it managed to keep Indian textiles out of Britain. Both countries were able to produce textiles because British textiles could not compete in India and the Indian product was kept out of the British market. However, in later years when British textiles were superior (because of the Industrial Revolution) and India was held by force, Britain was able to destroy the Indian textile industry by selling its cheaper products in the Indian market.

One can conclude from such examples that the international division of labour was not an agreement between equal parties open to review. Economic patterns and power relations sometimes date back to an ancient state of affairs. The significance of this point is that political authorities in the form of nation-states have a role in shaping where their population 'fits' in the division of labour.

Palan and Abbott (2005) have examined the various strategies that nation-states have pursued in order to shape comparative advantage and their place in the division of labour. Depending on their existing place in the global political economy and domestic political coalitions, some options are more feasible than others. Small- to medium-sized states bordering economic powerhouses might try a strategy of regional integration. Poor, small states could opt to fit into the division of labour by acting as tax havens or selling their flags to shipping lines that use them as flags of convenience (see Box 9.2). Some states can exploit their knowledge base and use social programmes to shield their workers, while others attempt to gain a cost advantage by suppressing the cost of labour.

Feminists note that employment in the labour market is segregated by gender. Particular tasks are assigned to men and other tasks are assigned to women. Women are clustered in poorly paid, unpaid and insecure forms of work. They are rarely able to reach positions of power. An example of this glaring inequality can be seen in photographs of G7 finance ministers, heads of state or business leaders. A woman's face rarely appears among the pictures of men in dark suits. Women are noticeable by their absence. Women are excluded from many occupations by a variety of obstacles and tools. These tools include the law, tradition, unequal educational opportunities, lack of public services and violence. From a gender perspective, the division of labour is created by unequal power relations and is reproduced on a worldwide basis (Peterson and Runyan, 1993).

MAJOR DEVELOPMENTS

There have been two major developments in the division of labour. The first has been the change and spread of different production processes. The way things are produced has gone through a number of changes and this influences how people fit into the work process. One major change was the introduction

---

Box 9.2 Flags of convenience

One strategy that some states have adopted for finding a place in the global division of labour has been to sell their sovereignty or state regulation to commercial interests. The flag of convenience (FOC) in the shipping industry is a prominent example. A FOC ship is one that flies the flag of a country other than the country of its ownership (International Transport Workers' Federation, 2012). For example, a ship owned in the US might fly under the flag of Panama. The FOC state allows shipowners from other states to register their ships in the FOC state. The ships sail under the flag of the FOC state and become subject to the labour, environmental and safety rules of that state. Leading FOC states are Panama, Liberia and the Marshall Islands. Even landlocked states such as Mongolia can become FOC providers.

The arrangement suits some states well because they earn a fee for every ship registered in their state. Shipowners benefit because they can lower their costs by avoiding labour, environmental and safety regulations, which impose financial costs. For example, a FOC ship can employ crews at much cheaper rates than crews on ships flagged in traditional maritime states such as the US or Britain. The disadvantages of this system are borne by seafarers who can endure difficult working conditions and non-payment of wages, traditional shipping states that lose business to FOC states, and any state wishing to regulate the maritime industry. FOCs can hide the identity of owners so that when a problem with a ship arises, such as an oil spill or the stranding of crew, it can be difficult to find the owners and hold them responsible for the incident.

of mass production in the early 20th century, while the second change occurred at the end of the century with the introduction of more flexible work organizations. The second major development has been the move from an international division of labour to a global division of labour. This has reduced, but not eliminated, the connection between type of work and geographical location.

Changes in the production process

Although the benefits of a division of labour were known before the 1800s, it was the Industrial Revolution and the application of modern factory management techniques that greatly boosted productivity. One man, Fredrick Taylor, had so much influence that a form of production was named after him – Taylorism, which refers to the practice of scientific management (Braverman, 1974, pp. 85–137). Similar to Smith, Taylor advocated the breaking down of production into individual tasks. He conducted detailed studies on the factory process and then recommended particular changes. In a famous case, Taylor used a stopwatch to time the shovelling of iron and made changes to improve the amount that could be shovelled by one person in a day from 12 to 47 tons.

The key to Taylorism was management control over worker time. Managers concentrated knowledge and power in their hands. Workers were viewed as beasts of burden who had to be instructed in particular tasks and closely supervised. The result was that workers were increasingly deskilled as they fitted into the factory system. Workers could be substituted into a series of simplified tasks.

The person most famous for successfully applying and elaborating on Taylorism was the car-maker Henry Ford. Ford engaged in the mass production of automobiles on factory lines. He standardized car models so that they could be made more quickly and cheaply. Advertisements for the Model T car promised customers they could have a car in any colour as long as it was black. The working conditions in Ford's factories were very difficult. He would often put the strongest workers at the beginning of the assembly line, thus forcing all others to keep up to the fastest pace. On a more positive note, Ford introduced the $5 a day wage, which was higher than what his competitors paid. The wage was designed to attract workers and also offered the possibility that workers might one day be able to afford the products they were producing. It opened the door to mass consumption to go along with mass production.

Some approaches to political economy, such as the Regulation School, label the post-1945 economic system in advanced industrialized countries 'Fordism' (Dunford, 2000). Fordism combined the model of mass production (the factory system) with mass consumption. Mass consumption was achieved by redistributing income from the wealthy to a broader base of citizens through programmes such as progressive taxation, old age benefits, public healthcare and education, and unemployment insurance. Organized labour played a role in the system as it negotiated wage increases for its members as productivity in the economy increased.

The Fordist system contributed to a boom in Western economies in the 1950s and 60s as the volume of consumer products exploded. However, by the 1970s, Fordism came under increasing pressure from inflation and the emergence of a new international division of labour. Competition from new producers in industrializing countries put pressure on national Fordist arrangements. In the 1980s, the Fordist method of production was increasingly challenged by what was variously called 'flexible specialization', 'lean production' or 'Toyotism' (after the Japanese car company). These new methods emphasized a form of production that was more flexible than Fordism. For example, just-in-time inventory systems meant that companies would not stockpile parts; they would order them and receive them just in time for production. Workers were encouraged to work in teams, learn a variety of skills and abandon traditional union structures in favour of work teams or company unions.

Today, we have a mixture of production methods in the global economy. Many automobile manufacturers have moved to Japanese production methods and more flexible specialization. However, the mass production factory system is alive and well in many old industries such as textiles and some newer service industries. For example, call centres where workers are closely monitored and follow particular scripts operate on a rigid Fordist factory model.

From the new international to the global division of labour

Beginning in the 1970s, a number of people noticed a new international division of labour (Frobel et al., 1980). This observation reflected the development of manufacturing in the newly industrializing countries (NICs), such as Brazil and Mexico and the 'four tigers' – Hong Kong, Singapore, Taiwan and South Korea. It seemed to be reversing the historical trend where non-Western states supplied raw materials for Western states.

As discussed in Chapter 7, a combination of factors helps to explain the geographical dispersal of corporate activity to other parts of the world (Dicken, 1998). Technological change made it possible to split up the manufacturing process and locate different operations in different countries. Improved transport and communication systems allowed for better control of this diffusion of manufacturing. Another factor was the combination of growing costs in developed states and low-cost production sited in developing states. The Fordist system in industrialized countries resulted in rising wage rates for labour. In industrializing states, labour costs were low and efforts were made to keep them low through labour suppression or the creation of export processing zones. Many states in the developing world pursued an active policy of supporting industrialization and exporting to the developed world.

In advanced industrialized states, the growth of manufacturing in developing states caused some concern. The Fordist compromise of distributing benefits to workers came under increasing pressure. Locked in cost competition, some workers were forced to accept wage reductions and some manufacturing operations closed down. Workers were urged to be more flexible in terms of working longer or more varied hours. Factories closed in many industrial areas such as the northeast of the US and a vigorous debate was launched about whether countries were 'deindustrializing'.

By the beginning of the 21st century, the process of globalization was facilitating the creation of a global division of labour. As outlined earlier in the chapter, geographic space was coming to be less and less a factor in determining the location of production. Patterns of inequality were still massive and growing, but pockets of different types of activity could be found in most parts of the world. To be clear, the concept of a global division of labour does not suggest that all the people of the world are involved in the same labour market. Indeed, even those sympathetic to the notion of global labour estimate that only 15 per cent of the world's population is actively engaged in such activity (Harrod and O'Brien, 2002, p. 13). Yet, this is a significant and growing group. More and more people are influenced by the global economy and must adjust their behaviour to take account of forces beyond national borders. Some specific groups benefit greatly from this trend and push for more rapid liberal globalization (see Box 9.3).

Another interesting dimension of the global division of labour is migration. People have migrated for thousands of years, but new forms of transportation and communication make it easier to travel long distances and allow migrants to maintain contact with their home

Box 9.3 Globalizing elites

A division of labour has implications for those people at the top of the income scale as well as the majority of people who live in poverty. Groups that benefit from a more liberal economic system and increasing capital mobility press for further liberalization and integration. A set of globalizing elites agitate for public policy that will allow them to continue to accumulate wealth at a rapid rate. They have political, economic and cultural orientations that favour global rather than national economic activity and lifestyles. Sklair (2001) has argued that groups of TNC executives, state and international bureaucrats, technical professionals, merchants and media officials form a transnational capitalist class. A major concern of these elites is to balance the continued opening of the global economy with the need for social stability (Gill, 2003). Globalization processes highlight and reinforce inequality, but they also provide marginalized groups with the opportunities to build alliances and challenge their subordinate position. Thus, the World Economic Forum, which serves as a meeting place for globalizing elites, is now challenged by the presence of a World Social Forum inhabited by non-elites seeking different forms of globalization.

community. There are about 215 million people (3 per cent of the world's population) living in countries other than the one of their birth (World Bank, 2011, p. vii). This includes people who have settled permanently in new countries, contract workers on limited stays, professionals working for TNCs, undocumented workers (illegal immigrants), refugees and asylum seekers. Although migrants are a small percentage of the world's population, they play a vital role in the global economy (see Table 9.1 for the rise in remittances globally).

In many developing states, the money that migrants send home from their employment in developed countries plays a significant economic role. Remittances are now larger than FDI and foreign aid in many countries. Major surges have flowed to emerging economies such as China, India and Mexico. The top recipients of officially recorded remittances for 2012 are India ($70 billion), China ($66 billion), the Philippines and Mexico ($24 billion each) and Nigeria ($21 billion). It is estimated that the value of remittances will increase from $406 billion in 2012 to $534 billion in 2015 (World Bank, 2012a). Table 9.2 provides statistics that show the increasing significance of remittance flows to developing countries.

There are a number of positive economic benefits associated with remittances sent by migrants to their home country. Remittances increase a country's foreign exchange and have a positive impact on savings and investment, leading to higher human capital accumulation, investment and entrepreneurship. Furthermore, remittances can be better targeted to the needs of the poor than official aid or FDI, and are positively correlated with reducing the level and severity of poverty.

Developed countries are becoming more and more dependent on migrant labour and immigration to fulfil their labour needs. Foreign workers are in demand for two reasons. First, the birth rate is so low in developed

Table 9.2 Remittance flows to developing countries, 2010–13 (billion dollars)

Inflows	2010	2011	2012	2013
All developing countries	334	373	403	418
East Asia and Pacific	95	106	107	113
Europe and Central Asia	32	38	48	52
Latin America and Caribbean	56	59	60	61
Middle East and North Africa	40	43	49	49
South Asia	88	97	108	111
Sub-Saharan Africa	29	30	32	32

Sources: World Bank (2013, 2015a)

states that their population is shrinking. Second, the population is rapidly ageing, which means that there will not be enough workers to pay for the pensions and healthcare demanded by the older generation. It is estimated that if Europe wants to retain a healthy ratio of workers to retired people, it will need to allow almost 159 million new immigrants into its territory by 2025 (*World Guide 2001/2002*, 2001, p. 21). Without increased immigration, almost 47 per cent of Europeans would be retired in 2025.

The increasing importance of migrant workers and immigration has raised a number of significant issues in the global political economy (Stalker, 2001). Migrant workers often have poor employment conditions and are subject to abuse or exploitation. Social tensions can arise in receiving states because native workers or citizens may feel themselves under economic or cultural threat from foreign workers. Since migrants play a crucial economic role in the states they leave and the states they work in, it is essential that mechanisms are developed to deal with such issues.

Table 9.1 Remittances from migrants, 2000–9 (billion dollars)

Year	Total	Developing countries	Developed countries
2000	131.5	81.3	50.2
2005	274.9	192.1	82.8
2009	416.0	307.1	108.9

Source: World Bank (2011)

KEY ISSUES

Migration is just one of many pressing issues surrounding the global division of labour. Here, we will focus on three others: the ways in which two huge, populous countries are becoming increasingly integrated into the global division of labour; the struggle over workers' rights in the global economy; and the relationship between workers' rights and global stability.

Global restructuring: the rise of China and India

A significant development in the global division of labour is the increasing integration of the world's two most populous countries, China and India, into the global economy. The adjustments required of workers in these and other countries as production and service provision move across state boundaries are substantial. They cause friction within and between countries.

China is the subject of immense attention because of the large share of FDI it attracts and the value of goods it exports to Western states. The label 'made in China' is found on an ever-increasing number of products. However, the rise of China as a centre of production is a complicated affair with a variety of implications.

Beginning in 1978, the Chinese communist government began a policy of selectively integrating some parts of its economy into the global economy. Special economic zones were created in several coastal areas to attract foreign investment and spur economic growth. The government later began a process of reducing the size of state-owned enterprises and forcing them to run on a more efficient basis. Although millions of jobs have been created in the special economic zones, millions of jobs have also been lost in the state sector and other parts of the economy. The majority of the people who lived in the countryside were excluded from the benefits of economic reforms. Foreign investment poured into the special economic zones and generated considerable growth. Indeed, China became the leading destination for FDI in the developing world in the 1990s.

The potential wealth and market share that China represents gives leverage to the Chinese government in its negotiations with foreign TNCs. For example, in return for the privilege of locating its search engine within China, Google agreed to censor websites objectionable to the Chinese government. Admitting that this censorship ran counter to its corporate ethics, Google claimed it would be worse not to offer Chinese users any information (Watts, 2006). Google joined Yahoo! and Microsoft in helping the government create the 'great firewall of China' by preventing Chinese citizens' access to sites dealing critically with Tibet, Taiwan and the Tiananmen Square massacre of 1989. Another example of Chinese state influence over TNCs was the ability of the Chinese government to extract a promise that European-based Airbus would set up production factories in China as part of a deal to sell planes to Chinese airlines.

China's ability to attract large amounts of foreign investment has increased employment and earned foreign exchange, but generates its own sets of problems. One issue is the impact on its own internal division of labour. The growth of special economic zones has created a growing gap between urban dwellers and those in the countryside. This, in turn, has caused the largest mass migration of people in history. Since economic reforms were introduced, it is estimated that over 150 million people migrated from rural to urban areas. This figure may rise to 500 million by 2020. One city in China, Shanghai, has two-thirds as many migrants from the countryside (three million) as there were Irish immigrants to the US over the 100 years from 1820 to 1930 (4.5 million) (Yardley, 2004). The mass movement of Chinese workers poses large problems for government authorities. Many migrants are exploited by employers who fail to pay wages. Many do not have access to adequate housing or healthcare services. In the countryside, economic conditions continue to stagnate, generating resentment against the growing inequality of economic development.

Although it is not possible to gather accurate statistics, unrest among peasants and workers in China appears to be increasing in the early 21st century (Cody, 2004, 2005). Peasants often confront local Communist Party officials who are unsympathetic to their plight. Workers are unable to form independent trade unions and must rely on the communist-controlled All China Federation of Trade Unions. In many cases, union officials represent the party's interest in pleasing foreign investors or they may even work for the company in question. Because of a lack of legitimate means to express dissent and articulate alternative working and living arrangements, worker and peasant frustration often explodes into violent and spontaneous demonstrations.

Another aspect of China's rapid integration into the global economy is the fact that the control of much of this production rests in the hands of foreign-controlled TNCs. Indeed, the increase in Chinese production is often simply the result of shifting economic activity from other parts of Asia. Asian and, to a lesser degree, Western investors have moved production out of East and South-east Asian countries into China. Computers formerly manufactured in Taiwan, textiles sewn in Hong Kong and electronics made in Japan are now made in mainland China. Whereas it is true that the US trade deficit with China has increased greatly, its trade deficit with Asia as a whole has not. This indicates that Asian manufacturers are using China as their assembly plant. The majority of exports out of China (60–70 per cent) are controlled by non-Chinese corporations or Chinese corporations subcontracting for foreign corporations. While Chinese corporations make profits and millions of Chinese workers have secured jobs, China has not yet been able to develop global brands as the Japanese did in the 1970s. It has primarily been other Asian (Taiwanese, Japanese, Hong Kong, South Korean) and Western TNCs that have reaped the profits of low Chinese production costs.

This has implications for the debate over whether or not Chinese manufacturing is undermining global labour standards. While Chinese suppression of independent labour unions does undermine labour standards in export industries, foreign TNCs must also accept some responsibility. Some foreign TNCs sign contracts with Chinese-based companies demanding they supply constantly cheaper products. The demand to 'roll back prices' leaves Chinese producers with very thin profit margins and an incentive to limit or reduce the amount of money paid to workers. The dilemma for Chinese companies is that raising prices to give more money to workers may well result in losing contracts from large Western retailers, such as Walmart. Thus, consumer demand in Western countries for cheaper and cheaper products gives an incentive for Western TNCs to demand less costly products, which squeezes the wage levels and working conditions of Chinese workers.

The rise of Chinese manufacturing also puts tremendous pressure on all those countries and workers producing labour-intensive products similar to China (Breslin, 2005). Western workers have felt the pinch of Chinese competition, but it is an even greater challenge to workers in developing nation-states. Mexico's strategy of using low wages to attract investment and become the assembly plant for North America is undermined by even lower cost Chinese labour. Attempts by Indonesia and the Philippines to attract foreign investment face an uphill battle against mainland China. The elimination of the Multifibre Agreement on textiles in 2005 means that many developing countries that had invested in textiles as a development strategy risk losing their economic activity to China. An emerging power like India must also pay attention to Chinese competition.

The story of global competition for wages does not end there, however, because even China is not immune to the threat of capital leaving for cheaper labour. In 2005 and 2006, foreign investors in the Pearl Delta region of China began to complain of a labour shortage for their factories. There were plenty of workers available, but the problem was that there were not enough workers of the preferred type. Factory owners wanted young women with a high school education willing to work for low wages in very poor working conditions. Increasing resistance to this type of work from Chinese women threatened the profits of some China-based businesses, raising the spectre that capital might move on to Vietnam or Cambodia (Yardley and Barboza, 2005). China's challenge is to manage its labour force so that it continues to attract investment in low-wage industries, but under conditions that do not alienate consumers concerned about labour abuses (see Box 9.4).

India, the world's second most populous country, has also become more integrated into the global economy since its government began a liberalization programme in the early 1990s (Jenkins, 2003). Whereas China has excelled as an assembly plant, India has enjoyed international success in the business services sector. Drawing on the skills of Indians who are well educated and proficient in English, TNCs have established businesses located in India that provide a wide range of services for Western companies. Call centres handle all manner of customer services such as dealing with customer complaints or booking airfares for Western airlines. Data processing activity for North American law or insurance companies can be shipped overnight to India and the completed work returned the next morning. Printing, editing and proofreading services for academic books can be done by Indians and shipped back to Britain.

The subcontracting of these types of services to India (and many other countries) has been termed 'outsourcing'. While Chinese production threatens to undermine blue-collar employment in industrialized countries, Indian outsourcing competes with white- and pink-collar employment. Service jobs can be shipped 'offshore' to cheaper Indian workers. In addition, the US government approved changes to its immigration laws in the 1990s, which permitted work visas for IT specialists to work within the US itself. The increased competition to US workers from Indian service sector workers led to the invention of a new slang term: 'Bangalored'. Bangalore is a city in India that has served as a centre of growth in the IT industry. To be 'Bangalored' means to lose one's job due to outsourcing.

> **Box 9.4** How do you make those Apples?
>
> Apple, consumers' favourite technology company, relies heavily on supplying people with cutting-edge electronics that respond to consumer demands and even create new desires. Central to its business model is the rapid introduction of new generations of technologies at affordable prices. On the eve of the launch of the new iPad in 2012, Apple was rocked by allegations from NGOs and in the media of its subcontractors' poor working conditions. Many of Apple's iPhones and iPads are made by Foxconn (a Taiwan-based company, whose official name is Hon Hai Precision Industry Co. Ltd), China's largest private sector employer. Foxconn had been reported to be a site of poor working conditions, which had prompted over a dozen workers' suicides. In response to increasing bad publicity, Apple agreed to a public audit of Foxconn by the Fair Labour Association (FLA). The FLA is an NGO working on labour issues. The FLA concluded that Apple's Chinese subcontractors posed 'serious and pressing concerns over excessive working hours, unpaid overtime, health and safety failings and management interference in trade unions'. In response, Foxconn pledged to reduce hours of work and increase wages for its employees (Duhigg and Greenhouse, 2012).
>
> The implications of these events will take some time to work out. An improvement in Foxconn employment conditions could set a positive precedent for Chinese factories and improve the lives of millions of workers. Alternatively, factories might relocate to new areas to maintain existing labour practices or they might not live up to the ones they have committed to. And what will the impact be on Apple consumers? Will they be content to accept increased prices and delays in product innovation that will result from improved working conditions?

The insertion of parts of India's economy into the global services market has generated political conflict both in the US and India. In the US, proponents of outsourcing stress the competitive advantages US companies can gain from cheaper global services.

Workers who have lost their jobs or feel threatened by increased economic insecurity attack outsourcing. During the 2004 US presidential election, the Democratic Party raised outsourcing as an issue of concern to workers and attacked the Republican Party for supporting corporate outsourcing strategies. In India, Hindu nationalist parties trumpeted high-tech successes as evidence of a rejuvenated and competitive country (Chakravartty, 2006). Other Indians worried that the government's emphasis on supporting high-tech and service industries came at the expense of helping the majority of India's population, which relies on small-scale agricultural production. These people highlight issues such as the large number of farmer suicides caused by rural desperation, and the poor working conditions in call centres, which require mainly female operators to work nights so that they can answer calls in the North American daytime. Thus, outsourcing became an election issue in India as well as in the US. In India, however, the concern was with the balance of the new economy with other areas of the economy.

The ongoing integration of up to two billion people into the global workforce generates immense challenges and opportunities. A deepening global division of labour simultaneously increases productivity and offers the possibility of people in the developing and developed world gaining from that increase. China's entry into the global economy has lifted millions of Chinese out of poverty and allowed Western workers to purchase many products at cheaper prices. However, these transformations also threaten social stability as inequality grows within countries and shifting manufacturing production reduces employment in some countries and regions. Workers from many different countries are pitted against each other in a competition for investment and wages. The challenge is whether states can develop mechanisms to redistribute wealth and manage social dislocation fast enough to maintain social order and harmony.

The integration of China and India into the global division of labour also raises questions from a power politics perspective. As China and India upgrade their economic capacity, they accumulate wealth and power. This change in absolute and relative capabilities may cause insecurity among their neighbours, leading to conflict. For example, South Korea and Japan may feel threatened by growing Chinese military power. The US might also see China as a potential military and economic rival. India has fought several wars with Pakistan and competes with that country for influence in Afghanistan. India and China also have a tense and competitive relationship. They have border disputes that have led to war in the past. As two of the largest developing countries, India and China are also rivals in seeking to attract foreign investment and as political leaders of the developing world. Whether one takes a perspective that focuses on social inequalities or state power, the absorption of China and India into the global division of labour is significant.

The struggle for workers' rights in a global economy

Over the past two decades, most international economic agreements, such as the revitalization of European integration through the single market project and monetary union, the North American Free Trade Agreement (NAFTA), the creation of the WTO and the attempt to negotiate a Multilateral Agreement on Investment at the OECD, have been designed to liberalize economic activity. In each of these cases, non-business social interests have attempted to influence the content of the agreements. However, the attempt to bolster labour rights in a globalizing and liberalizing economic world is extremely difficult. Although a wide range of groups have joined the struggle, they face two difficult questions (O'Brien, 2002). How do you regulate transnational capital? What is the appropriate relationship between equity groups located in different areas of the world?

The question of regulating capital concerns how people can create rules to place the activity of businesses that operate across state borders in a broader social context. How can they be prevented from undermining labour and environmental conditions? Corporate behaviour can be influenced through two different mechanisms. Firms can be regulated by states or by pressure in the market. With regard to state regulation, this can take place through the extraterritorial regulation of powerful states or the application of rules in multilateral institutions. Extraterritorial regulation involves a state demanding that corporations that have headquarters in their state or are engaged in economic activity in their state conduct global business according to the home state's rules. It sets the preferences of a particular state as the benchmark for corporate behaviour in other countries. In practice, this means that corporate activity must conform to the desires of particular interests in advanced industrialized states.

Depending on one's position on a particular issue, extraterritorial jurisdiction can have negative or positive effects. Most people would agree that developed states that prosecuted their corporations for using slave labour in foreign countries were doing a good thing. However, other prohibitions are viewed more negatively. Numerous states have objected to such activity in measures such as the US Helms-Burton Act of 1996 forbidding trade with Cuba. Since the US is engaged in economic warfare with Cuba, it threatens corporations that do business in the US with penalties if they trade with Cuba. Some Canadian executives of Canadian companies cannot enter the US because they would be arrested for the economic activity of their companies in Cuba.

Extraterritorial rules reflect the balance of power within a particular state rather than a consensus of the international community. Since the rules are set nationally and not negotiated between a group of states, they are idiosyncratic. The US's single-minded pursuit of economic warfare against Cuba is incomprehensible to most other states. However, because the US is such a powerful actor, its particular views have considerable impact. This is not a recipe for a global system with common rules.

It is because of the negative implications in unilateral extraterritorial regulation that multilateral arrangements involving a negotiated standard between numerous states are often viewed as preferable. However, multilateral agreements are difficult to negotiate and suffer from the accusation that they also benefit the strongest powers. This is illustrated in the debate about linking labour standards to the operation of the WTO.

Following the creation of the WTO, many elements of the international labour movement, such as the International Confederation of Free Trade Unions (ICFTU; now called the International Trade Union Confederation), sought to have their concerns addressed in the organization by incorporating labour rights into its principles. Labour's goal was to have core labour standards (or a social clause) brought into its purview (O'Brien et al., 2000, pp. 67–108). The social clause would have committed states to respect seven crucial ILO conventions (87, 98, 29, 105, 100, 111, 138). These conventions provide for:

1 Freedom of association and the effective recognition of the right to collective bargaining
2 Elimination of all forms of forced or compulsory labour
3 Effective abolition of child labour
4 Elimination of discrimination in respect of employment and occupation.

The union initiative to incorporate the conventions into the WTO emerged from a desire to make labour standards legally enforceable and not subject to the whims of individual states. In contrast to the ILO's reliance on moral argument, the WTO has the ability to enforce compliance. Labour unions, including the ICFTU and some of its prominent affiliates such as the American Federation of Labor & Congress of Industrial Organizations (AFL-CIO), pressured the US and the EU into raising core labour standards at the WTO. The unions argued that continued support for trade liberalization in developed states required a minimum floor for workers' rights.

The labour movement was unable to secure enforceable labour rights in international institutions mainly because of the opposition of a combination of liberal states, developing countries and business associations. Leaders in many liberal states argued that economic growth raises labour standards and any interference in trade for labour reasons would lower the gains from trade. Many leaders in developing states expressed a fear that labour standards would only be used as a form of protection by developed states against developing countries. Finally, businesses remain opposed, fearing both a rise in protectionism and a reduction in their profits.

In addition to resistance from state and corporate elites, there were elements of the labour movement that opposed both the idea that core labour standards should be part of the WTO and the existence of the WTO itself. For example, the linkage between labour standards and the WTO was rejected in two national conferences of Indian unions in March and October 1995. Delegates expressed fears that the social clause initiative was driven by protectionist desires in northern countries. The Indian union suggestion was that rather than working through the WTO, workers should push for a United Nations Labour Rights Convention and the establishment of National Labour Rights Commissions (*Asian Labour Update*, 1995).

Although unsuccessful at the WTO, unions have pursued other steps via the ILO. The first was the ILO's initiative to take the conventions setting out core labour standards and bundling them into the 1998 ILO Declaration on Fundamental Principles and Rights at Work. This declaration bound all states to respect core labour standards, but as mentioned above, it lacked any enforcement power. A second initiative has been the campaign at the ILO and the UN for a Social Protection Floor, which would set a minimum level of social protection for workers in all countries (Deacon, 2012). Once again, this is an important step in terms of setting goals, but there is considerable doubt whether states will implement such measures.

Today's global products can have supply chains that reach across the world and pass through a series of companies and their subcontractors. It can be difficult to know the labour and environmental conditions in which everyday products are manufactured and traded (see Box 9.5). In response to the failure of states to regulate TNCs and their subcontractors, efforts have been

---

Box 9.5 Forced migrant labour in Malaysia and Thailand

Forced labour can be found in a wide range of industries and countries whose products make it into global supply chains. In many cases, the labourers are migrants trapped by debt, forced to work in appalling conditions and vulnerable to violence. For example, some of the electronic devices sold in Europe and the US are assembled in Malaysia using migrant workers trapped in forced labour conditions. Workers from Bangladesh, India, Indonesia, Nepal and Vietnam working in Malaysian factories are vulnerable to having their passports confiscated by employers and landing in debt traps where they must continue working in poor conditions to pay off debts owed to recruitment agencies or employers. In Thailand, overfishing has increased competition, pushing down wages and working conditions. Fishing companies have increasingly turned to migrants from Burma and Cambodia to serve as cheap labour. In many cases workers are kept in bonded labour for years, constantly subject to poverty, illness and physical abuse (EJF, 2015). Their catch is turned into food for shrimp which are then exported around the world.

made to influence corporate behaviour through the introduction and enforcement of codes of conduct. This has spawned a series of campaigns against particular corporations by consumer and union groups. Such activity is part of a civil society campaign to 'Think globally and punish locally' (Rodman, 1998). In college campuses across the US, the largest student activist movement since the anti-apartheid campaign has formed around the issue of sweatshop labour. Students Against Sweatshops, a national movement, has lobbied for improved working conditions and labour rights in companies that supply products to universities. It has also put the question of ethics and the possibility of profiting from an ethical policy on the agenda of many corporations and in business publications.

Codes of conduct are meant to set basic principles for the behaviour of TNCs (and their subcontractors) with respect to their labour practices and environmental policies. In some cases, firms are willing partners in implementing such codes. For example, the code of conduct of the Levi Strauss jean company is reproduced in union literature as an illustration of a TNC working with the union movement (ICFTU, 1996a, p. 59). Levi Strauss is notable not just for its code of conduct banning labour exploitation, but also for its withdrawal in 1992 from states operating extreme forms of authoritarian industrial relations, such as Burma and China.

One prominent union strategy is to select a particularly serious abuse of workers' rights, highlight the abuses in the media and attempt to pressure governments to legislate, consumers to boycott and corporations to change behaviour. Good examples are the campaigns against child labour and labour conditions in South-east Asian toy factories (ICFTU, 1995a), and against child labour in the manufacture of footballs (ICFTU, 1996b). Prior to the start of the 1996 European Football Championships, the ICFTU revealed that footballs endorsed by FIFA, football's international governing body, were made in Pakistan using child labour. This involved cooperation between the ICFTU, Norwegian unions who supplied the camera crew, British unions in the country of the championships and Pakistani unions on site in the targeted country. The adverse publicity resulted in FIFA adopting a new code of practice and more attention being given to labour issues around a key social/sporting event.

The pressure from organized labour and consumer groups in developed countries has forced the hands of government and international organizations as well as TNCs. For example, in April 1995, US president Bill Clinton announced a voluntary code of conduct covering business ethics and workers' rights for US companies working abroad. The UN secretary-general brought together international organizations, corporations and civil society actors to launch the Global Compact initiative in 2000. It is designed to encourage businesses to adhere to internationally agreed principles on human rights, labour standards, environmental protection and anti-corruption. This initiative is discussed in more detail in Chapter 15.

Market-based solutions have recently been favoured because of the hurdles in establishing agreement between states. The proliferation of codes and the ensuing debate have focused a spotlight on the plight of workers in many countries (Pearson and Seyfang, 2001). Although one can point to the achievements of such activity, the fact is that it is a second-best strategy: it occurs because state regulation has failed (Kearney, 1999). Market activity is not seen as sufficient in national societies because of the inefficiency of effort required to launch continuing citizen campaigns. There are problems with collecting and distributing information, mobilizing citizens and the need for constant vigilance. A legal process and institution is needed to regularize activity and enforce general rules. If market-based activity is seen as inadequate for domestic purposes, why would it prove sufficient on a global scale?

In practice, there are a multitude of strategies from market to state-based initiatives seeking to address the labour standards issue. Some civil society actors have been successful in raising awareness, while the threat of state action (either unilaterally or multilaterally) has been useful to focus the minds of corporate and state elites. The challenge is to work out a suitable combination of these strategies (O'Brien, 2002).

The division of labour and global stability

It may seem strange to people living in the present era, but there was a time when the state of people's working conditions was thought to have an influence on international peace and security. Following the Russian Revolution and the end of the First World War, Western leaders were so worried about labour unrest contributing to conflict between states that in 1919 they created an international organization to deal with labour issues – the ILO. The goal of the ILO was to ameliorate working conditions so that labour unrest would subside and communist agitation would fall on infertile ground.

It is time to reconsider this relationship between labour unrest and global order. This can be done in both liberal and critical theoretical traditions. From a liberal perspective, labour can be viewed as one of many domestic interest groups that make international cooperation very difficult (Milner, 1997). From a critical perspective, labour is part of a broad social force that seeks to challenge the existing basis of international order (Cox, 1986). Numerous labour-oriented groups offer a challenge to the basic liberal principles that make up the global order (see Box 9.6). Here we'll consider just three groups of workers mobilizing to challenge the basis of global order: workers in the US, those in NICs and peasant farmers (O'Brien, 2000).

US workers

In the past 30 years, US labour has moved from being an unquestioning ally in the spread of US hegemony to being a growing obstacle to further liberalization and internationalization. US labour has not abandoned the state for worker internationalism, but is rethinking its position. This raises doubts about the social base in the US for maintaining leadership in the liberalization process.

In the immediate postwar era, US labour was firmly engaged in the politics of productivity (Maier, 1977). The politics of productivity involved subsuming class conflict by ensuring that growth and productivity gains were distributed across the economy. It reflected a belief that the proper technical management of the economy would create the conditions for prosperity, which would eliminate the need for harmful distributional battles. It was a method of neutralizing labour opposition by integrating unionized workers into a division of economic spoils. Internationally, organized labour played a crucial part in laying the groundwork for today's process of neoliberal globalization. US labour took a leading role in marginalizing radical workers' organizations in Latin America, Asia and western Europe (Cox, 1977; Radosh, 1969). This ground-clearing work facilitated the expansion of US business and resulted in labour becoming an actor in the globalization process (Herod, 1997).

However, the rise of neoliberal governments in the US and Britain, accompanied by a business offensive against workers, led to the ejection of labour from the governing coalition (Rupert, 1995a, pp. 167–207). This marginalization of moderate worker organizations corresponded with a movement by US elites to separate their destiny from the rest of the nation (Lasch, 1995; Reich, 1992). As the polarization of US society continues and the revolt of the elites is clearer, it becomes more practical for workers to look to the international realm for solidarity and assistance. In the US context, Rupert (1995b) has argued that the NAFTA debate may be a watershed in organized labour's acceptance of the dominant brand of liberalism. Not only did labour break with US corporations over the issue of linking

---

Box 9.6 Popular opposition to Greek austerity

The financial crisis that rolled over Greece between 2010 and 2012 shows how the best-laid international financial management plans can collapse in the face of public opposition. International solutions to Greece's debt problem negotiated between the government of Greece, the EU and the IMF reflected a consensus of political and financial elites in Europe and Greece. Indeed, Pasok and New Democracy, the leading parties in the Greek parliament, saw stringent austerity as the best path to regain solvency and stay in the eurozone. The austerity packages were severe. For example, cuts proposed in September 2011 included firing 100,000 public sector workers, immediate cuts to the pensions of farmers, sailors and telecommunication workers, and the creation of a reserve labour pool of 50,000 state employees working for reduced wages (Smith, 2011). The response from elements of the Greek population included peaceful and violent protests, demonstrations and a general strike. Austerity measures caused Greece to fall deeper into recession, with a considerable rise in unemployment. When elections were held in May 2012, the populace punished the governing parties and threw their support to parties on the left and right of the political spectrum that advocated a rejection of austerity and the debt deal. The international consensus negotiated to deal with Greek debt did not take worker responses into account and in the end was threatened by their opposition.

workers' rights to regional trade agreements, but it also openly opposed a Democratic Party leadership and a sitting Democratic president. A second notable change in the policies of organized labour was the attempt to work with environmental and consumer groups to forge a common position on this element of economic policy. Finally, the AFL-CIO was forced to cultivate relations with the emerging independent Mexican unions rather than rely on the Mexican government-sponsored Confederation of Mexican Workers. This had proved adequate for US workers' interest in the Cold War when the fight was against communism, but allies in the fight against transnational exploitation would have to be found in unions controlled by their members.

In what ways might a more oppositional US labour movement influence the global political economy? One method is by changing the agenda for international institution-building. At the multilateral level, labour organizations have complicated the WTO's plan to extend liberalization into new sectors and regions as they press for the inclusion of core labour standards (O'Brien, 1998). Labour organizations are pushing the IMF and the World Bank to revise the neoliberal content of their structural adjustment lending (ICFTU, 1995b). In the case of the World Bank lending to South Korea, this resulted in provisions aimed at offering unprecedented (if limited) protection for workers (World Bank, 1998). At the regional level, an alliance of convenience between labour and right-wing populism stalled US approval for the expansion of NAFTA. A second method is shaping the international economic environment through corporate policy. In concert with other social groups, labour has increased pressure on multinationals to change their investment locations or methods of conducting business. This is particularly evident in the campaigns for company codes of conduct to temper the poor labour and environmental practices mentioned above.

The recent, hesitant transformation of US labour may be part of a new internationalism for a broad spectrum of groups concerned with labour issues. A number of authors (Moody, 1997; Waterman, 1998) have raised the possibility of a new internationalism based on transnational networks of labour activists inside and outside unions. These networks form alliances with other social movements in the North and South to offer an alternative prescription for economic, political and social order.

Workers in the NICs

In the NICs, the 1997 financial crisis in East and Southeast Asia placed the issue of workers' rights and activities firmly on the analytical agenda. The Asian development model, sometimes sympathetically described as 'paternalistic authoritarianism' (Pye, 1988), was thought to prosper because, in contrast to Latin American authoritarian models, development was more egalitarian. Workers were often coerced, but they shared in the benefits of growth (in this view). Stability was ensured by growth. Suddenly, economic growth vanished, at least temporarily. Workers in South Korea faced the prospect of unemployment in a non-welfare state. The South Korean government was forced to create new welfare provisions in order to deal with potential unrest in the new democracy (Huck-Ju, 2001). In Indonesia, the economic collapse was more serious and eventually led to a transformation of the political system.

The social chaos arising from the financial meltdown in Asia and the reaction of workers to that chaos was a factor in determining regional and global stability. The World Bank recognized the danger of social disintegration when James Wolfensohn, its then president, announced that approximately 60 per cent of the $16 billion it had promised in financial assistance would be directed to 'protecting the poor and providing a social safety net' (*International Herald Tribune*, 1998). Social unrest was viewed as an imminent danger to internationally backed plans for financial restructuring. The threat to the IMF's and World Bank's rescue packages did not come from the political and economic elites of the target states, but from those who bear the costs of such restructuring – the working population.

Peasant farmers

As important as the role of workers in Asian states may be, there is another significant labour issue confronting the global political economy. To use McMichael's (1997) terms, it is the 'agrarian question'. The agrarian question concerns the implications of replacing peasant-based agriculture with capitalist agriculture. Although this was a subject of grave concern in Western states in the 19th century and attention to peasant affairs was also raised during social revolutions in China, Cuba and Vietnam in the middle of the 20th century, the agrarian question had not been posed again until recently. It has re-emerged in response to the threat that the liberalization of agriculture poses to billions of peasants around the world.

Slowly, but surely, a global peasant alliance emerged to challenge the dominant notions of liberalization, consumption and environmental destruction. The most dramatic event was the peasant and Aboriginal rebellion in the southern Mexican state of Chiapas in 1994 (Reding, 1994). Although the rebellion drew on a historical legacy of oppression, it was clearly linked to steps taken by the Mexican government to liberalize agricultural landholdings in the run-up to the NAFTA. Local concerns were linked to broader developments in the international political economy. The Zapatistas were quick to exploit modern technology to broadcast their cause worldwide and began the task of forging links with similarly minded groups in other parts of the world.

The Peoples' Global Action against 'Free' Trade and the World Trade Organization (PGA) is another example of a peasant-based anti-imperialist grouping. The PGA is an instrument for coordination, which brings together people's movements to oppose trade liberalization (PGA, 1997). The PGA organizes conferences approximately three months before the biannual Ministerial Conferences of the WTO. Conferences are used to update the PGA manifesto and coordinate global and local action against free trade. The conference committee for the February 1998 event included groups such as the Zapatista National Liberation Army from Mexico, Karnataka State Farmers' Association from India, the Landless Workers' Movement from Brazil and the Peasant Movement of the Philippines. The PGA is committed to nonviolent civil disobedience and a confrontational attitude in pursuit of its opposition to free trade. It represents a constituency firmly in opposition to dominant trends in the global political economy.

This analysis is not arguing that workers or peasants in the developing world will serve as the basis for a revolutionary movement to overthrow capitalism. There are certainly many peasants in the world, but the power they face in economic and military terms is immense. It is possible, however, to identify these groups as offering potentially significant resistance to the liberalization project. They represent a key force in world politics, but it is one usually hidden from view because of the standard IPE analytical categories. Analysis of the international order that ignores them would be incomplete and flawed.

CONCLUSION

The political fall-out from the financial and economic crisis of 2008–12 may once again raise the issue of worker welfare and political action onto the agenda. At the very least, the issue of inequality is once again on the political agenda (See Box 9.7). A person's place in the global division of labour has a great impact on how long they will live, how much they consume and what kind of health they can enjoy. The existence and growth of massive inequalities around the world is literally a question of life and death to millions of people. At the same time that such problems proliferate, people are active in forming themselves into trade unions, community associations, political parties and nongovernmental organizations to combat the negative effects of a growing global division of labour. They seek to increase equality and influence the division of labour to the benefit of the world's populations. Readers of this book are part of that process in their activity as citizens and consumers.

Box 9.7 Runaway inequality

In January 2014, Oxfam published a report on global inequality which argued that economic elites had captured political institutions in many countries and created a system which siphoned money to the top of the income scale. Some of its key findings included:

▶ Almost half of the world's wealth is owned by just 1 per cent of the population.
▶ The wealth of the 1 per cent richest people in the world amounts to $110 trillion. That's 65 times the total wealth of the bottom half of the world's population.
▶ The richest 85 people in the world (who could fit into one double decker bus) own as much as the bottom half of the world's population.
▶ Seven out of ten people live in countries where economic inequality has increased in the last 30 years.
▶ The richest 1 per cent increased their share of income in 24 out of 26 countries for which we have data between 1980 and 2012.
▶ In the US, the wealthiest 1 per cent captured 95 per cent of post-financial-crisis growth since 2009, while the bottom 90 per cent became poorer.

While people are divided into groups according to the division of labour in the global economy, they are also divided and shaped by another powerful structure – gender. Chapter 10 investigates how gender shapes and is shaped by the global political economy.

Further Reading

The classic work of Adam Smith on the division of labour is contained in the first three chapters of his *The Wealth of Nations* ([1776]1983). Ronen Palan and Jason Abbott outline a variety of strategies available to states seeking to find a place in the division of labour in *State Strategies in the Global Political Economy* (2005). Philip McMichael (1997) examines the pressing issue of agriculture and subsistence farmers in 'Rethinking Globalization: The Agrarian Question Revisited', *Review of International Political Economy*, 4(4): 630–62. An excellent source of articles on global labour issues is the open-access online *Global Labour Journal*, available at https://escarpmentpress.org/globallabour.

Chapter

10 | Gender

This book has already alluded to the gendered nature of the global political economy. Distinctions between men and women have played an important role in the history of the development of the global political economy (Part 2) and in all the key structures already examined in Part 3, namely, trade, production, finance and labour. Gender considerations are also relevant to the succeeding chapters, particularly those on development, the environment and security. The aim of this chapter is to take a systematic look at the gender dimension of the global political economy.

We begin by providing some definitions and background about gender and feminist approaches to IR and IPE. The next section outlines how and why attention to the relationship between men, women and the global economy is important for the study of political economy. The third section examines the integration of women into the world economy through a discussion of female employment trends. It follows this survey with an exploration of the internationalization of global gender policy through a focus on the evolution of global concern with the role of women in the world economy. The final section discusses three key gender issues in the contemporary economy: the feminization of poverty, the globalization of reproductive work and the impact of restructuring and globalization.

DEFINITIONS AND BACKGROUND

In everyday speech there is often a tendency to use the terms 'gender' and 'sex' interchangeably. This merging of the terms creates confusion between biology and social roles. It is now widely accepted that gender is a social construction and not a natural state. In the words of Jill Steans (1998, p. 10): 'gender refers not to what men and women are biologically, but to the ideological and material relations which exist between them.' This distinction is repeated by Peterson and Runyan (1993, p. 5), when they state: 'Unlike sex (the biological distinction between males and females) gender refers to socially learned behaviours that distinguish between masculinity and femininity.' The central point made in these definitions is that women and men are different biologically, but that this biological sex difference is not the same as the social distinctions made between men and women (see Box 10.1). To underscore this point, consider the various ways in which the meanings attributed to masculinity and femininity vary across cultures and across historical time. The innate biological makeup of men and women does not change, but the social expectations concerning appropriate behaviour, rights, responsibilities and resources are not static. While the roles ascribed to men and women vary across cultures and over time, this does not mean that they are arbitrary or random.

Box 10.1 Feminization as devalorization

Among the insights of a gender analysis are the extensive implications of feminization as devalorization. This means that the characteristics often associated with femininity are valued less than those associated with masculinity. Femininity is associated with caring rather than controlling, submissiveness rather than aggression, feeling rather than thinking, weakness rather than strength, home life rather than public life. With feminine attributes valued less than masculine attributes, anything that is feminized is then devalued. For example, labour markets are said to be increasingly feminized. This means more than just an increased number of women working in the labour market. It means that working conditions for the whole labour market are taking on the attributes of what was thought to be appropriate for female work – casual, informal, insecure, part-time and low-waged employment. The implications of devaluing the feminine are widespread because a whole series of groups, not just particular women, can be feminized. The characteristics of femininity can be applied to whole races, groups of men, immigrants, refugees or other groups that are kept in a subordinate position. Thus, feminists argue that denigrating the feminine can serve to support a whole series of hierarchies, not just those between men and women (Peterson, 2003).

Box 10.2 Gender inequality facts

▶ Of the approximately 775 million adults worldwide who lack minimum literacy skills, two-thirds are women.
▶ Youth and adult illiteracy is almost exclusively a developing country phenomenon.
▶ Of the 213 million women who become pregnant every year, 85 million have unplanned pregnancies.
▶ Despite a fall in maternal mortality globally between 1990 and 2013, every day around 800 women die from causes related to pregnancy and childbirth.
▶ Women's share of seats in national parliaments has increased worldwide since the early 1990s, but women still only account for 22.1 per cent of legislators in national parliaments.

Sources: IPU (2015); Sedgh et al. (2014); UNESCO (2015); WHO (2014)

There are some features, for example assigning women the primary role in childcare, that seem to be common in many societies. Moreover, the construction of masculinity as superior to femininity in terms of power and access to resources also appears constant throughout history (Peterson and Runyan, 1993, pp. 5–6).

A focus on gender is important because it makes us aware of a key axis of power in society. Gender roles fundamentally shape production, distribution and consumption activities within nation-states and across national borders. Gender thus plays a role in determining access to work, income, wealth, leisure, education, health, political power and decision-making (see Box 10.2). Comparative economic analysis reveals widespread discrimination on the basis of gender in education, health, economic opportunities and political

participation (see Box 10.3). It has been established that gender bias may reduce economic growth (Dreze and Sen, 1989), thus providing an economic incentive and political rationale for targeting gender inequality. Many national governments and international organizations are currently focused on addressing problems stemming from gender inequality. Current approaches to poverty and inequality focus on quantitative and qualitative measures (UNDP, 1995, pp. 72–86). A commitment to gender equality is necessary in order to transform the lives of women. It is the normative framework behind social and economic policies designed to reduce women's exclusion, invisibility and disempowerment.

The study of gender entered the discipline of IR and the sub-field of IPE through the work of feminist scholars. Unlike gender, which has a fairly settled meaning, no consensus exists on the definition of feminism. The absence of consensus on the definition of feminism is apparent in attempts to classify feminist theories. One classificatory scheme lists liberal feminism, Marxist feminism, radical feminism, socialist feminism, psychoanalytical and existential feminist thought, postmodern feminism and feminist critical theory (Steans, 1998, p. 16). Whitworth (1997, pp. 11–38), in her study of the application of feminist theory to IR, surveys a field comprising liberal feminism, radical feminism, feminist postmodernism and critical/feminist IR.

Box 10.3 Measuring the global gender gap

The World Economic Forum's *Global Gender Gap Report 2014* (2014) provides a cross-country comparison of the gender gap in 135 countries. Using four indices – economic participation and opportunity, educational attainment, political empowerment, and health and survival – the study used a scale of 0–1 to measure gender inequality, where 0 = inequality, 1 = equality. Countries were then ranked using this scale. The top five countries were Iceland (0.8594), Finland (0.8453), Norway (0.84374), Sweden (0.8165) and Denmark (0.8025). The bottom five countries were Mali (0.5779), Syria (0.5775), Chad (0.5764), Pakistan (0.5522) and Yemen (0.5145).

While recognizing the plurality of feminist discourses, it is possible to discern two zones of agreement relevant to analysis of the global political economy. First, feminist scholars recognize that gender differences are also differences of power, and these differences permeate all aspects of social life. A focus on the gender dimension of the global political economy allows us to examine the roles women and men play in productive and reproductive relationships. Second, feminist research is committed to 'making a difference'. The goal of some feminists is meliorative change, that is, change within the prevailing power structures, while others seek more revolutionary change and are interested in challenging the established order. At the heart of feminism is an agency of change. Whether committed to incremental change or emancipatory politics, feminist scholars recognize the close connections between activism, policy-making and academic research.

It has been argued that the feminist contribution to IR has been to highlight the ways in which the state and market are 'gendered by masculinist assumptions' (Youngs, 2004, p. 76). Feminists also show how the dominant approach 'ignores both women's realities and their active contributions to political and economic life' (Youngs, 2004, p. 76). Feminists have also demonstrated how a failure to examine gender 'obscures the interrelated social construction of male and female identities and roles' (Youngs, 2004, p. 76). These are important contributions and in the next section we review some

of the major theoretical issues that have arisen in the context of explanations of the gendered nature of the global political economy.

THEORETICAL PERSPECTIVES: GPE AS IF GENDER MATTERED

IR theorists are only one group of scholars seeking to explain the gendered nature of the global political economy. Economists, anthropologists, sociologists, political scientists and development specialists among others have all made relevant contributions. Indeed, it is arguable that these scholars have made more important and sustained analyses of global gender relations than IPE specialists. Research on gender and IPE has developed in two broad streams. On the one hand, it has evolved within the context of the conversation between IR theory and feminist scholars and in the internal debates in IPE as it strives to develop its identity. A second focus of research on gender and the global political economy emanates from feminist scholarship in the social sciences, particularly in economics and development studies. When feminist concerns first emerged in IR, they encountered a discipline that was gender blind. The three paradigms (realism, liberalism and Marxism) excluded consideration of women and gender issues. Gender issues were rendered invisible and illegitimate by the central assumptions contained in all three perspectives. Realism, with its focus on the activities of nation-states and its separation of the political and economic, is incapable of theorizing social relations of power. Liberalism, which admitted the existence of actors other than the state, was also dominated by a focus on the realm of state interaction and a separation between state and market. The traditional Marxist approach to class conflict did not distinguish between male and female workers, that is, it did not develop gender as an analytical category. One notable exception was the development of Marxist feminist analyses. For example, Maria Mies (1998) explored the connection between capitalism and patriarchy in her analysis of the international division of labour.

The emergence of IPE as a distinct sub-field of IR held out the promise that the limited agenda of conventional IR scholarship would be extended (Allen, 1999). As we have noted in Chapter 1, when IPE emerged as a distinct sub-field of IR it was constructed as a debate between the three IR paradigms. Although IPE promised to break out of the straitjacket of IR assumptions, many of these were carried into its own framework. Conventional IPE has limited (if any) engagement with feminist scholarship and gender issues. IPE directs attention to economic structures and processes and is open to investigating the importance of firms, social movements, civil society and international organizations, but usually not gender. While it would be correct to acknowledge that IPE scholars have extended the scope of IR, most significantly in giving serious consideration to the behaviour of non-state actors, it has nevertheless constructed a new and limited orthodoxy. The lament of Tooze and Murphy (1991) concerning the restrictions of orthodox IPE still resonates two decades later.

If conventional IPE was too restricted on the one hand, on the other critical IPE held promise as a site from which to engage in an exploration of gender in the global political economy. A number of studies in the 1990s noted the gender-blind nature of critical IPE but also thought that potentially favourable connections between critical IPE and feminist analyses could be developed. For example, Sandra Whitworth (1997, p. 31) argued that 'the most useful point of departure for a feminist IR theory is one which relies on socialist-feminist insights and critical theory more generally and takes into account gender relations'. And while recognizing the limitations of critical IPE, another feminist scholar claimed that critical global political economy was 'useful but not a sufficient starting point for thinking about gender relations and feminist politics' (Steans, 1999, p. 113). However, two more recent reviews of critical IPE scholarship argued that most of it fails to engage in any significant manner with gender (Griffin, 2007; Waylen, 2006). Despite the relative neglect by IPE scholars of gender relations, a vast and important literature examining the gender implications of international economic processes has developed.

There are a number of controversies and disputes in the political economy literature on the interrelationship between gender and global economic structures and processes. Instead of focusing on these various conflicts, we explore how attention to gender assists in providing compelling explanations of global economic processes (see Box 10.4). In this discussion, we take heed of the distinction between women as an empirical category and gender as an analytical category (Peterson,

> **Box 10.4** Significance of a gendered analysis
>
> A gendered analysis of the global political economy is important because it:
>
> ▶ enables analysts to focus on a more holistic political economy
> ▶ uncovers important subjects and brings these new topics to attention
> ▶ brings concern with development and poverty alleviation from the margins to a more central position
> ▶ remaps the conceptual landscape.

2005). It should also be emphasized that we do not assume that there is a single feminist position or that this summary of the important theoretical issues will cover all the themes that the various schools of thought consider vital.

In the first place, an assumption that the subject identities of men and women are identical is simply false. As we noted above, gender uncovers deep-rooted and systematic differences in power between men and women. A focus on gender uncovers the various ways in which power relations are constructed and maintained in the international economy. A political economy analysis that attempts to explain the real world cannot be based on concepts that are gender-blind. It cannot be taken for granted that activities are gender neutral. This point can be illustrated through an examination of the relationship between gender and trade. Research has shown that trade and trade policy affect men and women differently. A survey of the evidence claimed that 'trade policies continue to affect men and women differently due to gender inequalities in access to land, information, economic resources and decision-making' (Randriamaro, 2006, p. 11). The relationship between trade and gender is not a simple one; there are sector-specific differences and the results are influenced by geographic, cultural and other factors. Nevertheless, trade and trade liberalization have different impacts on women and men. For example, research has demonstrated the differential impact in agriculture and low-skilled, labour-intensive manufactured products (Korinek, 2005). Trade liberalization has been shown to have a positive impact on women's employment in manufacturing industries (Seguino, 2000). Another study of the relationship between trade liberalization and women's employment and earnings confirmed these results and concluded that trade liberalization is likely to be advantageous for women through job creation (Nordås, 2003). The results of these studies can be explained with reference to the price competitiveness of the relevant export sectors. These export sectors have higher rates of female employment since women's wages are lower than men's wages. It should be noted that the differential wage rates between men and women are built on existing gender inequalities. However, women are less likely to reap the benefits of agricultural trade liberalization due to persistent gender inequalities in access to land and limited property rights (Korinek, 2005, pp. 13–15; Randriamaro, 2006, pp. 20–3).

Another important consequence of exploring the political economy of gender is that it uncovers issues ignored in conventional (masculinist) political economy. As a consequence, it shifts attention away from a preoccupation with a limited range of questions and opens up space to consider issues that are marginalized, trivialized or simply ignored. From Cynthia Enloe's *Bananas, Beaches and Bases: Making Feminist Sense of International Politics* (1989) onwards, feminist scholars in IPE have engaged with subject identities and the constructions of masculinity and femininity in the global political economy. Among Enloe's subjects were women invisible to IPE scholarship, including flight attendants, chambermaids and nannies. Feminist scholars have investigated the 'problem of the missing body' (Youngs, 2000, p. 1). Attention to women's bodies and the construction of identities has influenced research on, for example, nationalism, security, sex, reproductive technologies and the environment.

With their focus on gender, feminist scholars have given development a higher profile in IR and IPE. It is arguable that development is a core structure of the global political economy and yet both conventional and heterodox IPE accounts tend to marginalize issues central to understanding development. Development is not only constituted through a range of competing discourses, it is linked in diverse ways to the operation of power internationally. A gendered lens on development has demonstrated that, prior to the invention and popularization of the concept of human security, analysis of development theory and practice brought to the fore key aspects of the contemporary human security paradigm.

Furthermore, gendered analyses of the political economy of debt, environmental degradation, financial crises, poverty and structural adjustment programmes (SAPs) have provided salient insights into globalization.

Feminist scholars have not only made women visible, they have reshaped the conceptual landscape. They have interrogated existing concepts and demonstrated their implicit masculinist assumptions, and developed new ways of thinking about political economy (Bakker, 1994; Young et al., 1984). Feminist economics has challenged many of the prevailing assumptions of neoclassical economics. First, feminist economists have argued that societal institutions are not neutral. In other words, the rationalist logic of 'economic man' is false and mistaken. Economic analysis cannot assume that all economic agents react in exactly the same fashion to price signals. This is because societal institutions are not neutral, and therefore do not provide the same starting point or incentive structures for men and women. For example, institutions such as property rights may restrict and shape the decisions of women (Deere and Doss, 2006).

Second, conventional economic analysis, with its focus on the market, disregards the full value of women's labour and economic contribution. Conventional economics takes unpaid reproductive labour as a given. This assumption masks the real cost of reproducing and maintaining the labour force. Thus, feminist economists have been engaged in strategies to make unpaid work visible and redefine what we mean by work so that it includes unpaid reproductive labour (Hoskyns and Rai, 2007). The invisibility of women's labour is exemplified by national account statistics, which are based solely on monetized values arising from market-based transactions. Feminist scholars have suggested a different classification of work: 'formal market work, informal market work, subsistence production, unpaid care work, and volunteer work' (UNIFEM, 2005, p. 23).

In empirical terms, it is safe to conclude that attention to gender is not only important, it is vital if a full account is to be given of transformation in the global political economy. Such analysis demonstrates how women and men enter into the global division of labour as gendered identities. Conceptual innovations are important in showing why gender analyses are crucial to explaining stability and change in the global political economy. A failure to examine gender relations in the international economy is a recipe for partial, inaccurate and irrelevant analysis. Policy conclusions following from such partial analyses will do little to address prevailing inequalities in the global economy.

MAJOR DEVELOPMENTS

Women enter the economy in a diverse variety of roles, for example as workers, consumers and entrepreneurs. Women are active economic agents in all the major sectors of economic activity – agriculture, industry and services. Chapter 9 introduced the concept of a gendered division of labour and discussed some of the specific consequences of this social arrangement. It highlighted the role that masculinist assumptions play in creating and maintaining inequalities. Here, we discuss two major developments relating to gender issues in the global economy. The first trend is the increasing integration of women into the workforce. We then turn our attention to the emergence of women as a distinct constituency in the global economy, and examine the evolution of concern about gender issues at the level of global public policy.

Women in the world economy: employment trends and prospects

Women have been active participants in economic activity in all human societies. However, women have not always been engaged in productive activity that is remunerated in monetary terms. Thus, while women's contribution to economic growth and development has been invaluable, it has not always been acknowledged and granted recognition by official agencies. The increasing participation by women in the paid workforce has increased the visibility of women's contribution to economic growth. As *The Economist* (2006) stated: 'Arguably, women are the most powerful engine of global growth.' The post-1945 period has witnessed an increasing integration of women into the workforce. This is not an even process, and women's labour participation rates reflect differing geographic patterns dictated by specific cultural and societal values and mores. A focus on women's income-earning capacities is frequently linked with the prospects for increasing

women's economic security. Nevertheless, it has become apparent that indicators showing increasing female participation in waged activity do not necessarily show decreases in gender inequality. In other words, while the level of participation is important, it is also necessary to examine the quality of employment. Therefore, in this survey of female participation in the labour force, apart from employment participation rates, we also examine employment by sector, the nature and status of employment, and wages.

Statistics reveal that more women are in paid employment than at any previous period in history. In 2012, of a total global labour force of 3.3 billion people, 1.3 billion were women (ILO, 2012, p. 15). However, women's share of the total employed labour force has not attained a steady upward curve, and was adversely affected by the global economic crisis (2008–12). In 2008, women made up 40.5 per cent of the global workforce (ILO, 2009, p. 9), while the figure quoted above shows that women's share of the global workforce has declined slightly to 39.9 per cent. While the historical trend reveals that the gap between men and women as part of the labour force, that is, those in work and those actively seeking work, has been decreasing, there are also stark regional variations (see Table 10.1). As Table 10.1 shows there are significant regional variations in women's labour force participation, with significantly lower participation rates in the Middle East and North Africa than in other regions. Differentials in labour force participation rates are also evident in unemployment rates. Female unemployment rates, traditionally higher than those for men in most countries and regions, were also adversely affected by the global economic crisis. Prior to the crisis in 2007 the gender gap in unemployment was 0.5 per cent, with female unemployment at 5.8 per cent and male unemployment at 5.3 per cent on average between 2002 and 2007. As a consequence of the crisis, by 2011 the gap had risen 0.7 per cent, with female unemployment at 6.4 per cent and male unemployment at 5.7 per cent (ILO, 2012, p. 4). In other words, the gender gap in global labour markets (employment, unemployment and labour participation rates) that had showed a degree of convergence in the decade prior to 2007 increased after the onset of the global financial crisis.

Employment trends are the result of short-term and long-term factors, which include general economic growth, sectoral employment shifts and wage differentials. One determinant of female participation in the

Table 10.1 **Male and female labour force participation rates (LFPR), 2002 and 2012**

	Male LFPR (5)	Male LFPR (%)	Female LFPR (%)	Female LFPR (%)	Gap (percentage points)	Gap (Percentage points)
Region	2002	2012	2002	2012	2002	2012
World	78.1	77.1	52.1	51.1	26.1	26.0
Developed economies and the EU	69.4	67.5	51.7	52.8	17.7	14.7
Central & south-eastern Europe (non-EU) & CIS	68.0	70.7	49.1	50.2	18.9	20.5
East Asia	81.4	79.4	69.1	66.4	12.4	13.0
South-east Asia & Pacific	82.8	81.8	58.4	58.8	24.4	49.5
South Asia	83.3	81.3	37.8	31.8	47.5	23.1
Latin America and the Caribbean	80.3	79.5	49.6	53.6	30.7	25.9
Middle East	73.8	74.3	17.2	18.7	56.6	55.5
North Africa	74.1	74.3	21.2	27.2	52.9	49.9
Sub-Saharan Africa	76.5	76.3	63.5	64.6	13.0	11.8

Note: CIS stands for the Commonwealth of Independent States, a regional organization whose participating countries are former Soviet republics. The gap refers to the difference between male and female ratios.

Source: Adapted from ILO (2012, p. 17)

workforce is the demand for female labour. A number of sector-specific factors account for trends in female participation in the labour force. The service sector has replaced agriculture as the main employer for women. In 2012, 47.4 per cent of women were employed in the service sector, compared with 36.4 per cent in agriculture and 16.2 per cent in industry (ILO, 2012, p. 57). These global figures conceal important regional variations.

Agriculture remains the main form of employment for many women in the developing world. Female employment share in the agricultural sector in sub-Saharan Africa is 62.5 per cent; in East Asia it stands at 39 per cent, it is 44.2 per cent in South-east Asia and the Pacific and reaches a regional high of 68.9 per cent in South Asia (ILO, 201, p.57). In all other regions, the service sector is the main source of employment for women (ILO, 2012). Across the globe women tend to be employed in a narrow range of occupations, increasing their vulnerability since the sectors in which women's work is concentrated are frequently characterized by low pay, informal working arrangements and inadequate social protection. This segregation of labour markets effectively maintains a gendered division of labour with women underrepresented in industry and more productive sectors.

The status of women's work cannot be inferred from the statistics on labour force participation and depend on the nature of employment and cultural factors in specific societies. Analysts have been concerned with the security of employment and the conditions of work (see the Key Issues section below for further discussion). It has been argued that women's employment is frequently temporary, part time and less secure than men's work (Mitter, 1986). In this context it has been noted that: 'The attractiveness of women as workers in labour-intensive export industries, whether they be domestically or foreign-owned, is related to the ease of shedding these workers, based in part on gender norms that relegate women's paid work to secondary importance after their domestic and care responsibilities' (UNRISD, 2005, p. 38). This casualization of work may lead to increased employment but frequently this employment is characterized by deteriorating working conditions. For example, enhanced employment in some industries comes at the cost of adequate occupational and health standards, and workers can be prevented from access to union representation and the opportunity to engage in collective bargaining. Furthermore, while women most often enter the labour market voluntarily in response to the economic opportunities offered through paid work, and as an avenue to enhance income and status, this is not always the case. For some women, entry to the labour market is the result of poverty and increased insecurity. The nature and conditions of work in occupations such as the sex industry and domestic service do not necessarily assist in enhancing women's empowerment. Therefore, we cannot conclude that all labour force participation is necessarily positive and beneficial.

One persistent issue regarding women's employment relates to wages and earnings. In all societies, women earn less than men on average. It has been estimated that globally women's earnings are 77 per cent of that of men and the gender pay gap is unlikely to close before 2086 if current policies remain unchanged (ILO, 2015a, p. 2). A UN report (2006, p. 54) noted: 'Closing the gap between women's and men's pay continues to be a major challenge in most parts of the world.' Various explanations have been given for the gender pay gap. It has been argued that women's income potential is stifled by the barriers limiting their progress up the career ladder at the same rate as men. Thus, women do not reach the higher-paid managerial positions (Lopez-Claros and Zahidi, 2005, p. 3). Another possible explanation lies in women's poor bargaining power and negotiating capacity (ILO, 2006). Other studies have focused on the relative influence of gender-specific factors, for example women's educational attainment and employment discrimination, versus overall labour market characteristics (Blau and Kahn, 2003). We can distinguish broadly between factors related to the employment profile of women and others related to wider social factors. On one hand, many women are clustered in low-wage occupations. Often these jobs are low waged because they are traditionally designated as women's jobs. And even in so-called 'female occupations', gender wage inequality is still prevalent, with men earning more than women (ILO, 2009). On the other hand, we can observe the impact of social provisions such as maternity leave and childcare facilities on the economic opportunities open to women and their relative earning capacities. But even where women are in high-wage professions, they do not earn the same as their male counterparts (see Box 10.5).

Gender and global public policy

In the past three decades, gender issues have moved from the margins to a more central position in the policy

---

> ### Box 10.5 The glass ceiling
>
> The term 'glass ceiling' refers to the situation where senior management positions are predominantly occupied by men and wage differentials between men and women remain wide at the top of the pay scale. Studies of the glass ceiling tend to focus on the failure of women to progress to top managerial positions. Obstacles to the recruitment and promotion of women are varied. Some are firm and industry specific, for example old boys' networks, male workplace cultures; others are societal, for example segregation in education, lack of childcare, parental leave and welfare provisions, which make it difficult for women to combine family life and career paths. Recent research confirms the existence of the glass ceiling (Barreto et al., 2009). One study of employment in Sweden identified 'gender differences in reward as a primary factor responsible for the glass ceiling effect' (Albrecht et al., 2003, p. 172).

---

statements issued by governments, regional organizations and multilateral agencies. Women did not just emerge onto the international agenda. Women's issues were 'brought into' the global public sphere as a result of conscious action. Specific human agency was behind the project designed to move women from a position of invisibility to one where their presence nationally and internationally was recognized. The project to 'bring women into the global political economy' was in part in recognition of their unacknowledged existence in economic activity and in part an effort to improve women's position. In the context of development policy, Naila Kabeer (1994, p. 1) notes that: 'One way of charting the emergence of women as a distinctive category in development discourse is to monitor their changing significance within the policy declarations and institutional structures of the major development agencies.' Here, we briefly discuss the roles played by international organizations in shaping the development of global policy on gender equity. We focus on the role of these organizations in the creation of global norms. This entails examining the ways in which shared expectations about appropriate behaviour were developed through the generation and dissemination of ideas, and the rule-making and standard-setting of these bodies.

Historical developments

From the perspective of the early 21st century, it is relatively easy to accept attention to gender as a 'natural' feature of global policy. However, the development of international policy should not be taken for granted. Although the UN created a Commission on the Status of Women in 1946, it had made limited progress by the 1970s. The progressive evolution of global gender policy can be traced to December 1972 when the UN General Assembly adopted Resolution 3010 (XXVII) proclaiming 1975 as International Women's Year. The impetus for International Women's Year came from civil society, and not from a national government. It arose from the Women's International Democratic Federation (WIDF), a Finnish NGO (Pietilä and Vickers, 1990, p. 73). The president of the WIDF in 1972 was Herta Kuusinen, who as a Finnish parliamentarian was also an observer at the annual session of the UN Commission on the Status of Women, and in that capacity was instrumental in getting the call for an International Women's Year onto the agenda. The resolution was later unanimously adopted by the General Assembly. The period between 1974 and 1995 is especially significant in the development of global policy on gender issues and the evolution of a new normative framework.

At the centre of these changes were four international conferences convened by the United Nations, as well as the International Decade for Women. In December 1975, the UN General Assembly proclaimed the period 1976–85 as the United Nations Decade for Women, which provided a focal point for activities within the UN system and raised the profile of women's issues at the international level.

The four key conferences were:

▶ the World Conference of the International Women's Year, held in Mexico City in June–July 1975
▶ the World Conference of the United Nations Decade for Women: Equality, Development and Peace, held in Copenhagen in July 1980 to review progress since 1975
▶ the World Conference to Review and Appraise the Achievements of the United Nations Decade for Women: Equality, Development and Peace, held in Nairobi in July 1985
▶ the Fourth World Conference on Women: Action for Equality, Development and Peace, held in Beijing in September 1995.

The first three conferences were at times fractious affairs, with divisions more apparent than common purpose (Newland, 1988). Nevertheless, these events were important in raising the profile of women's issues and in making gender concerns of utmost importance for development policy. The conferences had an enormous symbolic impact (Tinker, 1990, p. 31). They made women's concerns legitimate and forced national governments to take note of the impacts of their policies on women. The preparatory phases of the conferences and their outcomes were crucial in agenda-setting because they produced detailed research and voluminous literature. As part of the preparatory process for these conferences, governments were required for the first time to collect data that particularly revealed the gender-specific nature of economic, social and welfare policies. More accurate data enables more effective policies to be formulated in areas ranging from employment and income distribution to social security provision and welfare. Redefining work in the global economy effectively means recognizing both waged and unwaged work as essential to the social and economic wellbeing of countries. Moreover, the preparatory process of the conferences and the conference documentation were crucial in helping to identify and clarify women's needs and translate them into demands.

Each conference produced a report, which set the normative and policy framework for subsequent action:

▶ The 1975 Mexico City conference created the 'World Plan of Action for the Implementation of the Objectives of the International Women's Year'.
▶ The 1980 Copenhagen conference led to the 'Programme of Action for the Second Half of the United Nations Decade for Women: Equality, Development and Peace'.
▶ The 1985 Nairobi conference adopted the 'Forward-looking Strategies for the Advancement of Women to the Year 2000'.

These three documents were important in setting clear objectives and defined targets. For example, the mid-decade Nairobi conference in 1985 was convened to review and appraise the degree to which the targets established in the 'World Plan of Action', adopted at the Mexico City conference in 1975, had been attained, and to prepare a precise plan of action for the remainder of the decade. The review of action taken was not particularly encouraging, since it revealed that there had been, for example, limited improvement in the conditions of rural women. A redefined 'Programme of Action' was adopted in Copenhagen in 1980 to oversee efforts in the second half of the decade. Of the three documents, the 1985 'Forward-looking Strategies' is the most important in terms of serving as a blueprint for the advancement of women. The key objectives set out in the document concern women's interests in health, employment, family life, political life and human rights.

It has been argued that 'Perhaps the most far reaching impact of the conferences was the mobilization of women which they engendered' (Tinker, 1990, p. 32). Given the limited participation in UN conferences, their direct impact was also going to be limited. But parallel civil society meetings alongside the official ones provided an open market of ideas and increased the networking of women's organizations globally. The development of the UN Decade for Women and these conferences ensured that women in development became synonymous with the processes of change that were affecting women worldwide.

The full incorporation of gender equality into all stages and at all levels of planning was a slow and evolutionary process. While it is difficult to establish a precise moment at which gender issues became an integral part of the policy process, it is arguable that the Fourth World Conference on Women held in September 1995 in Beijing marked the widespread acceptance of gender mainstreaming (Hafner-Burton and Pollack, 2002). The 'Beijing Declaration and Platform for Action' (UN Women, 1995) set impressive commitments for governments and international organizations. In establishing a set of underlying principles, it explicitly invoked the mainstreaming of gender policies: 'It is essential to design, implement and monitor, with the full participation of women, effective, efficient and mutually reinforcing gender-sensitive policies and programmes, including development policies and programmes, at all levels that will foster the empowerment and advancement of women' (para. 19); and governments committed 'to implement the following Platform for Action, ensuring that a gender perspective is reflected in all our policies and programmes' (para. 38).

Normative and institutional change

While feminist critiques have shifted official policy at national, regional and global levels to consider the distinct interests of women, it is not, of course, the case

that the mainstreaming of gender issues has automatically led to the end of discrimination or to policies that are always pro-women. The concept of mainstreaming as used here refers simply to the diverse ways in which gender issues are now firmly on the agenda, and automatically included as part of the policy process (planning, implementation and monitoring), rather than placed as an afterthought. Thus, gender mainstreaming refers to the integration of gender perspectives with the goal of reducing gender inequality in all phases of decision-making (United Nations, 2001). There are three main features that characterize the current mainstreaming of gender in policy and practice.

The first feature is the normative commitment to gender equality. Since the adoption of the 'Beijing Platform for Action' in 1995, five documents have reinforced the commitment to gender mainstreaming at the international level:

1 the ECOSOC Agreed Conclusions, 1997/2, 'The Role of Gender Units and Focal Points in Gender Mainstreaming', July 1997

2 the UN secretary-general's communication on gender mainstreaming to heads of all major UN units, October 1997

3 resolution A/RES/S-23/3, 'Further Actions and Initiatives to Implement the Beijing Declaration and Platform for Action (Outcome Document)', adopted at the conclusion of the 23rd Special Session of the UN General Assembly, 5–9 June 2000

4 the Political Declaration adopted on 10 June 2000 at the conclusion of the UN General Assembly Special Session on Women 2000: Gender Equality, Development and Peace for the Twenty-First Century (also known as Beijing +5), 5–9 June 2000

5 the Economic and Social Council (ECOSOC) resolution 2001/41, 'Mainstreaming a Gender Perspective into All Policies and Programmes in the United Nations System', July 2001.

These documents are crucial in establishing a framework of gender equality for the work of the UN system. They build on previous important initiatives such as the Convention on the Elimination of All Forms of Discrimination Against Women (CEDAW) adopted by the UN General Assembly in 1979. These developments are not solely the result of activities by nation-states. They have been shaped by the activities of the international women's movement to shape global norms. A key strategy has been to frame women's issues in terms of the human rights discourse (Brown Thompson, 2002; Joachim, 2003).

The emergence and advancement of a norm of gender equality can be perceived in the ways in which international development policy is framed. In December 1961, UN General Assembly Resolution 1710 (XVI) inaugurated the (First) Development Decade. While it was a landmark event in bringing economic development to the forefront of world concern, it made no mention of gender issues. By the time the International Development Strategy (IDS) for the Third United Nations Development Decade was agreed in 1980, it was no longer possible to ignore the gender dimension of development policy. The IDS endorsed the programmes of the Mexico City and Copenhagen conferences and committed the UN to a substantial improvement in the status of women during the decade. Between 2000 and 2015 the consensus on global development policy was framed by the Millennium Development Goals (MDGs). The MDGs present an excellent example of the way in which global policy integrated gender concerns. While all eight MDGs (see Box 11.1) have implications for gender equality, three are explicitly focused on gender concerns. By 2000 when the MDGs were devised it was inconceivable that they would not explicitly address the subordination of women, yet had they been promulgated in 1960, it is unlikely that attention to gender would have gained any recognition. This integration into global public policy is further evidenced by the transition from the MDGs to the Sustainable Development Goals (SDGs). The MDGs will be replaced by the SDGs in 2015, and in the preparatory process gender equality has been earmarked as a key goal for the SDG era (see Box 10.6).

The second feature concerns the way that the normative developments detailed above have been reinforced by the increasing institutionalization of gender issues within the UN system. Gender analysis is now common in the specialized agencies of the UN. The Inter-Agency Network on Women and Gender Equality, established in 1996 and chaired by the secretary-general's Special Adviser on Gender Issues and Advancement of Women, is a focal point for gender mainstreaming activities in all branches of the UN system. The Office of the Special Adviser on Gender Issues and Advancement of Women (OSAGI) was established in 1997 and complements developments in the UN during the Decade for Women. The Committee on the Elimination of Discrimination

---

Box 10.6 Gender, the MDGs and the SDGs

MDG 3 stated 'Promote gender equality and empower women'. The formal target for achieving this goal is to 'eliminate gender disparity in primary and secondary education preferably by 2005 and to all levels of education no later than 2015'. Feminists would argue that gender equality initiatives must go beyond this one measure to address all the MDGs (www.mdgender.net). For example, MDG 1 stated 'Eradicate extreme poverty and hunger'. More women than men are among the extreme poor and women also have responsibility for managing the welfare of children who are also living in extreme poverty. Thus, if they are to succeed, initiatives to alleviate extreme poverty should be gender sensitive and adopt specific measures to improve the welfare of women and children. In response to such concerns, SDG 5 is much broader than its MDG predecessor. It states: 'Achieve gender equality and empower all women and girls' (SDG 5).

Against Women was established in 1982 and charged with the responsibility for supervising the implementation of CEDAW. Apart from this committee, other organizations have been created devoted to pursuing gender equality and ensuring that women play an active role in the development process:

- In 1976, a Voluntary Fund for the UN Decade for Women was established by the UN General Assembly, which was transformed into the United Nations Development Fund for Women (UNIFEM) in 1984. Currently, UNIFEM identifies four strategic areas to guide its work programme: reducing feminized poverty; ending violence against women; reversing the spread of HIV/AIDS among women and girls; and achieving democratic governance in societies.
- The UN International Research and Training Institute for the Advancement of Women (INSTRAW) was created in 1976.
- Within the UN, the Division for the Advancement of Women (DAW, part of the Division for Social and Economic Affairs) was created in 1988 as the central unit within the organization for all issues pertaining to women.

It would take until 2010 before the UN brought several aspects of its gender programmes under one institution (see Box 10.7).

The third feature is that gender has been mainstreamed within many international organizations. The establishment of gender departments or sections in many international organizations reflects not only the degree of institutionalization of gender issues but also the normalization of gender as a framework of analysis. Since the Beijing conference in 1995, many international organizations have raised the profile of gender issues in their research, analysis and operational activities. For example, although the ILO's mandate on gender equality is grounded in ILO conventions from the 1950s, including the Equal Remuneration Convention 1951 and the Discrimination (Employment and Occupation) Convention 1958, in the wake of the Beijing conference, the ILO director-general announced a policy on gender mainstreaming in 1999, and in 2001 the ILO adopted an 'Action Plan on Gender Equality and Gender Mainstreaming'. Another example is the World Health Organization (WHO). The WHO adopted a gender mainstreaming policy in 2002 (WHO, 2002), and has a specialist unit, the Department of Women, Gender and Health, to oversee WHO gender policy.

These changes are both a response to internal bureaucratic design and the result of external pressure. The normative shift has created a space for non-state actors to pressurize intergovernmental organizations. For example, women's groups in alliance with trade unions have been able to bring women's issues onto the agenda of the ILO. In 1996, the ILO adopted guidelines for employment in homework (Prugl, 1999). Homework is not housework, but work that companies have labourers do in their homes. It is usually performed by women working for very low pay. The fact that the ILO examined homework is a sign that feminist views and women's issues are making inroads into mainstream institutions.

In this context, the shift in policies at the World Bank presents an instructive case of the progress made in mainstreaming gender issues. The Bank was slow in integrating gender issues into its policies, and while by the end of the Nairobi conference in 1985 other aid donors had made provision to give attention to gender issues, it did not issue its first policy paper (*Enhancing Women's Involvement in Economic Development*) until 1994. Although a sole adviser on Women in Development had been appointed in 1977, and the Women in Development Office established in 1986, it was not until after the Beijing conference in 1995 that a concerted attempt was made to engage with feminist analyses of development. It should be noted that the World Bank's engagement with gender issues was also partly a response to pressure from civic associations. For example, women's groups had been in an extended dialogue

---

Box 10.7 UN Women

In July 2010, the General Assembly of the UN created UN Women, the United Nations Entity for Gender Equality and the Empowerment of Women. It merged the functions of four existing UN institutions:

▶ the Division for the Advancement of Women (DAW)
▶ the International Research and Training Institute for the Advancement of Women (INSTRAW)
▶ the Office of the Special Adviser on Gender Issues and Advancement of Women (OSAGI)
▶ the United Nations Development Fund for Women (UNIFEM).

The first executive director (2010–13) was Michele Bachelet, the former president of Chile. The current executive director is Phumzile Mlambo-Ngcuka, a former deputy president of South Africa. UN Women was created to address the lack of funding for women's issues and the need for a central body to work across the UN system on gender equity and empowerment.

Half the organization's key focus areas have an explicit economic aspect: economic empowerment, national planning and budgeting, and the SDGs; the others are human rights, peace and security, leadership and participation. Research and advocacy work in these areas are designed to raise issues of economic inequality and suggest measures to remedy disparities. For example, the national planning and budgeting focus advocates gender-sensitive budgeting to national governments. This form of budgeting entails considering explicitly the impact of budget decisions on gender issues and the adoption of budget measures that advance equity and empowerment for women.

with the World Bank (O'Brien et al., 2000, pp. 24–66). They had some success in convincing staff that development policies that ignore women are flawed. A more recent innovation in Bank policy occurred following the September 2006 annual meeting of the IMF and World Bank, at which Paul Wolfowitz, the Bank's then president, announced a new four-year $25 million plan called 'Gender Equality as Smart Economics' (World Bank, 2006a). The objective of this plan is to advance women's economic empowerment.

Transformations in the World Bank's policies, funding priorities and institutional arrangements have not automatically convinced its critics that it has effectively mainstreamed gender in its operations (Griffin, 2009). The record of the World Bank on gender mainstreaming is a topic for debate and the Bank's legitimacy in this area is questioned by groups that are yet to be convinced that the organization has a real, rather than a shallow, commitment to gender issues (Bessis, 2001). Critics contend that the World Bank's cognitive universe is neoclassical economics and as such its concern is with market efficiency. This contrasts with the gender justice objective of feminist economics (O'Brien et al., 2000, p. 47). The criticisms of the World Bank and its response are, of course, important but from the perspective of the argument here, the fundamental point is that the World Bank has not only had to respond to pressure to integrate gender concerns into its framework, but it is also sensitive to criticism concerning the ways in which it is mainstreaming gender.

KEY ISSUES

A gender perspective on the global economy reveals that men and women are impacted in different ways by changes in production, trade and financial flows. A gendered division of labour ensures that crises in the world economy are, in great measure, absorbed by poor and working-class women. We begin our discussion by presenting evidence related to the ways in which the global political economy impacts on poverty and women's capabilities. The discussion then analyses the globalization of reproductive work and highlights the various ways in which women's bodies are traded internationally. Finally, we explore three connections between gender, restructuring and globalization.

The feminization of poverty

The United Nations Millennium Declaration states that a key objective is 'to promote gender equality and the empowerment of women as effective ways to combat poverty, hunger, disease, and to stimulate development that is truly sustainable' (United Nations, 2000a). This statement represents a powerful global consensus linking poverty and gender inequality. While it is directed specifically at the developing world, the feminization of poverty is a phenomenon applicable to women worldwide. There are various alternative explanations to account for the apparent fact that women are more likely to be part of the very poor than men. Of the various factors accounting for female poverty, three have been given prominence in the literature: an increase in female-headed households; the continued existence of intra-household inequalities and systematic bias against women and girls; and the impact of neoliberal economic policies (Moghadam, 2005).

The increase in female-headed households

The term 'feminization of poverty' originated in the US in the late 1970s when researchers discovered an increase in female-headed households and a higher incidence of poverty among single mothers. US data since then has continued to reveal a link between poverty and female-headed households. However, the universal applicability of the thesis that female-headed households are more likely to be poor than male-headed households has been the subject of some controversy and contention. While research indicates a rising trend in female-headed households around the world, evidence on the impact of family structure on poverty is less conclusive. Some studies in the developing world have found that female-headed households are more vulnerable than other groups and have less access to income-generating opportunities (Appleton, 1996; Barros et al., 1997; Buvinic and Gupta, 1997). However, the contention that there is a link between female-headed households and poverty has been dismissed as 'impressionistic and anecdotal' (Quisumbing et al., 1995, p. 1). They argue that there is no strong evidence to support the claim that female-headed households are on average disproportionately represented among the poor. One review of the evidence suggests that there are cross-regional variations in the economic status of female-headed households (Moghadam, 2005). The importance of family structure on poverty is mediated by macro-social and political factors and women's access to employment. Another systematic review of the literature concluded that 'The evidence surrounding the incidence of poverty in female-headed households is (also) found to be country and case specific (Lampietti and Stalker, 2000). The importance of family structure on poverty is mediated by macro-social and political factors and women's access to employment. A recent study of poverty in Nigeria came to the conclusion that female-headed households are less likely to be poor than male-headed households (Oginni et al., 2013).

Intra-household inequalities

Research on the relationship between intra-household inequality and female poverty is more conclusive (Moghadam, 2005). Various studies have shown that in many societies (especially in South Asia), women are systematically discriminated against in the household. Women have unequal access to education, healthcare and nutrition and this unequal resource allocation negatively impacts their employment and income-generating opportunities. This intra-household inequality, when combined with existing social and economic structures of patriarchal dominance, exacerbates women's vulnerability and increases female poverty.

The impact of neoliberal economic policies

There has been a considerable amount of research on the human and social costs of neoliberal economic policies. Research in the 1990s and early 2000s focused on the impact of the Washington-consensus-type policies. For example, Marchand and Runyan (2000) explored the gender dimension of neoliberal restructuring. While many men have suffered from structural adjustment, women have been systematically and more dramatically impoverished. The costs of economic restructuring under SAPs are disproportionately borne by women. As governments attempt to balance budgets and engage in SAPs to make their economies more internationally competitive, women are often forced to pay the price by taking up tasks hitherto performed by the state or giving up their existing sources of income in order to concentrate on caring for their families'

immediate needs (Chang, 2000, pp. 124–9). In other words, SAPs are dependent on unpaid women's labour (Nagar et al., 2002). Furthermore, when food subsidies are reduced, women often cut back on their own nutrition in order to feed their children. As health and education are reduced, women often take on the additional burden of nursing family members, or girls are kept at home to help in domestic tasks rather than going to school. The move to export agriculture for foreign currency can cause peasant women to lose their land or force them into becoming seasonal workers. In desperation, many women export their labour through migration. It is widely accepted that women's lives are negatively impacted by loss of food security, additional burdens of work, application of user fees in healthcare and education, and increasing domestic violence resulting from the imposition of neoliberal policies. However, a study of the impact of structural adjustment in Niger and Senegal concluded that: 'It is a mistake (however) to assign a blanket impact for the SAPs where none existed' (Creevey, 2002, p. 110). Creevey argues that while SAPs in Niger and Senegal had a negative impact, some women were empowered as their businesses flourished in response to market liberalization measures. While most of the discussion has focused on the impact of structural adjustment on women in developing countries, women in relatively rich countries also bear a large burden in times of economic restructuring and deficit reduction (see Box 10.8).

This early work has been complemented by recent research that interrogates a more complex understanding of neoliberalism (Molyneux, 2008). This wider agenda has led to studies *inter alia* that explore the ways in which liberalization and privatization may have negative impacts in some contexts yet in others increase choice and employment opportunities for women (Rakowski, 2000); the ways in which development agencies have embraced women (Lincove, 2009); the subject position of women under neoliberalism (Roberts, 2015); and neoliberalism, gender and financial crisis (Griffin, 2015).

Globalization of reproductive work

The reproductive economy is the 'economy of families and the private sphere – where human life is generated,

Box 10.8 Gender and structural adjustment in the UK

In 2010, the newly elected Conservative / Liberal Democrat coalition government launched an austerity programme as its solution to Britain's economic downturn following the global financial crisis. Slashing government spending was seen as being vital to recovery. Similar to SAPs in many developing countries, the austerity programme forces women to absorb a disproportionately high share of the pain associated with the government cutbacks. Women workers make up two-thirds of public services, where large-scale job cuts and reduced benefits are being implemented. Women tend to be the heaviest users of the public services that are being cut, such as children's centres, legal aid and health services. Although the gendered nature of these cuts is recognized in the press and public debate, the government insisted that everyone is sharing the burden of adjustment (Stewart, 2012).

daily life maintained and socialization reproduced' (Peterson, 2003, p. 79). This private sphere is increasingly being globalized and marketized. Activities that formerly took place within the household can now be bought for money and provided through transnational structures. Three significant aspects are sex work, domestic services and the purchase of brides.

Sex work

The concept of an international political economy of sex (Pettman, 1996a, 1996b, 2003) is useful when exploring the connections between women, sex and the global political economy. Women's bodies in this international political economy of sex are tradable commodities. Women are exported from one country to another in much the same way as one would export a commodity such as wheat. Much of this export is designed to alleviate poverty in the sending country as the worker sends part of her pay cheque home to support her family. But this trade is based on implicit (and at times explicit) male violence. Central to the international politics of sex is the domestication of women and the sexualization of women's labour. Women are treated

as sexed beings on the basis of a heterosexual conception of sex. Women are assumed to be readily available for the gratification of heterosexual men's desires. The international political economy of sex and the attendant control over women's bodies is the context for domestic service, sex tourism, militarized prostitution and mail-order brides. A large number of women from developing countries are engaged in providing personal services to men and families in wealthier states. This can range from prostitution for a male clientele to providing cleaning, childcare and healthcare services in homes and institutions.

The global sex trade has expanded to include many women and children since the 1970s. Some are employed in their own countries servicing local and foreign men, while others are exported to foreign countries. Figures are difficult to come by since much of the industry is illegal but it is estimated to be worth billions of dollars per annum (Jeffreys, 2009). In 1998, one estimate of the significance of the sex sector in Malaysia, the Philippines and Thailand placed it at between 2 and 14 per cent of GDP (Lim, 1998, p. 7). It has been argued that 'much of the "foreign sex" trade is not so much individual or group sex tourism as militarised prostitution, grown up especially around huge foreign bases' (Pettman, 1996a, p. 201). Historical studies and social science research have established a close connection between militarization and prostitution. Occupying powers have traditionally expected local women to fulfil the 'needs' of their troops. This phenomenon is not solely a transnational one. Studies have documented the militarization of ethnic minority areas within national boundaries. Race plays a major role in the sexualization of local women, especially in border areas or areas that have histories of secessionist violence and large numbers of troops serving far from their homes (Chenoy, 2002; Moser and Clark, 2001).

The large sex trade in South-east Asia has its origins in the Korean and Vietnamese wars. US and allied soldiers taking time off from the conflicts sought out sex workers in countries such as Thailand and the Philippines (Barry, 1996, p. 132). Demand for prostitutes in these 'recreation' zones led to an upsurge in the sex trade. Once the Vietnam War ended in the mid-1970s, foreign tourists took the place of soldiers. These tourists tend to be Western and Japanese males who take advantage of the benefits of modern transportation to travel to other countries for sexual pleasure. The drawing power of prostitution for the tourist trade can be immense in some countries. For example, it is estimated that up to 73 per cent of tourists to Thailand are single males (not with a female partner) and that up to 3 per cent of all Thai women are engaged in some form of prostitution (Peterson and Runyan, 1993, p. 98).

This is a global business overlaid with racial stereotypes (Kempadoo, 1999) and designed to benefit men in developing and developed countries. Men purchase the services and keep the vast majority of the profits. They engage in activities that would be unacceptable or certainly much less available in their home countries. Some local men prosper as they secure revenues from pimping, through bribes to police or from hotels and bars. For foreign (usually Western) men visiting sex tourist countries, native women combine exotic cultural traits that make them the desired sexual partners. For example, Asian women are stereotyped as being more submissive and responsive to Western men's needs than the women of their own cultures.

This trade exacts a devastating price on the women and children who are involved. One cost has been the spread of sexually transmitted diseases (Ward and Aral, 2006) such as AIDS. This in turn drives a demand for younger and younger prostitutes in the mistaken view that customers will avoid the disease if they turn to younger victims. Physical and psychological damage to people engaged in the trade is also high. Those exported to other countries often live in conditions of slavery.

As noted above, one particularly egregious practice is child sex tourism. There are efforts to address this problem in several sectors. The global NGO network End Child Prostitution, Child Pornography and Trafficking of Children for Sexual Purposes campaigns to eliminate child prostitution, child pornography and the trafficking of children for sexual purposes. A number of Western states, for example Australia, Canada, the US and the UK, have introduced legislation to enable domestic courts to prosecute residents who have engaged in child sex tourism. For example, an American citizen or resident who engages in sexual activity abroad with a child under 18 can face 30 years in a US prison.

While this subsection has concentrated on the in-person sex trade, the proliferation of communication technologies means that people need not even be in direct physical contact to partake in the global sex industry. The most striking example of this is the explosion of the global pornography industry (see Box 10.9).

Box 10.9 Global Pornography Industry

Pornography has been called the world's most successful global media industry (Sarikakis and Shaukat, 2008). It has wide appeal across state borders, makes billions of dollars in revenue, drives technological innovation and touches the lives of millions as producers or consumers of the product. Precise data is difficult to find, but some estimates of just the online segment of the porn industry suggest:

⬤ 25 million porn sites worldwide
⬤ 12 per cent of all websites are porn
⬤ 30 per cent of all internet traffic is porn
⬤ Top three porn websites get as many page views as Wikipedia
⬤ 82 per cent of viewers are male
⬤ Worth up to $97 billion a year

(Rosen 2013)

An important aspect of the pornography industry is the degree to which other industries benefit from it. Hotels make millions from offering pay-TV porn in their rooms, cable TV companies charge for porn channels, internet providers offer access to porn sites, advertisers reach customers viewing porn. The rise in popularity of porn has influenced the broader culture from fashion to movies.

Serious concerns have been raised about the relationship of parts of the multibillion-dollar porn industry to organized crime, prostitution, sex trafficking, exploitation of women and child abuse.

Domestic services

Domestic work has also developed as a major international business drawing heavily upon women's labour (Pettman, 2003, p. 163). Women from developing countries are imported into western Europe, Canada, the US and the Middle East to help provide childcare, do housework or to assist in nursing elderly people at home or in hospitals (Yeates, 2009). The numbers of women engaged in this activity are large and the amount of money they contribute to their home economies through remittances is significant. Reliable figures are difficult to find and often dated, but here are some estimates. In 2011, it was estimated that nearly 600,000 Sri Lankan women were working as domestic servants abroad (Tidball, 2011). In 2010, 117,000 Filipino women were migrant domestic workers (UN Women, 2013). The flows of domestic migrant workers are South–South as well as North–South, with many Asian female migrants finding employment in the Middle East and Gulf region, in East Asia, and in Hong Kong, Europe and North America. The remittances sent home by these workers are significant for their families as well as their home state. While estimates vary, remittances from Filipino domestic workers amount to approximately 13 per cent of annual GDP.

This form of activity creates contradictory links between women in developing and developed states. Many women in developed states have been able to pursue careers similar to those of men in recent decades. The ability of some of these women from developed countries to attain professional success can depend on women from developing countries taking over some of their household responsibilities as maids and nannies (see Box 10.10). Young, educated women are more likely to obtain career benefits from globalization than others (Gottfried, 2004). However, in countries where there has been a reduction in welfare services or an absence of affordable day care (as in the US), these women must seek out a private solution to

the task of domestic work and childcare. One solution has been to hire foreign women to work as domestics. This can be done legally through employment agencies or illegally through less-established channels.

The purchase of brides

Another example of the transnational provision of domestic services is the exporting of wives. The mail-order bride has played a role in popular culture as amusing and humorous, in movies about the Wild West and in the 2001 film *Birthday Girl* starring Nicole Kidman as a Russian mail-order bride. However, the reality of the mail-order bride is far removed from fiction and fantasy. The international trade in mail-order brides is lucrative and reflects power differentials in the global political economy, with some countries cast in the role of suppliers and others as buyers (Pettman, 1996a, p. 194). In the contemporary transnational trade, mail-order brides usually originate from the developing world or economies in transition. However, the contention that mail-order brides are necessarily 'victims' has been countered by Nicole Constable, who prefers the term 'correspondence brides', and argues persuasively that attention has to be given to 'variations in the circumstances, forms of introduction, and actual experiences of couples who have met through correspondence and eventually married' (Constable, 2006, p. 2). When the specificity of these relationships is taken into account, it becomes apparent that correspondence brides need not always be viewed as victims of exploitation.

Gender and global restructuring

One of the earliest issues to gain the attention of feminist scholars was the subject of the gender implications of global restructuring. From pioneering studies of the impact of the new international division of labour on women (Mitter, 1986) to current concerns with globalization, political economists have examined the impact of changes in the international division of labour (Busse and Spielmann, 2003; Mies, 1998), international trade (Korinek, 2005; Randriamaro, 2006), global finance (Aslanbeigui and Summerfield, 2000; Porter, 2005) and global production structures on women's labour (Barrientos et al., 2004; Pyle and Ward, 2003). Here we briefly review some connections between globalization and women's economic activity.

Box 10.10 Professional women and illegal women domestic workers

The degree to which female labour from developing countries facilitates the lifestyles of women in upper-middle and professional classes in some developed states was very publicly illustrated in 1993. US president Bill Clinton was eager to bring women into his cabinet to show that he was reaching out to a wide group of Americans. However, his plans for diversity were upset by the fact that two of the professional women he approached (a corporate lawyer and a federal judge) had used 'illegal' immigrants for childcare (Marcus, 1993). Clinton's third woman candidate and eventual attorney-general, Janet Reno, was childless and did not face similar problems. In the UK, Attorney-General Baroness Scotland was fined £5,000 for employing a Tongan housekeeper who did not have a legal work permit (*The Times*, 2009).

Women have increasingly been integrated into global production through labour in TNCs, especially in EPZs – designated areas within a country, which are designed to attract foreign investment by providing financial incentives or regulatory relief from national laws. The number of EPZs grew from 845 in 1997 to 3,500 in 2006 and the number of employees exploded from 22.5 million to 66 million in the same period (Milberg and Amengual, 2008, p. 4). On average, 80 per cent of the workforce in EPZs is female.

Why is female labour so favoured in these zones? Factory managers might suggest that women are chosen because they have smaller fingers and can do more intricate work at a faster pace. Many women may be more skilled at dextrous work because of having developed skills such as sewing, but this is interpreted as a biological difference rather than a skill difference. Since it is not seen as a skill, it does not need to be rewarded by higher pay.

Another reason why women make up a large percentage of the workers in EPZs is because they are thought (often incorrectly) to be more compliant to managers' demands. Women have less of a history of unionization and are often willing to put up with very poor working conditions to support their families. It has been argued that the image of the compliant, docile female worker is a specific construction designed to serve the interests of states and TNCs. For example, a case study of a British TNC's operations in Malaysia in the 1990s argues that the pressures from global corporations and state authority structures within Malaysia have combined to produce the image of the low-waged, docile, diligent factory girl (Elias, 2005). Low-waged sewing jobs have been constructed in Malaysia as particularly suited to women, due to their manual dexterity, and particularly for Malay women whose traditions involved a great deal of sewing. Having many family members working in the same facility helps ensure that women comply with the behaviour and control methods already in place. This division of labour is based on a dominant structure of 'masculinist managerialism', a rationalized management system that depends on the creation of low-waged, pliable, female employment. Many women factory workers do not fit the docile and compliant stereotype and have been active in lobbying for better working conditions and the formation of independent trade unions. But since states attract TNCs by limiting space for labour organization, efforts at unionization are not encouraged. In Malaysia, highly feminized production sectors central to the government's export development strategy are also the sectors with the most restrictive anti-union policies (Elias, 2005, p. 207).

It can be argued that gender is a resource for globalizing capital. Women provide a source of low-cost labour for global capital, and are often exploited by it. This is the case with the Mexican maquiladora (Kopinak, 1995), as well as in traditional EPZs. The corporate desire to avoid demands of greater accountability for reproduction helps shape decisions for moving production facilities from richer countries to poorer, low-wage countries, outsourcing work and thus avoiding responsibility (Acker, 2004, pp. 27–8). TNCs continue to use the social construction of gender-role ideology and 'cultural sensitivities' to restrict choices and access to certain jobs and to provide unequal pay for women relative to men (Chow, 2003).

The incorporation of women into export-oriented work has had a number of contradictory outcomes. On the negative side, working conditions are often very difficult. Unions are often prohibited, working conditions and wages poor. Many workers are exposed to dangerous and unhealthy conditions as well as the threat of physical and sexual abuse (ICFTU, 1996a). In response to these issues, women have organized among themselves and participated in international campaigns to secure fair treatment from the TNCs that benefit from their labour.

However, working conditions vary widely in TNCs and can often be better than in local firms, providing opportunities for local women. These forms of employment have sometimes challenged local gender roles and provided women with better alternatives than preexisting work options. Some women are able to leave restrictive home environments and secure increased status and independence thanks to the incomes they earn in the factories. This has allowed many women to break free of patriarchal structures and gain some independence. The work available to women is, however, often less secure, less well paid and more demeaning than that available to men (Moghadam, 1999).

There are, in fact, a number of different patterns of work relations between women and TNCs in developing countries and one needs to be sensitive to this variety. In some cases, work may be relatively well paid, providing young women with an opportunity to accumulate some wealth and education. In other cases, working conditions are brutal and abuse is widespread.

The challenge is to expand the first type of employment and battle the second form through greater worker rights and economic development.

In response to the problems faced by many women in the global political economy, some academic analysis has called for the 'ungendering' of labour (Peterson and Runyan, 1993, p. 160). This would involve creating an environment where gender did not play a role in the form of work one chose to do. Such a scenario would involve women increasing their presence in male-dominated areas and men increasing their presence in female-dominated areas such as nursing and teaching. Such a transformation would require a shift in the balance of power between men and women and an acknowledgement of the value of the vast amount of work conducted by women that goes unpaid. One way of approaching this goal is for proper value to be attached to women's reproductive labour in systems of national accounts. The true cost of policies needs to be made visible. Another step would be for countries to support equal pay for equal or comparable work, national childcare policies and full reproductive rights.

The obstacles to change are great. Women must struggle against patriarchy in their own society, the strength of TNCs and the inequalities generated by capitalism, and with the difficulties of reforming a global system. However, the struggle for greater gender equality is one of the central issues in the development of a global political economy.

CONCLUSION

The global political economy is gendered. In other words, macroeconomic policies have differential impacts on men and women. Persistent and pervasive female poverty is one consequence of the power relations between women and men. While the relevant measures may be open to dispute, there is widespread agreement on the existence and consequences of gender inequality. How gender inequality is manifested and the impact this has on the lived experience of women and girls vary because gender inequality is constructed and maintained in a specific social context. Differences in political systems, cultural traditions and economic institutions all have an impact on gender inequality.

Although there is no single feminist perspective, feminist scholarship in the social sciences has explored the diverse ways in which gender is important in the global economy. Feminists have provided detailed empirical evidence showing the gendered nature of political and economic processes. They have also produced important critiques of the masculinist biases of conventional political economy.

This chapter has highlighted the integral connection between gender and development. Chapter 11 takes the concept and practice of development as its central focus.

Further Reading

The World Economic Forum's annual gender gap reports are invaluable; the latest is *Gender Gap Report 2014* (2014). The importance of a focus on gender for the study of IPE is explored in Penny Griffin's 2007 'Refashioning IPE: What and How Gender Analysis Teaches International (Global) Political Economy', *Review of International Political Economy*, 14(4): 719–36. Marianne H. Marchand and Anne Sisson Runyan (eds) *Gender and Global Restructuring: Sighting, Sites and Resistance*, 2nd edn (2010) interrogates the relationship between gender and neoliberal globalization. Nicole Constable's *Born Out of Place: Migrant Mothers and the Politics of International Labor* (2014) continues her fascinating ethnographic exploration of women and 'marginal' places in the global economy.

Attention to economic growth and development springs from a number of different motives. These include the eradication of global poverty, a reduction in inequalities in living standards and a lessening in global disparities of power and influence. A commitment to the pursuit of economic development as a means to eliminate poverty signals an aspiration that has been widely accepted by peoples and their governments worldwide. The World Bank's *Voices of the Poor* (Narayan et al., 2000) provides an excellent introduction to the reality of poverty in its various manifestations as experienced by poor people from many countries. Although some agreement exists on these objectives, there is no consensus on the methods and strategies necessary for the achievement of these goals.

This chapter is centrally concerned with the global pursuit of economic development since the end of the Second World War. It provides an introduction to a central issue in the contemporary global political economy through an assessment of the ways in which states and other actors have engaged with the challenge of aspirations for material improvement in the context of persistent global inequality. Despite universal acceptance of, and support for, economic development, it nevertheless remains a profoundly controversial concept. Proponents differ concerning its definition and the policies likely to bring it about. Critics of development question the very value of the enterprise itself. Many of these debates concerning development are themselves linked to other debates surrounding capitalism and modernity. In this chapter, we analyse development both as an aspiration or goal, and as a concrete set of practices.

The late 20th century's obsession with economic development (a fixation carried over to the 21st century) finds its roots in an earlier period. The origins of the quest for economic development are to be found in the onset of the era of modern economic growth begun in western Europe with the Industrial Revolution in Britain in the 18th century. Since Britain's successful industrialization, modernizing elites around the globe have attempted to emulate this feat (Kemp, 1983, pp. 1–17). The linkages between industrialization and military power further fuelled the drive for modernization (Sen, 1981). Until the Second World War, a country's industrialization was perceived almost solely as a national objective. This does not mean that there were no international implications but rather that economic growth, understood principally in terms of industrialization, proceeded without appeals for international assistance. This phase came to an end when, in the post-war era, the promotion of economic growth in poorer countries became an international issue. The quest for economic development, as it was now called, has been a significant feature of the postwar international system. A proclaimed objective of Third World elites, international organizations and Western governments, economic development has become an indisputable and undeniable right of peoples living in poverty. It has been claimed that: 'The development project brought all nations into line with the idea of national economic growth, even across the Cold War divide' (McMichael, 1996, p. 243).

This global consensus on development as a fundamental goal of nation-states and recognition of the inescapable international dimension of this process was foregrounded for a decade and a half (2000–2015) through the framework of the Millennium Development Goals (MDGs). At the United Nations Millennium Summit in 2000, world leaders adopted the Millennium Declaration, which established eight goals to be achieved by 2015 (see Box 11.1). In recognition of the normative success of the MDGS, in September 2011 the UN secretary-general established a UN System Task Force to support UN efforts to develop a post-2015 development agenda. Further political impetus was added to this process when at the Rio+20 Conference in 2012 it was agreed by UN member states that the post-2015 development agenda would be shaped by a set of sustainable development goals (see Box 11.2). It is noteworthy that the sustainable development goals (SDGs) build upon the MDGs. Thus the post-2015 development agenda marks an evolutionary process rather than major transformation.

This chapter begins by exploring the debates over several of the key terms encountered in discussions of international development. In the next section, we explore two major debates – internal versus external causation, and the role of the state. Under major developments, we discuss changes in approaches to development and development planning. The key issues considered in this

---

Box 11.1 The Millennium Development Goals

Goal 1. Eradicate extreme poverty and hunger.
Goal 2. Achieve universal primary education.
Goal 3. Promote gender equality and empower women.
Goal 4. Reduce child mortality.
Goal 5. Improve maternal health.
Goal 6. Combat HIV/AIDS, malaria and other diseases.
Goal 7. Ensure environmental sustainability.
Goal 8. Develop a Global Partnership for Development.

Source: www.unmillenniumproject.org/goals/gti.htm

Box 11.2 The Sustainable Development Goals

Goal 1. End poverty in all its forms everywhere.
Goal 2. End hunger, achieve food security and improved nutrition, and promote sustainable agriculture.
Goal 3. Ensure healthy lives and promote wellbeing for all at all ages.
Goal 4. Ensure inclusive and equitable quality education and promote life-long learning opportunities for all.
Goal 5. Achieve gender equality and empower all women and girls.
Goal 6. Ensure availability and sustainable management of water and sanitation for all.
Goal 7. Ensure access to affordable, reliable, sustainable and modern energy for all.
Goal 8. Promote sustained, inclusive and sustainable economic growth, full and productive employment and decent work for all.
Goal 9. Build resilient infrastructure, promote inclusive and sustainable industrialization and foster innovation.
Goal 10. Reduce inequality within and among countries.
Goal 11. Make cities and human settlements inclusive, safe, resilient and sustainable.
Goal 12. Ensure sustainable consumption and production patterns.
Goal 13. Take urgent action to combat climate change and its impacts.
Goal 14. Conserve and sustainably use the oceans, seas and marine resources for sustainable development.

Source: http://unsdsn.org/resources/goals-and-targets/

---

chapter are the organization of development, debt and debt relief, and the North–South conflict.

DEFINITIONS

Like many concepts in the social sciences, the concept of development remains ill-defined and contested. As Gertzl (1995, p. 1) asserts: 'There is no consensus as to what development means or requires.' Here, we discuss how people have interpreted the concept of development, and also the controversies surrounding the terminology to be applied to countries in the process of overcoming mass poverty. Development, as used in the literature, suggests both a process and a condition. It is a process, insofar as attention is given to the means whereby a society may transform itself so that it achieves self-sustaining economic growth. In the words of Dickson (1997, p. 16), development is 'an on-going process of qualitatively ameliorated social, political and economic change'. The term is also used to denote the condition reached by those societies that have made the successful transition to self-sustaining growth. It has also been seen as the condition in which 'individuals are more aware of, and have greater access to, (such) new technologies, and are induced to take advantage of their possibilities through the working of market forces' (Sundrum, 1983, p. 15). Thomas and Reader (1997, p. 91) define development as a 'multidimensional process involving change from a less to a more socially desirable state', which captures the idea of development as both a process and a condition.

Modern economic growth developed in western Europe and has been successfully exported almost exclusively to territories settled by Europeans. One unfortunate result of this has been a tendency to examine development as a process taking place almost exclusively in non-European areas of the globe. Thus, although in 1948 the gap in living standards between some European societies, for example Ireland, Portugal and Spain, and parts of the so-called developing world was fairly narrow, economic growth in Europe was never seen in terms of development. And when, after the fall of communism in Eastern Europe, attention turned to economic growth in the post-Soviet empire, these countries were categorized as transitional economies (or sometimes emerging markets) rather than as developing countries. Development, then, is, or shall we say became, the province of Africa, Asia, Latin America and the Caribbean, and the Pacific. For some writers, this geographical limitation is part of Western control of colonial and postcolonial peoples and territories (Escobar, 1995). In this view, the concept of development was created as a means of taming and controlling the Third World. This is an influential thesis but whether one is convinced by its claims rests on its further assertion that the development discourse is incapable of meeting its stated objective, that is, economic progress, since it is an instrument of control. We return to this issue later.

In the immediate postwar period, development was defined in terms of economic growth, where the standard measure was the gross national product (GNP) of a country. This approach emphasized economic variables and gave little if any attention to the social and cultural aspects of development. Moreover, because of its focus on aggregate growth, internal redistribution, that is, the different rates of growth of different regions, and the impact of growth on various social classes were not taken into account. Underlying this perspective was a naive faith in the so-called 'trickle-down effect'. Redistributive issues were perceived as second-order concerns. In other words, overall economic growth was necessary before attention could be given to dealing with inequality. This view was given scientific support by the Kuznets curve, which plotted the relationship between economic growth and equality (Kuznets, 1966). According to the Kuznets curve, an inverse relationship existed between growth and equity at early levels of development, with a more positive link developing as economic growth increased. This perspective, which equated economic growth with development, increasingly came under fire in the 1960s.

When Seers (1969) published his 'The Meaning of Development' article, it provided the first comprehensive alternative to the traditional definition. Seers contended that the development as growth model was too restrictive, and failed to address the multifaceted nature of development. He was particularly concerned with equity, and insisted that the definition of development should include social objectives such as employment, health and shelter. In this perspective, development was concerned with decreasing poverty and improving welfare indicators. Not only has the definition of development changed but the scope of traditional concerns has widened over time. Initially, development policies also failed to recognize the gender dimension, but since the publication of Boserup's (1989) pioneering study *Woman's Role in Economic Development* in 1970, increasing attention has been given to women's role in development. This is partly the result of academic research and writing and partly a response to grass-roots activism.

Many economists continue to measure development in terms of income – gross national income per capita (GNI); or production – gross national product per capita (GNP), or gross domestic product per capita (GDP). This should not be seen as a refusal to update their methods but rather reflects the advantages of using a single measure. Despite the various deficiencies that have been raised concerning GNI, GNP or GDP as indicators, they are standard, well-known measures that allow cross-national comparisons to be made. But critics of an economic definition have also developed criteria with which to measure development. Perhaps the best-known measure is the Human Development Index (HDI), pioneered by the United Nations Development Programme (UNDP). The HDI is based on a definition of development that takes into account social factors (see Table 11.1).

In 1990, the UNDP published its first *Human Development Report*, which argued that 'the real wealth of a nation is its people. And the purpose of development is to create an enabling environment for people to enjoy

Table 11.1 Social indicators of development for selected countries, 2013

HDI Rank	Life Expectancy at birth (years), 2013	Mean years of schooling (years), 2012a	Expected years of schooling (years), 2012b	Gross national income (GNI) per capita (2011 PPP $), 2013	Human Development Index Value
Very high human development					
1 Norway	81.5	12.6	17.6	63,909	0.944
2 Australia	82.5	12.8	19.9	41,524	0.933
3 Switzerland	82.6	12.2	15.7	53,703	0.917
4 Netherlands	81.8	11.9	17.9	42,397	0.915
5 United States	78.9	12.9	16.5	52,308	0.914
High human development					
50 Uruguay	77.2	8.5	15.5	18,108	0.790
51 Bahamas	75.2	10.9	12.6	21,414	0.789
51 Montenegro	74.8	10.5	15.2	14,710	0.789
53 Belarus	69.9	11.5	15.7	16,403	0.786
54 Romania	73.8	10.7	14.1	17,433	0.785
Medium human development					
103 Maldives	77.9	5.8	12.7	10,074	0.698
103 Mongolia	67.5	8.3	15.0	8,466	0.698
103 Turkmenistan	66.5	9.9	12.6	11,533	0.698
106 Samoa	73.2	10.3	12.9	4,708	0.694
107 Palestine, state of	73.2	8.9	13.2	5,168	0.686
Low human development					
1 Sierra Leone	45.6	2.9	7.5	1,815	0.374
2 Chad	51.2	1.5	7.4	1,622	0.372
3 Central African Republic	50.2	3.5	7.2	588	0.341
4 Congo (Democratic Republic of the)	50.2	3.1	9.7	444	0.338
5 Niger	58.4	1.4	5.4	873	0.337

a. 'Average number of years of education received by people aged 25 and older, converted from education attainment levels using official durations of each level.'

b.' Number of years of schooling that a child of school entrance age can expect to receive if prevailing patterns of age-specific enrolment rates persist throughout the child's life.'

Source: Data from UNDP (2014a), Table 1.

long, healthy creative lives' (UNDP, 1990, p. 9). This focus on human development goes beyond income. The UNDP invented the HDI as a basis for classifying countries. It is currently based on life expectancy, education (mean years of schooling, and expected years of schooling) and income. The most recent report (UNDP, 2014b) ranked 187 countries into four human development groups:

1 Those with very *high human development*, with an HDI index of 0.890, currently comprising 48 countries and including all of the countries usually identified as developed economies.
2 Those with *high human development*, with an HDI value of 0.783, currently comprising 53 countries inclusive of three members of the BRICS (Brazil, Russia and China).
3 Those with *medium human development*, with an HDI value of 0.614, currently comprising 42 countries and including the two remaining BRICS countries (India and South Africa).
4 Those with *low human development*, with an HDI value of 0.493, currently comprising 43 countries, it groups together many of the poorest countries in the world and is heavily concentrated in sub-Saharan Africa. For example, the 18 countries with the lowest HDI are all from Africa (UNDP, 2014b, pp. 33–36).

The use of GNI per capita versus the HDI is not just a statistical exercise. Because the HDI measures social factors, it will give higher rankings to societies that have a more equal distribution of wealth and invest in social services. In contrast, GNI per capita can rank highly those societies that have a large amount of wealth no matter its distribution among the population. Using UNDP data we can see that the HDI rankings of the top five countries ranked by GNI per capita are, with the exception of Singapore, more than ten places below their income scores (see Table 11.2). A country's relative ranking allows a government to claim it is doing well or for the opposition to attack a government for poor performance.

It is now widely agreed that development cannot be confined solely to economic growth. While there is agreement that development refers to economic, social and cultural variables, no consensus exists on either how we measure development or how it might be attained. To some extent the search for a consensual meaning is a fruitless one and we will conclude this

Table 11.2 Comparing HDI and GNI rankings

GNI per capita ranking	Country	HDI ranking
1	Qatar	31
2	Liechtenstein	18
3	Kuwait	46
4	Singapore	9
5	Brunei Darussalam	30

Source: UNDP (2014a)

discussion with two observations. First, development is more than mere economic growth and involves structural change and attitudinal change in a given society. It requires a structural transformation of the economy and a movement from a 'traditional' value system to a 'modern' one. Second, development consists of a set of material practices and a collection of ideas and statements. This controversy concerning the term 'development' is mirrored in debates concerning the terminology and classification of countries seeking to make the transition to the ranks of the advanced industrial countries.

Immediately after the Second World War, these countries were variously called 'underdeveloped', 'poor' or 'backward'. As more and more of these countries gained their independence, these terms came to be seen as derogatory and offensive. By the early 1960s, these terms were replaced by the term 'less developed country', but by the mid-1960s this term itself was held to be offensive and was replaced by the now ubiquitous term 'developing country'. Another term to describe a group of developing countries was coined in the 1950s and has also come under critical scrutiny. The term 'Third World' reflected more a political than an economic division in the world but came to be used interchangeably with that of 'developing country'. Various critics have argued that the term 'Third World' implies inferiority since third comes after first and second. However, such criticism is misplaced and signally fails to acknowledge the origin of the term. When Alfred Sauvy first used the term in 1952, he was making an analogy with the Third Estate in French civil society and emphasizing the revolutionary potential of the countries so classified. Thus, governments and many civil society organizations in the developing world have retained the use of this term since they do not attach a negative connotation to it. In the 1970s, it became fashionable to refer to the Third

World as the South since most of these countries were in the southern hemisphere. In the 1990s, this terminology was replaced by that of 'Global South', partly to indicate the fact that conditions of poverty and marginalization occurred in advanced industrial societies; thus, the term referred to people regardless of their geographic location. However, the term has become popularized in a manner that makes its usage no different from the term it replaced. It thus appears to be useful for the geographically illiterate, in that it reminds them that South does not mean the south of whatever country they find themselves in. But whether one uses developing, Third World, South or Global South, the grouping is invariably the same.

While the debate about terminology is not substantive, a further debate concerning divisions within this group of countries has greater political significance. The group defined as developing is large and heterogeneous, as we discuss below. The heterogeneity of the group has given rise to a debate on the criteria to be used in making divisions within the grouping, and the names to be given to these various sub-groups. Indeed, at various times it has been argued that instead of a singular category we should recognize a number of different types of countries that are not developed. Division into groups is an inherently subjective and political exercise. For example, following the first oil price rise in 1973, it became fashionable to talk about a Third World, a Fourth World and a Fifth World, ostensibly on the basis of their access to petroleum resources, but this was an ideological intervention at a time when the solidarity of the developing world threatened Western interests. In a similar vein, when, in the 1990s, financial analysts began to refer to developing countries that offered the opportunity for profitable investment as 'emerging markets', this signified a positive evaluation and was designed to speed the transfer of funds to these countries.

THEORETICAL PERSPECTIVES ON GROWTH AND DEVELOPMENT

The political economy of development has initiated a number of theoretical debates and controversies. Instead of detailing these various debates and issues

that have engendered such conflict, here we examine two of the enduring schisms discernible in discussions on development and link them with historical debates. Theorists and practitioners interested in the economic development of a particular state or region can be divided according to their views on two issues. The first concerns the relative importance of internal or external factors for the failure of a society to achieve development. The second issue is related to the comparative roles of the state and the market in promoting development. As will become apparent, these debates reflect and replay the inter-paradigm debate in IPE. Liberal theorists have tended to emphasize the role of internal factors in the success or failure of a state to achieve development. Writers influenced by the economic nationalist tradition have no consistent approach to this issue, with some agreeing with the liberal perspective and others agreeing with radical writers, who give greater weight to the role of external factors in inhibiting national development. It is not surprising that in the arguments concerning the relative importance of the state and market as agents of economic development, economic nationalist writers will emphasize the role of the state and liberal theorists will give more credence to market-related factors. Critical perspective writers, while focusing on the role of global capitalism, have tended to support state initiatives in this debate.

We spend some time exploring the first of these two issues before turning to the second. Proponents of what we term the 'internal causation theory' begin from the assumption that the absence of development in a particular society results from that society's failure to harness its resources in a way relevant to the demands of modern economic growth. The causes of underdevelopment are to be found in the underdeveloped society and the solution to underdevelopment is therefore to be found at the domestic level. This view was first and most systematically articulated in modernization theory.

Modernization theory originated in American sociology and economics, and adopted an evolutionary perspective on social change, taking the view that the currently underdeveloped societies were at an earlier stage of development than the advanced industrial countries. These poor countries could develop if they adopted similar attitudes and social structures to the developed world. Rostow's *The Stages of Economic Growth* (1960) presented the definitive statement of modernization theory's approach. He argued that there were five phases or stages of development that a country had to pass through. The movement from one stage to the next depended on raising standards of living and adopting modern values.

In contrast to this focus on internal causes of and solutions to underdevelopment, a different approach, which can be termed the 'external causation theory', is adopted by many practitioners and scholars. From this perspective, underdevelopment is the result of external forces that constrain a society's efforts to develop. The most widely influential example of external causation theory is dependency theory, which arose in the mid-1960s as a direct challenge to modernization theory. The dependency school began with analyses of Latin America (Dos Santos, 1970; Frank, 1967, 1969), but was extended to cover Africa (Amin, 1976) and the Caribbean (Beckford, 1972; Thomas, 1974). Dependency theorists argued that lack of development was not the result of poverty and the absence of modern values but was instead the direct consequence of economic exploitation. Whereas for modernization theorists development depended essentially on national efforts, for dependency theorists underdevelopment was the other side of development. Underdevelopment was a condition historically created by development.

Dependency theory argues that the development of some countries has resulted in the underdevelopment of others. Current advanced industrial societies only achieved this status through the expropriation of economic surplus from the currently underdeveloped societies. Moreover, whereas modernization theory predicted a successful transition to development for the underdeveloped world through the adaptation of specified practices, dependency theory argued that development was an impossibility within a capitalist international economic system. It was only by delinking or opting out that the poor would be able to prosper. Dependency theory contends that developing countries do not have any meaningful choices since they are controlled directly or indirectly by external influences.

From the perspective taken in this book, both internal causation and external causation theories are flawed. A complex phenomenon such as development is not attributable to forces arising from a single level of analysis. National societies are, as we have demonstrated in Part 2, integrally linked to an emerging global political economy. This observation severely weakens the internal causation perspective, which relegates external causes to, at best, a secondary role. Similarly, we have

presented evidence to show that external structures are mediated through internal processes in ways that are not automatic, thus raising serious questions about the external causation approach. Moreover, the relationship between external and internal variables is not fixed and their relative importance will vary according to national society and historical period.

Turning to the two variants of the approaches discussed, it should be clear that modernization theory's failure to address external structural constraints omitted a crucial set of considerations. Dependency theory was not only overly pessimistic but it overstated the impact of external conditions on domestic development, and could not account for differential rates of economic progress of countries faced with a similar external environment. While there are many cases in which developing countries have limited choice and are satellites or appendages of foreign companies or countries, one does not have to accept the simple dependency hypothesis since it overstates the constraints facing decision makers.

In short, development is neither solely an internal affair nor driven relentlessly by external pressures. Furthermore, the distinction between domestic and external policy is an analytical convenience that cannot be sustained when examining policy-making and economic development in poor, weak states with open economies. For many governments in the Third World, blaming the external environment is an easy option when domestic reform proves difficult. For most developing countries, efforts to improve the external environment will not bring the hoped-for rewards unless at the same time efforts are made to change internal policy-making. The stress on external change can be misguided and is frequently employed in an effort to avoid dealing with domestic problems. A thoroughly benign external environment cannot assist a dysfunctional domestic system. And it is arguable that a malign external environment can do less damage to a country that has a degree of flexibility and efficiency in its decision-making.

On the other hand, attention to internal issues should not blind us to the fact that not all problems are domestic in origin. There have been and continue to be external forces over which poor countries have limited control. All developing countries can be injured or overwhelmed by external events and forces for which they bear no responsibility, such as the oil crisis or global inflation. The international system imposes a hierarchy of hindrances and dangers that affect different countries in different ways but nevertheless do create barriers of injustice. However, there are many cases where the choices for Third World nations are not completely determined by outside forces, and these choices are neither trivial nor meaningless. The available choices may be sharply circumscribed by the weakness and poverty of the Third World and the options available may be heavily conditioned by the attitudes and assumptions of the advanced industrial countries, but even within these boundaries the possibility of better or worse decisions for each country has frequently remained open. Moreover, the persistent impact of nationalism, the growth of indigenous capacities and the impact of international organizations have increased the desire and ability of developing countries' elites to make their own decisions.

As enduring as the debate on the relative impact of external and internal variables is the debate between proponents of the market and those of the state as the critical actors in promoting development. While the debate concerning the relative merits of the state and the market continues to engage adversaries concerned with promoting development, we illustrate the key issues involved in the debate through an examination of a historical specific moment.

The success of the Asian newly industrializing countries (NICs) – Singapore, Taiwan, South Korea and Hong Kong, collectively known as the four tigers – spurred a debate concerning the reasons for their success. Between 1965 and 1980, these countries achieved impressive levels of economic performance characterized by fast growth, low inflation, macroeconomic stability and a strong fiscal position, high savings rates, open economies and thriving export sectors allied with improvement in welfare indicators such as life expectancy and literacy (see Table 11.3). In the 1980s and early 1990s, a second tier of East Asian countries – Indonesia, Malaysia, the Philippines and Thailand – appeared poised to repeat this success.

Two competing schools of thought developed – the neoliberal school, which emphasized the export-oriented industrialization (EOI) policies adopted by these states, and the developmental state school, which put most stress on the ability of the state to intervene successfully in the economy. Neoliberal scholars argued that the success of the NICs derived from their adherence to market discipline and promotion of export-led growth. Unlike the majority of developing countries, which developed highly interventionist policies, the NICs, in pursuing growth, had chosen to deregulate their economies. Success was the result of the pursuit of

Table 11.3 Economic and welfare indicators for Asian NICs

	Economic indicators					
	GNP/capita	Average annual CPI (%)	Export of goods and services % of GDP		Gross domestic saving % of GDP	
	1960–78	1970–8	1960	1978	1960	1978
Korea	6.9	19.3	3	34	1	28
Rep. of Taiwan	6.6	10.3	11	59	13	33
Hong Kong	6.5	7.7	79	98	1	15
Singapore	7.4	6.1	163	164	3	27

	Welfare indicators			
	Adult literacy (%)		Life expectancy	
	1975	1998	1978	1998
Korea	93	97.5	63	72.6
Rep. of Taiwan	82	–	72	–
Hong Kong	90	92.9	72	78.6
Singapore	75	91.8	70	77.3

Note: CPI = consumer price index.

Sources: World Bank (1980, p. 11); UNDP (2000, p. 157)

liberal economic policies, a climate conducive to foreign investment and a minimal role for the state (Hughes, 1988, 1989; World Bank, 1993). For successful industrialization, the government's role should be limited to the promotion of free trade, the provision of free labour markets, high interest rates to encourage savings, and conservative budgets. Neoliberals criticized the suspicious and at times hostile attitude to the international economy taken by most developing countries. These countries tried to limit interaction with external actors and promoted industrialization through a process of import substitution. Import substitution industrialization (ISI) denotes a high tariff policy in which the aim is to keep foreign products out, develop domestic infant industries and industrialize behind these high protectionist barriers. ISI policies tended to run into bottlenecks unless the developing country had a sufficiently large market. The costs of industrialization were immense, and the costs of imported technology and intermediate goods meant that, far from saving foreign exchange, the country was still running a large import

bill. Neoliberal theorists argued that successful industrialization in the NICs was based on a strategy diametrically opposed to ISI (see Table 11.4 for statistical support of the superiority of the NICs' export-led growth compared with Latin America's ISI growth). Instead of protecting the domestic market, these countries had taken an open view towards foreign capital and had promoted industrialization through exports rather than import substitution.

Proponents of the developmental state perspective (Amsden, 1989; Wade, 1990; White, 1988) did not dispute the export orientation of the NICs but argued that the state had played a crucial and determining role in East Asian industrialization. In the first place, these countries did not begin with a process of EOI but had undergone an ISI phase first. The crucial issue was not ISI versus EOI but rather the point at which governments switched from ISI to EOI. Moreover, EOI was not, as was claimed by neoliberal apologists, a recipe for laissez-faire economics; on the contrary, governments had been active in promoting EOI. In this perspective, the

Table 11.4 Comparison of Latin American and East Asian economies, 1965–80 (per cent)

	Annual rate of growth of real GDP		Annual rate of growth of manufacturing		Annual rate of growth of exports	
	1965–80	1980–9	1965–80	1980–9	1965–80	1980–9
Latin American countries						
Argentina	3.5	−0.3	2.7	−0.6	4.7	0.6
Brazil	8.8	3	9.8	2.2	9.3	5.6
Chile	1.9	2.7	0.6	2.9	7.9	4.9
Colombia	5.8	3.5	6.4	3.1	1.4	9.8
Mexico	6.5	0.7	7.4	0.7	7.6	3.7
Peru	3.9	0.4	3.8	0.4	1.6	0.4
Venezuela	3.7	1	5.8	4.9	−9.5	11.3
Latin America and Caribbean (average)	6	1.6	7	1.5	−1	3.6
East Asian countries						
Hong Kong	8.6	7.1	n/a	n/a	9.5	6.3
Indonesia	8	5.3	12	12.7	9.6	2.4
Korea	9.6	9.7	18.7	13.1	27.2	13.8
Malaysia	7.3	4.9	− 8	4.4	9.8	
Singapore	10.1	6.1	13.2	5.9	4.7	8.1
Thailand	7.2	7	11.2	8.1	8.5	12.8
East Asian (average)	7.2	7.9	10.6	12.6	10	10

Source: Data from World Bank (1989, 1990)

quality of government intervention and the choice of industrial policies and strategies were critical to economic success. With the exception of Hong Kong, government intervention was extensive in East Asia. Successful government intervention was based on a powerful set of policy instruments, a corporatist/authoritarian model of the state and the ability to restructure the economy towards high-tech production. The success of the NICs was the result of strong states governing the market. In other words, government intervention was vital in promoting economic development.

The strength of the neoliberal approach lies in its critique of ISI, and its weakness arises from its failure to give sufficient attention to historical factors. The strength of the developmental state model arises from its comparative analysis of political factors in the success or failure of economic policy, and its weakness lies in the difficulty of assessing the effectiveness of government intervention in development policy.

It is also worth noting a third approach to explaining East Asian development. This is the cultural approach, which emphasizes the role of Asian values. According to this perspective, the NICs succeeded because of the impact of Confucianism on their societies (see Box 11.3). What this argument fails to confront is the many centuries in which Confucianism appeared to be an obstacle to economic progress. It isn't clear how or why centuries of stagnation were suddenly transformed into economic success when the cultural component remained the same.

This debate between competing schools of thought was of profound importance to other developing countries, since the various perspectives had implicit or, indeed, explicit assumptions concerning the relevance or lessons of East Asian success for their economies. The liberal laissez-faire model was the easiest to follow and partly accounts for its success/emulation for/by many developing countries. This required countries to deregulate, privatize and dismantle governmental controls. Although this was not easy to do in societies where vested interests supported protectionism and governments depended on these vested interests, it was, theoretically, the easiest option. The second option required changes in governance structures and more fundamental societal change. The conditions for the creation of a developmental state were far from obvious. The third approach was the most pessimistic, since Asian cultural values could not easily be transferred to Africa, Latin America, the Caribbean or the Pacific.

> **Box 11.3** Confucianism and economic development
>
> The core values of Confucianism are derived from the concept of 'ren' (goodness, humanity), which describes the highest human achievement reached through moral self-cultivation. The implications for the individual include a collective orientation, reciprocity and knowledge through intuition. One result of the high priority given to these values in the business environment is a focus on the social and relational aspects of the business transaction. Trust developed through interaction in the public and private lives of partners is built to ensure the long-term nature of business relationships. Decision-making is less confrontational and involves consensus and cooperation, with mutual benefits being a high priority of all business deals. The importance of the family to Confucianism permeates business life, with companies becoming the second family of individuals. Paternalistic leadership encourages respect and long-term commitment on the part of employees (see Ornatowski, 1996).

MAJOR DEVELOPMENTS

From the foregoing it should be obvious that the pursuit of economic development has excited passions, aroused debate and affected billions of people in the postwar era. While each society will have its own periodization based on political and economic indicators, we outline two broad historical periods in the evolution of development as an issue in the global political economy. Undoubtedly, views about development and development practices have altered many times in the past five decades in response to the experiences of developing countries and a changing global economy. Arguably, however, a major change occurred at the beginning of the 1980s when, in McMichael's (1996) terminology, the development project was discarded in favour of the globalization project. The first period we discuss is one in which the nation-state was perceived as a key instrument in the search for economic growth and development, and development was conceived principally in national terms. In the second period, far greater emphasis has been given to the importance of market forces, and development has been conceived primarily in terms of the world market.

Development and national capitalism, 1947–81

Development in this period was conceived principally as a project of a strong and active government. In the Keynesian postwar compromise, states were expected to establish a balance between supply and demand for goods, encourage consumption, promote the growth of domestic industries and provide a safety net for their citizens in the form of social welfare. Keynesian economic theory sought a balance between non-intervention in the market by the state and guided control.

The political conditions for the nationalist development project were laid by the post-independence modernizing elites who were intent on securing economic growth as a mechanism to bolster their legitimacy. At the same time, many of these regimes were weak or corrupt or both. Thus, they pursued policies that supported their continued hold on power rather than those most likely to lift the majority of their population out of poverty. In a bid to protect both the regime and its sovereignty, many governments devised measures to increase the power of the state. A belief that the external environment was not conducive to development led, on one hand, to criticism of the international economy and the major international economic organizations and, on the other, to domestic policies of import substitution.

The quest for economic development was shaped and moulded by developments in the world economy and by the attitudes and actions of governments and international organizations. A number of changes in the international economy were to have a profound impact on the prospects for development in this first period. A striking characteristic of the international economy for most of this period was economic recovery and strong growth trends, especially among the advanced industrial countries. Between 1947 and 1971, the world economy experienced unprecedented growth. This growth began to falter in 1971 with the collapse of the Bretton Woods system of monetary management and came to an end after the first oil crisis of 1973–4. During this period, although many developing countries experienced high growth rates, most of this increase was consumed by high population growth. Moreover, the benefits from the

long boom of economic growth were limited for the developing countries. The postwar boom was based on the growth of manufactured exports and since most developing countries relied on primary commodities, the dynamism of the world economy was irrelevant to their prospects. But if their gains from postwar growth were meagre, the downturn in the world economy in the mid-1970s created an unfavourable economic climate. The first oil shock triggered, but was not solely responsible for, the onset of global recession in 1974. Non-oil-exporting developing countries were faced with a severely deteriorating balance of payments. It was in this period that Third World debt began to grow as governments borrowed to meet their obligations. The second oil shock of 1979 plunged many countries into severe balance of payments problems, and heralded the difficult times ahead. These events exposed the vulnerability of Third World economies and opened up divisions among them as the gap in the pace of growth between the middle-income and low-income countries widened.

The practice of development was also shaped by changing ideas about development. Early theories of economic development were concerned with establishing the characteristics of underdevelopment. Studies such as Myrdal's *Asian Drama: An Enquiry into the Poverty of Nations* (1968) helped to demonstrate the differences between the industrial world and the underdeveloped one. Without resorting to caricature, the standard view of an underdeveloped country saw it as one with a predominantly large population characterized by the absence of modern values. The theory of economic dualism developed in the 1950s asserted that developing countries were characterized by both a modern, dynamic sector and a traditional, stagnant sector. The task was to expand the small modern sector through investment. To the early development economists it seemed that development was a relatively simple matter of the application of certain techniques. At the beginning of this period there was also a belief in trickle-down economics. It was believed that economic growth would trickle down from the rich to the poor within societies. Over time, it became apparent that this optimism was ill-founded. During the 1960s, these views were increasingly challenged, as some analysts shifted the focus from the internal problems of developing countries to the negative impact of the external environment.

The orthodox position held at the beginning of this period came under sustained attack from a number of sources. Although there was agreement with the dominant position that industrialization provided the path to development, the view that underdevelopment arose from domestic failings was challenged by dependency theory. However, from the perspective of policy-making, it was the 'terms of trade' argument that made most impression. Simply put, the terms of trade thesis alleges that there is a persistent tendency for the value (or terms of trade) of primary commodities to fall vis-à-vis manufactured exports. This thesis was propounded by Raul Prebisch, the first secretary-general of the United Nations Conference on Trade and Development (UNCTAD), and was influential with policy makers in the developing world. The terms of trade thesis led to export pessimism and supported ISI policies, but it also led to two specific campaigns. First, it provided the economic rationale for preferential access for the manufactured exports of developing countries. If dependence on primary commodities condemned developing countries to a foreign exchange gap, it was logical to support their diversification into manufactured exports. Similarly, the terms of trade thesis provided the rationale for international commodity agreements as a mechanism to halt the decline in export earnings.

The downturn in the world economy in the mid-1970s and the failure of industrialization and trickle-down policies led to a new approach. The 'basic needs' approach, which gained support from the ILO and World Bank in the mid-1970s, rejected trickle-down

policies and argued for redistribution with growth, and also replaced the focus on industrialization with one giving greater attention to agriculture and the rural sector. Furthermore, gender considerations had been absent from orthodox development theory. During this period, research on gender and development began to show the necessity to bring such considerations to the forefront.

Another crucial feature of this period was the development of a Third World coalition to campaign for change in the international economic order. Modernizing Third World elites began to articulate a distinctive set of interests within the global economy. Although divided by levels of economic development, ideology, political systems, culture and an amazing diversity of domestic economic policies, the governing elites of developing countries were united in their demand for additional resources and reform of the international economic order. In the post-independence world, Third World elites were willing to assert their own vision of development. They did so through two main organizations. The Non-Aligned Movement, created in 1960, although mainly concerned with political issues, progressively addressed what it saw as the failures of the postwar liberal international economic order, and was instrumental in making reform of this order a key diplomatic issue in the 1970s. The Group of 77 (G77) became the chief vehicle through which Third World demands were aggregated and articulated (see Box 11.4

Box 11.4 G77 membership, 2015

Afghanistan, Algeria, Angola, Antigua and Barbuda, Argentina, Bahamas, Bahrain, Bangladesh, Barbados, Belize, Benin, Bhutan, Bolivia (Plurinational State of), Bosnia and Herzegovina, Botswana, Brazil, Brunei Darussalam, Burkina Faso, Burundi, Cambodia, Cameroon, Cape Verde, Central African Republic, Chad, Chile, China, Colombia, Comoros, Congo, Costa Rica, Cote d'Ivoire, Cuba, Democratic People's Republic of Korea, Democratic Republic of the Congo, Djibouti, Dominica, Dominican Republic, Ecuador, Egypt, El Salvador, Equatorial Guinea, Eritrea, Ethiopia, Fiji, Gabon, Gambia, Ghana, Grenada, Guatemala, Guinea, Guinea-Bissau, Guyana, Haiti, Honduras, India, Indonesia, Iran (Islamic Republic of), Iraq, Jamaica, Jordan, Kenya, Kuwait, Lao People's Democratic Republic, Lebanon, Lesotho, Liberia, Libya, Madagascar, Malawi, Malaysia, Maldives, Mali, Marshall Islands, Mauritania, Mauritius, Micronesia (Federated States of), Mongolia, Morocco, Mozambique, Myanmar, Namibia, Nauru, Nepal, Nicaragua, Niger, Nigeria, Oman, Pakistan, Panama, Papua New Guinea, Paraguay, Peru, Philippines, Qatar, Rwanda, St Kitts and Nevis, St Lucia, St Vincent and the Grenadines, Samoa, Sao Tome and Principe, Saudi Arabia, Senegal, Seychelles, Sierra Leone, Singapore, Solomon Islands, Somalia, South Africa, South Sudan, Sri Lanka, State of Palestine, Sudan, Suriname, Swaziland, Syrian Arab Republic, Tajikistan, Thailand, Timor-Leste, Togo, Tonga, Trinidad and Tobago, Tunisia, Turkmenistan, Uganda, United Arab Emirates, United Republic of Tanzania, Uruguay, Vanuatu, Venezuela (Bolivarian Republic of), Vietnam, Yemen, Zambia, Zimbabwe.

Source: www.g77.org/doc/members.html

for membership). The G77 lobbied UN organizations and, as the G24, brought a collective Third World voice to the World Bank and the IMF. During this period, the most intense and politically significant campaign occurred over proposals for a New International Economic Order (NIEO), which is discussed below.

The international political environment, and specifically the Cold War context, was also significant for most of this period. Western and communist states competed for the allegiance of Third World states and this competition was not solely political or strategic. It was also an engagement over economic ideology, markets and access to resources. Was capitalism superior to communism as the economic system likely to bring prosperity? Which side would have access to the strategic minerals in the developing world? Which side would find a lucrative market for its products? These questions framed the pursuit of development. Moreover, the Sino–Soviet split brought competition between Moscow and Beijing for Third World support. The West responded to the perceived threat of communism with reform of the World Bank and the GATT, and, in Latin America, the US sponsored the Alliance for Progress. But at the same time that limited reform efforts were underway and support was given for land reform, Western policy supported anti-communist governments rather than those committed to development. In other words, the containment of communism was more important than the eradication of poverty. This support for the security state apparatus resulted in the squandering of economic resources.

Development, neoliberalism and beyond, 1982–2015

The eruption of the Mexican debt crisis in 1982 signalled a shift in the development project. Importantly, it changed relations between developing countries and industrial countries, between developing countries and international organizations, and among developing countries. At the end of the 1970s, the second oil crisis and consequent recession hit many developing countries hard. It was apparent to astute commentators that development strategies at the end of the second Development Decade had failed. The World Bank began the process of structural adjustment lending in 1980, but it was the conditions created by the debt crisis that brought structural adjustment lending to the fore since it strengthened the conditionality imposed by the Bank and the IMF.

In August 1982, the Mexican government announced that it was unable to service its debt, thus bringing into the spotlight the severely indebted nature of many developing economies. The debt crisis was not only a problem for the international economy, it also had fundamental implications for the distribution of power and for ways of thinking about development. The debt crisis initially challenged not only developing economies but also the Western banking system. During this period, the debt crisis was the main issue of importance to the development prospects of the developing countries. The economic consequences of the debt crisis were disastrous for most of the developing world. The 1980s have become known as the 'lost decade' because of the overall decline in living standards and the increased numbers of people living in poverty. The debt crisis also led to a fall of investment in the developing world and a sharper concentration of investment in a limited number of countries. It contributed to widening income gaps domestically and internationally, increased differentiation among the developing countries, and reversed many of the gains made in the previous decade. Politically, the debt crisis put the Third World coalition under severe strain, partly because of the different levels of indebtedness, partly because of the uneven development that arose and partly because the response of Western creditors favoured the more politically and strategically important states. The debt crisis was also politically important since it increased the leverage of the multilateral financial institutions. The World Bank and the IMF were given prominent roles in finding solutions to the crisis and, as lenders of last resort, they were able to impose stringent disciplines on Third World debtors.

The debt crisis also heralded a major shift in the development paradigm. It swept away the basic needs and poverty alleviation approaches and replaced them with the neoliberal policy of structural adjustment (see Box 11.5). Although no single template exists for structural adjustment programmes (SAPs), they do have certain features in common. These include a curtailment of the role of the state in the economy, a bias towards the export sector, and a penchant for free markets. SAPs sought to shift developing countries from a reliance on ISI to EOI. This shift in policy is frequently referred to as the 'Washington Consensus' (Williamson, 1993),

---

Box 11.5 Structural adjustment: the case of Mexico

Following the financial crisis in 1994, the Mexican government and the IMF agreed a SAP. This was the second time in just over a decade that Mexico sought the IMF's assistance, since the 1982 debt crisis had already ushered in an adjustment package. On 1 February 1995, the IMF approved an 18-month standby credit for Mexico of up to US$17.8 billion in support of the government's 1995–6 economic and financial programme. The SAP attached to this loan had short- and long-term conditions. Structural adjustment was the long-term condition. In relation to its Mexican programme, the IMF (1995) stated: 'The domestic adjustment package, combining prudent fiscal and strong monetary and credit policies, a disciplined incomes policy, and further structural reforms, provides an appropriate policy response to current circumstances.'

SAPs have a number of common features. These include trade liberalization, privatization, deregulation, credit reduction and wage suppression. Critics of SAPs argue that growing poverty, unemployment, depression of wages, the undermining of rural livelihoods and the disintegration of societies are also common to them. The 1995 agreement consolidated and extended progress made in the area of IMF-imposed structural reform since 1982. It provided a reinforcement of the government's strategy for privatization, including privatization of basic infrastructure (rail, ports, airports, electricity generation and radio and telecommunications). Critics point to the adverse social effects that the SAPs had on Mexico, including over 50 per cent of all Mexicans living in poverty, more than a quarter of a million people losing their jobs by May 1995, a sharp decline in real wages and the government's banning of free wage negotiation. Some even claim that economic policies were the cause of the Chiapas uprising.

---

although the accuracy of this term to refer to a specific consensus that guided policy-making is disputed (Naim, 2000a, 2000b). An intense debate that remains unresolved arose concerning the impact of SAPs on the economy, the poor and women. Critics allege that SAPs hurt the poorest, increase women's burdens and provide no effective solution to debt (Bangura and Beckman, 1991; Pio, 1994; Sahn, 1994). Supporters have acknowledged the negative impacts of SAPs, but have argued that these can be addressed (Kahn and Knight, 1986; Sisson, 1986). Their main contention is that countries undergoing adjustment have performed better economically than those without SAPs.

As a consequence of the emphasis on rolling back the state, NGOs were given a greater role in development. Increasingly, NGOs have played roles as service providers, bringing welfare, development relief and social services to the poor. In those circumstances, where the state proved incapable of meeting basic needs, NGOs have been critical in supporting the material needs of people. This emphasis on the role of NGOs has been supported by national governments in the industrialized world and multilateral development agencies. It has been estimated that, in 1990, NGOs disbursed $1 billion in development aid but, by 1997, this figure had risen to $7.2 billion (UNDP, 2002, p. 102).

Furthermore, bilateral funds have been channelled through NGOs (Pinter, 2001, p. 201), while multilateral agencies have also increased funding to NGOs. The extent to which this increasingly close engagement between NGOs and official agencies is a positive development has been questioned by some analysts (Hulme and Edwards, 1997).

The failure of the demand for the NIEO suggested the difficulty faced by the Third World coalition as a force for change, but the impact of the debt crisis challenged its very raison d'être. The coalition survived the fragmentation and forces of disintegration and has re-emerged, although not as powerfully as in the 1970s, as the instrument through which a collective voice can be heard. It continues to insist that global inequalities remain relevant, and to coordinate positions before major conferences. Instead of arguing against the liberal system, as it did in the 1970s, it now seeks to ensure that developing countries are not discriminated against.

Until the end of the Cold War in 1989, the international political system was marked by continuing East–West tension and Sino–Soviet rivalry, with development needs sacrificed to political ends. The end of the Cold War in 1989 brought East–West competition in the developing world to a close. The end of communism has resulted in competition for investment and aid between former communist countries and traditional Third World countries. The end of communism also brought with it the end of the Soviet-style model and, given that China had effectively abandoned socialism since the onset of the Four Modernizations programme in 1979, development was now cast firmly in capitalist terms. However, the dangers of an open world market were all too visibly brought to the fore by the Asian financial crisis that erupted in mid-1997. It showed again how vulnerable developing countries were and how shallow much economic growth can be. The core Asian tigers were not as hard hit as the second-tier countries, especially Thailand and Indonesia.

This post-Cold War period has been noticeable for a modification in the neoliberal development paradigm. The Rio conference (known as the Earth Summit) in 1992 officially established sustainable development as the new approach to development. Although no agreed definition of sustainable development exists, that of the Brundtland Commission (World Commission on Environment and Development, 1987) is most widely used. The Brundtland Commission defined sustainable development as development that meets the needs of the present generation without jeopardizing the resources available to future generations. The end of the Cold War and the movement to sustainable development were important in the new focus given to governance issues. It is now widely accepted that governance is an important component of the search for development and, in this pursuit, democracy and democratization have come to occupy centre stage. This is a view of development far removed from the simple economic input model with which we began in the 1940s. Views have changed as the complexity of the task has become more apparent. But these changing views also represent the triumph of certain interests. The integration of sustainable development into the development paradigm as a core feature, renewed interest in poverty alleviation and a focus on governance resulted in an amelioration of the neoliberal approach or Washington Consensus. For some writers, the emergence of a post-Washington Consensus, while an improvement on the original model, remains too narrow and incapable of meeting the needs of the poor (Hayami, 2003; Öniş and Şenses, 2005).

The extent to which the 2008–9 economic crisis has forced a radical rethink of economic policy and a final abandonment of neoliberalism remains unclear. The impact of the crisis varied between and within coun-

tries although overall the assessment that 'developing countries are being severely hit through weaker trade, tighter global financing conditions and lower remittances' (UN, 2009, p. 1) was widely shared. The impact of the crisis has not been uniform in the developing world. Whether the focus is on employment, social protection (te Velde, 2009), trade (Meyn and Kennan, 2009) or remittances (Callí and Dell'Erba, 2009), the evidence suggests that the impact is varied, depending on external and internal factors.

Economic recovery in the post-crisis period has been uneven and its impact on developing countries and regions is therefore varied. As Table 11.5 shows, economic growth in the developed world has been weak with consequent falls in demand, private capital flows and FDI. Overall the consequences for employment and social protection have been negative in the post-crisis phase. The recovery of 2011–12 was not sustained, with the consequence that global unemployment increased to an estimated 201 million in 2014 (ILO, 2015b, p. 16). Rising unemployment and considerable underemployment in developing and emerging market economies has created a post-crisis world that is fragile and uneven and presents workers in the developing world with uncertain conditions. While in the immediate response to the crisis (2008–9) social protection was strengthened in many countries; in the period since 2010 governments in middle-income and low-income countries have tightened expenditure. For example, it has been estimated that in 2014, 82 developing countries will have contracted expenditure (ILO, 2015b, p. 6).

The flow of remittances provides an exception to the negative trend. The evidence on the impact of the global

Table 11.5 Economic growth by region, 2012–15

	World	Advanced Economies	Emerging Market and Developing Economies
2012	3.1	1.4	4.9
2013	3.0	1.3	4.7
2014*	3.7	2.2	5.1
2015*	3.9	2.3	5.4

Note: * = estimated.

Source: http://www.imf.org/external/pubs/ft/weo/2014/update/01/

economic crisis suggests that although faced with high transaction costs remittances were resilient during the global financial crisis and in its aftermath (Bettin et al., 2014; Sirkeci et al., 2012). This claim is supported by studies that show that historically remittances are stable or counter-cyclical (because they are driven by altruism or investment calculations. The World Bank (2014) estimated that officially recorded remittances to developing countries would reach $435 billion in 2014, climbing to $454 billion in 2015. Remittances grew by 3.4 per cent in 2013, 5 per cent in 2014, and were predicted to rise by 4.4 per cent in 2015.

KEY ISSUES

Developing countries continue to face a large number of issues in their quest for economic development. These issues are raised throughout the book: developing countries and the trade regime in Chapter 6, bargaining with TNCs in Chapter 7, the debt crisis in Chapter 8, the division of labour in Chapter 9, sustainable development in Chapter 12 and governance issues in Chapter 15. Here, we focus on three key issues that have dominated the global debate on development at the beginning of the 21st century and will continue to do so in the immediate future: the organization of development, debt relief and the North–South conflict.

The organization of development

Although the dominant view is that development will largely arise from national efforts, it is evident, as the previous section has shown, that development is also a process that is organized internationally. In other words, national development aspirations and efforts are shaped by international organizations, the policies of donor states and ideas concerning the meaning and practice of development. A major issue in the global political economy of development is the role of international organizations in this process. There are a number of controversies concerning the specific policies and general impact of multilateral development agencies and international financial institutions. Here, we provide a brief introduction to the role of the World Bank in the international organization of development.

The World Bank

The World Bank is the world's premier multilateral development agency. It comprises five organizations:

- the International Bank for Reconstruction and Development (IBRD)
- the International Development Association (IDA)
- the International Finance Corporation
- the Multilateral Investment Guarantee Agency
- the International Centre for the Settlement of Investment Disputes.

The Bank fulfils three main roles: it provides loans to countries; develops international norms; and resolves disputes. The most visible of these functions is the provision of loans to its member states. The IBRD provides loans and development assistance to middle-income countries and creditworthy poorer countries while the International Development Association provides long-term loans at zero interest to the poorest countries (see Tables 11.6–11.9). Through its research and development activities and the conditions it attaches to its loans, the World Bank contributes to the normative framework of international development. It also tries to resolve disputes between its members and between its members and private creditors.

While the World Bank attracted some form of critical scrutiny of its operations from the outset, it has been in the forefront of controversy since the early 1980s. This is the result of a number of factors, of which the most important are the impact of its adjustment policies on poorer countries in the 1980s and the

Table 11.6 IDA-IBRD commitments by region, fiscal year 2014

Region	IBRD (% share)	IDA (% share)
Africa	2	46
East Asia and Pacific	22	10
Europe and central Asia	25	4
Latin America and the Caribbean	25	2
Middle East and North Africa	14	1
South Asia	12	38

Note: Share of total commitments of $18,604 million

Source: World Bank (2014, p. 29)

Table 11.7 **IDA-IBRD disbursements by region, fiscal year 2014**

Region	IBRD (% share)	IDA (% share)
Africa	2	49
East Asia and Pacific	18	11
Europe and central Asia	35	4
Latin America and the Caribbean	30	2
Middle East and North Africa	9	2
South Asia	6	32

Note: Share of total disbursements of $18,761 million

Source: World Bank (2014, p. 29)

Table 11.8 **IDA-IBRD lending by theme, fiscal year 2014**

Theme	Percentage share of lending
Financial and private sector development	20
Rural development	16
Public sector governance	13
Human development	13
Urban development	11
Environmental and natural resource management	10
Social protection and risk management	9
Trade and integration	4
Social development, gender and inclusion	3
Economic management	2
Rule of law	1

Note: Share of total lending of $40.8 billion

Source: World Bank (2014, p. 57)

Table 11.9 **IDA-IBRD lending by sector, fiscal year 2014**

Theme	Percentage share of lending
Public administration, law and justice	22
Transportation	17
Energy and mining	16
Water, sanitation and flood protection	11
Education	8
Health and other social services	8
Agriculture, fishing and forestry	7
Finance	5
Industry and trade	4
Information and communication	1

Note: Share of total lending of $40.8 billion

Source: World Bank (2014, p. 57)

or irrelevant and misguided policies that made poor countries even more vulnerable to external shocks remains an issue of debate between supporters and critics of these policies. All sides are agreed, however, that the initial policies had consequences that were detrimental to the poorest, most marginalized sections of societies undergoing adjustment; for example, they increased the burdens on women. By the mid-1990s, the World Bank (1998) had come to accept many of the criticisms of these policies, and began designing safety nets for the most vulnerable groups in society. It also began to shift its lending priorities away from adjustment and towards the new goal of sustainable development. Under adjustment lending, it was believed that macroeconomic growth was the main target and poverty reduction would follow from a general improvement in the economy. The move to sustainable development lending has seen a greater focus on poverty reduction strategies but this is coupled with an increased emphasis on the role of the private sector in the promotion of development.

The role of World Bank lending remains controversial. Supporters argue that it provides developing countries with much-needed capital and that the projects it supports are vital in the fight against world poverty. In their view, these resources provide important supplementary assistance for the governments of developing countries and enhance the perceived stability of the economy to international investors. Supporters of

impact of its policies on the environment. When the World Bank abandoned its basic needs approach in the early 1980s and, in tandem with the IMF, began to focus on structural adjustment lending, it ignited a debate on its lending policies that has not lessened even though these policies have shifted significantly since they were first instituted. Adjustment policies pushed recipient countries to liberalize their economies and reduce the role of state intervention in economic management. Whether these were necessary reforms to counter decades of poor economic policies

World Bank policies think that the conditions it attaches to its loans provide a framework of sound financial management for the governments of its borrower nations (Muuka, 1998; Picciotto, 2003). On the other hand, critics accuse the Bank of putting profits before people and distorting development (Caufield, 1996; Danaher, 1994). To the critics, these resources are often insufficient, inadequate and ineffective. They contend that the specific conditionality imposed by the Bank privileges external interests over those of the recipients and is focused on repayment of the loan rather than improving welfare.

The World Bank espouses a liberal economic vision and it was conceived as an important instrument in the construction of a liberal economic order. As such, its policy prescriptions support the maintenance of liberal economic values. The Bank's normative framework of market principles and economic growth is opposed by radical critics and environmentalists, who believe that market-based approaches cannot effectively contribute to development and/or promote sustainability.

Another critical issue in terms of the organization of development concerns the democratic nature of the process. This is an issue that can also be illustrated with reference to the World Bank. In the context of the Bank, this issue is seen in two ways. First, democracy is discussed in relation to the formal decision-making provisions of the organization. The World Bank's decision-making system is one of weighted voting in which member states are allocated differential voting shares based on their financial contributions to the organization. The weighted voting system came under immense pressure from Bank critics and developing countries. The increased importance of the G20 in the wake of the global financial crisis hastened reform of voice within the Bank. Discussions at the G20 meetings in April and September 2009 addressed the issue of the governance of the Bank (and the IMF) and set in motion a reform process that resulted in increased voting power for developing country members of the Bank; and an additional executive director to represent Africa. Nevertheless, these reforms instituted in 2010 have been met with scepticism. A trenchant civil society assessment argued that 'the World Bank will continue to be overwhelmingly dominated by rich countries for decades. Inadequate reform stunts the Bank's legitimacy, limits its capacity to serve the interests of developing countries, and violates democratic principles' (Bretton Woods Project, 2010).

A further example of the controversy relating to the Bank's governance occurred with the appointment of Paul Wolfowitz, a neoconservative academic and politician with limited experience of development issues, as the Bank's president. During his short tenure in office (2005–7), Wolfowitz was the subject of frequent criticism. The debate over his appointment reflects an assumption in much of the literature on the World Bank that the executive head effectively dictates the organization's policies. This popular and persistent view is an oversimplification of power and influence in the Bank. For example, although Wolfowitz reorganized the bureaucracy, his main policy initiatives during his two years of office were concerned with devising an anti-corruption strategy. In 2012, another controversy over Bank leadership emerged as developing countries challenged the US's prerogative to appoint one of its citizens as president (see Box 11.6).

A second aspect of the debate on the democratization of the World Bank refers to its openness to influence from civil society groups and the populations subject to its policies. In the 1980s, development, environmental and women's groups launched a series of campaigns to make the Bank's decision-making more transparent and more accountable for the policies it implemented. As part of the voice reform package the Bank set out procedures to enhance its engagement with civil society. These included policy dialogue meetings, formal consultations, programmatic collaboration and grant-funding mechanisms. While the Bank has not responded in a manner that satisfies all its critics, it has become more open to scrutiny by external groups and has increasingly engaged in consultative processes to discuss its policies and proposed changes in its programmes.

As the above has demonstrated, there are conflicting views on the World Bank's role as a development agency. While it has been the target of criticism from the right of the political spectrum it has attracted most criticism from the left, as detailed above. Is it possible to adjudicate between the Bank and its critics?

1   To a large extent, the perspective one takes on the Bank is linked with the standpoint taken on economic aid (see below), capitalism and government intervention in the economy.

2   As the world's largest multilateral development agency, the Bank's profile means that it inevitably receives a significant amount of criticism. Thus, in

Box 11.6 North–South conflict over World Bank president' appointment

Since the founding of the IMF and the World Bank, Europeans have nominated the president of the IMF and Americans the president of the World Bank. Since both institutions use a form of weighted voting based on contributions, any deal between the US and Europe on the agency head carried the day.

In 2012, the US nominated an American international health expert, Jim Yong Kim, to be the Bank president. The Europeans supported the nomination since the US had previously backed their choice of a French woman (Christine Lagarde) to head the IMF after the previous director, who was also French (Dominique Strauss-Kahn), was forced out following allegations of sexual assault and attempted rape of a hotel maid. However, several developing countries insisted on a more open competition based on merit rather than nationality. In particular, Brazil and South Africa advocated the appointment of Nigeria's finance minister, Ngozi Okonjo-Iweala. Although Okonjo-Iweala's candidacy was unsuccessful, this marked the first time that there had officially been more than one candidate and the position was openly contested. It is estimated that under the weighted voting system, the Nigerian would only have received 19 per cent of the votes (Rushe et al., 2012). The case illustrated both a determination by developing countries to demand a greater say in the global governance of development and the continuing power of developed states to deny them that voice.

assessing the importance to be given to any critique, it is necessary to probe the existence of alternatives. In other words, what are the feasible alternatives in organizing the specific aspect of development?

3 Much criticism of the Bank is often out of date. Some critics appear unaware of its adaptability and produce critiques of policies or programmes that are no longer current. Therefore, in assessing any criticism of the Bank, it is important to ascertain its current relevance to Bank operations.

4 It is important to distinguish between the Bank's bureaucracy and its members. Criticism should be sensitive to the relationship between the Bank staff and its more influential members, because it is often the states behind the Bank that are setting policy.

5 The World Bank is a financial institution and any effective criticism must recognize the financial constraints under which it operates.

The World Bank has been in a seemingly endless process of remaking itself from its early days. At various times in its history its relevance as an institution of governance has been questioned. The creation by China in April 2015 of the Asian Infrastructure Investment Bank (AIIB) has once more led many to query the relevance of the World Bank. While World Bank president Jim Yong Kim has publicly stated that he plans to work closely with the AIIB and plays down the arrival of the AIIB as a rival to the World Bank, others have expressed concern that China has created the AIIB in a bid to supersede American hegemony by challenging a key institution underpinned by American power. The critical response of the Obama Administration to the AIIB and its failure to prevent major allies from joining the institution further supports the argument that the AIIB (and the new BRICS Development Bank) will herald a considerable loss of influence for the World Bank over the development agenda.

Debt and debt relief

Third World indebtedness has been a major problem since the debt crisis (see Chapter 8). Civil society organizations such as Make Poverty History and the Jubilee Debt Campaign have been important advocacy groups, campaigning for the cancellation of developing country debt. The severity and hence impact of debt on a country's economy can be measured either by the total external debt as a proportion of GDP or by the debt service ratio, that is, the relationship between debt service payments and export earnings. In many developing countries, total external debt is high compared with GDP and long-term debts outweigh the size of many countries' annual exports and thus their ability to generate income to repay their debts. The impact of debt is a severe constraint on development. It reduces the spending power of the indebted country and constrains their ability to fund education, health and other social programmes. Furthermore, it weakens incentives to invest in the debtor country and reduces economic growth.

In response to the pressure from civil society actors, Western governments and international financial agencies have embarked on debt relief programmes. The two most important multilateral debt relief mechanisms are the Heavily Indebted Poor Countries (HIPC) Initiative and the Multilateral Debt Relief Initiative (MDRI). Launched in 1996, the HIPC Initiative is a joint IMF–World Bank scheme, which brings together multilateral, bilateral and commercial creditors in a scheme to provide debt relief to poor countries. It was the first attempt to create a comprehensive debt relief framework for the world's poorest countries. The introduction of the HIPC Initiative was recognition that some debt cancellation would be required in order to move the poorest countries out of the poverty trap. Under the HIPC Initiative, countries that qualify for debt relief have their debt reduced in return for meeting certain performance criteria. The aim of the programme is to create a sustainable economic framework for heavily indebted countries. The operation of the HIPC Initiative has been criticized for an absence of transparency in its operations, for example when Nigeria was removed from the HIPC list in 1998. It has also been argued that the programme is too focused on the repayment of debt and not sufficiently focused on reducing poverty or improving economic growth (Oxfam International, 2000).

In 1999, in response to these criticisms, the HIPC Initiative was reformed. The Enhanced HIPC Initiative increased country coverage and intended to provide faster, deeper and broader debt relief and to strengthen the links between debt relief, poverty reduction and social policies. While debt reduction is not sufficient for debt sustainability, the initiative had become a vehicle for the transfer of additional funds to the HIPC (World Bank, 2006b).

The MDRI, created in 2006, provides for 100 per cent relief on eligible debt from the IMF, the World Bank, the Inter-American Bank and the African Development Bank to a group of low-income countries. Eligible countries are those that have reached or will attain the completion point under the HIPC Initiative (see Box 11.7). The MDRI is the result of a decision reached at the G8 summit at Gleneagles in July 2005. The MDRI is different from the HIPC Initiative in two respects. First, it is more comprehensive, in that it provides 100 per cent debt relief. Thus, it will free up more resources to be

> **Box 11.7** List of Heavily Indebted Poor Countries
>
> As of the end of September 2014, 35 countries have reached the completion point under the HIPC Initiative: Afghanistan, Benin, Bolivia, Burkina Faso, Burundi, Cameroon, Central African Republic, Comoros, Republic of Congo, Democratic Republic of Congo, Cote d'Ivoire, Ethiopia, the Gambia, Ghana, Guinea, Guinea-Bissau, Guyana, Haiti, Honduras, Liberia, Madagascar, Malawi, Mali, Mauritania, Mozambique, Nicaragua, Niger, Rwanda, Sao Tome and Principe, Senegal, Sierra Leone, Tanzania, Togo, Uganda and Zambia.
>
> Chad has reached the decision point under the HIPC Initiative but has not reached the completion point. Three countries are at the pre-decision point: Eritrea, Somalia and Sudan.
>
> *Source:* IDA/IMF (2014, p. 6)

dedicated to the fight against poverty. Second, debt relief is restricted to the IMF, the World Bank, the Inter-American Bank and the African Development Bank.

There is no doubt that the HIPC and MDRI programs have made a positive impact on the indebtedness of the eligible countries. HIPC has provided total debt relief of $76 billion (in nominal terms) and MDRI has provided total debt relief of $50 billion (in nominal terms). The debt stocks of the 36 post-decision-point HIPCs have fallen by over 95 per cent (World Bank, 2014). With 35 countries already having reached the completion point the debt reduction initiative is almost complete. Two severely indebted countries outside the umbrella of this scheme have yet to be fully assessed (IMF/World Bank, 2014).

The scheme has achieved a measure of success but challenges remain. The pre-decision countries have made limited progress in crossing the threshold and face challenging domestic environments. In the absence of a stable peace and improved governance they are unlikely to be able to meet the targets required to meet the decision point. There has been varied support from creditors, while the multilateral agencies and members of the Paris club have been effective participants. Moreover, for all countries there is a need to ensure that in the post-HIPC phase they will not slide back into indebtedness.

North–South conflict

It may appear odd to insist on examining the North–South conflict as a key issue in the contemporary political economy of development when so much attention is given (in the media and elsewhere) to the rise of the BRICS and other emerging countries. However, it should be apparent from the arguments in this chapter that the practice of international development is a distinctly political process in which consideration of power is central. In contrast to a liberal perspective that emphasizes the mutuality of interests between developed and developing countries, we perceive the simultaneous existence of common and competing interests. An integral feature of the international political economy of development, therefore, is constituted by what is termed the 'North–South conflict'. This refers to the existence of political differences and a diplomatic conflict between the governments of advanced industrial countries and those of developing countries. We have alluded to this conflict above and here we explore certain aspects of the historical evolution and contemporary manifestation of this aspect of international development. Within the global political economy, issues of dominance and dependence remain important and the answers to questions concerning who gets what, when and why are linked to the different ways in which interests are articulated. The answers to fundamental questions such as 'What is development? What are the best methods for promoting development?' cannot be divorced from the issue of exactly who gets to frame the answers to such questions. In other words, the central problem concerns the matter of who speaks for whom. This is a complex issue in which it is possible to identify a number of potential stakeholders. Although civil society groups involved in the promotion of economic development cannot be left out of any comprehensive answer to these questions, we focus our discussion at the level of official policy-making. States remain the key instruments of legitimacy in the global political order and development policies are officially implemented through agencies of the state. First, we will focus on the North–South conflict as an integral part of the international political economy of development through a brief exploration of its historical evolution. The ability of developing countries to exercise influence over international negotiations depends on the degree of solidarity they can achieve, and so we go on to assess the extent to which divisions among developing countries mean that they will be incapable of presenting a united front to the holders of power in the world economy.

The North–South conflict in a historical perspective

The dissatisfaction of developing countries with the liberal international economic order first surfaced in the 1950s with demands for reform of the international trading order and calls for increased economic aid. These demands were made with increasing stridency within the UN system after developing countries gained the majority in the United Nations General Assembly in 1960. A concerted demand for additional financial resources and increased market access for their exports followed the creation of UNCTAD in 1964 in Geneva. As part of the UN system, it became the principal forum for North–South confrontation over economic issues and the instrument through which the developing countries hoped reform would be undertaken. Between 1964 and 1973, UNCTAD spearheaded campaigns for increased market access for Third World manufactured exports, stabilization of international commodity prices and additional development assistance. UNCTAD's record during this period was mixed, with very limited gains.

The North–South conflict was given increased prominence in the 1970s with debate over a New International Economic Order (NIEO). Between 1973 and 1979, the NIEO dominated North–South discussions. Indeed, it can be argued that this period saw development with its highest international political profile. At the centre of NIEO demands were those pertaining to international commodity markets. The NIEO also encompassed reform of the GATT, the IMF and the World Bank. Developing countries argued that these organizations were controlled by the advanced industrial countries and failed to support developing country interests. A number of resolutions were passed by the UN General Assembly, of which the most important were the Declaration on the Establishment of a New International Economic Order (1974), the Programme of Action on the Establishment of a New International Economic Order (1974) and the Charter of Economic Rights and Duties of States (1975), creating the framework for the NIEO. These UN resolutions were seen by some scholars as important legal documents. They set out the mutual responsibilities of states, established a framework of action and the justification for a new order. The negotiations leading to the creation of an NIEO ended in failure. No single event or factor was responsible for this failure; however, the refusal of Western states to enter into serious negotiation was the most important reason for the collapse of the North–South dialogue.

For some analysts, the fragmentation of the Third World coalition in the 1980s led to the demise of the North–South conflict, and for others the rise of the BRICS and increasing differentiation among developing countries has effectively rendered the North–South conflict meaningless in the contemporary world. Our survey of the global political economy leads us to reject such conclusions as limited and limiting, based on a failure to situate North–South conflict as a structure of the international political economy of development. The North–South conflict arises from a real disparity in power and resources between rich and poor nation-states. Of course there is no singular experience shared by all developing countries as they engage with issues in international trade, finance, investment, climate change and environmental degradation, and migration. Nevertheless, in material terms the existence of a North–South divide arises from a perception of shared powerlessness. For the most part, Southern states lack instrumental (material) power resources. The North–South divide is fundamentally based on patterns of global inequality. The stark reality is that for Southern states the pursuit of economic development remains a key priority. While it is certainly the case that the North–South divide does not create a simple global dichotomy, there are fundamental socioeconomic differences across the divide. China is a pertinent example of a country that is both a rising power and a developing country. Indeed, China has taken on a role as a sponsor of development (see Box 11.8). Yet, while China has increased access to global decision-making through, for example, membership of the G20, it still feels constrained within existing global economic institutions.

Third World solidarity and fragmentation

The above discussion has not assumed commonality among developing countries but has noted the existence of a common bargaining platform. We have already noted the existence of significant differences among developing countries and the three main regions – Africa, Asia and Latin America. The concern of an international political economy of development is not with any organic unity but rather with the political expressions of unity and discord. Unity does not in itself lead to specific gains but it is an indicator of the extent to which developing countries can articulate a distinct vision in the global political economy. The historical record shows that Third World solidarity

---

Box 11.8 China as a development actor in Latin America

Although China is a key member of the developing world coalition and the BRICS, it also plays a growing and important role as a sponsor of development in other countries. Using its financial surpluses gained from its massive export industries, China has been investing in Asia, Africa and Latin America. In Latin America, China's impact has been immense. Key developments include China surpassing the US as the most important destination for South American exports and Chinese finance exceeding that provided by the World Bank and the Inter-American Development Bank combined (Ray and Gallagher, 2015). Chinese investment concentrates on building transportation infrastructure and resource extraction.

While Chinese investment gives Latin American governments more development options, it also brings numerous challenges. Chinese investment focuses upon gaining access to natural resources and Latin American exports to China are indeed dominated by the resource sector. Latin America primarily exports agricultural products such as soybeans and resources such as petroleum and metals (zinc, copper), while importing manufactured goods from China. This may be recreating the poor terms of trade that Latin America has experienced with Western states. Increased Latin American resources exports are also creating large carbon footprints and using vast amounts of water. Many of the Chinese development projects are located in indigenous and environmentally sensitive lands such as the project for a Nicaraguan canal to rival the Panama Canal. This raises the likelihood of environmental and social conflict over development strategies.

responds to changes in the global political economy and is not static.

Third World solidarity began to fragment in the 1980s primarily as the result of two developments. The debt crisis had a twofold impact on the coalition. First, it created a range of special interests as countries sought to battle their specific debt burdens and were given differential treatment within the international financial system. For example, while some countries welcomed wholesale debt reduction, others were concerned that such a strategy would undermine their creditworthiness. Second, the SAPs imposed by the World Bank and the IMF in promoting liberal economic thought severely curtailed the independence of developing countries. The severely indebted countries, as suppliants of Western economic assistance, were in no position to demand change in the international economic order. The second major development in the international system of the 1980s with an impact on the Third World coalition was the success of the NICs, since this exacerbated the differences among developing countries. But the scale of fragmentation is somewhat exaggerated and we still see and hear the collective voice of the developing world in many international negotiations. The important point is the degree to which they can articulate a different view.

The Doha Round of multilateral trade negotiations revived Third World solidarity not as a singular theme but in terms of the creation of various coalitions that were instrumental in giving developing countries a distinctive voice. Climate change negotiations provide another example of multiple developing country coalitions existing in the same negotiating space with some countries having multiple memberships in more than one coalition. Third World solidarity refers solely to the joint efforts by countries that identify as developing countries (Williams, 2005b). In this sense we can make two observations. A Third World coalition remains a part of the international debate on development. At all major international conferences, developing countries continue to try to present a common position. Furthermore, recognition that the G8 failed to include the voices of important developing countries was a key reason for the emergence of the G20 in 2008–9 as the prime forum responsible for coordinating a concerted response to the global economic crisis. Apart from the continuing existence of poverty and inequality, many countries identify with a collective Third World voice because of their lack of influence in international organizations. This inability to influence the international agenda is most starkly seen in the weighted voting decision-making process of the IMF and the World Bank. But it is also perceived in institutions such as the G8 leading industrial countries that meet periodically to make decisions concerning the future of the global economy. The G8 is a constant reminder that Third World governments do not shape the international agenda. In addition, the inability to successfully conclude the Doha Round at the WTO indicates the roadblocks that developing countries have encountered in moulding the global economic system.

Second, the historical record shows that as a counter-hegemonic force, the Third World coalition has been most important in presenting an alternative vision of development and a critique of the liberal economic order. It has not achieved important gains in material terms. Thus, in the future we should not expect any dramatic change in the ability of poor countries to wrest concessions from the richer nations.

CONCLUSION

In a powerful and influential critique of postwar development policy, Escobar (1995) argues that the development discourse began in 1949 with President Truman's inaugural presidential address in which he enunciated large-scale support for development. This perspective usefully alerts us to the role of external powers in constructing development and the importance of the international political climate. Escobar's view is, however, a limited one, since it removes autonomy from developing countries and makes them passive recipients of Western policy.

As we have seen, development is centrally concerned with material and normative issues. Whether the focus is on absolute poverty or relative poverty, it is apparent that poverty shapes the life chances of millions of individuals worldwide, constraining access to material and non-material goods and services. While development remains principally a national concern, it has, since the outset of the postwar development assistance regime, been inscribed on the international agenda. The organization, promotion and execution of national and international development policies are the result of structural change in the global political economy and the adaptation of state and non-state actors to these changes.

An important aspect of recent development theory and practice has been a debate about how economic growth can be reconciled with environmental sustainability. This echoes a broader concern in the field of IPE about the relationship between political economy and the environment. We examine the significance of the environment and its entanglement with political economy in Chapter 12.

Further Reading

The annual *Millennium Development Goals Report* is compulsory reading for anyone interested in international development. See *Millennium Development Goals Report 2012* (2014). Equally indispensable is the *Human Development Report*. See *Human Development Report 2013: The Rise of the South: Human Progress in a Diverse World*; and *Human Development Report 2014: Sustaining Human Progress: Reducing Vulnerabilities and Building Resilience* (2014b);

Amartya Sen's *Development as Freedom* (1999) is a classic that is worth reading. Emma Aisbett, 'Why are the Critics so Convinced that Globalization is Bad for the Poor?' in Ann Harrison (ed.) *Globalization and Poverty* (2007, pp. 33–85), is an excellent review of the debate on globalization and poverty. For a thoughtful and insightful view of how people globally view the post-2015 development agenda, see the UNDP publication, *A Million Voices: The World We Want* (2013).

In summarizing the significance of climate change for social and political affairs, activist and author Naomi Klein (2014) declares 'This Changes Everything.' She argues that the global capitalist system must give way to a new way of organizing intellectual, economic, social and political life or the consequences will be dire for the world's human population. Has everything changed, or should it? In this chapter we examine how the issue of the environment has been incorporated into IPE and the degree to which it poses a challenge to previous modes of thinking and acting. Is it simply another issue area or does it have the potential to change the very way we think about IPE?

The study of international political economy did not embrace the environment as a subject of study in its early years or incorporate insights from thinkers concerned with 'green' issues (Helleiner, 1996). There are two principal aspects to the integration of environmental concerns into IPE. First, a number of environmental problems have an impact on the global political economy, and some form of international agreement is necessary to cope with these problems. As Hurrell and Kingsbury (1992, p. 5) note: 'international cooperation is required both to manage global environmental problems and to deal with domestic environmental problems in ways that do not place individual states at a political or competitive disadvantage.' This intersection of environmental concerns and the international political economy can be termed the problem of 'international' or 'global governance'.

Second, global environmental change is intimately linked to national and international systems of production, distribution and consumption: 'The most important aspect of increased globalization derives from the complex but close relationship between the generation of environmental problems and the workings of the effectively globalized world economy' (Hurrell and Kingsbury, 1992, p. 3). This can be characterized as the problem of 'sustainability'. The historical process of capital accumulation and the pursuit of economic growth has contributed to current environmental degradation. Key issues concerning growth and development strategies, industrialization, international trade and North–South relations, for example, all require re-examination in the current historical conjuncture. In this context, it can be argued that modern global environmental challenges are characterized by three main features: uncertainty, irreversibility and uniqueness or non-substitutability (Pearce, 1990, p. 366). Since the 1992 United Nations Conference on Environment and Development (UNCED) in Rio, local and national authorities as well as international organizations, firms and NGOs have all in their various ways pledged allegiance in various forms to the concept of sustainable development. They have made numerous commitments to preserving environmental quality and combating environmental degradation. While it is not surprising that the rhetoric has surpassed the reality, this result nevertheless has to be explained rather than taken for granted.

Recent attention to environmental issues within IPE signifies scholarly attention to the subject, but often falls short of recognizing the intrinsic importance of the issue. It can be argued that the separation of economic activity from environmental consideration is an artificial distinction since the economy is embedded in nature. In other words, on one hand economic activity transforms the environment and on the other hand the resulting transformation of ecosystems impacts on societal development and these interactions have been taking place from the earliest human settlements. Placing ecological or environmental concerns at the centre of studies of the global political economy has the potential to transform the ways in which we think about key economic processes. Both the research program of historical ecology which 'traces the complex relationships between our species and the planet we live on, charted over the long term' (Crumley, 2006, p. 2), and that of ecological economics which 'addresses the relationships between ecosystems and economic systems in the broadest sense' (Costanza, 1989, p. 1) have provided important insights into understanding the political economy of environmental change.

This chapter explores the interface between environmental issues and the global political economy. It looks at the ways in which attention to environmental issues alters perceptions of and actions within the global political economy. The chapter begins by discussing some of the terms used in analysing the global political economy of the environment. Next, we consider IPE and environmental studies' explanations of environmental degradation. We then trace the evolution of the environment as an important issue in discussions on the international economy. The key issues considered in this chapter are: sustainable development, climate change and transnational land acquisitions.

DEFINITIONS AND BACKGROUND

Right from the start we are faced with the far from simple issue concerning whether the focus should be on environment or ecology. Without seeking to prejudge the issue, we will use the term 'environment' to discuss the issues with which we are concerned rather than 'ecology'. Within the literature these terms are sometimes used synonymously and at other times they are used in order to distinguish anthropocentric approaches from those that reject species hierarchy. The contention over the use of concepts has recently been highlighted by the introduction of the term Anthropocene (see Box 12.1).

Although used in various ways by different writers, the central difference between the terms appears to be that 'environmentalism' retains humans at the centre of its analysis, whereas 'ecologism' focuses on the interrelationship between humans and nature in a nonhierarchical manner. Given the widespread usage of the term 'environmentalism' to refer to the interactions between humans and the natural environment, this chapter will adopt the terms 'environment' and 'environmental' to denote the subject under scrutiny. At its simplest,

Box 12.1 The Anthropocene

The agreed term to define the current geological time period is the Holocene. However, although there is no agreement among scientists on the date from which we can chart its beginning, many scientists and commentators are increasingly using the term 'Anthropocene' to refer to the period in which we are currently living. The concept of the Anthropocene highlights the irreversible impact of human activities on the planet's ecosystems. Proponents of the concept argue that the period known as the Holocene is now at an end. The Anthropocene Working Group of the International Commission on Stratigraphy is currently considering whether the Anthropocene is a defined geological epoch within the geological time scale. Whether a formal Anthropocene can be defined it appears that the popularization of the term and its use in environmental circles indicates a strong desire to signify the impact of human activities on the environment. As Will Steffen contends, '[It] will be another strong reminder to the general public that we are now having undeniable impacts on the environment at the scale of the planet as a whole, so much so that a new geological epoch has begun' (Stromberg, 2013).

environment refers to the surroundings of a specific unit, that is, a unit or a system exists within a context and it is the context (that which surrounds the unit or system) to which the term 'environment' refers. In the context of the study of political economy, concern with the environment focuses on the impact of human activity on the natural environment. Attention is given to the use and misuse of natural resources and nature by humans. Environmental degradation therefore occurs when humans (ab)use nature in ways that both threaten the sustainability of the natural resource base and create unwanted problems such as pollution for human societies.

Defining environmentalism is difficult since it houses a variety of perspectives rather than a single approach. One attempt to combine diverse perspectives into identifiable schools of thought has been made by Clapp and Dauvergne (2011, pp. 3–17), who present a fourfold typology of worldviews of environment change: market liberals, institutionalists, bioenvironmentalists and social greens. A more conventional approach distinguishes between two broad strands (or ideologies) of environmentalism, although no agreement exists on the terminology to be used for this purpose. One useful and often cited distinction in the literature is that between 'light green' and 'dark green' perspectives, where the term 'green' refers to a positive and supportive attitude towards the protection and preservation of the environment. A light green approach is essentially reformist, accepting the major institutions of capitalist society and seeking to engender respect for the environment and preservation of the environment through strategies that do not disrupt modern economic growth and industrial society. On the other hand, the dark green or radical environmental approach begins from the assumption that fundamental practices will have consequences for future generations.

Other writers maintain a distinction between the two main strands of environmentalism but use different terms to convey the central distinction. O'Riordan (1976) distinguishes between technocentric and ecocentric positions, where 'technocentric' refers to approaches that attempt to accommodate sustainable development in the context of market incentives, whereas ecocentric positions challenge conventional economic goals and models. Dobson (1990, p. 35) distinguishes between environmentalism and ecologism, where environmentalism is characterized as 'a managerial approach to the environment within the context of

present political and economic practices', and ecologism 'presupposes radical changes' in humanity's relationship with the environment in order to care for it. Goodin (1992, pp. 7–8) makes a similar point when he distinguishes between an environmentalist posture, which is concerned with making environmental choices that serve human interests, and a green approach, which refuses to reduce nature to human or divine interests and posits an independent role for nature in the creation of value. For Eckersley (1992, p. 26), the key division is between anthropocentric and ecocentric approaches, where anthropocentric thinking 'offers opportunities for human emancipation and fulfilment in an ecologically sustainable society', while an ecocentric theory is one that 'pursues these goals in the context of a broader notion of emancipation that also recognizes the moral standing of the non-human world'.

Moving beyond approaches to environmentalism, we can recognize the existence of different ways of classifying issues of environmental concern. There are different approaches to classifying environmental problem sets. We can distinguish between:

- *physical changes:* such as atmospheric pollution, ozone depletion, climate change, marine pollution, loss of biodiversity
- *development activities:* such as energy production and use, tourism, agricultural production
- *aspects of the human condition and wellbeing:* such as population growth, health and security.

A different classification distinguishes between:

- *problems arising directly from human activity on the land:* for example deforestation, top-soil erosion and watershed failure
- *problems arising as the indirect result of waste:* for example greenhouse gases, ozone-depleting gases, nuclear contamination and toxic waste.

The first set of problems are relatively localized in their consequences, whereas the latter have direct global reach.

Furthermore, we can also distinguish environmental problems in terms of the situations faced by actors as they pursue cooperative or conflictual strategies, for example global commons, shared natural resources, transboundary externalities or linked issues (Young, 1994). Problems such as the depletion of the ozone layer, the potential for climate change as a result of the greenhouse effect, the loss of biodiversity, and deforestation and desertification are well documented. It is important to recognize that the impact of these trends and events on the physical fabric of the planet cannot be limited to environmental or technical considerations but are to be seen as essentially political in character, since 'the globality of environmental problems stems not merely from the replicated institutions which create them and the spread of environmental activism, but also from both the very transboundary nature of pollution and depletion problems and the reliance on co-operative mechanisms for problem solving' (Laferrière, 1994, p. 95).

Although there are some commonly accepted features of environmentalism (Box 12.2), the environmental problem is a complex and multifaceted one, with diverse political, social, economic and ethical dimensions. For example, while many environmental problems are indeed global in scope, it is an overstatement and a mistake to assume that all environmental problems possess this quality. To assume that all environmental problems are global can lead to the erroneous conclusion that environmental degradation translates into shared concerns, that we share a common future and have a common interest in combating environmental destruction. Such a conclusion is apolitical and abstracts from the power relations inherent in both the causation of ecological harm and the steps necessary to provide workable solutions.

THEORETICAL PERSPECTIVES: IPE AND ENVIRONMENTAL STUDIES

The upsurge of interest in the environment has resulted in the publication of numerous studies as analysts have explored the causal relationship between human practices and environmental degradation. These studies draw on differing understandings of the causes of environmental degradation and propose a range of appropriate responses to address the problems that have arisen. Theorists and practitioners interested in global environmental politics have conflicting views on the causes of and solutions to environmental degradation. Here, we explore two theoretical debates: one that has arisen in IR and IPE, and a second that is more familiar to students of environmental economics and environmental studies. We spend some time examining the debate between rival schools of thought in IPE (economic nationalism/realism, liberalism and Marxism) before turning to look at a debate based on differing conceptions of the relationship between humans and the environment (anthropocentric, environmental and ecocentric perspectives).

IPE debates

The traditional approaches to IPE, that is, economic nationalism, liberalism and Marxism, historically paid little or no attention to environmental issues. However, the emergence of the environment as an international political issue and the evident linkages between global environmental change and national and international systems of production, distribution and consumption have seen scholars working within these paradigms turn their attention to the analysis of global environmental politics. Most attention has been paid to the creation and maintenance of international cooperation on the environment, and the relationship between the global economy and the causes of environmental degradation. We first review the debate on international environmental cooperation before turning our attention to the political economy of sustainability.

Box 12.2 Five commonly accepted features of environmentalism

1 Environmental degradation is global in the sense that it affects everyone, and can only be managed effectively through global cooperation.
2 Environmental degradation can exacerbate intra-state and inter-state tensions.
3 There are complex linkages between the environment and the global economy.
4 Environmental issues are distinguished by uncertainty; that is, there is no guarantee that sometime in the future a finite natural resource will be replaced by technology.
5 Irreversibility is a key feature of environmental politics, for example once a species is extinct, it is impossible to make it reappear.

The economic nationalist or realist approach to international environmental cooperation is based on two main assumptions. Realists assume that nation-states act in terms of their national interests and that international cooperation is difficult to achieve and sustain, given the existence of competing national interests in an anarchical international system. With each state attempting to maximize its military and economic power, international cooperation on the environment, like any form of international cooperation, is inherently difficult since environmental interests will be subsumed by traditional political power goals.

The realist assumption that states are rational, self-interested utility maximizers leads to the conclusion that international cooperation on the environment will only be possible in situations where states perceive such cooperation to be in their interests. Moreover, realists contend that in an anarchical international system, cooperation on the environment will only be feasible on those issues and in those specific situations that support and maintain the interests of dominant states. Realist approaches are therefore sceptical about the possibility of extensive cooperation on environmental issues (Barrett, 1993; Blackhurst and Subramanian, 1992). There are, of course, many examples in environmental politics, either where states have failed to establish a basis for cooperation or where a cooperative arrangement has broken down, that provide support for the realist perspective. For example, the refusal of the US to ratify the Kyoto Protocol lends support to the realist argument. However, realist political economy is less well placed to explain why, in the absence of the dominant power in the world economy (the US), so many other states (192) have been willing to ratify the Kyoto Protocol.

The willingness of many states to ratify the Kyoto Protocol in the absence of the US is better explained by liberal IPE theories. Liberal IPE theories, although using the state as a key unit of analysis, begin from a recognition of the demands of interdependence. For liberal theorists, international environmental cooperation arises from the recognition of mutual or shared interests. A globalizing world economy creates networks of interdependencies and bonds of common interests among the various actors, thus facilitating international cooperation. Although states remain important actors, they are enmeshed in a network of transactions and interdependencies that limit and constrain their authority. Furthermore, environmental cooperation is made more feasible through the activities of non-state actors such as intergovernmental organizations, NGOs, scientific networks and firms.

There are a number of diverse critical and radical approaches to international environmental cooperation. Some radical writers argue that the rivalry between capitalist nation-states makes international environmental cooperation unlikely. Whereas realist writers emphasize the interests of states in maximizing power, and liberal theorists show how interdependence creates mutual bonds of interest, radical scholars focus on inequality and dominance in the international system. In this perspective, international cooperation is subsumed by the economic interests of dominant states and the capitalist class. International environmental cooperation is likely, but the forms of cooperation and the institutions created, since they are based on capitalism, will be incapable of providing effective solutions to environmental degradation. Some radical writers argue that in a hierarchical international power structure, the developed countries of the North dominate international decision-making, thus maintaining the historically established pattern of exploitation of developing countries in the South. Negotiations on international environmental issues will therefore reflect northern interests and southern concerns will be marginalized (Haas, 1990a, pp. 47–52).

While all three perspectives have something useful to contribute to analyses of international environmental cooperation, each perspective on its own is incapable of providing satisfactory answers to the range of issues and cooperative arrangements that arise in global environmental politics. The realist approach, for example, is flawed because its focus on states and emphasis on power are empirically unsustainable. A focus on states seriously limits analysis and omits consideration of important actors in the global political economy. Many analyses of global environmental politics have documented the critical roles played by international organizations, firms and NGOs.

Moreover, a number of studies have clearly demonstrated that international cooperation is possible and regimes can be created and maintained in the absence of a hegemon (Axelrod and Keohane, 1986; Keohane, 1984; Young, 1989, 1994). While liberal analysis, in admitting the importance of non-state actors, provides a more realistic account of environmental politics, liberal theories have a tendency to neglect the role of power in shaping institutions in the first place. They fail to give sufficient attention to considerations of structural inequalities. While radical theories show awareness of the importance of structural patterns of dominance and dependence, they frequently underestimate the importance of international actors. For example, international organizations are not mere epiphenomena with negligible impact on international relations, and the forms of bargaining that take place within such organizations do not merely reflect the distribution of power in the global system.

The second area of contention between the perspectives concerns the relationship between the global economy and environmental degradation. Since the issue of sustainable development will be discussed further below, at this point we only highlight some important differences between the three approaches. From an economic nationalist perspective, sustainable development will only arise if states perceive such policies to be in their interests. Since states exert control over national economies, the pursuit of sustainable development is dependent on states identifying this as a key goal. However, efforts to promote sustainability are likely to founder if economic growth remains the primary goal of political elites. As long as the elements of power are constituted through practices that degrade the environment, sustainable development will remain an aspiration rather than a reality.

In a liberal perspective, environmental degradation arises because of market failure, specifically the absence of mechanisms to provide a proper valuation of natural resources. The extension of market principles to the environment through, for example, the allocation of property rights and the inclusion of environmental values in pricing policies, will lead to a more efficient allocation of resources and environmental protection. In this view, sustainable economic policies are dependent on increased economic growth rather than its retardation. The problem is not growth per se but rather the forms that growth has taken to date. Indeed, economic growth and proper environmental assessments are crucial strategies for the promotion of sustainability.

Radical theorists locate the cause of environmental degradation in the development of capitalism. They argue that environmental degradation arises from capitalism and that current economic practices and value systems cannot promote sustainable policies since the capitalist system is inherently exploitative. As Redclift (1987, p. 56) has claimed: 'The concentration on

"growth" has served to obscure the fact that resource depletion and unsustainable development are a direct consequence of growth itself.'

Once again we can see that none of the perspectives provide a convincing explanation of the political economy of sustainability:

1   The ahistorical approach of realist IPE ignores the causes of environmental degradation since it fails to enquire into the ways in which historically constructed patterns of production and consumption have created the current environmental problems. Such an approach is incapable of challenging the processes of accumulation, production and reproduction central to capitalism and responsible for creating the environmental problems in the first place.
2   Liberal theories are deficient because they fail to deal adequately with power and power relations. Specifically, they are unable to represent structural forms of power.
3   NeoMarxist analysis, with its emphasis on the structural relationship between labour and capital and its location of environmental degradation in the political and economic structures of capitalist societies, does appear to represent an advance. But the historical evidence clearly shows that both capitalist and socialist regimes failed to protect the environment. The failure to implicate socialist development strategies in environmental degradation arises from a continued attachment to economic growth and a failure to recognize the ecological limits to growth. Another weakness of radical theories lies in the tendency to equate capitalism with industrialization.

This debate between the three traditional IPE paradigms serves to show the limitations of the traditional paradigms when applied to the study of the environment (see Table 12.1). While realists, liberals and Marxists do, as we have seen, have different foundations, they nevertheless all share a paradigmatic assumption of, and commitment to, the necessity and desirability of economic growth.

Environmental studies' debates

At this stage, it is necessary to move away from the established way of conceptualizing IPE as a contest between three perspectives, to focus on a different set of

Table 12.1 **Traditional IPE theories and the environment**

	Insight	Sustainable development	Shortcoming
Economic nationalism	State interests will frustrate international agreements	Unlikely, given desire for growth	Unable to confront issue of unrestrained growth
Liberalism	Interdependence increases incentives for environmental agreements	Better market signals will support it	Blind to role of state and corporate power in environmental change
Marxist, radical	Northern vs. southern interests, class interests	Degradation caused by capitalism	Ignores damage caused by socialist growth

values at the heart of environmentalism. The shared commitment to anthropocentrism of the three IPE paradigms results in their failure to engage with debates in environmental studies between proponents of technocentric solutions and supporters of ecocentric goals. Here, we will examine the contestation between environmentalism (technocentrism) and ecologism (ecocentrism) since it extends analysis of environmental degradation and sustainability.

The technocentric perspective is based on the assumption that the central objective of economic growth is to satisfy the needs of humans. This perspective is based on the superiority of Western cultural values and the transformational capacity of capitalism. Two variants of technocentrism can be identified – conservative and reformist. From the viewpoint of conservative technocentrism, modern economic growth is the basis for personal liberation and capitalism is the driving force for change. In this perspective, ecological change is necessarily attendant on economic growth but this does not mean that such change is negative. Writers in this perspective tend to emphasize the positive impact of economic growth and argue that humans have in the past found solutions to impending environmental problems. Capitalism, it is claimed, is an ingenious system that, through the search for profit, will naturally find market-based solutions to environmental problems. Indeed, some economists have argued that concern with environmental issues is misplaced, and any attempt to hold back progress in the name of environmentalism will result in economic catastrophe. Beckerman (1995) presented a fierce attack on controls on economic growth, in his polemical text *Small is Stupid*.

While the conservative technocentric position contests the claim that modern economic growth is responsible for environmental degradation, reformist technocentric writers have, principally through the development of the sub-field of environmental economics, tried to demonstrate the continued relevance of conventional economic theory to the study of environmental change. The reformist technocentric approach is rooted in environmental economics and begins from the assumption that environmental degradation is an accidental outcome of modern economic growth. It is thus a reformist rather than a radical position and argues that if the environment is fully priced, environmental degradation will be reduced.

From this perspective, environmental degradation arises from market failure. In order to protect the environment, it is essential to value the environment through determining the 'real costs' of resource use and then proposing the most efficient solutions. A tension exists among environmental economists between those who prefer the use of incentives and market-based solutions and those who argue in support of regulation and command and control measures. This tension can be perceived in discussions on global warming. Proponents of market-based solutions argue in support of tradable permits, whereas those who prefer interventionist solutions propose legislation restricting emission levels. Current national and international solutions to environmental change are largely based on this reformist perspective, and the policy debate is usually constructed in terms of market versus interventionist solutions.

This policy approach has been termed 'managerial environmentalism' (Levy, 1997). It recognizes the link between human activity and the environment but believes that an accommodation can be found between current economic activity and the long-term goal of sustainable development. Central to environmental managerialism are two features, the first being a commitment to business and the belief that capitalism and the environment are not antithetical, while the second includes a liberal internationalist belief in multilateral cooperation. This technocentric approach contrasts sharply with more radical ecocentric approaches (see Box 12.3).

The reformist technocentric approach has become an important part of contemporary discourse through the development of environmental economics. This is not to claim that concern about ecological limits to growth arose in this period for the first time. In the 1960s, a self-conscious subdiscipline of environmental economics began to emerge. At the centre of environmental economics is the idea that the economy is an open system. Environmental economics is based on a materials balance view of the economy, which begins from the assumption that the economy is an open system with three basic processes – extraction, processing and consumption. Resources (renewable and nonrenewable) are extracted from the environment and processed for consumption. All economic activities create waste that must either be recycled in the economic process or absorbed in the environment. The central issue therefore becomes that of maintaining economic growth without decreasing the assimilative capacity of the environment to absorb wastes. Environmental economics builds on the insights of neoclassical economics, and has successfully incorporated the environment into standard economic theory. It has moved from a position in which the economy is seen as closed to one that stresses the open nature of the system. But the overall assumptions are similar to those of its parent discipline. The objective of the economy is still to maximize the welfare of society. The fundamental economic problem remains the efficient organization of production and consumption.

In contrast, an ecological focus forces us to confront the changing relationships that have developed between human activity, natural systems and the built environment. Social systems and natural systems exist in a dynamic interactive context and interdependencies between the two systems mirror developments in both. From the work of anthropologists, we have extensive evidence of the myriad ways in which cultural beliefs, cultural artefacts, social structure and type of technology are intimately connected.

Unlike the technocentric perspective, an ecocentric perspective is founded on a rejection of continued economic growth and a critique of global capitalism. Writers within this approach are questioning of modern industrial growth and modern institutions. They reject anthropocentrism and argue instead for an ecological approach in which human needs are balanced by concern for all living organisms. Ecocentric theorists

---

Box 12.3 Technocentric and ecocentric approaches to sustainability

The ecocentric approach to sustainable development recognizes the environment as central to survival and progress. This can be compared with a technocentric approach, which is centred around humans and views nature merely as an instrument in sustaining human life. They can be compared in relation to a number of issues. These include:

▸ *Primary economic objectives*: economic growth (technocentric); zero economic growth (ecocentric)
▸ *Economic organization*: large scale (technocentric); small scale (ecocentric)
▸ *Market incentives*: green consumerism, economic instruments to regulate production (technocentric); limited consumerism, strong regulation of the economy (ecocentric)
▸ *Attitude to resource management*: conservationist (technocentric); preservationist (ecocentric)
▸ *Attitude to trade*: reconciliation of trade and environmental standards (technocentric); anti-trade and promotion of self-sufficiency (ecocentric)
▸ *Political project*: maintenance of nation-states and the status quo (technocentric); creation of small-scale communities as the basis of political authority (ecocentric)
▸ *Global governance*: reform of the existing international economic order (technocentric); resistance to industrialism, capitalism and modernity (ecocentric)
▸ *Ethical standards*: intergenerational and intragenerational equity (technocentric); ecological justice, equality for all life forms (ecocentric).

contend that the current emphasis in the organization of society is on human wants rather than human needs (Pepper, 1996, pp. 69–70). Human wants are socially derived and reflect the materialistic values of society, whereas human needs combine spiritual and material values to arrive at a balance between humans and the environment.

Ecological critiques of conventional economic theory point to a number of omissions in neoclassical economics, which render it incapable of providing solutions to global environmental degradation. According to ecologists, one key reason for the failure of neoclassical economics to provide a convincing analysis of environmental change stems from the omission of the fundamental laws of thermodynamics and ecology from its basic assumptions. Moreover, unlike conventional economics, the ecocentric perspective views the economy as a subsystem of the natural world and the environment rather than vice versa. Conventional economics tends to view the economy as an open system but ecologists see it as a closed system. Ecologists also object to what they perceive as the obsession with the short-term and marginal analysis of neoclassical economics. Instead of focusing on the short term, ecologists insist that we need to give more attention to the long run. This critique is related to the issue of discounting for the future, and ecologists argue that the future discounting assumptions of conventional economics are seriously flawed. Furthermore, in common with other radical critiques, the ecological perspective rejects the sterile, abstract reasoning of conventional economics and its embrace of arid mathematics. Conventional economic theory is based on constructing theorems based on questionable assumptions about human nature instead of integrating observed human or organizational behaviour into its analyses.

Although there are a number of strands of ecological economics, they all share two central ideas. These are a commitment to restricting or imposing limits on growth because of a belief that natural or ecological limitations to the earth's carrying capacity are real; and a rejection of anthropocentrism, that is, a belief in holism and an interactive relationship between all species. Three strands of ecological economics have made important contributions to the theorization of global environmental degradation. Steady state approaches focus on the issue of scale and attempt to maintain a link between the size of the economy and the overall system. Central to steady state theory is a determina-

tion to maintain the natural resource base for future generations. Radical ecology is indebted to Marxist insights and emphasizes the ways in which capitalism leads to overproduction and hence environmental degradation. Co-evolutionary approaches attempt to combine knowledge, values, social organization, technology and ecosystems. In this view, environmental degradation arises from the failure to respect the equilibrium of natural ecosystems and the neglect of the human/nature equilibrium.

MAJOR DEVELOPMENTS

Here, we focus on the evolution of the environment as an issue in the global political economy and the forms it has since taken. Over the past five decades, increased attention has been given to global environmental issues and there has been a proliferation of initiatives in the global political economy to address environmental degradation. The modern concern for the environment has gone through two phases. The first corresponds to the emergence of a new wave of environmentalism beginning in the 1960s, and the second is marked by the United Nations Conference on Environment and Development (UNCED, known as the Earth Summit) in 1992 and ushers in the mainstreaming of environmental issues on national and international agendas.

Bringing the environment in

Caldwell (1988) notes that there were three types of international environmental agreements in the first part of the 20th century:

1 *Wilderness and wildlife conservation:* included agreements such as the Fur Seal Treaty (1911) and the International Convention for the Regulation of Whaling (1946)
2 *Maritime pollution:* included the International Convention for the Prevention of Pollution of the Sea by Oil (1954) and the Convention on the High Seas (1958)
3 *Limiting the spread of nuclear weapons:* such as the Antarctic Treaty (1959) and the Treaty Banning Nuclear Weapon Tests in the Atmosphere, in Outer Space and Under Water (1963).

These efforts are important but they were not seen as part of an integrated concern with the environment.

Global concern with environmental degradation is a relatively recent phenomenon and stems from three sources.

1. UN international conferences

The international conferences convened by the United Nations were notable for their preparatory process, the resolutions passed and the follow-up process. The first significant one was the United Nations Conference on the Human Environment (UNCHE) convened in Stockholm in 1972. Called in response to lobbying by Scandinavian countries concerned by pollution, the conference agenda extended discussion beyond pollution. During the preparatory phase, the developing countries emphasized the link between development and the environment, laying the basis for the process that culminated in the UNCED in Rio 20 years later.

UNCHE recognized the environmental consequences of modern economic growth and these linkages were enshrined in the conference recommendations. Although these were subsequently ignored by governments, one notable impact of the conference was the creation of the United Nations Environment Programme, a permanent bureaucracy in the UN system to champion environmental issues.

The process begun in Stockholm culminated in 1992 when the UNCED held in Rio legitimized the environment as a concern for international economic diplomacy. The preparatory phase of the Earth Summit attracted significant attention from governmental and nongovernmental actors. Also, the high political profile of the disputes during the preparatory phase ensured maximum visibility for the conference proceedings. This became the largest conference ever held, in terms of the number of delegates present, and it also attracted the largest number of world leaders ever to convene in one place. The wide-ranging agenda gave rise to heated debate and produced Agenda 21, a document designed to provide a framework for future actions to halt environmental degradation. Agenda 21 also included a monitoring and implementation process. At the centre of the deliberations and conclusions of the Rio conference was the concept of sustainable development. The assembled delegates reached agreement that environmental degradation potentially could have profound ramifications for economic growth and prosperity.

Ten years after the Earth Summit, world leaders, civil society representatives, business leaders and journalists convened in 2002 in Johannesburg for the World Summit on Sustainable Development (also known as the Earth Summit 2002 or Rio+10). This provided an opportunity for the global community to assess the progress made in implementing the goals established at Rio. In the intervening decade, while the normative commitment to the environment remained strong, effective policy change was less evident. For example, a reduction in greenhouse gases had not been achieved despite the firm commitment made at Rio. Thus, instead of seeking binding treaties, the approach adopted at Rio+10 was to set targets.

2. Scientific knowledge

The second factor contributing to the emergence of the environment as an international issue was scientific knowledge. Probably the most significant advance here was the discovery of a hole in the ozone layer above Antarctica by a team of British scientists in 1985. The health implications of the ozone hole shocked populations and galvanized governments to act. In one sense, the image of the ozone hole was stark and readily comprehensible, and in another sense, the solution was reasonably straightforward. In saying this, we do not imply that it was easy to agree to a treaty, but rather that it did not involve a series of complicated linkages. But if the discovery of the ozone hole was part of a process of the expansion of knowledge, not all of this process was consensual. Haas (1990b) developed the concept of an 'epistemic community' to describe a collection of scientists and decision makers sharing a knowledge base. Epistemic communities have played a part in providing solutions to environmental problems.

Of equal importance to epistemic communities are the seminal books and articles that challenge conventional wisdom and alert publics to the linkages between environmental degradation and society. The publication in 1972 of *The Limits to Growth* by Dennis and Donella Meadows (1972) is one such contribution. Its controversial thesis was that the earth's finite resources would soon run out unless steps were taken to conserve energy use. Even though the projections made by the Meadows were subject to exhaustive tests and refuted by a range of experts, *The Limits to Growth* controversy was important in placing ecology on the agenda. A later report (Meadows et al., 1993), published after sustainable development had become a major feature of contemporary political debate, maintained a pessimistic vision of the earth's future.

3. Environmental disasters

A third factor contributing to awareness of the linkages between environment and the economy was a series of environmental mishaps in the 1960s, 70s and 80s. These included the *Torrey Canyon* disaster, Seveso, Bhopal (see Box 12.4) and Chernobyl. These incidents served to underline the fragility of human and marine life in the face of modern industrialization. They showed that modern production methods, industrialization and transport systems threatened health and safety rather than providing a welcome release from poverty. These disasters did not lead, except among a small group of people, to calls for abandoning economic growth but to a desire to find ways to reconcile growth and environmental sustainability.

These events were given impetus by two political developments. In chronological terms, the first was the emergence of the second wave of environmentalism in the US and western Europe in the 1960s. Some have argued that growing affluence among the middle classes contributed to the growth of an environmental movement in the West. While this is part of the explanation, environmentalism was also spurred by the disasters described above, and increasing scientific knowledge. Affluence, however, played a central role in the ability of these groups to organize effectively. Possessing unprecedented material resources

and high levels of education, the diverse environmental movement spawned effective advocacy and lobbying organizations and political parties that were in a position to influence the agenda of politics in western Europe and the US. The second development concerned the end of the Cold War, and the removal of the straitjacket of East–West tensions from international discussions of the environment. From the period of Gorbachev's glasnost, it became progressively easier to address environmental issues in a mature manner in the international arena.

Mainstreaming environmentalism

Following the Rio conference in 1992, environmental issues definitively moved from the margins to the centre of politics at domestic and international levels. This is not to say that politicians, the public and academics necessarily engaged with environmental issues in a manner likely to halt unsustainable practices. Rather, it signals a salience given to environmental issues in the sense that the environment became normalized in political discourse. The concerns of green parties and environmental activists are no longer regarded as outlandish or silly but have instead been co-opted to the orthodox political agenda. This enables a form of environmental management to become the standard approach, in which politicians, business groups and social movement activists are accorded the same legitimacy. More fundamental questions regarding the nature of economic growth in a world of finite resources

---

Box 12.4 Bhopal

On 2 December 1984 a gas leak occurred in a Union Carbide India Limited plant in Bhopal, India. An investigation revealed that a large amount of water was introduced into a pesticide tank where methyl isocyanate was stored. This caused a reaction that ultimately released a vapour cloud, which infiltrated homes overnight and, within days, killed 3,000 people. Over the next few years, 2,200 deaths were directly attributed to the 'irrespirable gases'. In the 30 years since the tragedy there has been no definitive figure on the exact number of people who have died as a result of the Bhopal gas leak. An estimated 150,000 people directly affected by the gas leak now live with chronic illnesses such as fibrosis, bronchial asthma, chronic obstructive airways disease, emphysema and recurrent chest infections. Pulmonary tuberculosis among the exposed population is notably higher than India's national average. In 1989 Union Carbide paid US$470 million to the Indian government to settle the victims' claims. However, many victims never received compensation; and many believe that the sum is inadequate. Bhopal is the worst chemical disaster in history.

Source: Greenpeace (2015); Union Carbide (2015); Bhopal Medical Appeal (2015)

are not addressed in this new approach to the environment. There are three main features that characterize the current mainstreaming of the environment.

The first feature of the mainstreaming of the environment lies in the development of environmental regulation at the domestic level. States in both the North and the South have established ministries wholly or partly responsible for the environment. These ministries have ushered in legislation to define acceptable limits of pollution, manage resources in a sustainable manner and prescribe penalties for activities that contribute to environmental degradation. There are, of course, disputes at the domestic level concerning the best mix of policies to be followed, and there are still groups that oppose environmental legislation. Nevertheless, it has become commonplace in many states to initiate environmental impact assessments as routine measures when planning new projects.

Second, environmental issues have been mainstreamed within many international organizations. To many critics, the so-called 'greening' of international institutions offers little if any real contribution to environmental sustainability (Horta, 1996; Rich, 1994). These are important criticisms but in this context the key issue is the change in the attitudes of international organizations from hostility, scepticism and in some cases apparently open cynicism (see Box 12.5) to an engagement with the arguments of environmentalists. For example, the World Bank's approach to the environment has undergone significant change (World Bank, 1995). Whereas once the Bank ignored environmental issues and made no attempt to assess the environmental consequences of its loans, the post-UNCED World Bank has consciously attempted to develop a green portfolio. It has adopted two different strategies to achieve its goal of sustainable development: instituted mandatory environmental assessments and systematic and routine environmental monitoring; and now disburses environmental loans. Its lending practices include one set of policies aimed at urban renewal and pollution control and another set of policies designed to promote biodiversity and reforestation.

The third feature of a mainstreaming of the environment in the global political economy can be seen in the behaviour of major firms. In response to the actions of environmental activists and the policies of government departments, business has shifted its profile and adopted an approach that emphasizes the sustainability of resources (Schmidheiny, 1992). Even some firms engaged in practices that at face value appear to be far removed from sustainable practices, such as mining and oil exploration and production, have embraced the concept of sustainable development. However, not all corporations have adopted this approach and many continue to operate in ways that maintain conventional practices and therefore contribute to environmental degradation (Clapp, 2001; Dauvergne, 2001). And some firms, in rejecting the sustainability thesis, find ways to oppose and denigrate the efforts of environmentalists (Beder, 1997).

Box 12.5 The Summers memo

Activists' suspicions that the upper reaches of the World Bank did not take environmental policy seriously seemed to be confirmed in December 1991 when an internal memo signed by Lawrence Summers, the Bank's chief economist, was leaked to the world's media (www.counterpunch.org/summers.html). The memo suggested that it would be economically more efficient if the Bank encouraged the migration of dirty industries to developing countries. Three reasons were advanced for this argument: health costs were lower in developing countries, many developing areas were underpopulated and could absorb more pollution, and many residents had more pressing concerns than whether the environment was attractive or the possibility that they might get a disease in old age.

In 2001, Lant Pritchett, then a junior economist at the Bank, claimed authorship of the memo (*Harvard Magazine*, 2001). He suggested that the leaked memo was incomplete and only an 'ironical aside' on the beneficial impacts of trade liberalization on developing countries. However, for many in the environmental movement, the memo was an example of an ethically deplorable and morally repugnant attitude to both environmental degradation and poor people. The memo and surrounding controversy highlighted how the logics of environmental protection and economic efficiency can clash.

KEY ISSUES

The extent to which the efforts of national governments and international organizations and firms seriously address the environmental crisis remains the subject of fierce debate. Within the contemporary global political economy, the politics of sustainability generates discussion on various issues. Conflicts arising from international trade, pollution control, the preservation of biodiversity and sustainable development have all figured prominently on the international agenda. Here, we focus on three significant environmental issues: sustainable development, climate change, and transnational land acquisitions. All three issues are at the centre of the debate between proponents and critics of environmental management.

Sustainable development

The problem with the term 'sustainable development' is its vagueness. It has proved difficult to formulate a definition that is comprehensible while retaining analytical precision. Sustainable development has been the subject of diverse definitions from a number of commentators (Pearce et al., 1989, pp. 173–85). As a result, it has come to mean very different things to ecologists, economists, planners and politicians. In its favour is the positive connotation implicit in the term. It is unlikely that any sane person or organization would willingly endorse unsustainable development or sustainable impoverishment, if that is not an oxymoron. Sustainable development is not necessarily identified with increased consumption and production but with an improved quality of life where the state of the natural environment is taken into consideration.

Of the many issues debated in the political economy of global environmental change, sustainable development is perhaps the most urgent. Sustainable development has, within a very short time, become a term to which everyone can subscribe but also attach a different meaning. The concept of sustainable development, like that of globalization, is hotly contested, with views ranging from those who reject the term as meaningless to others for whom it expresses the current development paradigm.

For some, sustainable development implies a commitment to sustainability with a consequent reduction in economic growth, while for others the concept of sustainable development is seen as integral to a new era of economic growth. While some analysts question the utility of a concept subject to multiple meanings, it should be pointed out that contestation over its meaning is not unique to sustainable development. This is a normal state of affairs regarding important concepts in the social sciences. In looking at the concept of sustainable development, it is vital that analysis moves beyond the clever but simplistic observation that sustainable development is a contradiction in terms. Without definitions of development or sustainability, such a conclusion is facile and incapable of wrestling with the core issues raised by sustainable development. In its various conceptualizations, sustainable development is a serious attempt to reconcile what at first sight appear to be contradictory objectives, and to meet the urgent test of fulfilling the needs of developing countries in their drive to eradicate poverty, and reducing the damage caused to the planet by unsustainable modes of production and consumption.

Different conceptions of development contribute to contending perspectives on sustainable development. Radical approaches reject capitalist development and argue that capitalism is responsible for both the creation and perpetuation of poverty and environmental degradation (Saurin, 1996). From this perspective, development requires rejection of the current international economic order, and a search for development models that emphasize small-scale, participatory development. In this view, the pursuit of economic growth can be counterproductive since such growth frequently stimulates policies that degrade the environment.

On the other hand, the dominant conception of sustainable development accepts the prevailing global political and economic structure, and locates development within the capitalist political economy. Within the dominant approach, economic growth per se is not a problem but an inescapable starting point. The report by the Trilateral Commission, *Beyond Interdependence*, states: 'Given the growth imperative evident in the material poverty of much of human kind, the only reasonable alternative is sustainable development' (McNeil et al., 1991, p. v). As this report suggests, economic growth is necessary in order to eradicate poverty. The World Bank, which has adopted sustainable development as its goal, has argued that it is poverty which is responsible for environmental degradation. In this view, economic growth provides the instruments through which societies can address environmental degradation.

In this debate between different approaches to development, history has shown convincingly that it is not the economic system, as such, but the importance attached to environmental values that is central. The radical critique is on firm ground when it draws connections between capitalist development and unsustainable modes of production and consumption. But it is surely on shaky ground when it assumes that a socialist (or non-capitalist) economic system automatically provides the conditions for sustainable practices. The evidences of the environmental disasters created by the communist regimes in Central and Eastern Europe are stark reminders of the fact that environmental pollution was in many cases far worse under these regimes than in the capitalist West. The objection that these were not true communist states is irrelevant.

It is irrelevant because one can equally claim that Western states are not examples of true capitalism. But, more importantly, these regimes provide a counter to the claim that capitalism creates environmental degradation, since whatever we call their economic systems, they were certainly not capitalist.

Differing conceptions of sustainable development also arise from contending views on the meaning of sustainability, and the measures by which sustainability is to be achieved. Crucial questions include the

following. Should sustainability be conceived in terms of a renewal of resources? How do we measure sustainability in relation to the needs of future generations? Should we use market-based solutions or command and control measures?

One of the sources of conceptual confusion surrounding the term is that no agreement exists regarding exactly what is to be sustained. The goal of sustainability sometimes refers to the resource base itself, and sometimes to the livelihoods derived from it. Some commentators refer to sustaining levels of production, while others emphasize sustaining levels of consumption. This difference is important, since development at the global level has become unsustainable largely due to the patterns of overconsumption and irresponsible production in the major developed countries. However, policies for sustainable development that have been put forward to date are essentially production oriented. The issues of consumption and ecological shadows generated in the North have been relatively under-examined (see Box 12.6).

Despite the controversy surrounding the term, a dominant approach to sustainable development is discernible in national and international policy-making circles. That is, current solutions to the problems of environmental degradation and poverty are framed

---

Box 12.6 Consumption and ecological shadows

Sustainable development requires changes in patterns of overconsumption and action to mitigate the damage of ecological shadows. The consumption problem arises because individuals in wealthy countries have dramatically increased what they consume and these consumption patterns are spreading to an ever-growing global population. Between 1960 and 2000, the world's population doubled but per capita consumption rose much faster – it quadrupled. The US and Europe, with only 12 per cent of the world's population, account for over 60 per cent of private consumption expenditures. Other countries are racing to imitate their lifestyles (Dauvergne, 2008, p. 4).

The politics of dealing with consumption is complicated by the phenomenon of global ecological shadows. Those engaged in overconsumption project the ecological costs onto peoples and environments distant from themselves. The people paying the cost are far away and relatively powerless. Dauvergne (2008) provides numerous examples of such practices:

▸ Japan and the US importing timber and beef from tropical rainforests in Southeast Asia and South America
▸ Europeans and North Americans shipping electronics to China for recycling
▸ China and India pursuing breakneck growth without regard to damage to the atmosphere
▸ companies introducing products without concern for long-term health effects
▸ countries exporting products domestically banned for safety reasons
▸ present generations polluting the air, oceans and land of future generations.

according to a consensual definition that ignores alternative conceptualizations. The dominant discourse has its origins in the Brundtland Commission, whose report, *Our Common Future*, defines sustainable development as 'development that meets the needs of the present without compromising the ability of future generations to meet their own needs', where 'needs' is defined as 'the essential needs of the world's poor', and 'development' is vaguely defined as the 'progressive transformation of economy and society' (World Commission on Environment and Development, 1987, p. 41). This definition of sustainable development has become, if not the standard definition, the one that is most widely used in policy-making circles. The evidence on critical thresholds (natural parameters) raised by reports such as *The Limits to Growth* is barely acknowledged, and the main limitations acknowledged are the 'present state of technology and social organization' (World Commission on Environment and Development, 1987, p. 16).

A number of common themes emerge in the debate on sustainable development:

1 Sustainable development appears to require an inescapable commitment to equity, specifically, intergenerational equity. There is general agreement on the principle of intergenerational equity. In other words, sustainable development policies should ensure that the welfare of future generations is no lower than our own.
2 Sustainable development requires an entrenchment of environmental considerations in policy-making and proponents of sustainable development focus on efficiency in resource use. Efficiency in resource use entails the internalization of environmental costs in pricing decisions. Looking more closely at the use of natural resources, and the pollution created as a result of economic production, efficiency is defined so that the full social costs of goods and services are reflected in the price of production inputs and consumer goods.
3 The literature on sustainable development has been concerned with the inter-country and intra-country effects of changes in economic policies. In the context of the global political economy, equity is normally discussed in relation to North–South issues. The advanced industrial states achieved their current living standards through a process of industrialization, which resulted in untold environmental

degradation. This option is now closed to the developing countries. However, the adoption of sustainable policies will be costly, and unless the advanced industrial countries are willing to provide major transfers of resources, the necessary policies are unlikely to be implemented.
4 A focus on sustainable development shifts the narrow focus on growth and obsession with GNP per capita and replaces it with greater attention to social aspects of development.

An implication of this approach is that those who consume the most have the greatest responsibly to take action.

Sustainable development is the current dominant solution to development. It seeks to combine the right to development with sustainability objectives. Politically, it is imperative that sustainable development is focused on economic growth, since to argue for a steady state in the developing world is unacceptable to the elites and masses in Africa, Asia and Latin America. The concept is a delicate balancing act and does not in itself suggest how one can reconcile these objectives should they come into conflict.

But progress has been made in the implementation of sustainable development. One major step has been in the mainstreaming of environmental assessments, especially in aid projects. It has become commonplace to give importance to the environmental consequences of new projects. But the rhetoric of sustainable development should not be confused with the reality of effective implementation. Independent assessments of lending by multilateral agencies counsel caution in the depth of commitment to meeting environmental objectives. Moreover, most private sector investment is exempt from such scrutiny since, although environmental ministries have mushroomed in the developing world, many of these agencies lack the resources and power to intervene effectively in support of environmental objectives.

A second major step has been increasing attention to participatory development. In the absence of genuine participation by stakeholders affected by development schemes and projects, it is highly likely that old-fashioned, unsustainable development practices will remain and may even be reinforced. In situations where the population has a clear stake in the programme or project, sustainability concerns are more likely to be implemented. Sustainable development has provided a site of contention and major policy initiatives as governments have tried to address environmental issues in the global economy.

Climate change

In mid- to late 2006, climate change became a major political issue, especially in the developed world. The release of the film *An Inconvenient Truth* in May 2006 and the publication of the Stern Review, *The Economics of Climate Change*, in October 2006 increased the visibility of climate change as an issue. The latest report of the Intergovernmental Panel on Climate Change (IPCC) unequivocally sets out the salience of the problem: 'Warming of the climate system is unequivocal, and since the 1950s, many of the observed changes are unprecedented over decades to millennia. The atmosphere and ocean have warmed, the amounts of snow and ice have diminished, sea level has risen, and the concentrations of greenhouse gases have increased' (IPCC, 2013, p. 2).

The IPCC's report notes that the scientific evidence is overwhelming and it claims that scientists are 95 per cent certain that humans are behind the planet's rising temperatures. This was an increase in the level of certainty which stood at 90 per cent in the previous (2007) report. The report further states that stabilising the climate system will require substantial and sustained reductions of carbon dioxide emissions, and those of other greenhouse gases.

In some respects, the international political economy of climate change provides an illustrative introduction to the ways in which environmentalism has been mainstreamed in contemporary political discourse:

1 The visible impact of global warming in terms of hurricanes, droughts and disruptions to weather patterns (as well as international commitments) has led many governments to initiate measures aimed at halting global warming. These include emission reduction schemes and the search for renewable energy sources.
2 There have been considerable efforts to organize responses to climate change at the international level. The Intergovernmental Panel on Climate Change (IPCC), established in 1988, was the first major signal that climate change had become an important international political issue. The United

Nations Framework Convention on Climate Change (UNFCCC; 1992) and the Kyoto Protocol (1997) established normative and policy frameworks.
3 It has become increasingly apparent that solutions to climate change depend heavily on the role of private sector actors.

Below we will examine three issues pertinent to exploring the international political economy of climate change: climate change negotiations, climate finance and climate security.

Climate change negotiations

Under the terms of the UNFCCC, states were mandated to 'gather and share information on greenhouse gas emissions, national policies and best practices; launch national strategies for addressing greenhouse gas emissions and adapting to expected impacts, including the provision of financial and technological support to developing countries; and cooperate in preparing for adaptation to the impacts of climate change'. (United Nations 1992). To fulfil these goals, the signatory states have held regular meetings, called Conferences of the Parties (COP), in order to develop global policy on climate change. To date, there have been 21 such meetings. At COP-1, held in Berlin in 1995, many of the subsequent difficulties in reaching a workable agreement were apparent. The most significant COP until 2015 was held in Kyoto in 1997 and resulted in the Kyoto Protocol to the UNFCCC. The Kyoto Protocol sets binding greenhouse gas (GHG) reduction targets for industrialized countries. Under the 'common but differentiated responsibility' principle, the Kyoto Protocol distinguishes between developed (Annex I countries) and developing countries (Annex II countries), with only the former subject to binding commitments. The Kyoto framework consists of three mechanisms:

1 *emissions trading*: allows countries to sell their unused emissions to countries that have exceeded their targets
2 *the clean development mechanism*: allows a country with a binding commitment under the protocol (Annex I) to implement an emission reduction project in developing countries (Annex II).
3 *joint implementation*: allows an Annex II country to earn emission reduction units through a project in another Annex II country.

Although adopted in December 1997, the Kyoto Protocol did not enter into force until February 2005 following ratification by Russia in November 2004. It could not enter into force until it was ratified by 55 countries accounting for 55 per cent of carbon dioxide emissions in 1990. It is widely agreed that the Kyoto Protocol is an inadequate instrument to halt climate change, and it was intended to remain in force until 2012 after which it would be succeeded by a new more effective agreement. However, it has proven difficult to negotiate a legally binding and acceptable post-Kyoto framework (see Box 12.7 for an account of an important moment of indecision in the post-Kyoto period).

Attempts to construct a post-Koto framework were stymied by a number of obstacles (Sjöstedt and Penetrante 2013 pp. 11-14). The sheer size of the negotiations i.e. the number of countries participating and the diversity of their economies contributed to the slow pace of negotiations. Furthermore, as the negotiations progressed new issues and new ways of approaching adaptation and mitigation measures surfaced thus adding complexity to an already complex negotiating process. Another central obstacle arose from patterns of conflict and alignment among states. For example, in the early years, the refusal of the US to engage with the Kyoto process in a meaningful manner under the Clinton and Bush administrations put the treaty in jeopardy. The North-South divide has also contributed to limiting progress. While on one hand there are various sub-groups of developing countries active in the negotiations e.g. the Alliance of Small Island States (AOSIS) there is also an attempt to present common positions via the G77. Moreover, as the negotiations have progressed, the industrialization and increased contribution to GHG emissions of newly emerging countries such as Brazil, China and India have led to new negotiating blocs in climate change talks (Hallding et al 2013; Hurrell and Sengupta, 202). Issues relating to additional economic aid, ccommon but differentiated responsibility, and free or cheap technology transfer continued to divide developed and developing countries. Opposition increased to accepting further binding commitments by developed countries in the absence of a quid pro quo from leading developing country emitters. The domestic politics of climate change in both rich and poor countries has been an effective stumbling block to further progress (Harrison and Sundstrom, 2007).

Another stumbling block to progress was the continued the role of climate science. Within the negotiating process the technical expertise required has hampered some delegations from participating in an effective manner. At the level of public support a continuing debate over climate science (Dessler and Parson, 2006) limited support for reform. Although most credible experts accept the findings of the IPCC, nevertheless there is a vociferous and at times politically influential minority who challenge the majority view. Climate 'sceptics' variously deny the existence of global warming, the adverse human impact on climate change, the speed of change and the possibility of devising appropriate climate policy. Labelled as 'climate deniers' by their opponents, a wide range of groups funded by the fossil fuel industry and conservative ideologues has sprung up to deny and discredit the work of climate scientists (Mann 2012).

Despite these obstacles, 195 countries agreed to a new climate deal at COP21 in Paris in December 2015. The Paris Agreement marks an historical moment in climate change negotiations. Countries committed themselves to limiting the planetary temperature increase to 1.5 C above preindustrial revolution levels, pledged to curb emissions levels, set a long term goal for zero net

Box 12.7 Earth Summit 2012

Twenty years after the first Earth Summit, a follow-up was held in Rio de Janeiro in June 2012. Bigger than its predecessor, the follow-up had less to show for its efforts. While the leaders of some states attended, the heads of the UK, Germany and the US did not. Environmental conditions had deteriorated since 1992, with global demand for natural resources 50 per cent higher, carbon emissions higher by 40 per cent and the global population forecast to rise from 7 billion in 2012 to 9 billion in 2050. Yet in the face of these and many other challenges, the summit's accomplishments were modest. State delegates agreed to work on new sustainable development goals but a split between Europe and the US on one hand and China, Brazil and India on the other over the nature of a 'green economy' prevented additional progress. While reaction to the summit was mixed, the event did not seriously address the pressing environmental crisis and served as an example of the increasing difficulty of negotiating global climate action.

emissions, instituted a review mechanism, recognized common but differentiated responsibility and established an obligation for developed countries to fund climate finance for developing countries. It was agreed that funding of at least $100 billion per year should be provided in climate finance. The plan is ambitious and could herald the end of development based on fossil fuels exploitation, which has driven growth since the 1700s. Yet, the pledge levels of countries are not sufficient to meet the goal of 1.5C warming, opposition from the fossil fuel industry remains intense and there is considerable doubt about whether countries will implement strategies to live up to their commitments. In particular, decisions in the US, India and China will be crucial for determining the fate of the Paris climate deal.

Climate finance

As previously noted, North–South issues are central to considerations of the international political economy of the environment. Climate finance as an issue in contemporary political economy fuses the development assistance regime with an emergent climate change regime. The nascent climate finance regime has been grafted onto the pre-existing regime of official development assistance. Climate finance has emerged from the recognition of a link between poverty alleviation, sustainable development and climate change. Climate finance programmes have arisen in response to demands from developing countries for climate-related aid. The pressing necessity of responding to the deleterious impact of climate change on livelihoods including agricultural productivity and health (for example, the rise of infectious diseases, malnutrition and hunger) has been recognized by governments, international organizations and civil society actors. The impact of climate change on developing countries is widely recognized. For example, the World Development Report 2010 estimates that the developing countries will bear between 75 and 80 per cent of the costs of damages associated with climate change (World Bank, 2010).

Notwithstanding this general agreement, the provision of climate finance has failed to meet the demand of developing countries and there are a number of attendant problems concerning the governance of climate finance. The link between climate finance and the development assistance regime has resulted in the replication of issues central to that regime. Thus, donors' interests are in maintaining control over resources and

establishing donor-supported norms, while recipients prioritise accessibility and the adequacy of funds.

The High-Level Advisory Group on climate financing established by the UN Secretary-General Ban Ki-Moon highlighted four sources of climate finance: public sources; development bank instruments; market-based finance; and private capital (United Nations Secretary-General, 2010). In the context of funding from bilateral and multilateral agencies a key issue has been related to additionality. The principle of additionality is enshrined in various documents, e.g. under the UNFCCC (Article 4.3), the Bali Action Plan (Paragraph 1(e)(i)) and the Copenhagen Accord (Paragraph 8). Annex I nations are obliged to provide 'new and additional' financial resources to poor countries (see UNFCCC, 1992, 2007b, 2009b). However, governments have been unable to agree on a baseline from which to measure 'new' and 'additional' finance. Furthermore no consensus exists on the funding necessary to assist countries to adapt to the threat posed by climate change. It has been argued that a key difficulty in arriving at an agreed estimate arises from the difficulty of separating development-related issues from climate-related ones. A UNFCC report noted, 'One of the specific challenges is that most of the measures identified are not only for the purposes of adapting to climate change but also have other development-related benefits' (UNFCCC, 2010, p. 9).

The Green Climate Fund (GCF) established in 2010 at COP-17 in Cancun, Mexico is designed to rectify criticisms of the adequacy of and accessibility to multilateral climate finance. Headquartered in Songdo, Incheon, Korea the GCF launched the mobilization process for funding in July 2014 and received $10 billion in pledges. In May 2015 the GCF surpassed the 50 per cent of pledges required to begin lending and is scheduled to begin deploying funds later in 2015 (Green Climate Fund, 2015). It is too early to tell whether the GCF will meet the hopes of its founders.

Climate security

In chapter 14 we explore the political economy of security. Here we make a connection between the IPE of security and the IPE of the environment by focusing on climate security. Attention to the connection between the environment and security emerged in the 1980s. Specialists on environmental security have been concerned with resource decline and environmental degradation as the source of actual conflict between states;

environmental degradation as a cause of diplomatic disputes, political tension or the deployment of military capability short of prolonged conflict; environmental degradation as a contribution to the breakdown of societal relations, especially in fragile states; resources and environmental services as a 'weapon' of war; environmental degradation as a consequence of war and conflict; environmental threats to economic security; environmental degradation linked to other forms of non-traditional security; environmental security and human security; security of and for the environment (Elliott, 2007, pp. 41–6).

Concern with climate change as a security issue was given prominence when the United Nations Security Council held a session in April 2007 on the impact of climate change on peace and security. Research on the linkages between climate change and security can be classified into two main perspectives. In the first perspective climate security is presented in terms of a threat. Such an approach was aptly captured by the representative from Papua New Guinea who, speaking during the debate in the UN Security Council on climate change and peace and security, claimed that 'the impact of climate change on small islands was no less threatening than the dangers guns and bombs posed to large nations' (United Nations Security Council, 2007). When perceived as a threat, climate security is framed in terms of conflict processes. Attention is given to the likelihood of conflict arising from climate-induced migration, degraded land and water resources, or state collapse.

The second approach to climate security focuses on vulnerability rather than conflict. Unlike the conflict perspective, which links its concerns with traditional approaches to security, the focus on vulnerability is indebted to the human security paradigm. Studies have examined the ways in which climate change can negatively impact health, limit access to food, increase poverty, lead to a loss of livelihood, increase dangers for migrants and heighten gender insecurities. The approach to climate security as vulnerability makes explicit linkages between climate change, economic processes and development.

Transnational land acquisitions

In the past decade the acquisition of large-scale agricultural land in the South by foreign corporations and countries has become a topic of intense debate. While this phenomenon is popularly known as 'land grab', other terms have been used including 'transnational land deals' (Anseeuw et al., 2012); 'investments' (Hallam, 2011) or 'large-scale land acquisitions' (Cotula et al., 2009). We will use the term transnational land acquisition (TLA) and following Cotula et al. (2011, p. 100) this can be defined as 'acquisition of land rights (whether through purchases, leases or other) for land areas over 1,000 ha'.

The rise in TLAs has been welcomed by some analysts who view them as providing the potential to increase much needed investment in the agricultural sector in the developing world (Arezecki et al., 2012). Advocates contend that it is a global win-win situation with land investments alleviating global food and energy shortages by making use of 'idle' lands in the South. Moreover, it can be argued that since most agricultural production will be exported, global and regional food trade will increase and satisfy world food demand.

Numerous critics have rejected this positive assessment and instead focus on the negative social and economic consequences of TLAs. McMichael (2012) has argued that current investments in farmland are attempts by new actors to create a global power transformation in food trade relations. TLAs have been criticized because of the unequal power relations they support and the distortion of local agriculture away from producing for the local market to export crop production, thus increasing the vulnerabilities of the poor (De Schutter, 2011).

Analysts differ over not only the definition of this phenomenon but also the scale of land affected. Estimates vary widely and the existence of the Land Matrix database has not brought any measure of agreement on the size and scale of the land purchases. Evidence on the geographic location of land purchases, their legal status and the implementation of agreements is scattered and based on a variety of sources (Scoones, 2013). It is difficult to measure the scale of TLAs because there is no common geographical pattern followed by investors or host countries, and no agreed reporting measures. Moreover, there is diversity among the investors with companies based in emerging countries such as Brazil and China, Gulf states and advanced industrial countries such as the US and the UK all engaged in TLA activity. TLAs are undertaken by transnational corporations, public or state-owned companies, banks, private equity funds, hedge funds and private–public partnerships. Despite this uncertainty there is never-theless general agreement that the vast majority of TLA activity is centred on Africa. It has been estimated that around 70 per cent of TLAs take place in Africa (Deininger et al., 2011, p. xiv).

There is a complex array of drivers behind the upsurge in land deals, and a variety of reasons have been given for the phenomenon. The foremost explanation centres on the search for food security by investing countries. Triggered by skyrocketing food prices of 2007/2008 and the resulting perceptions of food insecurity, oil-rich Gulf states and emerging Asian countries resorted to the acquisition of large-scale agricultural land, particularly in Africa. A combination of high food prices and export restrictions by major food exporters led many food importers to the conclusion that the global food supply system was unreliable and unstable. Faced with growing populations, water scarcity and dwindling agricultural land, emerging market economies and oil-rich states have pursued a strategy of reducing dependence on the global food market through the purchase of agricultural land overseas. This perception of food insecurity was the stimulus for explicit TLA policies developed by governments such as South Korea and Saudi Arabia.

If the search for food security appears to be the governing factor behind the land deals brokered by Gulf states and some Asian countries, the search for energy security seems to be the major motivation behind policies developed by emerging economies and advanced industrial countries. The search for renewable energy has stimulated the production and use of biofuels by developed countries such as the US and various EU member states, as well as emerging market economies such as Brazil, China, India and South Africa. This drive for energy security has increased the profit potential of biofuel producers, thus driving global competition for land even further. Another cause of the TLA surge has been the investment policies of a number of Western financial institutions. A combination of the global financial crisis and a subsequent search for safer investments coupled with rising land prices, projections of future increases in demand for food and biofuels, population growth, changing diets and environmental degradation has stimulated demand among financial institutions. Thus private investors seeking long-term gains have targeted land deals in the developing world.

The starting point for much of the literature on the environmental consequences of TLAs would concur with the claim that, 'The rate at which land grabbing consumes large quantities of physical space destabilises functioning in environmental and social systems alike' (Lazarus, 2014 p. 74). More specifically, critical scholars and civil society activists have pointed out that TLAs create severe social and environmental problems. One key issue pertains to land rights. It has been contended that such deals fail to protect the land rights of indigenous communities, small-scale farmers and local populations. For example, the land rights of indigenous communities are usually not protected because of pre-existing domestic property laws that view untitled but traditionally used lands as 'idle' and un-owned, hence government property (Wily, 2012, p. 752). Furthermore, since land deals are negotiated by governments and not by the people directly affected by the TLAs, small-scale farmers may subsequently be denied access to their natural resources (Cotula et al., 2009).

Second, 'land grabs' have been equated with major 'water grabs' as they are likely to affect future water availability in developing countries. Various researchers have concluded that TLAs have a negative impact on food security and water resources in host countries. For example, Rulli et al. (2015) argue that the amount of water 'grabbed' is excessive and undermines food security in host countries. TLA opponents argue that these new pressures on water resources will likely impact negatively on the livelihoods and food security of small farmers, pastoralists and fishermen. Third, researchers have warned that the commercialization of agriculture attendant on large-scale land investments may result in harmful distributional and gender effects (Behrman et al., 2011).

CONCLUSION

Given the extensive nature of the social, economic and political impact of environmental degradation, ecological concerns should form a central role in the study of the global political economy. The connections between economics and the environment, combined with the necessity of collective action to counter common resource problems, place contemporary environmental concerns at the centre of international relations. The causes of environmental degradation are complex and require careful understanding of the ways in which economic systems interact with the ecosystem.

This chapter has shown that no consensus exists on how we might best understand the processes of environmental degradation, or the solutions to the environmental crisis. At one end of the spectrum, neoclassical environmental economics requires the extension of market-based principles to areas of economic activity previously exempt. At the other end, radical ecological approaches to economic activity are based on the necessity for fundamental changes in economic structures, value systems and social behaviour.

The introduction of environmental issues to IPE poses questions concerning the adequacy of the three IPE approaches to explain environmental sustainability and environmental cooperation. In the absence of a specific green international political economy perspective (Dryzek, 1996), this chapter has examined the emergence of environmental problems, the different perspectives on the environment and various solutions to environmental problems. It has argued that the study of global environmental issues, which the existing IPE perspectives have failed to address adequately, should be supplemented through attention to debates in environmental economics and ecological economics.

The interaction of social systems, natural systems and the built environment are features of human history and it would be pointless to search for a position from which environmental degradation began. What we conceive as environmental degradation is essentially social, and one generation may accept something as natural that a subsequent generation may find unacceptable. A minor but pertinent example is that of cigarette smoke, which as little as 30 years ago in much of North America and western Europe was not seen as harmful to non-smokers. However, today it is generally accepted that secondary or passive smoking is detrimental to those who suffer its effects. It is likely that the struggle over environmental degradation and climate change will bring far greater changes in the way that people think about and act in the global political economy.

Both this chapter and Chapter 11 have highlighted the significant role that ideas play in shaping our perception of issues. How and what we think about development or the environment influences our actions on those subjects. Chapter 13 focuses our attention on the role of ideas in the global political economy.

Further Reading

An excellent textbook on the subject is Jennifer Clapp and Peter Dauvergne, *Paths to a Green World: The Political Economy of the Global Environment* (2011). Andrew Hurrell and Sandeep Sengupta (2012) 'Emerging Powers, North–South Relations and Global Climate Politics', *International Affairs*, 88(3): 463–84 provides an excellent review of the continuing relevance of the North–South divide in environmental politics. Gunnar

Sjöstedt and Ariel Macaspac Penetrante (eds) *Climate Change Negotiations: A Guide To Resolving Disputes and Facilitating Multilateral Cooperation* (2013) contains many useful essays concerning the difficulties encountered in global climate change negotiations. See *Law and Development Review* (2014) 7(2) for a special issue on 'Law and Development Perspective of International Land Acquisitions'.

Chapter

13 | Ideas

This chapter focuses on what Susan Strange called the 'knowledge structure'. She defined the knowledge structure as 'determining what knowledge is discovered, how it is stored, and who communicates it, by what means, to whom and on what terms' (Strange, 1988, p. 117). Our approach replaces the term 'knowledge' with that of 'ideas', which is a broader term that includes mental images about how the world operates. We are interested in the framework of ideas and knowledge that shape, and are shaped by, activity in the global political economy. Ideas and knowledge play a significant role in influencing actors' behaviour and in outlining the limits of the possible for states, corporations and individuals.

Previous chapters have highlighted the role of ideas in the global political economy. For example, in the 19th century, the age of imperialism was justified by racist ideas concerning the superiority of Europeans over non-Europeans. The material power of Western states at this time was the result of ideas that took concrete form in the technology of the Industrial Revolution. Today, ideas about free trade inspire and justify regional trade agreements and the WTO, while technological innovation drives the information revolution.

In this chapter, the definitional section outlines how the terms 'ideas', 'knowledge', 'information' and 'technology' are used. The theoretical section examines a number of approaches that highlight the role of ideas in the global political economy. These range from liberal theories, which see ideas as an independent variable that shapes behaviour, to poststructuralist approaches, which see language shaping all understanding of reality. The developments section examines the growth of the information revolution and society. It also considers how one particular idea – the Washington Consensus – came to dominate thinking about the global political economy and why it suffered some setbacks in the late 1990s. Key issues for this chapter are technological diffusion, patent protections for pharmaceuticals and financial deregulation.

DEFINITIONS

The ideas addressed in this chapter are thoughts about how the human, human-made and natural worlds do or should operate. By the human world we mean the interactions between people. Human-made refers to the physical creations of people, such as cities or machines. The natural world refers to the physical environment, including plant and animal life.

At their most general, ideas are thoughts or mental pictures about how the world works. The broad category of ideas includes a number of overlapping elements of thought. One variant is the 'worldview'. People adopt worldviews that contain assumptions about the forces that drive human nature and what constitutes appropriate action. Such a worldview can also be referred to as 'ideology', ideas inspired by a set of principles which then guide human action in diverse situations. Ideologies are usually associated with large-scale political projects such as communism, fascism, socialism, conservatism, libertarianism. However, worldviews are also embedded in what people accept as 'common sense'. Common sense refers to ideas accepted by the majority of the population that guide everyday behaviour. Common sense can vary widely over time and place and have a dramatic impact on how people live their lives. For example, it was common sense among many white people in the southern US in the early 19th century that the economy be based on slave labour. Common sense today in the same place rejects slavery as inhuman.

The category of ideas includes a number of related words that signify mental images in different forms. The term 'information' refers to news, data, facts or intelligence material. Information is a stream of facts about particular things. One can think of information about a country's economic performance, for example. Knowledge is slightly different, referring to an understanding of information that leads to it being used in a proper way or for a particular purpose. A person can have access to a great deal of information, but may lack knowledge because they do not know how to order or interpret the information. The word 'wisdom' is less widely used in today's technical and scientific world, but it refers to a type of knowledge that is gained from experience and reflection on life. It is often associated with the elders of a society and emerges from experience. A final way that ideas are used in this chapter (and the book) is in the form of concrete objects produced by knowledge. This is referred to as 'technology' and involves the technical know-how to produce or manufacture particular products or services.

THEORETICAL PERSPECTIVES: IDEAS ABOUT IDEAS

The traditional IPE approaches of economic nationalism, liberalism and Marxism did not give much weight to the independent role of ideas. They engaged in theoretical debate about how the world worked, but they

did not pay much attention to how ideas shaped the operation of the global political economy. However, since the early 1990s, a number of approaches to international relations have stressed the importance of ideas for understanding global political economy. They all suggest that the way people think about the world influences human action. However, they differ a great deal about the degree to which ideas are politicized and what kind of relationship they have to material interests. The field is also marked by some confusion because people use categories, concepts and labels in contradictory ways. Here, we outline the basics of key approaches, moving from liberal and conservative-constructivist approaches, which see an independent but limited role for ideas, to critical approaches, which link ideas to interests, to poststructural/interpretive-constructivist strategies, which begin with ideas and language as the basis for all understanding and action.

A rather modest liberal attempt at highlighting the significance of ideas is the literature on epistemic communities. An epistemic community is 'a network of professionals with recognised expertise and competence in a particular domain and an authoritative claim to policy-relevant knowledge' (Haas, 1992, p. 3). Members of an epistemic community articulate conceptions of a problem and propose solutions in keeping with science rather than the political interests of the state and other actors. They facilitate policy coordination between states by providing leaders with crucial information in an environment of uncertainty. They act as knowledge-brokers who can make a significant difference to the formation of international regimes. Through their control over ideas, knowledge communities exercise power and influence in international bargaining. The epistemic communities concept has been particularly important in helping us understand how scientists and scientific knowledge have been able to contribute to building international environmental regimes (Haas, 1992; Young, 1999, p. 126).

The epistemic approach has a number of limitations. One criticism is that it is unable to theorize the relationship between these communities and other groups such as interest groups or social movements. This has led some critics to charge that it is normatively biased in favour of expert groups over other possessors of knowledge and understanding (Toke, 1999). Other critics (Dunlop, 2000) have suggested that the epistemic communities 'other groups' problem causes this approach to miss how expert knowledge groups must engage in coalition-building in order to influence policy. A related criticism is that the epistemic communities literature does not offer an account of the ways in which knowledge can be used to support or justify existing policy positions (Litfin, 1994, p. 12). Furthermore, it has been argued that 'scientific communities are not necessarily consensual or impartial. Tensions and conflicts occur within epistemic communities' (Hurrell and Kingsbury, 1992, p. 19). Moreover, others claim that while scientists may possess relevant information, it is politicians who shape and determine policy. Thus, the policy outcome reflects the nature of social institutions, values and power rather than the activities of an epistemic community. The impact of epistemic communities may not always depend on their possession of the most reliable knowledge, since possessors of knowledge that is open to critique and contestation can also be influential in policy discussions. The fight over the state of climate change knowledge provides an example of how epistemic communities can be challenged by rival political interests (see Box 13.1).

Another shortcoming is that the notion of expert communities influencing state policy is confined to those areas where scientific consensus is widespread. This involves a limited number of cases, most of which are concentrated in the field where the term first emerged – the study of international environmental issues. In practice, expertise, even scientific expertise, is often divided or can be embedded in different social contexts in various countries. A good example is the disagreement between the WTO, the US and the EU over the safety of hormone-fed beef. Scientists from each side of the Atlantic may be able to agree about some of the technical issues, but the standards for acceptable risk are set by wider social processes (Skogstad, 2001).

The focus on epistemic communities took inspiration from, and contributed to, the constructivist turn in IR. Constructivists argue that knowledge and action are socially created (or constructed) and can be shaped to different purposes. Whereas rationalist approaches to IR and IPE examine actors' strategic interaction based on a set of presumed preferences, constructivists examine how those preferences came about in the first place and what impact they have on actors' perceptions and actions. For constructivists, the ideational aspect of social life is as important as the material world. In other words, there is both a social construction of reality and a construction of social reality (Guzzini, 2000, p. 149). In constructivist research, norms are central to explanation. While rationalist approaches to IPE tend to give primacy to material structures and to consider norms, rules and institutions as by-products that aid actors in their pursuit of their material interests, constructivist

---

Box 13.1 Challenging epistemic knowledge: the climate change fight

The Intergovernmental Panel on Climate Change (IPCC) was established in 1988 by the United Nations Environment Programme and the World Meteorological Organization (www.ipcc). It reviews scientific studies on climate change and issues reports summarizing the state of knowledge. Scientists from around the world work on IPCC projects on a voluntary basis. Reports are approved by the 195 countries that are members of the IPCC. The IPCC has published five assessment reports in 1990, 1995, 2001, 2007 and 2015. The reports summarize the scientific consensus on climate change and thus are an excellent example of the work of an epistemic community. They have been influential in highlighting the issue of climate change and the need for states to take action.

The epistemic community engaged in global warming science has faced a concerted political attack from those sceptical of its work and financial interests that would be harmed by policy initiatives designed to curb climate change, such as the oil industry (Sachs, 2010). This attack included hacking into the emails of research scientists, exaggerating scientific errors and alleging that climate scientists distort findings for financial gain. Most importantly, the anti-global-warming tactic was to cast doubt on the established science to prevent government action. Some science historians noted that the strategy of casting doubt on established science had previously been seen in corporate battles against the science of tobacco and smoking, acid rain, deterioration of the ozone layer and the dangers of second-hand smoke (Oreskes and Conway, 2010). Even scientific knowledge gets caught up in the battle of political economy interests.

approaches argue that intersubjective meanings are necessary in order for actors to interpret material power. Ideas are central in constructivist thought because objects, events and actors are only given meaning through intersubjective knowledge and practice. Constructivists claim that 'meaningful behaviour is possible only within an inter-subjective social context' (Hopf, 1998, p. 173). Normative structures give material power meaning and affect actors' interests and identities. The leading variant of this thought in the US has been labelled 'conventional constructivism'. It focuses on how norms and identities shape international politics (Checkel, 2004).

Working from a historical materialist tradition, neo-Gramscian authors have linked ideas with class interests. This critical approach is illustrated in the quote by Robert Cox (1986, p. 207) in Chapter 1: 'Theory is always for someone and for some purpose.' This means that theory and theorists are always linked to configurations of power and are not neutral. Powerful actors will find some sets of theories to their liking, while the weak or dispossessed are likely to find comfort in other theories. Developed states with advanced industries are more likely to advance the idea of free trade than states of weaker economies, which fear domestic businesses will disappear.

Thus, a contest over ideas is a key ingredient in establishing the hegemony of a state or social group. If group A can convince groups B and C that the self-interested proposals put forward by A will also benefit B and C, A will be able to further its interests by co-opting other groups. Hegemony comes about when one group convinces subordinate groups that their interests will be served by following the lead of the dominant actors. For example, US leadership of the Western world between 1945 and 1971 was accepted by other Western states as being in the common interest. This type of analysis leads scholars to focus on the ongoing battle to determine what is or is not the 'common sense' that frames political action. Rupert (1995b), for example, has examined how the 'common sense' that free trade is good for US workers came to be challenged in the NAFTA debate. When common sense breaks down or is challenged by another view of common sense, it is likely that politics will become more heated and fluid. The debate over ideas becomes crucial to wielding political power.

Another critical approach to using ideas in the study of IPE is poststructuralism. Poststructuralism comes to the social sciences from French philosophy and cultural studies. People adopting a poststructural perspective stress how 'reality' is interpreted in many different ways. It can also be labelled as 'interpretive constructivism', because it draws on linguistic theories of interpretation (Checkel, 2004, p. 231). Rather than a single poststructuralist theory, there are a number of poststructural approaches that concentrate on understanding how the language we use shapes our understanding and actions in the world (Belsey, 2002; Sarup, 1993). We use language, whether it be the spoken word, writing or visual images, to communicate our thoughts and represent reality. Yet, there is never a perfect fit between our language and the thing we are trying to describe. As a result, there must always be some doubt about the relationship between 'reality' and how we communicate reality. Some versions of poststructuralism suggest that we can never get close to reality or 'truth'.

How can these ideas apply to IPE? De Goede (2003) argues that applying poststructuralism to global finance politicizes formerly unquestioned or seemingly neutral financial structures and arrangements. For example, accounting standards, which are a technical form of language trying to represent 'reality', build a particular picture of reality that hides important elements. Standard accounting procedures do not incorporate the environmentally damaging impacts of economic activity and thus paint a very different picture than a set of standards operating from an ecological perspective. To take another example, debates about economic matters may be closed to the public because they require participants to master a particular language – neoclassical economics – before their views will be heard in elite forums. Thus, language is seen to both shape the conduct of global finance and privilege some voices over others. The contribution that this approach makes is that it 'denaturalizes' what is thought to be a natural state of affairs. Once this has been done, orthodox approaches to a particular order are vulnerable to challenge from other perspectives and interests.

An insight shared by a number of perspectives is that ideas become embedded in institutions (Goldstein and Keohane, 1993). Patterns of behaviour, legal codes and international organizations are created in a specific historic context and reflect the dominant set of ideas at the time they are created. The institutions embody the ideas that created them. The provisions of the ILO which allow for separate government, business and labour voting rights reflect the idea that these three social partners have different interests and require separate expression. US trade law is marked by elements of free trade and protectionism because it is composed of legislation that hails from the free-trading and protectionist eras. Yet, the story does not end there. Once institutions are created, they then become a site of conflict as new groups try to shape the institutions to reflect a different set of ideas and priorities (Cox, 1983).

In summary, there are a wide variety of approaches to examining ideas in the global political economy. Yet, they all stress the significant role that ideas and knowledge play in influencing and shaping all the other facets of GPE. This chapter draws on some of the insights advanced by these perspectives, but will ground the discussion of ideas by connecting them to the interests that advance particular sets of ideas and benefit from their adoption.

MAJOR DEVELOPMENTS

The postwar decades have witnessed two important long-term developments in the areas of knowledge production and dissemination. On the technological side, there has been the explosion of the information revolution and the creation of an information society. In the realm of worldviews, there have been equally dramatic developments, with shifts from embedded liberalism and Keynesianism to neoliberalism and the Washington Consensus to post-Washington Consensus uncertainty.

The information revolution and the information society

It has been claimed that the impact of information and communications technology (ICT) is fundamentally reshaping the global political economy (Castells, 1996). In April 1997, a report to the European Commission (1997, p. 16) noted:

> The Information Society is the society that is currently being put in place, where low-cost information and data storage and transmission technologies are in general use. The generalization of information and data use is being accompanied by organizational, commercial, social and legal innovations that will profoundly change life both in the world of work and in society generally.

The contention that the revolution in ICT has fundamentally transformed economic and social organization has not been accepted by all analysts, and we examine the extent to which technological change is leading to the creation of a 'new economy'. Apart from the impact of technology on economic and political relations, another important issue concerns access to technology. The *Declaration of Principles* adopted at the World Summit on the Information Society in December 2003 recognized the importance of access to IT in the construction of the new economy: 'The ability for all to access and contribute information, ideas and knowledge is essential in an inclusive Information Society' (United Nations, 2003, para. 24). We examine the problem of access in terms of the global digital divide below, but first we turn our attention to the impact of information on economic, social and political structures and processes.

The concept of a new economy has been central to debates concerning the political economy of the information revolution. The definition of the 'new economy' and related concepts such as 'knowledge economy', 'networked economy' or 'digital economy' are the subject of debate among social scientists. Given the different terminology and the absence of a consensus definition, we outline key features that appear in a number of definitions. A central element in the 'new economy' is the importance of knowledge and technology as key drivers of economic growth. It is argued that the role of science and technology applied to economic processes is unprecedented in human history. Closely allied with this emphasis on knowledge is the contention that services (and especially knowledge-based services) are the most important sources of added value in economic accumulation. The source for this change is to be found in technological innovations, such as the invention of the microprocessor, innovations in software development and the introduction of network technologies. The microprocessor has led to a fall in prices of computer equipment, software has made computers easier to use and the internet has revolutionized communication through its ability to connect people and systems. These technological developments, it is claimed, have had an impact on the macroeconomy in terms of low unemployment and low inflation.

The thesis of a new economy has come under sustained criticism. It has been dismissed as an invention of Wall Street and the media or as a myth designed to explain the performance of the American economy in the 1990s. As such, it is based on 'half truths, bad history and wishful thinking' (Madrick, 2001, p. 1). Other critics have attacked the conservative philosophy and implications of the new economy thesis. From this perspective, it is seen as an attack on trade unions and working people (Kotz and Wolfson, 2004), since the new economy thesis supports privatization, deregulation, de-unionization and flexible labour markets in order to create the required conditions for the innovation necessary for continued high-tech growth. The extent to which the changes in industrial practices are required by technology and whether or not they lead to economic growth and prosperity have also been questioned.

It is not necessary to subscribe to the new economy thesis to recognize the impact of knowledge and technology on political economic structures and practices. Equally, it is possible to note the changes brought by technological development at the same time as one rejects the new economy thesis. Instead of mediating in this debate (much of which has taken place in regard to the American economy), we briefly review some of the ways that ICT and knowledge can be said to be having a profound impact on the global political economy. At the centre of any analysis has to be an assessment of whether these changes are historically unprecedented. The authors of a comparative analysis of current changes and the innovations that took place during the Industrial Revolution conclude that the role of knowledge is not 'fundamentally' new. What is new 'is the type of technologies in which economy and society exist – digital technologies built around ICT' (Carlaw et al., 2006, p. 651). Thus, the key issue concerns the ways in which this particular form of knowledge is transforming traditional practices.

There are three ways in which the current application of knowledge is transforming the global political economy:

1 These technologies are transforming the ways in which we work. This is not solely a phenomenon of advanced capitalist states but refers to any society or segment of society that has access to ICT. For example, in India call centre operators work through the night so that they can respond to customers working during the day in North America.
2 Digital technologies are having an effect on the way we spend our leisure time, and directly on consumption patterns. These changes are visible in the ways people shop online, watch television or listen to music on iPods.
3 Advances in knowledge are having important effects on food and health technologies. The advances in biotechnologies are not only affecting the material world but also creating new ethical dilemmas, for example over stem-cell research or genetically modified food.

The term 'digital divide' refers to unequal access to digital technology; that is, some people are able to enjoy the benefits of digital technology and others are not. The term can be used in the domestic context to refer to unequal access across households or it can be used to refer to unequal access across national borders. In other words, globally we can observe multiple digital divides instead of a simple binary one. The Global Information Technology Report 2015 reports the existence of multiple digital divides internally and internationally (Dutta et al., 2015). However, in the context of the global political economy the digital divide is most frequently defined as 'the strikingly differential extent to which various forms of information technology are being exploited by developed, as opposed to developing countries' (James, 2001, p. 211). While the definition of the digital divide is reasonably straightforward, no agreed measurement exists. There have been a number of studies on the quantification of the digital divide. The International Telecommunications Union (ITU, 2006, p. 4) claims that 'over the last 10 years the digital divide between the developing and developed countries has been narrowing in terms of fixed telephone lines, mobile subscribers and Internet users.' On the other hand, UNCTAD's statistics (2005, pp. 10–11) reveal a continued high level of differentiation between countries. Differences in methodology account for these contrasting conclusions. The ITU's approach is to examine average per capita distribution of hardware (fixed lines, mobile lines) and number of internet users in developed and developing countries (see Box 13.2). The UNCTAD study challenged this approach by applying standard methods of inequality (Gini coefficients and Lorenz curves) to the cross-national data.

The significance of the digital divide lies in the benefits flowing from access to the goods and services produced by the information economy and conversely the costs of failing to keep pace with technological change. The importance of the digital divide therefore lies in its relationship to development. The salience of ICT for

---

Box 13.2 Internet statistics

▌ In 2000 there were 400 million internet users; by the end of 2015, 3.2 billion people are using the internet

▌ More than 80 per cent of households in the developed world have internet access

▌ 34 per cent of households in developing countries have internet access

▌ But only 7 per cent of households in least developed countries have internet access

▌ 78.2 per cent of Europeans have mobile broadband access, compared with 17.4 per cent of Africans

▌ Average monthly fixed-broadband prices are three times higher in developing countries than in developed countries.

Source: ITU (2015)

---

development has become an issue of interest to national governments and international organizations. An UNCTAD (2005, p. 8) report recognizes that the digital divide has 'significant consequences for social, economic and political development'. From an economic nationalist perspective, it becomes evident that an increasing digital divide between groups of states will increase the relative gains of those states with access to the information resources. Given the added value produced by ICT, this increases the gains of information-rich states. It has been argued that access to ICT is positively correlated with rates of economic growth (Becchetti and Adriani, 2003, p. 2; Andrianaivo and Kpodar, 2011). It is also the case that internal digital divides within developing countries accentuate social and economic disparities within such societies.

The digital divide need not remain a permanent feature of the global political economy and emphasis on differential access to technological resources need not obscure the impact that ICT can have on development. For example, ICT has an important role to play in meeting the challenges established by the MDGs (World Bank, 2003). The World Bank concluded that ICT 'is a powerful tool when used appropriately as part of an overall development strategy' (World Bank, 2003, p. 8). But it also cautions that 'ICT will only be helpful to the extent that users are able to use the technology and take advantage of the opportunities it creates' (World Bank, 2003, p. 8). However, without favourable economic,

political and regulatory environments, the promise of ICT will remain unfulfilled. The challenge lies in finding the right mix of private and public capital, political structures that incorporate the wide range of stakeholders (government, business and civil society), and targeted investment and regulation that foster innovation without replacing public monopolies with private ones. The Millennium Development Goals Report 2014 concluded that falling broadband prices and a rise in mobile broadband access increased internet use in the developing world (United Nations, 2014b, pp. 52–3).

The rise and stall of the Washington Consensus

The post-1945 era has seen a number of changes in the ideas that have guided dominant countries and economic institutions. Here, we focus on one prominent set of ideas – a bundle of liberal prescriptions for economic development labelled the 'Washington Consensus'. Our discussion highlights a number of key themes when considering the role of ideas in the global political economy. These themes are the relationship between ideas and interests, the relationship between ideas and practices, the multiple interpretation of ideas and the varied implementation of ideas.

The dominant approach of Western countries from the late 1940s until the early 1970s has been called 'embedded liberalism' (Ruggie, 1982). Domestically, states redistributed income through welfare policies and supported employment through government management of the economy. While there were wide variations between the Anglo-American forms of state, which supported minimal welfare provision, and the more social democratic states of northern Europe, with their elaborate welfare provision (Esping-Andersen, 1990), there was a shared commitment to state intervention to aid economic development. Internationally, the US and Britain led the development of international institutions that facilitated the liberalization of economic activity, but allowed for considerable domestic opportunity for states to pursue national development strategies.

In developing countries, the prevailing economic orthodoxy also favoured a strong role for the state. The state's proper role was seen as developing and nurturing national economic activity. Similar to developments in the West, there was a wide variety of developmental states, from those inspired and supported by the centrally planned model of the Soviet Union to East Asian states linking their prosperity to an export model of capitalism. What these various arrangements shared was the idea that the state played a crucial organizing role in assisting the developmental process. The developmental state perspective saw the international system as posing large challenges for national improvement. As outlined in Chapter 11, some intellectuals and state leaders feared that the existing system fostered dependency and that state action was required to redress inequalities.

Between 1980 and 1997, the notion of state-led development was eclipsed by an agreement among many financial, corporate and state elites that the secret to development was to give the freest rein possible to market forces to guide economic activity. The term 'Washington Consensus' was used as a shorthand for this view of economic development. Here, we examine what that consensus was, how that consensus came about, the impacts that it had and whether we are now in a transition to a new, not-yet-clear concept of development.

The 'Washington Consensus' is a term coined by John Williamson (1990) to capture a set of economic development policies that had broad support among officials and economists in the US government (especially the US Treasury), the IMF and the World Bank. He was writing specifically about policies with regard to Latin American development. These policies included fiscal discipline (balancing budgets), liberalizing trade, freeing exchange rates and interest rates, privatizing state industries, deregulation, tax reform to broaden the tax base, redirecting public expenditure to increase economic returns and redistribute income, and securing property rights.

The idea that economic growth would best be achieved by reducing state involvement in the economy was the hallmark of conservative governments in Britain (Thatcher) and the US (Reagan) in the early 1980s. The marrying of neoclassical economic propositions with the political project of implementing them is often referred to as 'neoliberalism'. The move to globalize the ideology of neoliberalism was facilitated by a number of developments:

1 The ideas of neoclassical economics were spread by an epistemic community of economists trained in neoclassical economics departments in the US.
2 The debt crisis of the early 1980s forced many developing countries to adopt a new policy paradigm.

The old developmental state model in countries such as Mexico and Brazil had drowned in debt and there was little alternative to neoliberal restructuring if these states wanted to attract FDI.
3 The US used the IMF to encourage states to adopt the main tenets of the Washington Consensus. Countries in debt that needed loans from the IMF were required to adopt structural adjustment packages that included many of the policies advocated in the Consensus, such as trade liberalization, reducing the role of the state, privatization, deregulation and fostering FDI.

The prescription of the Washington Consensus proved very powerful. Part of its power came from the fact that the major international financial institutions and the US government promoted it with vigour. Countries that adopted these prescriptions would be favoured by the IMF, the World Bank and the US, while countries that did not adopt them could expect problems. Another element of its influence was that the Consensus provided policy makers with a clear set of prescriptions for overcoming serious economic situations. State decision makers were told that if they implemented the package they could cure their economies. Many of the reforms were implemented by executive decree rather than needing the approval of legislatures and parliaments, making the adoption of the Consensus politically easy. A third element of strength was that with the onset of the debt crisis, the state developmental strategy appeared to be discredited. The collapse of the Soviet Union in 1989 further bolstered the sense that there was no alternative to accepting liberal economic policies.

Despite the influence of the concept of the Washington Consensus, it would be inaccurate to portray it as a universal set of principles that dominated the functioning of the global economy (see Box 13.3). One thing that curbed its influence was that it was actually implemented in a very different way in different countries. Some countries implemented the whole package, but most picked and chose from the original ten items. Countries subscribed to the general principle, but only implemented particular steps.

Another weakness of the Consensus is that even among its advocates, there were disagreements about its details (Naim, 2000a, 2000b). Some argued that countries in financial difficulties should undergo shock therapy, that is, they should implement a radical liberal

---

Box 13.3 The Occupy movement

The liberal ideas that dominated the Washington Consensus and inspired financial deregulation in the US and the UK faced a challenge from mass protests in 2011. Inspired by the crowds occupying public spaces such as Tahrir Square in Cairo, Egypt during the so-called 'Arab Spring', groups of people began to occupy public spaces around the world. The most visible was Occupy Wall Street, where people occupied Zuccotti Park near the financial centre of New York. Using social media, protest spread around the US and to other parts of the world (www.occupytogether.org).

Using slogans such as 'We are the 99%', the Occupy movement launched a critique of corporate and government elite power by focusing on the human costs of rising economic inequality. Although the movement had no central leadership and attracted a wide variety of participants, the demand to reduce economic inequality was central to its message. Protestors challenged government priorities of debt reduction and austerity by advocating economic redistribution and economic justice. Protest camps were eventually dismantled, but the ideological challenge remained. The movement had succeeded in changing the nature of the political discussion about the economy.

---

agenda immediately. Others suggested that such a strategy created economic damage and that reforms should be introduced at a gradual pace. Some argued that countries should also liberalize their capital markets by allowing foreigners to invest in stock markets and facilitating the movement of short-term capital into their countries. Others disagreed and did not include capital account liberalization in their view of the Washington Consensus.

A third brake on the domination of the Consensus was resistance from those groups that disagreed with its prescriptions. During its heyday in the late 1980s and early 1990s, the Consensus did command the allegiance of state and economic elites, but failed to gain the support of key social groups and movements. Environmentalists complained about the ecological damaged caused by unregulated liberalization, labour groups objected to the effects on wages and livelihoods and development groups questioned its effectiveness. Their ongoing opposition often prevented the full implementation of reforms.

Opposition to the Washington Consensus caused protests in the streets, but also changed and challenged the very meaning of the term. Whereas advocates viewed the term as indicating sound economic policies, opponents used the term to describe a broad approach to economic management that embodied a 'market fundamentalism'. 'Washington Consensus' became shorthand for all the liberal economic policies that seemed to be increasing inequality and poverty around the world. Despite his best efforts at clarification, Williamson could not enforce his view of the meaning of the term he invented.

By the end of the 1990s, the power of the Washington Consensus as a set of ideas had been eroded. Developments in Asia, Africa and the Americas posed a serious challenge to the consensus (Broad, 2004; Öniş and Şenses, 2005). While many neoliberals had claimed that the success of newly industrializing countries in Asia (South Korea, Taiwan and so on) could be attributed to the liberal market policies followed by these states, detailed research painted a different picture. These economies were market oriented, in the sense that they produced for a global market, but they had interventionist states that supported and guided national corporate activity. This undercut one element of the neoliberal case. A further blow came in 1997 when the East Asian financial crisis was seen to be caused by countries prematurely liberalizing their capital markets and exposing themselves to financial chaos. Although capital liberalization was not technically part of the original Washington Consensus, it was closely identified with a broad neoliberal policy stance. The actions of the IMF, which applied standard liberal prescriptions of belt-tightening, worsened the crisis and generated a great deal of criticism from both the left and the right. In Africa, numerous states that had experienced structural adjustment for almost 20 years continued to stagnate and had very poor economic growth. In the Americas, two states that had wholeheartedly adopted the prescriptions of the Consensus suffered financial crisis (Mexico in 1994, Argentina in 2001), leading many to question the wisdom of the original prescriptions.

Within the US itself, a series of corporate criminal scandals, such as the collapse of Enron, raised questions about the abuse of power by corporations in deregulated markets.

The response to these problems by the advocates of the Washington Consensus was to reply that its shortcomings were due to failures in policy implementation. The ideas were correct, but they had undesired effects because they were either partially or imperfectly put into practice. This led advocates of the original Consensus to broaden their focus to include the public institutions that are required to implement reforms. This prompted a new 'second generation' of reforms urged on developing countries, which include the creation of 'good governance' through the rule of law, transparency and eliminating corruption in public services. The basic elements of the Consensus remain in place, but they had to be supplemented by a wide series of measures reforming the governments and bureaucracies of developing countries (Krueger, 2000).

There are many ironies here:

1 The Washington Consensus was originally an attempt to curtail the role of the state, but it evolved into a concern about improving state structures. The new plan echoes the concerns of many of the pre-1980 developmental state theorists who emphasized the role of the government in assisting development.
2 One of the results of the implementation of Consensus policies was to weaken the state, but that state is required to be more active and efficient. The demand for state action is there, but the capacity has been reduced.
3 The prescriptions for development are now so extensive that they demand developing countries have all the features of developed states in order to begin the process of developing (Naim, 2000a, p. 522).
4 Although there is broad demand for state reforms, there does not seem to be any roadmap for meeting the demands being placed on developing countries (Naim, 2000a, 2000b; Santiso, 2004).

By 2005 there was agreement that a new 'post-Washington Consensus' might develop, but there was confusion about what it could entail. As suggested above, advocates of the original approach argued for a Consensus-plus model that focused on state reforms. Further to the left, others suggested that a social democratic model, which put more emphasis on demo-

cratic practices, increased regulation of the global economy and gave more attention to an equitable distribution of life chances, might supplant the Washington Consensus (Held, 2005). Even further to the left, others argued for abandoning the original Consensus and putting in place much more nationally oriented development strategies (Fine et al., 2001). The Washington Consensus was further undermined by the 2008 US financial crisis, which cast doubt on the wisdom emerging from Washington and the ability of unregulated markets to foster economic growth.

From embedded liberalism to post-Washington Consensus, ideas about the functioning of the global economy have influenced the behaviour of policy makers and other key actors. These ideas and prescriptions have also benefited or hurt the interests of various social groups. Thus, the struggle over ideas is also a struggle over power and wealth.

KEY ISSUES

Three key issues in the area of ideas and knowledge are the pace and extent of technological diffusion, the scope and enforcement of intellectual property rights (IPR) and the role of ideas and interests in the origins of the global financial crisis.

Technological diffusion

A vital issue for many countries, corporations and people is the phenomenon of technological diffusion. As a series of technological waves (see Box 13.4 for a discussion of a recent technological innovation) wash over advanced industrialized states, other states, corporations and people struggle to keep pace. Just as the Industrial Revolution conferred power on states, corporations and people who were able to harness industrialization at the expense of those who could not, the fear is that the information revolution may create similar inequalities. Inequalities and power differentials may be compounded because the states leading the information revolution tend to be those that emerged strongest from the Industrial Revolution. There are two further issues here. One concerns the diffusion of technology for production, while the other is the diffusion of technology through society as a whole.

Box 13.4 Cloud computing

One of the latest advances in ICT is the capacity to process, store and transmit data in the so-called 'cloud'. Cloud computing is an evolving technology and there is no agreed definition. One widely cited definition is that by the American National Institute of Standards and Technology:

> Cloud computing is a model for enabling ubiquitous, convenient, on-demand network access to a shared pool of configurable computing resources (e.g. networks, servers, storage, applications and services) that can be rapidly provisioned and released with minimal management effort or service provider interaction.
> (Mell and Grance, 2011, p. 2)

Whether the emphasis is on technology or political economy, it is predicted that cloud computing marks a significant technological innovation with far-reaching consequences for economic growth and development. A recent UNCTAD study noted that 'cloud computing and the economy based upon it are becoming increasingly important considerations for Governments and enterprises' (United Nations, 2013, p. 2). Although the market for cloud services is small it is rapidly expanding. Potentially, cloud computing offers developing countries new opportunities to catch up with the advanced economies because it reduces infrastructure costs and is easier and cheaper to maintain and upgrade than client-based computing. However, the UNCTAD report notes that the potential for enhanced efficiency and the hoped for benefits may not accrue. According to the report the scope for cloud adoption is low in developing countries, and the gap in cloud-related infrastructure between developed and developing countries is widening rather than narrowing (United Nations, 2013b).

Firms and countries producing products for the world market need up-to-date technology to ensure that their enterprises are as efficient as possible. However, corporations jealously guard their technology and demand financial compensation for sharing inventions. Accessing newer technologies became harder and more expensive following the insertion of IPR into the remit of the WTO. This limits the ability of developing countries or firms in developing countries to copy technology in their development process. Whereas rivals to Britain during the Industrial Revolution copied, stole and purchased technology in the race to catch up, today's legal environment makes the copying and stealing options much more difficult. Corporations possessing advanced technology tend to be based in advanced economies, as are many of the leading knowledge institutions (see Box 13.5). Countries already lagging behind in development face increasing technological barriers to catching up with wealthy countries.

On the other hand, there are some cases where technological advances can help states leapfrog the development gap. For example, the introduction of mobile phones in developing countries allows for the establishment of a communications infrastructure without the financial and resource investment required to lay the cables that provide the infrastructure for landline telephones.

Property rights and life (HIV/AIDS)

A second key issue in the field of ideas is the degree to which there should be private ownership over ideas that pertain to the necessities of life or life forms themselves. The issue is particularly pressing in the cases of patent protection for life-saving drugs and patent protection for microorganisms.

As outlined in Chapter 6, the issue of ownership of intellectual property became significant in global political economy after 1995 when the WTO was mandated to protect IPR. The WTO's Agreement on Trade-Related Intellectual Property Rights (TRIPS) states that 'patents shall be available for any inventions, whether products or processes, in all fields of technology, provided that they are new, involve an inventive step and are capable of industrial application' (GATT, 1994, Article 27, s. 1). The WTO's IPR provisions reflect a particular set of ideas about the relationship between private property and knowledge. In this view, companies or individuals that invest time and energy to create new intellectual products should have the legal right to prevent others from using or enjoying that knowledge, unless those other people first pay the inventor an agreed price. This policy is said to be justified on two grounds. One is that if intellectual property producers are not compensated properly, they will not produce the products people

Box 13.5 The uneven distribution of knowledge: patents and Nobel Prize winners

A cursory examination of the number of patents issued by country and the number of Nobel Prize winners per country illustrates how unbalanced the creation and control of knowledge are in the global economy. Patents are issued to protect the intellectual property of companies and individuals. Non-patent holders are prohibited from using this knowledge or must pay a licensing fee to the patent owner. As a rough measure, those countries with a large number of patents are accumulating more knowledge and inventions, while those with a low number will have to buy their knowledge and technology from others or wait until the patents expire. In 2011, over 121,000 patents were issued in the US and 48,256 in Japan. Only 3,786 were issued in China and 1,259 in India (US Patent and Trademark Office, 2011). Even if only a small percentage of patents leads to commercially viable products, China and India are likely to be at a severe technological disadvantage to the US and Japan.

A similar concentration of knowledge can be seen when examining the country of residence of Nobel Prize winners. Nobel Prizes are awarded each year to individuals or groups deemed to have made outstanding contributions to their fields. Over 60 per cent of the Nobel Prizes awarded in the fields of Chemistry, Physics, Physiology or Medicine and Economic Sciences since 1950 have gone to people based in the US. Just under a third of the US winners were also immigrants to the US (Wasow, 2006). This indicates that the US is home to many of the world's top knowledge institutions and that these institutions and the country draw in many leading scientists from around the world.

need. A second argument is that intellectual property is a work of labour and deserves to be rewarded just as the production of other products is rewarded. Patent protection for pharmaceuticals is usually for 20 years.

This approach to IPR serves the immediate interests of large corporations that dominate the fields of pharmaceuticals, computer software and entertainment. Indeed, the idea of having the WTO enforce IPR was originally put forward to the US government by the International Property Committee, which, in 1986, comprised the following companies: Bristol-Myers, Squibb, Digital Equipment Corporation, FCM, General Electric, Hewlett-Packard, IBM, Johnson & Johnson, Merck, Pfizer, Procter & Gamble, Rockwell International and Time-Warner (Sell, 2006, p. 194). The committee faced a dual task. First, the TNCs had to convince the US government that international protection of their property rights was a US priority. Second, the US had to convince or coerce other nations into accepting the same logic. However, even though the idea of stringent intellectual property enforcement was institutionalized in the WTO, the controversy was only just beginning.

A major issue with the WTO's IPR provisions was that they extended the patent for brand name drugs that can be used to treat infectious diseases. In particular, they solidified the grip of Western pharmaceutical producers over their production of antiretroviral drugs, which are used to treat HIV/AIDS (human immunodeficiency virus / acquired immunodeficiency syndrome). Patent protection means that generic drug producers are not allowed to make cheap copies. The difficulty arises because the majority of HIV/AIDS patients live in Africa where incomes are so low that they cannot afford life-prolonging brand name drugs. The cost of brand name antiretroviral treatment per patient for one year, depending on the drug cocktail, can range from US$2,738 to almost US$22,000, whereas the annual per capita income in sub-Saharan Africa is only US$601 (Floyd and Gilks, 1998; World Bank, 2006c). A strict interpretation of IPR would imply that approximately 26 million Africans suffering from HIV/AIDS are unable to access brand name drugs because they or their governments cannot afford the cost.

The clash between the notion of protecting private property rights and the human right to life and health sparked a large-scale intercontinental struggle over the WTO's IPR provisions and national legislation that implemented those provisions. The TRIPS Agreement allowed countries to make generic copies of life-saving drugs on public health grounds, but there were two shortcomings. First, a debate took place as to what drugs would qualify for this measure. Second, countries were allowed to make generic copies, but would not be allowed to import generic copies from other countries. Thus, countries with a pharmaceutical industry such as Brazil or India could make copies, but countries in sub-Saharan Africa, which did not have a domestic industry, were not allowed to import them from India or Brazil. On one side of the conflict were the WTO, northern pharmaceutical companies and the US government. On the other side were the governments of many developing states, generic drug producers and local and transnational NGOs. Campaigners in this second group were able to effectively contrast the desperate need of sick and dying people against the corporate profits of drug companies. The pressure to relax IPR built until WTO member states amended the TRIPS Agreement so that poor countries were allowed to import generic copies of antiretroviral drugs under the 2001 Doha Declaration on the TRIPS Agreement and Public Health.

The debate over the balance between protecting corporate interests and health rights revealed the glaring inequalities of the global political economy of health. The patents were mostly held by northern corporate interests, while many of the victims were in poor developing countries. Northern states were able to exert pressure on developing countries to agree to WTO provisions that went against the public health interests of their citizens. Moving away from a focus on HIV/AIDS, one can see the glaring mismatch between pharmaceutical research and development and global health needs. Pharmaceutical companies conduct research primarily into diseases of the affluent West, while placing little emphasis on diseases such as malaria that kill millions in the developing world. It is much more profitable for drug companies to fund research into impotence, baldness, toenail fungus or wrinkles. Although millions die from malaria, it is extremely unlikely that a new malaria drug would match Viagra's first-year sales of US$1 billion (Silverstein, 2002).

The move to globally enforce patent protection over products such as drugs, plants, seeds and even new uses for existing forms of life generates intense debates and new questions. Should corporations be given protection for the ideas and information they discover or generate? If so, should any limits be placed on their activity? Is it acceptable that TNCs patent life forms? Isn't this a form of biopiracy? (See Box 13.6.)

Ideas, interests and the global financial crisis

The US-centred financial crisis of 2008 destroyed trillions of dollars of wealth and plunged the world into a global recession. The origins of the crisis lay in the failure of governments, especially the US government, to adequately regulate financial industries. The question is: how did ideas of financial deregulation become so persuasive and why did they lead to crisis?

During the 1990s, a series of ideas took hold of the practitioners in financial markets and their regulators that the greatest amount of wealth would be created by financial markets subject to the least regulation. Left alone, financial markets were seen to be highly efficient and self-correcting. Market participants were capable

---

Box 13.6 Bioprospectors and biopiracy

Bioprospectors search the land, sea and sky to find natural ingredients for new drugs and industrial products. Examples of such ingredients are the venom of sea snails in the Philippines used for the painkiller Prialt and Easter Island soil used for the kidney transplant drug Rapamune (Elias, 2006). While many of these discoveries prove useful, the problem lies in the power relations and economic profits behind the bioprospecting sorties. The raw materials being exploited are usually found in developing countries. The research needed to turn them into marketable products is undertaken by northern corporations or universities. As a result, the patents are held by people in the developed world and the profits flow into northern multinationals or research universities. The benefits do not flow to the people living in the territory from which the natural ingredient originated. In addition, many of the indigenous people familiar with the local life forms do not have a Western sense of property rights and object to outsiders claiming rights to these life forms. From their perspective, northern institutions, which exploit life forms in developing countries, are engaged in biopiracy.

of self-regulation with minimal interventions by the state. Sound and profitable financial practices would win out over those that were questionable. While there might be some cases of inappropriate activity, these would be resolved in the marketplace. A fine example of this sentiment is provided by Alan Greenspan, the then chairman of the US Federal Reserve, when he argued against allowing the Commodity Futures Trading Commission to regulate derivatives: 'The primary source of regulatory effectiveness has always been private traders being knowledgeable of their counterparties. Government regulation can only act as a backup. It should be careful to create net benefits to markets' (Greenspan, 1998).

These were not new ideas, as particular elements of liberal theory had preached the virtue of minimally regulated markets for centuries. Yet, the repeated financial collapse of these markets, as in the case of the stock market crash of 1929, raises the intriguing question of why policy makers return to policies that have had disastrous consequences in the past. John Kenneth Galbraith (1975) suggested that the cycle of deregulation, financial crisis and reregulation is due primarily to the fading of memory. The consequences of financial disaster linger for a generation or two, but new generations repeatedly imagine that they have overcome the vices of previous eras. Some new technology (for example computers) or new technical methods (for example advanced mathematical formulae) convince a new set of financiers and regulators that they have discovered the secret of never-ending wealth creation. In reality, they have discovered nothing and simply repeat the mistakes of their predecessors, but in slightly different ways.

While such an explanation has some plausibility, one must look beyond the power of ideas themselves or the fading of the memory of regulators to explain the shift in financial regulation. The financial community was (and is) actively engaged in politics, continuously attempting to shift the regulatory framework to facilitate profit maximization. From 1998 until 2008, financial firms such as banks (both investment and commercial), insurance companies, hedge funds and property companies spent over $5 billion to purchase regulator influence. This included $1.7 billion in political contributions and $3.4 billion to pay an army of 3,000 registered lobbyists (Weissman and Donahue, 2009, p. 6).

The financial industry gave money to both Democrats and Republicans to ensure that, whichever party was in power, its interests were well represented. Although the Republican Party was ideologically more sympathetic to deregulation, key Democratic Party officials advanced a similar agenda or received large contributions from the financial industry. An example of the ability of financial firms to influence government activity was that the investment bank Goldman Sachs had its chief executive officer selected to be US Treasury secretary under both Democratic (Robert Rubin, 1995–9) and Republican (Henry Paulson, 2006–8) administrations.

The combined efforts of the financial industry were tremendously successful in revolutionizing their regulatory structure. Over the period of a decade, financial regulations were modified so that firms took on higher levels of risk under less government supervision (see Box 13.7). One set of initiatives allowed banks to increase in size, engage in new activity and appear more profitable than they actually were. Actions that fell into this category were:

- dismantling the barrier between insurance and banking industries
- allowing off-balance sheet accounting to hide debt
- allowing investment banks to adopt voluntary measures for setting their debt loads
- allowing commercial banks to set their own reserve requirements based on internal risk models
- facilitating mergers by dropping anti-trust regulations.

At the same time that banks were growing bigger and taking on more risk, the efforts to regulate non-bank financial institutions and instruments were blocked. Both the Democratic President Bill Clinton and then later the Republican-controlled Congress prevented the Commodity Futures Trading Commission from regulating risky derivatives. Federal regulators also refused to prevent predatory lending by financial institutions, objected to state-level governments taking such action and removed the possibility of clients suing financial institutions for such activities. Large mortgage institutions were encouraged to lend to more and more risky clients in the name of spreading home ownership. Federal regulators also refused to examine the conflict of interests ensnaring credit rating agencies who were being paid by the firms they were rating.

The notion that deregulated financial markets were positive and that the property boom was

---

Box 13.7 Twelve financial deregulation policies, 1998–2008

1 In 1999, Congress repealed the Glass-Steagall Act, which had prohibited the merger of commercial banking and investment banking.
2 Regulatory rules permitted off-balance sheet accounting, allowing banks to hide their liabilities.
3 The Clinton administration blocked the Commodity Futures Trading Commission from regulating financial derivatives, which became the basis for massive speculation.
4 In 2000, Congress prohibited regulation of financial derivatives through the Commodity Futures Modernization Act.
5 In 2004, the Securities and Exchange Commission (SEC) adopted a voluntary regulation scheme for investment banks that enabled them to incur much higher levels of debt.
6 Rules adopted by global regulators at the behest of the financial industry would enable commercial banks to determine their own capital reserve requirements, based on their internal 'risk assessment models'.
7 Federal regulators refused to block widespread predatory lending practices earlier in this decade, failing to either issue appropriate regulations or even enforce existing ones.
8 Federal bank regulators claimed the power to supersede state consumer protection laws that could have diminished predatory lending and other abusive practices.
9 Federal rules prevent victims of abusive loans from suing firms that bought their loans from the banks that issued the original loan.
10 Fannie Mae and Freddie Mac expanded beyond their traditional scope of business and entered the subprime market, ultimately costing taxpayers hundreds of billions of dollars.
11 The abandonment of anti-trust and related regulatory principles enabled the creation of too-big-to-fail megabanks, which engaged in much riskier practices than smaller banks.
12 Beset by conflicts of interest, private credit rating companies incorrectly assessed the quality of mortgage-backed securities; a 2006 law handcuffed the SEC from properly regulating the firms.

Source: Weissman and Donahue (2009)

---

increasing the stock of the nation's wealth was reinforced by the mass media. Financial institutions ran television commercials encouraging individuals to take out low rate mortgages or to remortgage their houses and use the money for consumption. Individual pensions based on market investments were sold as the guarantee of a good life in retirement. Dedicated financial channels, like CNBC, broadcast the glories of the financial markets on a 24-hour schedule and fed the need of market traders for instant information. Given its need to serve the financial community, it is not surprising that financial television network analysts and guests missed the story of the financial crisis until it overwhelmed them. The most devastating critique of the role of CNBC was not even presented in the mainstream news media, but appeared as a commentary on the Jon Stewart comedy show. Stewart (2009) contrasted the rosy and

wildly mistaken comments of financial experts on business television networks with the real-world stories of financial collapse and suffering.

Ideas in favour of financial deregulation and the explosion of credit/debt enjoyed considerable support from a wide variety of sources. The financial services sector grew from being 15 per cent of US GDP in 1980 to over 20 per cent in 2004. Even more striking was the fact that the financial services industry exploded as a source of corporate profits, leaping from 20 per cent in 1990 to 45 per cent in 2004 (Phillips, 2008, p. 31). While corporate profits soared, so did individual fortunes. The average pay of chief executive officers (led by the financial sector) ballooned from being 24 times that of the average worker's salary in 1965 to 71 times in 1989 to 262 times the average worker's salary in 2005 (Mishel, 2006). Stock options, shares and bonuses ensured that executive pay at financial firms skyrocketed, even if corporate performance was poor. Beyond highly paid executives, many ordinary people also benefited from credit easing. In an environment where real wages did not grow, individuals were able to use debt to fund consumption. Many individuals ran up credit card debt to purchase consumer goods, took on large mortgages in response to easy terms and borrowed against the value of their homes. In only seven years (2000–7), US households doubled their debt to $13.8 trillion (McKinsey & Co., 2009).

Because of the widespread reach of the financial and housing bubbles, there was widespread support for financial deregulation from the elite to the mass level. This helps to explain how those who benefited from a particular policy were eager to advance it in the public realm. However, the financial collapse was also facilitated by the flawed use of mathematical and technical models. Wall Street financial firms employ an army of professionals to guide and execute their market strategies. Many of these firms use PhDs in mathematics or economics from prestigious universities to create and implement mathematical strategies for seeking out the best investment returns. In a market that is presumed to be rational, the application of formal mathematical models will reveal the most efficient strategies. The mathematical models contributed to financial chaos for two reasons:

1 They focused on probabilities, but were unable to adapt to random or unforeseen developments (Taleb, 2004). They assumed that the future would be similar to the present, when the future always holds surprises. When those surprises came along, the financial strategies based on the models proved disastrous.
2 They assumed that market actors would act rationally. This assumption often holds in normal or good economic times, but once things began to deteriorate, market players were more likely to be motivated by fear and panic.

The revelation that the financial markets were not as rational, stable, predictable or self-policing as previously thought has led to an interrogation of the rational neoclassical model of economics. In response to the widespread failure of these markets, several economists have attempted to merge psychological variables into economic theory (Akerlof and Shiller, 2009; Lo, 2004).

It is a step back towards a more constructivist view of political economy.

Despite the questioning of neoclassical models and the principles of the Washington consensus, some questionable ideas remain entrenched. Mark Blyth (2013) has convincingly demonstrated both that the notion of austerity as a path to economic growth is mistaken and that it exercises a powerful hold over economic and political elites. The refusal of the IMF and European creditors to grant Greece debt relief in 2015 unless it committed to renewed austerity is an example of how some ideas combined with powerful interests can have a devastating impact on people's livelihoods and life chances.

CONCLUSION

Underlying the clash of ideas is a competition between different knowledge structures and worldviews among many actors in the global political economy. This contest over worldviews has intensified with the drift to the post-Washington Consensus. Rather than a single alternative to neoliberal views, there is a wide array of opposing views and philosophies. The common elements they share are a view that a neoliberal market should not be the only mechanism and ultimate decision maker in distributing resources or adjudicating between values, and that the power of TNCs needs to be curbed or regulated.

There are a number of alternative knowledge systems circulating in the global political economy. One set of understandings centres around indigenous knowledge. These belief systems have developed over many generations and posit a different understanding of human relationships with the natural world. Rather than being masters of information or abstract models, these systems draw on experience with nature and the wisdom embodied by elders or passed down through generations. As outlined in Chapter 12, many environmental movements also embody an alternative form of knowledge. Similar to indigenous perspectives, they see humans as being a part of nature rather than masters of nature. Chapter 10 highlighted the contributions of feminist knowledge, which challenges the model of atomistic rational actors. Feminists often advance an ethic of care rather than the pursuit of self-interest.

We can see these alternative forms of knowledge in action at the local level and on the global scale. Globally, the meetings of activists at the World Social Forum show a diversity of approaches. The slogan of the World Social Forum – 'Another World Is Possible' – offers a challenge to neoliberal ideas that claim exclusive knowledge of the path to development. These alternative forms of knowledge and the social forces and institutions that support them are engaged with dominant knowledge structures in a battle for common sense that would reorient the way the global political economy functions. Ideas and knowledge play a central role in the evolution of the global political economy. Worldviews and common sense guide how people react to developments and influence the actions they take. Although some worldviews dominate, as the Washington Consensus did in the 1980s and 90s, there are many alternative worldviews struggling to establish themselves. These worldviews can have significant distributional consequences because they tend to favour some social groups over others. Access to ideas in the form of knowledge and technology also has a significant role in the global political economy because it heavily influences economic growth and the life chances of people. As a result, the struggle over worldviews, technology and knowledge is a crucial aspect of the global political economy.

Chapter 14 shifts the focus away from the world of ideas to the world of physical violence. Although security, conflict and war are often studied under the umbrella of IR rather than IPE, there is a close and intimate relationship between political economy and global security.

Further Reading

The relationship between ideas, interests and power is explored in Robert Cox (1983) 'Gramsci, Hegemony and International Relations: An Essay in Method', *Millennium*, 2(2): 162–75. The case for considering the role of scientific experts in international policy making is made by Peter Haas (1992) in 'Introduction: Epistemic Communities and International Policy Coordination', *International Organization*, 46(1): 1–35. Gabriel Siles-Brügge (2013) 'The Power of Economic Ideas: A Constructivist Political Economy of EU Trade Policy', *Journal of Contemporary European Research*, 9(4): 597–617 demonstrates the explanatory power of constructivist IPE. Paul Krugman's *Depression Economics* (2008) provides a critique of the neoliberal ideas and practices behind the 2008 financial crisis. Mark Blyth's *Austerity: The History of a Bad Idea* (2013) examines the hold of a particular economic doctrine over policy makers and elites.

Chapter

14

Security

I PE and international security have developed as distinct sub-fields of IR and political science and are taught as separate subjects in many colleges and universities. Nevertheless, the intersection of political economy and security has long been recognized in studies of both sub-fields. Indeed, in one of the pioneering texts on IPE, the security structure is identified as a key structure of power in the international political economy (Strange, 1998). This chapter examines the global political economy of security and develops in a more explicit sense some of the security aspects of topics addressed elsewhere in the book. The security dimensions of some of these topics, for example development (Ballentine and Sherman, 2003), environment (Dalby, 2002) and gender (Hudson, 2009), have also been explored in the literature.

This chapter provides an introduction to the political economy of security through an examination of changing views on security, different approaches to the search for security in world politics and the links between economic structures and processes and security dynamics. It begins with a discussion of competing definitions and conceptions of security. We then consider the various ways in which the main approaches to IPE theorize the relationship between economics and security, and discuss key linkages between the economy and security concerns. Under the major developments section we consider changes in the global security structure since the end of the Second World War. The key issues considered in this chapter are economic statecraft, transnational crime and corporate espionage, and pandemics and disease.

DEFINITIONS: THREE VIEWS OF SECURITY

At its simplest, security refers to the protection from threats. However, the concept of security is contested and no consensus exists on its definition. The major point of contention is over the referent object of security, that is, what or who is being secured. Below we outline three approaches to security – the traditional state-centric approach, new security studies and human security – which define much of contemporary research and thinking on security.

The traditional state-centric approach

In the traditional approach to IR, the answer to the question 'Security for whom?' is not of much concern since the key object of study is the state and it is taken for granted that security refers to the security of the state. It is easy to see why the concept of security has usually been associated with the security of the state.

Writing in response to the carnage of the First and Second World Wars, as well as the threat of the Cold War, key IR thinkers have viewed the core of the field as being the issue of war and peace between states (Morgenthau, 1973). The international system is viewed as anarchic – it has no overarching authority, such as a government in domestic politics. Because of this anarchic condition, states are placed in competition with each other and must pursue power to achieve security. Thus, security has three central features:

1   Security and security studies are concerned with the preservation of the state from external (and internal) threats to its physical integrity and core values.
2   In an anarchical international system, state security is an issue of primary concern for policy makers and citizens. Indeed, it becomes the central priority since in the absence of an effective security policy, a state is likely to lose its sovereignty.
3   An emphasis on military might as the key determinant of security. In other words, security is defined almost exclusively in military terms.

It could be assumed that this traditional understanding of security, as state-based and concerned with military conflict, provides a simple and unambiguous basis on which states could pursue national security. This is not the case, however, and, as Wolfers (1952) argued, 'national security' is an ambiguous and pliable concept and goal. National security involves pursuing a policy that will reduce threats to a nation or the values the nation embodies. However, it is difficult to say which precise policies will increase security in any given situation. One problem that arises is the 'security dilemma', where the attempts of states to increase their security make everyone more insecure. For example, the attempts of State A to increase its security pose a security threat to State B. From the perspective of State A, its increased security (military) resources are simply for defensive purposes and do not therefore pose a threat to other states in the international system. However, from the perspective of State B, the increase in State A's security resources appears as a threat. State B then takes steps to respond to the threat, but this increases the insecurity of State A, which responds by taking measures that increase State B's insecurity and so on. A real-life example involves the Soviet Union and the US. The Soviet Union was threatened by the US monopoly of nuclear weapons after the Second World War. The

securing of nuclear weapons by the USSR initially made it feel more secure, but this increased US insecurity. The US took steps to increase its security, causing the USSR to do the same and have the same impact on the US. This led to an insecurity spiral and an arms race. Another difficulty with pursuing national security is that it can use up resources that might leave the nation more insecure. For example, a large military build-up might leave the nation economically vulnerable.

New security studies

At the end of the Cold War, this traditional concept of security was challenged by different perspectives that we will term 'new security studies'. Although they have different assumptions and methods, they were all developed as an explicit critique of the traditional definition and were concerned with proffering a new approach to analysis and policy. The first attack on the traditional concept emerged from writers who urged an expanded definition of security (Buzan, 1991). These writers accepted some key assumptions of the traditional approach but also provided a less exclusive conception of security, with a focus on social issues (Buzan et al., 1997). The assumptions concerning the state as the referent object of security and the importance of anarchy in creating insecurity were maintained, but they were modified in important ways:

1   It was recognized that, although the state is the primary referent object, the pursuit of national security does not always result in protecting individuals from threat.
2   It was acknowledged that the effect of international anarchy on security was not simple and straightforward. In other words, the condition of anarchy is mediated by systemic changes leading to different types of anarchy with different implications for the pursuit of national security.
3   There was a shift in perception of the nature and type of threat. Instead of security being defined in military terms, it was now seen in relation to five sectors: military, economics, the environment, societal and political. For example, while military security is concerned with violence between states, environmental security is concerned with threats arising from environmental issues such as conflict over resources or climate change.

The challenge provided by the conditions at the end of the Cold War served to undermine the settled consensus and led to a more radical approach. In their challenge to the traditional approach, proponents of critical security studies go further than those who seek to expand the concept of security. At the core of critical security approaches is a focus on the emancipation of the individual (Krause and Williams, 1997; Wyn Jones, 1999). Thus, critical security approaches replace the state as the referent object with the individual. They also reject the assumption of international anarchy as a pre-given feature of the international system. Finally, in promoting an alternative conception of security, this approach recognizes that threats to individual freedom come from a number of sources. Indeed, in a move that is directly counter to that of traditional theorists, critical security writers often posit the state as the key source of threat to individual security.

Human security

The concept of human security represents another approach that seeks to shift the focus away from the state-centric concerns of traditional security discourse. The term 'human security' was developed to capture a concern with the large number of threats to human life that existed beyond death caused by inter-state warfare. There were two elements to this approach. First, the end of the Cold War had reduced the threat of large-scale inter-state conflicts, but the incidence of intrastate conflict had become more prominent. Death from physical violence was more likely to be caused by civil wars or ethnic disputes within or across state boundaries than a formal war between states. Second, the easing of superpower tensions helped people recognize that death by starvation and disease was killing far more people than warfare. Issues such as the provision of food were increasingly seen as a security problem (see Box 14.1). Human security proponents thus seek to expand the agenda in order to bring the perspective of the individual and communities into focus and to address a range of threats to international security beyond those posed by other states.

The concept of human security was first introduced in the *Human Development Report 1994* (UNDP, 1994). This report set the tone for succeeding approaches to human security by focusing on a wide definition that takes a preventive, 'people-centred' approach. The UNDP definition focuses both on 'freedom from fear and freedom from want', thus covering safety from threats of hunger, disease and repression as well as protection from sudden and hurtful disruptions in the

---

Box 14.1 Food security

Although there are many definitions of food security, the UN Food and Agriculture Organization's (FAO, 1996) definition is widely accepted: 'Food security exists when all people, at all times, have physical and economic access to sufficient, safe and nutritious food to meet their dietary needs and food preferences for an active and healthy life.'

The issue of food security came to prominence in 2008 when, as a result of rising food prices, demonstrators took to the streets in over 40 countries to protest about high prices and food shortages. Following the collapse of Lehman Brothers in September 2008, the attention of the world shifted from the potential threat posed by the world food crisis to the ramifications of the global financial crisis. However, although world food prices declined in 2009, they nevertheless constitute a severe strain for many consumers in developing countries. The combination of the global financial crisis and the world food crisis has contributed to increasing poverty levels in the developing world. An influential report published by the UN Economic and Social Commission for Asia and the Pacific (ESCAP) states that the financial crisis has become a food crisis for 583 million people in the Asia-Pacific region (UNESCAP, 2009).

The human security implications of food insecurity are devastating. Food insecurity increases world hunger, resulting in a higher incidence of malnutrition, reduced spending on education and healthcare, and deepening poverty. The impact of food insecurity is felt most by the poor, especially the landless and female-headed households. Estimates from the FAO (2009) calculate that there are 923 million hungry people.

patterns of daily life. The report lists seven different elements of human security: economic security, food security, health security, environmental security, personal security, community security and political security (UNDP, 1994, pp. 24–5). Human security, conceived in these terms as the prerogative of the individual, effectively links security to human rights and human dignity.

Although the concept of human security has received considerable attention from scholars and policy makers, there is no consensus on a precise definition. Since its inception, the concept of human security has been defined and reinterpreted in numerous ways. While some groups have accepted the broad view of human security taken by the UNDP, others prefer a more narrow definition. A broad definition is provided by Kaldor (2007, p. 182), who defines human security as 'the security of individuals and communities rather than states and it combines human rights and human development'. In a similar vein, the Commission on Human Security (2003, p. 7) defines human security as the 'vital core of all human lives', without any specification regarding the content and context of this phrase on the grounds that 'different societies would interpret its meaning differently'.

On the other hand, the Human Security Centre's annual *Human Security Report* (2005, p. viii) takes the view that the concept should be confined to examining violent threats to individuals. In this approach, attention is paid to civil wars, terrorism, false imprisonment, torture by state officials (police, intelligence services), but not issues such as famine or development. Another limited definition is provided by Axworthy (2001), a former Canadian foreign minister and key architect of a distinctly Canadian approach to human security. The focus in this approach is less on the threats associated with underdevelopment and more on the insecurity resulting from violent conflict, while recognizing that such conflicts are not confined to inter-state conflict. Human security is thus defined in terms of freedom from fear.

In March 1999 the United Nations established the United Nations Trust Fund for Human Security (UNTFHS). UNTFHS finances activities undertaken by practitioners (either UN organizations or organizations approved by the UN) working to translate the human security approach into practice. The UNTFHS handbook (United Nations, 2009a) provides the underlying rationale and principles guiding its work.

THEORETICAL PERSPECTIVES: INTEGRATING SECURITY AND POLITICAL ECONOMY

Readers will recall from Chapter 1 that the three traditional IPE perspectives had very different views of conflict and cooperation. These views have had consequences for how people have studied and thought about the relationship between security and political economy. The dominant approach to economics – liberalism – has stipulated that the economic and political worlds are separate arenas dominated by different methods of behaviour. The economic world operates according to a set of economic laws, while the political world deviates from these laws. In the economic world, rational actors pursuing efficiency are rewarded, while the political world is marked by more emotional and irrational behaviour and rewards. As a result, economic liberals and liberals in IPE have tended to downplay or ignore the link between political economy and security. The one exception is that liberals have often argued that free trade and democratic politics are likely to increase peace between states. In contrast, power politics and critical approaches have tended to acknowledge the mutual influence of economics and security, but in different ways. Power politics approaches have viewed economic interests as subservient to security interests, while many critical approaches have viewed security issues as being heavily influenced if not dictated by economic interests.

Leading figures from the three traditional international political economy perspectives have all written on aspects of the relationship between security and political economy (Earle, 1986). Economic nationalists such as Hamilton and List argued that financial and industrial strength were prerequisites for military strength. In their view, it was the responsibility of the state to take action to protect national economic interests. Thus, Hamilton is often remembered for arguing that the US must protect its manufacturing base to bolster national power. List advocated a protectionist policy for Germany, alleging that free trade was only in the interest of the strongest economic powers.

Early liberal thought contained several approaches to the relationship between economics and security. Adam Smith usually criticized the overly protectionist policies of mercantilists, yet he acknowledged that there were circumstances where the interests of the state should trump commercial interests (Earle, 1986). For example, writing in the 1700s, Smith supported the British Navigation Acts, which stipulated that trade to Britain or its colonies must be carried in British ships. The purpose of these Acts was to ensure a strong merchant marine and Royal Navy, as well as protecting British economic interests. They were eventually repealed in the mid-1800s. While Smith supported a professional army and military defence of British interests overseas, some later free traders such as Richard Cobden adopted a more pacifist stance and campaigned against foreign interventions (such as the Crimean War).

A series of Marxist theorists and practitioners saw an intimate relationship between organized violence and political economy. To Marx and Engels, wars were both a ruse that ruling classes used to divert attention from domestic problems and an opportunity for workers to overthrow the ruling class should the war go badly (Neumann and von Hagen, 1986). States might engage in imperialism because of domestic economic needs and desires, but foreign adventures had the potential to weaken the security apparatus of the state and provide an opening for oppositional forces. Indeed, Lenin capitalized on Russia's disastrous performance in the First World War to launch and prosecute the Russian Revolution. In the 20th century, Marxists played a key role in launching revolutionary and nationalist wars in China, Vietnam, Africa and Cuba. Political power was seized and new economic systems were put in place following military defeat of their class opponents.

Scholarly interest in the relationship between economic activity and security has varied over time in response to the external environment. One issue of current concern to policy makers and scholars relates to defence procurement (see Box 14.2).

The shifting balance between security concerns and economics can be illustrated through the history of the US. Mastandumo (1998) argues that during those times when there has been no great external threat, US economic and foreign policies have been pursued on different tracks. However, during times of high threat, foreign and economic policies were integrated, with one serving the interests of the other. At some points during the Cold War, US economic policy was used to further foreign policy goals, while at other times foreign policy was used to advance economic goals. For example, when the US was concerned about Soviet expansionism, there was a tendency to support Japan and Europe through the Marshall Plan and open US markets to the exports of their allies. In the 1970s and 80s, foreign economic policy became more prominent as international monetary and trade issues were viewed as increasingly significant. Former allies were increasingly pressured to change their economic policies as security ties were seen as being less significant.

One of the cornerstones of much realist analysis of international relations has been a belief that issues of high politics are more important than issues of low politics (Keohane and Nye, 1977, p. 23). High politics is seen as those issues that relate to the military security of the state and low politics refers to other international issues, for example economic and environmental. However, even from a realist perspective, there is considerable justification for examining the relationship between security and political economy (Ripsman, 2005). As noted above, traditional mercantilist thought stressed that economic power is a prerequisite for military power. A state's military power is dependent on the economic resources at its disposal. Over time, the key economic resources relevant for the production of military forces and support for war-making efforts have changed but the connection between a strong domestic economy and national security has remained a key assumption of foreign and security policy. A state's economic strength can be defined in terms of 'the productive resources that its society possesses; labour, technology, natural resources, real capital (in the form of factories, power dams, railroads, inventories of materials and manufactures, and so on); and claims on the output of other societies inherent in reserves of international liquidity (gold, foreign currencies) and foreign investments' (Knorr, 1975, p. 46).

The contribution of economic resources to military potential will, of course, depend on the ways in which they are mobilized and the alternative uses of national economic product. The linkages between economic resources and national military power give rise to a number of dilemmas and policy problems. For example, to what extent should a state seek to organize production along nationalist lines or should it be open to foreign trade and investment? A nationalist policy may ensure the construction of domestic industries geared to national defence and ensure self-sufficiency in strategic goods. But such an economic nationalist policy may also be undertaken at a cost to efficiency and lead to a reduction in aggregate economic wealth. Such dilemmas

> ### Box 14.2 Defence procurement
>
> Defence procurement is an area where political economy and national security clearly overlap. It can be defined as the processes by which national governments procure military equipment and services. Defence procurement varies from state to state depending on the state of civil–military relations, the level of industrialization and technological development, global and regional tension, levels of threat perception and the general organization of military forces.
>
> Defence procurement is more than an exercise in commercial policy because the state plays a key role in the development of the defence sector and the complicated links between that sector and the rest of the economy. Distinctive elements of procuring military goods and services include:
>
> ▶ the role of the government as the key buyer and regulator
> ▶ the high cost of arms
> ▶ the importance of research and development
> ▶ the inflationary spiral of weapons production
> ▶ uncertainties related to the production process and the changing nature of external threats
> ▶ information asymmetries between the buyer and the supplier
> ▶ an oligopolistic market structure (de Fraja and Hartley, 1996; Rogerson, 1993).
>
> Governance issues play a major role in the defence procurement industry since secrecy and lack of transparency, often justified on security grounds, can lead to corruption and waste. In March 2009, US president Barack Obama estimated that changes in Defense department procurement policies could save the country over $40 billion (Gilmore, 2009). The high cost of weapons also makes defence procurement a political issue. For example, given that the UK suffered an intense economic slowdown between 2008 and 2010, does it make sense to spend billions of pounds on nuclear-armed submarines? The industrial–economic interests mixed with the political–diplomatic issues involved in purchasing weapons make defence procurement an especially contentious issue. Moreover, the relationship between defence procurement, military spending and economic growth is a subject of heated debate. In the context of developing countries, some analysts argue that governments should pursue strategies of military modernization and self-reliance in defence procurement. Other analysts contend that the development of weapons systems is economically wasteful (Balakrishnan, 2008; Singh, 2005).

form the centre of debates between neomercantilists and liberal theorists.

Just as some modern-day realists have examined the link between political economy and security, some liberals have suggested that peace is intimately connected to following liberal policies. Proponents of commercial liberalism, who focus on the influence of the market on domestic and transnational actors, contend that economic exchange reduces the likelihood of war among states (Moravcsik, 1997). From a liberal perspective, humans are rational, risk-averse actors who make decisions on the basis of personal gain and loss. On the basis of these assumptions, trade and investment across national borders provide positive benefits to states and thus the resort to war is likely to diminish economic and social welfare. In such circumstances, rational states will focus on the gains from economic intercourse

rather than the costs of war. The contention that liberal economic policies and a liberal international order are positively related with peace has long been a mainstay of liberal political theory (Howard, 2008). In the 1970s, these arguments were given added relevance with the development of interdependence theory (Keohane and Nye, 1977). Interdependence theory argued that under conditions of complex interdependence, there was an absence of issue hierarchy. Foreign policy is not simply reducible to a concern with national security; military force has limited utility and is ineffective in controlling outcomes; and when economic interdependence between states is high, it contributes to a search for peaceful solutions to conflicts and reduces the resort to violence.

There is an enormous body of theoretical and statistical literature that seeks to examine the commercial liberal proposition that peace is a product of economic interdependence. The results of these studies are mixed. Some studies provide statistical evidence in support of the claim (O'Neal et al., 1996; O'Neal and Russett, 1997), while other studies find no conclusive supportive evidence (Barbieri, 1996; Ripsman and Blanchard, 1996/7). This literature suffers from a number of ambiguities, with the most important being the failure to agree on a definition of economic interdependence.

A related liberal theory links the domestic political system with the possibility of international conflict. Going back to the thinking of Kant in the 18th century, liberals argue that a peaceful international system requires the presence of a large number of democratic states. The extensive democratic peace literature debates the connection between democracy and peace. Proponents of the link argue that democratic states do not engage in warfare with each other, while opponents dispute the data on which these claims have been made. Proponents of the democratic peace thesis argue that democratic states tend to resolve conflict over the bargaining table because of the constraints built into democratic political structures and the cultural values of peaceful resolution typical of democratic decision-making structures. However, they also insist that democracies are not constrained from waging war against authoritarian and totalitarian states (Russett, 1993). Critics contend that there is no conclusive evidence to prove that democratic states are peaceful in their relations with each other because they are democratic. Indeed, it may be the case that peaceful conditions produce democratic states rather than the reverse as the democratic peace thesis holds. It has also been suggested that the mathematical probability that democratic states would fight each other is small because historically there have been few democracies (Brown et al., 1996). It has also been argued that countries in the transition to democracy become more violent and prone to war (Mansfield and Snyder, 1995).

Critical approaches to international relations have argued that capitalism can promote violence and the existing structure of capitalism inflicts continuous violence on some groups of people. The notion of 'structural violence' is that the operation of the system itself causes people to be injured or killed (Galtung, 1969). For example, the world has enough food for everyone, but the system of distribution and payment is flawed so that millions of people regularly die from lack of nourishment. No individual or group is specifically targeted

nor is it intended that people die from starvation. Nevertheless, we have organized food production and distribution in such a way that people die on a regular basis from starvation. This violence is structural and inherent in the system as it is presently organized.

MAJOR DEVELOPMENTS

There have been dramatic changes in the global security structure since the end of the Second World War. We define a security structure as the overarching framework of material, institutional and ideational resources in response to perceptions of threat. A security structure thus comprises material and normative elements. Here, we will discuss two major changes in the global security structure. The first change was the creation after 1945 of a security structure dominated by a bipolar international system. This system featured the rise of the national security state and the military–industrial complex. The collapse of bipolarity and the ending of the Cold War triggered a new security structure. This post-Cold War security structure was less state-centric and has seen the rise of new security challenges.

The Cold War security structure

During the Cold War (1948–89), the meaning of security in international relations literature almost exclusively referred to the military preservation of the nation-state. Threats to national security were seen as emanating from external sources. Fundamental threats to territorial integrity or value systems were held to emanate from either real conflict of interests or ideological motivations or both. Given the dominant status of the US and the Soviet Union, the interests of these two superpowers were inevitably on a collision course according to experts who emphasize the Cold War as a clash of interests. The bipolar distribution of power inevitably led to a struggle for power. On the other hand, it is possible to conceive of the rivalry as the outcome of an ideological conflict between capitalism and communism. Whether the origins of the Cold War are rooted in a struggle for power, an ideological dispute or even the result of misperceptions, from the perspective of international political economy, the key issues relate to the ways in which this global conflict shaped political and economic systems and patterns of international economic intercourse.

Two issues are of particular importance in this respect. First, the central goal of states was conceived as self-preservation and the discourse of security placed emphasis on military weapons as the primary requirement for defence and security. As a result, there was increased military spending on both sides of the divide and an arms race. In this scenario, nuclear weapons became (and remain) the most important tool within a state's military arsenal. The existence of nuclear weapons gave rise to policies of deterrence (to avoid the use of these deadly weapons), non-proliferation (to halt the spread of this destructive tool) and the security dilemma. The cost of military armaments and the impact of defence spending on national economies were contributory factors to the search for arms agreements.

The second issue related to the impact of the bipolar security structure on international economic relations. One result of the Cold War was the creation of effectively two separate systems of international trade and payments. The bipolar security structure with opposing alliance systems gave rise to a Western system of free-market economies and a system of centrally planned economies. These two systems devised separate international organizations to regulate economic intercourse. For example, the World Bank and the IMF, among other institutions, played central roles in coordinating Western policy, while the Council of Mutual Economic Assistance was created to manage relations among centrally planned economies in the Soviet orbit. Another consequence of the Cold War security structure was the economic competition between the US and its allies and the Soviet Union in the developing world. The rivals were in competition not only over access to resources and markets but also over economic systems, as each tried to win converts to its economic ideology. In this sense, it was believed that national security was enhanced by 'capturing' states to the economic system preferred by the US or the Soviet Union.

The close relationship between the pursuit of security and the national economy during the Cold War can be seen in the rise of the military–industrial complex. In his final speech to the nation in 1961, US President Eisenhower (1961) warned his citizens that: 'In the councils of government, we must guard against the acquisition of unwarranted influence, whether sought or unsought, by the military industrial complex.' He was referring to the political influence exercised by the existence of a large military establishment and a massive arms industry. The outgoing president feared that the combined power of a military desiring new and more weapons systems and an arms industry eager to sell those weapons would influence public policy in a direction that would be against the national interest and personal liberty. In many ways this was a shocking statement. Eisenhower was not a left-wing radical. He was a war hero who had commanded the D-Day invasion of Normandy and was the first commander of NATO forces in Europe. And yet, this person, who was schooled in the military and rose to be president, highlighted the dangers of an expansionist military and arms industry to American democracy.

The origins of the military–industrial complex lie in the changing nature of warfare. Over a number of centuries, warfare transformed from an activity waged by a small number of people (knights, mercenaries or small professional armies) to one fought by nations and societies as a whole (Howard, 2009). The French Revolution mobilized a whole society that eventually served as the basis for Napoleon's conquest of Europe. The US Civil War was an early indication of the destruction to come from new weapons and the use of industrial strength and might to destroy an opponent. The First World War confirmed the trend of whole nations being mobilized for combat, while victory in the Second World War required the harnessing of large industries to produce tanks and ships in the US and USSR, as well as the creation of new super-weapons such as radar and nuclear bombs. Cold War security for the USSR and US rested on large militaries based in numerous countries and the deployment of advanced military technology. Military technologies ranged from the latest innovation in fighter aircraft to nuclear-powered, armed submarines to intercontinental ballistic missiles. The large corporations that supplied these technologies and the militaries that used them formed a relationship of mutual dependence as both sought to influence the procurement policies of their political leaders.

The post-Cold War security structure

The most significant change in the security structure since the end of the Second World War has been the end of the Cold War. It is not too dramatic to note that the world fundamentally changed with the collapse of the Berlin Wall and the demise of the Soviet Union. This change brought with it not only a rethinking of security relations but also changes in the dominant security discourse. The focus on the national security state was now challenged by considerations of a broader nature (discussed under 'New security studies' above). The end of the Cold War heralded an end to bipolarity and ushered in a unipolar world order with the US as the sole military superpower. Some analysts thought that the end of bipolarity signalled the opportunity to pursue a peace dividend. The peace dividend could arise by diverting finance that had previously been spent on armaments to peaceful purposes, and also by seizing the opportunity for international cooperation with the cessation of superpower rivalry.

In this new world order, the hope of many experts that an era of multilateral cooperation for security purposes would develop initially appeared to be well founded. In 1992, Boutros-Ghali, the UN secretary-general, proclaimed the Agenda for Peace, which committed the UN to identification of conflict at an early stage, peace-making efforts to bring parties to an agreement, and peacekeeping and peace-building. However, the conditions required to sustain the new multilateralism proved elusive. The imperatives of national security remained of vital importance to most states and the economic and political resources necessary to underwrite the new order were not forthcoming. As the financial and human costs of the new interventionism became evident, leading states were less inclined to support such policies. The casualties suffered by US forces in Somalia in 1993 proved an important turning point and paved the way for inaction in Rwanda, with its tragic consequences.

Another departure from Cold War politics was a growing willingness to address rather than ignore fundamental problems within the borders of war-torn states. This developed concurrently with a new focus on the security of the individual and on human rights. Recognition that the most direct threats to individuals frequently arise from their own governments ushered in the theory and practice of humanitarian intervention (Wheeler, 2000). Commitment to non-intervention in the affairs of states, which was sacrosanct in the previous four decades, made way for a more subtle interpretation, according to which, on occasions, the rights of individuals take precedence over the rights of repressive governments and the sovereign states they represent.

Humanitarian intervention proved controversial in theory and practice and is no longer the dominant framing of attempts to protect individuals.

The doctrine of the Responsibility to Protect (R2P) has effectively replaced humanitarian intervention as the appropriate policy response to situations of internal strife and human suffering. The R2P norm was brought to prominence in the report of the International Commission on Intervention and State Sovereignty (2001), and endorsed by world leaders at the United Nations World Summit in 2005 (United Nations, 2005).

External intervention in domestic conflict is a feature of the post-Cold War security structure because in this era wars within countries have exacted a heavy toll on humanity. Since 1945, three-quarters of all armed conflicts have been within countries and as many people have died in internal conflicts between 1980 and 2002 as in the First World War (Kahl, 2005, p. 77). These conflicts are supported by a particular global political economy, which nurtures such chaos and makes them difficult to resolve. Kaldor (1999) has labelled the wave of conflicts following the Cold War as 'new wars'. These wars take place in states with weak or nonexistent central authority, sometimes referred to as 'failed states'. The state is unable to retain its monopoly of violence, which leads to a proliferation of armed groups including renegade army units, para-militaries, local self-defence units, mercenaries and foreign troops. The state is unable to raise sufficient revenues for taxation or support the national economy. As a result, a great deal of economic activity grinds to a halt or becomes dominated by criminal gangs and mafias. Local strongmen use fear, insecurity and hatred of other populations to maintain power and engage in a population displacement policy through murder, ethnic cleansing or making particular regions uninhabitable.

Since new wars cause such damage to existing state structures and economic activity, local military forces finance their activities by extracting resources from the local population and tapping external sources of finance. The population as a whole must also turn increasingly to external actors for survival. Local warlords use a variety of tactics to raise funds from the local populations. They can force locals to sell possessions at cut-rate prices, collect protection money from terrified inhabitants, tax the movement of goods, loot local resources, hold prominent individuals hostage, and control criminal activity. Hard-pressed civilians may be forced to rely on humanitarian assistance from international organizations in the form of refugee camps, emergency shelter, food aid or development assistance in order to survive. Another source of external support comes in the form of remittances sent by family members working in more prosperous states.

External financial resources for local warlords come from a variety of sources. If these groups happen to control a valuable local resource, they can sell these products on the international market. Examples include cocaine from Columbia, heroin from Afghanistan, diamonds from Sierra Leone and cassiterite (tin) from the Democratic Republic of Congo (DRC; see Box 14.3). In some cases, large multinationals are crucial in facilitating the movement of these products to the global marketplace. Similar to civilian use of remittances, local ethnic militias can tap their diaspora communities for funds to purchase arms and supplies. Local warlords can also draw on the services of foreign governments. In some cases, this may involve explicit support from neighbouring states, such as Serbian and Croatian support for groups in Bosnia or Rwandan support for opposition groups in the DRC. In other cases, local warlords will divert international humanitarian aid by taxing convoys or charging exorbitant customs duties to allow access to local populations.

The issue of groups financing themselves through the sale of precious natural resources raises the broader issue of the relationship between competition for scarce resources and organized violence. Conflict analysts have noted a relationship between civil wars and two resource conditions (Kahl, 2005). The first condition is characterized by growing populations, environmental degradation and increased competition for renewable resources. In this scenario, ever-increasing numbers of people are caught in a downward spiral of destroying their local environment to meet survival needs, which increases political conflict and undermines long-term stability. A second condition occurs not when there is a shortage of natural resources, but when groups control highly valued resources such as diamonds, oil or minerals. In these cases, there is an incentive for other groups to engage in violence to control these resources. In addition, groups that control precious resources are likely to overinvest in their development and neglect other aspects of economic and political development. In the longer run, this leaves the economy and polity vulnerable to economic shocks.

A political economy approach to new wars suggests that while historical and identity issues are significant aspects of these engagements, the fuel sustaining them is to be found in the economic and political structures combatants have created (Griffiths, 1999). Nationalist and ethnic sentiments can be used to mobilize people, but localized acts of ethnic cleansing are often aimed at seizing the land and property of those being ejected. Local elites organize the confiscation of their former neighbours' property and create a new economic structure which serves their interests. Since the local

---

Box 14.3 Conflict minerals in the DRC

In the late 1800s, the population of the Congo suffered greatly as the world demanded rubber during the second Industrial Revolution. In the early 21st century, the Congolese suffer again as the world demands minerals for the electronics of the information revolution. Indeed, global consumption of 'conflict minerals' has fuelled ongoing mass murder and rape in the eastern areas of the DRC. Government military units as well as non-state militias and former rebel groups use force to control the mines and use the profit from the mines to fuel their military activity. The two primary minerals are cassiterite (the ore for tin) and columbite-tantalite (known as coltan, from which tantalum is extracted), which are both used in creating electronic goods such as laptops, mobile phones and MP3 players. Companies such as Apple, HP, Dell, Samsung and Blackberry risk having conflict minerals in their supply chain, thereby fuelling the conflict. States also profit from this trade, with Malaysia being the primary destination for Congo's tin ore, China processing the majority of tantalum and Rwanda facilitating the export of Congo's tin ore through its territory.

Steps could be taken to limit the trade in conflict minerals and prevent the financing of military groups engaged in murder and rape (Global Witness, 2010). Corporations could follow due diligence standards set out by the UN Security Council to ensure that conflict minerals are excluded from their supply chain. Major states could police their corporations and ensure that aid to the DRC is not diverted to militarizing economic activity.

economy collapses as a result of violent conflict, the general civilian population is often impoverished while criminal gangs control the import of products to satisfy local needs. The alleged solidarity within ethnic communities gives way to a reign of intimidation and corruption. Once the violence has begun, local warlords actively scuttle peace accords and block reconciliation because a return to legitimate state structures threatens their economic profiteering. Resolving the conflict requires attention to the newly established criminal economic interests.

Perhaps the most visible feature of the post-Cold War security structure is the threat of global terrorism. International terrorism is, of course, not new but the events of 11 September 2001, when al-Qaeda terrorists hijacked several US planes and used them as weapons against the World Trade Center in New York and the Pentagon in Washington DC, ushered in a heightened sense of insecurity and altered the security landscape in the advanced industrialized world. The terrorist atrocities of 11 September (commonly referred to as 9/11) led to a shift in the determinants of international security. It raised three key issues.

First, it raised the issue of the extent to which the source of military threat had shifted from state actors to non-state actors. Suddenly, a key threat was seen to emanate from non-state actors rather than states. The 9/11 attacks demonstrated that a relatively small non-state actor was capable of inflicting significant physical and emotional damage on even the strongest states. Non-state actors pose a particular problem for state strategists. They do not respond to conventional notions of deterrence because states have difficulty targeting small groups. Moreover, non-state actors make defence difficult because they use unconventional strategies, such as using civilian planes as flying bombs. Questions were raised about whether the modern infrastructure of advanced economies was uniquely vulnerable to new forms of warfare. Could a cyber attack knock out a country's communications systems and seriously damage a nations' economy? Might whole systems be thrown into panic by the effective targeting of power plants? Was it possible that a small nuclear suitcase bomb could be detonated in a large urban centre? Furthermore, conventional military retaliation has proved unsuccessful in a campaign against terrorists who do not accept international legal principles. As Cronin (2002/3, p. 38) argues, the threat of terrorism is a two-tiered challenge in which solutions are required that

'deal with the religious fanatics and the far more politically motivated states, entities, and peoples who would support them because they feel powerless and left behind in a globalized world'. A military response can at best be successful in the short term but is unlikely to be so in the longer term, where underlying problems related to poverty, poor governance and marginalization have to be solved in order to detach the terrorists from their support base. In short, only a human security approach can remove the enabling environment in which terrorists thrive. However, it can also be noted that because these actors do not control a state, it is difficult for them to sustain a long-term extensive campaign against opposing states (Goldman and Blanken, 2005). They may be able to temporarily disrupt a state or an economy with an attack, but those states and economies are durable and able to absorb occasional shocks. The attacks do not threaten the viability of their opponents.

Second, global terrorism has heightened personal insecurity and increased psychological vulnerability. In one sense, the fear that terrorists can strike anywhere and at any time has led to increased levels of security in many aspects of everyday life. International air travel has changed irrevocably. The bombs that brought down Air India Flight 182 over the Irish Sea in June 1985 and Pan Am Flight 103 in December 1988 over Lockerbie in Scotland did not lead to the type of surveillance and restrictions on cabin baggage that followed in the wake of the 9/11 attacks and the attempt by Richard Reid to detonate a shoe bomb on American Airlines Flight 63 in December 2001. A series of bombings, such as the October 2002 Bali nightclub explosion, the March 2004 Madrid train bombings, and the coordinated attacks on London underground trains and buses in July 2005, intensified the (Western) sense of insecurity. Key features of this contemporary terrorism are the transnational terrorist networks, the failure of the terrorists to issue authorities with a warning, the resort to the use of suicide bombers, and the random civilian targets chosen, raising fundamental questions concerning the ability of the state to protect its citizens.

Third, the onset of global terrorism has changed the political and security landscape of inter-state relations. Following the events of 9/11, combating terrorism became a key American security goal. President Bush famously declared a war on terror and reshaped American strategic priorities. The pursuit of international terrorists and states harbouring terrorists became a key priority. Other states also swiftly declared terrorism as a key security threat and antiterrorism legislation was enacted in many states to counter this new danger. Many states recognized a common enemy and developed joint counterterrorism strategies. As the international political landscape was transformed, discussion turned to the so-called 'clash of civilizations' and inherent conflict between militant Islam and Western values. Global terrorism has also changed military priorities and the deployment of resources. Following the 9/11 attacks, the US and its allies launched military action against the perpetrators of the attacks and the states deemed to be harbouring and supporting terrorists. Actions against the Taliban in Afghanistan succeeded in ousting the Taliban from power, but coalition forces failed to create a secure environment in that country. As the war progressed, the support of Western publics eroded. Despite, or perhaps because of, Western interventions in the Middle East, new terrorist threats continued to emerge (see Box 14.4).

KEY ISSUES

Traditional threats to security such as terrorism and nuclear war remain important in contemporary global politics. For many people, instruments of violence threaten their physical security on a daily basis. Here, we examine three issues relevant to the political economy of security. Economic statecraft links economic security and foreign policy and thus raises fundamental questions concerning economic instruments of state policy. Both transnational crime and corporate espionage illustrate the dark or covert side of GPE. Pandemics and disease are threats that can be viewed through conventional and human security perspectives and thus demonstrate the complex relationship between economics and security.

Economic statecraft and security

Economic statecraft is the use of economic resources to exert political influence by a state. Two issues have been most prominent in recent studies of economic statecraft: economic aid and economic sanctions.

Economic aid is generally seen in terms of 'carrots', that is, inducements for other states to behave in a particular manner. However, aid can be used as a stick if it is withdrawn. Sanctions are more clearly in the stick or coercion category. Both aid and sanctions have become controversial features of diplomatic practice.

Foreign aid can be categorized in a number of different ways. For example, a donor may classify the provision of aid in terms of bilateral development aid, economic assistance supporting political and security goals, humanitarian aid, multilateral economic assistance and military aid. Here, we are specifically concerned with bilateral development aid and economic

---

Box 14.4 ISIS as a new threat

A new dimension to the threat posed by terrorists emerged in 2014. The actions of the group known as the Islamic State of Iraq and al-Sham (ISIS) weakened conventional regional security and created further instability in an already volatile region as it captured territory in Iraq and Syria. With its public beheadings, mass killings of Christians and people of other faiths and the enslavement of women and children, ISIS worsened levels of human security in areas under its control. It used social media to promote its messages and successfully recruited men and women from around the world to its cause with foreigners making up around 50 per cent of its fighting force (Engel, 2015). The threat is not confined to Iraq and Syria since its recruitment campaign brings 'terror' to Western countries by planting jihadists in their midst. So-called self-starter terrorism where terrorists develop their acts independently but are influenced by the actions of ISIS (or al-Qaeda) became more frequent. Speaking in October 2014, the German chancellor Angela Merkel expressed the views of many Western leaders when she stated, 'To stand up against the IS terror is in the interest of the entire world, also in Germany's interest, as the jihadists are threatening our security as well' (*Economic Times*, 2014). The massacre of 130 civilians in Paris on 13 November 2015 demonstrated the ongoing ISIS threat to Western populations.

assistance supporting political and security goals. We are not explicitly concerned with the economic effectiveness of bilateral aid, humanitarian aid, multilateral aid or military aid. Our focus is on the use of economic aid as an instrument of statecraft, that is, bilateral development assistance that nominally has the objective of promoting economic growth, and aid specifically targeted to meet political and security goals. Of course, various donor motives are not completely separate. The objectives of promoting economic growth and poverty reduction, mitigating conflict and expanding democratic governance are perfectly compatible. For example, aid that results in improved economic growth can create the conditions for political stability and thus fulfil a political objective. Analysis of the allocation of aid shows conclusively the importance of political concerns in donors' motives (Maizels and Nisanke, 1984). For some analysts, key political goals are related to the preservation of order, stability and peace in the international system (Brandt Commission, 1983), while for others the main motive is more closely related to the national interests of donor states.

Changes in aid policy are the result of changing circumstances, changing norms governing the recipient–donor relationship and international development policy, and changing views about the efficacy of aid. Aid as an instrument of statecraft is viewed by donors within the overall context of their foreign relations with recipient countries, other potentially affected countries and competitor nations. During the Cold War era, aid was an important instrument of foreign policy. Both the US and its allies and the Soviet Union and its allies used economic aid as an instrument in the Cold War struggle, with Western countries' aid programmes targeted to supporting anti-communist regimes and aid from the communist bloc focused on supporting anti-Western sentiment in the Third World. Economic aid was deployed in the ideological conflict between the rival economic and political systems and to win votes in international organizations such as the UN. For the ex-colonial powers determined to maintain postcolonial spheres of influence, financial influence and national culture (especially in the case of France), aid was geographically concentrated in their ex-colonies. For example, French foreign aid went almost exclusively to ex-French colonies and British aid was concentrated on its ex-colonies.

In the post-Cold War environment, democracy promotion has emerged as a key goal of democratic states

and foreign aid as a suitable instrument with which to pursue this objective. Sizable funds have been specifically allocated to democracy promotion by aid agencies. For example, the US Agency for International Development budgeted $1,051 million in 2004 for democracy and governance/conflict (Tarnoff and Nowells, 2004). The political economy of aid and democracy has focused on the usefulness of this tool of economic statecraft. The evidence suggests that the results have been disappointing (S. Brown, 2005; Crawford, 2005). One reason for the failure of economic aid to promote democracy rests with the internal obstacles in the recipient states. It has been argued that the absence of a receptive political culture, chronic poverty and nonexistent institutions inhibit the efforts of donors to promote democracy in Africa (S. Brown, 2005, pp. 183–4). Donor shortcomings are another reason for the failure of democracy promotion (S. Brown, 2005, pp. 185–9). A study of the failed EU attempt to promote democracy in Ghana blamed EU member states for approaching democracy promotion in a narrow manner and being more concerned with fostering their self-interests than developing the norms and principles of democratic governance (Crawford, 2005). In a different but related manner, Cohen and Küpçü (2009) contend that US democracy promotion efforts have been hampered by a failure to adequately distinguish democracy from other strategic objectives such as development and humanitarian and public health assistance. A third reason rests with the tool of political conditionality itself (S. Brown, 2005, pp. 184–5). Political conditionality can be limited by constraints on the donor and recipient sides. Donors may have unclear objectives and are limited by the sovereignty of the recipient states from imposing their goals. On the recipient side, political conditionality is limited by the ability of local elites to evade demands for change, compliance by authoritarian rulers who appear on the surface to meet the demands for change while maintaining existing practices, and the capacity to shrug off demands for change if access to alternative sources of finance are available.

Economic sanctions, which were at one time a relatively non-contentious tool of foreign policy, have become a controversial issue in global politics. The political economy of economic sanctions has focused on the utility of sanctions as an instrument of foreign policy and the impact of sanctions on the target population. On both issues there are diverse opinions and competing research findings. On such a controversial issue, it is not surprising to note that there is no agreed definition of economic sanctions. Some scholars concerned with the usefulness of sanctions as an instrument of statecraft tend to support definitions that make reference to the purpose of sanctions. From this perspective, Doxey (1996, p. 9) defined sanctions as 'penalties threatened or imposed as a declared consequence of the target's failure to observe international standards or international obligations'. Other writers have tried to develop definitions that omit reference to the intent of the sanctions. Thus, Hufbauer et al. (2007, p. 3) define economic sanctions simply as 'the deliberate, government-inspired withdrawal or threat of withdrawal of customary trade or financial relations'.

Although economic sanctions have been dated to 432 BC (Dadkhah, 2006, p. 1386; Hufbauer et al., 2007, p. 9), they became prominent in the 20th century with the creation of the League of Nations. The Covenant of the League of Nations (and the UN Charter) allocates to collective economic sanctions an important role in the preservation of international peace and security. Since the end of the Cold War, states have increasingly turned to the use of economic sanctions. Between 1914 and 1989, there were 121 cases of economic sanctions, but between 1990 and 2000 there were 53 cases (Hufbauer et al., 2007, pp. 20–32). Sanctions have been utilized in relation to major contemporary issues such as ethnic cleansing, human rights abuses, nuclear proliferation and terrorism (see Box 14.5 for the example of Iran).

One of the main reasons why the evidence on the utility of sanctions is so inconclusive is because the motivations of the sender countries are not always clear. Governments impose sanctions for a variety of reasons. Some of these reasons are instrumental, that is, the sender seeks to impose costs on the target state such that the target will alter its behaviour and comply with the demands of the sender. However, sender states also impose sanctions for expressive or symbolic reasons. Sanctions imposed for expressive purposes serve to send a signal of disapproval to the target state but do not envisage compliance, or they have been imposed in order to meet the demands of a domestic interest group rather than to achieve their declared aims. Sanctions can also fail because the costs are too high. Costs incurred by domestic producers or allies weaken the resolve to maintain the economic measures. Furthermore, the success of sanctions is also dependent on the extent to which the target state can evade the coercive measures either through mobilizing domestic resources (political and economic) or by finding substitute suppliers of the embargoed goods. History is replete with examples of domestic mobilization against external intervention in the form of sanctions and sanctions busting.

Box 14.5 Sanctions against Iran

Iran has been a repeated target of economic and political sanctions. In 1979, the US imposed sanctions in response to the storming of its embassy by Iranian students. Concerns about Iran's nuclear weapons programme led to an intensification of sanctions in 2011. The EU, the US and Canada imposed a travel ban on Iranian officials involved in its nuclear programme or suspected of human rights abuses. A number of countries (including the US, the UK and Canada) also imposed a financial services boycott, which prevented their financial institutions from engaging in any activities with Iranian banks. In 2012, the EU joined the US in instituting an oil embargo preventing the import of Iranian oil. This was supplemented by an insurance ban on ships transporting Iranian oil.

The impact of these sanctions on Iranian policy is uncertain (Borger and Dehghan, 2012). Iranian oil exports were reduced by 50 per cent. Lower oil exports meant a reduction in foreign currency, which made it more difficult for Iranians to purchase foreign goods. Among the population at large, the impact was felt in rising food prices and a slowing economy. The economic impact is damaging, but the economy was not crippled. Politically, the outcome is even more uncertain. Will sanctions undermine support for the Iranian government and its nuclear programme or cause people to rally around the government in response to foreign attacks? During the first half of 2015 Iran negotiated an agreement with a group of international powers (US, France, Britain, China, Russia, Germany) to scale back its nuclear programme in return for the lifting of economic sanctions.

Given these caveats, it is not surprising that there is no consensus on the impact of sanctions. The most authoritative study (Hufbauer et al., 2007) rejects the claim that sanctions don't work. These authors argue that in the cases they examined between 1914 and 2000, sanctions were partially successful 34 per cent of the time (Hufbauer et al., 2007, p. 158). The reasons for success and failure were related to the type of policy change sought, the costs of enforcing sanctions, the extent to which sanctions were instrumental or expressive and conflicting aims among senders.

Prior to the upsurge in sanctions since 1990, there was limited interest in the potentially harmful consequences of economic sanctions on civilian populations. With the increased resort to sanctions in the post-Cold War period and a changing moral climate, debates concerning the legality and utility of sanctions have been complemented with concern over the possibly damaging impact of sanctions on target populations. A series of high-profile cases, most notably sanctions against Saddam Hussein's regime in Iraq, spurred interest in the humanitarian consequences of sanctions. It has led to a change in perception concerning the destructive nature of sanctions. Interest in the humanitarian impact of economic sanctions poses a number of issues and has given rise to contending views. A central issue concerns the extent to which foreign policy goals should take precedence over the human rights of target populations; and the circumstances under which humanitarian actors will decide on the unacceptable consequences of sanctions. It has been argued, on the one hand, that the unintended, harmful consequences of sanctions can be accepted as long as the desired political goal is achieved. On the other hand, it is contended that, given the close relationship between political goals and humanitarian objectives, the senders should cease their activities once it becomes apparent that the objectives cannot be attained (Weiss et al., 1997, pp. 18–19).

Transnational crime and corporate espionage

In the post-Cold War security structure, transnational organized crime has become recognized as a major threat to national security. It has been a major theme in US national security strategy since 1996 when President Clinton defined the fight against organized crime as a national security priority. There is no agreed definition of organized crime since a monolithic transnational criminal organization does not exist. The United Nations Convention against Transnational Organized Crime adopts a broad definition. It defines an organized criminal group as a 'structured group of three or more persons, existing for a period of time and acting in concert with the aim of committing one or more serious crimes or offences ... in order to obtain directly or indirectly a financial or other material benefit' (United Nations, 2000b, Article 2a). Organized criminal activity covers a wide range of illegal activities including drug trafficking, trafficking in persons, trading in human organs, money laundering, illicit traffic in weapons, theft of art and cultural objects, corruption and bribery of officials, environmental crime and the use of legal networks for illegal business activities (see Box 14.6).

The expansion of transnational criminal activities has been linked to the end of the Cold War and the intensification of globalization. Criminal networks have taken advantage of weak central governments in the former communist world, and the increase in ethnic conflict in central and eastern Europe, to expand their activities. Economic globalization has provided the conditions for the massive expansion of transnational organized crime. Economic liberalization, technological change and the transformation of transport systems have facilitated the growth of transnational criminal activity (Serrano, 2002, p. 25). The liberalization of trade and finance has provided avenues for the operation of criminal gangs. Communication and information technology has not only provided the infrastructure to allow these groups to coordinate their activities, it has also opened up new avenues of illegal activity such as internet fraud. The expansion of transport networks has increased the flow of legal and illegal goods.

Transnational organized crime poses a security threat in traditional and human security terms. It poses a direct threat to the political stability of weak states, and an indirect one to stronger states. Transnational organized crime poses a direct threat to governance and state institutions through increasing corruption in government and subverting good governance. The ensuing lack of legitimacy can undermine governmental and state authority. Moreover, links between transnational criminal groups and terrorists pose a direct threat to all states. In areas where governmental control is weak, transnational organized crime can inflame regional conflict and destabilize regional relations

Box 14.6 Transnational crime: the MS-13 and M-18 gangs

Poverty, underdevelopment, misguided criminal justice policies and global mobility have acted together to transnationalize criminal economic activity. Particularly violent examples of this are the MS-13 (Mara Salvatrucha) and Mara 18 gangs (Arana, 2005). In the early 1990s, these gangs were local groups in a poor part of Los Angeles and composed mainly of refugees from El Salvador's civil war. Following the Los Angeles riots of 1992, US criminal and immigration policies became more severe. Thousands of Central Americans were arrested and deported. The US gang deportations transnationalized their criminal activities and destabilized the states of El Salvador, Honduras and Guatemala. They are estimated to have 70,000–100,000 members. The gangs quickly expanded their activity in drug trafficking, car theft, prostitution, human trafficking and contract killing. Although Central American states rounded up and imprisoned thousands of gang members, membership remained high because of a lack of economic opportunities for young people. The gangs returned to the US more dangerous than when they had departed. They now engage in a wide range of criminal activity, often extremely violent, across Central and North America.

through illegal cross-border activity, which can lead to the creation of territorial zones outside the control of the central government; or through the supply of illegal weapons to combatants. The economic activities of transnational criminal groups also pose a traditional threat to the security of the state. An interdependent global economy provides opportunities for money laundering and tax evasion. Transnational organized criminal activities can threaten legal markets, destroy legitimate businesses and expand illegal markets, resulting in a negative impact on economic growth and development. Poor economic performance often results in situations where a large illegal economy has been allowed to flourish.

Transnational crime also has serious implications for human security. It can have a damaging impact on state capacity by limiting the government's revenue, with a resultant decline in spending on infrastructural projects and social services. Thus, there is a direct impact on human security when services such as education and health are curtailed. Moreover, activities such as the supply of illegal drugs, trafficking in persons for sexual exploitation, forced labour or the harvesting of body parts are obviously injurious to the persons subject to such activities. Furthermore, transnational crime is accompanied by increased violence, loss of individual autonomy and consequent increased insecurity.

Corporate espionage is a term that refers to companies spying on other companies to gain commercial advantage (Javers, 2010). In this section we broaden the investigation to examine how corporations have colluded with state intelligence organizations, how states

have used their intelligence organizations to assist their corporations and how corporations have engaged in security activity against civic associations. A noticeable trend is a merging of state and corporate interests as states and corporations collaborate on espionage projects. A question of concern is whether corporate activity in the intelligence field poses a threat to democracy.

One side of the problem concerns companies cooperating with state intelligence agencies to monitor citizens or suppress dissent. In Chapter 5 we mentioned corporate actions to curb Wikileaks through denying the use of servers or refusing to process financial payments such as donations. A series of revelations in 2013 indicated that some high tech companies were actively working with US intelligence services to subvert internet privacy (Greenwald et al., 2013). For example, Microsoft was accused of working with the US National Security Agency (NSA) to facilitate its monitoring of web chats on Microsoft's Outlook.com portal and facilitated access to its cloud storage service SkyDrive. It has been further alleged that the NSA had direct access to the systems of several major internet companies such as Skype, Apple, Google, Yahoo and Facebook. The NSA is also rumoured to have worked with major high tech companies to place 'back doors' in their electronic systems to allow easy access to security services. This has allowed NSA in the US and GCHQ in the UK to gain access to emails, banking and medical records on a vast scale.

The close relationship between internet companies and security services poses a challenge for these corporations. On one hand they are often legally required to cooperate with intelligence services; on the other, their cooperation with these services places their businesses at risk if consumers lose faith in the security of their communications. Foreign companies and customers may be reluctant to use US companies if they are aware of the extent to which their data is shared with US intelligence agencies.

Another way that high tech companies can assist governments to suppress political dissent is through selling their products to state agencies interested in monitoring or eliminating online dissent and activism. The Citizenship Lab at the University of Toronto has reported on the use of products made by a California company, Blue Coat Systems (Markoff, 2013). Blue Coat's products can be used to filter content and detect particular web applications. The Canadian study revealed that Blue Coat systems were being used in Syria, several other Arab states, China, Indonesia, Venezuela and a number of other states with poor human rights records.

The flip side of companies working for intelligence agencies is state intelligence agencies working on behalf of or against particular corporate interests. In some cases states are prepared to defend their corporations against attacks from other corporations or states while in other cases they act to support a particular economic model (see Box 14.7). In October 2012, speaking to the Business Executives for National Security, the US Secretary of Defense announced that the government would defend US private sector computers against cyber attacks of foreign powers (Nakashima, 2012). This came in the wake of a cyber attack against Saudi Arabian oil company Aramco in which a virus replaced crucial files with a picture of a burning US flag. In other cases it is feared that state-sanctioned hackers are attacking foreign corporate interests. For example, in May 2014 the US government filed an indictment against a group of Chinese military hackers alleging that they had attacked Westinghouse Electric, SolarWorld, US Steel, Allegheny Technologies and the US Service Workers (Arthur, 2014). The charges added credence to private sector reports that China-based hackers had attacked a series of iron, steel, chemical, high technology and media companies dating back to 2006. A stranger example occurred in December 2014 when the North Korean government was accused of hacking Sony in retaliation for filming a comedy (*The Interview*) that made fun of an assassination attempt on North Korea's leader.

The third side of this issue is corporations engaged in espionage against civil society groups. Many corporations have chief intelligence officers tasked with identifying threats to the corporation, including threats from non-profit civil society groups. Beyond using public sources to accumulate intelligence, corporations may hire ex-military or intelligence service members to investigate or infiltrate civil society groups. Activities that have been documented include computer hacking, wiretapping, voicemail hacking, theft of computers, disinformation campaigns and investigating activists' private lives. Consulting companies hired by the US Chamber of Commerce to combat the non-profit Chamber Watch suggested a wide range of strategies and a proposed budget of $2 million a month to combat that public interest group monitoring the Chamber's activities (Ruskin, 2013). Another example of such activity is Burger King's infiltration of the Student/Farmerworker Alliance which had been lobbying for a

---

Box 14.7 Canadian intelligence services and the resource economy

Canada offers another example of a country where corporate and state interests seem to have become fused, at least in the natural resource sector. In the autumn of 2013 it was revealed that Canada's electronic spies, the Communications Security Establishment Canada (CSEC), had been involved in monitoring Brazil's Ministry of Mining and Energy. They were able to access the Ministry's email, electronic and telephone communications. The Canadian government also convenes regular meetings bringing together federal agencies, spy and police forces with corporate officials to review threats to energy infrastructure, challenges by environmental groups to energy projects, and economic and corporate espionage (Lukas and Groves, 2013). Even the domestic police force seems bent to service the natural resource sector with the Royal Canadian Mounted Police declaring the existence of a radical 'anti-petroleum' movement threatening the Canadian natural resources development strategy (McCarthy, 2015).

raise for migrant farm workers harvesting tomatoes bound for Burger King (Schlosser, 2008).

By their nature corporate espionage activities take place behind a curtain of secrecy and it is difficult to gauge their prevalence and extent. However, it is clear that corporations and state intelligence agencies do interact to monitor the activities of other corporations, states and civil societies. It is a significant element of the covert or underside of the global political economy.

Disease, pandemics and security

The detection and control of pandemics and infectious diseases that might lead to pandemics have emerged as important security issues, with implications for traditional security and human security concerns. The link between health and security has been made by scholars from the human security (Curley and Thomas, 2004) and traditional security paradigms (Peterson, 2002/3). Both sets of scholars have focused on the risks posed by new diseases such as HIV/AIDS, emerging infections like severe acute respiratory syndrome (SARS) or re-emerging diseases such as drug-resistant tuberculosis or malaria.

Health is an intrinsic aspect of most definitions of human security because health is a critical component of wellbeing and poor health threatens the quality of life an individual may attain. Brower and Chalk (2003, pp. 7–10) discuss six ways in which the international transmission of disease poses a threat to human security:

1 Disease is a direct threat to human life.
2 Disease can erode a state's legitimacy by undermining public confidence if state authorities fail to respond adequately to outbreaks of disease or pandemics.
3 Disease can threaten a state's economic capacity through its impact on public health spending and the productivity of the workforce.
4 Disease can negatively impact a state's 'social order, functioning and psyche' (Brower and Chalk, 2003, p. 9).
5 Infectious diseases can promote regional volatility and instability through mass population movements, economic dislocation and defence underpreparedness.
6 Through biowarfare or bioterrorism, diseases can become a security threat.

Instead of viewing health as a human security problem, some scholars have demonstrated the compatibility of health with traditional approaches to security. From this perspective, infectious diseases are a national security issue. Infectious diseases can affect national security either directly or indirectly. Since health is a key component of national power, infectious diseases may undermine national power and hence alter the balance of power or contribute to economic, social and political instability. Moreover, infectious diseases may contribute to or exacerbate inter-state conflicts. Infectious diseases can also play a direct role in military conflict through the release of biological warfare (Peterson, 2002/3). Price-Smith (2009) combines both human security and traditional perspectives in his approach to the security implications of infectious disease. He argues that there are three crucial linkages between disease and national security: disease may present a direct threat to state security by undermining state capacity; it has the potential to foster economic and political discord; and warfare gives rise to the proliferation of infectious disease.

Whether a traditional or human security perspective is adopted, scholars locate the newfound interest in the security dimensions of health in the post-Cold War security structure. The end of the Cold War was pivotal in creating more open borders and enhancing the movement of people. But the forces of globalization – specifically trade and commerce, and travel and tourism – have contributed to the rapid spread of infectious diseases (Cecchine and Moore, 2006). For example, the rapid movement of the SARS virus in 2003 from China and Southeast Asia was facilitated by air travel. In a globalized world, national borders are incapable of fully securing individuals within the nation-state from the transnational spread of infectious disease. While it may be argued that state borders have never been an effective barrier against the spread of disease, increased interdependence and the resultant mass movement of people have increased the risk of the spread of disease across national borders.

Much of the literature on the security implications of diseases focuses on infectious diseases rather than on non-contagious diseases, since it is easier to present such diseases as a threat. Thus, variants of the influenza virus have been particularly susceptible to this treatment. Both H5N1 (avian flu) and H1N1 (swine flu) have captured media attention around the world and governments have been forced to respond to these diseases as security threats. Clearly, not all infectious diseases pose a security concern but there is sufficient evidence concerning the security implications of diseases and epidemics to suggest their impact on national, regional and international security. Perhaps the disease that has been the subject of the greatest attention from academics and policy makers is HIV/AIDS (human immunodeficiency virus/acquired immunodeficiency syndrome) (see Box 14.8).

The security implications of disease and the problems created for international cooperation were highlighted by the SARS crisis of 2003. In late 2002, SARS broke out in China and created a national health emergency as well as a global health crisis. The Chinese government failed to deal adequately with the crisis. The disease was first notified to the Chinese Ministry of Health in January 2003 but the government failed to notify the WHO. When cases were reported in late February and early March in Canada, Singapore, Thailand and Vietnam, the Chinese government remained silent. China was finally forced to admit the scale of the crisis as the result of international pressure, especially the activities of the WHO. The spread of the virus not only threatened the health of individuals in Southeast Asia; it also had detrimental impacts on the stability

and prosperity of these countries. This episode demonstrated the security implications of disease. As two commentators noted: 'the impact of SARS quickly moved beyond a health issue, to become a political and economic threat as well as a major foreign policy challenge' (Curley and Thomas, 2004, p. 23).

In 2014 an Ebola outbreak in West Africa once again raised the issue of global security and the political economy of health. The WHO was slow to respond to the epidemic, leaving the task to overwhelmed NGOs such as Médecins Sans Frontières. Europeans and Americans expressed concern as cases threatened to move into their territory. One of the reasons why the disease proved to be so threatening is that the public health systems at the centre of the disease in Sierra Leone, Guinea and Liberia had been devastated by years of structural adjustment. IMF programs demanded the cutting of government services, reduction of government workers, salaries and decentralization of healthcare systems. When Ebola arrived, the local health-systems were too weak to adequately respond (Kentikelenis et al., 2015). The IMF reacted to Ebola by promising additional funding, but the damage had been done.

For only the second time in its history, the United Nations Security Council considered a public health

---

Box 14.8 The securitization of HIV/AIDS

In 2001, HIV/AIDS expanded from a health issue to also being a security issue when the UN General Assembly and the UN Security Council held special sessions on the pandemic. It was the first time in history that a health issue had been placed on the agenda of the Security Council. The speech of James Wolfensohn, then World Bank president, to the UN Security Council encapsulates the securitization of HIV/AIDS. He informed delegates:

> Many of us used to think of AIDS as a health issue. We were wrong. AIDS can no longer be confined to the health or social sector portfolios. Across Africa, AIDS is turning back the clock on development. Nothing we have seen is a greater challenge to the peace and stabilities of African societies than the epidemic of AIDS … We face a major development crisis, and more than that a security crisis. For without economic and social hope we will not have peace, and AIDS surely undermines both.
>
> (Cited in Brower and Chalk, 2003, p. 31)

Singer (2002) presents a conventional and alarming interpretation of HIV/AIDS as a security threat. He posits a number of security implications of AIDS, including:

▶ a direct weakening of the military
▶ increased state vulnerability as the result of declining state capacity
▶ state failure
▶ an upsurge in new combatants and renewed civil conflict
▶ a hollowing out of the capacity of international peacekeepers.

issue on its agenda. At the conclusion of its discussion the link between infectious disease and security was clearly expressed in UN Security Resolution 2177 (18 September 2014). The resolution recognized that the Ebola crisis was 'undermining the stability of the most affected countries concerned and, unless contained, may lead to further instances of civil unrest, social tensions and a deterioration of the political and security climate'. Further, the resolution determined 'that the unprecedented extent of the Ebola outbreak in Africa constitutes a threat to international peace and security' (United Nations, 2014c).

The securitizing of health can bring a higher profile to the problems of disease and pandemic. However, this process also carries risks. If the security threat is perceived in traditional terms, there is the possibility that responses will also be traditional. Military responses may edge out public health responses. Patients could become targets, compassion replaced by violence.

CONCLUSION

Chapter 1 noted how various disciplines have tended to evolve without much reference to developments in other fields. Some approaches to security and international political economy have been equally insular. Despite this, many theoretical approaches have noted the intersection of security and economic issues. At the broadest level, the international security system limits the free exchange of goods and services because of inter- and intra-state conflict. Political economy developments also influence the relative security of various national and subnational populations. The introduction of new concepts of security, such as human security, has encouraged analysts to think about the multiple threats to individuals. Issues of disease, hunger and environmental degradation (see Chapter 12) pose equally serious physical and psychological threats to human survival as direct physical violence. In these areas, political economy variables, which influence the distribution of food, the manufacture of vaccines and the exploitation of the environment, have a clear impact on human security.

Consideration of security and political economy leads us to another topic central to the interests of political scientists and international relations specialists – governance. In previous chapters, we have examined how rules are made and how governance is exercised over the complex global economic activity. This is the focus of Chapter 15.

Further Reading

The strategic studies implications of some key political economists is considered in Edward Mead Earle's 'Adam Smith, Alexander Hamilton, Fredrich List: The Economic Foundations of Military Power' and Sigmund Neumann and Mark von Hagen's 'Engels and Marx on Revolution, War and the Army in Society', both in Peter Paret (ed.) *Makers of Modern Strategy: From Machiavelli to the Nuclear Age* ([1943]1986), pp. 217–61, 262–80. Norman Ripsman and Peter Dombrowski outline how political economy influences international security in *Guns and Butter: The Political Economy of International Security* (2005). The human security concept was initially publicized by the UNDP's 1994 *Human Development Report: New Dimensions of Human Security*. It is available at http://hdr.undp.org/en/ reports/global/hdr1994/. See UNODC's *The Globalization of Crime: A Transnational Organized Crime Threat Assessment* (2005) for an excellent introduction to the breadth and scope of transnational crime. It is available at http://www.unodc.org/documents/data-and-analysis/tocta/TOCTA_Report_2010_low_res.pdf.

Governing the Global Political Economy

The subject of this chapter is global governance. While previous chapters of the book have given some attention to global governance, this chapter explores the concept in greater detail. Specific attention is given to understandings of governance, multiple levels of governance, contemporary issues facing the global political economy and the attendant challenges ahead for global managers and citizens. First, we explore the term 'global governance'. We then debate the role of the state in global governance. The major developments we highlight are the proliferation of governance levels and actors. The key governance challenges facing the global political economy are development and economic growth, equality and justice, and democracy and regulation. Overall, we paint a picture of an increasingly globalized world, with states, firms and citizens struggling to create, manage and distribute wealth and power (O'Brien, 2003).

DEFINITIONS

The term 'global governance', like that of globalization, is also subject to a variety of meanings. It has been used in an analytical sense to refer to an approach to world politics distinct from traditional IR theorizing, with its focus on the activities of states, and also in a normative manner to refer to a positive political project in world politics (Dingwerth and Pattberg, 2006). Some writers contend that global governance constitutes a specific discourse of international politics whose function is to legitimize specific liberal solutions to practical problems (Brand, 2005).

By 'global governance', we mean the overarching system that regulates human affairs on a worldwide basis. Another term would be the system of 'world order' (Cox and Sinclair, 1996). The mechanisms and rules of global governance are created by the actions and agreements of key actors in the global system. The primary political actor is the state, but other actors such as corporations and civic associations can also influence and participate in global governance. A striking feature of global governance in the past 50 years has been the increasing role played by international (that is, inter-state) organizations in facilitating governance. More recent developments have been the growing role of corporations and the mobilization of citizens through civic associations.

THEORETICAL PERSPECTIVES: WHITHER THE STATE?

The growth of the global political economy has sparked intense debate about the future of the state. Are global flows of finance and trade overwhelming the autonomy of states? Are states increasingly powerless or do they retain the ability to shape the world to benefit their citizens? In various chapters in this book we have suggested that states vary in their nature over time and between places. For example, Chapter 5, on the 20th century, discussed the evolution of the welfare state into a competition state. It argued that states were increasingly positioning their citizens for global competition rather than ensuring their welfare on a universal basis. We also charted the role of offshore finance and regulation in transforming the state. In a similar manner, Chapter 11, on development, noted the change from national capitalism to more neoliberal forms of state. In Chapters 6, 7 and 8, on trade, production and finance, we highlighted the various constraints and policy options available to states in the South and North. We have stressed the different possibilities open to stronger and weaker states. Chapter 14, on security, highlighted the growth of the national security state and charted its transformations in the post-Cold War security structure.

Despite these varieties in state form, the state as an institution retains a pivotal role in creating and maintaining governance in the global system because of the centrality of the connection between law and political authority. The state is the central legal actor and primary representative of individuals in the international system. Agreements binding the population of a country can only be made by a state. While its representative function is often imperfect, the state is the only institution that can make a legitimate claim to represent all the people within its territory. Attempts to reform global governance must work through the state system.

Not all states are equally important in the process of global governance. The most developed and wealthy states are the most significant because they can veto changes or coerce other states to follow particular sets of policies. Thus, the US is a central actor because of its wealth and power. Changes in US domestic politics can have a significant influence on the processes of global governance. For example, the election of a Republican

to the US presidency in 2000 made international agreement to slow climate change much more difficult. President George W. Bush had much closer ties to the oil industry than his Democratic predecessor and successor. Many suggestions for slowing global warming threatened the profits of US oil companies and were not welcomed by the Republican president. Since the US is one of the world's largest producers of the pollutants that contribute to global warming, a treaty without its participation is not very effective. Barack Obama, Bush's successor, has moved in a different direction and directly engaged the world on climate change issues. However, a US Congress hostile to climate change action continues to make it difficult to take concrete action. In a similar way, on different issues, the position of the EU and its member states is crucial to securing or blocking changes in global regulation.

Other states in the system are important for different reasons. The early 21st century has seen the emergence of a number of developing countries taking on a leadership role (see section on BRICS below). For example, China's views carry increasing weight because of the size of its population relative to other countries and its recent modernization. China's population is estimated to be 1.3 billion of the global total of 7 billion. In military terms, it is a force to be considered because of its large army and nuclear weapons. In economic terms, the Chinese state controls access to what is potentially the largest market when it reaches a sufficient stage of development. China is also cash rich, having accumulated millions of dollars through its export industry. Thus, corporations and states tread more lightly when they deal with China than with small, less powerful states. It is much easier to exert pressure on a small country such as Nicaragua with respect to universal human rights than on China.

Another example of a developing state whose views can carry some weight is South Africa. The South African state has a great deal of legitimacy to speak on behalf of oppressed people in Africa and the developing world because of its struggle to overthrow apartheid. In addition, because South Africa is a democratic state, its views carry more weight in global discussions than the views of a similar-sized authoritarian state. An interesting example of the role that the South African state played in challenging the existing form of global governance was its campaign to challenge the patent protection afforded to multinational drug companies that produce anti-AIDS drugs. The South Africans made a moral argument for violating the patent protection that is enshrined in the WTO.

Despite the importance of the state to global governance, some groups have moved away from concentrating all their efforts on influencing state power. The major explanation for this is that the ability of the state to offer protection from the harmful aspects of globalization seems to have been reduced. The populations of the weakest states in the developing world have been at the mercy of Western states and large corporations for many years. Recently, however, it appears that even advanced industrialized states seem less able to protect their citizens from increasing global competition. This has been described by one observer as the state shifting its role from providing welfare for its citizens to preparing the population for increased competition (Cerny, 2000). The state does not shrink or disappear, but changes its role. The process of globalization is seen to have made it more difficult to support the traditional welfare state, which cushioned the effects of competition (Mishra, 1999).

The view that the state is losing power has been widely challenged. Some have suggested that globalization is exaggerated, by arguing that the degree of internationalization as measured by percentages of trade and investment flows has precedents in the early 1900s (Hirst and Thompson, 1996). Citing the persistent differences between North American, European and Asian models of capitalism, students of comparative politics dispute that there has been a movement to policy convergence (Garrett, 2000). These scholars deny that the state is weaker or is unable to protect its citizens. They suggest that if political forces advocating social protection gather the political will and organize themselves properly, the government can be pointed in the direction of social protection. From this perspective, globalization has very little to do with increasing inequality or decreasing social protection.

Controversies about the relative importance of the state continue to rage and observable trends point in different directions. On one side, it is possible to see that most states around the world, in stark contrast to the 1970s, actively seek multinational investment. This indicates that, in relative terms, corporations have become more important to states. Second, in contrast to earlier decades, states seem more intent on furnishing those companies with an attractive environment than with regulating their activity. Some have referred to states engaging in 'beauty contests' in an effort to attract foreign investment (Palan and Abbott, 2005). Of course, the balance of power between any particular state and any particular firm will vary depending on their position in the global economy. On the other side, the financial crisis of 2008–9 saw a resurgence in state regulation as governments bailed out the financial industry and considered imposing new regulations on global finance. Suddenly, global finance looked very weak and states looked strong. Once again, however, it is important to note that only particular states were able to reassert authority, while many poor and weak states were not.

MAJOR DEVELOPMENTS

One of the most important issues facing students of, and practitioners within, the global political economy is the management of change. In other words, what determines changes in the rules under which a particular form of global governance operates? For example, how do actors with a commitment to environmentalism shift the system in a direction that puts a higher emphasis on environmental protection? The relatively brief history of world orders or global governance warns against expecting rapid change and highlights the link between crisis and changes in governance. Dramatic transformations in governing relations between states have tended to follow large-scale wars. For example, in the aftermath of the Napoleonic Wars at the beginning of the 19th century, the European state system was managed by the Concert of Europe. The next large change in organizing the international system followed the terrible destruction of the First World War. The League of Nations and a number of other international organizations and treaties were created to try to improve governance and maintain peace. The Second World War marked the end of that system and ushered in a new world order in 1945. Many of today's international organizations such as the UN, the IMF, the World Bank and NATO date back to this era. The end of the Cold War between the US and the Soviet Union in 1989 resulted in the strengthening of existing Western institutions rather than the creation of a new form of international organization.

Large-scale changes in reforming or replacing existing global governance structures are unlikely unless there is a devastating crisis in the international system. With the relatively peaceful end to the Cold War, the chances are low that a new world war will erupt in the near future to cause major change in global governance. It is more likely that wholesale change would come about as a result of a severe financial crisis that plunged the world into economic depression. Financial collapse would force decision makers to change the existing system or replace it with a new set of rules. Since such a collapse would impoverish millions and probably lead to violent conflict within and between states, it is not a method of changing global governance that many people would choose. Such a scenario is only attractive to those who have nothing to gain from the existing system. Some feared that the financial crisis in the US in 2008 might be just such an event. The crisis has not led to wholesale changes in the governance architecture. The G20 has taken the lead in responding to the global economic crisis and its efforts to date signal piecemeal rather than radical reform of the international financial system. While there has been intense debate concerning the failure of regulation and the loopholes in financial management that triggered the crisis, proposed reforms do not indicate major changes to governance arrangements.

In the absence of change on a grand and destructive scale, we must look to particular developments in governance institutions and particular actors to foster innovations that might gradually guide the globalization process in a more positive direction. Here, we will highlight the proliferation of new governance arenas and actors that are shaping global governance.

Proliferation of governance levels

A striking feature of governance in the global political economy is the numerous levels on which it takes place. While the state remains important, as outlined above, governance is taking place on a number of other levels. Foremost among these are governance at the subnational, regional and global levels. Some elements of governance have also shifted away from the state into the private/corporate realm, but this will be dealt with in the following subsection. The term 'multilevel governance' helps us to think about the vertical power relationships, while terms such as 'international regimes' get us to focus on the relationships at the international level.

'Multilevel governance' is a term that emerged from studies of the EU (Marks et al., 1996). It posits that authority and policy-making in Europe are shared across subnational, national and supranational levels. National governments must be mindful of EU treaties and the operations of EU institutions. For example, the European Commission has the power to roll back national subsidy or state aid programmes and members of the eurozone must live with the monetary policy of the European Central Bank. National governments are also sensitive to the demands and interests of subfederal governments, regions and cities (see Box 15.1). In studies of urban politics, multilevel governance is taken even closer to the local level as studies can examine governing arrangements at the inter-urban, city and even neighbourhood levels (Kearns and Forrest, 2000).

The focus of multilevel governance is the vertical relationship of power and politics running up and down between different levels. Are national states losing power to regional integration projects such as the EU or the NAFTA? Conversely, are national states losing influence in relationship to subnational levels such as regional or provincial governments? Central to these studies is the notion that, even though governance is taking place across a number of levels, the people involved are bounded by some form of community. Thus, although there are many political differences in the EU and problems negotiating common policies, there is a sense of a common European community and a common set of institutions, whether that is the European parliament or the euro.

As regional trade and economic groupings have multiplied in most parts of the world, the issue of multilevel governance has become more pressing (Boas et al., 2005; Coleman and Underhill, 1998). How is it possible to coordinate policies across subnational, state and regional levels? A related problem is: How do these regions relate to global governance? Are regions compatible with global rules? This issue is most visible in reconciling trade rules. An example of this was the case of hormone-treated beef cited in Chapter 6. A European view of appropriate risk clashed with an American view of the supremacy of science. To take another example, the American desire for formal institutions in regional agreements runs counter to Asian preferences for informal arrangements and minimal institutions. Thus, the problems of multilevel governance can be extended up past the regional level to international institutions such as the WTO.

At the international level, many approaches focus on world or international organizations and their ability to

Box 15.1 Cities in the global economy

IPE usually focuses on states, but cities are also significant economic actors on the global stage. While the process of economic globalization has geographically dispersed many economic functions, some activities such as specialized professional services, financial services, high-level management and corporate head offices have become concentrated in leading 'global cities' (Sassen, 2006). Key international financial and business centres include New York, London, Tokyo, Paris, Frankfurt, Chicago, Zurich, Amsterdam, Sydney, Toronto and Hong Kong. These cities have been joined by key centres in developing countries, such as Seoul, Singapore, São Paulo, Mexico City, Mumbai, Buenos Aires, Shanghai and Beijing. Surrounding the well-paid, internationally connected professionals living in highly priced apartments is an army of low-paid service workers cleaning buildings, working in retail, running the transportation services, preparing food and taking care of domestic tasks. The wealth generated in these cities can unbalance national economies and politics as the cities exert increasing influence. Conflicts can emerge between city elites and other residents or between the interests of the city and the rest of the national economy. For example, house prices in global cities can rise so high that low-wage workers must commute hours to work. Alternatively, the finance industry of a global city may take precedence over manufacturing or agriculture in other parts of the economy.

address global problems (Hewson and Sinclair, 1999). International organizations are often best placed to address collective action problems at the global level. Greater international cooperation is vital to tackle the range of problems identified in this chapter. These organizations are significant because they provide both the forum for negotiating globalization rules and the mechanisms for monitoring and enforcing rules.

In the field of IR, the governance arrangements put in place by states in particular issue areas are often referred to as 'regimes'. Regimes are 'implicit or explicit principles, norms, rules and decision-making procedures around which actors' expectations converge in a given area of international relations' (Krasner, 1983, p. 2). Regimes are ideas and rules about how states should behave. A vast literature explains the conditions under which regimes are created, maintained and destroyed. Most approaches see regimes as being created through state-to-state negotiations, with states acting as self-interested, goal-seeking actors pursuing the maximization of individual utility (Hasenclever et al., 1997). In other words, states create regimes because they believe that a regular pattern of cooperation will bring them benefits. In many cases, states participate in regimes that are not ideal because the cost of conflict outside the regime is greater than the bad deal they get inside the regime (Keohane, 1984). For example, developing states may object to many aspects of the trade regime, but they prefer to be members than to operate outside the main trading institution.

We can identify a number of ways through which regimes influence behaviour. Some regimes have a strong legal framework that compels states to obey rules by the threat of economic sanctions. The WTO is an excellent example. It has the Dispute Settlement Body, which adjudicates trade conflicts based on the rules contained in the agreements that created the WTO. Countries in violation of the rules must change their policies or face economic sanctions from the states they have injured. Even powerful states obey these rules because they have an interest in a predictable system of rules that fosters increased trade and economic activity. The WTO puts the value of free trade above other goals, leading to conflict with those people who feel that free trade undermines environmental standards. In this case, liberal values and market mechanisms are privileged over other approaches. Environmental protection must take place in the context of free trade.

The distribution of money and provision of credit can also be used to foster compliance with particular rules. This is the approach used by the World Bank and the IMF. These organizations lend money to states that are in need of funds to weather an economic crisis or to assist in long-term development strategies. The loans are usually conditional on the recipients undertaking certain policies. These policies have varied over time, but usually ask states to liberalize their economies so that they earn money to pay back the loans. Institutions that disperse money are influenced by their largest financial contributors. In the case of the World Bank and the IMF, voting rights are distributed in proportion to the financial contributions of member states. At the IMF, the G7, which represents just over 700 million people, controls 43 per cent of the votes. In contrast, the five largest least developed countries, with a population of about three billion people, control only 8.7 per cent of IMF votes (see Table 15.1). Because the US is the largest contributor to the IMF and the World Bank, it has the largest share of votes and influence. Thus, policies that the US advocates are the most likely to be spread through this channel of influence in the global governance process. For example, IMF loans to South Korea during the East Asian financial crisis stipulated that South Korea open up its manufacturing and financial industries to foreign investors, many of whom were from the US.

At other times, states' behaviour can be influenced by appeals to morality. This is the approach used by the ILO. The ILO conducts research on labour issues and highlights the abuse of workers' rights through reports and investigations. It facilitates negotiations between states to set minimum standards for countries to follow and publicizes failure to comply with the standards. The organization's work is based on the belief that states may change their behaviour if they face international condemnation. Although the ILO has been operating for almost 100 years, its ability to influence states' behaviour is limited by its lack of enforcement measures. Many states ignore its reports and advice.

Expertise can also be used to convince actors that it is in their best interests to behave in a particular way. For example, organizations such as the OECD and the IMF issue reports on the economic policy of particular states and suggest how they should adapt to globalization. Reports do not order states to change their policies, but they advise that a particular change will help foster economic growth. These institutions tend to offer liberal approaches to economic restructuring and until very recently were unlikely to advocate policies that might protect society by reducing the influence of unregulated markets.

A final element that influences behaviour is the structure of the global system itself. This is known as 'structural power'. Drawing on theories of the privileged power position of business in a national context, Gill and Law (1993) argue that the internationalization of economic activity has increased the direct and indirect power of business in relationship to the state. The nature of the system makes particular types of behaviour more likely and punishes some forms of behaviour more harshly than others. For example, states must pay attention to the desires of international investors if they want to attract capital for investment or keep their national wealth and businesses from fleeing to other locations. This encourages state leaders to move their economies in a more liberal direction.

It is important to note that, in the system of global governance, the institutions that are tasked with liberalizing the global economy and increasing the role of the market are more influential than those seeking to protect society from economic failures. On the market liberalization side, the IMF and the World Bank are able to use the provision of finance for influence and the WTO has its important Dispute Settlement Body. However, the ILO, which protects labour standards, is confined to an advocacy role. Other institutions with social mandates, such as UNICEF, which assists poor children, and the WHO, must work within the economic policies advocated by the liberal institutions. The structure of governance seems to favour the increasing power of the market at the expense of social values. Returning to Polanyi's (1957) view of the dislocating effects of the liberal market, this is likely to lead to social turbulence and conflict over the rules of global governance.

Table 15.1 **IMF voting rights versus share of world population**

Country	IMF votes (%)	World population (%)
United States	16.74	4.5
Japan	6.23	1.8
Germany	5.81	1.1
France	4.29	0.9
United Kingdom	4.29	0.9
Italy	3.16	0.8
Canada	2.56	0.5
G7 total	43.08	10.5
China	3.81	19.2
India	2.34	17.5
Brazil	1.72	2.8
Indonesia	0.85	3.5
Nigeria	0.72	2.5
Five LDCs total	9.44	45.5

Source: IMF (2015); Worldometers (2015)

Proliferation of actors

In addition to the state and inter-state agreements, two other actors and realms of activity have become prominent in discussion of global political economy governance: the corporation and global civil society.

In the early 1990s, some observers argued that the growing power of TNCs in relation to the state necessitated a revision of international relations and international business theory. Drawing on a study of investment relations in Brazil, Malaysia and Kenya, Stopford and Strange (1991) argued that state–firm and even firm–firm bargaining was becoming more important to the international system. States are increasingly interested in attracting foreign investment and firms are increasingly capable of influencing government investment policy. Thus, a key feature of how rules are created and enforced in the global economy is the negotiation conducted between states and firms.

A good example of how corporations can influence global governance is provided by the insertion of intellectual property rights (IPR) into the WTO. IPR include things such as copyright protection for books and music, as well as patent protection for inventions and scientific discoveries. They do not really fall under the umbrella of free trade because their enforcement does not increase the flow of goods between states. However, in the 1980s, many Western corporations in industries such as pharmaceuticals, computer software, films and music became concerned that competitors were copying their products. An association of leading US TNCs, including Du Pont, General Electric, IBM and Monsanto, convinced the US government that IPR should be protected in trade agreements. Eventually, the corporations were able to have rules that they largely drafted inserted into the WTO (Sell, 1999; Sell and Prakash, 2004). These are some of the rules that the government of South Africa fought against in an attempt to provide affordable drugs to combat the large numbers of deaths from AIDS in southern Africa (Lanoszka, 2003; Thomas, 2002).

In addition to the trend of increasing corporate influence over state policy makers, one can also point to the rise of private authority. Private authority exists where firms exercise decision-making power over a particular issue area and this activity is viewed as legitimate. Cutler et al. (1999) have identified six mechanisms for the exercise of private authority: industry norms; coordination service firms, for example bond rating; production alliances; cartels; business associations; and private regimes. They argue that private firms are increasingly exercising authority in particular issue areas in the global economy. Studies of the telecommunications industry, insurance business, accountancy and cartels support the notion of private authority (Strange, 1996). A recent study of the relationship between private actors and the UN system has argued that increased private sector participation in the multilateral system is having varied but significant impacts on the ways these institutions function (Bull et al., 2004).

It is important to note that recognizing the role and significance of corporate activity does not imply that state power is unimportant or that all corporations behave in the same way. One can acknowledge the role of corporate activity in global governance, while agreeing with Doremus et al. (1998), who argue that there are differences in behaviour between corporations from different states, and that states often support the behaviour of corporations headquartered in their territory. Corporations have an interest in influencing the terms of global governance, even if their particular interests are not identical.

In their pursuit of profits, corporations will attempt to influence the structures of global governance. Not all corporations will have the same immediate goals or follow the same tactics. Indeed, business conflict theory (Skidmore-Hess, 1996) advises us to expect clashes of interest between corporations in international as well as domestic realms. Corporations from particular states or sectors may demonstrate distinctive characteristics. Firms that are internationally competitive will have different preferences from those that are not internationally competitive. Despite or because of these differences, corporations will attempt to shape governance structures by influencing state, international organization, corporate and civil society behaviour. The role of the corporation in international relations has grown to such an extent that attempts to understand or influence global governance must take the role of corporations into account.

In addition to resource-rich corporations, voluntary citizen organizations operating in global civil society are playing an increasing role in influencing the principles of global governance (Khagram et al., 2002). Indeed, in the 1980s and 90s, prominent civic actors played the role of unofficial opposition to global governance agencies and inter-state agreements. They stressed an agenda that puts citizen autonomy and security at the centre of governance questions. Peace groups have opposed particular weapons systems and military strategies. The campaign to ban the production and use of landmines is a prime example. Development, women's, environmental and labour groups have opposed the dominance of liberal policies emanating from international economic institutions. Citizen action across state borders to overcome the anti-democratic actions of their own states has been described as 'democratic internationalism' (Gilbert, 1999).

The global civil society sphere is the space where civic actors meet to engage in debate and political activity in an effort to shape the direction of global and national society (Scholte, 2000b). It is primarily composed of voluntary, non-profit associations. To differentiate them from profit-seeking NGOs such as corporations, this chapter uses the term 'civic associations'. The most visible organizations tend to be those working in high-profile areas, such as Greenpeace and Friends of the Earth in the environmental field or Amnesty International in the human rights area. However, there are many other forms of organizations in civil society. For example, the International Trade Union Confederation claims a representative (175 million members) as well as advocacy role. Religious organizations are also very active. In terms of numbers of formal organizations, the bulk of activity takes place in relatively uncontroversial forms such as industry associations and scientific knowledge organizations (medicine, sciences, communications) (Boli and Thomas, 1999, p. 41). Aggregating visible NGOs with less visible local activity, one can point to the emergence of fluid social movements around issues such as development, human rights, peace and women's issues.

The global civil society arena is occupied by several actors that do not share the characteristics of being non-profit, voluntary, equity-seeking civic associations. One prominent group is composed of business associations. These associations seek to create an environment where corporations can maximize profits. A prominent example is the International Chamber of Commerce. In addition to lobbying state and civil society actors, it attempts to foster an environment that encourages self-regulation (Schneider, 2000).

Although it goes against the grain of our understanding of domestic civil society, there are civic associations that lack civility. Civility, or the agreement to manage interaction according to a common set of rules and

without recourse to violence, is a hallmark of domestic notions of civil society. Those who choose not to be bound by such rules are considered to be outside the bounds of civil society. An example would be a criminal organization such as the Mafia (see also Chapter 14 for a discussion of transnational organized crime). In the global system, there is less agreement about common rules and much less enforcement than in most national societies. As a result, there is a greater space for uncivil groups to operate alongside peaceful civic associations. Examples include organized crime, violent ethnic nationalists and terror organizations. They are shunned by the majority of civic associations, but they exist in a similar space. They are a major influence in the illicit side of global political economy – the covert world (see Box 15.2).

While there are many different groups with specific agendas, most politically active groups would describe themselves as pursuing the objectives of equity or social justice. Equity and justice could be sought in respect to gender relations (women's groups), distribution of resources (development groups), quality of life (environmental groups) or human security (human rights). There are, of course, differences between members of civil society, just as there are conflicts between states or corporations. Organized labour is challenged by NGOs claiming to speak on behalf of the informal sector. Women's groups in the developing world have an ambivalent and sometimes conflictual relationship with feminist groups in the developed world. Environmentalists seeking radical changes to the doctrine of economic growth are in conflict with more conservative conservationist groups. Various NGOs claim to speak on behalf of social movements or constituencies, but the plethora of groups and lack of transparency make it difficult to determine the legitimacy of their claims.

Although the precise nature of global civil society is debatable (Amoore and Langley, 2004; Lipschutz, 2005), it is less contentious that transnational civic actors have an influence on world politics and interstate relations. Scholarly attention has tended to focus on human rights, environmental and women's groups' attempts to influence norms and values in the global system (Keck and Sikkink, 1998). International NGOs seeking social transformation operate on a number of levels to influence global governance: they create and activate global networks, participate in multilateral arenas, facilitate inter-state cooperation, and act within states to influence policy and enhance public participation (Alger, 1997). Even in areas often considered to be the sole

---

Box 15.2 The covert world

The covert world is an integral yet often neglected element of the global political economy (Cox, 2002b). It encompasses the illegitimate, illegal and barely visible actions of states, corporations and civic associations. Activities of prime importance include:

▶ the drug trade, which funnels narcotics to customers in the US and Europe
▶ the sex trade, which supplies vulnerable women and children to satisfy the desires of wealthy clients
▶ the smuggling of people to supply undocumented workers to staff construction, health and domestic services at a low cost
▶ the trade in human organs, providing new or better lives for those who can pay
▶ the small arms trade, which floods the world with handguns, rifles and machine guns
▶ the service of mercenaries to provide state or corporate security.

The covert world responds to and complements the overt world of legal global political economy relations:

▶ Chaotic economic relations and the withdrawal of state regulation or service provision provide opportunities for covert activities. The economic collapse of regions such as the former Soviet Union or Mexico provides the people desperate enough to become caught up in human trafficking.
▶ The reduction in the welfare state, combined with an ageing population in Western states, creates a demand for the private provision of health and domestic services at low cost.
▶ The breakdown in state security provides the demand for corporations to hire private security firms and even for states such as the US to privatize elements of warfare in countries such as Iraq.
▶ The globalization of finance and the creation of offshore financial centres provide the opportunities for illegally obtained money to be transported and laundered.
▶ The Cold War and since then the war on terror provide the excuse for security services to engage in illegal activities to fund and run security operations.
▶ Actors in the covert world respond to the incentives of the overt world to provide illegal services, often through the use of violence against defenceless people.

---

domain of states, such as international security, civil society groups can play a role in shaping the agenda and contributing to policy change (Price, 1998).

At the minimum, we can say that civic actors increasingly serve a role as disseminators of information, mobilizers of public opinion, and articulators of dissent and protest. Ignoring their role, as the architects of the Multilateral Agreement on Investment did (Mayne and Picciotto, 1999), is likely to lead to governance breakdown. Civic associations can be instrumental in undermining the legitimacy of international organizations, even as states continue to support them.

If global governance is to push ahead, one would imagine that some form of accommodation is required between the three different types of key actors (state, corporate and civic). For example, a trade regime would have to simultaneously be sensitive to the interests of developing states for increased equity, corporate interests for expansion and profit, and social interests for restricting human and environmental exploitation. This is an enormously complicated task. An example of such an approach is the UN's Global Compact, established in 2000 (Box 15.3).

Rise of the BRICS

In Chapter 3 we discussed the regions of the world economy in the 15th century. At that time China was likely the largest, most advanced and powerful of the world civilizations, but other thriving centres existed in Japan, Southeast Asia, India, Africa, the Americas and

---

Box 15.3 The Global Compact

The Global Compact asks corporations to incorporate ten principles drawn from the Universal Declaration of Human Rights, the ILO's Declaration on Fundamental Principles and Rights at Work, the Rio Declaration on Environment and Development and the United Nations Convention Against Corruption, into their corporate practices. It is designed to identify and disseminate good practices, and asks leaders of some of the world's most prominent corporations to publicly commit themselves to good labour and environmental practices.

It simultaneously addresses the concerns of some corporate, state and civic associations. From a developing country point of view, the initiative is tolerable because it is aimed at influencing the policy of multinational corporations rather than restricting state policy or punishing developing states for poor labour conditions. This is preferable to the WTO enforcing standards because it removes the threat of northern protectionism. From the corporate viewpoint, it is tolerable because regulations are voluntary and allow continued expansion of the global economy and accumulation of profits. They can claim to be good corporate citizens without being bound by compulsory regulation. For some civic actors, it represents a limited advance in enshrining some principles of social protection. It is a small step that might lead to more binding forms of regulation. Others reject this approach, claiming the Global Compact threatens the integrity of the UN as corporations attempt to 'bluewash' their record by association with the UN (Transnational Resource and Action Center, 2000).

This example of the Global Compact is informative for our efforts to understand global governance reform for three reasons. First, it illustrates that the concerns of civic actors about the damaging aspects of globalization are being taken seriously by other actors in the system. The UN is responding to public unease about the costs of globalization. Second, it highlights the failure of existing global governance arrangements. Existing global governance mechanisms seem unable to improve social standards. Finally, the Global Compact illustrates just how difficult it is to create new governance arrangements. The cost of freer markets is creating more public resistance, but many states and corporations resist instruments that would require better labour, environmental or social standards.

Europe. The 16th–20th centuries witnessed European colonialism and imperialism, with European power amplified by the Industrial Revolution of the 19th century. The US and white settler colonies such as Australia, Canada, New Zealand and South Africa built upon the economic and political advantage flowing from European colonialism and industrialization.

The early 21st century is characterized by a rebalancing of the global economy with increased economic growth and development among a significant number of developing countries. This shift in the balance of global economic power from the United States and Europe to a number of fast-growing and large developing countries is transforming the global economy and structures of global economic governance. While it is debatable whether these developments amount to a paradigm shift (Ingram, 2011, p. 10), it is apparent that in key areas of the global economy such as trade, finance and investment, Western powers can no longer dictate outcomes. The idea that an economic and political counterweight to Western states is emerging is best captured by the concept of the BRICS. The acronym refers to five large developing countries from different parts of the world that have enjoyed some measure of economic success – Brazil, Russia, India, China and South Africa. Initially the BRICs was a term coined by Jim O'Neill of Goldman Sachs in 2001 (O'Neill, 2001) to denote the rapid economic growth of Brazil, Russia, India and China. The transition from BRICs to BRICS was made when the foreign ministers of the BRICs agreed in September 2010 to invite South Africa to the third BRICS summit (Sanya, China) in April 2011. Together the BRICS have a population of almost three billion, or about 40 per cent of the world's population. These economies account for rising shares of global GDP, manufacturing and trade, including a significant expansion of trade among the developing countries (South–South trade). These shifts are driven by growing economic integration and interdependence among economies, particularly through new global production and supply chains that incorporate inputs from many different countries. However, they are a very diverse group. Their economies have different strengths – natural resources in the case of Russia, South Africa and Brazil, information technology and services in India, manufacturing in China and to a lesser extent in Brazil. They have different political systems – authoritarian one-party rule in China, authoritarian rule with the trappings of democracy in Russia, vigorous democracies in India, Brazil and South Africa. They also differ in levels of social provision and inequality (see Table 15.2).

The rise of the BRICS challenges the established structures of global economic governance in two important ways. First, a clash of interests and values arises because rising powers seek both an increased share of the gains from economic exchange and greater control over international decision-making. Demands for a greater voice in the International Monetary Fund and the World Bank arise from their challenge to the dominance of Western powers in these institutions. Moreover, the rise of the BRICS has led to increased contestation over norms. For example, the OECD consensus on development assistance has been challenged by the arrival of new donors (especially China) in ways that have been perceived as disruptive to the existing norms and values and consequently viewed as undermining the system. Secondly, the rise of the BRICS has led to a diffusion of preferences, with many more voices demanding to be heard. This makes reaching agreement in complex international negotiations even more difficult than previously. This has had an impact, for example, on the slow progress of the Doha Round of trade negotiations.

A combination of a shared interest in development and a desire to influence the global economy has led to attempts by the BRICS to institutionalize their relationship through the development of a framework of cooperation. Since 2009 the BRICS have convened an annual high-level summit meeting (see Table 15.3).

These summit meetings and the creation of other fora for consultations are an attempt to demonstrate that the BRICS are not simply a subset of emerging economies but also a group with common interests. In addition to the summit meetings, foreign ministers; finance/economic ministers; agriculture ministers; and trade ministers meet regularly to discuss issues of mutual interest. For example, the BRICS' foreign ministers meet regularly in New York at the United Nations, and the foreign and economic ministers meet at the joint IMF/World Bank annual meetings. A major institutional initiative was taken at the sixth BRICS summit in July 2014 with the Agreement on the New Development Bank (BRICS, 2014b). This decision brought to fruition a process begun at the fourth BRICS summit in 2012 when leaders made a commitment to create a development bank. The Indian banker K. V. Kamath has been named as the head of the bank, which will be headquartered in Shanghai. Furthermore, the BRICS have created a number of second-track diplomatic activities including collection of comparative statistical data and a forum for business leaders.

The strongest challenge to Western leadership comes from China. With its large population, industrialized economy and massive trade surpluses, China is seeking to carve out a new international role. An example of these efforts occurred in October 2014 when representatives from 21 countries gathered in Beijing to launch the $50 billion Asia Infrastructure Investment Bank (AIIB). Funded primarily by China, its purpose is to channel funds to Asian economies for infrastructure development. The institution fills a number of roles. First, it provides an additional source of funds to Asian

Table 15.2 **BRICS key indicators (with US for comparison) 2011–14**

	Population (millions)	GDP (Billions US$)	GDP per capita (Billions US$)	HDI ranking	Gini Coefficient
Brazil	201	2,246	11,171	.774 (high)	52.7
Russia	144	2,096	14,604	.778 (high)	39.7
India	1,211	1,626	1,416	.586 (low)	33.9
China	1,357	9,185	6,768	.719 (medium)	37
South Africa	52	382	7,810	.658 (medium)	65
US	320	16,800	53,042	.914 (very high)	41.1

Source: Data compiled from BRICS, 2014a; UNDP, 2015; World Bank, 2015b; US.gov. A Gini score of zero expresses perfect equality (everyone has the same income) whereas a Gini score of 100 is at the opposite end where one person has all the income.

Table 15.3 **BRICS summits**

Date	City	Country
2009	Yekaterinburg	Russia
2010	Brasilia	Brazil
2011	Sanya	China
2012	New Delhi	India
2013	Durban	South Africa
2014	Fortaleza	Brazil
2015	Ufa	Russia

countries. Second, its lending will have fewer or different conditions than the US-led World Bank or the Japanese-chaired Asian Development Bank (ADB). For example, although the Bank claims it will be 'lean, clean and green' (aiibank.org) and that it is committed to sustainable development, it may be more likely to fund coal energy projects than the World Bank or the ADB. Third, it allows China, which had been frustrated by the operation of the World Bank and the ADB, more influence over development lending.

In April 2015, Chinese authorities announced that 56 other countries had been accepted as prospective founding members of the bank due to begin operation at the end of that year (see AIIB, 2015). Prospective members include the other BRICS states (Brazil, Russia India, South Africa), key Western states such as Australia, France, Germany and the United Kingdom, and all major Asian economies with the exception of Japan. Conspicuously absent is the United States and some of its closest allies (Canada, Japan and Mexico). The fact that China was able to create the bank and that so many states wanted to join despite US resistance is an indicator of the growing influence of China in the global political economy. Alongside the BRICS, decision to start their own development bank, the AIIB is another example of developing countries exerting more influence on the global economy.

TWENTY-FIRST-CENTURY CHALLENGES

Inhabitants of the global political economy face numerous challenges in the 21st century. Here, we outline three pressing governance issues: economic development and growth, equality and justice, democracy and regulation.

Development and growth

World leaders have pledged to eradicate extreme global poverty by 2015. The Millennium Declaration (United Nations, 2000a, para. 11) states that 'we will spare no effort to free our fellow men, women and children from the abject and dehumanising conditions of extreme poverty'. Such an achievement would have been truly staggering and no one seriously believed that this objective would be fulfilled. Nevertheless, as the MDGs are replaced by the SDGs there has been noticeable progress in some areas. It would be overly cynical to refuse to acknowledge that some targets have been met. For example, targets achieved include reducing extreme poverty by half, and the proportion of people having access to improved drinking water has also been met. Furthermore, some targets such as reducing preventable deaths from malaria and tuberculosis are close to being achieved (United Nations, 2014b).

Nevertheless, the fate of most of humanity remains desperate in a world of plenty. In the early 21st century, modern economic growth has still not been dispersed to the majority of the world's seven billion inhabitants. The challenge of economic development became an international issue in the years immediately following the Second World War and was driven by the leaders of newly independent states. In order to maintain their hold on power, political elites were obliged to respond to what was frequently referred to in the 1960s as the 'revolution of rising expectations'. Some 40 years after the UN proclaimed the First Development Decade, prospects remain bleak. One of the major challenges is therefore to meet the development needs of people living in Third World countries. What exactly does this entail at the current historical conjuncture? And what conditions are currently considered necessary to bring this change about?

In Chapter 11, we examined the changing meaning of the concept of development, and showed how the focus has shifted from a concentration on economic growth to a consideration of social factors. In the absence of an agreed definition of development, we can nevertheless suggest certain key features of the concept as it is currently understood. An improvement in material capabilities remains central to most conceptions of development. At the heart of national and international development efforts is the objective of raising material living standards. In effective terms, this translates into the provision of basic necessities such as adequate foodstuffs, clean water, electricity, shelter, improved transportation and better sanitation. It will, in time, lead to the consumption of a wider range of products, but in essence development consists in satisfying basic needs. Of course, clean water, electricity and so on are meaningless outside the context of human beings. Directly linked to the provision of these needs are another set of equally basic services without which people will be un-able to fulfil their life chances. These include education and healthcare. But development has increasingly come to mean the attainment of non-material values. In this respect, we need to think about the ability of people to make their own decisions and to have greater control over their own lives. Amartya Sen (1981), the Indian Nobel laureate, developed his theory of entitlements to show that famine arose not because of the absence of food but in circumstances where those starving lacked the bundle of resources that enabled them to have access to food. Development clearly entails increased participation and the empowerment of marginalized groups.

Early efforts at promoting development were gender blind, but we are aware that one of the main challenges of development in the 21st century will be to ensure that women are fully integrated into national development strategies. For a number of reasons this remains a daunting task. The problems facing women in developing countries remain the subject of analysis and policy prescriptions (Datta and Kornberg, 2002). In the light of the experience of women in advanced industrial countries, the mainstreaming of gender will not in itself lead to equality. Although women in Western developed societies have achieved legal equality, they continue to experience many forms of discrimination and structural exclusion. In terms of formal equality, women in the West have made the most significant gains but the concept of the glass ceiling is well understood, and is an actuality for many women. The 'glass ceiling' refers to the existence of an invisible barrier that limits women from attaining the highest positions in many sectors and firms. Thus, the battle to produce development policies that will support women's livelihoods in the developing world remains a daunting task.

How are the mechanisms of global governance responding to the challenge of economic development? As will have been apparent from previous chapters, the answer to this question depends on the perspective of the observer. We have rehearsed many of these arguments already and so we will not repeat them here. There are a number of identifiable problems of governance that the various perspectives will have to address

and it is to these that we now turn. The first problem we will discuss is that of coordination of various initiatives. There are a number of agencies – national, regional and international – attempting to promote development, but no means of coordinating the various activities that exist at present. Indeed, governmental, intergovernmental and nongovernmental actors can pursue diverse and conflicting objectives within a single country or region. Moreover, no system of allocation exists to ensure that resources are delivered where they are most needed and duplication of effort is avoided.

A second problem also relates to the overall framework in which economic development is promoted. In Chapter 8 we discussed the global financial system and raised problems of regulation. We have seen a number of financial crises, most notably in Mexico, East Asia and Argentina, which have reversed decades of progress. In the absence of reform of the international financial architecture, hard-won gains can be lost within a matter of days. Are global governance mechanisms or national regulations up to the task of curbing the destructive impacts of runaway finance?

A third problem lies in the seeming inability of states to move forward together on the issue of climate change. Post-Kyoto agreement has proved elusive, with some states such as Canada abandoning their international commitments and other states divided along North–South cleavages over targets for reductions and resource transfers. Is it possible to reconcile the economic growth needed for development with measures to safeguard the environment through existing global governance mechanisms? It is proving difficult to curb runaway consumption (see Box 15.4).

National governance has been identified as a crucial issue in the promotion of development and it is now widely accepted that in the absence of effective governance mechanisms there will be limited achievement of development goals. However, at the moment, there is an absence of consensus concerning how good governance is to be pursued. Lectures from developed countries on good governance ring hollow when political motives still play such a large part in the foreign aid policies of leading donor nations.

Equality and justice

Current discussions may lead one to conclude that global inequality is unique to globalization, which it is

Box 15.4 How many planets do we need?

The practice of pursuing a life of high consumption in the North and the desire to replicate these living standards in the South highlight the tension between economic growth, development and environmental sustainability. In 2012, the world's population was engaged in an ecological overshoot of 50 per cent, meaning that it would take the earth a year and a half to replenish all the renewable resources we consume in a year. Alternatively, we can say that the human population uses a planet and a half of resources for one planet. If every country consumed resources at the same rate that Americans do, we would require four planets (WWF, 2012). This suggests that the nature of economic growth and consumption will have to change if a majority of the world's population is to achieve a reasonable level of development and the planet remain healthy.

claimed is wreaking havoc on the development prospects of Third World countries, and creating an underclass in advanced industrial societies. As we have seen in this book, the global economy and international economic exchange have always created winners and losers. To point to the historical existence of a phenomenon is not, however, to claim that it is unimportant. It makes us aware that these issues have been of concern to people for a very long time. At the beginning of the 21st century, the search for equality and justice is as pressing as ever. The 'Human Development Report 1994' noted 'a breathtaking globalization of prosperity side by side with a depressing globalization of poverty' (UNDP, 1994, p. 1), and it is the existence of such glaring disparities that drives part of the agenda for greater social equity.

Governments around the world and international institutions will have to give greater attention to social justice issues in the coming decades. To some extent, the dominance of neoliberal ideology masked issues of equity and justice in its naive faith in market solutions. At the end of the 20th century, these issues began to be taken more seriously and there was evidence of a move away from the Washington Consensus, as discussed in Chapter 13. The search for equality and justice is being driven by the impact of changes in the global economy and the reaction of various groups to these

developments. The process of globalization is leading to increasing inequality within and between nations. In other words, the challenge of inequality is not to be seen simply in terms of differences between states but also in terms of internal inequality. Thomas (2000, p. 11) reminds us that: 'two-thirds of the global population seem to have gained little or nothing from the economic growth that has occurred as a result of globalization to date'. Globalization is affecting income inequality within countries and it has the potential to adversely affect the standards of living of workers in developed countries (Kitching, 2001, p. 266).

If left unchecked, this will give rise to greater tensions and instability within and between nations. One example of the response to increasing inequality within many advanced industrial societies has been the rise of ethno-nationalist parties blaming foreigners for loss of employment and a range of social ills. As governments have cut back on public spending, reduced social safety nets and increased privatization, the poor and disadvantaged in industrial countries have become even more marginalized. Centre-left and centre-right governments have increasingly lost the ability to appeal to large segments of those left behind by economic and technological change. The result has been an increase in support for right-wing, populist parties. Of course, while this phenomenon is occurring in a number of countries, there is nothing automatic about these developments and the success of these parties also depends on domestic circumstances. Moreover, the timing of increased support reflects developments in local politics.

The link between domestic politics, global processes and the search for international solutions is illustrated in the continuing debate over migration in advanced industrial societies. A crisis over asylum seekers erupted in western Europe and Australia in 2000–2, and continues to make political headlines. Indeed, in 2015 the scale of refugees fleeing from Syria turned this simmering issue into a major political crisis for the European Union. The controversy over refugees is partly a consequence of rising inequality between states and rising levels of inequality in affluent societies. There is a perception that among the refugee flows are so-called 'economic migrants' seeking a better life and responding to the lack of opportunity in their home countries. The existence of glaring disparities between rich and poor nations will continue to fuel a trade in people-smuggling and illegal migration. The uncharitable reception of asylum seekers also reflects the attitude of those who feel that they are currently losers in the process of globalization. They resent what they see as scarce resources being spent on foreigners. The solution to this problem does not lie in individual initiatives by single governments but requires international cooperation.

While it is important to remember that shifting patterns of equality are not to be seen in simple North–South terms, the impact of change in the global political economy is experienced differently and much more harshly within the South. While globalization has the potential to create significant benefits for developing countries, these countries will only gain if they institute effective management systems at the domestic level and attain support from international agencies. Unless states find ways to cope with the adjustment and social costs attendant on further integration into the global economy, they will be unable to reap the benefits of globalization (Cook and Kirkpatrick, 1994, p. 64). We can see evidence of major variations among regions in the developing world: while Africa seems to be falling further behind, the countries of Southeast Asia appear to have benefited from their incorporation into the global economy. This is obviously not a straightforward process as the Asian financial crisis demonstrated, but the economies in Asia hardest hit by the crisis are now returning to higher growth rates.

By influencing the location and distribution of wealth and productive power in the world economy, globalization defines and reshapes global patterns of hierarchy and inequality. The challenge for global governance in the 21st century is to devise structures to reverse persistent inequality and widening income disparities that lead to a more unstable and unruly world. The extent to which national and global leaders currently have the understanding and political will to respond creatively to these challenges remains open to doubt. One set of actors within the global political economy has prioritized issues of equality and justice. Many national and transnational civic associations are actively involved in seeking to promote a social justice agenda. We will illustrate this movement by reference to one campaign.

As noted in Chapters 8 and 11, the debt crisis has had a profound impact on the developing world. Efforts to reduce Third World debt provide an example of the struggle currently being waged to address social justice in the context of the global economy. One of the key actors in this struggle is a civic organization known as the Jubilee Debt Campaign (previously known as Jubilee 2000). Members of the Jubilee Debt Campaign base their strategy on the belief that total debt remission is both economically feasible and ethically defensible. As two of their proponents ask: 'How many more deaths are needed before [debt] unsustainability is recognized and treated?' (Dent and Peters, 1998, p. 15). The aim of the Jubilee Debt Campaign is to inject justice into an economic system given over to profit and stability. The coalition has used a diverse range of tactics to grab the attention of world leaders. These range from normal lobbying tactics to mass actions designed to hit the international headlines. For example, Jubilee activists have engaged in street protests at G7 summits, including forming a human chain around the meeting site of the 1997 G7 Denver Summit (Michael, 2001, p. 11). The campaign has not succeeded in its aim of total debt cancellation for all poor countries, but the Heavily Indebted Poor Countries Initiative was a response by creditor governments to calls for debt cancellation. Subsequent G7 decisions on debt, such as the decision at the Cologne Summit in 1999 to cancel $27 billion and the Multilateral Debt Relief Initiative agreed at the G8 Gleneagles Summit in July 2005, reflect the influence of the coalition. The Jubilee Debt Campaign is part of a larger movement of citizens seeking the promotion of global security, democracy and justice. It has been joined by another anti-poverty movement – the Global Call to Action Against Poverty (see Box 15.5).

Another component of this search for justice in the global economy is the fair trade movement. Advocates of fair trade argue that the current trading order is fundamentally biased against the developing world and seek to initiate a more just trading order. This position usually takes two forms. One central concern relates to the prices paid to producers in the developing world, and the campaign is for more equitable prices. In this scenario, the market confines poor countries to export goods whose prices are vulnerable to fluctuations and also historically low. The other issue of concern relates to labour standards. In this view, international trade is unfair because the internationalization of production leads to the exploitation of workers in the developing world (Sengenberger and Wilkinson, 1995, p. 112). Trade is an important part of this process since production is largely for export.

Democracy and regulation

The increasing globalization of the world economy has been accompanied by increasing global regulation. For

Box 15.5 The Global Call to Action Against Poverty

The Global Call to Action Against Poverty (www.whiteband.org) is a coalition of groups around the world that mounted an intense mobilization campaign to call attention to global poverty issues and solutions in 2005. In the UK and several other developed countries, it took the form of the Make Poverty History campaign. The Make Poverty History initiative ran stark television commercials featuring film and music personalities marking the death of a person in poverty every few seconds. The campaign urged supporters to wear white armbands as a sign of their concern. Letter-writing campaigns and large-scale meetings were used to put pressure on political leaders in developed states to make global poverty alleviation a priority.

The Make Poverty History campaign advocated a number of changes to the operation of global governance (www.makepovertyhistory.org). On the trade front, it demanded increased access for developing countries to developed countries' markets and increased protection for developing countries. With regard to debt, the campaign called for the cancellation of debt for all those countries unable to pay. On finance issues, the demand is for more and better aid, while undemocratic conditionality on loans should be eliminated. Fighting corruption is a final element in the campaign. These campaigns had some success in raising poverty issues in 2005, but the struggle to implement this alternative global governance agenda continues.

example, since the early 1990s, international institutions such as the IMF, the World Bank and the WTO have taken on a more prominent role in governing the global economy. Rules and norms are needed to guide state, corporate and citizen activity in this environment. However, new forms of regulation raise difficult issues about democratic control over the regulators and the process of creating rules and norms. The impression that existing regulatory structures serve the needs of the rich and powerful has led to considerable public unease about global governance.

A good example of this unease can be found in the area of financial regulation. Following the 1997 East Asian financial crisis, a wide range of actors called for a new form of financial architecture that would safeguard the public interest. During financial crises, the regulations governing capital mobility and debt seemed to privilege the owners of capital and punish poor people in developing countries. During 2002, a series of financial scandals at a number of large US companies such as Enron raised serious questions about the degree to which accounting regulations and stock market practices hurt the public interest because they facilitated corporate theft and plunder. Public unease over the direction of the global economy was heightened by these regulation failures.

In April 2000, Joseph Stiglitz, a former chief economist and senior vice-president of the World Bank, wrote:

Next week's meeting of the International Monetary Fund will bring to Washington DC many of the same demonstrators who thrashed the World Trade Organization in Seattle last fall. They'll say the IMF is arrogant. They'll say the IMF doesn't really listen to the developing countries it is supposed to help. They'll say the IMF is secretive and insulated from democratic accountability. They'll say the IMF's economic 'remedies' often make things worse – turning slowdowns into recessions and recessions into depressions.

(Stiglitz, 2000)

Stiglitz concedes that the demonstrators do have a point – an opinion in sharp contrast with the views of most mainstream commentators. Stiglitz's comments go to the heart of the current challenge to global governance institutions. A critical issue we have touched on at various times in this book is the subject of the legitimacy of institutions of global governance, and this issue will remain important in the early part of the 21st century. There is currently official and popular dissatisfaction with many global governance institutions, and one of the challenges ahead will be to find ways to ensure that these institutions meet current tests of democratic control. Rapid financial innovation continuously raises new challenges for regulatory authority (Box 15.6). As complexity increases, the regulatory systems increasingly appear to be captured by specialized financial interests. The result can be regulatory failure as in the case of the US financial crisis of 2008–9.

Few theorists or practitioners would disagree with the claim of a former UN secretary-general that: 'Respect for democratic principles at all levels of social

---

Box 15.6 Bitcoin – a new currency for a new age?

Communications technology has facilitated the emergence of new forms of currency, the most prominent of which is Bitcoin. Bitcoin markets itself as 'money for the internet generation' (http://www.bitcoin.com). Its origins lie in open software distributed by someone using the pseudonym Satoshi Nakamoto in 2008. It can be thought of as a decentralized digital currency. Coins are created as payment to people who manage the system. It is decentralized in that it is run by the Bitcoin community rather than a central bank or a government. The system is anonymous so the identifes of the purchasers are not known. It allows peer-to-peer transactions, avoiding the services of banks or credit card companies, so transaction fees are very low. Payments can be sent around the world, very quickly, anonymously and at minimal cost. For some people, this liberates them from relying on the services of governments and financial institutions. For others, the advent of Bitcoin has raised fears about its use by criminals and concerns over its stability and volatility.

---

existence is crucial in communities, within states, and within the international community' (Boutros Ghali, 1995, p. 2). While consensus exists concerning the spread of democracy, none is forthcoming concerning the reasons for the upsurge of interest in global democracy. The final two decades of the 20th century witnessed a sharp increase in the number of democratic states giving rise to what has been termed the 'third wave' of democratization (Huntington, 1991). As a result of democratization processes in Asia, Africa, Latin America and Europe, democracy has become an unquestioned global norm. There has been a burgeoning literature on the causes of democratization, the theory and practice of democracy, and the global order and democracy. But democracy remains an aspiration for many of the world's peoples, a goal proclaimed by almost all politicians wherever they reside and a crucial political value in the 21st century. It is difficult to envisage a serious political party or politician that did not claim attachment to the values embodied within democratic constitutions. The reality may well fall far short of the ideal and it may be that the date for a transition to democracy is postponed into the future, but across the globe democracy has triumphed as the preferred form of government. Democracy thus stands as a crucial test of the legitimacy of political arrangements in the contemporary world. In other words, institutions lacking in democratic features are held to be illegitimate and, by extension, unjust. The ramifications of the triumph of democracy are evident in subnational, national and international politics. There has been a diffusion of democratic norms – at the core of recent protests against the international economic institutions, the central issue is one of democratic governance.

The changing global economic order poses fundamental questions for the exercise of global democratic governance. Three disjunctures in the global system challenge the image of increasing global democracy presented above:

1 A key aspect of globalization has been the creation of new non-state centres of authority (Cutler et al., 1999; Hall and Biersteker, 2002). One feature of this is what can be termed the 'privatization of regulation' (Cutler, 1995; Sinclair, 1994). Policy decisions taken by, for example, financial institutions can have profound effects on the policies of governments and intergovernmental organizations.

2 There are limitations on state sovereignty, in the sense that the authority and power of national authorities is undermined by the creation of regional and global organizations. In other words, international organizations are not to be conceived as solely the instruments of states. Another centre of authority is to be found in the increased influence of international organizations. Through the expanded mandate of organizations like the EU and the WTO, their member governments and their citizens are increasingly subject to new forms of regulation over which there is little direct control.

3 The development of international economic law is creating a system in which political authority is migrating to regional and global centres without a proper system of checks and balances.

One response to these developments is to claim that these international economic organizations (IEOs) remain firmly intergovernmental, and are therefore democratic because they are accountable to their member states. It can be argued that this claim fails to recognize shifting authority patterns and structures in a changing world order. For example, both through the impact on state preferences and directly on the bureaucracy of such organizations, non-state actors influence the agendas and functioning of global institutions. Any assessment of the role of IEOs must therefore begin from a recognition of the transformation in multilateralism (O'Brien et al., 2000). No longer can multilateralism be conceived solely in state-centric terms; that is, states are no longer the only salient actors in the construction of multilateral regimes. In this perspective, IEOs are assessed not solely on their ability to fulfil the needs of states but rather on whether they meet the aspirations of social movement actors as well as states. It is within this context of change that the democratic credentials of IEOs have to be assessed. From this perspective, representation can be conceived as concern for the interests of stakeholders. Institutions of global governance will fail to meet the test of democratic control in the absence of transparent procedures, access for nongovernmental groups, and mechanisms through which policy can be explained and justified to the range of stakeholders.

Some political theorists (Held, 1995) have attempted to project national democratic institutions onto the international stage to remedy the problem of democratic deficits in a globalizing era. Attempts to have international parliaments seem premature, given the decentralization of the international system. An alternative approach has been developed by Coleman and Porter (2000), who have suggested the application of six criteria to judge the degree of democracy surrounding a particular institution or regime. The criteria are: transparency, openness to direct participation, quality of discourse, representation, effectiveness and fairness. They argue that international governance arrangements can be modified to improve performance on these measures without rebuilding domestic institutions such as legislatures at the international level. For example, transparency can be increased by providing clear and timely information about an institution's operations.

Participation in the policy process can be increased by greater consultation with a wide range of interests. The quality of discourse can be improved by launching education campaigns and fostering debate around key issues. Representation concerns can be mitigated by creating institutional linkages with concerned parties.

Effectiveness may be increased by streamlining decision-making processes and developing institutional autonomy. Fairness would be bolstered by procedures deemed to be legitimate and policy outcomes that were sensitive to the distribution of costs and benefits.

CONCLUSION

This chapter focused attention on one of the themes running through the book, namely the issue of governance. In Part 2, we examined governance structures (or the lack of them) in various historical periods. In Part 3, examining key frameworks in the contemporary global political economy, we noted the importance of governance institutions for the functioning of the global economy. In this chapter we outlined how governance is accomplished in the contemporary global political economy, and discussed the actors involved in this process. The second section provided a brief introduction to three key challenges to institutions of governance. We have not suggested solutions to these challenges but have raised some of the difficulties in addressing these issues.

As globalization intensifies, the fate of peoples around the world is increasingly interconnected. Despite rapid advances in technology and production, the world faces daunting challenges of inequality, environmental degradation and democratic governance. Attention to, and action in, the global political economy is needed now more than ever.

Further Reading

A good overview of the extensive regime literature can be found in Andreas Hasenclever et al., *Theories of International Regimes* (1997). An early contribution to the private authority literature is Claire Cutler et al. (eds) *Private Authority and International Affairs* (1999). Ngaire Woods outlines the role of the IMF and World Bank in global governance in *The Globalizers: The IMF, The World Bank and Their Borrowers* (2007). *Global Governance* is a journal devoted to a wide range of global governance issues.

Bibliography

Abbott, F. M., Breining-Kaufmann, C. and Cottier, T. (eds) (2006) *International Trade and Human Rights: Foundations and Conceptual Issues* (Ann Arbor, MI: University of Michigan Press).

Abdelal, R. (2009) 'Constructivism as an Approach to International Political Economy', in M. Blyth (ed.) *Routledge Handbook of International Political Economy (IPE): IPE as a Global Conversation* (London: Routledge).

Abdelal, R., Blyth, M. and Parsons, C. (2010) *Constructing the International Economy* (Ithaca, NY: Cornell University Press).

Abernethy, D. B. (2000) *The Dynamics of Global Dominance: European Overseas Empires 1415–1980* (New Haven, CT: Yale University Press).

Abu-Lughod, J. L. (1989) *Before European Hegemony: The World System AD 1250–1350* (New York: Oxford University Press).

Acker, J. (2004) 'Gender, Capitalism and Globalization', *Critical Sociology*, 30(1): 17–41.

African Development Bank and Global Financial Integrity (2013) 'Illicit Financial Flows and the Problem of Net Resource Transfers from Africa: 1980–2009', http://www.gfintegrity.org/storage/gfip/documents/reports/Africa NetResources/gfi_afdb_iffs_and_the_problem_of_net_resource_transfers_from_africa_1980-2009-web.pdf, last accessed 17 October 2015.

AIIB (2015) 'Prospective Founding Members', http://aiibank.org/members.html, last accessed 13 May 2015.

Aisbett, E. (2007) 'Why are the Critics so Convinced that Globalization is Bad for the Poor?', in A. Harrison (ed.) *Globalization and Poverty* (Chicago: University of Chicago Press).

Akerlof, G. and Shiller, R. (2009) *Animal Spirits: How Human Psychology Drives the Economy, and Why It Matters for Global Capitalism* (Princeton, NJ: Princeton University Press).

Albrecht, J., Bjorkland, A. and Vroman, S. (2003) 'Is There a Glass Ceiling in Sweden?' *Journal of Labor Economics*, 21(1): 145–77.

Alger, C. F. (1997) 'Transnational Social Movements, World Politics and Global Governance', in J. Smith, C. Chatfield and R. Pagnucco (eds) *Transnational Social Movements and Global Politics: Solidarity Beyond the State* (Syracuse, NY: Syracuse University Press).

Allen, M. (1999) 'Women, Bargaining and Change in Seven Structures of World Political Economy', *Review of International Studies*, 25(4): 453–74.

Amin, S. (1976) *Unequal Development* (New York: Monthly Review).

Amoore, L. and Langley, P. (2004) 'Ambiguities of Global Civil Society', *Review of International Studies*, 30(1): 89–110.

Amsden, A. H. (1989) *Asia's Next Giant: South Korea and Late Industrialization* (New York: Oxford University Press).

Andrews, D. M. (1994) 'Capital Mobility and State Autonomy: Towards a Structural Theory of International Monetary Relations', *International Studies Quarterly*, 38(2): 193–218.

Andrianaivo, M. and Kpodar, K. (2011) 'ICT, Financial Inclusion, and Growth: Evidence from African Countries', Working Paper 11/73 (Washington, DC: IMF).

Anseeuw W., Boche, M., Breu, T., et al. (2012) 'Transnational Land Deals for Agriculture in the Global South. Analytical Report based on the Land Matrix Database', https://www.oxfam.de/sites/www.oxfam.de/files/20120427_report_land_matrix.pdf, last accessed 17 October 2015.

Appleton, S. (1996) 'Women-headed Households and Household Welfare: An Empirical Deconstruction for Uganda', *World Development*, 24(12): 1811–1827.

Arana, A. (2005) 'How the Street Gangs Took Central America', *Foreign Affairs*, 84(3): 98–110.

Arezecki, R., Deininger, K. and Selod, H. (2012) 'The Global Land Rush', *Finance & Development*, March: 46–49.

Arthur, C. (2014) 'Department of Justice Indictment Confirms Existence of Projects such as "Titan Rain" and Pattern of Attacks against US Firms', *Guardian*, 19 May.

Asian Labour Update (1995) 'Towards a UN Labour Rights Convention, Conclusions of the National Consultation Concerning the Social Clause in World Trade Agreements', *Asian Labour Update*, 20: 11–12, 17.

Aslanbeigui, N. and Summerfield, G. (2000) 'The Asian Crisis, Gender, and the International Financial Architecture', *Feminist Economics*, 6(3): 81–103.

AU/ECA (2015) 'Illicit Financial Flows: Report of the High Level Panel on Illicit Financial Flows from Africa' (Addis Ababa: African Union / UN Economic Commission for Africa).

Axelrod, R. and Keohane, R. (1986) 'Achieving Cooperation Under Anarchy: Strategies and Institutions', in K. Oye (ed.) *Cooperation Under Anarchy* (Princeton, NJ: Princeton University Press).

Axworthy, L. (2001) 'Human Security and Global Governance: Putting People First', *Global Governance*, 7(1): 19–23.

Azreki, R., Deininger, K. and Harris, S. (2012) 'The Global Land Rush' *Finance & Development* 49(1): 46–49.

Baker, D. (2006) 'The Political Economy of Fascism: Myth or Reality, or Myth and Reality?' *New Political Economy*, 11(2): 227–50.

Bakker, I. (ed.) (1994) *The Strategic Silence: Gender and Economic Policy* (London: Zed Books).

Balakrishnan, K. (2008) 'Defence Industrialisation in Malaysia: Development Challenges and the Revolution in Military Affairs', *Security Challenges*, 4(4): 135–55.

Baldwin, R. E. and Thornton, P. (2008) *Multilateralising Regionalism: Ideas for a WTO Action Plan on Regionalism* (London: Centre for Economic Policy Research).

Ballentine, K. and Sherman, J. (2003) *The Political Economy of Armed Conflict: Beyond Greed and Grievance* (Boulder, CO: Lynne Rienner).

Bangura, Y. and Beckman, B. (1991) 'African Workers and Structural Adjustment: The Nigerian Case', in D. Ghai (ed.) *The IMF and the South: The Social Impact of Crisis and Adjustment* (London: Zed Books).

Banjo, S. (2014) 'Inside Nike's Struggle to Balance Cost and Worker Safety in Bangladesh', *Wall Street Journal*, 21 April.

Bannock, G. (1971) *The Juggernauts* (London: Weidenfeld & Nicolson).

Baran, P. A. and Sweezy, P. M. (1966) *Monopoly Capital* (New York: Monthly Review Press).

Barbieri, K. (1996) 'Economic Interdependence', *Journal of Peace Research*, 33(1): 29–49.

Barnett, R. J. and Muller, R. E. (1975) *Global Reach* (London: Jonathan Cape).

Barraclough, G. (1967) *An Introduction to Contemporary History* (New York: Penguin).

Barreto, M., Ryan, M. K. and Schmitt, M. T. (eds) (2009) *The Glass Ceiling in the 21st Century: Understanding Barriers to Gender Equality* (Washington, DC: American Psychological Association).

Barrett, S. (1993) 'International Cooperation for Environmental Protection', in R. Dorfman and N. S. Dorfman (eds) *Economics of the Environment*, 3rd edn (New York: W. W. Norton).

Barrientos, S., Kabeer, N. and Hossain, N. (2004) 'The Gender Dimension of the Globalization of Production', Working Paper 17 (Geneva: policy integration department, ILO).

Barros, R., Fox, L. and Mendonca, R. (1997) 'Female-Headed Households, Poverty, and the Welfare of Children in Urban Brazil', *Economic Development and Cultural Change*, 45(2): 231–57.

Barry, K. (1996) *The Prostitution of Sexuality* (New York: New York University Press).

Bath, V. (2012) 'Foreign Investment, the National Interest and National Security: Foreign Direct Investment in Australia and China', *Sydney Law Review*, 34(5): 5–34.

BBC (2012) 'Tax Havens: Super-Rich "Hiding" at Least $21tn', 22 July, http://www.bbc.com/news/business-18944097, last accessed 15 May 2015.

BBC (2015) 'Obama Plans Tax on US Firms Overseas to Fix Roads at Home', 2 February, http://www.bbc.com/news/business-31085912, last accessed 15 May 2015.

Becchetti, F. and Adriani, F. (2003) *Does the Digital Divide Matter? The Role of Information and Communication Technology in Cross-Country Level and Growth Estimates* (Rome: Centre for International Studies on Economic Growth).

Beckerman, W. (1995) *Small is Stupid: Blowing the Whistle on the Greens* (London: Duckworth).

Beckford, G. (1972) *Persistent Poverty* (New York: Oxford University Press).

Beder, S. (1997) *Corporate Spin: The Global Assault on Environmentalism* (Melbourne: Scribe).

Behrman, J., Meinzen-Dick, R. and Quisumbing, A. (2011) 'The Gender Implications of Large-Scale Land Deals', IFPRI Discussion Paper 010506, http://cdm15738.contentdm.oclc.org/utils/getfile/collection/p15738coll2/id/124877/filename/124878.pdf, last accessed 17 October 2015.

Bello, W. (2000) 'Why Reform of the WTO is NOT the Agenda', www.zmag.org/CrisesCurEvts/Globalism/notreformbello, last accessed 26 January 2007.

Belsey, C. (2002) *Poststructuralism: A Very Short Introduction* (Oxford: Oxford University Press).

Bennett, A. L. and Oliver, J. K. (2002) *International Organizations: Principles and Issues*, 7th edn (Upper Saddle River, NJ: Prentice Hall).

Bergman, S. M. (2013) 'The Global Supply Chain: Our Economy, Security and Health Depends on It', *Huffington Post*, 27 January, http://www.huffingtonpost.com/stanley-m-bergman/global-supply-chain_b_2561493.html, last accessed 17 October 2015.

Bernard, M. (1994) 'Post-Fordism, Transnational Production and the Changing Global Political Economy', in R. Stubbs and G. R. D. Underhill (eds) *Political Economy and the Changing Global Order* (Basingstoke, UK: Macmillan).

Bernards, N., O'Brien, R. and Zhang, F. (2015) 'Labour and Tax Justice' (South Africa : Rosa Luxemburg Stiftung), available at: http://www.rosalux.co.za/wp-content/uploads/2015/10/OBrien-Futures-Commission-01_2015.pdf, last accessed 2 December 2015.

Bessis, S. (2001) 'The World Bank and Women: "Instrumental Feminism"', in S. Perry and C. Schenk (eds) *Eye To Eye: Women Practising Development Across Cultures* (London: Zed Books).

Best, J. and Paterson, M. (2010) *Cultural Political Economy* (London: Routledge).

Bettin, G., Presbitero, A. F. and Spatafora, N. (2014) 'Remittances and Vulnerability in Developing Countries', Working Paper 14/13 (Washington, DC: IMF).

Bhopal Medical Appeal (2015) 'What Happened', http://bhopal.org/what-happened/, last accessed 17 October 2015.

Biersteker, T. J. (1992) 'The Triumph of Neoclassical Economics in the Developing World', in J. N. Rosenau and E. O. Czempiel (eds) *Governance Without Government: Order and Change in World Politics* (Cambridge: Cambridge University Press).

BIS (2014) 'Triennial Central Bank Survey: Global Foreign Exchange Market Turnover in 2013' (Basel: Bank for International Settlements; Economic and Monetary Department).

Blackhurst, R. and Subramanian, A. (1992) 'Promoting Multilateral Cooperation on the Environment', in K. Anderson and R. Blackhurst (eds) *The Greening of World Trade Issues* (London: Harvester Wheatsheaf).

Blau, F. and Kahn, L. (2003) 'Understanding International Differences in the Gender Pay Gap', *Journal of Labor Economics*, 21(1): 106–44.

Block, F. L. (1977) *The Origins of International Economic Disorder* (Berkeley, CA: University of California Press).

Bloom, R. (2003) 'Few Investors Will Celebrate Today's Tech Boom Anniversary', *Globe and Mail*, 10 March.

Blustein, P. (2001) *The Chastening: Inside the Crisis that Rocked the Global Financial System and Humbled the IMF* (New York: Public Affairs).

Blyth, M. (2013) *Austerity: The History of a Bad Idea* (Cambridge: Cambridge University Press).

Boas, M., Marchand, M. and Shaw, T. M. (eds) (2005) *Political Economy of Regions and Regionalisms* (Basingstoke, UK: Palgrave Macmillan).

Boli, J. and Thomas, G. M. (1999) *Constructing World Culture: International Nongovernmental Organizations since 1875* (Stanford, CA: Stanford University Press).

Bonacich, E., Alimahomed S. and Wilson, J. (2008) 'The Racialization of Global Labor' *American Behavioral Scientist* 52(3): 342–355.

Borger J. and Dehghan, S. (2012) 'Iran Sanctions Will Halve Oil Sales But May Still Not Succeed', *Guardian*, 28 June.

Boserup, E. (1989) *Woman's Role in Economic Development* (London: Earthscan).

Bouchon, G. and Lombard, D. (1987) 'The Indian Ocean in the Fifteenth Century', in A. Das Gupta and M. N. Pearson (eds) *India and the Indian Ocean 1500–1800* (Calcutta: Oxford University Press).

Boutros Ghali, B. (1995) 'An Agenda for Peace' (New York: UN).

Bowles, P. and Wang, B. (2008) 'The Rocky Road Ahead: China, the US and the Future of the Dollar', *Review of International Political Economy*, 15(3): 335–53.

Brand, U. (2005) 'Order and Regulation: Global Governance as a Hegemonic Discourse of International Politics?' *Review of International Political Economy*, 12(1): 155–76.

Brandt Commission (1983) *Common Crisis: North–South Cooperation for World Poverty* (London: Pan).

Braudel, F. (1979) *The Perspective of the World: Civilization and Capitalism 15th–18th Century*, vol. 3 (New York: Harper & Row).

Braudel, F. (1994) *A History of Civilizations* (New York: Allen Lane).

Braverman, H. (1974) *Labor and Monopoly Capital: The Degradation of Work in the Twentieth Century* (New York: Monthly Review).

Breslin, S. (2005) 'Power and Production: Rethinking China's Global Economic Role', *Review of International Studies*, 31(4): 735–53.

Bretton Woods Project (2010) 'Analysis of World Bank Voting Reforms', http://www.brettonwoodsproject.org/2010/04/art-566281/, last accessed 17 October 2015.

BRICS (2014a) 'Joint Statistical Publication 2014' (Rio de Janeiro, Brazil: IBGE), http://brics.ibge.gov.br/downloads/BRICS_Joint_Statistical_Publication_2014.pdf, last accessed 8 May 2015.

BRICS (2014b) 'Agreement on the New Development Bank' (Fortaleza, Brazil) 15 July, http://brics6.itamaraty.gov.br/media2/press-releases/219-agreement-on-the-new-development-bank-fortaleza-july-15, last accessed 13 May 2013.

Bridges Trade BioRes (2009) 'Trans-Atlantic Beef Hormone Dispute Heats Up Once Again', 9(1): 1–11.

Broad, R. (2004) 'The Washington Consensus Meets the Global Backlash', *Globalization*, 1(2): 129–54.

Brower, J. and Chalk, P. (2003) *The Global Threat of New and Reemerging Infectious Diseases: Reconciling US National Security and Public Health Policy* (Santa Monica, CA: Rand).

Brown, D. (2005) 'Conspicuous Consumption, Fashion and Style in the Global Marketplace', in P. A. O'Hara (ed.) *Global Political Economy and the Wealth of Nations: Performance, Institutions, Problems and Policies* (London: Routledge).

Brown, M. E., Lynn-Jones, M. and Miller, S. E. (eds) (1996) *Debating the Democratic Peace* (Cambridge, MA: MIT Press).

Brown, S. (2005) 'Foreign Aid and Democracy Promotion: Lessons from Africa', *European Journal of Development Research*, 17(2): 179–98.

Brown Thompson, K. (2002) 'Women's Rights Are Human Rights', in S. Khagram, J. V. Riker and K. Sikkink (eds) *Restructuring World Politics: Transnational Social Movements, Networks and Norms* (Minneapolis, MN: University of Minnesota Press).

Bull, B., Bøås, M. and McNeill, D. (2004) 'Private Sector Influence in the Multilateral System: A Changing Structure of World Governance?' *Global Governance*, 10(4): 481–98.

Busse, M. and Spielmann, C. (2003) 'Gender Discrimination and the International Division of Labour', HWWA Discussion Papers 245 (Hamburg: Institute of International Economics).

Buvinic, M. and Gupta, G. R. (1997) 'Female-Headed Households and Female-Maintained Families: Are They Worth Targeting to Reduce Poverty in Developing Countries?' *Economic Development and Cultural Change,* 45(2): 259–281.

Buzan, B. (1991) *Peoples, States and Fear,* 2nd edn (Hemel Hempstead, UK: Harvester Wheatsheaf).

Buzan, B., Waever, O. and de Wilde, J. (1997) *Security: A New Framework for Analysis* (Boulder, CO: Lynne Rienner).

Caldwell, L. (1988) 'Beyond Environmental Diplomacy: The Changing Institutional Structure of International Cooperation', in J. E. Carroll (ed.) *International Environmental Diplomacy* (Cambridge: Cambridge University Press).

Callí M. with S. Dell'Erba (2009) 'The Global Financial Crisis and Remittances: What Past Evidence Suggests', Working Paper 303 (London: ODI).

Carlaw, K., Oxley, L. and Walker, P. (2006) 'Beyond the Hype: Intellectual Property and the Knowledge Society/Knowledge Economy', *Journal of Economic Surveys,* 20(4): 633–58.

Carlson, L. J. (2000) 'Game Theory: International Trade, Conflict and Cooperation', in R. Palan (ed.) *Global Political Economy: Contemporary Theories* (London: Routledge).

Carr, E. H. (1939) *The Twenty Years' Crisis 1919–1939: An Introduction to the Study of International Relations* (London: Macmillan).

Casson, M. (1991) 'Modelling the Multinational Enterprise: A Research Agenda', *Millennium,* 20(2): 271–85.

Castells, M. (1996) *The Rise of the Network Society* (Oxford: Blackwell).

Caufield, C. (1996) *Masters of Illusion: The World Bank and the Poverty of Nations* (New York: Henry Holt).

Caves, R. E. (1974) 'The Causes of Direct Investment: Foreign Firms' Share in Canadian and UK Manufacturing Industries', *Review of Economics and Statistics,* 56(3): 279–93.

CBC (2014) 'Federal Pension Board Used Offshore Scheme to Skirt Foreign Taxes', 5 November, http://www.cbc.ca/news/politics/federal-pension-board-used-offshore-scheme-to-skirt-foreign-taxes-1.2824959, last accessed 26 February 2015.

Cecchine, G. and Moore, M. (2006) *Infectious Disease and National Security: Strategic Information Needs* (Santa Monica, CA: Rand).

Cerny, P. G. (1993) 'The Deregulation and Re-regulation of Financial Markets in a More Open World', in P. G. Cerny (ed.) *Finance and World Politics: Markets, Regimes and States in the Post-Hegemonic Era* (Aldershot, UK: Edward Elgar).

Cerny, P. G. (1995) 'Globalization and the Changing Logic of Collective Action', *International Organization,* 49(4): 595–625.

Cerny, P. G. (2000) 'The Competition State', in R. Stubbs and G. R. D. Underhill (eds) *Political Economy and the Changing Global Order,* 2nd edn (Toronto: Oxford University Press).

Chakravartty, P. (2006) 'White-Collar Nationalisms', *Social Semiotics,* 16(1): 39–55.

Chamberlain, M. E. (1985) *Decolonization: The Fall of European Empires* (London: Basil Blackwell).

Chang, G. (2000) *Disposable Domestics: Immigrant Women Workers in the Global Economy* (Boston, MA: South End).

Chang, H.-J. (2002) *Kicking Away the Ladder* (London: Anthem Press).

Charles, A. (2014). 'Department of Justice Indictment Confirms Existence of Projects such as "Titan Rain" and Pattern of Attacks Against US Firms', *Guardian,* 19 May.

Checkel, J. (2004) 'Social Constructivisms in Global and European Politics: A Review Essay', *Review of International Studies,* 30: 229–44.

Chenoy, A. M. (2002) *Militarism and Women in South Asia* (New Delhi: Kali).

Cheru, F. (2002) 'Debt, Adjustment and the Politics of Effective Response to HIV/AIDS in Africa', *Third World Quarterly,* 23(2): 299–312.

Chicago Tribune (2012) 'McDonald's Food You Can't Get Here', 15 June, www.chicagotribune.com/ business/ct -biz -mcdonalds -food -around -the world,0,5168632.photogallery, last accessed 13 December 2012.

Chin, C. (2008) 'Labour Flexibilization at Sea', *International Feminist Journal of Politics,* 10(1): 1–18.

Chinguno, C. (2013) 'Marikana Massacre and Strike Violence Post-Apartheid', *Global Labour Journal,* 4(2): 160–6.

Chow, E. N. (2003) 'Gender Matters: Studying Globalization and Social Change in the 21st Century', *International Sociology,* 18(3): 443–60.

CIA (2014) 'World Factbook' (Washington, DC: Brassey's), https://www.cia.gov/library/publications/resources/the-world-factbook/, last accessed 17 October 2015.

Clapp, J. (1998) 'The Privatization of Global Governance: ISO 1400 and the Developing World', *Global Governance,* 4(3): 295–316.

Clapp, J. (2001) *Toxic Exports: The Transfer of Hazardous Wastes from Rich to Poor Countries* (Ithaca, NY: Cornell University Press).

Clapp, J. (2006) 'WTO Agricultural Negotiations: Implications for the Global South', *Third World Quarterly,* 27(4): 563–77.

Clapp, J. and Dauvergne, P. (2011) *Paths to a Green World: the Political Economy of the Global Environment,* 2nd edn (Cambridge, MA: MIT Press).

Cody, E. (2004) 'In China, Workers Turn Tough', *Washington Post,* 27 November.

Cody, E. (2005) 'For Chinese, Peasant Revolt is a Rare Victory', *Washington Post,* 13 June.

Cohen, B. J. (2007) 'The Transatlantic Divide: Why are American and British IPE so Different?' *Review of International Political Economy,* 14(2): 197–219.

Cohen, E. A. (1996) 'A Revolution in Warfare', *Foreign Affairs,* 75(2): 37–54.

Cohen, M. A. and Küpçü, M. F. (2009) *Revitalizing US Democracy Promotion: A Comprehensive Plan for Reform* (Washington, DC: New America Foundation).

Coleman, W. and Porter, T. (2000) 'International Institutions, Globalisation and Democracy: Assessing the Challenges', *Global Society*, 14(3): 377–98.

Coleman, W. and Underhill, G. (eds) (1998) *Regionalism and Global Economic Integration* (London: Routledge).

Commission on Human Security (2003) *Human Security Now* (New York: Commission on Human Security).

Conrad, J. ([1902]1999) *The Heart of Darkness* (New York: Penguin).

Constable, C. (2006) 'Brides, Maids, and Prostitutes: Reflections on the Study of "Trafficked" Women', *PORTAL: Journal of Multidisciplinary International Studies*, 3(2): 1–25.

Constable, N. (2014) *Born Out of Place: Migrant Mothers and the Politics of International Labor* (Berkeley, CA: University of California Press).

Cook, P. and Kirkpatrick, C. (1994) 'Globalisation, Regionalization and Third World Development', *Regional Studies*, 31(1): 55–66.

Cooper, R. N. (1987) *The International Monetary System: Essays in World Economics* (Cambridge, MA: MIT Press).

Coote, B. (1992) *The Trade Trap* (Oxford: Oxfam).

Costanza, R. (1989) 'What is Ecological Economics?' *Ecological Economics* 1: 1–7.

Cotula, L., Vermeulen, S., Leonard, R. and Keeley, J. (2009) 'Land Grab or Development Opportunity? Agricultural Investment and International Land Deals in Africa' (FAO, IIED and IFAD), http://www.fao.org/3/a-ak241e.pdf, last accessed 17 October 2015.

Cotula, L., Vermeulen, S., Mathieu, P. and Toulmin, C. (2011) 'Agricultural Investment and International Land Deals: Evidence from a Multi-Country Study in Africa' *Food Security* 3(S1): 99–113.

Cox, R. W. (1977) 'Labor and Hegemony', *International Organization*, 31: 385–424.

Cox, R. W. (1979) 'Ideologies and the NIEO: Reflections on Some Recent Literature', *International Organisation*, 33: 370–95.

Cox, R. W. (1983) 'Gramsci, Hegemony and International Relations: An Essay in Method', *Millennium*, 12(2): 162–75.

Cox, R. W. (1986) 'Social Forces, States and World Order: Beyond International Relations Theory', in R. Keohane (ed.) *Neorealism and its Critics* (New York: Columbia University Press).

Cox, R. W. (1987) *Production, Power, and World Order: Social Forces in the Making of History* (New York: Columbia University Press).

Cox, R. W. (1996) 'Civilisations in World Political Economy', *New Political Economy*, 1(2): 141–56.

Cox, R. W. (2002a) 'Reflections and Transitions', in R. Cox and M. Schechter (eds) *The Political Economy of a Plural World: Critical Reflections on Power, Morals and Civilization* (London: Routledge).

Cox, R. W. (2002b) 'The Covert World', in R. Cox and M. Schechter (eds) *The Political Economy of a Plural World: Critical Reflections on Power, Morals and Civilization* (London: Routledge).

Cox, R. W. and Sinclair, T. (1996) *Approaches to World Order* (Cambridge: Cambridge University Press).

Craig, G. A. and George, A. L. (1983) *Force and Statecraft: Diplomatic Problems of Our Time* (New York: Oxford University Press).

Crawford, G. (2005) 'The European Union and Democracy Promotion in Africa: The Case of Ghana', *European Journal of Development Research*, 17(4): 571–600.

Creevey, L. (2002) 'Structural Adjustment and the Empowerment (or Disempowerment) of Women in Niger and Senegal', in R. Datta and J. Kornberg (eds) *Women in Developing Countries: Assessing Strategies for Empowerment* (Boulder, CO: Lynne Rienner).

Croce, B. (1941) *History as the Story of Liberty* (London: George Allen & Unwin).

Cronin, A. K. (2002/3) 'Behind the Curve: Globalization and International Terrorism', *International Security*, 55(1): 30–58.

Crosby, A. W. (1996) *Ecological Imperialism: The Biological Expansion of Europe, 900–1900* (Cambridge: Cambridge University Press).

Crumley, C. (2006) 'Historical Ecology: Integrated Thinking at Multiple Temporal and Spatial Scales' in A. Hornberg and C. Crumley (eds) *The World System and the Earth System: Global Socioenvironmental Change and Sustainability Since the Neolithic* (Walnut Creek, CA: Left Coast Press).

Curley, M. and Thomas, N. (2004) 'Human Security and Public Health in Southeast Asia', *Australian Journal of International Affairs*, 55(1): 17–32.

Curtin, P. D. (2000) *The World and the West: The European Challenge and the Overseas Response in the Age of Empire* (Cambridge: Cambridge University Press).

Cutler, C. (1995) 'Global Capitalism and Liberal Myths: Dispute Settlement in Private International Trade Relations', *Millennium*, 24(3): 377–97.

Cutler, C., Haufler, V. and Porter, T. (eds) (1999) *Private Authority and International Affairs* (Albany, NY: SUNY Press).

Dadkhah, K. M. (2006) 'Sanctions, Economic', in T. M Leonard (ed.) *Encyclopaedia of the Developing World*, vol. 3 (New York: Routledge).

Dalby, S. (2002) *Environmental Security* (Minneapolis: University of Minnesota Press).

Danaher, K. (ed.) (1994) *50 Years Is Enough: The Case Against the World Bank and IMF* (Boston, MA: South End).

Darwin, J. (1988) *Britain and Decolonisation: The Retreat from Empire in the Post-War World* (Basingstoke, UK: Macmillan).

Datta, R. and Kornberg, J. (eds) (2002) *Women in Developing Countries: Assessing Strategies for Empowerment* (Boulder, CO: Lynne Rienner).

Dauvergne, P. (2001) *Loggers and Degradation in the Asia-Pacific: Corporations and Environmental Management* (Cambridge: Cambridge University Press).

Dauvergne, P. (2008) *The Shadows of Consumption: Consequences for the Global Environment* (Cambridge, MA: MIT Press).

Davies, N. (1982) *The Ancient Kingdoms of Mexico* (London: Allen Lane).

Davis, M. (2001) *Late Victorian Holocausts: El Niño Famines and the Making of the Third World* (London: Verso).

Deacon, B. (2012) 'The Social Protection Floor', CROP Poverty Brief, October, www.crop.org/ storypg.aspx?id=598& MenuNode=63395886862835845 5&zone=12, last accessed 19 December 2012.

Dean, J. W. and Globerman, S. (eds) (2001) *Dollarization in the Americas?* (Boulder, CO: Westview).

Deere, C. D. and Doss, C. R. (2006) 'The Gender Asset Gap: What Do We Know and Why Does it Matter?' *Feminist Economics*, 12(1/2): 1–50.

DEG (2015) 'DEG 2014 Year End Home Entertainment Report', http://degonline.org/resource/deg-2014-year-end-home-entertainment-report/, last accessed 17 October 2015.

Deininger, K., Byerlee, D., Lindsay, J., Norton, A., Selod S. and Stickler, M. (2011) 'Rising Global Interest in Farmland: Can It Yield Sustainable and Equitable Benefits?' (Washington, DC: World Bank).

Denemark, R. and O'Brien, R. (1997) 'Contesting the Canon: International Political Economy at UK and US Universities', *Review of International Political Economy*, 4(1): 214–38.

Dent, M. and Peters, B. (1998) 'Poverty and Debt in the Third World: Confronting a Global Crisis', *Conflict Studies*, 310: 1–24.

Dessler, A. E. and Parson, E. A. (2006) *The Science and Politics of Global Climate Change: A Guide to the Debate* (Cambridge: Cambridge University Press).

DFAT (2015) 'TPP Market Snapshot', http://dfat.gov.au/trade/agreements/tpp/Pages/trans-pacific-partnership-agreement-tpp.aspx, last accessed 17 October 2015.

Diamond, J. (1997) *Guns, Germs, and Steel: The Fates of Human Societies* (New York: W. W. Norton).

Diao, X., Diaz-Bonilla, E. and Robinson, S. (2003) *How Much Does it Hurt? The Impact of Agricultural Trade Policies on Developing Countries* (Washington, DC: IFPRI).

Dicken, P. (1992) *Global Shift: The Internationalization of Economic Activity*, 2nd edn (London: Paul Chapman).

Dicken, P. (1998) *Global Shift: Transforming the World Economy*, 3rd edn (New York: Guilford).

Dicken, P. (2007) *Global Shift: Mapping the Changing Contours of the World Economy*, 5th edn (New York: Guilford).

Dickson, A. K. (1997) *Development and International Relations* (Cambridge, UK: Polity).

Dinesh, K. and Little, D. (2004) 'International Apparel Trade and Developing Economies in Africa', *International Journal of Social Economics*, 31(1/2): 131–42.

Dingwerth, K. and Pattberg, P. (2006) 'Global Governance as a Perspective on World Politics', *Global Governance*, 12(2): 185–203.

Dobson, A. (1990) *Green Political Thought* (London: Routledge).

Dodd, R. and Mills, P. (2008) 'Outbreak: US Subprime Contagion', *Finance and Development*, 45(2): 14–18.

Dommen, C. (2002) 'Raising Human Rights Concerns in the World Trade Organization: Actors, Processes and Possible Strategies', *Human Rights Quarterly*, 24(1): 1–50.

Doremus, P., Keller, W. W., Pauly, L. W. and Reich, S. (1998) *The Myth of the Global Corporation* (Princeton, NJ: Princeton University Press).

Dos Santos, T. (1970) 'The Structure of Dependency', *American Economic Review*, 60(21): 231–6.

Doxey, M. P. (1996) *International Sanctions in Contemporary Perspective*, 2nd edn (Basingstoke, UK: Macmillan).

Doyle, M. W. (1996) *Empires* (Ithaca, NY: Cornell University Press).

Drache, D. and Froese, M. D. (2006) 'Globalisation, World Trade and the Cultural Commons: Identity, Citizenship and Pluralism', *New Political Economy*, 11(3): 361–82.

Dreze, J. and Sen, A. K. (1989) *Hunger and Public Action* (Oxford: Clarendon).

Dryzek, J. (1996) 'Foundations for Environmental Political Economy: The Search for *Homo Ecologicus*', *New Political Economy*, 1(1): 27–40.

Duhigg, C. and Greenhouse, S. (2012) 'Electronic Giant Vowing Reforms in China Plants', *New York Times*, 29 March, www.nytimes.com/2012/03/30/business/apple-supplier-in-china-pledges-changes-inworking-conditions.html?emc=eta1, last accessed 15 May 2012.

Dunford, M. (2000) 'Globalisation and Theories of Regulation', in R. Palan (ed.) *Global Political Economy: Contemporary Theories* (London: Routledge).

Dunlop, C. (2000) 'Epistemic Communities: A Reply to Toke', *Politics*, 20(3): 135–44.

Dunning, J. (1973) 'The Determinants of International Production', *Oxford Economic Papers*, 25(3): 289–336.

Dunning, J. (1981) *International Production and the Multinational Enterprise* (London: Allen & Unwin).

Dunning, J. (1985) *Multinational Enterprises, Economic Structure and International Competitiveness* (Chichester, UK: John Wiley).

Dunning, J. (1988) *Explaining International Production* (London: Unwin Hyman).

Dunning, J. (1991) 'Governments and Multinational Enterprises: From Confrontation to Cooperation', *Millennium*, 20(2): 225–39.

Dutta, S., Geiger, T., and Lanvin, B. (eds) (2015) 'The Global Information Technology Report 2015: ICTs for Inclusive Growth' (Geneva: World Economic Forum and INSEAD).

Eamon, J. (2010) *Broker, Trader, Lawyer, Spy: The Secret World of Corporate Espionage* (New York: Haprer Collins Business).

Earle, E. M. (1986) 'Adam Smith, Alexander Hamilton, Fredrich List: The Economic Foundations of Military Power', in P. Paret (ed.) *Makers of Modern Strategy: From Machiavelli to the Nuclear Age* (Princeton, NJ: Princeton University Press).

Eckersley, R. (1992) *Environmentalism and Political Theory* (London: UCL Press).

Economic Times (2014) 'ISIS Poses Major Threat to Global Security: Angela Merkel', 4 October, http://articles.economictimes.indiatimes.com/2014-10-04/news/54626675_1_german-chancellor-angela-merkel-jihadists-berlin-wall, last accessed 17 October 2015.

Economist, The (2006) 'A Guide to Womenomics: The Future of the World Lies Increasingly in Female Hands', 12 April, www.economist.com/node/6802551, last accessed 19 December 2012.

Eichengreen, B. (1996) *Globalizing Capital: A History of the International Monetary System* (Princeton, NJ: Princeton University Press).

Eichengreen, B. (2011) *Exorbitant Privilege: The Rise and Fall of the Dollar and the Future of the International Monetary System* (Oxford: Oxford University Press).

Eisenhower, D. D. (1961) 'Farewell Address', 17 January, www.eisenhowermemorial.org, last accessed 5 March 2009.

EJF (2015) *Pirates and Slaves: How Over-Fishing in Thailand Fuels Human Trafficking and the Plundering of our Oceans* (London: Environmental Justice Foundation).

Ekins, P. (1989) 'Trade and Self-reliance', *Ecologist*, 19(5): 186–90.

Elahi, K. (2004) 'Microcredit and the Third World: Perspectives from Moral and Political Philosophy', *International Journal of Social Economics*, 31(7): 643–54.

Elias, J. (2005) 'The Gendered Political Economy of Control and Resistance on the Shop Floor of the Multinational Firm: A Case Study from Malaysia', *New Political Economy*, 10(2): 203–22.

Elias, P. (2006) 'Bioprospectors Raise Ire as They Patent More Life Forms', *Detroit News*, 21 January.

Elliott, L. (2007) 'Environment and Security: What's the Connection?' *Australian Defence Force Journal*, 174: 39–52.

Elms, D. K. (2008) 'New Directions for IPE: Drawing from Behavioral Economics', *International Studies Review*, 10(2): 239–65.

Elster, J. (1985) *Making Sense of Marx* (Cambridge: Cambridge University Press).

Emmanuel, A. (1972) *Unequal Exchange* (London: New Left Books).

Engel, P. (2015) 'ISIS is Revolutionising International Terrorism Recruitment', *Business Insider Australia*, 9 May, http://www.businessinsider.com.au/isis-is-revolutionizing-international-terrorism-2015-5, last accessed 20 May 2015.

Enloe, C. (1989) *Bananas, Beaches and Bases: Making Feminist Sense of International Politics* (London: Pandora).

Escobar, A. (1995) *Encountering Development: The Making and Unmaking of the Third World* (Princeton, NJ: Princeton University Press).

Esping-Andersen, G. (1990) *The Three Worlds of Welfare Capitalism* (Princeton, NJ: Princeton University Press).

EUbusiness (2012) 'Europe Ends Beef Trade War with US, Canada', 14 March, www.eubusiness.com/ news-eu/us-canada-trade.fon/, Last accessed 20 January 2013.

European Commission (1997) 'Building the European Information Society for Us All: Final Policy Report of a High Level Group' (Brussels: European Commission, Directorate-General for Employment, Industrial Relations and Social Affairs).

Faiola, A. (2008) 'The End of American Capitalism?' *Washington Post*, 10 October.

Fanon, F. (1963) *The Wretched of the Earth* (New York: Grove).

FAO (Food and Agriculture Organization) (1996) 'Rome Declaration on World Food Security and World Food Summit Action Plan' (Rome: FAO).

FAO (2009) 'The State of Food Insecurity in the World 2008' (Rome: FAO).

Feldstein, M. (1992) 'The Case Against EMU', *The Economist*, 13 June, 19–22.

Financial Times (2014) 'The Future of the Renminbi', 30 September 2014.

Fine, B., Lapavitas, C. and Pincus, J. (eds) (2001) *Development Policy in the Twenty-First Century: Beyond the Post–Washington Consensus* (London: Routledge).

Finlayson, J. A. and Zacher, M. W. (1981) 'The GATT and the Regulation of Trade Barriers: Regime Dynamics and Functions', *International Organization*, 35(3): 561–602.

Finnemore, M. and Sikkink, K. (1998) 'International Norm Dynamics and Political Change', *International Organization*, 52(4): 887–917.

Floyd, K. and Gilks, C. (1998) 'Cost and Financial Aspects of Providing Anti-Retroviral Therapy', background paper for the online conference 'Anti-Retroviral (ARV) Treatment in Developing Countries: Questions of Economics, Equity and Ethics', www.worldbank.org/aids-econ/ arv/index.htm#Readings, last accessed 30 May 2006.

Fontana, M., Joekes, S. and Masika, R. (1998) 'Global Trade Expansion and Liberalisation: Gender Issues and Impacts', BRIDGE Report 42 (Brighton, UK: Institute of Development Studies).

Forslund, D. (2014) 'The Bermuda Connection: Profit Shifting and Unaffordability at Lonmin 1999-2012' (Cape Town: Alternative Information and Development Centre).

Fortune (2014) 'Global 500 2014', http://fortune.com/global500/, last accessed 20 May 2015.

Fraja, G. de and Hartley, K. (1996) 'Defence Procurement: Theory and UK Policy', *Oxford Review of Economic Policy*, 12(4): 70–88.

Frank, A. G. (1967) *Capitalism and Underdevelopment in Latin America* (New York: Monthly Review).

Frank, A. G. (1969) *Latin America: Underdevelopment or Revolution* (New York: Monthly Review).

Frank, A. G. (1998) *ReOrient: Global Economy in the Asian Age* (Berkeley, CA: University of California Press).

Freedman, L. (1985) *The Evolution of Nuclear Strategy* (London: Macmillan).

Frieden, J. (1981) 'Third World Indebted Industrialization: International Finance and State Capitalism in Mexico, Brazil, Algeria and South Korea', *International Organization*, 35(1): 407–31.

Frieden, J. (1987) *Banking On the World* (New York: Harper & Row).

Frieden, J. and Martin, L. (2003) 'International Political Economy: Global and Domestic Interactions', in I. Katznelson and H. V. Milner (eds) *Political Science: The State of the Discipline* (New York: W. W. Norton).

Frobel, F., Heinrichs, J. and Kreye, O. (1980) *New International Division of Labour* (Cambridge: Cambridge University Press).

Fukuyama, F. (1992) *The End of History and the Last Man* (New York: Free Press).

G20 (2000) 'Meeting of the G-20 Finance Ministers and Central Bank Governors, Montreal', 25 October, http://www.g20.utoronto.ca/ministerials.html, last accessed 19 October 2015.

Galbraith, J. K. (1975) *The Great Crash 1929* (London: Penguin).

Galbraith, J. K. (1996) *Money: Whence It Came and Where It Went* (Boston, MA: Houghton Mifflin).

Galtung, J. (1969) 'Violence, Peace and Peace Research', *Journal of Peace Research*, 6(3): 167–91.

Gamble, A., Payne, A., Dietrich, M., et al. (1996) 'Editorial Statement', *New Political Economy*, 1(1): 5–11.

Gamier, D. (2005) *Ayutthaya: Venice of the East* (Bangkok: River).

Garber, P. (1989) 'Tulipmania', *Journal of Political Economy*, 97(3): 535–60.

Garrett, G. (2000) 'Shrinking States? Globalization and National Autonomy', in N. Woods (ed.) *The Political Economy of Globalization* (Basingstoke, UK: Macmillan).

Garside, J. (2012) 'Apple's Factories in China are Breaking Employment Laws, Audit Finds', *Guardian*, 30 March, www.guardian.co.uk/technology/2012/mar/30/apple-factories-china-foxconn-audit, last accessed 15 May 2012.

GATT (1994) 'Annex 1 C (Trade-Related Aspects of Intellectual Property Rights)', *Marrakesh Agreement Establishing the World Trade Organization* (Geneva: WTO).

Geddes, B. (2003) *Paradigms and Sand Castles: Theory Building and Research Design in Comparative Politics* (Ann Arbor, MI: University of Michigan Press).

Gereffi, G. and Fernandez-Stark, K. (2011) 'Global Value Chain Analysis: A Primer' (Durham, NC: Center on Globalization, Governance & Competitiveness, Duke University), http://www.cggc.duke.edu/pdfs/2011-05-31_GVC_analysis_a_primer.pdf, last accessed 17 October 2015.

Gereffi, G. and Korzeniewicz, M. (eds) (1994) *Commodity Chains and Global Capitalism* (London: Praeger).

Germain, R. (1997) *The International Organization of Credit: States and Global Finance in the World-Economy* (Cambridge: Cambridge University Press).

Gerth, H. H. and Mills, C. W. (eds) (1958) *From Max Weber: Essays in Sociology* (New York: Oxford University Press).

Gertzl, C. (1995) 'The New World Order: Implications for Development', Briefing Paper 35 (Canberra: Development Bulletin).

Gilbert, A. (1999) *Must Global Politics Constrain Democracy? Great Power Realism, Democratic Peace, and Democratic Internationalism* (Princeton, NJ: Princeton University Press).

Gilbert, J. (2015). 'Debt Dispute between Hedge Funds and Argentina at Impasse', *New York Times*, 5 January, http://dealbook.nytimes.com/2015/01/05/debt-dispute-between-argentina-and-hedge-funds-at-impasse/?_r=0, last accessed 4 May 2015.

Gill, S. (ed.) (1993) *Gramsci, Historical Materialism and International Relations* (Cambridge: Cambridge University Press).

Gill, S. (2003) 'Globalizing Elites in the Emerging World Order', in S. Gill, *Power and Resistance in the New World Order* (Basingstoke, UK: Palgrave Macmillan).

Gill, S. and Law, D. (1988) *The Global Political Economy* (Baltimore, MD: Johns Hopkins University Press).

Gill, S. and Law, D. (1993) 'Global Hegemony and the Structural Power of Capital', in S. Gill (ed.) *Gramsci, Historical Materialism and International Relations* (Cambridge: Cambridge University Press).

Gilmore, G. (2009) 'Obama Cites $40 Billion in Defense Procurement Budget', *American Forces Press Service*, http://archive.defense.gov/news/newsarticle.aspx?id=53627, last accessed 17 October 2015.

Gilpin, R. (1981) *Change and War in World Politics* (Cambridge: Cambridge University Press).

Gilpin, R. (1987) *The Political Economy of International Relations* (Princeton, NJ: Princeton University Press).

Global Witness (2010) 'The Hill Belongs to Them: The Need for International Action on Congo's Conflict Mineral Trade', www.globalwitness.org, last accessed 28 May 2012.

Goede, M. de (2003) 'Beyond Economism in International Political Economy', *Review of International Studies*, 29(1): 79–97.

Goede, M. de (2006) *International Political Economy and Poststructural Politics* (Basingstoke, UK: Palgrave Macmillan).

Goldin I., Knudsen, O. and van der Mensbrugghe, D. (1993) *Trade Liberalisation: Global Economic Implications* (Paris: OECD).

Goldin, I. and Reinert, K. (2007) *Globalization for Development: Trade, Finance, Aid, Migration and Policy* (Washington, DC: The International Bank for Reconstruction and Development / World Bank).

Goldman, E. O. and Blanken, L. J. (2005) 'The Economic Foundations of Military Power', in P. Dombrowski (ed.) *Guns and Butter: The Political Economy of International Security* (Boulder, CO: Lynne Rienner).

Goldstein, J. and Keohane, R. (eds) (1993) *Ideas and Foreign Policy: Beliefs, Institutions and Political Change* (Ithaca, NY: Cornell University Press).

Goodin, R. E. (1992) *Green Political Theory* (Cambridge, UK: Polity).

Goodman, J. and Ranald, P. (eds) (2000) *Stopping the Juggernaut: Public Interest Versus the Multilateral Agreement on Investment* (Annandale, NSW: Pluto).

Gordenker, L. and Weiss, L. (1999) 'Pluralizing Global Governance: Analytical Approaches and Dimensions', in L. Weiss and L. Gordenker (eds) *NGOs, the UN and Global Governance* (Boulder, CO: Lynne Rienner).

Gott, G. (2000) 'Critical Race Globalism? Global Political Economy and the Intersections of Race, Nation and Class', *University of California Davis Law Review*, 33: 1503–18.

Gottfried, H. (2004) 'Gendering Globalization Discourses', *Critical Sociology*, 30(1): 9–15.

Graham-Harrison, E. (2015) 'Greece Needs Further Debt Relief After Third Bailout Deal in Five Years, Says IMF Chief', *Observer*, 16 August, http://www.theguardian.com/world/2015/aug/15/greece-needs-more-debt-relief-imf-lagarde, last accessed 5 September 2015.

Grant, A. (2013) 'Does Studying Economics Breed Greed', *Psychology Today*, https://www.psychologytoday.com/blog/give-and-take/201310/does-studying-economics-breed-greed, last accessed 30 April 2015.

Graz, J. C. (2001) 'Beyond States and Markets: Comparative and Global Political Economy in the Age of Hybrids', *Review of International Political Economy*, 8(4): 739–48.

Green Climate Fund (2015) 'GCF Reaches Effectiveness, Can Begin Allocating Resources Ahead of Paris Climate Conference', 21 May, http://news.gcfund.org/wp-content/uploads/2015/05/GCF_press_release_21_may_2015.pdf, last accessed 17 October 2015.

Greenaway, D. and Hine, R. C. (1991) 'Introduction: Trends in World Trade and Protection', in D. Greenaway, R. Hine, A. O'Brien and R. Thornton (eds) *Global Protectionism* (Basingstoke, UK: Macmillan).

Greenpeace (2015) *Bhopal Disaster*, http://www.greenpeace.org/usa/en/campaigns/toxics/justice-for-bhopal/, last accessed 20 May 2015.

Greenspan, A. (1998) 'The Regulation of OTC Derivatives', testimony of Chairman Alan Greenspan before the Committee on Banking and Financial Services, US House of Representatives, 24 July, http://www.federalreserve.gov/boarddocs/testimony/1998/19980724.htm, last accessed 17 October 2015.

Greenwald, G., MacAskill, E., Poitras, L., Ackerman, S. and Rushe, D. (2013) 'How Microsoft Handed the NSA Access to Encrypted Messages', *Guardian*, 12 July.

Grieco, J. M. and Ikenberry, G. J. (2003) *State Power and World Markets: The International Political Economy* (New York: W. W. Norton).

Griffin, P. (2007) 'Refashioning IPE: What and How Gender Analysis Teaches International (Global) Political Economy', *Review of International Political Economy*, 14(4): 719–36.

Griffin, P. (2009) *Gendering the World Bank: Neoliberalism and the Gendered Foundations of Global Governance* (Basingstoke, UK: Palgrave Macmillan).

Griffin, P. (2015) 'Crisis, Austerity and Gendered Governance: A Feminist Perspective', *Feminist Review*, 109(February): 49–72.

Griffiths, H. (1999) 'A Political Economy of Ethnic Conflict and Ethno-Nationalism and Organized Crime', *Civil Wars*, 2(2): 56–73.

Grimwade, N. (2000) *International Trade: New Patterns of Trade, Production and Investment* (London: Routledge).

Griswold, D. (2003) 'Free-Trade Agreements: Stepping Stones to a More Open World', Trade Briefing Paper 18 (Cato Institute Centre for Trade Policy Studies), www.freetrade.org/pubs/briefskbp-018.pdf, last accessed 17 October 2015.

Gruffydd Jones, B. (2005) 'Africa and the Poverty of International Relations', *Third World Quarterly*, 26(6): 987–1003.

Guardian (2015a) 'Tsipras Declares End to "Vicious Cycle" of Austerity after Syriza Wins Greek Election – As It Happened', *Guardian*, 26 January.

Guardian (2015b) 'The Guardian View on HSBC Files: A Damning Dossier', *Guardian*, 9 February, www.theguardian.com/commentisfree/2015/feb/09/guardian-view-hsbc-files-damning-dossier, last accessed 26 February 2015.

Guzzini, S. (2000) 'A Reconstruction of Constructivism in International Relations', *European Journal of International Relations*, 6(2): 147–82.

Haas, P. (1990a) *Saving the Mediterranean* (New York: Columbia University Press).

Haas, P. (1990b) 'Obtaining International Environmental Protection Through Epistemic Consensus', *Millennium*, 19(3): 347–63.

Haas, P. (1992) 'Introduction: Epistemic Communities and International Policy Coordination', *International Organization*, 46(1): 1–35.

Hafner-Burton, E. and Pollack, M. A. (2002) 'Mainstreaming Gender in Global Governance', *European Journal of International Relations*, 8(3): 339–73.

Hall, P. and Soskice, D. (eds) (2001) *Varieties of Capitalism: The Institutional Foundations of Comparative Advantage* (Oxford: Oxford University Press).

Hall, R. and Biersteker, T. (eds) (2002) *The Emergence of Private Authority in Global Governance* (Cambridge: Cambridge University Press).

Hallam, D. (2011) 'International Investment in Developing Country Agriculture - Issues and Challenges', *Food Security*, 3(S1): 91–98.

Hallding, K, Jürisoo , M., Carson, M. and Atteridge, A. (2013) 'Rising Powers: The Evolving Role of BASIC Countries', *Climate Policy*, 13(5): 608–631.

Halliday, F. (1983) *The Making of the Second Cold War* (London: Verso).

Hamilton, A. ([1791]1991) 'Report on Manufactures', in G. T. Crane and A. Amawi (eds) *The Theoretical Evolution of International Political Economy: A Reader* (Oxford: Oxford University Press).

Harmes, A. (1998) 'Institutional Investors and the Reproduction of Neoliberalism', *Review of International Political Economy*, 5(1): 92–121.

Harrison, K. and Sundstrom, L. M. (2007) 'The Comparative Politics of Climate Change', *Global Environmental Politics*, 7(4): 1–18.

Harrod, J. and O'Brien, R. (eds) (2002) *Global Unions? Theory and Strategy of Organised Labour in the Global Political Economy* (London: Routledge).

Harvard Magazine (2001) 'Toxic Memo', May/June, www.harvardmagazine.com/on-line/050171.html, last accessed 3 January 2013.

Harvey, D. (2011) *The Enigma of Capital and the Crisis of Capitalism* (Oxford: Oxford University Press).

Hasenclever, A., Mayer, P. and Rittberger, V. (1997) *Theories of International Regimes* (Cambridge: Cambridge University Press).

Hayami, J. (2003) 'From the Washington Consensus to the Post–Washington Consensus: Retrospect and Prospect', *Asian Development Review*, 20(2): 40–65.

Hayek, F. A. von (1944) *The Road to Serfdom* (London: George Routledge & Sons).

Heckscher, E. (1919) 'The Effect of Foreign Trade on the Distribution of Income', in H. S. Ellis and L. A. Metzler (eds) (1949) *Readings in the Theory of International Trade* (Homewood, IL: Irwin).

Held, D. (1995) *Democracy and the Global Order: From the Modern State to Cosmopolitan Governance* (Cambridge, UK: Polity).

Held, D. (2005) 'At the Global Crossroads: The End of the Washington Consensus and the Rise of Global Social Democracy?' *Globalization*, 52(1): 95–113.

Helleiner, E. (1996) 'International Political Economy and the Greens', *New Political Economy*, 1(1): 59–77.

Helleiner, E. (2005) 'The Strange Story of Bush and the Argentine Debt Crisis', *Third World Quarterly*, 26(6): 951–69.

Helleiner, E. (2008) 'Political Determinants of International Currencies: What Future for the Dollar?' *Review of International Political Economy*, 15(3): 354–78.

Henry, J. S. (2012) 'The Price of Offshore Revisited', *Tax Justice Network*, http://www.taxjustice.net/cms/upload/pdf/Price_of_Offshore_Revisited_120722.pdf, last accessed 22 June 2015.

Herod, A. (1997) 'Labor as an Agent of Globalization and as a Global Agent', in K. Cox (ed.) *Spaces of Globalization* (New York: Guilford).

Herod, A. (2001) *Labor Geographies: Workers and the Landscapes of Capitalism* (New York: Guilford).

Heron, T. (2006) 'The Ending of the Multifibre Arrangement: A Development Boon for the South?' *The European Journal of Development Research*, 18(1): 1–21.

Hewson, M. and Sinclair, T. J. (1999) 'The Emergence of Global Governance Theory', in M. Hewson and T. J. Sinclair (eds) *Approaches to Global Governance Theory* (Albany, NY: SUNY Press).

Higgott, R. (1998) 'The Asian Economic Crisis: A Study in the Politics of Resentment', *New Political Economy*, 4(1): 333–56.

Hirst, P. and Thompson, G. (1996) *Globalization in Question* (Cambridge, UK: Polity).

Hobsbawm, E. J. (1987) *Industry and Empire: From 1750 to the Present Day* (Harmondsworth, UK: Penguin).

Hobson, J. (1902) *Imperialism: A Study* (London: George Allen & Unwin).

Hobson, J. M. (2004) *The Eastern Origins of Western Civilization* (Cambridge: Cambridge University Press).

Hochschild, A. (1999) *King Leopold's Ghost: A Story of Greed, Terror and Heroism in Colonial Africa* (New York: First Mariner).

Hoogvelt, A. (1997) *Globalisation and the Postcolonial World: The New Political Economy of Development* (Basingstoke, UK: Macmillan).

Hopf, T. (1998) 'The Promise of Constructivism in International Relations', *International Security*, 23(1): 171–200.

Horta, K. (1996) 'The World Bank and the International Monetary Fund', in J. Werksman (ed.) *Greening International Institutions* (London: Earthscan).

Hoskyns, C. and Rai, S. M. (2007) 'Recasting the Global Political Economy: Counting Women's Unpaid Work', *New Political Economy*, 12(3): 297–317.

Houlder, V. (2013) 'Offshore Wealth Grows Despite Crackdown on Tax Havens' *Financial Times*, 30 May.

Howard, M. E. (2008) *War and the Liberal Conscience* (New York: Columbia University Press).

Howard, M. E. (2009) *War in European History* (New York: Oxford University Press).

HSBC (2011) 'The World in 2050: Quantifying the Shift in the Global Economy', HSBC Global Research, January.

Huck-Ju, K. (2001) 'Globalization, Unemployment and Policy Responses in Korea: Repositioning the State?' *Global Social Policy*, 1(2): 213–34.

Hudson, N. F. (2009) *Gender, Human Security and the United Nations: Security Language as a Political Framework for Women* (London: Routledge).

Hufbauer, G. C. and Elliott, K. (1994) *Measuring the Costs of Protection in the United States* (Washington, DC: Institute for International Economics).

Hufbauer, G. C., Schott, J. J., Elliott, K. A. and Oegg, B. (2007) *Economic Sanctions Reconsidered*, 3rd edn (Washington, DC: Peterson Institute of International Economics).

Hughes, H. (ed.) (1988) *Achieving Industrialization in Asia* (Cambridge: Cambridge University Press).

Hughes, H. (1989) 'Catching Up: The Asian Newly Industrializing Economies in the 1990s', *Asian Development Review*, 7(2): 128–44.

Hulme, D. and Edwards, M. (eds) (1997) *NGOs, States and Donors: Too Close For Comfort?* (Basingstoke, UK: Macmillan).

Human Security Centre (2005) 'Human Security Report' (Oxford: Oxford University Press).

Huntington, S. P. (1991) *The Third Wave of Democratization in the Late Twentieth Century* (Norman, OK: University of Oklahoma Press).

Hurrell, A. and Kingsbury, B. (1992) 'The International Politics of the Environment: An Introduction', in A. Hurrell and B. Kingsbury (eds) *The International Politics of the Environment* (Oxford: Clarendon).

Hurrell, A. and Narlikar, A. (2006) 'A New Politics of Confrontation? Brazil and India in Multilateral Trade Negotiations', *Global Society*, 20(4): 415–433.

Hurrell, A. and Sengupta, S. (2012) 'Emerging Powers, North–South Relations and Global Climate Politics', *International Affairs*, 88(3): 463–484.

Hymer, S. (1976) *The International Operation of National Firms* (Cambridge, MA: MIT Press).

Hymer, S. (1979) *The Multinational Corporation: A Radical Approach* (Cambridge: Cambridge University Press).

ICFTU (International Confederation of Free Trade Unions) (1995a) *From the Ashes: A Toy Factory Fire in Thailand* (Brussels: ICFTU).

ICFTU (1995b) 'Rethinking the Role of the IMF and World Bank: ICFTU Proposals to the Annual Meetings of the Board of Governors of the IMF and World Bank', Washington, DC, 10–12 October.

ICFTU (1996a) *Behind the Wire: Anti-Union Repression in the Export Processing Zones* (Brussels: ICFTU).

ICFTU (1996b) *No Time to Play: Child Workers in the Global Economy* (Brussels: ICFTU).

IDA/IMF (International Development Association / International Monetary Fund) (2009) 'Heavily Indebted Poor Countries (HIPC) Initiative and Multilateral Debt Relief Initiative (MDRI) – Status of Implementation', www.imf.org/external/np/pp/2007/eng/082807.pdf, last accessed 17 October 2015.

IDA/IMF (2014) 'Heavily Indebted Poor Countries (HIPC) Initiative and Multilateral Debt Relief Initiative (MDRI) - Statistical Update', https://www.imf.org/external/np/pp/eng/2014/121214.pdf, last accessed 17 October 2015.

Ietto-Gillies, G. (2012) *Transnational Corporations and International Production: Concepts, Theories and Effects*, 2nd edn (Cheltenham, UK: Edward Elgar).

IFPI (2015) 'IFPI Digital Music Report 2015', http://www.ifpi.org/downloads/Digital-Music-Report-2015.pdf, last accessed 17 October 2015.

Iliffe, J. (1995) *Africans: The History of a Continent* (Cambridge: Cambridge University Press).

ILO (International Labour Organization) (1998a) 'Labour and Social Issues Relating to Export Processing Zones' (Geneva: ILO).

ILO (1998b) 'Export Processing Zones Growing Steadily', 28 September, www.ilo.org/ global/about-the-ilo/newsroom/news/WCMS_007997/lang--en/index.htm, last accessed 13 December 2012.

ILO (2006) 'Global Employment Trends: BRIEF', January 2006, www.ilo.org/public/english/employment/strat/download/getb06en.Pdf, last accessed 26 January 2007.

ILO (2009) 'Global Employment Trends For Women' (Geneva: ILO).

ILO (2012) 'Global Employment Trends for Women' (Geneva: ILO).

ILO (2015a) 'Women and the Future of Work: Beijing+20 and Beyond' (Geneva: ILO).

ILO (2015b) 'World Employment and Social Outlook: Trends 2015' (Geneva: ILO Research Department).

ILO (2015c) 'World Social Protection Report 2014/15' (Geneva: ILO).

IMF (International Monetary Fund) (1995) 'IMF Approves US$17.8 Billion Stand-By Credit for Mexico', 1 February, www.imf.org/external/np/sec/pr/1995/pr9510.htm, last accessed 17 October 2015.

IMF (2008) 'World Economic Outlook Database, October' (Washington, DC: IMF).

IMF (2012a) 'World Economic Outlook Database, April' (Washington, DC: IMF).

IMF (2012b) 'IMF Members' Quotas and Voting Power, and IMF Board of Governors' (Washington, DC: IMF).

IMF (2015) 'IMF Members' Quotas and Voting Power, and IMF Board of Governors' (Washington, DC: IMF).

Ingram, J. (2011) 'Foreword' in The North–South Institute (ed.) 'Canadian Development Report 2011, Global Challenges: Multilateral Solutions' (Ottawa: The North–South Institute), pp. 7–14, http://www.nsi-ins.ca/publications/canadian-development-report-2011-2/, last accessed 17 October 2015.

International Centre for Trade and Sustainable Development (2012) 'US–China Clean Energy Rift Deepens Over Wind Tower Countervailing Duty Announcement', *Bridges Weekly Trade News Digest*, 16(22): 5–6.

International Commission on Intervention and State Sovereignty (2001) *The Responsibility to Protect* (Ottawa: International Development Centre).

International Herald Tribune (1998) 'World Bank Targets the Next Asian Danger: Growing Social Unrest', 2 February, p. 4.

International Transport Workers' Federation (2012) 'What are Flags of Convenience?' http://itf.global.org, last accessed 14 May 2012.

IPCC (2013) 'Working Group I Contribution to the IPCC Fifth Assessment Report; Climate Change 2013: The Physical Science Basis; Summary for Policymakers', http://www.ipcc.ch/report/ar5/wg1/, last accessed 17 October 2015.

IPU (2015) 'Women in National Parliaments', http://www.ipu.org/wmn-e/world.htm, last accessed 17 October 2015.

ITU (International Telecommunications Union) (2006) 'World Telecommunication/ICT Development Report 2006: Measuring ICT for Social and Economic Development' (Geneva: ITU).

ITU (2011) 'ICT Facts and Figures', www.itu.int, last accessed 29 May 2012.

ITU (2015) 'ICT Facts and Figures: The World in 2015', http://www.itu.int/en/ITU-D/Statistics/Documents/facts/ICTFactsFigures2015.pdf, last accessed 17 October 2015.

Jackson, J. H. (1969) *World Trade Law and the GATT: A Legal Analysis of the General Agreement on Tariffs and Trade* (Indianapolis, IN: Bobbs-Merrill).

Jackson, J. H. (2006) *Sovereignty, the WTO, and Changing Fundamentals of International Law* (Cambridge: Cambridge University Press).

James, J. (2001) 'Bridging the Digital Divide with Low-Cost Information Technologies', *Journal of Information Science*, 27(4): 211–17.

Javers, E. (2010) *Broker, Trader, Lawyer, Spy: The Secret World of Corporate Espionage* (New York: Harper Collins Business).

Jeffreys, S. (2009) *The Industrial Vagina: The Political Economy of the Global Sex Trade* (New York: Routledge).

Jenkins, R. (2003) 'International Development Institutions and National Economic Contexts: Neoliberalism Encounters India's Indigenous Political Traditions', *Economy and Society*, 32(4): 584–610.

Joachim, J. (2003) 'Framing Issues and Seizing Opportunities: The UN, NGOs, and Women's Rights', *International Studies Quarterly*, 47(2): 247–74.

Joekes, S. P. (1987) *Women in the World Economy: An INSTRAW Study* (Oxford: Oxford University Press).

Julian, C. C., Ahmed, Z. U. and Xu, J. (eds) (2014) *Research Handbook on the Globalization of Chinese Firms* (Cheltenham, UK: Edward Elgar).

Julius, D. (1990) *Global Companies and Public Policy: The Growing Challenge of Foreign Direct Investment* (London: Royal Institute of International Affairs/Pinter).

Kabeer, N. (1994) *Reversed Realities: Gender Hierarchies in Development Thought* (London: Verso).

Kahl, C. H. (2005) 'Plight or Plunder? Natural Resources and Civil War', in P. Dombrowski (ed.) *Guns and Butter: The Political Economy of International Security* (Boulder, CO: Lynne Rienner).

Kahn, M. S. and Knight, M. D. (1986) *Fund-Supported Adjustment Programs*, Occasional Paper 42 (Washington, DC: IMF).

Kaldor, M. (1997) *Restructuring the Global Military Sector: New Wars* (London: Pinter).

Kaldor, M. (1999) *New and Old Wars: Organized Violence in a Global Era* (Stanford, CA: Stanford University Press).

Kaldor, M. (2007) *Human Security: Reflections on Globalizaiton and Intervention* (Cambridge, UK: Polity).

Kant, I. ([1795]1991) 'Perpetual Peace: A Philosophical Sketch', in H. Reis (ed.) *Kant: Political Writings* (Cambridge: Cambridge University Press).

Kaplinsky, R. (1991) 'TNCs in the Third World: Stability or Discontinuity?' *Millennium*, 20(2): 257–68.

Kar, D. and Spanjers, J. (2014) *Illicit Financial Flows from Developing Countries: 2003-2012* (Washington, DC: Global Financial Integrity), http://www.gfintegrity.org/wp-content/uploads/2014/12/Illicit-Financial-Flows-from-Developing-Countries-2003-2012.pdf, last accessed 17 October 2015.

Kearney, N. (1999) 'Corporate Codes of Conduct: The Privatized Application of Labour Standards', in R. Mayne and S. Picciotto (eds) *Regulating International Business: Beyond Liberalization* (Basingstoke, UK: Macmillan).

Kearns, A. and Forrest, R. (2000) 'Social Cohesion and Multilevel Urban Governance', *Urban Studies*, 37(5/6): 995–1017.

Keck, M. and Sikkink, K. (1998) *Activists Beyond Borders: Advocacy Networks in International Politics* (Ithaca, NY: Cornell University Press).

Kemp, T. (1983) *Industrialization in the Non-Western World* (London: Longman).

Kempadoo, K. (1999) (ed.) *Sun, Sex and Gold: Tourism and Sex Work in the Caribbean* (Lanham, MD: Rowman and Littlefield).

Kennedy, P. (1987) *The Rise and Fall of the Great Powers: Economic Change and Military Conflict from 1500 to 2000* (New York: Random House).

Kentikelenis, A., King, L., McKee, M. and Stuckler, D. (2015) 'The International Monetary Fund and the Ebola outbreak', *Lancet* 2(3): 69–70.

Keohane, R. O. (1984) *After Hegemony* (Princeton, NJ: Princeton University Press).

Keohane, R. O. (1989a) 'A Personal Intellectual History', in R. O. Keohane (ed.) *International Institutions and State Power: Essays in International Relations Theory* (Boulder, CO: Westview).

Keohane, R. O. (ed.) (1989b) *International Institutions and State Power: Essays in International Relations Theory* (Boulder, CO: Westview).

Keohane, R. O. (2002) 'Introduction: From Interdependence and Institutions to Globalization and Governance', in R. O. Keohane, *Power and Governance in a Partially Globalizing World* (London: Routledge).

Keohane, R. O. and Nye, J. (1977) *Power and Interdependence: World Politics in Transition* (Boston, MA: Little, Brown).

Keynes, J. M. (1936) *The General Theory of Employment, Interest and Money* (London: Macmillan).

Khagram, S., Riker, J. V. and Sikkink, K. (2002) 'From Santiago to Seattle: Transnational Advocacy Groups Restructuring World Politics', in S. Khagram, J. V. Riker and K. Sikkink (eds) *Restructuring World Politics: Transnational Movements, Networks and Norms* (Minneapolis, MN: University of Minnesota Press).

Kindleberger, C. P. (1969) *American Business Abroad* (New Haven, CT: Yale University Press).

Kindleberger, C. P. (1986) *The World Depression 1929–1939* (Berkeley, CA: University of California Press).

Kindleberger, C. P. (1993) *A Financial History of Western Europe*, 2nd edn (Oxford: Oxford University Press).

Kirschner, J. (2008) 'Dollar Primacy and American Power: What's at Stake?', *Review of International Political Economy*, 15(3): 418–38.

Kitching, G. (2001) *Seeking Social Justice through Globalization* (University Park, PA: Pennsylvania State University Press).

Klein, N. (2001) *No Logo: Taking Aim at the Brand Bullies* (New York: St. Martins).

Klein, N. (2014) *This Changes Everything: Capitalism vs. the Climate* (Toronto: Alfred A. Knopff).

Knorr, K. (1975) *The Power of Nations* (New York: Basic Books).

Kock, K. (1969) *International Trade Policy and the GATT, 1947–1967* (Stockholm: Almqvist and Wiksell).

Kopinak, K. (1995) 'Gender as a Vehicle for the Subordination of Women Maquiladora Workers in Mexico', *Latin American Perspectives*, 22(1): 30–48.

Korinek, J. (2005) 'Trade and Gender: Issues and Interactions', Trade Policy Working Papers 24 (Paris: OECD).

Kotz, D. M. and Wolfson, M. H. (2004) 'Déjà Vu All Over Again: The "New" Economy in Historical Perspective', *Labor Studies Journal*, 28(4): 25–44.

Kovach, H., Neligan, C. and Burall, S. (2002/3) *Power Without Accountability?* (London: One World Trust).

Krasner, S. D. (1976) 'State Power and the Structure of International Trade', *World Politics*, 28(3): 317–48.

Krasner, S. D. (ed.) (1983) *International Regimes* (Ithaca, NY: Cornell University Press).

Krause, K. and Williams, M. C. (eds) (1997) *Critical Security Studies: Concepts and Cases* (London: UCL Press).

Krol, K. (2008) 'Trade, Protectionism, and the U.S. Economy: Examining the Evidence', Cato Institute Trade Briefing Paper, http://object.cato.org/sites/cato.org/files/pubs/pdf/tbp-028.pdf, last accessed 14 June 2015.

Krueger, A. (ed.) (2000) *Economic Policy Reform: The Second Stage* (Chicago: University of Chicago Press).

Krugman, P. (ed.) (1986) *Strategic Trade Policy and the New International Economics* (Cambridge, MA: MIT Press).

Krugman, P. (1987) 'Is Free Trade Passé?' *Journal of Economic Perspectives*, 1(2): 131–44.

Krugman, P. (2005) 'The Chinese Connection', *New York Times*, 20 May.

Krugman, P. (2008) *Depression Economics* (New York: W. W. Norton).

Kuznets, S. (1966) *Modern Economic Growth* (New Haven, CT: Yale University Press).

Kwa, A. (2003) *Power Politics in the WTO* (Bangkok: Focus on the Global South).

Laferrière, E. (1994) 'Environmentalism and the Global Divide', *Environmental Politics*, 3(1): 91–113.

Lall, S. (1991) 'Multinational Enterprises and Developing Countries: Some Issues for Research in the 1990s', *Millennium*, 20(2): 251–6.

Lall, S. and Streeten, P. (1977) *Foreign Investment, Transnationals and Developing Countries* (London: Macmillan).

Lampietti, J.A. and Stalker, L. (2000) 'Consumption Expenditure and Female Poverty: A Review of the Evidence: A Policy Research Report on Gender and Development', Working Paper 11 (Washington, DC: World Bank, Development Research Group / Poverty Reduction and Economic Management Network).

Landes, D. S. (1998) *The Wealth and Poverty of Nations* (New York: W. W. Norton).

Landes, D. S. (2003) *The Unbound Prometheus* (Cambridge: Cambridge University Press).

Lanoszka, A. (2003) 'The Global Politics of Intellectual Property Rights and Pharmaceutical Drug Policies in Developing Countries', *International Political Science Review*, 24(2): 181–97.

Lasch, C. (1996) *The Revolt of the Elites and the Betrayal of Democracy* (New York: W. W. Norton).

Lavelle, K. C. (2005) 'Moving in from the Periphery: Africa and the Study of International Political Economy', *Review of International Political Economy*, 12(2): 364–79.

Law and Development Review (2014) Special Issue: 'Law and Development Perspective of International Land Acquisitions', *Law and Development Review*, 7(2).

Lazarus, E. D. (2014) 'Land Grabbing as a Driver of Environmental Change' *Area* 46(1): 74–82.

Lee, D. (2012) 'Average U.S. Family's Wealth Plunged 40% in Recession, Fed says', *Los Angeles Times*, 11 June, http://articles.latimes.com/2012/jun/11/ business/la-fi-family-worth-20120612, last accessed 13 June 2012.

Lenin, V. I. ([1917]1969) *Imperialism: The Highest Stage of Capitalism* (New York: International).

Lever, H. and Huhne, C. (1986) 'The Demand for Credit and the Supply of Credit', in H. Lever and C. Huhne, *Debt and Danger* (Boston, MA: Atlantic Monthly).

Levy, D. (1997) 'Environmental Management as Political Sustainability', *Organization and Environment*, 10(2): 126–47.

Levy, D. L. (2005) 'Offshoring in the New Global Political Economy' *Journal of Management Studies*, 42(3): 685–693.

Lim, L. L. (ed.) (1998) *The Sex Sector: The Economic and Social Bases of Prostitution in Southeast Asia* (Geneva: ILO).

Lincove, J. A. (2009) 'Are Markets Good for Girls? The World Bank and Neoliberal Education Reforms in Developing Countries', *Whitehead Journal of Diplomacy and International Relations Winter*, X(1): 19–35.

Lipschutz, R. D. (2005) 'Power, Politics and Global Civil Society', *Millennium*, 33(3): 747–70.

List, F. ([1885]1991) 'Political and Cosmopolitical Economy', in G. T. Crane and A. Amawi (eds) *The Theoretical Evolution of International Political Economy: A Reader* (Oxford: Oxford University Press).

Litfin, K. T. (1994) *Ozone Discourses: Science and Politics in Global Environmental Cooperation* (New York: Columbia University Press).

Lo, A. (2004) 'The Adaptive Market Hypothesis: Market Efficiency from an Evolutionary Perspective', *Journal of Portfolio Management*, 30th Anniversary Issue: 15–29.

Lopez-Claros, A. and Zahidi, S. (2005) *Women's Empowerment: Measuring the Global Gender Gap* (Geneva: World Economic Forum).

Lukas, M. and Groves, T. (2013) 'Canadian Spies Met with Energy Firms, Documents Reveal', *Guardian*, 9 October.

Lynch, D. A. (2010) *Trade and Globalization: An Introduction to Regional Trade Agreements* (Lanham, MD: Rowan & Littlefield).

Macalister, T. and Goñi, U. (2012) 'Argentinian President Moves to Nationalise Spanish-Owned Oil Assets', *Guardian*, 16 April.

Macdonald, K. (2014) *The Politics of Global Supply Chains: Power and Governance Beyond the State* (Cambridge, UK: Polity).

Mackay, C. (1852) *Memoirs of Extraordinary Popular Delusions and the Madness of Crowds*, 2nd edn, 2 vols (London: Office of the National Illustrated Library).

Madeley, J. (1992) *Trade and the Poor* (London: Intermediate Technology).

Madrick, J. (2001) *The Business Media and the New Economy*, Research Papers R-24 (Cambridge, MA: Harvard University, Joan Shorenstein Center on the Press, Politics and Public Policy).

Maier, C. S. (1977) 'The Politics of Productivity: Foundations of American International Economic Policy after World War II', *International Organization*, 31(4): 607–33.

Maizels, A. and Nisanke, M. K. (1984) 'Motivations for Aid to Developing Countries', *World Development*, 12(9): 879–900.

Mann, M. (2012) *The Hockey Stick and the Climate Wars* (New York: Columbia University Press).

Mansfield, E. S. and Snyder, J. (1995) 'Democratization and War', *Foreign Affairs*, 74(3): 79–97.

Marchand, M. and Runyan, A. (2000) *Gender and Global Restructuring* (London: Routledge).

Marcus, R. (1993) 'Woman Chosen as Attorney General', *Washington Post*, 12 February, p. 2.

Markoff, J. (2013) 'Rights Group Reports on Abuses of Surveillance and Censorship Technology', *New York Times*, 16 January.

Marks, G., Hooge, L. and Blank, K. (1996) 'European Integration from the 1980s: State-Centric vs Multi-level Governance', *Journal of Common Market Studies*, 34(3): 341–78.

Marshall, R. (1993) *Storm from the East: From Genghis Khan to Khubilai Khan* (London: BBC Books).

Martin, L. L. (ed.) (2015) *The Oxford Handbook of the Political Economy of International Trade* (New York: Oxford University Press).

Marx, K. and Engels, F. ([1848]1977) 'The Communist Manifesto', in D. McLellan (ed.) *Karl Marx: Selected Writings* (Oxford: Oxford University Press).

Mastandumo, M. (1998) 'Economics and Security in Statecraft and Scholarship', *International Organization*, 52(4): 825–54.

Matthews, A. (2008) 'The European Union's Common Agricultural Policy and Developing Countries: The Struggle for Coherence', *Journal of European Integration*, 30(3): 381–99.

May, C. (2005) 'Intellectual Property Rights', in D. Kelly and W. Grant (eds) *The Politics of International Trade: Actors, Issues, and Regional Dynamics* (Basingstoke, UK: Palgrave Macmillan).

May, C. (2015) *Global Corporations in Global Governance* (London: Taylor & Francis).

Mayne, R. and Picciotto, S. (eds) (1999) *Regulating International Business: Beyond Liberalization* (Basingstoke, UK: Macmillan).

McCarthy, S. (2015) '"Anti-Petroleum" Movement a Growing Security Threat to Canada, RCMP Say', *Globe and Mail*, 17 Feb.

McClanahan, P. (2013) 'Why the WTO Agreement in Bali has Finally Helped Developing Countries', *Guardian Poverty Matters Blog*, 6 December, http://www.theguardian.com/global-development/poverty-matters/2013/dec/06/wto-agreement-bali-helped-developing-countries-india, last accessed 17 October 2015.

McKinsey & Co. (2009) 'Will Consumer Debt Reduction Cripple the Economy?' www.mckinsey.com/mgi/publications/us_consumers/, last accessed 17 October 2015.

McLeod, R. H. and Garnaut, R. (1998) *East Asia in Crisis: From Being a Miracle to Needing One?* (London: Routledge).

McMichael, P. (1996) *Development and Social Change: A Global Perspective* (Thousand Oaks, CA: Pine Forge).

McMichael, P. (1997) 'Rethinking Globalization: The Agrarian Question Revisited', *Review of International Political Economy*, 4(4): 630–62.

McMichael, P. (2012) 'The Land Grab and Corporate Food Regime Restructuring', *Journal of Peasant Studies*, 39(3/4): 681–701.

McNamara, K. R. (2008) 'A Rivalry in the Making? The Euro and International Monetary Power', *Review of International Political Economy*, 15(3): 439–59.

McNeill, J., Winsemius, P. and Yakushiji, T. (1991) *Beyond Interdependence: The Meshing of the World's Economy and the Earth's Ecology* (New York: Oxford University Press).

McNeill, W. (1982) *The Pursuit of Power: Technology, Armed Force, and Society since AD 1000* (Chicago: University of Chicago Press).

Meadows, D. and Meadows, D. (1972) *The Limits to Growth* (London: Earth Island).

Meadows, D., Meadows, D. and Randers, J. (1993) *Beyond the Limits: Global Collapse or a Sustainable Future* (London: Earthscan).

Mell, P. and Grance, T. (2011) 'The NIST Definition of Cloud Computing: Recommendations of the National Institute of Standards and Technology', US Department of Commerce; NIST Special Publication 800–145, http://csrc.nist.gov/publications/nistpubs/800-145/SP800-145.pdf, last accessed 17 October 2015.

Meyn, M. and Kennan, J. (2009) 'The Implications of the Global Financial Crisis for Developing Countries' Export Volumes and Values', Working Paper 305 (London: ODI).

Michael, M. (2001) 'Jubilee 2000: Drop the Debt, Not the Campaign', *Dollars and Sense*, Mar/Apr(234): 11.

Mies, M. (1998) *Patriarchy and Accumulation on a World Scale: Women in the International Division of Labour* (London: Zed Books).

Milanovic, B. (2005) 'Globalization and Goals: Does Soccer Show the Way?' *Review of International Political Economy*, 12(5): 829–50.

Milberg, W. and Amengual, M. (2008) *Economic Development and Working Conditions in Export Processing Zones: A Survey of Trends* (Geneva: ILO).

Mill, J. S. ([1859]1980) *On Liberty* (Harmondsworth, UK: Penguin).

Milner, H. (1997) *Interests, Institutions and Information: Domestic Politics and International Relations* (Princeton, NJ: Princeton University Press).

Mishel, L. (2006) 'CEO-to-Worker Pay Imbalance Grows', *Snapshot*, 21 June, www.epi.org, last accessed 17 October 2015.

Mishra, R. (1999) *Globalization and the Welfare State* (Cheltenham, UK: Edward Elgar).

Mitter, S. (1986) *Common Fate, Common Bond: Women in the Global Economy* (London: Pluto).

Moghadam, V. M. (1999) 'Gender and Globalization: Female Labour and Women's Mobilization', *Journal of World-Systems Research*, 5(2): 367–88.

Moghadam, V. M. (2005) *The 'Feminization of Poverty' and Women's Human Rights*, SHS Papers in Women's Studies / Gender Research 2 (Paris: UNESCO).

Molyneux, M (2008) 'The "Neoliberal Turn" and the New Social Policy in Latin America: How Neoliberal, How New?' *Development and Change*, 39(5): 775–797.

Moody, K. (1997) *Workers in a Lean World: Unions in the International Economy* (London: Verso).

Moravcsik, A. (1997) 'Taking Preferences Seriously: A Liberal Theory of International Politics', *International Organization*, 51(4): 513–53.

Morgenthau, H. J. (1973) *Politics Among Nations: The Struggle for Power and Peace*, 5th edn (New York: Alfred A. Knopf).

Morris, D. (1989) 'Free Trade: The Great Destroyer', *Ecologist*, 19(5): 190–5.

Moser, C. O. and Clark, F. C. (eds) (2001) *Victims, Perpetrators or Actors? Gender, Armed Conflict and Political Violence* (New York: Zed Books).

Mote, F. W. (1999) *Imperial China: 900–1800* (Cambridge, MA: Harvard University Press).

Murphy, C. and Nelson, D. (2001) 'International Political Economy: A Tale of Two Heterodoxies', *British Journal of Politics and International Relations*, 3(3): 393–412.

Muuka, G. N. (1998) 'In Defense of World Bank and IMF Conditionality in Structural Adjustment Programs', *Journal of Business in Developing Nations*, 2, http://www.ewp.rpi.edu/jbdn/jbdnv202.htm, last accessed 17 October 2015.

Myrdal, G. (1968) *Asian Drama: An Enquiry into the Poverty of Nations* (London: Penguin).

Nagar, R., Lawson, V., McDowell, L. and Hanson, S. (2002) 'Locating Globalization: Feminist (Re)Readings of the Subject and Spaces of Globalization', *Economic Geography*, 78(3): 57–84.

Naim, M. (2000a) 'Fads and Fashion in Economic Reforms: Washington Consensus or Washington Confusion?' *Third World Quarterly*, 21(3): 505–28.

Naim, M. (2000b) 'Washington Consensus or Washington Confusion?' *Foreign Policy*, 118: 87–103.

Nakashima, E. (2012). 'Cyberattack on Mideast Energy Firms was Biggest Yet, Panetta Says', *Washington Post*, 11 October.

Narayan, D., Patel, R., Schafft, K., et al. (2000) *Voices of the Poor: Can Anyone Hear Us?* (New York: Oxford University Press).

Narlikar, A., Daunton, M. and Stern, R. M. (eds) (2012) *The Oxford Handbook on the World Trade Organization* (Oxford: Oxford University Press).

Narlikar, A. and Tussie, D. (2004) 'The G20 at the Cancun Ministerial: Developing Countries and their Evolving Coalitions in the WTO', *The World Economy*, 27(7): 947–966.

Naughton, J. (2010) 'WikiLeaks Row: Why Amazon's Desertion has Ominous Implications for Democracy', *Observer*, 12 December, www.guardian.co.uk/ technology/2010/dec/11/wikileaks-amazon-denialdemocracy-lieberman, last accessed 7 May 2012.

Needham, J. (1954–1995) *Science and Civilisation in China*, vols 1–6 (Cambridge, UK: Cambridge University Press).

Neumann, S. and von Hagen, M. (1986) 'Engels and Marx on Revolution, War and the Army in Society', in P. Paret (ed.) *Makers of Modern Strategy: From Machiavelli to the Nuclear Age* (Princeton, NJ: Princeton University Press).

Newland, K. (1988) 'From Transnational Relationships to International Relations: Women in Development and the International Decade for Women', *Millennium*, 17(3): 507–16.

Nikiforuk, A. (1996) *The Fourth Horseman: A Short History of Plagues, Scourges and Emerging Viruses* (Toronto: Penguin).

Nordås, H. K. (2003) 'The Impact of Trade Liberalization on Women's Job Opportunities and Earnings in Developing Countries', *World Trade Review*, 2(2): 221–31.

Nordstrom, H. and Vaughan, S. (1999) *Trade and Environment* (Geneva: WTO).

Norris, P. (2001) *Digital Divide: Civic Engagement, Information Poverty, and the Internet Worldwide* (New York: Cambridge University Press).

O'Brien, R. (1998) 'Shallow Foundations: Labour and the Selective Regulation of Free Trade', in G. Cook (ed.) *The Economics and Politics of International Trade* (London: Routledge).

O'Brien, R. (2000) 'Labour and IPE: Rediscovering Human Agency', in R. Palan (ed.) *Global Political Economy: Contemporary Theories* (New York: Routledge).

O'Brien, R. (2002) 'The Varied Paths to Minimum Global Labour Standards', in J. Harrod and R. O'Brien (eds) *Global Unions? Theory and Strategy of Organised Labour in the Global Political Economy* (London: Routledge).

O'Brien, R. (2003) 'Paths to Reforming Global Governance', in R. Sandbrook (ed.) *Civilizing Globalisation* (Albany, NY: SUNY Press).

O'Brien, R. (2009) 'North American Regional Report: Neoliberalism Wounded', *Global Social Policy*, 9(1): 127–33.

O'Brien, R., Goetz, A. M., Scholte, J. A. and Williams, M. (2000) *Contesting Global Governance: Multilateral Economic Institutions and Global Social Movements* (Cambridge: Cambridge University Press).

Odell, J. (2001) 'Case Study Methods in International Political Economy', *International Studies Perspectives*, 2(2): 161–76.

OECD (1998) 'Harmful Tax Competition – An Emerging Global Issue', http://www.oecd.org/tax/transparency/44430243.pdf, last accessed 22 June 2015.

OECD (2010) *Trade, Policy and the Economic Crisis* (Paris: OECD).

OECD (2012) 'Foreign Direct Investment: Main Aggregates', OECD International Direct Investment Statistics, OECD iLibrary, www.oecd-ilibrary.org/content/ data/data-00338-en, last accessed 16 December 2012.

OECD (2015) 'Base Erosion and Profit Shifting', http://www.oecd.org/ctp/beps.htm, last accessed 27 February 2015.

Oginni, A, Ahonsi, B. and Ukweiji, F. (2013) 'Are Female-Headed Households Typically Poorer than Male-Headed Households in Nigeria?' *Journal of Socio-Economics*, 45(August): 132–137.

Ohlin, B. (1933) *Interregional and International Trade* (Cambridge, MA: Harvard University Press).

Ohmae, K. (1990) *The Borderless World* (London: Fontana).

O'Neal, J. R., O'Neal, F. H. and Maoz, Z. (1996) 'The Liberal Peace: Interdependence, Democracy, and International Conflict, 1950–1985', *Journal of Peace Research*, 33(1): 11–28.

O'Neal, J. R. and Russett, B. M. (1997) 'The Classical Liberals Were Right: Democracy, Interdependence, and Conflict, 1950–1985', *International Studies Quarterly*, 41(2): 267–93.

O'Neill, J. (2001) 'Building Better Global Economic BRICs', Global Economics Paper 66 (London and New York: Goldman Sachs)–, http://www.goldmansachs.com/our-thinking/archive/archive-pdfs/build-better-brics.pdf, last accessed 13 May 2015.

Öniş, Z. and Şenses, F. (2005) 'Rethinking the Emerging Post-Washington Consensus', *Development and Change*, 36(2): 263–90.

Oreskes, N. and Conway, E. (2010) *Merchants of Doubt: How a Handful of Scientists Obscured the Truth on Issues from Tobacco Smoke to Global Warming* (New York: Bloomsbury Press).

O'Riordan, T. (1976) *Environmentalism* (London: Pion).

Ornatowski, Gregory K. (1996) 'Confucian Ethics and Economic Development: A Study of the Adaptation of Confucian Values to Modern Japanese Ideology and Institutions', *Journal of Socio-Economics*, 25(5): 571–590.

Oxfam (2009) 'Tax Haven Crackdown Could Deliver $120bn a Year to Fight Poverty', 13 March, https://www.oxfam.org/en/pressroom/pressreleases/2009-03-13/tax-haven-crackdown-could-deliver-120bn-year-fight-poverty, last accessed 17 October 2005.

Oxfam (2012) Working for the Few: Political Capture and Economic Inequality, https://www.oxfam.org/sites/www.oxfam.org/files/bp-working-for-few-political-capture-economic-inequality-200114-en.pdf, last accessed 4 May 2014.

Oxfam International (2000) *Debt Relief and Poverty Reduction: Failing to Deliver* (Oxford: Oxfam).

Oxfam International (2002) *Rigged Rules and Double Standards: Trade, Globalisation, and the Fight against Poverty* (Oxford: Oxfam).

Pakenham, T. (1991) *The Scramble for Africa 1876–1912* (London: Abacus).

Palan, R. (1998) 'Trying to Have Your Cake and Eating It: How and Why the State System Has Created Offshore', *International Studies Quarterly*, 42(4): 625–44.

Palan, R. (2000) 'The Constructivist Underpinnings of the New International Political Economy', in R. Palan (ed.) *Global Political Economy: Contemporary Theories* (London: Routledge).

Palan, R. (2002) 'Tax Havens and the Commercialization of State Sovereignty', *International Organization*, 56(1): 151–76.

Palan, R., Abbott, J. and Deans, P. (2005) *State Strategies in the Global Political Economy* (London: Pinter).

Parker, G. (1996) *The Military Revolution and the Rise of the West 1500–1800* (Cambridge: Cambridge University Press).

Pauly, L. W. (2000) 'Capital Mobility and the New Global Order', in R. Stubbs and G. R. D. Underhill (eds) *Political Economy and the Changing Global Order*, 2nd edn (Toronto: Oxford University Press).

Pauly, L. W. and Reich, S. (1997) 'National Structures and Multinational Corporate Behaviour: Enduring Differences in the Age of Globalization', *International Organization*, 51(1): 1–30.

Pearce, D. (1990) 'Economics and the Global Environmental Challenge', *Millennium*, 19(3): 365–87.

Pearce, D., Markandya, A. and Barbier, E. (1989) *Blueprint for a Green Economy* (London: Earthscan).

Pearson, R. and Seyfang, G. (2001) 'New Hope or False Dawn? Voluntary Codes of Conduct, Labour Regulation and Social Policy in a Globalizing World', *Global Social Policy*, 1(1): 49–78.

Penrose, E. T. (1968) *The Large International Firm in Developing Countries: The International Petroleum Industry* (Cambridge, MA: MIT Press).

Pepper, D. (1996) *Modern Environmentalism: An Introduction* (London: Routledge).

Persaud, R. B. (2001) 'Racial Assumptions in Global Labor Recruitment and Supply', *Alternatives*, 26(4): 377–99.

Peterson, S. (2002/3) 'Epidemic Disease and National Security', *Security Studies*, 12(2): 43–81.

Peterson, V. S. (2003) *A Critical Rewriting of Global Political Economy: Integrating Reproductive, Productive and Virtual Economies* (London: Routledge).

Peterson, V. S. (2005) 'How (the Meaning of) Gender Matters in Political Economy', *New Political Economy*, 10(4): 499–521.

Peterson, V. S. and Runyan, A. S. (1993) *Global Gender Issues* (Boulder, CO: Westview).

Pettman, J. J. (1996a) *Worlding Women: A Feminist International Politics* (London: Routledge).

Pettman, J. J. (1996b) 'An International Political Economy of Sex', in E. Kofman and G. Youngs (eds) *Globalization: Theory and Practice* (London: Pinter).

Pettman, J. J. (2003) 'International Sex and Service', in E. Kofman and G. Youngs (eds) *Globalization: Theory and Practice*, 2nd edn (London: Continuum).

PGA (1997) *First Conference of the Peoples' Global Action against 'Free' Trade and the World Trade Organization* (Manila: Peoples' Global Action Secretariat).

Phillips, K. (2008) *Bad Money: Reckless Finance, Failed Politics, and the Global Crisis of American Capitalism* (New York: Viking).

Phillips, N. (2005) '"Globalizing" the Study of International Political Economy', in N. Phillips (ed.) *Globalizing International Political Economy* (Basingstoke, UK: Palgrave Macmillan).

Phillips, N. and Weaver, C. (eds) (2011) *International Political Economy: Debating the Past, Present and Future* (London: Routledge).

Picciotto, R. (2003) 'A New World Bank for a New Century', in C. Roe Goddard, P. Cronin and K. C. Dash (eds) *International Political Economy: State–Market Relations in a Changing Global Order*, 2nd edn (Boulder, CO: Lynne Rienner).

Pietilä, H. and Vickers, J. (1990) *Making Women Matter: The Role of the United Nations* (London: Zed Books).

Pinter, F. (2001) 'Funding of Global Civil Society Organisations', in H. Anheier, M. Glasius and M. Kaldor (eds) *Global Civil Society 2001* (Oxford: Oxford University Press).

Pio, A. (1994) 'The Social Impact of Adjustment in Africa', in G. A. Cornia and G. K. Helleiner (eds) *From Adjustment to Development in Africa: Conflict, Controversy, Convergence, Consensus?* (New York: St. Martins).

Polanyi, K. (1957) *The Great Transformation* (Boston, MA: Beacon Hill).

Pomeranz, K. and Topik, S. (1999) *The World that Trade Created: Society, Culture and the World Economy, 1400 – the Present* (London: M. E. Sharpe).

Porter, T. (2005) *Globalization and Finance* (Cambridge, UK: Polity).

Price, R. (1998) 'Reversing the Gun Sights: Transnational Civil Society Targets Land Mines', *International Organization*, 52(3): 613–44.

Price-Smith, A. T. (2009) *Contagion and Chaos: Disease, Ecology, and National Security in the Era of Globalization* (Cambridge, MA: MIT Press).

Prugl, E. (1999) *The Global Construction of Gender: Home-Based Work in the Political Economy of the 20th Century* (New York: Columbia University Press).

Pye, L. W. (1988) 'The New Asian Capitalism: A Political Portrait', in P. L. Berger and H. M. Hsia (eds) *In Search of an East Asian Development Model* (Oxford: Transaction).

Pyle, J. L. and Ward, K. B. (2003) 'Recasting our Understanding of Gender and Work during Global Restructuring', *International Sociology*, 18(3): 461–89.

Quisumbing, A. R., Haddad, L. and Pena, C. (1995) 'Gender and Poverty: New Evidence from 10 Developing Countries', Food and Nutrition Division Discussion Papers 9 (Washington, DC: International Food Policy Research Institute).

Radice, H. (ed.) (1975) *International Firms and Modern Imperialism* (London: Penguin).

Radosh, R. (1969) *American Labour and United States Foreign Policy* (New York: Random House).

Rakowski, C.A. (2000) 'Obstacles and Opportunities to Women's Empowerment under Neoliberal Reform', *Journal of Development Studies*, 16(1): 115–138.

Randriamaro, Z. (2006) 'Gender and Trade', BRIDGE Report (Brighton: Institute of Development Studies).

Ratha, D. and Mohapatra, S. (2007) 'Increasing the Macroeconomic Impact of Remittances on Development', Development Prospects Group (Washington, DC: World Bank).

Ravenhill, J. (ed.) (2014) *Global Political Economy*, 4th edn (Oxford: Oxford University Press).

Ray, R. and Gallagher K. (2015) 'China–Latin American Economic Bulletin', Discussion Paper 2015-9, Global Economic Governance Initiative, http://www.bu.edu/pardeeschool/files/2015/02/Economic-Bulletin-2015.pdf, last accessed 26 June 2015.

Redclift, M. (1987) *Sustainable Development* (London: Routledge).

Reding, A. (1994) 'Chiapas is Mexico', *World Policy Journal*, 11(1): 11–25.

Reich, R. (1992) *The Work of Nations* (New York: Vintage).

Ricardo, D. ([1817]1992) *The Principles of Political Economy and Taxation* (London: J. M. Dent, Everyman's Library).

Rich, B. (1994) *Mortgaging the Earth: The World Bank, Environmental Impoverishment and the Crisis of Development* (London: Earthscan).

RIPE (2009) Special Issue: 'Not So Quiet on the Western Front: The American School of IPE', *Review of International Political Economy*, 16(1).

Ripsman, N. M. (2005) 'False Dichotomies: Why Economics is High Politics', in P. Dombrowski (ed.) *Guns and Butter: The Political Economy of International Security* (Boulder, CO: Lynne Rienner).

Ripsman, N. M. and Blanchard, J.-M. F. (1996/7) 'Commercial Liberalism under Fire: Evidence from 1914 and 1936', *Security Studies*, 6(2): 4–50.

Ripsman, N. and Dombrowski, P. (2005) *Guns and Butter: The Political Economy of International Security* (Boulder, CO: Lynne Rienner).

Risso, P. (1995) *Merchants and Faith: Muslim Commerce and Culture in the Indian Ocean* (Boulder, CO: Westview).

Roberts, A. (2015) 'Gender, Financial Deepening and the Production of Embodied Finance: Towards a Critical Feminist Analysis', *Global Society*, 29(1): 107-127.

Robinson, R. (1972) 'Non-European Foundations of European Imperialism: Sketch for a Theory of Collaboration', in R. Owen and B. Sutcliffe (eds) *Studies in the Theory of Imperialism* (Bristol: Longman).

Rodman, K. A. (1998) 'Think Globally, Punish Locally: Non-state Actors, Multinational Corporations and Human Rights Sanctions', *Ethics and International Affairs*, 12: 19–41.

Rogerson, W. P. (1993) 'Economic Incentives and the Defense Procurement Process', Discussion Paper No. 1078 (Evanston, IL: Northwestern University).

Rosen, D. (2013) 'Is the Internet Killing the Porn Industry?' *Salon*, 20 May, http://www.salon.com/2013/05/30/is_success_killing_the_porn_industry_partner/, last accessed 26 June 2015.

Rostow, W. W. (1960) *The Stages of Economic Growth* (Cambridge: Cambridge University Press).

Roubini, N. (2009) 'The Almighty Renminbi?' *New York Times*, 14 May.

Rubin, R. (2014) 'Cash Abroad Rises $206 Billion as Apple to IBM Avoid Tax', *Bloomberg Business*, 12 March, http://www.bloomberg.com/news/articles/2014-03-12/cash-abroad-rises-206-billion-as-apple-to-ibm-avoid-tax, last accessed 14 march 2015.

Rubin, R. (2015) 'Profit Shifting: Moving Profits to Cut US Taxes', *Bloomberg QuickTake*, 3 February, http://www.bloombergview.com/quicktake/profit-shifting-avoid-tax, last accessed 14 March 2015.

Rubinstein, A. (2006) 'A Sceptic's Comment on the Study of Economics', *Economic Journal*, 116(March): c1–9.

Ruggie, J. G. (1982) 'International Regimes, Transactions and Change: Embedded Liberalism in the Postwar Economic Order', *International Organization*, 36(2): 379–415.

Ruggie, J. G. (1998) *Constructing the World Polity: Essays on International Institutionalization* (New York: Routledge).

Rulli, M. C., Saviori, A. and D'Odorico, P. (2015) 'Global Land and Water Grabbing', *PNAS*, 110(3): 892–897.

Rupert, M. (1995a) *Producing Hegemony: The Politics of Mass Production and American Global Power* (Cambridge: Cambridge University Press).

Rupert, M. (1995b) '(Re)Politicizing the Global Economy: Liberal Common Sense and Ideological Struggle in the US NAFTA Debate', *Review of International Political Economy*, 2: 658–92.

Rushe, D., Stewart, H. and Mark, M. (2012) 'World Bank Names US-nominated Jim Yong Kim as President', *Guardian*, 16 April, www.guardian.co.uk/ business/2012/apr/16/world-bank-president-jim-yongkim, last accessed 11 June 2012.

Ruskin, G. (2013) 'Spooky Business: Corporate Espionage against Non Profits' (Washington, DC: Essential Information), http://www.corporatepolicy.org/spookybusiness.pdf, last accessed 19 February 2015.

Russett, B. M. (1993) *Grasping the Democratic Peace: Principles for a Post-Cold War World* (Princeton, NJ: Princeton University Press).

Sachs, J. (2010) 'The Phony Attack on Climate Science', *Project Syndicate*, www.project-syndicate.org/ commentary/the-phony-attack-on-climate-science, last accessed 25 May 2012.

Sahn, D. E. (1994) 'The Impact of Macroeconomic Adjustment on Incomes, Health and Nutrition: Sub-Saharan Africa in the 1980s', in G. A. Cornia and G. K. Helleiner (eds) *From Adjustment to Development in Africa: Conflict, Controversy, Convergence, Consensus?* (New York: St. Martins).

Samson, M. (1995) 'Towards a "Friday" Model of International Trade: A Feminist Deconstruction of Race and Gender Bias in the Robinson Crusoe Trade Allegory', *The Canadian Journal of Economics / Revue canadienne d'Economique,* 28(1): 143–158.

Samuelson, R. (2009) 'Chinas Dollar Deception', *Washington Post,* 6 April.

Santiso, C. (2004) 'The Contentious Washington Consensus: Reforming the Reforms in Emerging Markets', *Review of International Political Economy,* 11(4): 828–44.

Sarikakis, K. and Shaukat, Z. (2008) 'The Global Structures and Cultures of Pornography: The Global Brothel', in K. Sarikakis and L. Shade (eds) *Feminist Interventions in International Communications* (Lantham: Rowman and Littlefield), pp. 106–126.

Sarup, M. (1993) *An Introductory Guide to Post-structuralism and Postmodernism,* 2nd edn (Athens, GA: University of Georgia Press).

Sassen, S. (2006) *Cities in a World Economy,* 3rd edn (Thousand Oaks, CA: Pine Forge Press).

Saurin, J. (1996) 'International Relations, Social Ecology, and the Globalisation of Environmental Change', in J. Vogler and M. F. Imber (eds) *The Environment and International Relations* (London: Routledge).

Sazanami, Y., Urata, S. and Kawai, H. (1995) *Measuring the Costs of Protection in Japan* (Washington, DC: Institute for International Economics).

Schechter, M. G. (2002) 'Critiques of Coxian Theory: Background to a Conversation', in R. W. Cox and M. G. Schechter *The Political Economy of a Plural World: Reflection on Power, Morals and Civilization* (London: Routledge).

Schlosser, E. (2008) 'Burger with a Side of Spies' *New York Times,* May 7.

Schmidheiny, S. (1992) *Changing Course: A Global Business Perspective on Development and the Environment* (Cambridge, MA: MIT Press).

Schneider, V. (2000) 'Global Economic Governance by Private Actors: The International Chamber of Commerce', in J. Greenwood and H. Jacek (eds) *Organized Business and the New Global Order* (New York: St. Martins).

Scholte, J. A. (2000a) *Globalization: A Critical Introduction* (New York: St. Martins).

Scholte, J. A. (2000b) 'Global Civil Society', in N. Woods (ed.) *The Political Economy of Globalization* (Basingstoke, UK: Macmillan).

Schutter, O. de (2011) 'How Not to Think of Land-Grabbing: Three Critiques of Large-Scale Investments in Farmland', *Journal of Peasant Studies,* 38 (2): 249–279.

Schwartz, H. (1994) *States Versus Markets* (New York: St. Martins).

Scoones, I., Hall, R., Borras, S. M., et al. (2013) 'The Politics of Evidence: Methodologies for Understanding the Global Land Rush', *Journal of Peasant Studies,* 40(3): 469–483.

Sedgh, G., Singh, S. and Hussain, R. (2014) 'Intended and Unintended Pregnancies Worldwide in 2012 and Recent Trends', *Studies in Family Planning,* 45(3): 301–314.

Seers, D. (1969) 'The Meaning of Development', *International Development Review,* 11(4): 2–6.

Seguino, S. (2000) 'Gender Inequality and Economic Growth: A Cross-country Analysis', *World Development,* 28(7): 1211–30.

Sell, S. (1999) 'Multinational Corporations as Agents of Change: The Globalization of Intellectual Property Rights', in C. Cutler, V. Haufler and T. Porter (eds) *Private Authority and International Affairs* (Albany, NY: SUNY Press).

Sell, S. (2000) 'Structures, Agents and Institutions: Private Corporate Power and the Globalisation of Intellectual Property Rights', in R. A. Higgott, G. R. D. Underhill and A. Bieler (eds) *Non-state Actors and Authority in the Global System* (London: Routledge).

Sell, S. (2006) 'Big Business, the WTO and Development', in R. Stubbs and G. R. D. Underhill (eds) *Political Economy and the Changing Global Order,* 3rd edn (Oxford: Oxford University Press).

Sell, S. and Prakash, A. (2004) 'Using Ideas Strategically: The Contest Between Business and NGO Networks in Intellectual Property Rights', *International Studies Quarterly,* 48(1): 143–75.

Sen, A. K. (1981) *Poverty and Famines: An Essay on Entitlement and Deprivation* (Oxford: Clarendon).

Sen, A. (1999) *Development as Freedom* (New York: Alfred A. Knopf).

Sengenberger, W. and Wilkinson, F. (1995) 'Globalisation and Labor Standards', in J. Michie and J. G. Smith (eds) *Managing the Global Economy* (Oxford: Oxford University Press).

Serrano, M. (2002) 'Transnational Organized Crime and International Security: Business as Usual?' in M. Berdal and M. Serrano (eds) *Transnational Organized Crime and International Security: Business as Usual?* (Boulder, CO: Lynne Rienner).

Servan Schreiber, J. J. (1968) *The American Challenge,* trans. R. Steel (New York: Athenaeum).

Shillington, K. (1995) *History of Africa* (New York: St. Martins).

Shrybman, S. (1990) 'International Trade and the Environment: An Environmental Assessment of the General Agreement on Tariffs and Trade', *Ecologist,* 20(1): 30–4.

Sil, R. and Katzenstein, P. (2010) 'Analytic Eclecticism in the Study of World Politics: Reconfiguring Problems and Mechanisms across Research Traditions', *Perspectives on Politics,* 8: 411–31.

Siles-Brügge, G. (2013) 'The Power of Economic Ideas: A Constructivist Political Economy of EU Trade Policy', *Journal of Contemporary European Research,* 9(4): 597–617.

Silverstein, K. (2002) 'Millions for Viagra, Pennies for Diseases of the Poor', www.planetaportoalegre.net/publique, last accessed 30 May 2006.

Sinclair, T. (1994) 'Passing Judgement: Credit Rating Processes as Regulating Mechanisms of Governance', *Review of International Political Economy*, 1(1): 133–60.

Sinclair, T. (2005) *The New Masters of Capital: American Bond Rating Agencies and the Politics of Creditworthiness* (Ithaca, NY: Cornell University Press).

Singer, P. W. (2002) 'AIDS and International Security', *Survival*, 44(1): 145–58.

Singh, B. K. (2005) 'The Political Economy of China's Defence Modernisation', *Strategic Analysis*, 29(4): 680–705.

Sirkeci, I., Cohen, J. H. and Ratha, D. (eds) (2012) *Migration and Remittances during the Global Financial Crisis and Beyond* (Washington, DC: World Bank).

Sisson, C. A. (1986) 'Fund-Supported Programs and Income Distribution in LDCs', *Finance and Development*, 231(March): 33–8.

Sjöstedt, G and Penetrante, A. M. (2013) 'Strategic Facilitation of Climate Change Negotiations', in G. Sjöstedt and A. M Penetrante (eds) *Climate Change Negotiations: A Guide to Resolving Disputes and Facilitating Multilateral Cooperation* (London and New York: Routledge), pp. 3–40.

Skidmore, D. (1997) *Contested Social Orders and International Politics* (Nashville, TN: Vanderbilt University Press).

Skidmore-Hess, D. (1996) 'Business Conflict and Theories of the State', in R. W. Cox (ed.) *Business and the State in International Relations* (Boulder, CO: Westview).

Sklair, L. (2001) *The Transnational Capitalist Class* (Oxford: Blackwell).

Sklias, P. (1999) *Non-Governmental Organisations and the International Political Economy, with Special Reference to the European Union's Development Policy* (Athens: Nubis).

Skogstad, G. (2001) 'The WTO and Food Safety Regulatory Policy in the EU', *Journal of Common Market Studies*, 39(3): 485–505.

Sky, J. (2015) 'Opinion: Financial Crime is Routine in Major Banks', *Deutsche Welle*, http://www.dw.de/opinion-financial-crime-is-routine-in-major-banks/a-18246158, last accessed 1 May 2015.

Smith, A. ([1776]1983) *The Wealth of Nations* (New York: Penguin).

Smith, H. (2011) 'The Future of Greece Rests on a Phone Call', *Guardian*, 18 September, www.guardian.co.uk/world/2011/sep/18/greece-debt-phonecall, last accessed 14 February 2012.

Smythe, E. (2000) 'State Authority and Investment Security: Non-State Actors and the Negotiation of the Multilateral Agreement on Investment at the OECD', in R. A. Higgott, G. R. D. Underhill and A. Bieler (eds) *Non-State Actors and Authority in the Global System* (London: Routledge).

Soderbaum, F. and Shaw, T. M. (eds) (2003) *Theories of the New Regionalism* (Basingstoke, UK: Palgrave Macmillan).

Spero, J. (1981) *Politics of International Economic Relations* (London: Unwin Hyman).

Spruyt, H. (1994) *The Sovereign State and its Competitors* (Princeton, NJ: Princeton University Press).

Spruyt, H. (2000) 'New Institutionalism and International Relations', in R. Palan (ed.) *Global Political Economy: Contemporary Theories* (London: Routledge).

Stalker, P. (2001) *The No-Nonsense Guide to International Migration* (Oxford: New Internationalist).

Steans, J. (1998) *Gender and International Relations* (Cambridge, UK: Polity).

Steans, J. (1999) 'The Private is Global: Feminist Politics and Global Political Economy', *New Political Economy*, 4(1): 113–28.

Stearns, P. N. (1993) *The Industrial Revolution in World History* (Boulder, CO: Westview).

Stern Review (2006) *The Economics of Climate Change* (London: HM Treasury).

Stewart, H. (2012) 'Wealth Doesn't Trickle Down: It Just Floods Offshore, Research Reveals', *Guardian*, 21 July.

Stewart, J. (2009) 'CNBC Financial Advice', 4 March, www.thedailyshow.com/watch/wed-march-4-2009/cnbcfinancial-advice, last accessed 23 December 2012.

Stewart, S. (2012) 'Public Sector Cuts Will Hit Women Hard, Thinktank Warns', *Observer*, 18 March.

Stiglitz, J. (2000) 'The Insider: What I Learned at the World Economic Crisis', *The New Republic*, 17 April, www.tnr.com/article/politics/the-insider, last accessed 23 December 2012.

Stilwell, F. (2002) *Political Economy: The Contest of Economic Ideas* (Oxford: Oxford University Press).

Stopford, J. M. and Strange, S. (1991) *Rival States, Rival Firms: Competition for World Market Shares* (Cambridge: Cambridge University Press).

Strange, S. (1982) 'Cave! Hic Dragones: A Critique of Regime Analysis', *International Organization*, 36(2): 337–54.

Strange, S. (1985) 'Protectionism and World Politics', *International Organization*, 39(2): 233–59.

Strange, S. (1986) *Casino Capitalism* (Oxford: Blackwell).

Strange, S. (1987) 'The Persistent Myth of Lost Hegemony', *International Organization*, 41(4): 551–74.

Strange, S. (1988) *States and Markets* (London: Pinter).

Strange, S. (1991) 'An Eclectic Approach', in C. Murphy and R. Tooze (eds) *The New International Political Economy* (Boulder, CO: Lynne Rienner).

Strange, S. (1994) 'Rethinking Structural Change in the International Political Economy: States, Firms and Diplomacy', in R. Stubbs and G. R. D. Underhill (eds) *Political Economy and the Changing Global Order*, 2nd edn (Toronto: Oxford University Press).

Strange, S. (1996) *The Retreat of the State: The Diffusion of Power in the World Economy* (Cambridge: Cambridge University Press).

Strange, S. (1998) *Mad Money: When Markets Outgrow Governments* (Manchester: Manchester University Press).

Strange, S. (2002) 'I Never Meant to Be an Academic', in R. Tooze and C. May (eds) *Authority and Markets: Susan Strange's Writings on International Political Economy* (Basingstoke, UK: Palgrave Macmillan).

Stromberg, J. (2013) 'What Is the Anthropocene and Are We in It?' *Smithsonian Magazine*, January, http://www.smithsonianmag.com/science-nature/what-is-the-anthropocene-and-are-we-in-it-164801414/?no-ist, last accessed 17 October 2015.

Stubbs, R. (1999) 'War and Economic Development: Export-Oriented Industrialization in East and Southeast Asia', *Comparative Politics*, 31(3): 337–55.

Stubbs, R. and Underhill, G. (eds) (2005) *Political Economy and the Changing Global Order*, 3rd edn (Toronto: Oxford University Press).

Sundrum, R. M. (1983) *Development Economics: A Framework of Analysis and Policy* (Chichester, UK: John Wiley).

Swann, D. (1992) *The Economics of the Common Market*, 7th edn (London: Penguin).

Swinnen, J. (2007) 'Global Supply Standards and the Poor: Some Empirical and Theoretical Insights', paper prepared for presentation at the 2007 Farrell Lecture at the University of Guelph, http://www.researchgate.net/profile/Johan_Swinnen/publication/240638074_Global_Supply_Chains_Standards_and_the_Poor_Some_Empirical_and_Theoretical_Insights1/links/0a85e52e963bcb05ef000000.pdf, last accessed 17 October 2015.

Syal, R., Bowers S. and Wintour, P. (2013) '"Big four" Accountants Use Knowledge of Treasury to Help Rich Avoid Tax', *Guardian*, 26 April, http://www.theguardian.com/business/2013/apr/26/accountancy-firms-knowledge-treasury-avoid-tax, last accessed 14 March 2015.

Syal, R. and Wintour, P. (2012) 'MPs attack Amazon, Google and Starbucks over Tax Avoidance', *Guardian*, 3 December, www.guardian.co.uk/business/2012/dec/03/amazon-google-starbucks-tax-avoidance/, last accessed 13 December 2012.

Taleb, N. (2004) *Fooled by Randomness* (New York: Random House).

Tarnoff, C. and Nowells, L. (2004) 'Foreign Aid: An Introductory Overview of US Programs and Policy', CRS Report for Congress, http://pdf.dec.org/pdf_docs/ PCAAB191.pdf, last accessed 17 October 2015.

Tax Justice Network (2012) 'The Price of Offshore Revisited', www.taxjustice.net, last accessed 22 July 2012.

Taylor, I. (2005) 'Globalization Studies and the Developing World: Making International Political Economy Truly Global', *Third World Quarterly*, 26(7): 1025–42.

Te Velde, D. W. (2009) 'The Global Financial Crisis and Developing Countries: Synthesis of the Findings of 10 Country Case Studies', Working Paper 306 (London: ODI).

Thomas, C. (2000) *Global Governance, Development and Human Security* (London: Pluto).

Thomas, C. (2002) 'Trade Policy and the Politics of Access to Drugs', *Third World Quarterly*, 23(2): 251–64.

Thomas, C. and Reader, M. (1997) 'Development and Inequality', in B. White, R. Little and M. Smith (eds) *Issues in World Politics* (London: Macmillan).

Thomas, C. Y. (1974) *Dependence and Transformation* (New York: Monthly Review).

Thompson, W. R. (2000) *The Emergence of the Global Political Economy* (New York: Routledge).

Thorne, C. (1978) *Allies of a Kind: The United States, Britain, and the War against Japan, 1941–1945* (London: Hamish Hamilton).

Tidball, S. (2011) 'Migration of Sri Lankan Women as Housemaids to the Middle East', *Third Annual Interdisciplinary Conference on Human Trafficking,* Paper 12, http://digitalcommons.unl.edu/cgi/viewcontent.cgi?article=1011&context=humtraffconf3, last accessed 17 October 2015.

Tilly, C. (1999) *Coercion, Capital, and European States ad 990–1992* (Oxford: Blackwell).

Times, The (2009) 'Brown Spares Baroness Scotland, But Tells Her to Apologise "Profusely"', 22 September.

Tinker, I. (1990) 'The Making of a Field: Advocates, Practitioners, and Scholars', in I. Tinker (ed.) *Persistent Inequalities: Women and World Development* (Oxford: Oxford University Press).

Toffler, A. (1980) *The Third Wave* (New York: Morrow).

Tokarick, S. (2008) 'Dispelling Some Misconceptions about Agricultural Trade Liberalization', *Journal of Economic Perspectives,* 22(1): 199-216.

Toke, D. (1999) 'Epistemic Communities and Environmental Groups', *Politics*, 19(2): 97–102.

Tooze, R. and May, C. (2002) 'Authority and Markets: Interpreting the Work of Susan Strange', in R. Tooze and C. May (eds) *Authority and Markets: Susan Strange's Writings on International Political Economy* (Basingstoke, UK: Palgrave Macmillan).

Tooze, R. and Murphy, C. (eds) (1991) *The New International Political Economy* (Boulder, CO: Lynne Rienner).

Transnational Resource and Action Center (2000) 'Tangled up in Blue: Corporate Partnerships at the United Nations', http://s3.amazonaws.com/corpwatch.org/downloads/tangled.pdf, last accessed 17 October 2015.

Trans-Pacific Partnership (2011) 'Leaders Statement', https://www.whitehouse.gov/the-press-office/2011/11/12/trans-pacific-partnership-leaders-statement, last accessed 14 March 2015.

Union Carbide (2015) 'Bhopal Gas Tragedy Information', http://www.bhopal.com, last accessed 17 October 2015.

United Nations (1992) 'United Nations Framework Convention on Climate Change', Doc. FCCC/INFORMAL/84 (New York: United Nations).

United Nations (2000a) 'The Millennium Declaration', UN General Assembly Resolution 55/2, adopted 18 September 2000.

United Nations (2000b) 'United Nations Convention against Transnational Organized Crime and the Protocols Thereto', www.unodc.org/documents/treaties/UNTOC/ Publications/TOC%20Convention/TOCebook-e.pdf, last accessed 17 October 2015.

United Nations (2001) 'Gender Mainstreaming: An Overview' (New York: United Nations, Office of the Special Adviser on Gender Issues and Advancement of Women).

United Nations (2003) 'Declaration of Principles. Building the Information Society: A Global Challenge in the New Millennium', World Summit on the Information Society, UN Doc: WSIS-03/ GENEVA/DOC/4-E.

United Nations (2005) 'World Summit Outcome 2005', UN General Assembly Resolution A/RES/60/1, 24 October, paras 138, 139, https://www.ifrc.org/docs/idrl/I520EN.pdf, last accessed 17 October 2015.

United Nations (2006) 'The World's Women 2005: Progress in Statistics' (New York: United Nations, Department of Economic and Social Affairs, Statistics Division).

United Nations (2009a) 'Human Security in Theory and Practice: Application of the Human Security Concept and the United Nations Trust Fund for Human Security' (New York: United Nations, Human Security Unit Office for the Coordination of Humanitarian Affairs United Nations).

United Nations (2009b) 'The World Financial and Economic Crisis and its Impact on Development: Report of the Secretary-General' (New York: United Nations).

United Nations (2013a) 'World Economic Situation and Prospects 2013' (New York: United Nations).

United Nations (2013b) 'Information Economy Report 2013: The Cloud Economy and Developing Countries' (New York and Geneva: United Nations).

United Nations (2014a) 'World Economic Situation and Prospects 2014' (New York: United Nations).

United Nations (2014b) 'The Millennium Development Goals Report 2014' (New York: United Nations).

United Nations (2014c) 'UN Security Council Resolution 2177', UN Doc. S/RES/2177, http://www.un.org/en/ga/search/view_doc.asp?symbol=S/RES/2177%20(2014), last accessed 17 October 2015.

United Nations Secretary-General (2010) 'Report of the Secretary-General's High-Level Advisory Group on Climate Change Financing', http://www.un.org/wcm/webdav/site/climatechange/shared/Documents/AGF_reports/AGF%20Report.pdf, last accessed 17 October 2015.

United Nations Security Council (2007) 'Security Council Holds First Ever Debate on Impact of Climate Change on Peace, Security Hearing over 50 Speakers' (UN Security Council SC/9000).

UNCTAD (1999) 'World Investment Report 1999: Foreign Direct Investment and the Challenge of Development' (New York: United Nations).

UNCTAD (2005) 'The Digital Divide: ICT Development Indices 2004' (Geneva: United Nations).

UNCTAD (2011) 'World Investment Report 2011' (Geneva: United Nations).

UNCTAD (2013) 'Trade and Development Report 2013' (New York and Geneva: United Nations).

UNDP (1990) 'Human Development Report' (Geneva: UNDP).

UNDP (1994) 'Human Development Report' (Geneva: UNDP).

UNDP (1995) 'Human Development Report' (Geneva: UNDP).

UNDP (2000) 'Human Development Report' (Geneva: UNDP).

UNDP (2002) 'Human Development Report' (Geneva: UNDP).

UNDP (2007/8) 'Human Development Report' (Geneva: UNDP).

UNDP (2012) 'Human Development Report' (Geneva: UNDP).

UNDP (2013a) 'Human Development Report 2013: The Rise of the South: Human Progress in a Diverse World' (Geneva: UNDP).

UNDP (2013b) *A Million Voices: The World We Want*, https://www.worldwewant2015.org/bitcache/9158d79561a9de6b34f95568ce8b389989412f16?vid=422422&disposition=inline&op=view, last accessed 19 October 2015.

UNDP (2014a) 'Human Development Statistical Tables', http://hdr.undp.org/en/data, last accessed 8 May 2015.

UNDP (2014b) 'Human Development Report 2014: Sustaining Human Progress: Reducing Vulnerabilities and Building Resilience' (Geneva: UNDP).

UNDP (2015) 'Human Development Report', http://hdr.undp.org/en/content/human-development-index-hdi-table, last accessed 8 May 2015.

UNESCAP (2009) 'Sustainable Agriculture and Food Security in Asia and the Pacific' (Bangkok: Escap).

UNESCO (2015) 'Statistics on Literacy', http://www.unesco.org/new/en/education/themes/education-building-blocks/literacy/resources/statistics, last accessed 8 May 2015.

UNFCC (2010) 'Synthesis Report on the National Economic, Environment and Development Study (NEEDS) for Climate Change Project', FCCC/SBI/2010/INF.7.

UNICEF (1999) 'The Progress of Nations' (New York: UNICEF).

UNIFEM (2005) 'The Progress of the World's Women 2005: Women, Work and Poverty' (New York: United Nations Development Fund for Women).

UNODC (2005) 'The Globalization of Crime: A Transnational Organized Crime Threat Assessment', https://www.unodc.org/documents/data-and-analysis/tocta/TOCTA_Report_2010_low_res.pdf, last accessed 17 October 2015.

UNRISD (2005) 'Gender Equality: Striving for Justice in an Unequal World' (New York: UNRISD).

UN Women (1995) 'Beijing Declaration and Platform for Action', *Fourth World Conference on Women*, 15 September (New York: UN Women).

UN Women (2013) 'Contribution of Migrant Domestic Workers to Sustainable Development' (Bangkok: United Nations Entity for Gender Equality and the Empowerment of Women).

US Patent and Trademark Office (2011) 'Patents by Country, State and Year – All Patent Types' (Washington, DC: USPTO).

Vaitsos, C. (1975) 'Power, Knowledge and Development Policy: Relations between Transnational Enterprises and Developing Countries', in G. K. Helleiner (ed.) A *World Divided: The Less Developed Countries in the International Economy* (Cambridge: Cambridge University Press).

Van Staveren, I. Elson, D., Grown, C. and Cagatay, N. (eds) (2007) *The Feminist Economics of Trade* (London: Routledge).

Verité (2014) *Forced Labour in the Production of Electronics Goods in Malaysia.* (Amherst, MA: Verité), http://www.verite.org/sites/default/files/images/VeriteForcedLabor-MalaysianElectronics_2014_0.pdf, last accessed 5 May 2015

Verma, A. (2003) 'Global Labour Standards: Can We Get from Here to There?' *International Journal of Comparative Labour Law and Industrial Relations*, 19(4): 515–34.

Vernon, R. (1966) 'International Investment and International Trade in the Product Cycle', *Quarterly Journal of Economics*, 80(2): 190–207.

Vernon, R. (1971) *Sovereignty at Bay* (London: Penguin).

Vernon, R. (1977) *Storm over the Multinationals: The Real Issues* (London: Macmillan).

Wade, R. (1990) *Governing the Market: Economic Theory and the Role of Government in East Asian Industrialization* (Princeton, NJ: Princeton University Press).

Wade, R. H. (2003) 'What Strategies are Viable for Developing Countries Today? The World Trade Organization and the Shrinking of "Development Space"', *Review of International Political Economy*, 10(4): 621–44.

Wade, R. and Veneroso, F. (1998) 'The Asian Crisis: The High Debt Model vs the Wall Street-Treasury-IMF Complex', *New Left Review*, 228: 3–22.

Waley-Cohen, J. (1999) *The Sextants of Beijing: Global Currents in Chinese History* (New York: W. W. Norton).

Wallach, L. and Woodall, P. (2004) *Whose Trade Organization? A Comprehensive Guide to the WTO* (London: New Press).

Walmart (2015) '2015 Global Responsibility Report', http://www.corporatereport.com/walmart/2015/grr/2015_WALMART_GRR.pdf, last accessed 17 October 2015.

Walter, A. and Sen, G. (2008) *Analysing the Global Political Economy* (Princeton, NJ: Princeton University Press).

Walton, S. (2002) 'The Danger of Global Finance: A Reassessment of the Asian Crisis', *Journal of Asia-Pacific Affairs*, 4(1): 107–21.

Ward H. and Aral S. O. (2006) 'Globalisation, the Sex Industry, and Health', *Sexually Transmitted Infections*, 82(5): 345–347.

Wasow, B. (2006) *Losing the Genius for Openness* (Washington, DC: Century Foundation).

Waterman, P. (1998) *Globalization, Social Movements and the New International-isms* (London: Mansell).

Watson, M. (2005) *Foundations of International Political Economy* (Basingstoke, UK: Palgrave Macmillan).

Watts, J. (2006) 'Backlash as Google Shores up Great Firewall of China', *Guardian*, 25 January.

Waylen, G. (2006) 'You Still Don't Understand: Why Troubled Engagements Continue Between Feminists and (Critical) IPE', *Review of International Studies*, 32(1): 145–64.

Weber, H. (2004) 'The "New Economy" and Social Risk: Banking on the Poor?' *Review of International Political Economy*, 11(2): 356–86.

Weingast B and Wittman, D. (2006) 'The Reach of Political Economy', in B. Weingast and D. Wittman (eds) *The Oxford Handbook of Political Economy* (Oxford: Oxford University Press).

Weiss, L. (1998) *The Myth of the Powerless State* (Ithaca, NY: Cornell University Press).

Weiss, L. (1999) 'State Power and the Asian Crisis', *New Political Economy*, 4(3): 317–42.

Weiss, L. (ed.) (2003) *States in the Global Economy: Bringing Domestic Institutions Back In* (Cambridge: Cambridge University Press).

Weiss, T. G., Cortright, D., Lopez, G. A. and Minear, L. (1997) 'Economic Sanctions and their Humanitarian Impacts: An Overview', in T. G. Weiss, D. Cortright, G. A. Lopez and L. Minear (eds) *Political Gain and Civilian Pain: Humanitarian Impacts of Economic Sanctions* (Lanham, MD: Rowman & Littlefield).

Weiss, T. G., Forsyth, D. P. and Coates, R. A. (2001) *The United Nations and Changing World Politics* (Boulder, CO: Westview).

Weissman, R. (2007) 'Sovereign Wealth Funds', *New York Times*, 3 December.

Weissman, R. and Donahue, J. (2009) *Sold Out: How Washington and Wall Street Betrayed America* (Washington: Essential Information and Consumer Education Fund).

Wendt, A. (1987) 'The Agent–Structure Problem in International Relations Theory', *International Organization*, 41(3): 335–70.

Whalley, J. (2006) 'The Post-MFA Performance of Developing Asia', NBER Working Paper 12178 (Washington, DC: National Bureau of Economic Research).

Wheeler, N. J. (2000) *Saving Strangers: Humanitarian Intervention in International Society* (Oxford: Oxford University Press).

White, G. (ed.) (1988) *Developmental States in East Asia* (London: Macmillan).

Whitworth, S. (1997) *Feminism and International Relations* (Basingstoke, UK: Macmillan).

WHO (2002) 'Integrating Gender Perspectives in the Work of WHO: WHO Gender Policy' (Geneva: WHO).

WHO (2014) 'Maternal Mortality', Fact Sheet No. 348, http://www.who.int/mediacentre/factsheets/fs348/en/, last accessed 17 October 2015.

Wiener, J. (2005) 'GATS and the Politics of "Trade in Services"', in D. Kelly and W. Grant (eds) *The Politics of International Trade: Actors, Issues, and Regional Dynamics* (Basingstoke, UK: Palgrave Macmillan).

Wilkins, M. (1970) *The Emergence of the Multinational Enterprise* (Cambridge, MA: Harvard University Press).

Williams, E. (1944) *Capitalism and Slavery* (Chapel Hill, NC: University of North Carolina Press).

Williams, M. (1994) *International Economic Organisations and the Third World* (London: Harvester Wheatsheaf).

Williams, M. (1999) 'The World Trade Organization, Social Movements and "Democracy"', in A. Taylor and C. Thomas (eds) *Global Trade and Global Social Issues* (London: Routledge).

Williams, M. (2005a) 'Civil Society and the World Trading System', in D. Kelly and W. Grant (eds) *The Politics of International Trade: Actors, Issues, and Regional Dynamics* (Basingstoke, UK: Palgrave Macmillan).

Williams, M. (2005b) 'The Third World and Global Environmental Negotiations: Interests, Institutions and Ideas', *Global Environmental Politics*, 5(3): 48–69.

Williamson, J. (1990) 'What Washington Means by Policy Reform', in J. Williamson (ed.) *Latin American Adjustment: How Much Has Happened?* (Washington, DC: Institute of International Economics).

Williamson, J. (1993) 'Democracy and the Washington Consensus', *World Development*, 11(8): 1329–36.

Wilson, W. ([1918]1986) 'The Fourteen Points', in J. A. Vasquez (ed.) *Classics of International Relations* (London: Prentice Hall).

Wily, L. A. (2012) 'Looking Back to See Forward: The Legal Niceties of Land Theft in Land Rushes' *Journal of Peasant Studies*, 39(3/4): 751–775.

Winham, G. R. (1986) *International Trade and the Tokyo Round Negotiations* (Princeton, NJ: Princeton University Press).

Wolf, E. R. (1982) *Europe and the People without History* (Berkeley, CA: University of California Press).

Wolfers, A. (1952) '"National Security" as an Ambiguous Symbol', *Political Science Quarterly*, 67(4): 481–502.

Wollstonecraft, M. ([1792]1992) *A Vindication of the Rights of Woman* (London: Penguin).

Woods, N. (2007) *The Globalizers: The IMF, The World Bank and Their Borrowers* (Ithaca, NY: Cornell University Press).

World Bank (1980) 'World Development Report' (New York: Oxford University Press).

World Bank (1989) 'World Development Report' (New York: Oxford University Press).

World Bank (1990) 'World Development Report' (New York: Oxford University Press).

World Bank (1993) *The East Asian Miracle: Economic Growth and Public Policy* (Oxford: Oxford University Press; Washington, DC: World Bank).

World Bank (1996) 'World Development Report' (New York: Oxford University Press).

World Bank (1998) 'Partnerships for Development: A New World Bank Approach' (Washington, DC: World Bank).

World Bank (2001) 'Global Development Finance' (Washington, DC: World Bank).

World Bank (2002) 'The World Bank Annual Report 2002' (Washington, DC: World Bank).

World Bank (2003) 'ICT and MDGs: A World Bank Group Perspective' (Washington, DC: World Bank, Global ICT Department).

World Bank (2006a) 'Gender Equality as Smart Economics: A World Bank Group Gender Action Plan (Fiscal Years 2007–10)' (Washington, DC: World Bank).

World Bank (2006b) 'Debt Relief for the Poorest: An Evaluation Update of the HIPC Initiative' (Washington, DC: World Bank, Independent Evaluations Group).

World Bank (2006c) 'Key Development Data and Statistics: Sub-Saharan Africa', http://devdata.worldbank.org, last accessed 30 May 2006.

World Bank (2008) 'Annual Report 2008' (Washington, DC: World Bank).

World Bank (2010) 'World Development Report 2010' (Washington, DC: World Bank).

World Bank (2011) 'Migration and Remittances Factbook 2011' (Washington, DC: The World Bank).

World Bank (2012a) 'Developing Countries to Receive over $400 Billion in Remittances in 2012, Says World Bank Report', 20 November, www.worldbank.org/en/news/press-release/2012/11/20/developingcountries-to-receive-over-400-billion-remittances-2012world-bank-report, last accessed 20 February 2013.

World Bank (2012b) 'Annual Report 2012' (Washington, DC: World Bank).

World Bank (2013) 'Development and Migration Brief 21', http://siteresources.worldbank.org/INTPROSPECTS/Resources/334934-1288990760745/MigrationandDevelopmentBrief21.pdf, last accessed 17 October 2015.

World Bank (2014) 'HIPC MDRI', http://www.worldbank.org/content/dam/Worldbank/Feature%20Story/Debt/HIPC_Fall2014_ENG_CRA_web.pdf, last accessed 17 October 2015.

World Bank (2015a) 'Development and Migration Brief 23' (Washington, DC: World Bank), http://siteresources.worldbank.org/INTPROSPECTS/Resources/334934-1288990760745/MigrationandDevelopmentBrief24.pdf, last accessed 17 October 2015.

World Bank (2015b) 'World Development Indicators, Distribution of Income 2015', http://wdi.worldbank.org/table/2.9, last accessed 8 May 2015.

World Commission on Environment and Development (1987) *Our Common Future* (Oxford: Oxford University Press).

World Economic Forum (2014) 'The Global Gender Gap Report 2014' (Geneva: World Economic Forum).

World Guide (2001) *World Guide: An Alternative Reference to the Countries of Our Planet* (Oxford: New Internationalist).

Worldometers (2015) Countries in the World (Ranked by 2014 Population), http://www.worldometers.info/world-population/population-by-country/, last accessed 17 October 2015.

WTO (1998) 'International Trade Statistics 1998' (Geneva: WTO).

WTO (2001) 'Doha Ministerial Declaration' (Geneva: WTO).

WTO (2006) 'World Trade Report 2006" (Geneva: WTO).

WTO (2007) 'World Trade Report 2007' (Geneva: WTO).

WTO (2008) 'International Trade Statistics 2008' (Geneva: WTO).

WTO (2009a) 'World Trade Report 2009' (Geneva: WTO).

WTO (2009b) 'Regional Trade Agreements', www.wto.org/english/tratop_e/region_e/region_e.htm, last accessed 17 October 2015.

WTO (2011a) 'World Trade Report 2011—The WTO and Preferential Trade Agreements from Co-existence to Coherence' (Geneva: World Trade Organization).

WTO (2011b) 'International Trade Statistics 2011' (Geneva: WTO).

WTO (2012) 'World Trade Report 2012' (Geneva: WTO).

WTO (2013) 'World Trade Report 2013' (Geneva: WTO).

WTO (2014a) 'International Trade Statistics 2014' (Geneva: WTO).

WTO (2014b) 'Public Stockholding for Food Security Purposes' (WT/L/939).

WTO (2014c) 'Agreement on Trade Facilitation: Protocol amending the Marrakesh Agreement' (WT/L/940).

WWF (World Wide Fund for Nature) (2012) '2012 Living Planet Report', http://wwf.panda.org/about_our_earth/all_publications/living_planet_report/2012_lpr/, last accessed 17 October 2015.

Wyn Jones, R. (1999) *Security, Strategy, and Critical Theory* (Boulder, CO: Lynne Reinner).

Yardley, J. (2004) 'The New Uprooted: In a Tidal Wave, China's Masses Pour from Farm to City', *New York Times*, 12 September.

Yardley, J. and Barboza, D. (2005) 'Help Wanted: China Finds Itself with a Labor Shortage', *New York Times*, 3 April.

Yeates, N. (2009) *Globalizing Care Economies and Migrant Workers: Explorations in Global Care Chains* (Basingstoke, UK: Palgrave Macmillan).

York, G. (2009) 'How Zimbabwe Slew the Dragon of Hyper-inflation', *Globe and Mail*, 23 March, B1.

Young, K., Wolkowitz, C. and McCullagh, R. (eds) (1984) *Of Marriage and the Market: Women's Subordination Internationally and Its Lessons*, 2nd edn (London: Routledge & Kegan Paul).

Young, O. (1989) 'The Politics of Regime Formation: Managing Global Resources and the Environment', *International Organization*, 43(3): 349–77.

Young, O. (1994) *International Governance: Protecting the Environment in a Stateless Society* (Ithaca, NY: Cornell University Press).

Young, R. (ed.) (1999) *The Effectiveness of International Economic Regimes: Causal Connections and Behavioral Mechanisms* (Cambridge, MA: MIT Press).

Youngs, G. (2000) 'Introduction', in G. Youngs (ed.) *Political Economy, Power and the Body* (Basingstoke, UK: Macmillan).

Youngs, G. (2004) 'Feminist International Relations: A Contradiction in Terms? Or: How Women and Gender are Essential to Understanding the World "We" Live In', *International Affairs*, 80(1): 75–87.

Zakaria, F. (1994) 'Culture is Destiny: A Conversation with Lee Kuan Yew', *Foreign Affairs*, 73(2): 109–26.

Index